The Diary of George Templeton Strong

The Diary of George Templeton Strong

Edited by
ALLAN NEVINS *and* MILTON HALSEY THOMAS

Abridged by
THOMAS J. PRESSLY

University of Washington Press
Seattle and London

Library of Congress Cataloging-in-Publication Data

Strong, George Templeton, 1820–1975.
    The Diary of George Templeton Strong.

    Includes index.
    1. Strong, George Templeton, 1820–1975—Diaries.
2. United States—Politics and government—19th century.
3. New York (N.Y.)—Social life and customs.   4. United
States—History—Civil War, 1861–1865—Personal
narratives.   5. New York (N.Y.)—Biography.
6. Columbia University—History—19th century.
I. Nevins, Allan, 1890–1971.   II. Thomas, Milton
III. Pressly, Thomas.   IV. Title.
F128.44.S83   1988   974.7'103'0924   87–23154

ISBN 0–295–96511–8
ISBN 0–295–96512–6 (pbk.)

CONTENTS

ILLUSTRATIONS

following page 202

INTRODUCTION

In 1835, a fifteen-year-old undergraduate at Columbia University named George Templeton Strong began a diary that he was to continue until his death forty years later. It is our good fortune that Strong was exceedingly conscientious in making entries in his diary for most of the days from 1835 to 1875, and also that he was a person of such broad interests that his entries cast light on many different facets of life during those four decades.

Strong was a lawyer and his diary describes his taking and passing the bar exam in New York State in the 1840's, his work on numerous legal cases, his reactions to judicial decisions, and various other matters related to the practice of law in the middle of the nineteenth century. He was also a trustee of Columbia University and a vestryman of Trinity Episcopal Church. Many diary entries are devoted entirely or in part to the appointment of professors, the apportionment of funds, and other university affairs, plus analogous events at Trinity Church. He was a lover of music, and one gets the impression that he attended virtually every concert and every opera performed in New York City, sometimes with extended critical evaluations in his diary. Theater did not draw as much comment from Strong as did music, but even so there are many notations of plays Strong attended, usually with his wife. He was a reader of books—liked *Vanity Fair,* did not care for *Jane Eyre,* considered *Trois Mousquetaires* "amusing trash"—and he made frequent comments about his reading of other novels, of historical writings, and of works of science.

Prominent throughout the diary are Strong's descriptions and analyses of economic conditions and politics. He chronicles the ups and downs of the business cycle, noting its effects on his own financial prospects and on the prospects of relatives and friends. He was a close observer of local, state, and national politics, and his pages are filled with pungent comments on the political scene and on individual political figures.

The themes that come to dominate political and economic life in the United States by the 1850's also become dominant in Strong's own life and in his diary: the worsening relations between North and South, conflicting views over the institution of slavery, and the relations between blacks and whites. Through the pages of his diary we see the change from Strong in the 1830's, the Whig opponent of Democrats Andrew Jackson and Martin Van Buren, to Strong by the 1850's, the ardent supporter of the Union against the Southern secession movement and subsequent Confederate States of America. As a patriotic supporter of the Union during the Civil War, Strong became treasurer of the United States Sanitary Commission, that all-purpose organization which performed the many tasks assigned in later wars to a host of groups such as the Red Cross, the USO, and the Medical Corps of the various armed services.

Through Strong's work in the Sanitary Commission he met and visited President Abraham Lincoln on two occasions, and was present in the East Room of the White House for Lincoln's funeral. One of the many interesting subthemes in the diary is Strong's increasingly favorable evaluation of Lincoln as national leader and as human being, the evaluation reaching its peak shortly after Lincoln's assassination: "His name," Strong wrote in the entry for May 14, 1865, "is Faithful and True. He will stand in history beside Washington, perhaps higher." Strong met and was favorably impressed with Lincoln's successor, Andrew Johnson, but later came to oppose Johnson's Reconstruction policies for not protecting the Union and black Southerners from the actual or potential machinations of white Southern "rebels and traitors."

Behind all the specific events recorded in the forty years of diary comments, we can glimpse George Templeton Strong the person: his attraction and marriage to Ellen Ruggles, his concern for her and for their children, his gift for friendship, his frequent sick headaches (migraine?), his interest in hydropathy, and his fascination with fires, which led him to visit and comment upon what must have been the majorty of all fires within a two- or three-mile radius of his home, qualifying him as, in the language of our own day, a genuine "sparkie."

The sequence of events that led to the publication of Strong's *Diary* was described by the two editors in their Preface to the four volumes in which the *Diary* was published in 1952; relevant portions of that Preface are reprinted in the pages following this Introduction. After its publication in 1952 the *Diary* quickly became a classic source for historians, a sort of Northern counterpart to *The Children of Pride* and other first-hand accounts by nineteenth-century white Southerners. I have assigned various portions of the *Diary* as reading for my undergraduate and graduate history courses for some thirty-five years now, and I have been impressed with its continuing appeal for successive, and quite different, "student generations."

The present one-volume abridged edition is designed to make portions of Strong's *Diary* accessible to general readers, students, professional historians, and anyone else interested in a vivid description of life in the United States from the 1830's to the 1870's. The selections included here comprise from one-fifth to one-fourth of the material in the four-volume 1952 edition of the *Diary*. In making the selections I have sought to reflect the chronological scope and the wide diversity of topics that characterized the original edition.

This one-volume edition was first projected a number of years ago after Ted Cuningham, one of the editors at the Macmillan Company who had worked on the 1952 edition, joined the staff of the University of Washington Press. For making this edition possible, my deep appreciation goes to Ted Cuningham, to Don Ellegood, the director of the University of Washington Press, and to their skilled and efficient colleagues, including Naomi Pascal, Julidta Tarver, Veronica Seyd, and Pamela Chaus.

THOMAS J. PRESSLY
University of Washington
July 1987

FROM THE PREFACE
TO THE ORIGINAL EDITION

T o write a truly great diary, one should keep its composition secret and should intend no early publication of its contents. If a man is known to be keeping a journal, his friends and acquaintances may play up to it; if he wishes it published in his own time, he must be over-discreet in his entries. It is fairly plain that George Templeton Strong's friends did not suspect him of being a note-taking chiel, and perfectly clear that his diary contained much that would have forbidden its uncensored publication in 1875, the year of his death. His family rightly laid the great record of more than four million words away. For fifty years it was closely guarded by his heirs. Only in 1927, when Mrs. George Strong Derby lent it to the museum of the American Red Cross, did its existence become known to more than a few. Even then it failed to arouse much interest, and for some years no student attempted to explore its riches.

A natural train of circumstances drew the diary to the attention of the present editors. Mr. Henry Waters Taft late in life began a history of the law firm which, founded in 1818 by George Washington Strong and John Wells, had during the next century engaged the talents of the diarist George Templeton Strong, his partners Marshall S. Bidwell and Charles E. Strong, and his successors John L. Cadwalader, George W. Wickersham, and Mr. Taft himself. In writing his history, Mr. Taft learned of the diary and obtained permission from John R. Strong of New York and Hasket Derby II, now of Portland, son and grandnephew of the diarist, to use it. His interesting volume on the record of this brilliant line of attorneys, entitled *A Century and a Half at the New York Bar, Being the Annals of a Law Firm*, was privately printed in 1938. In that year Mr. Taft mentioned to President Nicholas Murray Butler of Columbia University that he had temporary possession of a diary containing a wealth of information on Columbia affairs, and Dr. Butler conveyed word of the find to the editors.

George Templeton Strong III, of Larchmont, New York, whose father John R. Strong died in 1941, and Hasket Derby II willingly consented to the publication of the journal, giving the editors complete freedom in their treatment of it.

The diary, kept in uniform blank-books, is now bound in four morocco volumes, fourteen by nine inches in size, which contain an aggregate of more than 2,250 pages. The number or words is perhaps nearer four and a half million than four million. Strong wrote his record in a minute hand, no larger than the type of our footnotes, beautifully regular, fine-lined, and clear. Hardly a hundred times in these volumes have we found a word undeciperable. At first the diarist used quill pens, whose deficiencies he often bewailed, and when gold pens grew popular in the 1850's he doubtless turned to them. Ordinarily he made his entries just before going to bed, first at his parents' home on Greenwich Street and later at his own residence on Gramercy Park. It is one merit of the record that he kept it up to date, seldom indulging in John Quincy Adams's practice of deferring it until a day of leisure enabled him to write in the arrears. His impressions were thus kept vivid; many a concert, political meeting, or evening party was described an hour after it ended.

The task of the editors has been both onerous and fascinating, sometimes irritating, frequently exhilarating. The first requisite was a drastic reduction of the bulky record. All diaries inevitably contain much that is ephemeral and trivial: comments on the weather, notes on random walks and pointless episodes, mentions of unidentifiable or uninteresting people, and jottings of commonplace ideas. We have not only excluded such dull matter, but have omitted prosy theological disquisitions, dealt sternly with lectures, sermons, and vestry sessions, and kept the notation of routine legal business to a minimum. In two fields we have held our selections within strict limits in the expectation that future books of a special nature will do ampler justice to the materials. Strong's interest in Columbia, as student, alumnus, and trustee, is well illustrated in these volumes; but enough remains unused to fill a valuable supplementary monograph. And though we give numerous excerpts from his discriminating criticism of concerts, oratorios, and operas, again an interesting volume of musical comment could—and some day will—be compiled from the diary.

With these two exceptions, these pages contain, we believe, the parts of Strong's narrative of greatest interest to the general public. We have tried to include all that bears significantly upon the cultural, social, and political history of the times. Many interesting personal entries, dealing with the diarist's family circle, have been left out; but these would make another kind of story.

In preparing the diary for publication, our fundamental rule has been to treat it precisely as any conscientious publishing house would treat an important manuscript by a living author. The text has been carefully respected; so far as words and sentence structure go, except for a few insertions of an article or preposition, the record stands exactly as Strong wrote it. But spelling and punctuation have been made fairly consistent, conforming to modern usage; orthography of proper names has been corrected and made uniform; Greek phrases have been put into English; abbreviations like "Col: Coll:" have been written out; and minor errors like the use of "farther" for "further" have been corrected. Omissions within entries have been indicated by the usual ellipses, but in the interest of space-saving and appearance of the printed page, especially in the Civil War volume, we have avoided an excess of dots and allowed selected passages to appear as entire entries.

Fidelity to the text has, of course, involved the retention of many outspoken passages. Strong had a way of indulging, sometimes semi-humorously, sometimes quite seriously, in heated attacks on individuals, groups, and societies; he used the diary now and then to blow off steam. His violent assaults upon Yankees, Negroes, Southern rebels, Britons, Irishmen, Frenchmen; his scathing remarks about conservative Columbia trustees, Roman Catholics, Low-Church Episcopalians, Jews, Unitarians, Presbyterians, and other sects; his contemptuous excoriation of many of the cruder manifestations of social and political democracy—all this gives salt to the great document he left. Sometimes the salt may seem a little stinging. But if hasty and unfair judgments are included, it is not because the editors approve them, but because they have historical value. . . .

ALLAN NEVINS
MILTON HALSEY THOMAS
Columbia University
January 1952

DRAMATIS PERSONAE

(Adapted from the 1952 four-volume edition of Strong's Diary)

HENRY JAMES ANDERSON (*Harry*), graduate of Columbia (1818) and the College of Physicians and Surgeons, was professor of mathematics in Strong's time; later they were on the board of trustees together. Spending much time in European travel after his retirement as professor of mathematics in Columbia College in 1843, Anderson was converted to Catholicism in Italy. A trustee of Columbia from 1851, he and Strong constantly met at board sessions. "Cautious, rational, and judgmatical," wrote Strong; "clear-headed, money-making, real-estate-buying, demonstrating." He was the "incarnation of a right angle," but he could also refine tiny points and torture arguments like a medieval scholastic.

CHARLES ANTHON (*Bull, Taurus, Charley,* etc.), Jay Professor of the Greek and Latin Languages at Columbia, the best-known member of the faculty of his time and something of a terror to the students, was the son of a German-born surgeon-general in the British army long stationed at Detroit, and a French mother. He was graduated from Columbia in 1815, practised law briefly, and in 1820 began his long teaching career at the college, to which he added in 1830 the rectorship of the Columbia Grammar School. A powerful, irascible man, he was a self-taught classicist who never married, shunned society, and over a period of forty years turned out an incredible number of grammars, lexicons, dictionaries, and heavily-annotated editions of Greek and Latin authors.

GEORGE CHRISTIAN ANTHON, Columbia 1839, son of the rector of St. Mark's and nephew of Professor Charles "Bull" Anthon, with whom he did not get along, was Strong's frequent companion and chess-antagonist in college and later. He joined the students in Strong's office for a time, but later abandoned the law for teaching. The intimacy between Strong and the nephew of his awesome old Latin and Greek professor deepened in the 1850's. Anthon, still unmarried, was one of the most frequent diners at the Strong home and often accompanied the young couple to the opera, concerts, and art exhibitions. When his brief tenure of the professorship of Greek at New York University ended with a summary dismissal in 1851, Strong defended him stoutly, even composing his answer to the Council's charges, though he privately considered him not entirely equal to filling the chair. In the fall of 1853 Anthon began teaching in the Columbia Grammar School under the supervision of his uncle. The close-knit triumvirate of Anthon, Charles E. Strong, and the diarist persisted through the war years. Though his war activities took so much of Strong's time and energy, he still found hours to spend with "G.C.A.," whose temperamental vagaries were often trying in the nerve-straining days, but whose loyal friendship was nonetheless a comfort. Anthon was also devoted to Mrs. Strong, sharing her interests in music and art; he frequently escorted her to opera and concert when her husband was busy with Sanitary Commission or Trinity Church affairs. Anthon ruptured his friendship with Strong in a fit of pique. A highly temperamental man, he long refused to repair the breach. When Strong sent him a friendly message, he disregarded it for three years on the excuse that the bearer had made some untactful remarks about water-proof overshoes when delivering it! As for Charles Anthon, his death on July 29, 1867, was a blow to all sons of Columbia.

FREDERICK A. P. BARNARD. When Strong refused to be considered for the presidency of Columbia College, this former president of the University of Mississippi was easily elected to the place (1864). A son of Massachusetts and of Yale, Barnard was then fifty-five. He was deaf as a post, and prosily loquacious. But Strong was convinced from the outset that he was a man of vision, judgment, and courage, and never had reason to change the opinion. Barnard was the best president Columbia had thus far had. Although the diarist suffered under Barnard's endless flow of talk, more otiose he thought than Mendelssohn's Introduction to the *Lobgesäng*, he delighted in the man's progressive ideas. "But for his two infirmities, deafness and prolixity, he would be very near perfection as president of Columbia College," wrote Strong.

HORACE BINNEY, JR., the eldest son of the eminent Philadelphia attorney and statesman, himself a brilliant attorney practicing with his father and active in municipal affairs, was related to Strong by marriage to his cousin, Eliza Johnson. The Civil War brought Strong and his cousin-by-marriage into much closer relation than they had known through exchange of family visits. Like the diarist, eleven years his junior, Binney took time from his busy law practice to work for the Union cause in many ways. He became a member of the Sanitary Commission in the summer of 1861, to Strong's satisfaction; organized the Philadelphia auxiliary group, brought Philadelphia's leading professional and business men to the support of the work, and exerted a steadying influence on the whole undertaking. Strong wrote that "he was so simple, modest, and retiring that few recognized the value of his quiet, hard work for the country."

JOHN A. and MORGAN DIX. Despite a distinguished early career as soldier in the War of 1812, member of the "Albany Regency," New York's secretary of state, and United States Senator, and despite great abilities, John A. Dix was in political exile until the outbreak of civil war. Southern slavery men hated him. He was forced to turn to law practice and railroad management. Meanwhile, his gifted son Morgan was advancing in the Episcopal Church, becoming assistant minister of Trinity in 1855 and assistant rector four years later. Strong greatly esteemed and liked both men.

JOHN A. DIX. The general was a man whom Strong almost unreservedly admired. The diary records most of his important activities—his part in organizing the Union Defense Committee in New York in 1861; his rapid organization of regiments for the front; his command in Maryland in the critical days after Bull Run, when that state was precarious; service at Fortress Monroe; and his measures as head of the Department of the East after the Draft Riots. The general, nearly sixty-seven when the war ended, made a good minister to France 1866–1869, and an excellent governor of New York 1873–1875.

MORGAN DIX. Strong was deeply gratified when the young assistant rector of Trinity Church was unanimously elected to the rectorship on the death of the Rev. William Berrian in November, 1862, and a month later to Berrian's place on the Columbia College board of trustees. The Rector's sister, "the handsome, buxom, bouncing . . . Miss Kitty," pleased the diarist, too; in fact, he liked the whole Dix family. News of the Rector's engagement, at the age of forty-five, to a woman more than twenty years his junior struck the diarist almost speechless. He could not believe the report until it was confirmed by the young lady's family; however, he disagreed with those who took a pessimistic view of the union. Describing the wedding, Strong wrote that "Morgan Dix looked like a beatified saint and, as it were, phosphoresced from brow to boots." The bride, whom he found intelligent and interesting rather than pretty, was soon included in Strong's approval of all the Dixes.

THOMAS EGLESTON. Strong's ardent desire to see Columbia College expand into a university made him a sturdy champion of the plan for a School of Mines which Egleston (then at the Smithsonian Institution) published in 1863. From the partnership of four men, Egleston, Charles F. Chandler, Francis Vinton, and Strong, the School was born. A graduate of Yale and the Ecole des Mines in Paris in 1860, Egleston was in his early thirties at the time. The diary throws much light on his unselfish devotion to the great undertaking.

HAMILTON FISH. First governor, then United States Senator, Fish was already counted among the most eminent of Columbia's alumni, and became chairman of the board of trustess in 1859. He united ability, character, wealth, and family prestige. But in the Gibbs controversy his ingrained caution made him play a wobbling part, and Strong was justly critical of his wishy-washy course: "O Piscicule, Piscium minimicule!" As scion of two wealthy and aristocratic families, the Fishes and the Stuyvesants, Hamilton Fish was a man of power and influence. But Strong found him too cautious, chilly, and precise-minded to be agreeable, and thought him lukewarm in the Union cause—indeed, in every cause. Fish had more public prestige than any other Columbia trustee. His services to the college were many and great, though he had a tendency to be "perturbed and dissatisfied about everything." In 1869 he took the Secretaryship of State for what he thought would be a few weeks, and remained eight years, making one of the ablest records in the history of the office.

WOLCOTT GIBBS. Just two years younger than Strong, this grandson of Oliver Wolcott had come through Columbia College on the diarist's heels. Then he had given himself the finest possible training in chemistry, studying three years under the best German and French masters. In the decade of the 1850's he was teaching in New York, first at the College of Physicians and Surgeons, and then at the Free Academy (which became City College). He was just the man for the chair of natural and experimental philosophy and chemistry vacated by James Renwick. Strong writes: "Gibbs is a cast-iron man who would take little trouble for me, or any one else, *I think*. But his transcendent abilities and energy must be secured for Col: Coll: if any exertion of mine can put him there." They became warm friends. Their friendship grew closer still when the chemist (who also had a medical degree) became a member of the executive committee of the Sanitary Commission. It was Gibbs, too, who deserved most of the credit for the idea which flowered into the Union League Club in New York, which Strong helped to establish. Until 1863 he held a chair in City College; then he went to Harvard.

FRANCIS LIEBER. At the beginning of the 1850's Lieber filled the chair of history and political economy at the South Carolina College. Strong pronounced him in 1850 "a clever man, but not quite so clever as he thinks himself." In 1853 Lieber produced two learned volumes called *On Civil Liberty and Self-Government;* three years later, having failed of election to the presidency of his college, he resigned and came north; and in 1857, with the backing of Strong and Samuel B. Ruggles, he was made professor at Columbia. The Civil War gave national and international scope to Lieber's political wisdom. He was consulted by the Union government in the formulation of rules of war, and his opinions were adopted. The War Department's General Orders No. 100, "Instructions for the Government of Armies in the Field," was an issue in revised form of Lieber's most famous treatise on this subject. Nothing of the kind existed in any language before this publication. It was accepted by military authorities of other countries and became the basis of international rules for the conduct of war. When the Civil War ended, this distinguished political scientist had reached the age of sixty-five, and his powers were flagging. Unable to interest Columbia students or maintain discipline, he was saved from dismissal by being transferred to the School of Law. Here again he was so useless that only his death in 1872 forestalled compulsory retirement. Strong credited him with learning, ability, and dignity, but thought he lacked common sense. "He is such an *owl,* so wise and lazy, and so puffy with self-importance. . . ."

GOUVERNEUR MORRIS OGDEN. Lawyer, Trinity vestryman, graduate and trustee of Columbia, and arch-reactionary, this "simple-hearted, sincere, thick-headed, addlebrained son of Adam" led the battle against Wolcott Gibbs, and wrote a pamphlet on the controversy which Strong characterized as "feeble and flat, verbose, wooden, and stupid." Ogden was one of the most important of the Columbia trustees, and as treasurer of the college, a watchdog on its expenditures; the diary reveals him as conservative, intelligent, and gloomy.

SAMUEL B. RUGGLES. Strong's father-in-law, Yale graduate at fourteen, one of the ablest and most public-spirited citizens of New York during a long generation, and the best member of the Columbia board of trustees, labored hard throughout the 1850's to make Columbia College efficient and progressive. In this endeavor he had the diarist's ardent cooperation. The two bore the brunt of the fight for Wolcott Gibbs. This decade also witnessed the tragic collapse and painful rebuilding of Ruggles's financial fortunes. Ruggles, busy in many public fields, remained well throughout the war. He conferred often with his friend Seward and lobbied for important legislation. In 1863, going to Berlin to attend an International Statistical Convention, he used the opportunity to promote the Northern cause in Prussia. Like Strong, he became a warm admirer of Lincoln, and when the President was shot made a statement remarkable for so kindly a man: "The one consolatory fact connected with Lincoln's death is that he cannot pardon his murderer." Ruggles was American delegate to the International Monetary Conference at Paris in 1867, and to the International Statistical Congress at Berlin in 1869. On October 22, 1872, he suffered a paralytic stroke of which Strong gives a vivid account. But he recovered and continued his public labors, surviving Strong, and doing more than any other trustee to make Columbia great. It was he who cabled Professor John W. Burgess, when the trustees approved the new School of Political Science on June 7, 1880: "Thank God, the University is born."

CHARLES EDWARD STRONG (*Charley*), 1824–1897, George's first cousin once-removed, had two years at Yale and was graduated from Amherst in 1843, immediately entering the Strong office; from this time the cousins were in intimate association, socially and in business, until parted by death. They had many qualities in common: modesty, interest in literature, industry, and conscientious devotion to duty. Charles's marriage to Eleanor Burrill Fearing in 1850 pleased both George and Ellen Strong. The two young couples saw much of each other. Upon the cousin and partner of the diarist fell the heavy burden of the Wall Street law office whenever the combined needs of the Sanitary Commission, Columbia College, and Trinity Church absorbed nearly all of George Templeton Strong's energies. The diary reflects the almost perfect harmony of opinion and outlook between the two men. "Charley" shared with George Anthon the diarist's most intimate friendship. His daughter Kate ("little

Miss Puss") was Strong's god-daughter; she came close to filling the place of his own daughter lost at birth. When, in 1866, Mrs. Eleanor Strong and little Kate went to Europe to live and Charles sold the home on East 22nd Street that he had built in 1852, George Strong was full of sadness and foreboding. Charles's trips abroad to visit his wife and daughter in the following years, Eleanor's long illness, the growing up of Kate and her engagement to an English captain all caused the diarist anxiety and unhappiness.

ELLEN RUGGLES STRONG. Memories of his wife's nearly fatal illness and loss of her first baby in the spring of 1849 haunted the diarist during her second pregnancy in 1851. His relief and joy at the birth of John Ruggles Strong in the autumn of that year were unbounded. The birth of a second son, George Templeton Strong, Jr., in May, 1856, caused less anxiety and brought great happiness. Mrs. Strong, with her keen interest in music, theatre, art, literature, and friends, made their home a gay, stimulating place. The diarist's pride in his wife reached even greater heights as the war revealed unsuspected qualities in her. She threw herself wholeheartedly into war work and when, in the spring of 1862, she won her husband's reluctant permission to serve on some of the Sanitary Commission's hospital ships in Southern waters, she astonished him by her physical endurance and her executive ability as much as she worried him with her disregard of danger. "What a plucky little thing she is!" he wrote; and how proud he was of her "stepping naturally into command of our volunteer corps of nurses" on the ships. Mrs. Strong made frequent and protracted visits to Washington during these years, meeting notable personages and getting an inside view of the political machinery. The diarist often indulged in praise of his wife. Once he wrote: "Her social faculty is great. She acts on people of diverse temperaments and tastes just as a bit of platinum sponge acts on a current of mixed oxygen and hydrogen—makes them react on each other and become luminous—by a special unaccountable gift of catalysis." The Church Music Association could hardly have been the success it was without her skillful rallying of New York society to its support.

GULIAN C. VERPLANCK. As lawyer, political veteran, and litterateur, nobody in New York was more warmly liked than Verplanck; but his Copperhead tendencies led to his deposition from the presidency of the Century Club—a step which Strong half approved, half lamented. His death in 1870, at the age of nearly eighty-six, removed one of the land-marks of New York life. "He is a great loss to our Vestry," wrote Strong, "and to sundry other boards and trusts, and to what *literate* society we have in New York. Had he only lived in Boston, he would have been famous."

The Diary of George Templeton Strong

1837

*S*trong bought a new blank book for his journal of 1837, and his daily entries grew markedly in length. He recorded briefly that his father escaped the traditional New Year's call-making by having "a very convenient 'bad cold' " and staying at his office all the morning of Monday, January 2. George himself "prudently and wisely made no visits at all." He wrote on January 4 that he was not sorry to see the last of the holidays, for "a period of leisure is pleasant only as a change, and . . . we soon feel inclined to desire another change, that is, back to studying again." College events thereafter occupied most of the diary. On the night of January 25 a magnificent display of aurora borealis was visible in the city, and next day a time-honored trick was played in the astronomy class: "We got Professor Anderson astraddle of one of last night's columns of light, and he shot off into infinite space; of course we heard no more of the appointed recitation." The semi-annual examinations occasioned the usual bouts of studying and apprehensions of failure, but when the medals were awarded, Strong stood at the head of his class. Preparations continued actively for the semi-centennial anniversary of the college in April. This celebration commemorated the charter of 1787, which had restored Columbia as an independent successor to King's College after three unsuccessful years as part of the University of the State of New York. The students had originated the idea of a celebration and had interested the alumni association, a casual organization headed by old General Edward W. Laight of the class of 1793.

When the year opened, the country seemed prosperous, and speculation and commercial expansion were giving multitudes an illusion of wealth. But

astute men saw trouble on the horizon. Jackson's Specie Circular of the previous
summer, requiring that all payments on public lands be made in hard money,
had distressed the banks which were financing Western land speculation; a
financial crisis in England caused British creditors to call in their American
loans; and poor crops had lowered the purchasing power of many farmers.
Late in March, the failure of a large cotton firm in New Orleans involved
other houses. Panic overspread the South and West, and debts there became
uncollectible. Frantic efforts by Philadelphia and New York banks to stem the
tide were fruitless. Merchandise fell thirty per cent in a few weeks; stocks
dropped in even greater degree; and on May 10 the New York banks suspended,
those of other Eastern cities at once following the example. Anxiety, bank-
ruptcy, and want overspread the whole land.

January 7. . . . Went to the library and returned the books I took out
a fortnight ago. I have only read Dibdin through, and some parts of the
others. Dibdin is very interesting, full of anecdote and information, but
the author is perfectly crazy, mad, on the subject of "large paper" and
"tall copies," and insane about "fine old Morocco bindings," etc. I took
out three volumes of the *Harleian Miscellany*. . . . Up to Appleton's for a
copy of Southey's poems. Not to be had. Hunted about a good while and
as a last resort went into that rascally citadel of humbug, [W. A.] Colman's, though I had made up my mind not to enter the place again.
Succeeded in catching a copy at the moderate price of $6.50. . . . Spent
the evening on Southey and Aeschylus.

January 13. . . . Stopped in Appleton's on my way from college and
ordered a copy of Bacon's works in four volumes folio and a very handsome edition indeed, price $20. . . .

January 15, SUNDAY. I have been thinking today about taking
Italian lessons of Signor Foresti,[1] one of the Italian exiles just arrived
here, after eighteen years' imprisonment in Spielberg for republicanism
and patriotism. If it were any other time of the year I would, but now
with revision just about beginning and the examination at no very great
distance, I don't see how I can spare the time.

---

[1] Eleuterio Felice Foresti, LL.D. Bologna 1809, had the misfortune to be an
ardent liberal in a most reactionary period of his country's—and Europe's—history;
nevertheless, during his exile here he continued his leadership in Italian movements
and was finally welcomed back in 1858 as U.S. consul at Genoa, where he died the
same year; he was professor of Italian at Columbia from 1839 to 1856.

January 20. . . . Came home with [Henry Partridge] Fessenden. He mentioned to me a piece of business which has lately been going on among the Seniors which surprised me not a little. The night before last, eight or nine of the class went to Barber's residence in Greenwich Street to serenade him. They sang a song composed for the occasion, each verse ending with Fia-a-a-a-a-*ay*! thereby giving the professor a practical demonstration of their progress in elocution. They then proceeded to the nearest druggist's and purchased a delectable compound of ipecac, castor oil, salts, and all conceivable nastiness, adding to it a quantum of a solution of tincture of asafoetida, so as to make the whole of the consistence of mud. Three times did Fessenden ring the bell to leave this diabolical compound for the professor, and each time he saw the professor himself coming with a stick to open the door, and he therefore beat a retreat. At last they gave a black boy sixpence to give the parcel to the professor; it was wrapped in two or three papers and formally directed to the professor as a "donation from the Senior class." The unfortunate black boy took it to the door, the professor nabbed him, and applied the cudgel lustily. The boy yelled "Help! Murder!" and so on, the students ran, the watchman gave chase, and there was quite a combobbolation. The president begs that they will desist from their persecution of the poor man.

January 21. Splashed, slid, and stumbled to college, and on my way home stopped at Wiley & Long's to purchase what I have long been most anxious to read, a translation of *Faust*. I have been nearly all day at it and hardly know whether to like it or not. It is not quite equal to my expectations, but has some splendid passages in it.

January 31. . . . Dr. [John] Neilson gave me this morning a regular exhortation. He tells me I don't take enough exercise, stoop too much in writing, sit still too much, and so on. He is right. If I go on as I have for the last three months, I verily believe it will put a very peremptory stop to my studying. I have taken little or no exercise and have often, after sitting the whole afternoon, sat at the desk, without ten minutes intermission, from 6:30 to 12. He says I must have a standing desk made.

Great news from Boston. "Totty" No. 2, Master George Strong Derby, made his entree into the light of heaven on Sunday at four A.M., in fine health and spirits. Eloise is well. . . .

February 10, FRIDAY. . . . Some rascal has put into the papers a notice of the death of Prof. Renwick, "after an excruciating illness, which he bore with Christian fortitude." I have no doubt that Douglass is at the bottom of it. Renwick stands it very well, more good humoredly than was to have been expected. Our class entered the room to the Dead March, and [Edward] Anthony asked him whether we were to attend the funeral or not. It has made quite a talk.

February 13. . . . They say that [John Beekman] Fish is the author of the notice of Prof. Renwick's death. He has applied for a dismissal, which has been refused. . . .

February 14. We had a row last night. A mob, with the usual discretion of all mobs, attacked Mr. Eli Hart's store in Washington Street and destroyed three hundred barrels of flour, because flour is high, and they wish to lower its price.

February 16. . . . I had a long talk with Fish today. He has got both [James Gordon] Bennett and one of [James Watson] Webb's clerks to declare that he was not the person who brought the notice. Their description of the person who brought the notice answered very well to Douglass, and in spite of Douglass's asseveration, I fancy he is at the bottom of the business after all. . . .

February 20. . . . My standing desk arrived today. It is an excellent article, no doubt, but it maketh the bones ache to study at it.

March 12, SUNDAY. Went to Cedar Street Church in the afternoon, for the last time, as it is to be begun to be pulled down this week.

March 17. . . . Went over to Chittenden's. Started off with him for a walk. We traveled up Broadway and along the railroad, some distance beyond that abode of sweet savors, the big glue factory on the Middle Road [Fifth Avenue]. Came home through the Bowery, a little tired.

We don't take near exercise enough generally; this week I mean to do a month's walking. To do anything in the world, we don't want mental strength merely, but physical abilities also; an educated mind in a weak carcass is like a powerful engine on board a leaky steamboat. Our walk was a very pleasant one. Chittenden has not lost one jot or tittle of his propensity for political life, and it was of that we talked. And we built castles in the air, of such architecture as has rarely been equalled. But who can tell? May not their substratum be a little more solid than it seems just now? Chittenden has energy and independence; I have perseverance; and who knows but twenty years hence we may amuse ourselves by talking over our daydreams of eminence and fame? I myself have but few political ingredients in me. I want decision and resolution. Chittenden has them both; he is a good speaker and I am not, and he, if he enters on public life, will not long remain unnoticed. I find that Chittenden is rather vacillating between two courses of life, one to remain here and the other to move westward. There he would find it easier to gain distinction than here, but when gained it is a far less valuable acquisition. Most sincerely do I hope that he'll do no such thing. We have been so much together for the last few years that if he were to leave the city I should find the change most disagreeable; for his own sake, too, I hope he'll stay, for I have no great opinion of the West, taken as a whole. He's a fellow whose equal I have never met with yet, sound minded and warm hearted, and afflicted neither with puppyism nor any of the absurdities of which nine-tenths of the youths of Gotham are so deeply enamored. He has been a fine friend to me through college and I shall fight for him tooth and nail wherever I can find a chance to do it.

Evening. . . . The books I bought this morning at Wiley & Putnam's arrived in good order, *videlicet*, a set of Sismondi, four volumes, and Sidney's works, one volume, both fine copies and both very valuable, especially the former.

March 20. In the afternoon went to Pike's and got one of those camera lucidas for taking views, a good purchase but a horribly dear one. . . .

March 23. Shelley in the afternoon. Rather humbuggical, I think. I agree with Backus about his poetry; it passes for more than it is worth, especially his "Cenci," which is great stuff, and his "Queen Mab," which is as flimsy and hyperbolical in composition as it is detestable in sentiment. Setting its sentiments aside, it does not compare in point of poetic fancy with "The Culprit Fay" or half a dozen other pieces which are not generally half so much read. Shelley in fact, like Byron, is rather a proscribed author; he is read by stealth and hence is read with more pleasure. Strike out from Byron's works those sentiments which make them in many cases forbidden fruit, and the fact that they are now open to all, free from censure, would deprive them of half their charm. At present it is fashionable, manly, to admire Byron and Shelley, and therefore they are admired by those who have no more poetic feeling than a horse, and five out of ten have not read the very author whom they glorify. . . . It is amazing to read the life of Shelley prefixed to any edition of his works and generally to read all the laudatory articles on him and Byron. To be sure he seduced women without number, to be sure the atheism and profligacy in his works has been a fountain of destruction to hundreds and so will continue to be; to be sure he displayed depravity in every shape conceivable, and no one can deny that he was a curse to the world while he lived and that his writings still propagate the infection after his death and go on raising up other Byrons and other Shelleys to do the same good office by mankind, but still "He had a good heart." What utter humbug! It reminds me of the fellow in the Pickwick Club who was tried for pummeling his wife when he was tipsy, and whose counsel said "it was only an amiable weakness." Shelley and Byron no doubt had some good qualities—they would be strange beings if they had not—but the tree is known by its fruit, and on these trees the rotten fruit predominated.

March 24. Occupied myself after breakfast in arranging my books, which require an overhauling about twice a year, and then went to church, it being Good Friday. Heard a doleful sermon from a dolorous-looking parson. . . .

March 25, SATURDAY. . . . Crossed over to Jersey City with Chittenden for a ramble, and after roaming about a little while over that doleful region, where they are making the site of a future metropolis, we at last found a more civilized road running north, and on this we entered. Vacant building lots—everything of that kind which forms the outskirts of a city —are dreary, desolate, and dolorous to a very great degree, neither city nor country, but a detestable approximation to both. But ten times more so is a recently manufactured district elevated from a salt water bog into a collection of building lots, public squares and so on, and of that nature is two-thirds of the country around Jersey City. . . .

Read [John] Todd's *Student's Manual* this morning, or rather looked over it. Very utopian, I think. This evening read *The Pilot*, which I like, though it has the same fault with all Cooper's novels that I ever read, viz., not quite attention enough to probability.

March 27. . . . Read Cooper's *Prairie*, which is still more improbable than the *Pilot*, though interesting and spirited.

March 29. . . . In the afternoon attended an ΑΔΦ meeting at Columbia and in the evening read *Frankenstein* and Observerized. *Frankenstein* I have tried vainly to get hold of for the last two years, till Chittenden got it out of the Mercantile Society Library for me. It is a genuine production of the German school, the material well selected and well wrought up into one of the most unearthly and ghastly pieces of *diablesse* I ever heard of. But it is woefully deficient in probability. Matter of fact, real probability is not to be looked for, the very design of the book precluded it, "Dr. Darwin and the German Physiologists" to the contrary notwithstanding, but the book wants poetic probability also; it has not the truth of fiction. How does this monster acquire in a couple of years an elegant English style, considerable skill in logic, and sufficient acquaintance with the history and manners of mankind to enable him to converse and reason at least as well as his sapient creator Frankenstein? Where does the soul come from that enables the master to do this under any circumstances, or after any time for study? Does the "Modern Prometheus" create spirit as well as matter, or does the authoress mean to imply that the soul is matter, or that it is a nonentity? There the daughter of Mary Wollstone-craft and the wife of Percy B. Shelley shows herself. Again the hero is a fool. Why doesn't he shoot the monster in some of their tête-à-têtes? Nothing could be easier. Why does he not take measures to give him his quietus when followed through England by him? (There, by the way, is another piece of improbability.) Why does he not comply with his wishes and save himself and his family from destruction by giving the monster a mate, and thus producing a race of high-souled, generous devils who, if we may judge from the specimen shown us, are very glorious fellows indeed? And finally, why is Frankenstein such an infernal, cold-blooded, cowardly villain as to suffer Justine to be executed for a murder of which he knows her to be innocent?

What is the object of the book? The obvious "moral," I think, is a warning against a thirst for knowledge carried to excess. But that is not Shelleyish enough. The object of the authoress seems to have been to show what the soul becomes when deprived of all communication with other human beings. To show that all men if isolated like Frankenstein's devil would become as high-minded and noble as the conclusion of the book shows him to be. "Vain wisdom all, and feeble philosophy." In plainer language—all humbug. . . .

March 30. . . . Called at George Anthon's. Found him hard at work making out the catalogue of [Professor] Anthon's library[2] (some five thousand volumes!). George is a little too much awed by the mighty Taurus, who I fancy finds him a very convenient worker now and then. . . .

Afternoon. Went up to Chittenden's and enjoyed a good laugh with him and Backus. Cut up *Lalla Rookh* in a very bloodthirsty manner and gave Backus a fair field for once. He never enjoys himself quite so much as when massacring a modern poet or a lovelorn novel writer. . . .

Heard a capital story today about Philip Hone (Senior). He was show-

[2] This fine classical library, numbering 6,500 volumes at Anthon's death in 1867, was sold to Cornell University, which opened the following year.

ing his library to some foreign gentleman and wanted to find some book, but could not succeed. At last he gave it up in despair and turned to the foreigner who was assisting his search. "Don't trouble yourself, sir," said he. "It's not to be found—never mind—*nunquam animus.*"

April 7. College. . . . Got off at the second hour. Walked up with the two Wards to see the library Samuel Ward[3] has brought out from Germany with him. Looked over Mr. Ward's picture gallery and then went into the library. In point of show it is certainly the finest I ever saw, a great majority of the books being in the finest possible condition as to binding and typography. Indeed I never saw anything comparable in the way of binding to many of the books there. It is certainly a superb and valuable library. In point of mathematical works, one of the finest in the country, I suspect, Mr. Ward having bought up all Lagrange's library. I noticed a superb Baskerville Bible, a complete set of the *Gentleman's Magazine,* sets of many reviews, magazines, etc., transactions, without number, of societies in England, France, Italy, and Russia. It is particularly rich in German literature, and almost equally so in French and Spanish. It is a splendid collection though I fancy more for show than use.

Afternoon. Bought the first volume of Capt. Marryat's *Snarleyyow,* not quite up to his former books, though amusing. . . .

Terrible state of things out of doors. Merchants failing by the dozen. Some fear that all the banks will stop payment. We are on the eve of a

[3] Sam Ward, Columbia 1831, brother of one of Strong's Ward classmates and cousin of the other, was a fabulous nineteenth century character. His father was a banker and Columbia trustee, and one of his sisters was Julia Ward Howe; the family lived in a mansion at the corner of Bond Street and Broadway. Sam was prepared at the Round Hill School at Northampton, and after graduating from college spent several years in a Grand Tour of Europe, on which he paused long enough at Tübingen to write a dissertation on higher mathematics in Latin which brought him a Ph.D. At this time he was having a gay whirl in New York society, writing for magazines and acting as literary broker for his friend Longfellow; in 1838 he married the daughter of William Backhouse Astor (Columbia 1811), the richest man in the United States. Before long misfortune crowded upon him: his father died and the firm of Prime, Ward & Co. failed; his wife died and a second marriage resulted in estrangement from the Astors; his second wife tired of his financial reverses and left him. In 1849 Sam joined the gold rush to California and is said to have made and lost a fortune there; by the middle fifties he was back in New York in the brokerage business, and just before the war accompanied William H. Russell, correspondent of the London *Times,* on his famous tour of the Confederacy. After the war he found his real vocation—as a lobbyist in Washington in which he was a tremendous success; he was called "The King of the Lobby" and Lord Rosebery extended his title of "Uncle Sam" to "the uncle of the human race." After losing his money again, he went to England to live with the Roseberys, and died on a visit to Italy in 1884.

change, a revolution in business matters, but it is a change that cannot be effected without shaking the whole fabric to the very foundation. I trust it will stand, but——

April 10. Met Charley [Anthon], who talked very fiercely about the Semi-Centennial, being, I take it, somewhat huffed about the lamentable and untimely death of his Greek ode. His nephew [George] tells me that he had avenged the ode by perpetrating a poem on the Semi-Centennial of six hundred lines, cutting up president and professors, making them sing songs and do no pretty conduct for a professor!

Professor Anthon had taken a dim view of the celebration from the start—Strong felt that it was because he had not been permitted to run it—and when his plan for a Latin play to be given at the Park Theatre under his direction was turned down, he was wrathful indeed. The Greek ode he wrote for the occasion went unread; he was sulking in his rooms.

Took a long rambling walk nearly out to the Shot Tower. Being two-thirds famished, we stopped to get some grub in the Bowery. Found it to be a very loaferish place—pie tasted of potato peelings and coffee was a dirty infusion of tobacco—accommodations to correspond. Cleared out in a hurry, leaving pie and coffee to take care of themselves. Minus eighteen pence for this speculation.

April 12. Another luxurious, warm, delicious, glorious day. Hurrah for the Constitution! Hurrah for the Semi-Centennial!!! and hurrah most especially for the clear weather I trust we shall have on the truly tremendous occasion. Went up to college as usual. The business of decorating the chapel doth verily flourish like a green bay tree. There are busts and statues ad infinitum, the only fault that can be found with them is the overwhelming majority of plaster over marble. Then there are portraits of all the great men and all the little men that can be scraped together, from Washington to McVickar. Then there are paper flowers by the shipload and a big pasteboard column extending through the staircase, from the first floor even to the garret. . . . Moreover, by the spirit of humbug! I must not forget the gilded chandeliers nor the portrait of Bishop Onderdonk, nor must I pass over a really admirable portrait of Prex in commencement robes (there shines forth the spirit of William Alexander Duer, LL.D.!), nor a representation of McVickar which may lay first claim to the title of "admirable" since it has made him look like a decent, sensible man. Then there's a whole forest of greenhouse plants . . . red and blue curtains alternately all round the chapel. Mirrors in each pier! The chapel looks for all the world like an old dame of sixty dressed in her granddaughter's French finery. Really I question whether the venerable dust hole was ever so thoroughly aroused before. . . .

After college went over to Brooklyn and enjoyed a very pleasant amble. Came back by a delightful back road which I never traveled before. Very warm, grass green and birds singing. . . . Came home and read Charles Lamb, which is a genuine and real acquisition to my library. . . .

Terrible lot of failures today, Mr. Hull and Abraham Ogden among them. Awful bad times. The merchants going to the devil *en masse*. Hope they'll carry nobody else after them. They say the Locofocos are going to come down on the Bank for specie, but that's no go, for the whole party (taking out some half dozen men) can't raise $1000 among them. Their strength lies in dock loafers and scavengers to whom bankbills are a rarity and whose circulating medium consists of coppers and sixpences and "such small beer." No bills to claim specie with are to be found in their pockets, even if they have any pockets to put them in. . . .

April 13. Got up with a dreadful headache and sickness in the stomach. Felt more like going to bed again than dressing and going to the Anniversary. . . . Conquered the feeling, though with difficulty, and started for college. The weather, which had been miserably cloudy and with every prospect of rain, cleared off bright and pleasant by half-past eight. Very warm and a finer day we could not have had.

Found Chittenden in the Prex's room and Prex himself in silk tights and a new coat, looking very tremendous. Got my secretary badge which we officers (whew!) of the Philolexian are to wear on this terrific occasion. . . . The AΔΦs met in Vermilye's lecture room. . . . The students kept pouring in meantime and so did the alumni, etc., in great abundance; the Green soon presented a very animated appearance. The [New York] University AΔΦs soon made their appearance in full force, and I must not forget the Grand Order of Digamma, a new special society manufactured expressly for the occasion by Messrs. Cooper and Douglass. Cooper is of course piqued at not having sufficient deference paid to his immense talents and at not being respectfully solicited to favor the AΔΦ by becoming one of its members. . . .

At ten o'clock the bell tolled and the procession began to form, a task of no small difficulty. At length we succeeded in getting into an approximation to decent order and moved off at twenty minutes past ten precise . . . the whole procession occupying something like five blocks. . . . We moved slowly, through Park Place, Broadway, Chambers, and Hudson

Streets to St. John's Park, and then through the park to the church. . . . I never saw a church so full, the aisles crowded, the very windows overflowing, and as hot as the inside of Tartarus in July. . . .

Eastburn's speech was glorious, both in matter and manner. I had expected something good, but nothing equal to this. He handled the subject in the right way. He avoided all the cock and a-bullical stuff that some men would have delighted in, about the "glories of Alma Mater" and so on, but he struck a happy mean between the depths of Prose and and the heights of Poetry, i.e., the heights of humbug. . . . Then came the "Rex tremendae majestatis et Benedictus" by Mozart, which made a terrible noise, and then came Mr. [William] Betts with his poem. I have no doubt that it was very good, but I could not hear it, nor could anyone else. The poor man was dreadfully scared, too, and his hand trembled and his voice faltered and altogether everyone said it was a flunk. This was followed by the *Te Deum* [of Haydn] which I never heard more agreeably performed. . . . Prex then proceeded to utter the honorary degrees. I don't recall all the names, but there were [Fitz Greene] Halleck, [William Cullen] Bryant, and George Griffin!!!![4]

Renwick then appeared on the stage and ejaculated that the students were to form a procession and return to the college, so we made our way out of the church and assembled in St. John's Park, where after a great deal of fun and hurrahing for Giles M. [Hillyer, student marshal] and so on, we succeeded in forming a sort of half-procession, half-mob and marched toward the college. The students were all glorious and more than one potato and apple was cabbaged from the barrels in front of the groceries we passed, to pelt with, so that our whole line of march presented quite an uproarious appearance. . . .

Read Charles Lamb all afternoon. I never got hold of a style which I think is quite equal to it, and it is truly, as they call it, "inimitable."

Started after tea for college. . . . About eight o'clock, at which time I succeeded in forcing my way through the crowd into the chapel, to half-past nine all the rooms were perfectly jammed; a single small ring around the president for introductions was the only space that could be found. At ten it was just possible to move about.

[4] Fourteen honorary degrees in all were conferred, mainly on clergymen and lawyers; George Griffin was the godly partner of Strong's father. A third Knickerbocker author, whom Strong does not mention, received the A.M. with Halleck and Bryant: Charles Fenno Hoffman, a non-graduate of the class of 1825.

I must not forget that the Sophomore Class had their dinner today and that four of them got most magnificently drunk, [Richard Stockton] Emmet, [Edward Rogers] Bell, [James William] Walsh and Charles E. Anthon; the former pugnaciously cocked, fought everyone, swore like a trooper, and ended at last by tumbling down and breaking his head. Bell was loafing about all evening, most delightfully cocked, until Dugan kicked him out of the college for calling him a —— liar. Walsh was philanthropically cocked and went about hiccuping and running over with the milk of human kindness and declaring his love, affection, and esteem for everybody he met.

But the music was magnificent and the feminines were enchanting and I felt altogether altitudinarious, especially the "Marche Moses" and "La Bayadère." They played delightfully, the finest music I ever heard by all odds, and I thought at one time there seemed strong symptoms of a cotillion in the chapel. Praeses was in such a supremely good humor that I don't think he would have thought of objecting. If he don't get an affection of the spine from excess of bowing he will be fortunate. Renwick, too! his mouth was not straight once during the evening. It was a gay scene. One of Frederic Anthon's bean-pole sisters stuck the Philolexian society badge in her hair for a headdress and one of the McVickars' thousand and one daughters or nieces mounted the Alpha Delta Phi collar round her neck. Mac himself was likewise exceeding glorious.

Refreshments I did not try for. They say that the Freshmen monopolized them, the little cormorants! They deserve the horsepond.

The AΔΦ paid their respects to the president as a society in the course of the evening. At about eleven the students began moving around the chapel in a circle, to the tune of *Hail, Columbia* by the band (I wish that I could hear such music every evening), and we soon took our leave. The students were tremendously uproarious as soon as they got on the Green, and as for myself I was very festive, too, and joined in their three cheers with all my heart and headed for home where I arrived safe a little before twelve. . . .

April 14. . . . Afternoon. . . . Junior dinner. Walked up with Frederic Anthon to the Athenaeum Hotel. . . . Had a royal time. Cooper was tremendously drunk and smashed the glasses, had a row with the waiter, got on the table and delivered an oration, and so on. . . . Drank but little myself. I was cautious, for I scarcely know how much wine I can swallow without making a fool of myself, and moreover I have not acquired much taste for it, nor do I care to. Expected to sit till eleven, but came off at eight and walked home with Backus, who was very tipsy. . . .

April 15. Spent a couple of hours in the college library. Fixed up some portraits under the direction of the Praeses. Came home. Journalized. Read *Pickwick Club.* Capital. All Smollett's humor and none of his vulgarity.

April 17, MONDAY. College. Everything much as usual. Philology with the Philologian. R. H. Douglass and Daniel Lord of the sophs called this afternoon; Lord appears to be a fine gentlemanly fellow.

Had learned some of Horace this afternoon, imagining that that was the lesson for tomorrow. By the way, we're to read Aeschylus and that detestable Horace this session. . . . Found myself mistaken, so all that I had spent on the Horace was lost time. Had an immense deal to do this evening but everything went so contrary I was constantly tempted to give it up in utter desperation. First there was the mistake about Horace, then before I got fairly under way on Aeschylus, who should make his appearance but that good-natured old proser, Dr. McElroy, who favored us with a sitting of three mortal hours. Endured it for a season and then went downstairs to find some place to study. Out of the frying pan into the fire. David Lambert and his brother Henry from the West were downstairs. I was in the room before I saw them and was fairly nabbed. Cleared out at last.

Got through my Aeschylus and wrote a composition which kept me till one o'clock. On Southey, and containing a rowing up on the subject of his political tractorism that would have made Byron look tickled. . . .

April 18. . . . Bought a copy of Byron this afternoon. Byron, from what I've seen of his poetry, is not such an incarnate Satan as he's cracked up to be. I don't think his wit is generally enough appreciated. One scene in the beginning of "Don Juan" is glorious, and Donna Julia's scolding oratory brought tears of laughter out of my eyes. Pity that poem is contraband. Cut out a few "improprieties" and it's glorious.

April 19. Recited in Horace. State of things in Wall Street worse than ever. The whole city going to the devil in a pecuniary point of view.

April 21. . . . *Afternoon.* Wall Street. The blackness of darkness still hangeth over it. Failure on failure. . . .

April 22, SATURDAY. . . . Went up to Chittenden's . . . and with him to the Academy of Design. . . . There are two rooms open and the exhibition is infinitely superior to what it was last year. [Daniel] Huntington

of the University has several good pictures there and so has [Cornelius]
Ver Bryck. . . .[5]

Philip Hone has gone to the d—l, figuratively speaking, having lost
pretty much everything by his son, by Schenck & Co. (of Matteawan factory) and by some speculation moreover, all of which have eased him out
of not much below $200,000. What will become of his sons now? for they
have nothing to prop their conceit but their father's cash, and now that
that is gone, what will become of them?

April 25. . . . *Evening*, AΔΦ. Some of the best singing that an AΔΦ
meeting ever heard. . . . Had no idea of the beauty of German songs.
Heard one or two from the Wards, who are very Germanic in their
tastes. They were really beautiful—have more of the "real gift" of music
about them than a dozen appoggiaturing Italian airs. Italian music is like
filagree work compared with them, to my ear at least.

April 26. . . . Went to the Academy of Design. Saw Chittenden by
appointment, and Ver Bryck of the University. Some deuced good pictures there. There's a portrait of the daughter of Morse of New Haven, a
splendid painting, and according to Chittenden, a good likeness. There's
a portrait of [Arthur] Cleveland Coxe, full length, tolerable. A couple
of Yankee pictures by [William Sidney] Mount,[6] perfect, expression and
everything true to life; they are "Farmers Nooning," half asleep under a
haystack, one kicking his heels, and one boy half asleep himself tickling a
nigger with a straw, the nigger being sound asleep. It is insurpassable.

There is Prex's portrait [by Henry Inman] in all its glory, and a
portrait of Mrs. Duer just above it and two very handsome Spanish-
looking female portraits one on each side. Huntington's paintings are
both very good indeed. I like them as well as any there. There are some

[5] Daniel Huntington was just at the beginning of his long career as a painter of
portraits, landscapes, genre and historical pieces, which was to bring him to the
presidency of the National Academy of Design. Ver Bryck, Huntington's brother-in-
law, was an esteemed young painter of landscapes and allegories who died at the age
of thirty. They were residents, but not members, of New York University. The first
chancellor of that institution, Rev. James M. Mathews, having sunk all their funds in
an imposing marble Gothic building on Washington Square, the university was
obliged to turn most of it into a rooming-house, and Professor S. F. B. Morse was
the nucleus of a famous colony of artists and bohemians. A vivid picture of this group
is to be found in Theodore Winthrop's novel, *Cecil Dreeme* (1861).

[6] William Sidney Mount (1807–1868) of Setauket and Stony Brook, Long Island,
had progressed from sign-painting to portrait-painting and delightful scenes of
American genre, and became National Academician in 1832.

(and not a few) of the most abominable daubs that ever were hung at a tavern door. I'm surprised they should have ever got into the Academy.

April 27. . . . Matters very bad out of doors. Confidence annihilated, the whole community, big and little, traveling to ruin in a body. Strong fears entertained for the banks, and if they go, God only knows what the consequences will be. Ruin here, and on the other side of the Atlantic, and not only private ruin but political convulsion and revolution, I think, would follow such an event. My father looks and talks and evidently feels very gloomily on the subject. For myself, I feel very philosophic, on my own account. I firmly believe that in a moral point of view it would be all for my good to have to push my own way, entirely unsupported, and I think I am competent to do it. I have no very extravagant tastes that I know of, unless perhaps in the way of books, but I can't accuse myself of wasting money on dress or billiards, or horses or on sprees, or any other follies of that nature. . . .

As for the banks, they are losing from five to fifty thousand dollars daily in the way of specie and everyone seems to have the same fears, though almost everyone is afraid (and I'm glad to see it) to give them utterance. Where in the name of wonder is this all to end?

May 1, MONDAY. . . . Arthur Tappan has failed! Help him, ye niggers![7]

May 2. . . . Matters worse and worse in Wall Street as far as I can learn; everyone discouraged; prospect of universal ruin and general insolvency of the banks, which will be terrible indeed if it takes place. Workmen thrown out of employ by the hundred daily. Business at a stand; the coal mines in Pennsylvania stopped and no fuel in prospect for next winter—delightful prospects, these.

May 3. . . . Went up to the office at six. Fresh failures, Talbot Olyphant & Co., among them. So they go—smash, crash. Where in the name of wonder is there to be an end of it? Near two hundred and fifty failures thus far! Bush & Hillyer have stopped, but Giles [Hillyer] is as extensive as ever.

Locofoco meeting in the Park this morning—and such a meeting! It looked like a convention of loafers from all quarters of the world.

May 4. . . . Terrible news in Wall Street. [John] Fleming, late president of the Mechanics Bank, found dead in his bed this morning. Some say prussic acid; others (and the coroner's jury) say "mental excitement"

[7] Tappan was the great abolitionist and philanthropist, a founder of Oberlin College and lavish donor to Lane Theological Seminary, the American Tract Society, and anti-slavery causes.

and apoplexy. Anyhow there's a run on the bank—street crowded—more feeling of alarm and despondency in Wall Street than has appeared yet. The bank is to be kept open till five o'clock; politic move, that. Fears entertained that tomorrow the attack will be general on all the banks; if so they'll go down and then all the banks from Maine to Louisiana must follow—universal ruin. People talk ominously about rebellions and revolutions on this side of the Atlantic, and if they come on this side, political disturbances will soon break out on the other.

There are matters of no little weight depending on the doings of Wall Street for the next four or five days. I wish I were ten or fifteen years older.

Afternoon. Studied till five. Went to the office. Things look no better. If my father would only bear up a little under this state of things, it would be better for him. But he's not calculated for such times. They oppress his spirits and weaken his nerves.

May 5. . . . Something like twenty failures yesterday! . . .

May 6. . . . There's a run on the Dry Dock Bank and the other banks have refused to sustain it! At least they are to have a meeting this night to decide definitely on the subject and there's scarcely a chance of their decision being favorable. Uncle Benjamin [Strong], the president, is almost dead with excitement and misery. He is personally involved to his utter ruin, so at least my father fears. He called this evening and had a kind of private consultation with my father. There's scarce a chance of the bank's going on.

May 7, SUNDAY. St. Paul's this morning and afternoon. Regular tirade against the ladies from [the Rev. John Frederic] Schroeder this morning, very tremendous indeed, how their extravagance was ruinous and their frivolity detestable, and so forth. My father was at Uncle Benjamin's all the afternoon and evening. The bank will not open tomorrow morning. It is very hard for him, in his old age, and he feels it deeply.

May 8. Not feeling very thorough on Anthon's stuff, I got leave of absence from the president and went down to Wall Street. There was a crowd round the bank ready to recommence the run on it, eagerly waiting for ten o'clock to begin it. But the only notice the bank took of ten o'clock was to close its windows also, much to the consternation of the multitude. The crowd increased rapidly and I expected a fight, but they were at last dispersed by the Mayor [Aaron Clark], who made them a speech and told them that the other banks would redeem the Dry Dock bills. The mob dispersed incontinently for their cash; it was the best means that could have been thought of for scattering them. . . .

This affair of the Dry Dock Bank has gone better than I expected, but I fear it will prove the entering wedge to split up all Wall Street. The other banks are generally blamed for not sustaining it, and justly so.

Only imagine that [Uncle Benjamin] should actually have come to such a situation as to be afraid of personal insult if he go into the street! Yet so it is. What can be more dreadful? I can scarcely realize it—as kind and good-hearted and benevolent a man as ever breathed, his character unimpeached and unimpeachable, yet obliged to secure his house from attack and afraid of showing himself. These wretched banks and credit systems and paper wealth; they have done all this.

May 9. . . . As I expected, there's a run on all the banks, the depositors drawing out the specie as fast as the tellers can count it. They are in a dangerous situation most certainly, and if they break we shall have a revolution here. I don't see how they can help breaking; this run must increase every day and they can't possibly stand it more than three or four days longer.

Studied hard all afternoon. George Anthon called at seven and then I went up to Gurley's where those books are to be sold. Never saw books go so low. Bought about $25 worth of them for which I paid between $9 and $10. They sold for nothing, in fact.

Let me see what were my purchases. Browne's *Vulgar Errors*, a very fine folio edition; Hobbes, *Leviathan*, ditto, and moreover the *editio prin-ceps*; and Camden's *Annals*, also folio and all three in the very best of strong solid old binding I bought for $4 and one or two shillings. I have been asked $6 for a very inferior copy of the first alone! Quevedo, trans-lated by l'Estrange, I got for twenty-five cents, a little collection of Greek Epigrams for six cents! Prior's *Poems*, the earliest edition, a very magnif-icent folio, I got for $1.50! I had not the remotest idea of getting it, for I took it for granted it would bring $6 or $7, and even then very cheap. A very handsome quarto Catullus in fine binding and excellent type and paper I got for 95 cents, and lastly a folio Philostratus, Greek and Latin, for $3. Many other books that I would have given a good deal to have went in the same style and I could have laid out fifty dollars easily and got ten times the worth of my money, but I was afraid that in these hard times I should find it difficult to raise the wind for what I did get.

I understand that the banks are now in session to devise means of support. It will be of no use.

May 10.   Extensive news in this morning's paper. The banks (except three) have concluded to stop specie payment! ! ! Glory to the Old General! Glory to little Matty, second fiddler to the great Magician! Glory—ay, and double patent glory—to the experiment, the specie currency, and all the glorious humbugs who have inflicted them on us.

Commerce and speculation here have been spreading of late like a card house, story after story and ramification after ramification till the building towered up to the sky and people rolled up their eyes in amazement, but at last one corner gave way and every card that dropped brought down a dozen with it, and *sic transit gloria mundi*! How people have grown rich of late! I often wondered when I heard how Messrs. A. B. C. and D. were worth a million apiece and how people were now worth half a million at least before they could be called more than paupers. I often wondered where all the money had come from and how such a quantity of wealth had found its way into the country. But here's the result of it. No matter.

Went to college. The military out, in Park Place and in front of the City Hall. Wise precaution, that. McVickar losing terribly. Saw him this morning coming up from Wall Street. He looked half dead. . . .

Afternoon.   The Bank of America, Merchants, and Manhattan, which had resolved to try and hold out a little longer, have closed. Immense crowd and excitement in Wall Street, but the military prevent any disturbance.

Went to the Long Room for my purchases of last night. Glorious haul. George Anthon called this afternoon. Walked up a little way with him. Had a $3 bill in my pocket, paper money and a drug now, so went up to Appleton's and laid it out on an edition of Wordsworth.

May 11, THURSDAY. . . .   Went to Cooley's where the library of [President] Edward Dorr Griffin of Williamstown College was selling. Great many clergymen there, this being the season of anniversaries, and therefore probably selected for the sale. Books brought their full value. Bought nothing of any importance but a copy of Roscoe's *Lorenzo de Medici.*

May 23. . . .   Went with Backus to Stebbins's where I saw an eyeglass that fit my eye exactly; must have it, foppish and baboonish though it looks. . . .

We had our foot ball on the Green today and were just beginning to enjoy some good sport with it, when the old Praeses put his veto on it and knocked up our sport tetotaciously. Deuce take him.

1844

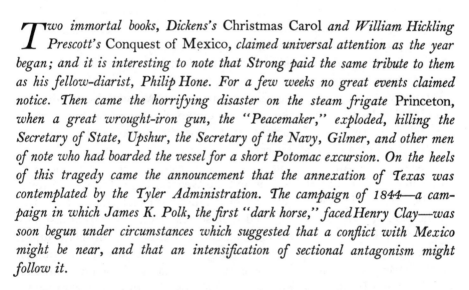

Two immortal books, Dickens's Christmas Carol *and William Hickling Prescott's* Conquest of Mexico, *claimed universal attention as the year began; and it is interesting to note that Strong paid the same tribute to them as his fellow-diarist, Philip Hone. For a few weeks no great events claimed notice. Then came the horrifying disaster on the steam frigate* Princeton, *when a great wrought-iron gun, the "Peacemaker," exploded, killing the Secretary of State, Upshur, the Secretary of the Navy, Gilmer, and other men of note who had boarded the vessel for a short Potomac excursion. On the heels of this tragedy came the announcement that the annexation of Texas was contemplated by the Tyler Administration. The campaign of 1844—a campaign in which James K. Polk, the first "dark horse," faced Henry Clay—was soon begun under circumstances which suggested that a conflict with Mexico might be near, and that an intensification of sectional antagonism might follow it.*

January 1, MONDAY. . . . There seems to have been an unusual turnout today; the shrines of Wall Street were left desolate for the ten thousand temples of womankind. . . . For my own part, I did no homage to Juggernaut. Went to the office as usual and worked away famously, wrote and whistled and chalked out a week's work for Deane. . . .

Read Prescott's *Mexico* this afternoon. Very clever book it is, and it can't help being among the most interesting of histories. There's a little striving after fine writing now and then visible that's rather a nuisance, but on the whole I like the book much.

January 5. Just got to the end of a visit from Pete. His chief and engrossing topic at present is the atrocious conduct of that ungentlemanly ruffian the Vicomte Bertrand at the soirée last Friday, where he had the cold-blooded villainy to call for a cigar and some brandy and adjourn to the kitchen to enjoy them. He's the Cesare Borgia of the nineteenth century. Well, if people will invite these fancy characters to their houses because they're counts, it serves them right to meet with a little cavalier treatment. People who look on their entertainers as low-bred republican *canaille* are apt to show it. . . .

January 6. . . . Read Kent assiduously on the delicate and inflammatory subjects of tenancy by the curtesy, reduction into possession of choses in action, and other collaterals of the *vinculum matrimonii,* exposing myself to that combustible course of reading mainly in reference to that amiable and amatory intestate Mr. Vyse, whose vicious old concubine is going to make herself as troublesome as she conveniently can and will probably try to make herself a dowager by brevet, prove herself a widow by prescription, or kind of post mortem Mrs. Vyse, connubialized *nunc pro tunc.*

January 21, SUNDAY. . . . Visit from George Anthon. I shouldn't be astonished if he were to wake up some cloudy morning and find himself multiplied by two, for I surmise that, like the immortal Panurge, he "hath a flea in his ear and desireth to be married." . . .

From what [Anthon] tells me, there's reason to fear that the next diocesan convention in September and the General Convention in October will be scenes of renewed attacks on Catholicism and church authority on the part of those who disgraced themselves at the ordination last July and of their backers and fellows in faction at the subsequent convention; and that they are organizing and straining every nerve to secure a triumph for their party at the next. Shame on them! —a party whose only common principles and bonds of union are personal hostility to their bishop and a fidgety antipathy to everything that implies submission, humility, and reverence. Many of its members are governed by very different motives, to be sure; but to think that clergymen should condescend to associate themselves as leaders of a "religious party" with such men as John Duer, a swindler to the extent of $200,000, and "Sir Pandarus Dogdraught" Webb, the unblushing and notorious author of more outrages on honesty, morality, and public decency than any man I at this moment remember. . . .

January 27. . . . Last night I found myself growing blue again, but the unexpected entry of Coryat's *Crudities,* arrived per the last steamer, set me all right again, and with that most comical book and with Dickens's clever (but mighty absurd) extravaganza, the *Prose Christmas Carol*, I've been very comfortable and strong of heart ever since. *Dissipantur inimici;* the blue devils are scattered, and I trust that I shall "live to my dying day in despite of mine enemies."

Delightful book is Mr. Dickens's. He's not dead yet, though *Martin Chuzzlewit* is flat and the *American Notes* a libel on this model republic of enlightened freemen.

February 2. . . . Read the article attributed to Dickens in the *Foreign Quarterly* on American poets, over which all the papers are going into severe paroxysms of patriotic wrath. Don't see why they can't keep cool. That we have no national school of poetry is very true, but it's our misfortune and not a fault, for we've no materials to make one out of. We've neither a legendary past nor a poetic present. Large mountains, extensive prairies, tall cataracts, long rivers, millions of dirty acres of every cosmographical character don't "constitute a state" for purposes of poetry; but "men, high-minded men" and their memories. . . . That except Halleck and Bryant and Longfellow, we've no poets is a fact that the *Foreign Quarterly* man seems to regard as a great critical discovery and which our independent press in general are calling heaven and earth to witness is a most foul and bare-faced slander begotten by British envy, but which I suppose to be a very undesirable matter. I think that in the course of time, when the various hostile and prosifying causes that are enumerated in the article in question (and certain others) have ceased to operate, we shall have our poets, and that we have as fair a chance of producing the next Dante or Milton or Shakespeare as any other nation, in the course of the coming five centuries, which is about a reasonable period to assign for the advent of the next of that stamp.

February 15. . . . Have been reading with delight and astonishment the argument in the Supreme Court of the United States in the Girard will case delivered by—(silence for two minutes and a half, followed by a flourish of trumpets and three claps of thunder in G-sharp)—DANIEL WEBSTER!

How long is it since I've seen or heard anything from any one of our quacking flock of "statesmen" and politicians that I cared to read again or to remember? This, I do believe, is the first, and though the immortal Daniel is said to be slightly heathenish in private life, and though it is but a forensic argument after all, it gives one hopes of the republic to find a man wide awake to his political reputation and thoroughly conversant with the thoughts and feelings of the Sovereign *Demos*, the dispenser or withholder of his highest earthly good, venturing to leave legal technicalities and deal with a subject in the light of realities and truths that I thought were most odious to the taste of the free and enlightened masses.

How it must have bored Horace Binney to hear truths that he doubtless recognizes from the bottom of his heart, hurled at him to the demolition of the argument he'd been building up, by authorities ingeniously dovetailed, and his own convictions diligently smothered into silence.

Likewise I have been reading Macaulay. He's a clever humbug—a fluent, plausible, elegant, perspicuous sophister. His review of Gladstone is in some points unmatchable. Whether his profound ignorance of the views of Gladstone's friends on church matters as exhibited in his confident crowing over the state arguments that would disgrace a boy of fifteen who had a clear view of the battleground, or his presumption in daring to tamper in such a spirit of meddling vanity with the awful truths or diabolical falsehoods (whichever they are) that his subject embraces be the more stupendous is a full, great, doubtful question. I'd like to ask the man, just for my own satisfaction, what he means by being such a lying idiot. Such was the man whom Rabelais (or somebody else) didn't wish to hear repeat the Creed, lest it should weaken his faith. . . .

February 17, SATURDAY. Croton water bathing pipes just burst, to the consternation of the household who are engaged in solemn consultation somewhere in the basement, up to their necks in water, I suppose. It hasn't flooded my premises, though I think the fatal breach is somewhere inside the wall thereof, which will probably lead to the destruction of my domestic peace and literary seclusion by an irruption of hod-carrying, plaster-mongering Goths, vandals, and Mongrel Tartars. Shall I sue the architect, the plumber, or the Mayor, Aldermen & Co.? . . .

February 22, THURSDAY. Today the nation celebrates "Pa's birthday" —a fact of which I received very early notice, having been waked by the brazen uproar of a vigorous military band under the window, out of my precious morning nap, doubly precious from my having sat up near all night to despatch an urgent injunction bill. . . .

February 28, WEDNESDAY. . . . Saw Fowler this morning and M. M. Backus this afternoon—both well and in good health and sound condition —no expression of "hang you, you think yourself better than me, but you a'nt a bit of it" about either of 'em, which is a gratifying thing. It's very hard that a man can't lead an eremitical life and decline making a pig of himself at claret and whiskey punch parties and a donkey of himself by philandering with his friends' wives without being set down for a super-fine piece of stolid self-conceit that thinks himself too good to associate with other people.

February 29, THURSDAY. News this afternoon of a frightful occur-rence at Washington: the explosion of one of the *Princeton's* Paixhans, killing Upshur, Secretary of State; Gilmer, Secretary of the Navy; Virgil Maxcy, Solicitor of the Treasury; Commodore Kennon, a high officer in Gilmer's department; David Gardiner of Southampton, and others of less note. I suppose there's scarcely an instance on record, of late times at least, in which so many high official characters under one government have been destroyed by the same blow. James II of Scotland died alone. And after all the brag that's been made touching those guns, which were lallied about as if they were sufficient alone to defend the nation against the English navy, it's a most dismal issue for the invention. Col. [Thomas Hart] Benton and [Commodore Robert Field] Stockton were both badly hurt.

March 1, FRIDAY. . . . It was this atmosphere of laziness that set me to reading Tennyson, I suppose; but apart from that, he's on the whole a favorite of mine, and if they'd publish an edition of his poems expurgated of their spooneyism, affectation, and grimace, I'd import a large paper copy with india proofs (for a collection of "dainty" little vignettes would be indispensable to make it a complete thing) and have it bound in very light green morocco and it would be quite a nice little pet book. In fact, of the English *Di Minorum Gentium* he's about the cleverest. . . .

March 16. . . . The Vestry of Trinity Church have concluded to com-plete the tower, to put on the spire, I mean, at once. So saith gossip rumor. *Vivat* said vestry.

The College Green is to be cut up into city lots on College Place and Murray Street, on some authority. The trustees should be bound over to keep the peace without delay. Goths are they, and vandals and a horde, or board, of barbarous blackguards. If they think of cutting down those trees, I'll assassinate 'em in detail or blow up the president's room at their next meeting.

March 19. . . . United States stocks are *down* "full fathom five" on the strength of the rumors touching the Texas project. No wonder. If consummated it may probably lead to war, and if its opponents are dis-posed to make trouble, to a Dissolution of the Union. For that it's an utterly unconstitutional measure, there can be no doubt. It is not an exercise of the treaty-making power and cannot lawfully be done by that power—nor is it within the compass of both Houses; it can be legitimately accomplished only by direct action of the People, from whom the powers of those bodies and the Constitution under which they act, are derived. To say that President and Senate have power to *incorporate us with another nation,* because they've power to make binding treaties with foreign powers, is to say that one member of a partnership can add a dozen members to it, of his own free will, *because* he can bind the firm by signing notes and making bargains. It's an act of Sovereignty of the most fundamental character, which in a Popular government that has not expressly clothed its Representatives with the power, can be done only by the fundamental authority, the People itself.

April 10, WEDNESDAY. Hurrah for the Natives! They've elected Harper by a majority of 4,000 and stand two to one in the Common Council. Such a revolution is unheard of; the Locos are perfectly stunned and the Whigs not much better off. Such a blow hasn't fallen on the Hibernian race since the days of Earl Strongbow or Boynewake at the latest.

I'm just from the Native Headquarters, the Aboriginal gathering place. Not an exile of Erin ventures to show his nose in the neighborhood and the row and the bonfires and the popping of small arms of every denomination and the incessant whizz of rockets from the roof of "Military Hall" are altogether imposing and tremendous. . . .

April 24. . . . Got in a fine copy of Holinshed (first edition) this afternoon. I've strong hopes of Purchas's *Pilgrims* through Bartlett & Welford, and then I shall consider myself to have laid a very fair foundation for an Englysshe Librarie.

As for the bibliomaniacal introuvables of Caxton, DeWorde, Pynson & Co., it's idle to think of acquiring anything more than a specimen or so of each of them, and not even that unless chance throws cheap copies in one's way. The technical bibliomania, the pure, abstract *Delirium Dibdinianum* that rages after those things simply as book varieties, independently of any interest attaching to the edition, I never was smitten with to any great extent, and if I had Earl Spencer's fortune I never should have got together Earl Spencer's library. . . .

Yet are some Caxtons and Pynsons genuine black diamonds that I'd bleed freely for. The *Morte d'Arthur* for example, Pynson's Froissart (mine's imperfect) and divers other stars that twinkle far beyond human reach in the profoundest depths of the book firmament, I should enjoy greatly. But a sale catalogue of these books with the prices is generally a mere monument of folly, for there's nothing to recommend nine-tenths of them but the childish merit of rarity. They are rare now because they were always worthless. Rarity adds to the value of what's good, but alone it's nothing.

Went to the anti-annexation of Texas meeting tonight at the Tabernacle. It was very full and much more interesting than I'd expected to find it. Albert Gallatin presided and spoke with more force and more physical strength than one would have anticipated from his appearance, for he's very old and looks very infirm. Sedgwick and Field also spoke, neither of them with any very startling degree of eloquence. The principal source of fun arose from Mike Walsh and a tail of about twenty who had come down express to make a row and did all they could to provoke one. They were in a decided minority, however, and their impertinent blackguardism only made the meeting applaud the louder and feel the more magnanimously hostile to Tyler Texas. . . .

April 25, THURSDAY. . . . Started for the Greenwood Cemetery with Templeton at four o'clock and walked there, traversed the grounds, and walked back by half-past seven, a pretty fair afternoon's walk, and I confess to a pair of feet a little exacerbated and one or two extensor muscles a little sore. Beautiful place it is, and they're hard at work improving it, putting it all in good order. When it's brought to the same high state of civilization with Mt. Auburn, it will far surpass it. I'm glad to see that what Pugin calls the "revived Pagan style" doesn't prevail very extensively there. I only noticed one pair of inverted torches and not a single urn or flying globe or like silliness, only not profane because it may be supposed to be unmeaning. This recurrence to heathen taste and antichristian usage in architecture or art of any sort is or should be unreal and unnatural everywhere, but in such a place as that, it's disgusting. But when churches are modelled after Parthenons—even to the bulls' heads and sacrificial emblems on the frieze—of course it's not wonderful that people will cover their tombs with the symbols of Paganism.

I used to be very indignant at any assaults on classical literature, and to be sure one may well be so at the pseudo-utilitarianism that generally prompts the attack. Anything that may be said about waste of time, useful knowledge, greater advantage of familiarity with living languages and all that, is sheer twaddle. But whether their cultivation and study may not be objected to on other grounds entirely, whether it's not an utterly false basis for education that they supply, whether it's not wrong to poison the minds of boys of fourteen with Ovid and Lucretius, whether much of the degeneration of Christendom is not traceable to the revival of their study, are questions that it might be worth while for people to think about.

April 27. If John Tyler originated this Texas project, he's a more sagacious shepherd of the people than I gave him credit for being. There's no chance of the annexation's being effected just now, I think, but it may well bring about a general moving of the waters that will upset all calculations as to the coming election and knock all the existing "interests" into hotchpot. I give the immortal John a chance of making himself conspicuously absurd for another four years. Stranger things have happened since Adams's time than even the reëlection of John Tyler would be.

After all, while Mississippi and Pennsylvania and certain other sovereign states continue to be stars in our galaxy, I don't know that we need turn the cold shoulder to Texas—or New South Wales (*that's* colonized with a strong infusion of Anglo-Saxon blood and there's some of the superlative ichor of Anglo-Americanism there, too).

A general act of amnesty to all our expatriated citizens in the new member of the Confederacy would remove one serious obstacle.

The Treaty now before the Senate was published this afternoon. If I were a senator, as unfortunately for the republic I'm not, I should insist on the following supplementary or additional clauses:

I. The Republic of Texas shall, at its own proper cost and charges, procure to be printed a sufficient number of copies of *The Whole Duty of Man*, Paley's *Moral Philosophy Abridged*, *God's Revenge against Murder and Adulterie*, *Fichte on the Distinction between the Ego and the Non Ego*, as applicable to questions of Meum and Tuum, and some approved practical treatise on the law of larceny, swindling, embezzlement, and the picking of pockets, and shall cause the same to be distributed gratuitously among its citizens within six months from the ratification of his treaty.

II. The Republic of Texas shall, within the same period, enact a statute making assassination with the bowie knife or repeating pistol to be felony, and no person shall receive from the Executive of said Republic more than fifteen pardons for offences against such statute, but on the sixteenth conviction for violation thereof, shall be punished by fine or imprisonment in the discretion of the jury by whom he is convicted.

III. The Republic of Texas shall build her own penitentiaries, tread-mills, and other penal establishments.

IV. The Republic of Texas shall not be entitled to send any Representative to Congress who shall have become a citizen thereof after having been sentenced to be hanged in any state or territory of the Union.

With those improvements and one or two more, the Treaty would
deserve a more respectful consideration unquestionably than it is now
entitled to. . . .

April 30. Splendid night it is, clear, cool and everything glowing
in a flood of moonlight. Walked uptown by irresistible necessity. No one
can stay in the house under such circumstances. Went to the Academy of
Design this afternoon. This year's exhibition is but a shabby affair; more
than the usual number of libellous portraits, and a decided preponderance
of the signpost school of art in the other pictures. There are two or three
good landscapes by [Asher Brown] Durand and a very nice portrait by
[Henry Peters] Gray of Mrs. Kem[ble] Paulding, I believe, and at this
moment I can think of nothing else that's worth walking up that intermi-
nable flight of stairs for.

That reminds me that the Generalissimo of No. *56* is going to have
his portrait taken by Mount, the artist selected for the sake of Suffolk
County, I s'pose, for I don't think much of his powers in that line.[1] Gray's
the best portrait painter we have. It should be a grand historical piece
representing an examination on Graham's *Practice* with a bevy of future
chief justices and attorney generals, *videlicet* our hopeful students, as
examinees, including that last most precious addition to our numbers
Mr. somebody Phillips[2] (son of the parson's) who is in sober sadness the
most unadulterated snob I ever met: a perfect "artist's dream" of snobbi-
ness, snobblaginous in all his details of blackguardism. I've known blackguards before that were perhaps equally hircine and porcine, but none
that could stand comparison with him for a moment as to the *in toto
attingunt* of the combined elements of blackguard, spooney and snob.

May 1. Fine weather, to the great comfort of the locomotive public.
Never knew the city in such a chaotic state. Every other house seems to
be disgorging itself into the street; all the sidewalks are lumbered with
bureaus and bedsteads to the utter destruction of their character as thor-
oughfares, and all the space between the sidewalks is occupied by long
processions of carts and wagons and vehicles omnigenous laden with

[1] George Washington Strong's portrait by William Sidney Mount was exhibited
the following spring at the National Academy of Design.

[2] This seems to have been John Mason Phillips (New York University 1841),
son of Rev. William Wirt Phillips, D.D., minister of the First Presbyterian Church.

perilous piles of moveables. We certainly haven't advanced as a people beyond the nomadic or migratory stage of civilization analogous to that of the pastoral cow feeders of the Tartar Steppes.

May 7, TUESDAY. . . . Just back from another visit to the Academy of Design. That man [Francis William] Edmonds is certainly a most clever painter. Durand's pictures improve on acquaintance; so do Montgomery Livingston's landscapes. The rest is stuff.

> Hey-hey - de country's risin'
> For Henry Clay and Frelinghuysen.

Good nomination was Frelinghuysen's, astute decidedly; Clay, being by the admission of his friends a good deal of a runner, will run none the worse for having a deacon to ride him. But the Democracy is in a most "unhandsome fix." Their convention meets on the 27th, and if Van Buren's science in wire-pulling and managing the mechanism of the party procures his nomination, the game's up for them, and barring accidents, Clay's as sure of dining in the White House on the 4th of March in the year of grace 1845 as ever he was of doing his man at brag or poker. If they select any other champion, it's a matter of hopeless uncertainty to calculate the chance. Yet whom can they bring out except Van Buren, but at the certain sacrifice of the electoral vote of New York? In short, their game's very extensively disorganized, their pieces don't support each other, and their only salvation will be in sacrificing a castle and risking everything else in some desperate demonstration from an unexpected quarter. . . .

Well, I don't think I shall allow myself to suffer much anxiety or distress of mind, whatever the issue may be.

> In the year Eighteen hundred
> And forty and four
> There are darkies as many
> As ever before.

May 8. . . . Great row in Philadelphia. Queer city that, the most anarchical metropolis on this side the Atlantic. The military won't do anything because they're afraid they won't get their pay; the fire department won't do anything because the military won't help them; and as for the police, if one of them gets a rap in the row he's trying to quiet he treats it as a personal matter and throws himself into the arms of the party that's opposed to his man, and lays about him like a trump. . . .

This breeze was Natives *vs.* Hibernians, and the latter had the best of it: seem to have been decidedly gamey, and to have shot down their men with as little compunction as a sportsman lets slap into a mob of black-birds, and to have been desperate and sanguinary and savage enough to do anything. I would not live in such a hornets' nest as the City of Brotherly Love appears to be. One can't look out of his window without the risk of being knocked down by some stray bullet or other that was intended for somebody else entirely, or fired on speculation, without meaning anything against anybody in particular.

This'll be a great thing for the Natives, strengthen their hands amazingly if judiciously used. It wouldn't be wonderful if it should lead to some flare-up here. There's latent irritation enough which won't be much mollified by the exaggerated versions of this business, bad enough at best and in matter of fact, but magnified into a second St. Bartholomew's on both sides that will be recounted and expatiated on in every alley and bar-room and ganglion of rowdyism from Madison Square to the Battery. . . .

May 11, SATURDAY. . . . The City of Brotherly Love is reduced to a state of quietude by dint of hostile demonstrations from the Governor of the Commonwealth and eloquent appeals to the public by the Fathers of the City. Such a pitiable scene of feebleness, irresolution, and old-grannyism in general as the civic potentates of that place have enacted for the amusement of posterity isn't to be found anywhere, unless in Dickens's description of the No-Popery riots in *Barnaby Rudge*. Captain Fairlamb and General Cadwalader must settle it between 'em which is to succeed Henry Clay, for the country never can forget the services of those great military chieftains. The charges of the "City Troop," first up the street, second down the street, and third off the ground entirely, form a combination of manoeuvres that outsaxify Saxe's wildest "reverie." An amusing commentary on the whole affair is the resolution adopted by acclamation at the grand meeting held after all the damage had been done, that the majority of rioters consisted of small boys too young to know how naughty they were; and that all parents and guardians were requested to keep said small boys at home, send 'em early to bed or hide their stockings. Doubtless it was a sensible practical person that moved that resolution.

It's some consolation that Philadelphia is worse governed than we are. Some apprehensions are entertained of a flare-up among our own virtuous and independent masses, but every precaution's taken to put a stop to any such proceeding at a very early stage and I don't think our shepherds of the people would think it discreet to wait for an opinion in

writing from the Attorney General before they authorized the military to
fire on the mob. . . .

May 12, SUNDAY. . . . Walked uptown tonight. Looked at Grace
Church. They won't consecrate it this fall, I think, from present appearances. [James] Renwick [Jr.] is a clever fellow and his church looks very
well on paper, but I fear the practical embodiment of his conception, the
church itself, will be a botch. He's hampered for money and the plan's an
ambitious one and the effect of the structure will probably be that of an
·attempt at the sumptuous on slender means, which is always undignified,
and generally unsuccessful. . . .

May 13. Went through Trinity Church this morning with George
Anthon. The spire is commenced and rising rapidly; that steam engine
shows its true value now that the stone has to rise 140 feet. From the
wilderness of cunningly carved stones that lie about I infer that the spire
is to be more ornate than was at first designed, as an innovation which
will be generally conceded to be an improvement. The tower has settled
to a considerable extent and produced some ugly starting, springing and
gaping about the south front window, but Upjohn's a man of unlimited
resources, and he'll remedy that somehow; if he has to shove up the
tower again with jackscrews. The stained glass so far as it's yet visible
does very well for native American manufacture.

May 19, SUNDAY. Feel today neither particularly happy nor particularly unhappy, I can't certainly determine which, for did I not last
night hear the Symphony in C minor by one Ludwig Van Beethoven,
No. 67, played *ad unguem* by the Philharmonic? Haven't I been fairly
tingling all day with the remembrance of that most glorious piece of
instrumental music extant, the second movement? (Twice played, by the
by, the first *encored* symphony on record.) . . .

The first movement, with its abrupt opening, and the complicated
entanglement of harmonies that makes up the rest of it, is not very satisfactory or intelligible to me as a whole, though it abounds in exquisite
little scraps of melody that come sparkling out like stars through a cloudy
sky, but the second and fourth movements (the third a'nt much) are
enough to put Beethoven at the head of all instrumental composers if he'd
never written another note. They're just one succession of points and
yet each is as perfect, each seems as if it had been a single effort of the
composer's genius that gave it birth. There's nothing in them like the
mere aggregation of distinct though original and beautiful passages that
one notes in Rossini's music, for example.

The introduction of the subject of the second movement by the violins and its instantaneous ringing repetition by the full orchestra is matchless; so is the stately opening of the fourth. But it's idle to write about it. If I were asked for an explanation of the symphony, and to tell the exact train of thought that produced it, I should be at a loss. The first general purport of its story would seem to be, for the first movement, weariness, sorrow, and perplexity; energies preying on themselves for the want of an object for life and the disheartening sense that earnest minds feel at a certain stage of their development of the worthlessness of all that they're doing and living for, and their need of something that may wake them up to real and energetic existence. Then, in the second, is the glorious birth of the new principle of love, ambition, or some yet higher element and its exulting and triumphant progress in freshness and vigor, on to the victory and full function of the end and aim which seems to be the subject of the finale. . . .

Between the second and third parts Vieuxtemps made his appearance and played variations on themes from *Norma*, on one string with the orchestra, about the most satisfactory piece of violin music I ever heard. "Casta Diva" in particular was most exquisitely played, and with a delicacy and expression beyond what I ever heard the voice give it.

The second part was Mendelssohn's *Midsummer Night's Dream*, beautiful thing it is; some trash or other by Vattelina, and Weber's *Ruler of the Spirits*, a very effective overture. . . .

May 27. . . . I find that Mrs. Lewis L.'s anticipated offspring has flashed in the pan and proved a total failure likewise. The story is that some castoff Unfortunate Female of that most unfortunate male, her husband, recently made her appearance with much clamor and obstreperousness and several small children at the residence of that gentleman during his absence and threw an entirely new light on his ante-nuptial habits and practices, new to his wife at least, and that the vexation and annoyance thereby occasioned brought to pass the result aforesaid. Isn't it execrable? Yet if pretty, amiable, intelligent, and accomplished women will condescend to unite themselves with men who've led such lives as common fame and his own hard face give Mr. L. the credit of having led, they've not much to complain about; they must make the most they can of the fashionable name and the foreign graces that formed the consideration of the contract. . . .

Wonder how the grand Democratic Palaver is getting on at Baltimore about this time. They've a pretty tangled skein to wind and I suppose the consumption of cobblers and brandy smashes, loud lying and hard swearing throughout today has kept the dealers in those commodities pretty actively employed. On the whole, two to one on "the little red fox of the Empire State." He's about as available as anybody they can put forward, and if the Texas plot be really knocked on the head, which blessed consummation of the scheme there's reason to hope has taken place, the sole shadow of a chance of nomination that John Tyler ever possessed is gone. Don't much care; "country's risin', Clay and Freling-huysen, quite surprizin', give the Loco pisen," and so on. It don't matter much which Loco is selected to be made a martyr of. . . .

Whether the jacobinical spirit and the antipathy to law and order and the overthrow of everything worth preserving, which is the un-conscious principle of the one party, and the temper and final result of its unchecked development, be worse than commercial, speculating, bank-swindling, money-worshipping *primum mobile* of the other is a question.

Certainly since the downfall of Federalism there has been no con-servative party in the country which has ventured to avow any higher aim than the cultivation of tariffs and credit systems, trade and manu-factures.

Its unchecked development would make us a commercial aristocracy which is mean enough everywhere, but here 'twould be a fluctuating mushroom aristocracy and the meanest the world has seen yet.

May 28, TUESDAY. . . . Came across a bibliographical black swan this morning: a copy of [Daniel] Horsmanden's quarto concerning the nigger plot of [1741–1742], fine copy, too, and uncut (though I never could appreciate the importance of that), the only copy of the book I ever saw or heard of. Gave orders to have it bought in; hope I may get it.[3]

Started after dinner with Templeton for a walk to Weehawken. . . . Hoboken's a good deal cut up and built up, but pleasant still; pity it's haunted by such a gang as frequent it; its groves are sacred to Venus and I saw scarce any one there but snobs and their strumpets. Walked on in momentary expectation of stumbling on some couple engaged in what Schroeder would call "the commission of gross vulgarity."

Crossed the dyke and walked out to Weehawken. The "William Tell

[3] This book, *A Journal of the Proceedings in the Detection of the Conspiracy founded by some White People, in Conjunction with Negro and other Slaves, for Burning the City of New York in America, and Murdering the Inhabitants. . .* (New-York, 1744), fetched $300 at the sale of Strong's library in 1878, the highest price paid for any book in the sale.

Cottage" of Mary Rogers memorability is shut up and deserted, probably found to be haunted.

Nothing decisive yet from the Baltimore council fires. Van Buren stock seems rather down and the "Jack Casses," as the adherents of that very great statesman are disrespectfully termed, are understood to be full of hope and hilarity. *He'd* be beat most signally if nominated; his Louis Philippe toadying would kill him dead the first month of the campaign.

May 30. News arrived this morning of the issue of the Baltimore Convention, the result of the agonizing throes of the last three days. For President, James K. Polk and for Vice-President, Silas Wright.

There's no telling what a day may bring forth, *a fortiori*, no telling what the chance and change of the next six months may result in, but I can't think that the nominees will get much good of their nomination.

Poor Martin Van Buren! It's his final exit from the busy scene of politics, there's no doubt of that. He's laid on the shelf for good. The tidings went northward by this evening's boat and they'll reach the cabbage gardens of Kinderhook in an hour or two. Doubtless Matty received a dismal and ominous letter from Ben Butler last night, telling him to keep up his spirits, but expatiating largely on the ingratitude of party men, the demoralization of the Democracy and the great blessings of private life and rustical retirement: and now he's waiting for the decisive news that the night boat will bring in a fever of fidgety desperation.

June 3. . . . Item: Silas Wright's backed out of his proffered Vice-Presidency, disgracefully declining the crown of martyrdom, and [George Mifflin] Dallas of Pennsylvania is the chosen victim. . . . Item: Polk and Dallas are a severe dose for the Northern Democracy; if Van Buren would consent to run, as he certainly won't, I believe they'd be tempted to make a schism in the party.

June 16. . . . Bad business, this, in the Diocese of Pennsylvania. They say that in the Philadelphia bar-rooms some new modifications of mint julep have become popular under the name of "Onderdonks." I do believe that Philadelphia lies in some special manner under the dominion of the "Prince of the Power of the Air." Everything goes wrong there: insolvent government, swindling banks, burnt churches, drinking bishops, rapes, murders, and riots all seem to flourish and abound there as in their appointed abiding place and own natural home. As for the Bishop [Henry Ustick Onderdonk], if the reports that are current here as to certain eccentricities of his be true, he'll unquestionably be refused permission to resign and his career will be terminated by a degradation, and probably that is the best course for the church that can be adopted. . . .[4]

June 17. . . . Looked in at Trinity Church. They're pushing it fast; possibly next Easter may see it consecrated, but I profoundly doubt the probability thereof. . . .

The present taste for . . . pointed architecture and the other increasing "retrograde" tendencies in art and literature that one sees the signs of every day may be very important matters if they're not a mere temporary caprice of popular taste and one of the phases of fashion. But even if they are so, and their result should be but trifling, it must be good so far as it goes. All things are bound together, and the study of medieval art must tend, at least, to revive some of the medieval habits, thoughts, feelings, and principles, an infusion of which the age is sadly in want of. . . .

June 23, SUNDAY. . . . What I've read and thought on the subject of late has led me to the conclusion that the present Catholic movement in England and in this country cannot produce any permanent and important changes except as a transition state towards the higher positions which alone can produce a lasting Reformation, as preparing the way for a movement the first principle of which shall be the abjuration and utter defiance of everything that appertains to enlightened Protestantism, without apology or circumlocution. Catholicism can't be built up again without offending the prejudices of the nineteenth century, and it's idle to think of a compromise.

June 26. . . . I've just heard a rumor that infatuated old John Tyler was married today to one of those large, fleshy Miss Gardiners of Gardiner's Island. Poor, unfortunate, deluded old jackass; it's positively painful to think of his situation, and the trials that lie before him. . . .

June 29. . . . Went up to Pike's this morning with Anthon to look at some electromagnetic apparatus of his that's reported to be sovereign for sick headache, and we shocked ourselves and sent currents of the mysterious fluid marching and countermarching through our several systems with most scientific gravity and perseverance. It's certainly a very nice and ingenious contrivance, but whether a sick headache will bow before it is a doubtful question. It may have been fancy, or the fine weather, or

[4] The Right Reverend Henry Ustick Onderdonk (1789–1858), A.B., A.M., M.D. and D.D. (Columbia), M.R.C.S. (London), Bishop of Pennsylvania, wrote to the House of Bishops in 1844 confessing his habitual use of intoxicating liquor and offering his resignation, which was accepted. They also voted to suspend him from the ministry, but two years before his death the suspension was removed.

unaccustomed eupepsia, but I certainly felt extremely fresh, vigorous, and bright after my dose of magnetism.

Had a call from [Mancer Mark] Backus this afternoon: he's in better health and spirits than I've seen him for some time, all which he devoutly attributes to matrimony, and like most foxes who've lost their tails, he counselled me with much earnestness to do likewise and lose no time about it. It seems he's not studying for the "ministry" at all, but is an associate editor of a certain weekly organ of some schism or other called *The Evangelist*, the critical and literary department whereof would seem to be entrusted to his special care and conduct. To such base uses may we come at last. . . .

Went to Pike's again, with Backus, and bought one of his machines and have just been galvanizing all my finger joints nearly out of their sockets. It's a most mysterious effect to come of such slight means.

June 30, SUNDAY. Heard a certain Mr. Southard[5] this morning, good sermon of its kind, but I'm not partial to the sentimental style of pulpit oratory that always has such an effect on the soft-hearted tailor that sits on the other side of the aisle, and always makes him to blow his sympathetic nose so fervently. It's an especially unhappy way for a young clergyman to get into; they can raise such a fuss among all the young women and old women so easily that they're in danger of adopting it to the exclusion of all manlier tones: and they get so petted and coddled up for it that unless some signal good fortune save them, they're apt to sink into clerical coxcombs—"pet parsons"—and they are without any exception the most miserable creatures on earth. Heard Wainwright this afternoon, and took a long walk tonight. The air is like October's.

Tried the galvanic apparatus again this afternoon, for the premonitories of a headache. The headache took itself off, but whether I'm to thank Pike for the deliverance must be resolved by future experiments. If it can vanquish a well-developed assault of that my fiercest and fellest temporal foe, I'll present Pike with a gold snuff box and a duly authenticated certificate of the most surprising cure on record.

July 2, TUESDAY. Walked uptown tonight. Stopped at the Society

[5] The Rev. Samuel Lewis Southard, Jr. (Princeton 1836), who erupts later into this diary, was the son of the Hon. Samuel Lewis Southard (Princeton 1804), sometime U.S. Senator, Secretary of the Navy, and Governor of New Jersey. The son went to the General Theological Seminary, was ordained to the Episcopal ministry in 1842 and became rector of Calvary Church in New York. After the big row there in 1849, he was located in Boonville, Missouri. Deposed from the ministry in October, 1859, he died December 7, 1859, at St. Louis from an overdose of chloroform.

Library. Read the July number of *Brownson's Quarterly Review*. He's a strange being, but he has two most uncommon characteristics that redeem a multitude of sins. He has a proper estimate of the relative values of Truth and Trade, and furthermore, when he's satisfied he's in a false position he's not ashamed to confess it and seek a better. I shall certainly subscribe to his *Review*.

In this number he avows himself to be (for the present) a Roman Catholic and seems to have satisfied himself (for the present) that the Anglican Church forfeited its claim to the title of Catholic at the Reformation.

July 6. . . . Isaac Greene Pearson is the architect of Phillips's new schism-shop in the Fifth Avenue [the First Presbyterian Church], and from what I can hear of the plan, it's going to prove an abortion, and just such a travesty of a Gothic church as one might expect from a bankrupt Unitarian amateur builder of meeting houses.

Another rumpus in the Protestant city of Philadelphia. Extras out, and "at the time our reporter left" the church of St. Philip Neri beleaguered by a mob of Natives. If the people facetiously called "authorities" of that city permit a recurrence of the late outrages without shooting down at least a hecatomb, they richly deserve to be hanged by some special act of *ex post facto* legislation. . . .

July 8. . . . Joe Smith's killed. Wonder whether that'll kill Mormonism; probably not. Jolly fight in Philadelphia, civil war raging, mob pelting the military, not with paving stones, but with grapeshot and scrap-iron out of ten-pounders; the state of things in that city is growing worse and worse every day. I shan't be caught voting a "Native" ticket again in a hurry.

July 14, SUNDAY. A most stewing night this is; if I were not a counsellor I would be a salamander.

Attorneys *are* poor creatures, a most inferior order of creation. What a snob I've been for the last three years without knowing it!

¶ Will be published shortly a New Work of great interest entitled: "Incidents of Travel, by a Counsellor at Law." In three vols. 8vo. price six cents.

CONTENTS: *Chap. I*, TUESDAY. Steamboat *Troy*. Reflections on the progress of science and the march of steam. Leave at seven. Gardiner Howland, Ogden Hoffman, his friend Dorr, and Clarence Livingston, nice party. . . . Beautiful run up the river. Overslaugh in a disgusting state.

Proposal to erect a statue of John Tyler in the act of writing his last veto, on the shallowest spot. Albany: Congress Hall. Noyes. Bad supper of doughy bread and a muddy fluid humorously termed coffee. Adjourned to the piazza for a comfortable smoke, and retired after being composed into a proper frame therefor by two several orations delivered by me.

Chap. II, WEDNESDAY. Journey through the great desert from Albany to Schenectady, thence to Utica. Climate torrid exceedingly. Weather showery. Railroad in every respect shockingly bad. Utica at two; feeding time; piggish character of the car dinner. Joe Blunt and Clinton DeWitt the lovely representatives of the New York bar. John Astor,[6] F. Cunningham and Emott of Poughkeepsie. Dalliba and Dick Varick.

Call on Mr. Clerk Denio and take an evening saunter with Dorr and Clarence Livingston out to "Deerfield."

Chap. III, THURSDAY. . . . At court. Examiners appointed: Noxon, Hand of somewhere, and Benton of Little Falls. Spend the day in lounging and loafing. Attorneys examined after dinner . . . Listened to it for an hour; pretty sharp work—too minute entirely. Forty-nine, all admitted. Evening. . . . Examination [for counsellor] commenced at eight in one of Baggs's parlors: class of twenty-five. Hand and Benton both examined rather lightly; one asked me some questions about uses, the other about trespass on the case—all very smooth and I thought that was the end of the matter, but it was only the beginning, for old Noxon took up the thumbscrews and I quaked with exceeding fear when I found what kind of an ordeal he was going to make us pass. His way of doing things was severe and searching enough. My share of his attention related chiefly to pleading and evidence and though I answered one or two questions somewhat at random, I believe I got through fairly enough, so I judge at least from the remarks that he and Comstock and somebody else were reported to me to have made touching and concerning my distinguished self and my profound acquirements.

Got through a little before twelve and went to bed with a headache. Friday. . . . Went to court. Everybody admitted. Took a pretty warm walk a couple of miles out on the railroad and then along the beautiful Mohawk.

[6] John Jacob Astor (1822–1890), the son of William Backhouse Astor, was educated at Columbia (A.B. 1839), Göttingen and the Harvard Law School, and practised law briefly, but his lifework was the management of family real estate in New York. For a decade he was a Columbia trustee whom Strong rated highly.

October 16, WEDNESDAY. . . . Looked in upon Trinity Church this morning. They've got up the first flying buttress on the south side of the chancel, very light and pretty it is; also, I observe indications of cleaning up dirt and carting off rubbish that give hopeful promise of the commencement of paving and finishing inside. The church looks like Westminster Abbey, or the Cathedral of Cologne completed on three times the original scale after the churches I've been looking upon in Philadelphia, the city of ugly buildings *par excellence*. There's not a church in it but's downright *hideous*.

October 19. . . . Whether this attack that's now going on in Philadelphia against our diocesan [Bishop Benjamin T. Onderdonk] with such strange and ominous stillness comes from the same quarter or not, I don't know. I rather suppose it does not. It's the office I respect and not the man. I don't know him personally and if these charges be sustainable, in the name of heaven let things take their course. But I devoutly hope the matter will pass over quietly and be dismissed by the House of Bishops and that we shall be spared the excitement and pain of a second edition of the Pennsylvania case.

October 23, WEDNESDAY. . . . Looked in at Trinity; got hold of the tower key by a lucky chance and went up into the spire with Anthon, second time I've been up. It's now rather over 200 feet, I believe; glorious view of the city and parts adjacent. Terrible breakneck process getting up and rather worse coming down again. Found one way on the upper scaffolding above the aisles of the nave where for the first time we had a view of the ceiling of the nave and the clerestory windows as far as completed, eight, I think, in the north side, and four or five on the south. Both are lovely. . . .

October 27. . . . The movement against our bishop, whatever it may precisely be, still kept very close. A paragraph in the *Express* of Friday morning alluding to it, contradicted "by authority" in yesterday's paper and in the *American*. Were there anything in it, the Bishop has enemies enough who'd be too happy to push matters to a crisis, so I'm disposed to hope the best from their inactivity. . . .

November 8, FRIDAY. The verdict's against us, and a new trial can't be got. The state's given up, now, and to be sure it's time, for Polk's majority is running hard on 5,000. It's no use to think about the matter any longer. There's a bare possibility that Delaware and the other states yet to come in may alter the aspect of affairs, but it's hardly worth considering, and the vote of New York has settled the question and the illustrious Polk is President-Elect.

And the Whig Party is defunct, past all aid from warm blankets, galvanic batteries, and the Humane Society; it's quite dead and the sooner it's buried the better. What form of life will be generated from its decomposition remains to be seen.

Two causes have mainly brought all this to pass: Native Americanism, and the great difference between the candidates in conspicuousness and vulnerability. Everybody could talk about Clay's long career as a prominent politician and find something in it to use against him fairly or falsely, while his opponent was impregnable from the fact that he'd never done or said anything of importance to anybody and the attempts made by the Whigs to injure his personal political character only recoiled on their own heads. Henceforth I think political wire-pullers will be careful how they nominate prominent and well-known men for the Presidency; they'll find it safer to pick up the first man they may find in the street. . . .

November 10, SUNDAY. . . . I omitted on Wednesday to chronicle the fact that Bishop Onderdonk was on that day "presented" in due form by Bishops Otey, Polk, and Meade for (*sit venia loquendi* the lying charge) "licentiousness," the presentment, or charges, served on him, and the House of Bishops notified to assemble for a judicial session in this city thirty days hence.

The "actor" seems to be the Reverend Mr. [James Cook] Richmond. He was left off the missionary committee at the last Convention and was weak enough to let his irritation and wounded vanity show themselves most plainly in all he said and did thereafter till the adjournment. This has made him just fit for the purpose of the Reverend Henry Anthon, who, I can't doubt after what I've heard, is the real mover in the matter, and with him [Thomas J.] Oakley, [John] Duer, John Jay!!! and I fear the whole of that unhappy minority.

It is in short, and really and truly painful is it to believe the fact so, the last desperate effort of the malignant, bitter, partisan hostility of those people to the Bishop that has brought this false and foul accusation into the light of day, and Richmond is the tool used for work too dirty even for Dr. Anthon, and after his attack on McVickar in the last convention I thought nothing was too mean and miserable for him to put his hands to when the Bishop or the Bishop's friends could be injured by it. But this dirt is to be thrown at a higher mark and may fall on the head of him who aims it, and a prudent man is the doctor.

1848

*T*he happiest year of Strong's life begins gloomily enough in his record. On the 26th of January the name of Miss Ellen Ruggles appears in the diary for the first time, although it is almost certain that the "beautiful sunshiny face" that haunted him at the office and around town on April 16, 1847, after the Ruggles soirée of the night before, was none other than hers. Strong remarked then that he was not in love but didn't care to be nearer to it than he was. Nevertheless he took plenty of time to think it over, and confided nothing to his journal. The party at Mrs. John Austin Stevens's December 28, 1847 (barely noted at the time but vividly recollected a decade later) and the soirée in January of this year evidently revived the whole matter, but still he wrote nothing until March 4, when the situation was well in hand. From that point we let him tell his story in full.

This was an eventful year; the year of a formal peace with Mexico, of the organization of the Free-Soil Party, of the great Whig victory in electing Taylor to the presidency, and of the discovery of gold in California. To Strong, however, it was a year of one event which transformed his life.

January 26, WEDNESDAY. . . . Have been dissipating on chloroform lately. It seems an innocent kind of amusement not followed by any reaction or other unpleasant symptoms. N.B. I think it altogether probable that its use may be instrumental in bringing to light important truths in the science of "psychology," or rather in that department of physiology which relates to the connexion between mind and matter, the functions of the nervous system and so forth.

Nothing else new except the opera and the people one sees there—the "Ruggleses" and so on. Miss Ellen Ruggles is *rather* worth cultivating. . . .

January 27. . . . Am sitting here waiting for Sam Whitlock who promised to come and see me tonight—poor fellow, what a bore it must be for him, this condemnation to a black patch over one eye for life.

January 29. . . . George Jones[1] looked in to turn over engravings, then walked up and had an hour or two at the club. Tayler Lewis, Verplanck, Hoppin, Dorr, Leupp and Gray, *cum multis aliis*. Walked downtown with Verplanck. Legend of the corner of Canal Street and the woodchuck killed there one moonshiny night in June, 1815.

January 30, SUNDAY. . . . *"Lassati sumus in via iniquitatis"* and of all its paths and byways this is surely the most rugged and the least attractive. But it is well for me that I have got into this rather than another. A taste for wicked *pleasures* I might find myself too weak and worthless to resist or even wish to conquer. But sinful self-denial and ungodly sorrow, penance and mortification and the renouncing of worldly pleasure for the sake and service of evil, I think I am able to contend against. Christian asceticism may look unpromising, but this *dämonische ascese*, this cutting off the right arm and plucking out the right eye in order to be as wrong and unhappy as possible, this renouncing the happiness of earth because one thinks it probable he can't get the moon, is unreasonable, intolerable, and not to be endured.

Think I'll write "confessions of a chloroform-smeller" some of these days after the manner of the English Opium Eater, though I've as yet but little to confess. It's curious stuff, is chloroform—and very curious indeed are its temporary effects on one's system. The dreams are so strange it fills one's mind with, the apparent duration of its effects so much longer than one's watch indicates. The sensations of a week are crowded into two minutes.

Last time I dosed myself I heard most distinctly the performance of a part of Mozart's *Requiem*—the "Dies Irae" chorus and part of the "Tuba Mirum" accompaniment by an orchestra and, as I noticed at the time, not a very good one. I remember listening most attentively and noticing that in

---

[1] This is probably George Frederic Jones (1822–1882), who was in college with Strong, married Lucretia Stevens Rhinelander, and was the father of Edith Wharton; and not George Jones (1811–1891), then of the *Tribune* and later a founder of the *Times*. The Centurions mentioned are Professor Tayler Lewis of New York University, Gulian C. Verplanck, William Jones Hoppin (Yale 1832), Henry Crawford Dorr (Brown 1839), Charles M. Leupp and Henry Peters Gray, the artist. Dorr was a younger brother of Thomas Wilson Dorr (Harvard 1823), the Rhode Island insurgent.

many points my memories of the music were wrong. I may add, as showing that perchloride of formyle is not a power of inspiration or a supernatural means of arriving at truth (like Mesmerism) that as compared with the dream concert my memories of the music were right.

February 1. . . . Consulted a horse doctor about Tornado this morning. Tornado, I fear, has chronic podagra. Rather think I've got or am getting a typhus fever, for I'm uncomfortable to a degree and can't sleep at night. Longfellow's *Evangeline*, quiet and beautiful; under obligations to the "recommender" of it, confound her.

February 5, SATURDAY. . . . Just in from the Mendelssohn "Commemoration" Concert at Castle Garden. Went with Charley and Pedrillo and Johnny Parish. It was unparalleled in one respect—the crowd. Tickets had been sent out gratis, and I suppose eight thousand people availed themselves of the opportunity of testifying their musical taste and their respect for the departed composer. There were just as many people as the place would hold, and it was a fine sight to behold. Almost a compensation for the heat and press and prodigious discomfort of the whole transaction. Certainly there was no other compensation, for though the music was very discreetly selected (including the second movement of the *Eroica* and the glorious "Sleepers awake—A voice is calling" chorale from *St. Paul*) it was played so vilely that I scarcely cared to listen to it. . . .

February 10, THURSDAY. . . . Opera: Biscaccianti. The Bostonians may puff her till they crack their cheeks, demonstrate till they're tired that she's taller than Jenny Lind and prettier than Jenny Lind and acts better than Jenny Lind and is therefore a fitter subject for a furor than Jenny Lind, but it's altogether of no use. She's excessively slow, sings and acts with visible effort and painful straining for effect, and has been provided by nature with a voice and a face and a manner that Bostonians may admire but I do not. Habicht seems to have constituted himself her especial champion and defender.

At the club frequently of late in the course of my walks downtown from the opera; pleasant hour there last night.

Reading, last two volumes of Campbell's *Chancellors*—gossiping and pleasant. Queer novel, *Jane Eyre*—not a book I *like* at all, but very full of cleverness and character. Lamb's books—haven't yet got them home. Application from Duyckinck on behalf of Professor [Henry Hope] Reed of Philadelphia for leave to print some of Coleridge's marginal scribblings.

Visit from Dr. Berrian today with divers data and statistics to show the propriety of building a new chapel of Trinity Parish uptown—doubtless a desirable thing to do, for the tide of uptown emigration has left the church and its present chapels almost bare of parishioners. . . .

February 13, SUNDAY. . . . Not much to write that's new or entertaining just now. Remsen party Thursday night: great crowd—found the transaction a bore. "Evangeline" dancing the polka most indefatigably.

I do hate to see women who are worthy of better things, who have heads at least if not hearts, whirling and spinning and ricocheting across a ball room, profaned by the touch and breath and look of somebody who's not worthy to come within a hundred yards of them. For the *real* "dancing girls," whose organs of saltatory locomotion have been cultivated to such a development and perfection as to render the head and heart quite secondary and subordinate parts of their physical organization, if not to obliterate and destroy them quite (like the stamina and pistils of an artificial hothouse rose), it don't matter at all. They are merely fulfilling their vocation, acting out the part in life they've chosen and for which they've laboriously qualified themselves. But for those who are fit for better things, it's a sin and a shame. Neither brains nor hearts. I wonder why those J. people, for instance, don't decompose as other people would if deprived of those important viscera. Probably they avail themselves of antiseptics. . . .

Darley's outlines to the Rev. Mr. Somebody's *Margaret*[2]—spent an hour yesterday in Maunsell Field's office examining them. Very exquisite indeed, as good in their way as anything of Retzsch's, possibly better in respect of the character and individuality of all the faces and figures, and the "native Americanism" of the accessories and still life. Admirable as Retzsch's productions undoubtedly are, most of them look like a series of tableaux by the same people in different costumes. That's a dictum of Hoppin's and the most sensible thing he ever said, for though I denied it stoutly at first, it is, on consideration, perfectly true.

February 17. . . . Lamb's book home at last. Coleridge's notes are quite interesting, at least when read in Coleridge's autograph. Duyckinck has acknowledged my civilities in the premises by the present of a copy of *Arcturus*, so I've just been writing him a letter expressing my gratitude,

[2] Rev. Sylvester Judd (1813–1853), Yale 1836, Unitarian minister of Augusta, Maine, had a brief but important career as a humanitarian preacher and lecturer; his religious and social views were set down in his two novels, *Margaret* (1845) and *Richard Edney and the Governor's Family* (1850). F. O. C. Darley's book, *Compositions in Outline . . . from Judd's "Margaret,"* was not published until 1856. Maunsell Bradhurst Field (Yale 1841), New York lawyer and diplomat, was co-author with G. P. R. James of a novel, *Adrian; or, The Clouds of the Mind* (1851), and wrote a valuable book of memoirs.

as I conscientiously could for his good intentions—and for nothing else—
the contents of the periodical as a whole, and with the exception of one or
two piquant articles by Dr. Hawks, being very great stuff, indeed. Literature pursued as an end, for its own sake, and not for the truths of which it
may be made the vehicle, is a worthless affair, and those who cultivate it
for itself alone are always unreal, and unless they have ability and original-
ity far above their fellows, are pretty sure to degenerate into puppyism and
pedantry. Where such a litterateur is feeble himself and is dealing with and
laboriously commenting on and striving to magnify the writings of people
like himself, his productions are apt to be among the most pitiful specimens
of human infatuation that are to be found anywhere. And Mr. Duyckinck
and Mr. [Cornelius] Mathews, criticizing and comparing and weighing
with the nicest accuracy the relative merits and demerits of the small fry
of authors, foreign and domestic, exhibit and illustrate in their own persons
the ridiculous side of humanity with painful force and clearness. However,
there are some principles maintained in the book; it is pervaded by the
cant of progress instinct with the lies of "liberality" and enlightenment
and the like twaddle.

Arcturus would unsex woman and destroy the Idea of Womanhood
on Earth by removing their "disabilities" and "elevating" them into a race
of disagreeable, effeminate men in petticoats. It holds capital punishment
cruel, barbarous and unnecessary, the diffusion of useful information a
panacea for all social evils, and so forth—anybody can gulp its doctrines
on all other subjects from those specimens.

February 22, TUESDAY. . . . Rumors of a peace with Mexico made by
Scott on his own responsibility—generally credited. Senate will probably
ratify it in a hurry and be glad to be done with conquering. . . .

News that John Quincy Adams has been seized with paralysis.

February 24. J.Q.A. died yesterday. The indomitable old boy has
been put down at last. Other news is there but little. Peace rumors confirmed—ratification of some sort of treaty thought to be certain, though
no party is quite satisfied with the terms and conditions of the preliminaries
said to have been agreed on. There strikes seven, so I must go and array
myself for an evening in Union Place to meet some Boston woman or
other whose name I don't remember, and enough people besides, I suppose,
to make up some sort of tea squall.

February 27. . . . Lamartine—*Harmonies Poétiques*—the first French
Poetry I've yet read with respect. In spite of the difficulty of giving dignity

and earnestness to anything written in that dialect, these poems express solemn and pious feeling with reverence and sincerity. Just finished "Le Retour"—"*On regrette la vie avant d'avoir vécu.*" Fine enough.

March 4, SATURDAY. Afternoon, 26 minutes and 1/2 past three P.M. Bright sunshine and a lovely day, though somewhat sloppy and slushy under foot, for we'd quite a heavy little snowstorm Thursday night. Thermometer 34° at this present writing. Rather particular as to the details of the current half-hour for I find myself just now in an Abnormal State, very new and strange. Have thought once or twice on former occasions that I was experiencing this sort of thing, but it was all a mistake. I've never had the disorder before but in a mild form; it's been slowly coming on for the last three months and has now assumed a very threatening character. Perhaps I shan't journalize any more, for if this bubble should burst (as I hope and sometimes believe it will not) I think I should die on the spot. At least I should not want to survive the rage, mortification, and bitter disgust of such a state of things. Never mind that, however, just now. . . .

March 6. Eleven P.M. Just in from my expedition to Union Place and I sit down here to write in the first flush of real happiness and joy I've known for years—the first I've *ever* known—that I may have something tangible to recall it by hereafter.

Walked downtown nearly wild. Heaven help me if I'm under a delusion, and make me grateful if this be real and true; for if so, I believe the game can and will be won and I shall be—there are no words in the English or any other language to express this.

God bless, keep, preserve, protect, and defend her forever!

"Fashionable" and "artificial"!!!!! The sagacity of some people is marvelous.

Case stands over till Thursday night—possibly Friday. What an idiot I was not to settle it tonight. But if if if if if if if IF this be all a dream of mine!

March 13, MONDAY. Here endeth the life and history of the G.T.S. hitherto known in the pages of this journal. Another person bearing the same name and residing at the same place here beginneth the Chronicle of his Life—and humbly hopes that it will be a very different kind of life from the dreary, desolate, objectless, worthless existence the shabby details whereof are contained in the miserable pages that go before.

1848

Reminiscences of the Transition period and new birth.

March 7, TUESDAY. Pleasant morning, gradual assault of the blues, nervousness, uneasiness, and all kinds of horrors. Evening. Buffet. Madame de Staël. Walk up with Charley, stop at Florence's, eat oysters, drink ale—if possible, more desperate than before. Conclusion that I'm a presumptuous fool settled in my own mind irrevocably and without appeal. Came home, read Longfellow, conscientious effort to be philosophical and heroic ending in total failure.

March 8, WEDNESDAY. Warm, mild, lovely day, which I thought at the time disgusting. Call from Jem Strong. Appleton's, last *Dombey*, great doubt and perplexity whether 'twould do to send it up. Another chase after an English *Jane Eyre*—unsuccessful. Rush up to Colman's to look for an engraving mentioned by Jem Strong; couldn't find it; back to Wall Street. Wilbur and Brush, intense desire to throw 'em out of the window. J.Q.A.'s funeral—disgusting crowd. Home. Mrs. Stevens: walk her and M. to Trinity Church. Afternoon: sat in Wall Street, did nothing but boil inwardly till I nearly burst. Evening: walked on the Fourth Avenue to nobody knows where and back again; considered the question of cabling— decided against it. Half moon over Cheever's meetinghouse; very pretty, quiet, mild spring evening it was. Met Samuel B. Ruggles, Esq., as I came down Broadway. Club: "Delineators"—Ellsworth—Dorr—Charley. Long and very distrait talk with old Verplanck on a variety of subjects. Home.

March 9, THURSDAY. Rain and wind—very desperate state of things. Terribly grand, gloomy, and peculiar conversation with Charley which makes me laugh now, though I didn't perceive how funny it all was at the time. Evening: carriage to Professor Nicoll's lecture at the University; found my friends by special good fortune and joined 'em. Lunar surface, great craters, Tycho, lunar mountains upside down, "innate depravity of human nature." Walk home through the rain in a consolatory frame of mind.

March 10, FRIDAY. Morning. Master's office, Maurice, James J. Jones, W. T. J., Raddi and Garrigue after German duplicates. Evening: to Union Square. Fouqué—Hoffman—Tennyson—*Couriers*—St. Peter's— Raffaello—*pieta curia advisari vult*—"continuance" to tomorrow night.

Saturday March 11th A.D. *1848*. Call at No. 8 Wall Street at eleven-thirty—at Bank of Commerce at twelve-thirty. Long conference and cross examination. Frank Griffin referee. Afternoon: Wall Street—to the *Herald* office and back. Evening: Union Square. *Victoria!* God make me grateful enough for it and enable me to bear myself henceforth as becomes the depositary of so precious a trust and so unspeakable a blessing.

Yesterday: church in the morning. Charley and Johnny Parish. Haight preached, I believe. Walked a little way up Broadway thereafter. Afternoon: sat still in this chair and did nothing. Evening: walked to Union Square. Overtook Johnny Parish and he joined me, evidently in great wonder as to where I could be going. Mr. and Mrs. Tighe—Mr. and Mrs. Henry R[uggles?].

Today: announcements. Carried two round to Delmonico's and took his breath away with the news. Walter Cutting—Henry Cram—walked with him on the Battery from eleven to twelve in sheer reckless, indolent happiness, spurning Wall Street with my heels. George Gibbs—letters—dinner—Mamma in great felicity, for she went to Union Square this morning; my father was there tonight and he's as happy and pleased as possible. That was all that was yet wanting to make this *perfect.*

* * * *

April 9, SUNDAY. Have been meaning to take out the journal every day since my last entry, but my efforts have been unavailing. Not that there has been anything to chronicle—there has been nothing but a monotony of happenings. But this state of things is so new and strange, this last month of my life has been so utterly different from all the months that have gone before it, and worth so much more than all of them together, that I have felt as if I ought to preserve some trace of it for my journal.

Perfect, entire happiness—so new and strange to me that I dread day to day and almost from hour to hour that it must end. Happiness that teaches one gratitude to God and faith in him, and so enables me to shake off my nervous fear that it cannot last. Happiness that I can dwell upon and luxuriate in freely and unrestrained, because it includes the anticipation of a life no longer cold and selfish and objectless and indolent, but henceforth to be built on joyful self-denial and hearty labor for a worthy end. Happiness that it bewilders me to look upon—that I know I do not even yet fully realize and appreciate—the happiness of loving and being generously loved by a beautiful, high-principled, noble-hearted, frank, affectionate, good girl possessed of everything that refinement and cultivation and taste and intelligence can adorn womanhood withal.

Who'd have thought this six months ago? Even yet I can scarcely believe it myself.

I've not had much to journalize about. For the mornings, I've spent them in diligently dodging all work and labor that was not inevitable. . . . Home at half-past five regularly; dress and omnibus to Union Square. Back again rather late than otherwise—quite too late to cultivate the journal.

Of course I'm not such an ass as to look forward to the life before me as one of mere abstract felicity. There are chances and changes to be feared, and at best there will be oceans of cares and anxieties that I'm an utter stranger to as yet and of which I am like to be more than commonly sensible—the care about money matters first of all—to be fought with and to be mastered.

That same care about the *Diva pecunia* is the only one that besets me at present, though I know that as far as human calculations and arrangements are worth anything, I've a right to feel at ease on that score. But it has become so momentous all of a sudden, after having always been so entire a matter of indifference, about which I never felt anxiety, fear, or foreboding that I can't quite yet treat the matter rationally and philosophically. Till a month ago I don't think it would have given me three days' abiding unhappiness to have a cypher for my worldly estate in possession and expectancy; on some accounts I should rather have enjoyed the perfect Diogenes independence of such a state of things. Now things are rather changed. And our start in life will probably be on rather a larger and more expensive scale than I should have wished, if my tastes alone had been in question.

Never mind—I think we may fairly count on things coming out right.

At Grace Church this morning Ellen confirmed by Bishop [Alonzo] Potter of Pennsylvania. After dinner walked downtown, and here I am, and I shall march uptown again presently, so I must be expeditious with my chronicling.

Plenty of news of late. French Revolution No. 3. Democratic influenza running through Europe. French provisional government—absurdity, sentimentality, and melodramatic monkeyism of every kind; decrees that "everybody shall have everything, and secondly everything else is hereby abolished." Louis Philippe run away. Lamartine, Louis Blanc, Ledru-Rollin, and so on in his shoes. Wish all this could have been postponed a year, for it has nipped in the bud our projected summer expedition to the Old World. Death of old [John Jacob] Astor. William B. his grand residuary legatee. Affliction has fallen on the Oxonian Bristed, and great tribulation on all the tribe of the Langdons.[3] Henry Cram engaged to Miss [Katherine] Sergeant at last!

April the 15th A.D. *1848:* I sometimes think it can never be—something will befall before then. But even at the worst, one era of my life has past and is gone and can never return. I never again can return. I never again can be what I have been.

If this were all to come to naught, I should never return to the quiet, desolate, vacant, objectless, "respectable" life of the last five years. I should either die at once or leave the country instantly, no matter how, and go no matter where and never return. I'm waked up now, for good or evil, according as the event shall show (for I dare not think of the event as certain), and I shall doze and dream and stupefy no more.

I'd sooner join a settlement of the gregarious blue baboons of South Africa than live on in the dismal way I've been living of late.

Half-past four, and I must stop scribbling. Heaven prosper this to us both and give me the will and the power henceforth to fulfil aright my new obligations to show myself worthy of being its instrument and make the life of her whom its mercy has given to me as beautiful and happy and honored as it ought to be.

April 20. 12 M., "noon of night," that is. Just in from Union Square. Ancestors called there this evening. Also Mr. and Mrs. Abbott Lawrence of Boston "happened in"—both possessed of a full appreciation of their own estimable qualities. Out this morning with my glorious little Ellen making calls on divers people. Mercy on us: I'm terrified at that "my" in the last line. Things temporal are uncertain—"many a slip" and so forth. I dread to tempt the destinies to mischief by a premature use of the pronoun possessive.

Prussia's a republic and Europe generally has gone mad.

April 24, Monday night or Tuesday morning—uncertain which, for my watch is wrong and as to my clock, it ran down somewhere about the 11th of March last and has not been wound up to this day. "In" from Union Square. Isn't my little Ellen Ruggles a noble little girl!

I'm horribly bored. Mrs. Mary Jones, the "Madame Josephine Weiss" of polite society—the female impresario of the "dancing girls"—has sent

[3] The "Oxonian Bristed" was the Rev. John Bristed (1778–1855), physician, lawyer, author, and cleric, who married Magdalen (Astor) Bentzon, daughter of John Jacob Astor. Fitz-Greene Halleck lampooned Bristed in *Fanny* with the foregoing title, but the reverend gentleman's name does not appear on the rolls of that university. Col. Walter Langdon of New Hampshire married Dorothea, another of Astor's daughters.

us cards for tomorrow night's saltatory *soirée*. That don't seem as if it were a sufficient reason for my feeling prompted to shoot myself or take passage for New Holland or write a note uptown to announce that our —— must be —— yet I feel as if I could do any one of them. Brooded over the prospect in constantly increasing blackness of spirit all the way downtown, and I'm now boiling over with wrath and disgust and desperate ill humor. But I know the notion or prejudice or vexation or dislike or whatever it may be called is unreasonable and that I'm a fool. Whatever Ellen does is right, *ipso facto*. But I wish Mrs. Mary might be seized with apoplexy tomorrow morning and recover and be restored to perfect health just two minutes after her invitations had been irrevocably countermanded.

Yesterday was Sunday. At Grace Church: very momentous day it was, of the transaction whereof I will not write while I'm in my present most unchristian frame of mind. Prussia isn't a republic after all.

Wish I had the man here that invented the polka—I'd scrape him to death with oyster shells. Probably, though, he's dead already, and polking everlastingly through another and a *worser* world, and so beyond my vengeance. . . .

April 28.   At Wenzler's studio this morning. Portrait prospers, and gains ground daily, and will be a good portrait exceedingly. Poor little Ellen quite unwell and obliged to end the séance prematurely—better though this evening. . . .

Jones *soirée* was not honored by either of us. Broadway Theatre last night. *Romance and Reality* and *Used Up*—much fun in both. Still suffer from the debilitating effect of excessive cachinnation. . . .

Orders given to commence excavating in Twenty-first Street Wednesday night at 23 minutes past seven P.M. Hibernia came to the rescue yesterday morning; twenty "sons of toil" with prehensile paws supplied them by nature with evident reference to the handling of the spade and the wielding of the pickaxe and congenital hollows on the shoulder wonderfully adapted to make the carrying of the hod a luxury instead of a labor commenced the task yesterday morning.

What the object may be of putting us into a forty-foot house, and how soon such an establishment is going to reduce us to an insolvent state, and whether it is or is not absurd in me to acquiesce in this lamblike way I've not yet clearly settled in my mind. All that deliberation and consideration on those and other cognate subjects I've left to the Two Governors, on whose judgment I perfectly luxuriate in relying, for it saves me a deal of perplexity and anxious thought.

The wedding is to be noisy to a degree—perfectly vociferous. I don't care tenpence. If any one had told me six months ago that I should be utterly indifferent to such a prospect I should have looked at him with serene incredulity, and if he'd repeated the statement offensively, should have kicked him with violence for his impudent mendacity.

It's a shame I should so neglect my journal *now*, for though I've a right to expect and do expect that hereafter will be a happier time than this (rather), still I know that I shall always dwell on the memories of this time and cherish them most dearly, even as I now think of the month or two that preceded the 11th of March and try to remember every little matter connected with their history, and half wish I could live through the same scenes again—anxious and unhappy as I was then.

If I could but rid myself of this dead weight of responsibility that so presses on me, even when I'm happiest! Yet I know I need feel no special uneasiness, that I've less reason than most men for forebodings about embarrassment and difficulties and anticipatory cares about expense and pecuniary perils, that I'm (at the worst) as competent as most men to care for a household and fight my way through life without "prospects" or assistance *ab extra*. My own personal tastes, views, and wishes are sufficiently modest and subdued, and work and vigilance, with the help of Heaven, will enable me to gratify the *additional* tastes and wishes that I'm now bound to look after and provide for. Ellen isn't one of the people who live by satin and rosewood alone, but she likes elegance and comfort, and she has got to be suited and satisfied, and she shall be if I can bring it to pass. For myself—I've spent money on myself lavishly enough heretofore and I'm tired of that kind of thing; "there's nothing in it," as Sir Charles Coldstream says, and I can make my precious self comfortable enough on $250.00 a year and rather enjoy the novelty of the proceeding.

April 30, SUNDAY AFTERNOON. Sixteen days yet. Grace Church this morning—dinner—downtown with George Gibbs. Dr. Wainwright preached.

Just striking five and I'm in a fidget to be back in Union Square, and here's a whole fortnight (and more, too) to be got rid of somehow before the 15th of May shall make its advent on this earth. It strikes me that I'm in love—a little. And tomorrow I've got to do some work—that there's no escaping from—and I'd rather take a dose of physic. Never mind—I'll live through it all in some way or other, I suppose.

May 3, WEDNESDAY AFTERNOON. Bright and clear, after a rainy

morning. Indefatigably busy (comparatively speaking, that is). Collins—
Maurice—Prince—Dickinson—Peck—Glover and so forth. Tomorrow I
must spend at Flushing superintending a foreclosure where there is going
to be vexation and bother without end, fifty things probably going
wrong, for all which I don't care tenpence. At Mrs. Rebecca Jones's
party last night with Ellen, Heaven bless her.

May 8.   Home an hour earlier than usual, for I had to leave Union
Square at eight and come down to a most prosy vestry meeting of Trinity
Church, which I should have cut if Bishop [William Heathcote] De
Lancey and Dr. [Benjamin] Hale hadn't both called to urge my attendance for the sake of Geneva College, which has sent in a humble "sifflication" to Trinity Church to be "liberally endowed"—they are not particular
how, as long as it's arranged "liberally," but they'd rather prefer un-
encumbered improved real estate in the city of New York.

It has been fearfully hot and showery for the last few days. Sunday
was perfectly withering. I've got a slight cold too, which is a bore, as
the cards are out today for the 15th.

Poor dear, good, innocent little Ellen, thinking so much of me and so
grateful for every little attention I'm able to show her. It really seems
incredible that I should have gained such an unprecedented combination
of all sorts of excellence as she is and entirely and absolutely. Thank
Heaven that she thinks of me as she does, and long may she think so—
but that she should condescend to love me is marvellous. It's the unspeakable and most undeserved blessing of heaven and I must show my
gratitude for it by making her happiness the one great object of my life.

Enter conscience and common sense with a bucket of cold water and
a knout. "Mr. G. T. S., you are more thoroughly in earnest in what you
have been thinking and writing than ever you were on any other subject
in all your life, we believe and admit. But don't you know what a miserable, selfish, thoughtless, good-for-nothing vagabond you really are?
Don't you know that five years hence or ten years hence your Wife will
be an everyday affair and not the lovely novelty that she is now; and that
there will be cares and anxieties and worriments and vexations and
temptations to bad humor or little unkindnesses or nameless neglects or
little insignificant unamiabilities that you would *now* die sooner than
admit the possibility of your committing? Won't you be lazy and tempted
to neglect her, bored and cross and careless about her feeling it, selfish
and unaccommodating and unwilling to sacrifice your comfort to hers?

Now if you forget your feelings of this time and of the months that have passed, and all that you have said and promised—and all that she has done and is to do for you—if you ever forget this and cease to keep it all fresh and a living spring of action in your heart *we shall not forget a bit of it*. And if you ever thoughtlessly or willfully, by look, word, or deed, slight or neglect her or ever cease for one minute to think of her as she deserves or treat her as you are bound to treat her, then look out for yourself; for as we have thrown cold water on your dream of a whole life of uninterrupted and undiminished fervent, romantic adoration, so we shall come down with the knout of retributive vengeance on one solitary failure of the care and gentleness and kindness and affection that you've promised and are ever bound to show."

Very sagacious and true, but I survive the cold water and I believe I shall not incur the knout. If Ellen's face and form were her chief excellence, I could well fear that I should gradually find my love growing less fervent as time fades her beauty, and cares and anxieties unfelt before might make me less mindful of my pledge to cherish and care for her; but thank Heaven it is not so, and if ever I fail in my duty to make her comfort and happiness my daily care, may Heaven abandon me as I shall most justly deserve.

May 13, SATURDAY. Half-past three P.M. So one era of my life is ending—all the old ways and habits and associations are obsolete now and to be laid on the shelf.

In all the happiness of this time there's now and then something like a feeling of self-reproach. "How *can* I abandon all these old usages and leave this dirty, rat-infested loaferine Greenwich Street and everything that I've grown up among and got used to, and yet feel no sorrow about it; give up all my old friends here, the row of houses on the opposite side of the way that I've known so long, the lookout on shabby brick walls from the windows of this room, this inconvenient old house where alone I can remember living, and yet change cheerfully?" It seems to me as if I were parting from my oldest and best friends for ever and ought to be unhappy about it: but somehow I a'nt a bit. Which, under the circumstances, is not so very remarkable after all.

This morning was bright and pleasant, but clouds have come back now, and there's reason to fear more rain. Improved the sunshine by a walk uptown to Mantello's and Dunlap's, bouquet-hunting, and then went to Wall Street and looked sagacious and did nothing at all.

Preliminary mass meeting of *bridesmaids and groomsmen* came off

Thursday night. Monday at twelve-thirty all hands reassemble at No. 24 Union Place.

Now may Heaven help me to do my duty and bear myself as I should in my new estate! That's all I ask—with that blessing I may reasonably count on every other as its necessary consequence.

Miss MARY C., only daughter of Chester Childs, Esq., of this city.
On Monday, the 15th inst., by Rev. Dr Taylor, GEORGE TEMPLETON STRONG, to ELLEN, daughter of Samuel B. Ruggles, Esq.
On Monday evening, the 15th inst., by the Rev. Dr. Fisher.

Gloria Deo in Excelsis — et in Jenâ Pax

July 26, WEDNESDAY.   I've been too busy and too happy to journalize of late, but there's a leisure hour of warm weather before me just now, and it seems natural to take out my journal—though I hope and believe it will never again seem natural to cover its pages with the morbid, monotonous, melancholy whinings and maunderings of the last two or three years. There's too much to do and too much to enjoy to admit of any philosophizing and sentimentalizing about my nervous system and the other favorite and pleasing topics of the pages that go before.

Retrospect. May 15th. Defection of Walter Cutting by reason of the death of his brother-in-law Wilson. Jem R[uggles] took his place. Grace Church. Rev. Thomas H. Taylor. Reception—slight *déjeuner* and *soirée dansante*. All very jolly and very brilliant and very preëminently successful. Mrs. Dillon and Madame Trobriand. Day was unsurpassable —bright sunshine and cool. Church quite full; poor little Ellen behaved like a Joan of Arc, or any other heroine. Tuesday at eleven we took a carriage and drove over to Mrs. Post's; left there Saturday afternoon. Particularly pleasant time—several nice drives; one stampede of three cows, two horses, one heifer, and a cat. Poor Ellen sick on the Saturday, to my unspeakable dismay, but able at last to come to town. Monday was the day of Mrs. Davis's party in honor of Mrs. Rives; then came the Kean blowout in honor of Mrs. S. June 13th was our expedition to Lydig's at West Farms. Sunday afternoon, drive to High Wood (James Gore King's) [at Weehawken]. June 18th to Mrs. James Strong's place

—memorable as an awfully hot time. Poor Ellen sick the day after and confined to her bed for two or three days. Divers pleasant sprees in a small way at the Broadway Theatre: *School for Scandal, Romance and Reality, Old Heads and Young Hearts,* etc.

Friday afternoon last we went to Rockaway, where Jerry V[an] R[ensselaer] got us a very nice room. Maj. Gen. Scott and Mrs. Scott and the (rather pretty) young ladies—Mrs. Brooks, Tucker, the Hamersleys, Mrs. Robert Cutting, and so on. Very nice time, including one surf bath and two drives, one of them (with Charley and Mrs. V. R. on the beach) it is consolatory to remember in this warm weather. To town yesterday at three P.M.

Letter from Sharon announcing that a room is engaged for us, so thither we go next Monday. Tomorrow afternoon we may perhaps betake ourselves to Whitestone (Powell's) for a day or two.

The house-building plans have undergone a series of mutations. First there were to have been three houses on the four lots. Then Aunt O[livia Templeton] concluded that she would not live in anything so big, and insisted on a single lot. Then the remaining three lots were to have been divided between the two other houses, but when plans and estimates came in my father became refractory and struck for a single lot, too. Now our architectural arrangements are ordered as follows.

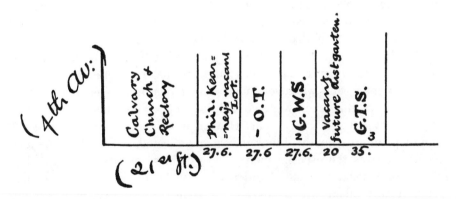

Nos. 1 and 2 have got the start and are going on fast. No. 2 advances more slowly. Mr. Ruggles very kindly gives us a stone front and a kind of architectural bay window for Ellen's boudoir or snuggery on the west side. The house will cost a clean $25,000, of which fact I don't think my

father has yet a full realizing sense. As to furnishing, I've called in a
little $2000 investment which will do something, and for the balance I
trust to economy of income during the coming year, and those comprehensive words "somehow or other."

Going into so large a house and starting on so grand a scale is not in
accordance with my "private judgment." But they tell me I'm safe and
I hope it will prove so. If I had not the most prudent, sensible, economical,
managing little wife that ever was heard of I should be in despair.

In all my happiness there's but one drawback—a sad kind of indefinite
foreboding that it is too great to last, a feeling that in this world people
cannot expect more than a short interval of contentment and prosperity
and perfect happiness like what I'm now enjoying.

Our first plan for the winter was life at a hotel, but we found the
extravagance and discomfort of that system quite too severe, and so to
housekeeping we go in October in a house of Mr. Ruggles's on the
Fourth Avenue till our own shall be finished. . . .

Very hard at work in Wall Street ever since I was married; last great
job a partition bill for the benefit of the Beekman estate, which nearly
drove me demented. No longer listless and weary and bored in Wall
Street—there's need of work now, and I have worked, diligently and
with all my heart, and have found comfort in working. How this confounded New Code is going to work does not yet appear, but I fear it
will touch me in what has now become a tender spot, the profits of the
trade. Never mind, if that fail utterly there will be (so far as one can
count on things temporal) $3,000 a year and a house. Heretofore I've
made near $2,500 per annum, and I ought to make something now.

And anyhow, and whatever may befall, I've got a Wife that's worth
all the dollars that ever were coined and that I love better and prize
higher every day and every hour. Heaven bless and preserve her! What
I'm going to write now will look unreal and affected, but is what I believe
and feel. It was the especial mercy and goodness of God that gave her
to me, for when I won her I did not know the thousandth part of her
worth. I was taken with a sweet face, sense, amiability, and ladylike
manners, and knew of nothing more. And a couple of months' experience
of married life has shown me that there might well have been, along
with all this and nowise inconsistent with it, fifty terrible drawbacks that
would have made me by this time utterly wretched. Some of them I took
it for granted I should find, and should have to bear with, and I supposed
then that they would be trifles though, and see *now* that they would have

been calamities I ought to have dreaded. I supposed I should have fashionable extravagance to contend against—in the place of the sound practical sense and economy I've found—and though I knew she had a kind of reverent feeling for religion and things connected with it, I never suspected her of the piety and high principle that put me to shame every day. No, it was no wisdom and prudence and sagacity of mine that picked her out from the crowd of people that filled Mrs. Stevens's drawing rooms on the night of the 27th of December last, but the special mercy of Heaven that gave me infinitely more than I hoped to find and gave me withal the *duty* and happy, honorable labor, of watching over her to the end of our lives—the office of its minister to make all her days to come as cheerful and contented and bright as they ought to be.

July 29, SATURDAY. Went to Whitestone with Ellen Thursday evening, in the *Washington Irving*. She stays there till Monday and I am going up and down as of old. As of old, and yet I hardly know the place or recognize myself, for I see everything with different eyes now. For the last three summers I've looked on that region with downright disgust. The miserable depression that haunted me in town overwhelmed me there, where I had no resource but a solitary lounging walk and a cigar, and nothing prevented my putting a decisive stop to my daily and nightly voyagings and my dismal evenings and more dismal monotonous listless Sundays but the certainty that our people would go nowhere else, and that if I stayed away, Mamma would abridge her sojourn or perhaps spend the summer in town. But I don't think I could have borne it this summer. Now I see things rather differently. Ellen seems to be pleased and happy there—contented everywhere, she is. Mr. and Mrs. Binney and the infant B. and the Johnsons. . . .

We go to Sharon Tuesday. Would give at least one joint of my little finger to stay away—not only because I've no great surplus of time and am ravenous to be working, but for other reasons. It will be a useful trial, however, of a fault of temper that I'm very conscious of, and it shall be submitted to with as good grace as may be.

July 31, MONDAY. In from Flushing with my dear little wife this morning. Spent yesterday there very pleasantly. . . . Today is drizzly and foggy and warm and the air of the city generally and of Greenwich Street in particular is not aromatic. Bidwell off tomorrow morning for the Red Sulphur. I'm off P.M. for that rendezvous of rheumatic old men and fortune-hunting young ones, Sharon Springs. . . .

September 2, SATURDAY. Month's rustication at Sharon has just ended. Left yesterday morning at eight and came down the river in the *Oregon* last night. Have found my unwonted holiday pleasant decidedly, though toward its end I began to feel a yearning for Wall Street like that of a banished patriot for his native land. Not without some apology neither, for I wanted to be working again, and moreover Charley has been stewing in town all through the month and my conscience smote me a little for not relieving him sooner. One or two bores there were, especially in the earlier part of the season, due mainly to my own faults of temper. I'm wanting in the easy good nature that carries me pleasantly through a month's companionship with all sorts of people good and bad. . . . D'Oremieulx of West Point—capital person; said to be engaged to Miss Laura Gibbs. Miss Chanler, very lively; Miss Kean with her rueful admirer Gerry, and Lieut. Griffin; Hamilton Fish and his whole ichthyological collection; Brandegees big and little; Henry Lloyd and wife, the latter quiet and rather nice; Parishes, Johnny P. included; Vanderpool; Johnstons—Miss Margaret J. clever but not particularly agreeable—something wrong in her composition, I don't know what. Christie and Lupp, very conversable; Penningtons, very fast; Beldens very nice, except that fat piece of usurious vulgarity vainly striving to look virtuous and to be elegant, viz., the papa, and except also the mamma, who has plenty of sense and of seeming good nature, but is entirely too strong-minded, too long-headed, and too long-winded for my taste. Miss Teresa Griffin; Major Van Buren and Mrs. V. B. and little Matty; O'Sullivan elder and younger; old Dr. Rodgers and Miss Fanny, painfully slow; Mrs. Borland, very nice; Clement Moore & Co., the sons a compound of imbecility deep beyond all fathoming, with an appetite for chambermaids beyond all precedent—the two Miss M's very nice indeed; Dr. and Mrs. Mütter; Kennedy of Baltimore, very pleasant; Mr. and Mrs. Van Rensselaer—the W. Rhinelanders, Giacasso Rhinelander included; Hudson and Munson, *Arcades ambo*; the Fowlers—loquacious mamma, daughters that I didn't exactly like, and De Grasse (2d son) a very fine fellow; James Suydam; Col. Duane, sublimely slow; Remsen and wife; Mr. and Mrs. Wurts; pretty little Miss Marié and her very nice mamma and brother; Mrs. Habicht, and others. I can't remember any more just now.

Sharon's a pretty place, in the midst of a pretty country. The natives seem to be a primitive race: they crowded up to the Pavilion on "hop" nights to see the dancing, and flattened their noses hour after hour against the windows with a patient perseverance in admiration worthy of a party

of South Sea Islanders paying their first visit on board a man-of-war. My
own amusements were limited. Was with Ellen a good deal—God bless
her. She gave up waltzing, except with the girls, because she thought I
didn't like it, the first day we reached Sharon. Indeed, I shouldn't have
liked it, by a great deal. I walked about the country a little and we took
a drive every now and then, to Prospect Hill or the "Palisades"—one
drive with Griffin and Miss K. was highly entertaining—and one moonlight expedition, with little Miss Marié, on a most sultry night was
refreshing. There was a good deal of music. Ellen was principal per-
former and was persecuted to sing to the utmost limit of her good nature.
One of the Boston Bigelow girls played nicely and Major Searle accompanied himself on the guitar occasionally, to his own great delectation.

September 10, SUNDAY EVENING.   Have walked downtown this beautiful moonshiny night to see how Mary is getting on in her solitude here
in Greenwich Street, for all the balance of the household and Aunt Olivia
beside betook themselves to Whitestone again yesterday afternoon. So
here am I once more of an evening in this my little library and at the
same old table, and everything looking so natural and as it used to look
that I might almost fancy the last six months a pleasant delusion, only
that instead of the lamp that used to be lit so punctually for me I've a
couple of candles, and that the table is lumbered up with all sorts of
things and in such an entirely chaotic condition that it is apparent that
some unwonted cause has been at work and reduced it to its present
state of neglect and confusion.

"No more that clock repeats the hours," for it has run down. Its
seven used to be the signal for Hempel, Eitheiler, Adler, and Buffet; at
eight I used to look out for the boys coming down from the law examination in the library upstairs and wonder whether some of them wouldn't
come in for a cigar; half-past nine—Charley, if he was here, would insist
that he must go uptown; ten I used to make the signal for going into the
front room for a few minutes, to try experimental chords and fancy
modulations on the organ; half-past eleven generally found me at this
journal and warned me to shut it, lock it up, and march off to bed.

All that's over. It was a dreary monotony enough, and one or two
years more of it would have ruined me utterly; my faculties were rusting,
temper souring, feelings preying on myself for want of a dinner, and oh,
how wretched I was for the past two or three years and how happy I am
now! But it's strange how the thought that it's gone and over and never

can come back makes one feel toward any period of past life; what a beautiful melancholy light it sheds over times and things that were insignificant, dull, or downright disgusting while they lasted. It's like the change that distance works in the clouds—mere uncomfortable masses of damp, dingy fog, but when seen from far off, inaccessibly distant, becoming exquisite in form and glorious in coloring, beyond any object of this lower earth.

Great fire in Brooklyn last night and this morning—some three hundred houses burned. At Calvary Church twice today. Poussin, the minister of Republican France, taking tea in Union Place when I came off —quite an agreeable kind of person. At the Astor Place Opera House twice last week, *Elisir d'Amore* and *Fille du Régiment*, both pleasant— Donizetti's comic music lively and pretty—those operas worth a dozen *Lucias* and *Lucrezias*. Gramercy Park houses prospering, and I shall be in the little Fourth Avenue establishment in two or three weeks. How I shall furnish the *Schloss am Square* when it's finished, without borrowing, is an inscrutable problem about which I think it prudent not to trouble my head at present. This New Code is going to *tell*, I think, most powerfully, on "the Law and the Profits" and to reduce all professional incomes to a standard of Arcadian simplicity corresponding with the unsophisticated and primitive rudeness of the system introduced by it. . . .

September 14. . . . Took dear little Ellen to Flushing in the *Washington Irving* last night, came down this morning, and am going up again at five. . . .

September 18, MONDAY. Pleasant fall weather. Spent Saturday and yesterday at Flushing. Weather was cool and autumnal, and we were very comfortable, barring a sick headache on Saturday, and the charcoal and magnesia treatment to which I resorted in order to get rid of it. . . .

Charley in town this morning: he has been having a grand time at Catskill. How I wish we could have gone! I never appreciated the *maladie du pays* before, but the memories of the Mountain House and the region around it haunt me perpetually now, I suppose because it's the only place I'm familiar with where nature's to be seen in something like ruggedness and mountain grandeur. The drive up the Mountain House road in the shadow of the mountain rising high and almost perpendicularly on the right with its dark growth of pines and hemlocks, and far up, hundreds of feet above, a single tree just catching the last rays of the sun that's setting behind the mountain and glowing there like a mass of arborescent gold, relieved against the clear autumnal blue sky and giving deeper gloom by the contrast to the solemn shadows that have settled on all the woods below—it seems to me as if I'd give a year of life to be traveling up there with Ellen this evening and to have her quite well and strong enough for a little rambling and scrambling on the mountain for two or three days of sunshine and pleasant weather. . . .

September 20. At Niblo's last night (Astor Place). *London Assurance,* clever comedy, played middling well. Driven nearly desperate by the mosquitoes all the rest of the night as the small hours drew on. I commenced promenading the room with my eyeglass on my nose, candle in one hand and handkerchief in the other, "deer stalking" on a small scale. Game shy—bagged three mosquitoes and one cockroach and finally sunk into slumber a little before four. Desperately tired and altogether good for nothing all today; superintended the removal uptown of sundry household gear, sweeping out most of the chairs from this apartment and the bureau from my dormitory on the second story. We shall soon be in our little Fourth Avenue house. Ellen's rooms at No. 24 Union Square are being stripped and dismantled and most of her furniture is already removed to our future quarters. It made me quite unhappy to see the rooms sacked that have always looked so bright and comfortable. . . .

September 25, MONDAY AFTERNOON. So tired that I feel as if rising from this chair were a physical impossibility. Poor little Ellen is decidedly ill: no worse thing the matter than influenza, I hope, but that is no mild affliction when it comes with fever and restlessness and all pervading weariness and pain for its symptoms. She wasn't well on Saturday, but the indomitable little woman would be up and busy with her little household arrangements at No. 54 Union Place, so yesterday she had to lie still and suffer for it, and today she's no better at all. Spent all yesterday at No. 24 with her except a short walk to Twenty-first Street and up the Third Avenue in the morning and an expedition to this place and back in the evening, and as I had little sleep for the past two nights (only an hour or so last night) I feel most abjectly tired just at present. Dr. Johnston has been invoked, and I trust he'll do his office so far as to alleviate her troubles and give the poor little girl the comfortable, refreshing sleep that her feverishness has denied her for the past two days. . . .

Haven't been very energetic this morning, though I tried to get my-

self into working order by a stimulating cup of coffee at Delmonico's—
the first time I've so sinned against my liver for some months. . . .

Bought a pew in Calvary Church, Saturday, of Isaac S. Hone—$550.
Poor old Jesse Oakley unaccountably blew his brains out Saturday in the
little room adjoining the Supreme Court clerk's office. Inspected the
little Fourth Avenue house t'other day—the area of the future domestic
circle, if two points can constitute a circle. Furnishing nearly completed
and everything looking supremely spruce. We were to have taken possession Thursday, but poor Ellen's indisposition will probably retard us.

September 30, SATURDAY AFTERNOON. My little wife not well yet—
better and worse by turns all through the week—and this morning better
decidedly than she has been since her illness began, but I'm afraid that
when I go uptown this evening I shall find her down again and as wretched
as ever. . . .

Tom Griffing I saw yesterday. He seems improved by his campaign,
though it was not a very eventful one and involved little consumption of
powder except in Mexican snipe shooting. . . .

Thackeray's *Vanity Fair*. Not a "work of genius," as some people
call it, by any means, but a remarkable book written on a new principle
and likely to have many imitators in this age—the principle being the
exclusion of any sort of *idealism* in character, plot, or catastrophe. Its
title is an apt one, "a novel without a hero." And now that "heroism,"
in every sense but the melodramatic, is at a discount, people will naturally
feel best satisfied and most at home with a class of fiction that has no
characters or features or notions in its structure that rise much above
their own experience of the world themselves; they will prefer a Hogarth
to all the romantic scene painters in the world. And it is a preference
that no one need quarrel with. Every commonplace man, woman, and child
on earth has hopes and fears and destinies and trials and latent powers of
good and evil that no human artist can do justice to. The elements of
what we called Romance are but a cheap substitute, after all, for the
awful interest of everyday realities. The greatest painters of the most
glorious period of art found their noblest ideals in portrait, and the considerations which explain their triumphant use of individual portraiture
of the human face in their greatest and most strictly ideal works, and their
infinite superiority over our modern painters with their (so-called)
original insipidities of their own creation apply for aught I can see with
tenfold force to the painter of character in novel or drama. *Every* character
is ideal. . . .

1854

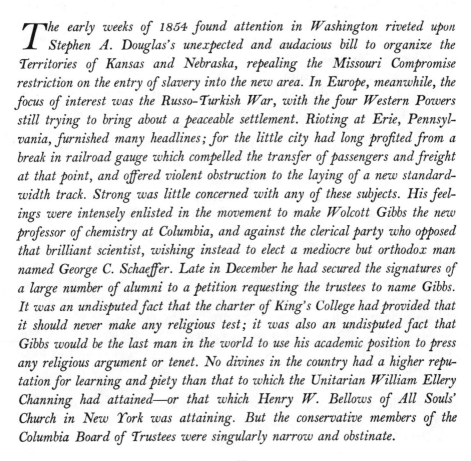

*T*he early weeks of 1854 found attention in Washington riveted upon
Stephen A. Douglas's unexpected and audacious bill to organize the
Territories of Kansas and Nebraska, repealing the Missouri Compromise
restriction on the entry of slavery into the new area. In Europe, meanwhile, the
focus of interest was the Russo-Turkish War, with the four Western Powers
still trying to bring about a peaceable settlement. Rioting at Erie, Pennsylvania, furnished many headlines; for the little city had long profited from a
break in railroad gauge which compelled the transfer of passengers and freight
at that point, and offered violent obstruction to the laying of a new standard-
width track. Strong was little concerned with any of these subjects. His feelings were intensely enlisted in the movement to make Wolcott Gibbs the new
professor of chemistry at Columbia, and against the clerical party who opposed
that brilliant scientist, wishing instead to elect a mediocre but orthodox man
named George C. Schaeffer. Late in December he had secured the signatures of
a large number of alumni to a petition requesting the trustees to name Gibbs.
It was an undisputed fact that the charter of King's College had provided that
it should never make any religious test; it was also an undisputed fact that
Gibbs would be the last man in the world to use his academic position to press
any religious argument or tenet. No divines in the country had a higher reputation for learning and piety than that to which the Unitarian William Ellery
Channing had attained—or that which Henry W. Bellows of All Souls'
Church in New York was attaining. But the conservative members of the
Columbia Board of Trustees were singularly narrow and obstinate.

January 8, SUNDAY. . . . Went last evening with Mr. Ruggles and George Anthon to Professor Charles Anthon's for a council over the affairs of the College, and particularly Gibbs. First time I've spoken to "Bull" since 1838, for some six years before which time he was the object of my reverent admiration and dread, an awful, unaccountable divinity, most frequently malevolent. Spent a couple of hours with him very pleasantly, then to Charles King's awhile, and then home. Was reading in this library at one or thereabouts, when an alarm of fire and the sight of a fine rich column of smoke lit up with a very angry red light rolling off toward the southwest, seemingly not far off, sent me on a brisk trot down the Fourth Avenue and Broadway, through the frosty air and along the silent streets of a January midnight. No one was stirring anywhere, but now and then a pedestrian on the same errand as mine. Fire was in Tripler Hall and Laffarge's Hotel, very showy and splendid. . . . When I came off at a little before four, the fire was rampant and volant throughout all the building, and this morning it appears badly burnt up and burnt out. Fires are epidemic this season, three bad ones within a month: Harpers', the *Great Republic*, and this half-million hotel. . . .

Of course, the leading idea of the past ten days has been Gibbs. No time to go into particulars, but there will be "a murder grim and great" before his defeat and all the chain of consequences are disposed of. Result of election uncertain and unpromising. We meet tomorrow at two; the committee will report simply the papers in its hands, without recommending anything. And it may be that the *Fossil* party, having a majority (Hoffman can't come down from Albany), will insist on an election at once. If so, we must talk against time or use any other lawless weapon chance may provide. But I don't think they'll be disposed to take that course—and that Schaeffer won't be elected is far less uncertain than that Gibbs will.

Certain resolutions will be offered that will make the fur fly a little, the ayes and noes being called for, and an intimation made of a committee of inquiry from the legislature if they are voted down. . . .

January 9. . . . Now for Columbia College. We met at two P.M. Mr. Ruggles offered his resolutions, and a storm followed such as was foreseen. All the six clerical members of the board pronounced distinctly and expressly against them and *against Gibbs* on the sole ground of his religious belief, and the resolutions were "indefinitely postponed" on motion of Dr. Spring. Election postponed to a week from Tuesday. Gibbs's election no longer to be hoped, but I think Schaeffer may be defeated, who is utterly unfit for the place. Wainwright, Haight, and one or two men of Gibbs's opponents won't vote for Schaeffer, if they can help it.

Vestry meeting tonight. Very ill-tempered and vicious, a mere series of squabbles without result.

I am most thoroughly disgusted with the action and language of the clerical members of the board of Columbia College, including the three members of the clerical staff of Trinity. The resolutions offered and objected to by them were, in substance, that inasmuch as the original charter and the subsequent acts of the legislature since the Revolution prohibited any religious qualification for office in the College, members of the board cannot rightfully or lawfully object to any candidate for the vacant professorship on account of his religious creed. One would think it a truism, a mere formal assertion, that men with the enlightened conscience of a professed theologian cannot lawfully do that indirectly by ballot and *sub silentio* which the law of the land and this special contract with the state forbids them to do directly and avowedly; that if it was conceded to be wrong, unlawful, and a breach of trust to adopt a resolution that Unitarianism or Deism or Roman Catholicism should debar a man from office in the College, it was quite as wrong to debar him from that office on that avowed ground without that resolution.

Yet these gentlemen, churchmen and dissenters, all avowed distinctly that they would not vote for any Unitarian candidate, whatever might be his qualifications for the place.

I asked Haight and Wainwright: Suppose Gibbs went to Trinity Church, would you not vote for him? Their answer was *"Yes, most gladly"* —or if he went to the Presbyterian Church. But they say this is *not* establishing a religious test, or violating the provisions under which they hold office. . . .

Wainwright, Spring, and Knox during the meeting of the board, and Haight in talk after the adjournment, were *explicit* on this subject.[1] And the unutterable illogicality of their talk! Confusion of practical immorality with the soundness or error of the tenets in matters of religion to which the enactments in question refer. Confusion between what one *can* do and what one can *lawfully* do. Ignoring of any responsibility except to the Supreme Court on a *quo warranto*. These are thy *priests*, O, Israel!

[1] The Rev. Jonathan M. Wainwright, Provisional Bishop of New York; the Rev. Gardiner Spring, minister of the Brick Presbyterian Church; the Rev. John Knox, pastor of the Middle Dutch Church; and the Rev. Benjamin Isaacs Haight, assistant minister of Trinity Church; all conservative trustees.

Although the Kansas-Nebraska bill passed the Senate on March 3 by the decisive majority of twenty-three, it had aroused a terrible storm of anger in the North and West, and the vote in the House was uncertain. Opposition there had become intense. On March 21 a sudden manoeuvre by Brockholst Cutting of New York sent it to Committee of the Whole; an unhappy fate, for debate in that body was unrestricted, and it might be delayed by talk on all kinds of subjects. The irate Southern Democrats made Cutting feel the weight of their wrath, and Strong's diary contains a record of the excitement in New York City when it seemed likely that the young Congressman might be pressed into a duel with John C. Breckinridge of Kentucky. Feeling between the slavery and anti-slavery forces was growing, and free-soilers of the North were rallying all their forces to prevent any further expansion of the institution they detested. At the same time, the international scene was becoming darker. The Crimean War was now fully begun. All efforts to bring Turkey and Russia to an agreement had failed, and France and Britain were resolved to permit no dismemberment of the Ottoman Empire. Dislike of the Czar and his tyranny was strong among all liberals of Western Europe; the French emperor was hopeful that he could strengthen his still-insecure regime by some glorious victories in the East; and the British government was anxious to safeguard its communications with India. By the end of March, 1854, forces were being gotten in readiness to defend Turkey against Russia, or if necessary to invade the Czar's domains. Nearer home, certain difficulties with the Spanish authorities in Cuba led many to fear a conflict with Madrid. The steamer Black Warrior, voyaging between New Orleans and New York, touched at Havana. Because of some irregularities in her papers, she was seized by the Spanish port officials. Radical Southern leaders like John Slidell and John A. Quitman demanded drastic action, and for a few tense weeks war seemed a distinct possibility. Finally the steamer was released and the tension ended—but the Southern desire for the annexation of Cuba remained keen.

The crisis in Columbia College affairs was now approaching its climax. All the principal newspapers had taken a hand. The Tribune on February 3 had violently assailed the conservative trustees for their "illiberality" in "trampling on rights secured by the most solemn sanctions of the law" and trying "to establish a religious test as a condition of office." The Evening Post on February 2 had raised the question whether it was proper to place an institution of learning in the hands of men almost exclusively of one religious *sect. The* Courier and Enquirer *printed a spirited expostulation. Senator Hamilton Fish was detained in Washington until the final vote was taken on the Kansas-Nebraska bill in the upper chamber; after that he was free to come to New York. Both parties plied him with letters; Ruggles urging him to take a stand for justice and law, while Gouverneur Ogden complained to him that the anti-Gibbs forces were being subjected to intimidation and outside pressure. But Fish sat stubbornly on the fence.*

March 27. At Albany Mr. Ruggles read some proof sheets of the Gibbs document to Hoffman, who of course bestowed some gas on Jonathan [Wainwright] the next time he encountered that venerable man. This led to a breakfast: Potter, Jonathan, Ruggles. Jonathan in perplexity. "If this thing can only be settled without trouble, there will never be any question of the same sort." "Haight and I can't take the back track so suddenly." "Do be sure that Fish and Hoffman attend the next meeting." "Don't let Gibbs resign if he's elected." "Tell him he may be sure of the most cordial support, laboratory, assistants, anything he wants." "Above all, don't let him be defeated." O, Jonathan, Jonathan! What must be the vital power of the church that lives in spite of such organs and ministers?

March 30, THURSDAY. Snowstorm nearly all day. . . . No [Cutting-Breckinridge] duel after all. People think now that there won't be any duel, and that all the talk is smoke and gas, or both. Miss Jenny Field (David Dudley Field, the codifier's daughter) took tea with Ellie and saintly Miss Ellen Rodgers, who goes to Lisbon Saturday with her diplomatic brother-in-law O'Sullivan.

The Gibbs manifesto printed at last. The conclusion of that job is a comfort. I've so read and reread drafts and copies, first proofs and second, of that document, that I'm disqualified to form any opinion as to its effect on others, or its merit and value. But it seems to me a very compact, clear, unanswerable paper. There can be no doubt that it is full of thought, and that there is in it much that will bear expansion and is capable of development, and that may perhaps need explanatory or rhetorical dilution to make it generally intelligible.

March 31. Very filthy drizzle all day. No prospect of any duel at Washington after all. With all its high moral sense, I think the public is disappointed, like a mob at an execution, balked by a reprieve. Gibbs manifesto sent out today among the trustees. Can't foresee its effect, can't name a single vote we shall gain by it, and do not think we shall lose any, but it's dubersome. . . . Mr. Ruggles went to Albany this afternoon and hopes to bring Hoffman down Monday, which hope is, I think, vanity. I don't know whether I wish Gibbs may be elected or not. It's a tolerably even balance of interest.

April 1. . . . Most pleased with Dr. Kane's volume of Arctic experiences. [2] It's far more attractive than any narrative of northern voyages and discovery that I've met. Franklin's first journey has a strong tragic interest, but this far surpasses it in clearness and picturesqueness of description and conveys a much more distinct image of the perils and marvels of the polar ice. . . .

Governor Seymour has vetoed the Maine Liquor Law. Whether he's right or wrong is a question on which an off-hand opinion is clearly presumptuous, for the questions involved are deep and dubious. I've no sort of sympathy with the temperance fanatics—rather a prejudice against them. But I am sure it would be better for mankind if alcohol were extinguished and annihilated. Has or has not society the right to make it contraband, as it forbids the sale or storage of gunpowder within certain limits, as it . . . assumes a right to confiscate and destroy a beauteous print brought into the custom-house from Paris? I don't know. If the popular voice demands this kind of legislation, we shall have it, and with the support of popular sentiment it will be enforced. Otherwise, the law will probably not be enacted, and if enacted will certainly not be enforced. The democratic despotism of a majority is a formidable element of injustice and oppression, but it is the power to which we are subject and which will determine this question.

Hamilton Fish is in town and will probably be present at the Columbia College meeting Monday afternoon. We are like to have a refreshing season there. Result uncommonly dubious. If Mr. Ruggles brings Hoffman down from Albany, and if Morris be absent, Gibbs will pretty surely be elected. Whether that be desirable or not desirable, I can't say. Should he be elected, we are only entering on the battle. Our fight has been thus far nothing but a preliminary skirmish. Should he be defeated, we may stand in a better position for the contest as to the strengthening or enlargement of our educational work, the conversion of the second-rate college into a university. And it may be well for us to gain this advantage by the loss of an individual agent clearly the best in his own department.

April 3, MONDAY.   All is lost save our honor. The trustees of Columbia

[2] Elisha Kent Kane's book, *Arctic Explorations: The Second Grinnell Expedition in Search of Sir John Franklin, in the Years 1853–1855*, published in two volumes, told an heroic story so ably that it reached almost every American home.

College met at two P.M. Present, beside the members usually attending, Governor Fish, Ogden Hoffman, and G. W. Morris. Absent, that sagacious man Jonathan the Bishop. Some interlocutory business done: question about the effect of John C. Stevens's thirty-foot excavation in an alleged bed of quicksand underlying the college; the possible tumbling into the gulf of McVickar's house and Charles Anthon's, not to speak of the whole college building up to Church Street being endangered should this traditional quicksand begin to run out. When that matter and some other affairs had been disposed of, the professorship came up. We went into ballot, and the result was as follows, to wit: (I put down names because each is certain and unmistakeable.)

For Wolcott Gibbs	*For one Richard McCulloh*
Charles King	Rev. Dr. Berrian
S. B. Ruggles	Rev. Dr. Haight
Ogden Hoffman	Rev. G. Spring
H. J. Anderson	Rev. John Knox
Edward Jones	Rev. G. H. Fisher
Robert Ray	William Betts
William H. Hobart	T. L. Wells
Clement C. Moore	G. G. Van Wagenen
G. T. Strong	G. M. Ogden
(9)	G. W. Morris
	Dr. Beadle
	(11)

Hamilton Fish voted for Professor Bache, virtually a blank, as Bache was not in nomination and would not take the place. His expectation no doubt was that the vote would be 10 to 10 and that by this inoperative vote he would keep the question open, retain the balance of power, and after moving for postponement (which he told me he meant to propose after the first ballot) dictate terms to both sides. But the defection of Beadle defeated this very politic purpose. Beadle has no doubt been converted by Knox and Fisher, in whose churches he is a deacon or a ruling elder or something else.

There was no fuss when the result was announced. Betts moved a resolution that McCulloh was elected, a piece of surplusage which he withdrew when Mr. Ruggles asked the ayes and noes on its passage. Spring proposed an inauguration and an inaugural address, but backed out when King suggested that this business had better be hushed up and that any parade of our choice might be impolitic.

We adjourned early. Had a long discourse with King, Hoffman, Anderson, and Mr. Ruggles thereafter. O *Piscicule—Fecisti ridiculi— Piscium minimiscule!* . . .

Beadle's defection may have been effected by the influence and exertions of Knox and Fisher, or perhaps by the very decided churchmanship of the printed manifesto.

We're now just on the beginning of a shindy: legislative inquiry, open controversy, war to the knife. King says that McCulloh will certainly accept the appointment. Seems to me not so certain. . . .

Fish says that when Colonel Benton is interrogated as to the probable fate of the Nebraska bill he replies: "Did you ever see a dog, sir, in the month of July or August, which had been shot through the head about a fortnight before? The condition of that animal, sir, after that accident, is the condition of the bill you mention. Putrefaction, sir, and decomposition, and tendency to annihilation, characterize alike the dead dog and 'the dead bill.' "

Strong's disgust and disappointment over the rejection of Wolcott Gibbs were violently felt. "This Columbia College business half tempts me to turn Roman Catholic," he wrote on April 4. "The clerical morality of that church is certainly not below that of the Anglican Church, or of Protestantism generally. And its music is far better and higher." Feeling, like Ruggles, that a good legislative inquiry was needed, he expressed fear that Fish was using his strong influence at Albany to prevent one. Great excitement was felt among the alumni, among whom the attorney Silas Weir Roosevelt (class of 1842; an uncle of the future President Theodore Roosevelt) and George James Cornell (class of 1839) headed a movement to censure the trustees. A pamphlet war began to rage and attracted wide attention. Ruggles's well-written manifesto, "The Duty of Columbia College to the Community, and its Right to Exclude Unitarians from the Professorships of Physical Science," scattered broadcast by the efforts of Moses H. Grinnell and others, evoked from Gouverneur Ogden a reply: "A Defence of Columbia College from the Attack of Samuel B. Ruggles." An investigation by a committee of the state Senate in due time took place. A dozen of the trustees declined to answer its inquiries;

and it finally reported that while some of the individual members might have been guilty of a breach of trust, the college could not be said to have violated its charter.

April 14, GOOD FRIDAY.   To church at Trinity, where Hobart preached. Yesterday afternoon an April shower, this afternoon another, preceded by the deathliest cold chill wind and congealed before it reached us into a snowstorm which continues at the date of these presents, viz.: about midnight.

General war in Europe avowed at last; the Queen and Louis Napoleon have announced to England and France that they are at war with Russia. Probably we're entering on a historical period that will affect the map of Europe ten years hence.

Also, there is war in Columbia College, and all the signs of a coming shindy, far more bitter and vehement than anything yet. Mr. Ruggles's pamphlet is circulating far and wide, scattered by Moses H. Grinnell, backed by George Cornell and a batch of alumni. It excites attention and almost unanimous approval. The Harvard people (Mr. Ruggles is just back from Cambridge) are enthusiastic about its merits. Only Agassiz says he don't want this battle fought from within the Church. *I do.* If it's wholly without the Church, the field is not worth fighting for. From imperfect telegraphic despatches received last night, it would seem that the legislature has appointed a joint committee of inquiry, "with power to send for persons and papers," and has passed Cornell's bill giving the chairman of any such committee power to attach and imprison for contempt, or for refusal to answer a question. I anticipate a rumpus if this resolution has actually passed both houses, and it is clear that it has passed the Senate. Irreconcilable breach and "the rigor of the game" must follow. Bellows takes the same view with Agassiz, and objects to the "churchmanship" of the letter. Thank God he does. . . .

It is an immense fact that a *majority* of the churchmen in the board and H. J. Anderson (Roman Catholic) voted for Gibbs; that all the dissenters, Spring, Knox, Fisher, and Beadle, voted against him, in solid phalanx. . . .

April 15.   Easter eve. . . . At Columbia College from 1 to 2:30 with King, Knox, and Betts; meeting of our "Centennial" Committee, called at Knox's request, who thought the alumni meeting required some action by the committee, or some statement of facts to be laid before the ad-

journed meeting a week hence. Betts's self-complacency led him to think
otherwise, and King and I saw no reason for any action. . . .

Our next meeting, first Monday of May, will be stormy, I think.
McCulloh has accepted. Glad of it. But it don't raise my opinion of the
man. Perhaps the Association for the Advancement of Science, about to
meet at Washington, may so express itself as to change his views. . . .

April 17. . . . In the matter of Columbia College there is nothing new,
except that the Senate has appointed a committee (Brooks, Hopkins, and
Danforth) on its own account—the House non-concurring; and that the
committee will probably act notwithstanding the non-concurrence. Unless
there be much caution and circumspection, this will do far more harm
than good. And I don't clearly see how it can do much real good in any
way. . . .

News from across the Atlantic. The tocsin is clearly sounding for
instant battle on the largest scale, with the most tremendous material
agencies, and the most momentous interests depending on the issue.
These months are important in the history of the century, perhaps of the
age.

(Though Gurowski's vaticinations do not amount to a great deal, I
used to hear him talk precisely the same talk which is written down and
elaborated in *Russia As It Is,* hour after hour, and used to be bored
thereby.)

But this is a serious controversy for the Old World, and for mankind, if it be vigorously prosecuted as it has begun. That the civilization
of Western Europe, continental Europe, at least, is effete and worn out,
like that of the Roman Empire, I can't doubt. Should the ultimate triumph
of Russia introduce a new element, Cossack or Slavonic or whatever it
may be, into the social life of the Old World, shattering and destroying
all its present organizations, the disruption may well prove a blessing.
And this seems to be what politicians hold up as the consequence of
allowing Russia to go unopposed, and the reason for resisting her progress southward to the Dardanelles. As to the propriety of kicking Islam-
ism out of Europe as it kicked itself in, four hundred years ago, I've no
doubt.

The French and English forces at Malta or somewhere else have been
exchanging musical compliments, the French regimental bands playing
"God Save the Queen," the English, "Partant pour la Syrie." Very
appropriate and significant in the latter, considering why, for what
object, and in what spirit, "Dunois, the young and brave" departed

thither. Alas for the old, undoubting, fraternal league of all the nationalities of Christendom against pagans and misbelievers! Godfrey and Tancred and Saint Louis were indifferently posted up as to the balance of power.

John Bull goes joyously into the battle. But I think he will be tired before it is done (though I don't know but his rulers contemplate nothing more than a partition with their enemy of the spoils of their ally). Suppose he sinks or captures every Russian ship of war now afloat, drives the Czar across the Danube and out of the Principalities, bombards Odessa, Sebastopol, and Cronstadt, occupies St. Petersburg itself, how much nearer is he to victory and the conquest of peace? . . .

April 21. . . . . European news vague, contradictory, and unreliable. Its utter uncertainty throws some light on the value of history in matters of detail. What the Russians have done since they crossed the Danube on the extreme left of their line and got into the notorious swamps of the Dobrudja, whether they've taken divers fortalices and strong places, Hirsova included, or have not, whether there is any demonstration against Kalifat or not, are questions no man can answer.

As was foreseen, the tempest of Saturday and Sunday was fruitful of disaster. More than one shipwreck on the Jersey shore, and sad destruction of life. The *Powhatan,* stranded within three hundred feet of the beach, broke up slowly, and every one of her two or three hundred passengers and crew perished in the surf.

As to Columbia College, I hear that the caucus of alumni that has been sitting from day to day through the week has adopted a scheme of action for the meeting tomorrow, and that a string of resolutions will be offered far from complimentary to the trustees. There is room for doubt whether this proposed action can be carried out, though a large majority of the older alumni incline to adopt it. The graduates of the last three or four years will probably be numerously represented, and will be generally in favor of cooperating with the trustees in a celebration. Ogden and Betts now say that they won't attend the meeting at all, from which I infer that their efforts to collect backers have failed and that they have found they will have no material to work with. Ogden has met with decided rebuffs from several persons to whom he has made application, as Dick Emmet and G. W. Wright, for instance. . . .

Have been looking into Maurice's *Theological Essays* tonight. Some things seem profoundly good and true, others (at the first glance) shallow and wrong. There seems to be much vigor and life in the "Broad Church" platform of F. D. Maurice, Charles Kingsley, and their backers. Am disposed to think their views more likely to *tell* on men and to be felt in the Church than those of either the High Church or the Evangelical party.

April 22, SATURDAY. . . . The alumni meeting was a great success. Very large and respectable, 125 present, thirty-four classes represented; Robert Kelly, Sedgwick, James A. Hamilton, John Jay, Russel, Cornell, Ike Fowler, Henry Nicoll, Rev. A. S. Leonard (converted and now adverse to the trustees), Dick Emmet, John Hamersley, Richard H. Ogden, W. T. Johnson, and so on, present and of one mind. They tried to gag Worthy Romaine, but couldn't. He declined the honorable appointment of associate secretary to take down the names of all present, and made a great speech, which the reporters tried to take down but abandoned at last, because it did not clearly appear on which side he was talking or what ideas he meant to convey. Then Weir Roosevelt took up his parable and made a speech which Anthon reports to have been clear and creditable, moving a long string of resolutions concocted in caucus during the week. Russel seconded them and made a long and vigorous talk, pitching energetically into the trustees. Leonard objected that what was done could not be undone and that it was entirely idle to pass resolutions about it (not so unreasonable a suggestion), but expressly declared himself hostile to the position taken by the trustees. Only a certain Rev. Coffee, who probably wants a D.D., and little lithping niminy-piminy Gillespie, who wants a professorship, took sides distinctly with the board. Jay offered substitutes for two of the resolutions and seems to have supported them very well, and the original resolutions thus modified were carried by about 90 votes to 30. It seems that the purport of the resolutions is to condemn and censure the policy of the board, to thank the minority, to recommend those members whose conscientious convictions interfere with the execution of their trust to resign their seats, to decline cooperation for the present with the board in any celebration, and to appoint a pretty strong committee of about thirty to ask the board about the programme of the celebration and the policy of its future administration, and report their answer to a future meeting of the alumni. On the whole, a very emphatic rebuke.

April 23. The alumni resolutions in this morning's *Herald* are better than I expected; appear to have been framed with care and accuracy and present no salient points for attack. And a list of the men who adopted them shews an array of very weighty and respectable names, Trinitarian and Unitarian. I think this is a shot that will tell a little. But it won't be as effective as Gould and Peirce and Lovering seem to suppose. . . . I hope for nothing from this demonstration, except a strong skirmish which may move all parties to increased energy and activity in moving uptown and enlarging the usefulness of the College. . . .

April 24, MONDAY. Meant to have been wildly energetic in business today, but it passed away somehow in confabulation with Mr. Ruggles, Cornell, Knox, and George Anthon over the Saturday's alumni meeting, which is conspicuous in this morning's papers, and was in fact an important demonstration. Mare's nest discovered; Betts, "Professor of Law," is also trustee. The Revised Statutes forbid any tutor or professor in an incorporated college to be a trustee of the same. Did Betts's acceptance of this professorship after Kent's death vacate his seat as trustee? If it did, Professor McCulloh is not elected. There was a tie on the ballot supposed to have resulted in his election, or rather no majority for any one candidate. It was Gibbs 9, McCulloh 10, Bache 1; eleven votes necessary for a choice. And was not Gibbs in fact elected on some of the earlier ballotings? I've not time to look back.

Rumor of an answer to Mr. Ruggles's pamphlet. Can't find out by whom, or where it can be seen. . . .

April 25. Combat thickening in Columbia College. People *vs.* Carrique in 2d Hill seems to make it clear that Betts's acceptance of the law professorship vacated his seat as trustee; *ipso facto*, that every vote he has given is a nullity. Very well for our professor of law. I hope the alumni committee which meets Saturday will suggest this little complication to the board. . . .

The pamphlet vehemently approved in all quarters. The college is like to be a "Bishop without a Church." Unless it is equal to self-sustainment in infinite absolute space, without support from its alumni or from any portion of the community, it would seem to be in a bad way.

April 26. News from Europe. No fighting yet in the Baltic; uncertain reports of Russian defeat in the Principalities and on the south side of the Danube.

May 1, MONDAY. Much complaint by the English press of delay in bringing troops into the seat of war and of inaction of the naval force in the Baltic and the Black Sea. John Bull thinks his screw-steamers and bomb-ketchers have only to bark once, and his enemies are scattered. He errs, I think; at least he is not entitled to expect so speedy and easy a victory. This looks like a grim fight. . . .

Columbia College meeting at 2 P.M. W.T.J. had written King a letter calling his attention to the fact that one if not two seats in the board are vacant by operation of law, which King read apropos of the question of approving the minutes. But King was borne down by Fisher and others and nothing came of it. . . .

May 4.   Bilious. George Anthon dined here, and went with Ellie to the Crystal Palace, today "reinaugurated" under the auspices of Barnum. [3] Their report is claptrap, humbug, barrenness, and probable failure.

May 5.   It seems that Gouverneur Ogden and some unknown confederates are meeting to devise an answer to Mr. Ruggles's letter, and Gouverneur considers it an outrage that that business should be thrown on him.

May 6, SATURDAY.   Gouverneur Ogden has come out with a "defence" which reached me at dinner. It seems very feeble and flat, verbose, wooden, and stupid.

Went with Charlie to Century Club at eight. George Curtis, Marbury, Tracy, Durand, H. P. Gray, Bob LeRoy, Verplanck, Suydam, Ehninger, Cozzens, D. D. Field, O. S. Strong, Robert Kelly, Slosson, Schell, Van Winkle, and so on. Oysters and lobster salad and probable dyspepsia.

May 8.   I think Gouverneur Ogden's pamphlet like to do no execution. Cornell, Dr. Hobart, and others pronounce it a failure; William Waddington (Gouverneur's friend) and Anderson express the same conviction; and their first impressions are significant.

May 9, TUESDAY.   Got out of bed at six this sunshiny morning, breakfasted, and omnibussed down to the South Ferry, with a view to a Long Island Railroad train which the very timetable on the wall of the ferry office certified to start at 7:30. Found on crossing that it started at 7 and had gone. Also that the next train, announced in like manner for 9 A.M., had been recently postponed to 10 A.M. So I had two and a quarter hours before me to be killed in South Brooklyn. I improved the occasion by a walk to the Atlantic Dock, and took a first inspection of my "41 and 42" premises, unhappily under mortgage; on which mortgage I shan't pay off quite as much this spring as I meant to pay.

To Jamaica at last, and took a waggon to Rockaway; selected rooms,

[3] P. T. Barnum, who had a well-earned reputation for making money, had been induced by some of the stockholders to become a director of the languishing Crystal Palace enterprise. When he reluctantly consented, he was chosen president. It was already moribund, but he did what he could to arouse new interest. In his autobiography he remarks that "it was temporarily galvanized and gave several lifelike kicks."

loafed down to the beach, looked at the surf and sand hills and beach grass. Less stern and sad, I think, than the solemn cliffs of Nahant. May I not visit *that* place again! What followed so close on my last visit has colored my memories of our summer's sojourn there with tints of darkness and death, and has made that a place forbid. And, independently of all that, Nahant is full of stern and gloomy influences to which I don't want to be subjected. The glittering beach of Rockaway is cheerful compared with those austere ramparts of rock. The roll and break of the sea I watched this morning seemed inspiring and joyous when I remembered the sullen heave and subsidence of the sea on Pulpit Rock and East Point.

May 13. Looked at a *microscope* of Ross's, only $350, which I yearn to possess.

Went through the Astor Library yesterday for the first time. It is good and promises still better things.

May 15, MONDAY. Nebraska battle still raging at Washington with most dubious result. The meeting in the Park Saturday afternoon was a failure according to the *Herald* and the *Journal of Commerce*; a most stern, earnest, and unprecedented demonstration, according to the *Times*, the *Tribune*, and the *Courier*. Which is right, I don't know.

May 16. Fine weather. Dozed in the library chair till twelve, in a state of headache, then downtown and did some work, considering. Nebraska controversy still boisterous and bitter; the final, decisive explosion seems to be postponed to Saturday, when the bill will pass. Pierce seems to be trying to get up a war with Spain by way of diverting attention from this particular issue.

May 22. Long buttonholing talk with Professor Anderson today. He's more fully with the minority than I expected to find him—and condemns that murderous outlay on the Botanic Garden, and the consequent paralysis of the college for at least another generation, as heartily as I do.

Nebraska battle still undecided, but no one doubts the bill will pass the House. I'm resisting awful temptations to avow myself a Free-Soiler. Think I shall come out on the platform at last, a unit in the great Northern party the consummation of this swindle will call into being. I've never denied or doubted the wrong of slavery, assuming the fundamental dogmas of our polity to be right and true. I have denied that wrong because I could not affirm that all men were born free and equal. And I am no nearer the capacity to affirm that proposition. *Don't believe* all men so born. But if that be the conventional theory of our social institutions, we are entitled to enforce it and claim its benefits where its violation will do mischief. If North and South alike affirm the proposition, either may fairly insist on its consequences and corollaries; if that be our fundamental law, anyone may claim that it be consistently carried out, whatever he may think of its soundness.

May 23, TUESDAY. Nebraska bill passed the House at two A.M. by a small majority. Senate will concur in the amendments. . . .

On May 30, while the free-soil press pealed its denunciation, President Pierce signed the ill-omened Kansas-Nebraska Act. By this heedless piece of legislation, Douglas had immensely deepened the chasm between the two sections and accelerated the march toward civil war. Already the forces of freedom in the North were preparing to assist in filling Kansas with anti-slavery settlers. Passage of the law was quickly followed by an explosion in Boston. The Negro Anthony Burns, a Virginia slave who had taken up residence in Massachusetts, was arrested, arraigned before a federal commissioner, and delivered over to the authorities for transportation to his former home. Rioting broke out; an attempt at rescue was frustrated; and the city, crowded with indignant men from half of New England, went into mourning. It required the united force of city police, state militia, and federal troops and sailors to carry the poor black man back into bondage. The Northern States, in their indignation over the Kansas-Nebraska Act, were soon framing Personal Liberty laws.

Strong was amusing himself this spring by scientific and literary studies. He had ordered a powerful microscope from England, with object-glasses and accessories. The cost was formidable. "But I take intense interest and delight in that sort of investigation," he wrote, "and I think it wholesome. One gets relaxation by this total change of work—and truer appreciation of the marvels around him. 'Increased Defining Power' is further insight into the marvels of God." He read John Henry Newman's University Education *with admiration: "Full of thought and truth, its reasoning and conclusions real, clear, and deep." If Newman had lost a little in polish of style by leaving Oriel College for Ireland, he had gained in other respects. Echoes of the Wolcott Gibbs case continued to rumble around the horizon. On June 5, the Columbia trustees held a meeting at which Betts, attorney, clerk of the board, and professor of law, announced that he had a painful statement to make. Referring to the communication from the alumni law committee respecting his status, he*

*declared that although he believed their conclusions wrong, he had suffered
"agony" since they had raised the question, and believed it his duty to resign
both his law professorship and his post as trustee. Ruggles then wisely took the
initiative, and moved that he be re-elected as trustee; which was done.*

June 10, SATURDAY. The order of *Know-Nothings* seems to have
become a material fact. Late elections at Washington and Philadelphia
shew it to be a potent agency. "Street-preaching" rows here and in
Brooklyn prove it aggressive and bellicose and capable of using not only
the ballot box but the carnal weapon. Every recent indication of Northern
sentiment points to vigorous reaction against the Nebraska bill and the
formation of a strong anti-slavery party at the North. Should the next
move of the Administration be war with Spain, as predicted, there will
be an energetic and immense minority dissenting.

June 18, SUNDAY. The conjunction of Barnum and Jullien at the
so-called "Musical Congress with 1,500 performers" naturally produced
one of the grandest humbugs on record. Went with Ellie, George Anthon,
and Miss Tote. The last-named two dined here, as did Jack Ehninger,
but after sitting down with them, I had to retire to the library for a
headachy nap. The crowd was enormous. It is estimated at fifteen thousand
by some and forty thousand by others. I've no opinion at all as to the accuracy of either estimate. But for some time after taking our seats I was
seriously exercised about the possibilities of falling galleries and panic-
stricken multitudes, and was tempted to evacuate the building at once.

The building is most defective, acoustically. Sound passes off into
dome and transepts and is not reverberated by its flimsy walls of sheet
iron and glass. Solos were inaudible; an occasional emphatic note or two,
or a phrase from the orchestra, kept one *au courant.* To those who did
not know *The Messiah* and so on, the solo pieces must have been a great
mystery. Beside the unfitness of the building, there was the great mass
of muslin and broadcloth behind the solo singers (the orchestra and
chorus) which absorbed instead of reflecting their voices. And the incessant shuffling in and out of the vast crowd that was marching into and
about the building was sufficient to drown the voice of any but Stentor
or Boanerges. Four choruses from *The Messiah* (including the Hallelujah,
which was encored!!!, and the first chorus, "All flesh shall see it together,")
certainly gave to them all new power, and clearer expression of their
meaning. That first chorus of *The Messiah,* it seems to me, may perhaps
be the most awful embodiment of thought extant in music, with the

possible exception of the "Hallelujah." The rest of the concert was mostly trash. Overture to *William Tell* was unheard except the sharply cut, martial finale. We watched Jullien leading its opening movement and wondered what he could be doing, till a familiar squeak or two very high up in the scale indicated that the orchestra was at work on this overture. Wagner's *Tannhäuser* Overture was rather better—audible, and seems nice. Of the Symphony in C minor only the third movement and part of the finale were played; the former half audibly, the latter very vilely.

As to the grand "Fireman's Quadrille," words can't express its clap-trap. It's a pleasure to see humbug so consistently, extensively, and cleverly applied: military bands beginning to play in the distance, drawing nearer and finally marching into the orchestra; red and blue fire visible through the windows of the dome; a clamorous chorus shouting "Go it, 20," "Play away, 49," "hay-hay," and so on. The audacity of the imposition reconciled one to its grossness. But Jullien is a genius after all. There were taking points, even in this atrocious production; e.g., a very clever appropriation of phrases from the second movement of Beethoven's *devilish* A Symphony, and some admirable pieces of instrumentation meant to imitate the thundering, quivering, shuddering rush and roar of falling walls. Friday and Saturday nights the performances have been less ambitious and the audiences much smaller, though the price was reduced. I doubt the success of the speculation. I doubt whether the stock ever struggles much above 21. I sympathize with those who bought at par and held on for a rise at 175. The building seems all but gutted. Its character has changed. It is now merely an extension of Barnum's Museum.

June 20. After the everlasting rains of the spring, we are entering on a period of drowth. The sun sets, a well-defined, coppery disk like a red-hot penny in a dark room, and all the western sky is curtained with dull, coppery haze. Cholera is in town, and pretty active—fifty-odd deaths last week. But many of these cases were doubtless aggravated diarrhœa and cholera morbus, and all are thus far confined to the lowest and filthiest classes, whose existence from one day to another in their atmosphere of morphic influences is a triumph of vital organization and illustrates the vigorous tenacity of life (under the deadliest conditions) bestowed on the human species. But we may well be destined to undergo an epidemic this summer. Coleridge's Cologne was not more fetid or mephitic than this metropolis. The stinks of Centre Street lift up their voices. Malarious aromata rampage invisible through every street, and in the second-rate regions of the city, such as Cherry Street, poor old Greenwich Street, and so on, atmospheric poison and pungent foetor and gaseous filth cry aloud and spare not, and the wayfaring man inhales at every breath a pair of lungs full of vaporized decomposing gutter mud and rottenness. Alas for our civic rulers, whose office it is to see that this be not so. . . .

Old Davenport's very promising young son, George, seems to have gone suddenly to the dogs. An only son, his father full of pride (ill-concealed under censures of his extravagance) in his appetite for books and music, married within the year, he seems to have taken all at once to drink and gambling, to borrowing from everybody, swindling his clients, and to reckless shortsightedness and dishonesty that looks like monomania. I'm sorry for his steady-going old Presbyterian father, and also for Charley Strong, though victimized to the extent of only $115, which he's not like to see again. I should have loaned the young gentle-man very readily anything my bank account would conveniently stand, had he come to me, for we all had the fullest confidence in him. His father has made himself penniless to meet a $2,500 embezzlement, monies advanced by some society, of which he was treasurer and master, George "Counsel," for an investment on mortgage, and fraudulently stopped *in transitu.* His wife, the daughter of a Connecticut parson, went home to her father. Poor little woman, how desolate she probably is this evening! She left today and I suppose is now in the midst of the eager, indignant home circle, feebly striving to palliate, and excuse, and suggest doubts, with all the weapons of her poor little loving woman's wit; or more probably, as it's past twelve, trying to go to sleep in her own little room of former times, and thinking of her dirty little swindling scamp of a husband, in the sure and certain hope that he'll yet put down calumny and shew himself the greatest and best of men.

July 6. Wall Street all agog with the fraud on the New Haven Railroad Company by its President Robert Schuyler, whose failure was announced last week.[4] A swindle of near two millions, by no nameless money-making speculator, but by one of our "first" people in descent and social position and supposed wealth. . . . This swindle of Schuyler's is a great disaster and may well be the first crack that preludes general

[4] Robert Schuyler, president of the New York & New Haven Railroad, had signed hypothecated stock certificates to the value of about two millions. He absconded and efforts at pursuit failed.

crash and collapse. It has already, as its immediate consequence, weakened all confidence in a very large class of securities.

July 19. . . . Cholera has become somewhat threatening. The Board of Health makes daily reports. As yet, the cases are not very numerous, and the type of disease seems not specially malignant. Nineteen reported yesterday, I think, and two or three less today. . . .

July 26. Still fearfully and wonderfully hot. Cholera makes some progress, but less than one would expect, for this is said . . . to be the severest July since 1822. But many are a little out of order intestinally; cholic inflammation of the bowels and "cholerine" abound. . . .

We went to Rockaway Friday morning. Blistering heat. Waited at Jamaica some hours and dined there, then went to the Pavilion more comfortably. That evening did not promise much. Crowd, heat, bad fare, and mosquitoes, said to be exceptional and anomalous. Since then things have looked up a little, but the fare is indisputably villainous. Stayed over Saturday and Sunday. Saturday morning I took a long walk on the beach with my shoes and stockings off and pantaloons rolled up the knee. Result—pair of blistered legs that nearly deprived me of the power of locomotion the next day. Not only were they superficially *scalded*, but every now and then cramps came in the calf, so that I could not use the limb for a few minutes.

Came to town Monday; up Tuesday afternoon; down again this morning.

Saturday night the crowd was immense; lots of people were turned away without mercy. The Baxters came along with a large party, but three of them had to make their way back to Jamaica—the rest found accommodations on the floor somewhere. Mr. Ruggles slept on a sofa in Ogden Hoffman's cottage.

People at the Hotel: Carson Brevoort and wife, Mr. and Mrs. Cousinery, Mrs. Edward S. Gould and musical daughter, the Gerards, Le Barbiers, Mr. and Mrs. Meletta, *cum multis aliis*, mostly of a second and third rate type. . . .

Columbia College meeting Monday thinly attended. Van Wagenen read the proposed answer of the board to the queries of the Senate committee, which was ordered printed for examination. It denies categorically that any religious test has been imposed. Then Betts produced the long-expected result of his labors over the proposed remodeling of the college course. Long, prosy, and feeble, warm water at its tenth dilution. I thought Betts had more virility.

1856

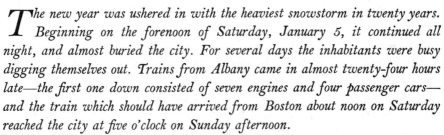

*T*he new year was ushered in with the heaviest snowstorm in twenty years. Beginning on the forenoon of Saturday, January 5, it continued all night, and almost buried the city. For several days the inhabitants were busy digging themselves out. Trains from Albany came in almost twenty-four hours late—the first one down consisted of seven engines and four passenger cars—and the train which should have arrived from Boston about noon on Saturday reached the city at five o'clock on Sunday afternoon.

The principal topics of the day were the protracted speakership contest in Congress and the alarming civil strife in Kansas. The struggle in the House, which had disturbed business and disgusted the country, finally ended on February 2, after nearly two months of deadlock, with the election of the Republican candidate, Nathaniel P. Banks. This was hailed in the North as the first great victory for freedom over slavery. In Kansas two rival regimes confronted each other: one the regular government under Wilson Shannon, who had been sent out by Pierce as the second territorial governor, and who was supported by a legislature elected by fraudulent means; the other an irregular "government" chosen by the free-soil settlers, who had made Charles Robinson of Lawrence their "governor." Violence simmered in the territory, and something near open warfare was expected in the spring. John Brown had reached Kansas in the autumn of 1855, and was soon to place a bloody imprint on its history. Feeling in the North against the Pierce Administration continued to grow, even the Democrats having little use for the President. Already it was certain that the Republicans would make a strong bid for control of the govern-

ment. Discussion of the campaign began early; and on February 18–20, 1856, a national Know-Nothing convention nominated Millard Fillmore and A. J. Donelson. Opponents of the Know-Nothings declared that this premature action would give ample opportunity for exposing the dangerous nature of nativism.

At last the war in the Crimea was ·drawing to an end. The Russians, who had lost more than a hundred thousand men in the fruitless defense of Sebastopol, realized that victory was out of the question. Napoleon III was tired of the long and costly struggle, and the British were quite willing to see it end. In February, 1856, the Treaty of Paris was signed. By it the Allies gained just one clear result—Russian warships were to be excluded from the Black Sea. Even this agreement, as time showed, was to be respected only for fifteen years. But the integrity of the Ottoman Empire had been preserved, and Britain's sea route to India was safe.

January 5. Today I enjoyed an hour of intercourse with the Rev. Eleazar Williams, believed by many three or four years ago to be the oppressed and suppressed successor of Louis XIV *de jure*. Wainwright came to me in the summer of 1854 about a deed conveying land to him and his successors in office, which was to be held on some vague trust, either for Eleazar personally or for a mission church he was organizing. The deed was waste paper, and so I advised the Bishop. The premises were thereupon given to him (Wainwright) absolutely, it seems, and it's now a question whether his heirs . . . shall transfer the premises to Eleazar individually or to some representative of the Church. . . . Bishop Potter has been called upon to direct what disposition shall be made of it, and he refers the question to Gouverneur Ogden and me as commissioners. Eleazar's manner impresses me favorably.

January 8, TUESDAY. This is a stern winter. Saturday's snowstorm was the severest for many years past. The streets are like Jordan, "hard roads to travel." One has to walk warily over the slippery sidewalks and to plunge madly over crossings ankle-deep in snow, in order to get uptown and down, for the city railroads are still impracticable and walking (with all its discomforts) is not so bad as the great crowded sleigh-caravans that have taken the place of the omnibi. These insane vehicles carry each its hundred sufferers, of whom about half have to stand in the wet straw with their feet freezing and occasionally stamped on by their fellow travelers, their ears and noses tingling in the bitter wind. . . .

May 8, THURSDAY. Ogden Hoffman, it's now said, left assets insufficient to pay his undertaker's bill, and debts beside. . . .

The distinguished citizen, well known in financial circles and formerly connected with the city government, to whom the newspapers are alluding as in some mysterious scrape with a woman, is none less than old Cornelius W. Lawrence.[1] It's a scrape of near twenty years' antiquity. The woman was the mistress of one Brown, who also kept the Red House at Harlem, a noted sporting place, and who afterwards married her. It seems the gentleman and lady have been living on Lawrence ever since he committed this indiscretion and bleeding him freely, cupping him by atmospheric pressure of threatened exposure and so on.

May 14, WEDNESDAY. Some uneasy feeling about possible complication with England in the matter of Nicaragua, Colonel Walker, and the Padre Vijil whom Pierce is about to recognize as Walker's legate *a latere.* J. J. Post badly beat in Superior Court in a suit growing out of some indiscreet invasions of other people's freeholds by him and his agents in the improvement of his own premises on Broadway. Columbia College meeting this afternoon (special) over the report of Building Committee on plans for the new college uptown, and over a project of Dillon's to open a new avenue between Fifth and Sixth from "Reservoir Square" to "Central Park." No definite conclusion was reached on the subject, and we were going to adjourn when Gouverneur Ogden rose solemnly to lug in the twopenny business of the last meeting (the action of the faculty on the offences of one Romeyn, a disorderly Sophomore, whose father's petition for his reinstatement after dismissal by the faculty was referred to the President at our regular May meeting). Gouverneur was aggrieved because the President, who has been ill, was not prepared to report any action and wanted a special meeting next Monday. Betts and Tom Wells were ready to record his motion, or any other motion indirectly attacking King, but Bishop Potter came out very manfully and distinctly in support of discipline, even Bradford was compelled to decline supporting his friend's demonstration, and Gouverneur backed out. But there may well be a serious shindy over that little matter. In the faculty there certainly will be, for King is in vast wrath against Bull Anthon, who has stimulated the disturbance to the utmost of his powers.

May 16, FRIDAY. Yesterday spent in a state of virulent, outrageous, unprovoked dyspepsia and headache, which I endured in Wall Street,

[1] Cornelius W. Lawrence had made a small fortune as partner in Hicks, Lawrence & Co., an auctioneer firm, and had been mayor of New York 1834–35.

having promised Ellie to go with her and Johnny to see the Düsseldorf pictures again in the afternoon. She called for me, and we inspected those works of art. Hanslein was astonished, bewildered, and delighted. Hübner's picture of the "Wounded Poacher" fixed his attention especially.[2] Didn't dine; couldn't go and hear the Rev. John Lord's lecture on Gregory VII in the evening. Spent it in cutting the leaves of *Modern Painters*, volume IV. Went for Ellie to Mr. Ruggles's and brought her home at ten-thirty in a very bilious condition indeed. There are many fine, original, brilliant, suggestive things in this fourth volume, but I fear Ruskin is writing a little too fast. Many passages occur in it that are unlike anything in the first and second or in the *Seven Lamps*, passages of rhetoric and fine writing embodying commonplace thought, of vehement, ornate diction not justified by force or beauty in the meaning they convey, passages in which he seems conscious that he is reputed eloquent and must sustain his reputation. Looked over his pages tonight with Mr. Ruggles, whom I found here on my return from an expedition to Canavan's after chloroform. Mr. Ruggles's delight with Ruskin was unqualified by acquaintance with the better things he has done. . . .

Yellow fever abundant and malignant at Quarantine, according to Cyrus Curtiss; reminiscences of its last year's ravages at Norfolk; general uneasy anticipation of its planting itself here this summer; popular notion that it's working northward in a specially malignant form.

War with England, apprehension whereof has become prominent within the last forty-eight hours. Ruin, of course, to all New Yorkers.

This was a gloomy spring to thoughtful Americans, as Strong's diary suggests. Kansas was suffering under a veritable reign of terror; American filibusters under William Walker were engaged in lawless killing and property-destruction in Central America; the Administration had carried its quarrel with Great Britain to a point which made sober citizens fear war; and the Senate, where sectional passion had reached a new climax, witnessed the most disgraceful scene of its history in the assault of Preston Brooks of South Carolina upon Charles Sumner of Massachusetts.

Twisting the lion's tail, always a popular American amusement, was politically profitable to any party in power in a campaign year. The Democratic Administration had no reason to treat British infringements of American neutrality leniently, and the British representatives in America had put them-

[2] Rudolf J. B. Hübner (1806–1882), German painter.

selves sadly in the wrong in enlisting men for the Crimean campaign. All winter and spring rumors that Minister Crampton was to be recalled or dismissed were rife on both sides of the Atlantic. The request of Secretary Marcy that he be recalled, which was kept partially secret, was unpalatable to the British government. The foreign minister, Lord Clarendon, refused to call Crampton home, and declared to our Minister in London, Buchanan, that he must hear from the envoy and the three British consuls before replying to Marcy. Finally the Pierce Administration lost patience. Marcy, on May 27, sent a decisive note to Lord Clarendon. He would accept the British assurances that no disregard of American neutrality had ever been planned, but he must dismiss Crampton, and revoke the exequaturs of Consuls Barclay, Mathew, and Rowcroft. On May 28 the dismissals duly took place. For a few weeks men feared that Great Britain would send Minister Dallas home in retaliation (he had replaced Buchanan in London); but British opinion took a moderate stand, Gladstone made an able speech in criticism of Clarendon's policy, Dallas was kept at his post, and the risk of a breach between the two nations disappeared.

Meanwhile, horrifying events had taken place almost simultaneously in Kansas and the Senate. May 20 found a proslavery force under an irresponsible Federal marshal invading the town of Lawrence, headquarters of the free-soil element in Kansas. This large "posse," armed with five cannon, destroyed the printing office whence the free-soil newspaper was issued, fired the substantial stone hotel, and pillaged stores and residences. The outrage was intended to strike terror to the growing free-soil population—a population heavily reinforced this spring and summer by immigration from the East and Middle West. May 20 was also the day on which Senator Sumner concluded his abusive speech called "The Crime Against Kansas." Full of billingsgate and personal calumny, it aroused general indignation. Two days later Preston S. Brooks of South Carolina entered the nearly empty Senate chamber, approached Sumner busily writing at his desk, and rained heavy blows on his head with a guttapercha cane. This indefensible action seemed to many Northerners a fitting accompaniment to the partial destruction of Lawrence. All opposition to slavery, many said, was to be overborne by the use of violence.

May 18. Trinity Sunday. The separation of Paulding and his wife is avowed now. The lady and her two children stay with Wolcott Gibbs for the present at least. Paulding and his wife's brother, Jem Mauran, have had a rough and tumble fight in the New York Hotel, and Paulding was licked. Samuel Whitlock is dangerously ill at Staten Island with remittent fever. . . . War and yellow fever continue to be sources of alarm. I fear this is to be a dismal summer.

May 19. Fine weather, rather an active day. The war-chill (it's by no means a war-fever) has knocked stocks down to fearful depths, and Beardom rejoices with exceeding great joy. Jacob Little is of a cheerful countenance.[3] Ellie continues well, cramp her chief trouble. Went with her tonight to hear the Rev. John Lord's lecture on Innocent III (at the corner of Twenty-third Street and Fourth Avenue, the new medical college). Quite a clever lecture, though inferior I'm told to the others of his series on the papacy. Hearty recognition of some truths about medieval times that are unpopular with Protestants, mixed up with crude incon-sistent ultra-Protestant commonplaces of censure and denunciation. Some-what superficial, too, I think, though Mr. Ruggles ranks him so high. Denouncing St. Francis of Assisi and St. Dominic for the filthy corrup-tions and degeneracies of the mendicant orders is like describing the rise of Methodism and making Stigginses of Wesley and Whitefield. After the lecture, I went to the Century to announce that I could not attend the dinner in honor of Dr. Cogswell next Thursday. Found George Anthon here on my return, en route for a little sociable party of one hundred and fifty at Bob LeRoy's.

May 20. Samuel H. Whitlock is to be buried on Thursday, the first of that happy hopeful dozen of law students who took the world so easily and found my father's office so pleasant a rendezvous between 1838 (?) and 1843, that has finished his course on earth and gone forth to the silent world toward which we are all walking, toward which every pulsation is a step. Sad to think of Sam Whitlock's *past* nonchalant gaiety and good nature with Cram and Pete Strong and Post and George Anthon. Sadder to remember his enviable vigor and enterprise, walking, leaping and climbing years ago when we were together at Catskill.

May 22, THURSDAY. George Anthon dined here. After dinner little Lucy [Derby] and her mamma and Aunt Mary came in, and I performed on the magic lantern, to the delight of the two babies, Lucy and Johnny. News tonight that Charles Sumner of the Senate has been licked with a loaded cane by a certain honorable Carolinian Brooks for his recent rather sophomorical anti-slavery speech. I hold the anti-slavery agitators wrong

[3] The notorious stock market manipulator, whose *coups* with Morris Canal securities in 1835 and Erie Railroad stock in 1840 marked a new era in speculation.

in principle and mischievous in policy. But the reckless, insolent brutality of our Southern aristocrats may drive me into abolitionism yet.

May 23. Much angry feeling about the assault on Sumner at Washington. It will strengthen the Free-soilers and Abolitionists, and it's reasonable and right it should strengthen them, for it's an act of brutality and blackguardism that ought to tell against its authors and endorsers. Jay told me of it as we rode home from Whitlock's funeral Thursday.

May 26. Seven thirty P.M. I should be a graceless hound if I were not deeply thankful for today. It has been a nervous time, but Ellie has got through her troubles, thus far at least, very far better than I hoped. Last night I spent mostly in the library and got a brief, disturbed doze in the big chair and got no sleep but did not suffer severely till about four this morning, when I marched down to Fourteenth Street after Dr. Peters with awful misgivings. It was one of the loveliest spring mornings that ever dawned. Brought him back with me a little before five, and he soon began administering chloroform, pretty freely I thought, producing much alleviation, but nothing like insensibility nor even any apparent confusion of thought or difficulty of speech. From the time he came in, there was a very steady crescendo of suffering, and the last four or five paroxysms were piteous and terrible to see. Much worse agony I never witnessed. It ended a quarter before eight, when her nine-and-a-quarter-pound baby (George Templeton Strong, Jr.) came into the world, screeching an indignant protest against his change of domicile. . . .

The baby is a man-child, pronounced by all who've seen him to be a prodigy of infantine loveliness, in which decision I acquiesce, distrusting my own private judgment. He's certainly less flatulent, colicky, querulous, and quarrelsome than Johnny was at his age (twelve hours and a fraction), and has borne his honors meekly thus far, not puffed up with adulation or with wind. It's said he's going to look like the maternal side of the house. Well, may Heaven defend him and his mamma.

May 28. Never was the country in such a crazy state as just now. Civil war impending over Kansas; the Administration blundering us into the misery and ruin of war with England, in a quarrel about which no mortal feels interest enough to induce him to spend five dollars; North and South farther alienated than ever before. I believe civilization at the South is retrograde and that the Carolinas are decaying into barbarism. Brooks comes on Sumner at his desk unawares, stuns him with a cudgel, and belabors the prostrate orator till the cudgel breaks and splinters, and Southern editors and Congressmen talk about the "chivalry," "gallantry," and manliness of the act, and they're getting up a testimonial for Brooks in Charleston. If Brooks belonged to the House of Commons, he'd be convicted and sentenced to a degrading imprisonment of two years, within six weeks from the date of his offence, if the blood of all the Howards and De Veres were in his veins. If Herbert, who shot the Irish waiter at breakfast the other day, were an English peer, he'd be hanged like Earl Ferrers.

The baby, thus far so quiet, seems disposed to discourse a little tonight.

Crampton is probably dismissed, and the glove thrown down. If England isn't wiser than we are, she will take it, and there will be a breach of the peace. Collision on the coast of Nicaragua may make it inevitable.

May 29, THURSDAY. No new vagaries from the wild men of the South since yesterday. The South is to the North nearly what the savage Gaelic race of the Highlands was to London *tempore* William and Mary, *vide* Macaulay's third volume; except that they've assumed to rule their civilized neighbors instead of being oppressed by them, and that the simple, barbaric virtues of their low social development have been thereby deteriorated.

A few fine specimens have given them a prestige the class don't deserve. We at the North are a busy money-making democracy, comparatively law-abiding and peace-loving, with the faults (among others) appropriate to traders and workers. A rich Southern aristocrat who happens to be of fine nature, with the self-reliance and high tone that life among an aristocracy favors, and culture and polish from books and travel, strikes us (not as Brooks struck Sumner but) as something different from ourselves, more ornamental and in some respects better. He has the polish of a highly civilized society, with the qualities that belong to a ruler of serfs. Thus a notion has got footing here that "Southern gentlemen" are a high-bred chivalric aristocracy, something like Louis XIV's noblesse, with grave faults, to be sure, but on the whole, very gallant and generous, regulating themselves by "codes of honor" (that are *wrong*, of course, but very grand); not rich, but surrounded by all the elements of real refinement. Whereas I believe they are, in fact, a race of lazy, ignorant, coarse, sensual, swaggering, sordid, beggarly barbarians, bullying white men and breeding little niggers for sale. The exceptions prove no more that's in favor of the class than Lochiel or "Fergus McIvor" can prove in favor of Highland civilization. Or a parallel might be drawn between the South Carolina statesman and fire-eater, and the Irish politician descended from Brian Boru, proud of his own beautiful Ireland, oppressed by Saxons, ready to give satisfaction to any political opponent, full of gas and brag and bosh. But it would be unfair to the Celtic gentleman.

May 30. Very busy day downtown. Charley came in after dinner with some papers that wanted attention, and I had to hurry down to Wall Street. On my way up at eight, I stopped at the Tabernacle, where the citizens of New York were summoned to meet and declare their sentiments about Sumner and the South. A vast crowd, earnest, unanimous, and made up of people who don't often attend political gatherings.[4] Significant that John A. Stevens called the meeting to order and old Griswold presided; men not given to fits of enthusiasm or generous sympathy, unlike to be prominent in anything wherein the general voice of the community does not sustain them. Evarts read the resolutions, which seemed discreetly framed and not intemperate. The meeting was prepared to swallow much stronger language. The roar of the great assemblage when Sumner's name occurred, and its spontaneous outburst of groaning and hissing at the sound of "Preston S. Brooks" impressed me. They seemed expressions of deep and strong feeling. I guess the North is roused at last. After the resolutions were read, Daniel Lord began a forcible-feeble speech, and I made my way out through the crowd as best I could.

Charley has just been here, and it seems the crowd multiplied after I left, and a separate meeting was organized outside with George W. Blunt for orator.

May 31, SATURDAY. The Sumner meeting last night is admitted by the *Herald* to have been an imposing demonstration. Mr. Ruggles made an emphatic speech after Lord finished; wish I'd known he was among the orators of the evening. Few dissenters from the action of the meeting, among them Cram, influenced, I guess, by his Southern connections (Henry A. Wise and others), and Mrs. ——, who's thinking of the nice Southern men she'll meet at Newport this summer and can't tolerate the idea of non-intercourse.

June 1. Much discourse about Sumner and the South. Shall we pro-

[4] New York businessmen had long tended to sustain the South. Since the Kansas-Nebraska Act they had taken a different attitude, and now they felt outraged. S. B. Ruggles advised Southerners to think twice. "There are more free men within one mile of this platform than in the whole state of South Carolina."

claim non-intercourse with Southerners? Shall the New York Club, for example, blackball three gentlemen who belong to "the Chivalry" and are now in nomination, and shall I omit to call on Mr. Frank Hampton and Sally, his wife, when they come here? My present impulse answers both questions in the affirmative, but I see that it's a doubtful matter. Suppose we say: "Gentlemen, we can't get along with you, we had better separate into two confederacies and fight openly, for public war is better than private personal broils and assaults." But the idea of dissolution and division is intolerable. Union is a necessity. Schism is ruin to both fragments of the nation. Do not our preponderance in material wealth, intelligence, and every element of political power enable us to assert that union must and shall exist, that there shall be no decomposition, that we will maintain the Union against Southern folly?

June 3.   Long thundershower in progress, heavy and hot. Ellie has been sitting up half the day, so I hope she sleeps unconscious. . . . Nominating convention of the Democracy parturient at Cincinnati and in puerperal convulsion. It may bring forth Pierce, Douglas, Buchanan, or somebody else, as our Southern rulers shall determine, and I doubt if the North be even yet sufficiently irritated to unite in defeating their nominee. F. B. Cutting tells me, however, that he thinks the Sumner affair will decide the election against the Democracy. It will certainly weaken that party at the North, and it will be politic for them to promote Brooks's expulsion, and so pacify more or less the present strong feeling against the Administration.

June 6, FRIDAY.   Buchanan nominated at Cincinnati. It might have been much worse. Northern divisions will make him the next President. Pierce is served right. The South has used him sufficiently and thrown him away, enjoyed the fruits of his treason and kicked him out of doors. He'll find cold comfort at home when he goes there; his neighbors have just been hanging him and Brooks in effigy. Only one course is left for him, and that is to throw all the weight of executive power and patronage into the scale of the North during the ten months of power that remain to him; to strengthen the United States troops in Kansas and direct them to make war on Missouri, if it shew its grimy nose across the border, to adopt every measure of violence and extremity the most ultra Northern politician could suggest. So may he yet secure a few friends who will be willing to associate with him and recognize him in his approaching days of insignificance, and he cannot make himself more infamous than he is already by any new exhibition of baseness. . . .

Report that some officious friend has informed old Lydig that Judge Daly, his son-in-law elect, is subject to epilepsy (informed him by anonymous letter, it's said), and that Lydig and his whole house are urging Miss Maria to break off her engagement, which she stoutly refuses to do, and that there is "a time" about it. I don't believe the judge's epilepsy amounts to anything very serious, and I think Miss Maria had better maintain herself in her present position.

June 7. . . . Democratic ticket is Buchanan, and Breckinridge (F. B. Cutting's antagonist) for Vice-President.

June 8, SUNDAY. Extracts from Southern papers indicate that Mr. Brooks's brutality is endorsed and sanctioned by the South; that the feeling of the North on that subject and our strong, unanimous condemnation of Carolinian chivalry and Virginian ethics irritate and annoy and gall the gentlemen whose vocation is to breed niggers and flog them; and that they seek, therefore, to relieve their own minds and strengthen their own convictions by greater vehemence in assertion and bluster. In forming an opinion about the moral tone of the South as illustrated by its judgment on this matter, it ought to be remembered that slavery, which lies at the bottom of Southern institutions, society, and property, which enables the Southern gentleman to buy comforts for his wife and food for his children, on which Southern girls marry, and families depend, and which is interwoven with and supports the whole fabric of Southern life, is condemned as a wrong and a sin by the whole civilized world. Wrongly condemned, it seems to me, but still condemned and censured from London to Vienna. Our political theories of right and wrong are decisive that it is an iniquity; we start with the so-called self-evident truth that all men are born free and equal. The South has all the culture, civilization, intelligence, and progress of the nineteenth century against it, unanimous in declaring that it lives on oppression and robbery. Great allowance should be made for the soreness and bitterness that a consciousness of this fact must produce.

June 10. The Bank of New York is evacuated by Oothout and Halsey and their retinue of steady-going clerks and tellers and is to be pulled down. It's the last surviving monument of old Wall Street. The Union Bank, with its two squat doric columns, is leveled and won't be missed. In Broadway there is considerable demolition, including Masonic Hall, a very notable old landmark, and both corners of Pearl Street. . . .

Kansas meeting last night. Bleecker presided. Large and loud-mouthed committee to get money for Sharps's rifles and so on. Talk in the *Tribune* about invading Missouri. All rather resembling overt acts of treason. Perhaps the outrages in Kansas are in fact such as justify rebellion, but all accounts from that quarter are so discordant and unsatisfactory that no one has sufficient evidence of that fact, which is now, moreover, *sub judice*—under investigation by a congressional committee. So the right of insurrection is not yet established here; we at the East are not yet in a position that allows us to become revolutionary. If we proceed to organize civil war, we fight at infinite disadvantage, not merely because the whole militia of Kentucky, Tennessee, and Missouri can at once be brought to bear on the field of action, but because law and the Constitution are words of power which would make our opponents invincible. Reaction throughout the North would be instantaneous, and the Black Republican Party would become a byword like the Hartford Convention.

June 11.   Rumor that Miss Maria Lydig has turned Roman Catholic, which I don't believe; also that the paternal Lydig distinctly and expressly forbids her alliance with Judge Daly, and that the young lady intends to have her own way and will be married this summer, which is not improbable.[5]

June 12.   I'm full of sorrow and contrition tonight. A poor little mouse had been caught alive and unharmed, which I tended very carefully through the evening, and supplied with food and water. Its little eyes and whiskers were delightful, and I fully intended to set it at large in the street in front of somebody else's dwelling house after making it the subject of a slight scientific experiment, often heretofore tried on myself and rather pleasurable than otherwise—inebriation by chloroform. So he was "taken up tenderly, lifted with care" by the tail and lodged beneath a spacious bell-glass with a rag wet with a sufficient dose of that beneficent fluid. First he ran about vigorously, then his footing grew uncertain, then he tumbled down and kicked. Then I lifted the bell-glass and took him out, and he kicked more feebly and lay still and did not come to. I became alarmed. I exhausted the remedial agents within my reach, cold water, artificial respiration, and friction of the extremities. Ammonia and galvanism were not at hand. But it was unavailing. "The vital spark had fled." It makes me unhappy, for though mice are vermin, I hate to kill them. . . .

We shall have news from England in a day or two and shall know

[5] An unfounded story; New York generated many rumors.

what John Bull says about our insult in the Crampton matter.[6] Probably there will be a period of great depression and alarm thereupon.

June 13. Walked uptown with Mr. Ruggles. Looked in for five minutes at the convention (Free-Soil section of the Know-Nothings), busy making a President in the Apollo Room at Broadway. Heard some very sound and wholesome talk from a rather raw Connecticut Yankee named (I believe) Perkins.

Signs of the times: the Honorable Hannibal Hamlin, Senator and Democrat, announces to the Senate his defection from the Democratic party and hostility to the Cincinnati platform. The New York *Herald's* hose-pipe of dirty water begins to be directed uncertainly, and to splash not the North alone, but North and South impartially. It talks now of "nigger-drivers" as well as nigger worshipers. The trumpet of that respectable paper is giving forth an uncertain sound, and I guess Bennett and Hudson & Co. will be talking Billingsgate in support of the Northern candidate within two months.[7]

June 16, MONDAY. Another perfect summer day, of splendid sunshine and clear, bracing air. Stopped awhile on my way downtown to contemplate the ruins of the old "Peale's Museum" building in Broadway near Murray Street, which tumbled down spontaneously just before I arrived there. The house adjoining on the south side has just been demolished, and this edifice, being too weak to stand alone, began to settle and crack on Saturday evening. Proper precautions were taken, and Broadway was made no thoroughfare at that point, so nobody was hurt when the crash came. . . .

The "Vigilance Committee" has reappeared in San Francisco.[8] Dangerous and bad, but it might be worse. Not unlikely that within a few years this community will require a like organization, a "protoplasm" of new social agencies that will gradually take definite form and replace the old debilitated and inefficient instruments of law. But the transition process is fearfully critical and may lead straight to anarchy.

June 17. News from England looks bad, and we've yet to learn the

[6] That is, Secretary Marcy's rather abrupt dismissal of Minister Crampton, which was condemned by much of the press and many public men.

[7] Bennett's *Herald*, long sympathetic with the South, turned to support Frémont in the campaign.

[8] A new crisis had been produced in California by the murder of the trenchant reform journalist, James King of William, on May 14, 1856, by an ex-convict and cheap politician named James Casey. The "law and order" men of San Francisco tried Casey and his accomplice Cora and on May 22 put them to death.

effect of Crampton's dismissal. Dallas will receive a *vade in pace*, the two nations will cease to be on speaking terms, there will be an awful panic here, and that subtle mischief-maker, Louis Napoleon, may take advantage of our rift to intrigue us somehow into actual war.

The Philadelphia Convention nominates for President John C. Frémont, for Vice-President Dayton of New Jersey. *Hurrah for both.* I shall vote the Republican ticket, if alive and capable of locomotion to the polls next fall. Northern discords and splits will defeat that ticket beyond question, but I want it to have a respectable minority in its favor. I belong to the insurgent plebeians of the North arming against a two-penny South Carolina aristocracy—to the oppressed Saxons assailing our modern Front de Boeufs and De Bracys in their strongholds. . . .

It is said Miss Maria Lydig and Judge Daly are to be married next week; that papa is resolute in the most emphatic protest against the match, won't witness the ceremony himself, and won't allow any of his family to attend it.

June 21, SATURDAY. Ellie has been making visits today. Called on Miss Maria Lydig, who's *not* at her father's, but at her aunt's, Mrs. William Remsen's, in Waverley Place. I'm sorry that lady's wedding takes place under a cloud, but lithotomy alone can get a crotchet out of her papa's system, when it has once established itself there.

June 23. Frémont promises to run pretty well. Fillmore in town; nobody cares much.[9] Foreign news not warlike.

June 24. Saw George Cornell, returned from his South American expedition, wherein he has made a good operation for himself, Cram, and Townsend, but not quite so good as he expected. The Park pretty well filled with loungers, loafers, policemen, awaiting the arrival of Fillmore's triumphal procession; not much sign of enthusiasm, though. The masses take both Frémont and Buchanan rather coolly. What little sign there is of life and excitement is for Frémont.

June 25. Fillmore procession yesterday generally pronounced a failure and a "fizzle." The Frémont "ratification meeting" tonight at the Tabernacle will do better, I hope. Little chance of his success, it seems to me, though that sanguine man, Anthony Bleecker, declares Frémont will carry every Northern state by unheard-of majorities. There is a great hurrahing out of doors in the distance, which comes, I suppose, from some

[9] Ex-President Millard Fillmore returned from Europe to meet a reception from Know-Nothings (with many Whig allies), who had already nominated him for President.

enthusiastic band of peripatetic Frémonters in procession; "deluded souls that dream of" nice little places in the Custom House and jobs and pickings and stealings. Frémont won't be President, my dear, deceived, enthusiastic, short-sighted brothers. You are bellowing to no purpose, disquieting yourselves in vain. Better for you to go home and to bed, and husband your vital forces and bellow for Buchanan on the first opportunity. The *Aristocratuli* of the South still have power for a time and times. Their day is not yet come. Ten years hence there will be some Frémont who can make it worth one's while to hurrah for him, but *you*, my unknown vociferous friends and fellow-citizens, are premature. You don't perceive that "the Republican party" is a mere squirm and wriggle of the insulted North, a brief spasm of pain under pressure and nothing more.

June 26. Severely hot. Frémont meeting last night very imposing in character and numbers. The new Republican Party calls out many who have long eschewed politics. It will probably sweep this state and nearly all the Northern states. Reasonably efficient today. Decision of the Court of Appeals on the great case of Schuyler's over-issued stock of the New Haven Railroad Company, adverse to the spurious stockholders (or a large class of them), much discussed. Very acute, wise, and sound, I think. Generally approved, except by the Board of Brokers.

June 29. News from England: things in an uneasy state, with room for anxiety; but Bull is less obstreperous than was to have been expected. San Francisco is in anarchy to any government by established law. The "Vigilance Committee" has acquired the highest judicial office. It has solemnly hanged two notorious scoundrels and arrested several more, one of whom, the illustrious Yankee Sullivan, removed his case from the jurisdiction of the committee by severing an artery in his arm and bleeding himself to death. The committee treats habeas corpuses as a nullity, and the governor is trying to organize a hostile force. If it be true, as it is said, that a reaction is setting in, and that there will be a formidable resistance to this new development of Lynch Law, a civil war is unlikely. But the committee claims to represent all the respectability, property, and honesty of San Francisco, and if so, I hope its experiment may succeed. One like it will have to be tried in New York within ten years.

July 2. We went to the concert of the "Mendelssohn Union." Heard Mendelssohn's "Music to Athalie" and "Walpurgisnacht" by a large and capitally drilled chorus, with piano accompaniment. Solo parts well filled also; good voices, and evident careful study of the music, rare in these amateur performances. On the whole, the execution of the music was most unusually satisfactory and creditable. The Walpurgis affair did not impress me very much, but the Athalie must be a very splendid work—of that there can be no doubt even on a first hearing. I did not think Mendelssohn could sustain himself on a high level through so long a composition, nor that he could write anything so free from manner, and so full of beautiful melodic feeling. I hope I may hear it again.

Kansas battle beginning in the House. Indications that Douglas and others are scared by the storm their selfish folly has raised. Should things be compromised and smoothed over, the Northern party will accomplish little next November. I hope such may be the result; that is, that the mischief may be so far repaired as to make a sectional contest unnecessary.

News from England seems pacific, but can civil war between North and South be postponed twenty years longer? I fear we, or our children, have got to pass through a ruinous revolutionary period of conflict between two social systems before the policy of the U.S.A. is finally settled. The struggle will be fearful when it comes, as it must sooner or later, for an amicable disunion and partition of territory is an impossibility. In those days will the price of gunpowder rise suddenly? One thing seems clear; the North can hardly fail to have the moral support of England and the whole civilized world enlisted in its favor.

July 6. The Washington statue, *"statua gentilissima del gran commendatore,"* unveiled on the morning of the Fourth.[10] I think the horse and his rider very creditable to their artist, particularly the former. They look raw and brassy now, but I'm told the weather will bronze them. . . .

July 8. To meeting of [Columbia] trustees—barely a quorum. Resolution to buy the Deaf and Dumb building carried *nem. con.*, and without debate. It seems a prudent measure, and I hope we may abandon our present dormitory next fall.

Political matters unchanged. We're in a pretty uneasy and uncomfortable state, in which violent convulsion is possible at any moment; for example, there may well be some collision at Washington that would bring forward delegations from both North and South to support and uphold their respective representatives. The West is said to be decided that Kansas shall *not* be a slave state, if the physical power of the West can prevent it; so there may be civil war in these days. On good authority I hear that its possibility was urged in the Philadelphia Convention by

[10] This bronze monument in Union Square—one of the first equestrian statues in the United States—was by Henry Kirke Brown, with a base by J. Q. A. Ward.

Frémont's Western supporters as a reason for making him the candidate of the Northern party, his military experience and energy qualifying him above McLean to lead the North in civil war. This alienation of North and South is an unquestionable fact and a grave one. Straws shew how the wind blows. Here is Mrs. Hampton in the city, and I'm hesitating whether Ellie shall bestow a piece of pasteboard on the wife of a South Carolinian.

July 14, MONDAY. The Rev. Hawks, very limp and moist, loafed in after tea, and favored us with a Southside view of the present political issues; and a very clear, strong, and plain-spoken confession of faith it was. Don't dispute many of the Dean's propositions myself. It would be a rather strong measure to hang Sumner and Seward with Brooks and Douglas, but it might be expedient. . . .

Today cruelly hot. Tonight hotter, and but feebly mitigated by sea-breeze. Charley at Newport. Attended Hackley's examination of the Freshmen of Columbia College awhile this morning. Not so bad as I expected, though bad enough.

July 15. House of Representatives has disposed of the Brooks and Sumner case. The motion to expel Bully Brooks failed for want of a two-thirds vote, but the majority in favor of expulsion was considerable, so the *Cheval*, or *Hoss* (his nearest approach to a chivalric title) made an allocution to his Southern admirers and refractory Northern liegemen and indignantly resigned his seat. It's said that Butler is to leave the Senate and that this caitiff will be instantly promoted to Butler's seat.[11] Even South Carolina can hardly be so blind and drunken with insolence and folly. Reasonable men and gentlemen, North and South, must be unanimous as to Brooks's harangue, which has rarely been equaled for bad taste, self-importance, and brutality.

He said "even the North must allow that if he chose to strike a blow now, it would be followed by revolution"—and took credit for with-holding his lightnings. He said almost *totidem verbis* that had Sumner resisted vigorously, he would have killed him, and admitted by implica-tion that he went armed to his brutal work and prepared to be murderer as well as bully should occasion require. Yet it's said he was welcomed, as he left the House in his majesty, by the congratulations and embraces of Southern "gentlemen," and the kisses of Southern ladies, who crowded the galleries and rushed into his arms. Poor things, they are hero-wor-shipers by virtue of their sex, and if the true divinity is absent or under a

[11] This was not done; but Brooks was at once re-elected to the House.

cloud, they must be excused for bowing down before some braying Mumbo-Jumbo whose brag and finery eclipse all competitors.

Vivat Frémont—I fear I shall come out a "damned Abolitionist" after all.

July 16.   George [William] Curtis is going about speechifying at political meetings in the cause of Frémont, and pretty effectively, it seems. Theodore Winthrop(!!!) active in the same work. It is clear that the "Black Republican" party commends itself much to educated and intelligent people at the North, particularly of the sort that commonly declines any concern in "mere" political matters. I don't think its principle has made its way down to the masses yet, or is taken hold of by them (unless in the New England states), though the working-class is deeply and directly interested in this controversy. Next fall will shew whether I am right. Perhaps some considerable part of the German vote may be cast for Frémont.

July 24.   One of our civic scourges, an organ-grinder, is putting his broken-winded engine of torture through "St. Patrick's Day in the Morning," just so far off that I daren't shy anything at him for fear of stirring up the wrong man. . . .

Brooks *vs.* Burlingame of Massachusetts: Brooks challenged the Massachusetts man, who accepted and named Clifton House (Niagara) as the place of meeting. Bully Brooks instantly backs out. Publishes a statement putting his withdrawal on the ground that he'd be assassinated if he came North, but intimates that if Burlingame will challenge him (and give him choice of weapons) he may accept. General opinion is that Bully Brooks has shewn the white feather.

Anson Burlingame's stinging attack upon Preston Brooks in the House had resulted in a challenge. The Massachusetts Congressman, who had been reared on the Michigan frontier, accepted it; but he insisted that they should meet on the Canadian side of Niagara Falls, and Brooks feared that he could not pass through hostile Northern territory with safety. The duel was thus averted, both men laying claim to credit in the affair. Burlingame's course heightened his popularity in the North.

The campaign of 1856, remarkable for its fervor and its bitterness, was now reaching a climax of excitement. The Democrats had held their national convention in Cincinnati in June, with the civil conflict still raging in Kansas. Since the platform endorsed the Kansas-Nebraska Act, the logical nominee would have been its author, Stephen A. Douglas. But the popular condemnation of the law was so widespread in the North that he was an unacceptable candidate. The choice, therefore, fell upon James Buchanan, "available" because he had been safe in England while the Kansas quarrel was gaining heat. For Vice-President the Democrats nominated John C. Breckinridge of Kentucky, who was counted upon to carry his own state and neighboring Tennessee— neither of which the party had won since Jackson's day. The Republicans, meeting in an enthusiastic convention in Philadelphia on June 17, the anniversary of Bunker Hill, had drawn up a platform which called for exclusion of slavery from all territories, and for the construction of a Pacific Railroad. It included the Declaration of Independence, an appeal to radical sentiment at the North. For President the delegates had nominated the dashing explorer John C. Frémont, son-in-law of Thomas Hart Benton. It was evident that the battle between the two principal parties would be close. The Democrats rallied all their forces, Southern planters uniting with New York merchants and conservatives of New England and the Middle West. Douglas gave full support to Buchanan, and large sums of money were contributed by Northern businessmen fearful that a Republican triumph would spell secession and civil war. The Republicans, for their part, appealed to the idealism of the young men of the North and West and to popular resentment over the high-handed course of the proslavery men in Kansas and Washington. During the summer a group of Southern governors met at Raleigh, North Carolina, and proclaimed that their states would leave the Union if Frémont were elected. This and similar threats were denounced by the Republican press as an attempt to blackmail the electorate.

August 1. Spent most of the day in the Trust Company with Ludlow and Moses Taylor, as a Committee of Examination. All correct and prosperous as far as we could discover, but such an investigation is little more than a formality. Six months' hard work over ledgers and vouchers might enable us to report positively that Kearny and David Thompson had not cheated the company out of $100,000 or so, but no less amount of labor is of any real use.

August 4, MONDAY. Our brethren of the South are surely mad. Think of the Virginian Wise telling Mrs. Ritchie (Mowatt)[12] who told

[12] Henry A. Wise, governor of Virginia 1856–1860, and a man of fire-eating propensities; Anna Cora [Ogden] Mowatt, the noted actress, who in 1854 had married William F. Ritchie, editor of the Richmond *Enquirer*.

Mr. Ruggles, who told me, that "if Frémont were elected, he would never be permitted to reach Washington." Their brag and bluster can't well be paralleled, unless by a Chinese edict meant to intimidate the foreign barbarians. One thing is very clear and very important, that in Kentucky and Missouri and possibly in Virginia itself, there are germs of insurrection among the "poor trash," the plebeians who don't own niggers. Such a movement once formed and recognized must triumph sooner or later, and nigger emancipation and the downfall of the nigger-breeding (and mulatto-breeding) aristocracy of those states must follow.

Poor Edward Curtis is dead, after two years and a half of seclusion in the Flushing Asylum, during which there has never been any hope of his restoration or material improvement.

August 5.   My old college friend, G. M. Hillyer, seems to be in trouble. He's a Natchez newspaper editor (I used to be confident that he and N. W. Chittenden would be rival candidates for the presidency as soon as they reached the constitutional age), and one of his "cotem-poraries" publishes a card printed as a specimen of the courtesy of "The Chivalry" in this morning's *Times,* certifying Giles to be "a liar, a coward, a poltroon, and a scoundrel." Poor Giles! Long talk with Charles Kuhn this afternoon over the affairs of the nation. My platform is substantially this:

1. Slavery is not a wrong per se. If it were so, the states in which it exists ought to right it. We are not called on to interfere with it, sup-posing it a wrong, any more than we are bound to attack the serfdom of Russia or the iniquities of Naples. And there are so many practical diffi-culties in the way of righting it that the people who are in that case bound to act, the South, may be pardoned for pausing and hesitating and acting reluctantly. . . .

2. The practical working of the institution (whether it be in itself a wrong or not) includes iniquities that are probably curable by legislation, but are, perhaps, of its essence—inseparable: the selling asunder of families, remediless cruelty and oppression, enforced concubinage, incest, and so forth.

3. It practically demoralizes and degrades the whole community where it exists.

4. It operates against the material development and the progress in civilization and wealth of such community, and is guilty of the difference between Virginia and New York.

5. Any interference by Northern states or individuals with the legal

institutions of the Southern states, which is calculated to produce disaffection or disorder in their servile class, being not merely gratuitous, but most perilous to the insecure social system of those unhappy communities, ought to be repressed most sternly. The North would be merely acting in good faith if it made such interference a capital crime.

6. Congress has no power over any feature of the institution as it exists in a Southern state.

7. But it has power to legislate for the territories, and it may and should exclude from those territories while under its jurisdiction an institution which has thus far only done harm wherever it exists. When those territories have been set up in business for themselves, they may legislate as they please, and introduce slavery into their system if they are fools enough to do it.

Pity I'm not in the Senate of the United States!

Hydropathy was still one of the medical crazes of the period, though it had reached its apogee in the 1840's. Its founder was Vincent Priessnitz, a peasant of Austrian Silesia, who first healed himself and then many of his neighbors by copious use of the springs and streams abounding in his mountain region. Wealthy and fashionable people began to flock to him. He made his patients give up all stimulants, eat plain food, take plenty of exercise in the open air, and use large quantities of water both internally and externally. Naturally his regimen restored many debilitated people to health. He found an American apostle in Henry Gardiner Wright, an enthusiastic young man whom Bronson Alcott had brought back with him from England, and another in Dr. Joel Shew, who edited the Water Cure Journal and Herald of Reform. *The principal English exponents of the system were James M. Gully and Sir W. E. Wilson. Hydropathic establishments, modeled more or less on Priessnitz's original institution at Grafenberg in Silesia, sprang up in great numbers in Germany, France, and the United States. Many of them prospered, and they made a distinct contribution to medicine and sanitation. The cooling bath in fevers and the wet-sheet pack have become recognized implements of medical practice, while hydropathy did much to popularize the morning tub and the drinking of large quantities of water. Two of the principal establishments in the United States were the Brattleboro Water Cure House, and Dr. Shew's house at Lebanon Springs, N. Y.; Dr. Shew also founded the world's first urban water cure in New York City. As Brattleboro offered many cool charms*

*in addition to the hydropathic establishment, Strong had good reason to take
his family there for a summer visit. He left New York early in August, and
after suffering a minor train wreck, the same evening "was welcomed on the
piazza of Wesselhoeft's Hydropathic Asylum by Ellie and Miss Rosalie and
Mr. Ruggles."*

August 13, WEDNESDAY.   I tried all the various forms of the Aqua
Pumpi treatment: plunge bath, sitz bath, half bath, wave bath, douches
of every grade of intensity, and lastly "packing," not a pleasant way of
spending an hour. The packed patient . . . looks just like the pictures of the
gravid female white ant.

Brattleboro is a charming, thrifty New England town, set in a lovely
region of hills. "The country hunches up a good deal" in these parts.
Chesterfield Mountain on the other side of the Connecticut is a goodly
protuberance. The town has its town hall, academy, lots of meeting-
houses, an ambitious opposition water-cure wherein the Honorable
Bayard Clarke and that busted speculator Davison are somehow interested,
two hotels, nice shops, fine houses, droves of the ugliest curs, shoals of
women that ain't attractive, an undue percentage of elderly young ladies
in spectacles, several small thriving factories, plenty of sumptuous old
maples, and running water *ad libitum*. Our hospital or hotel—it's both—is
a queer, low, disjointed building, with ways unlike those of any hotel I've
known, combining usages appropriate to a German watering-place, an
insane asylum, and a penitentiary. Fare good of its kind and abundant. We
are mostly graminivorous. Walks, cold baths, and open air made me eat
as I have never eaten before; mountains of hominy and bowls of milk
vanished before me. I rose at six and turned in at ten, at which hour a
stern Teuton always came into the funny little parlors and silently put
out the lamps. Place agreed with dear little Ellie and the babies, too. . . .

Mr. Ruggles came up Thursday evening and left Saturday. Walter
Cutting also was added unto us. Mr. Ruggles varied the rather monotonous routine of the place by a row with that insufferable old hog, Count
Gurowski, who stays at the opposition "Lawrence Water Cure," and is,
of course, ubiquitous, all-seeing, malignant, mischievous, and abominated.
(I dropped the man's acquaintance, intelligent and instructive as he is,
years ago.) We went across the street to a "hop" at the other house, and
old Gurowski, after several unsuccessful attempts, caught Ruggles's eye
and came up with his usual obsequious Kalmuck purr. Mr. Ruggles told
him he would have no intercourse with him. The Count wanted to ex-

plain, but Mr. Ruggles waved him off in a majestic manner and told him he could do that "tomorrow." Next morning came a challenge in form— only the bearer was a little German waiter girl and a non-combatant. George C. Anthon took charge of the case, and the result was that the Count was very sorry for some things he had said and regretted them extremely, and so it was all satisfactorily settled.

August 14. Nothing new today but my own virtuous simplicity of manners. Yellow fever stock is falling like Nicaragua or Lucifer, son of the morning. None of it in town, and fewer cases at Quarantine. *Per contra*, the most astounding and terrific legends of its prevalence at Bath, New Utrecht, and Fort Hamilton; how everybody is running away, and no one lives there any more but people in the black vomit stage who are too much prostrated to run; how you can nose the poisoned deadly air of those villages a mile before you reach them; how all the dogs and cats are saffron colored, and so forth. But men are very susceptible of panic when the word epidemic is whispered to them. On the Battery tonight, the sudden recollection that the cool sea-breeze I was enjoying came from somewhere near the Quarantine, over nine miles of moonlit saltwater, quickened my walk for a moment.

August 30. Saw George [William] Curtis, wholly wrapt up in the Frémont campaign, wherein he does good and active service, speaking almost every night with great approval and with much more ability than I gave him credit for. Partly for money, I suppose (from some "Central Committee" or other), but somewhat for love of the cause, which commends itself to his Eastern proclivities, and of his pretty Miss Shaw, whose papa is a vehement Free-Soiler. Fillmore seems rather to lose ground. Frémont rather gains. His enemies help him by the bitter malignity of their personal attacks, which will surely decide some thousands to vote in his favor. Were I a moderate Know-Nothing or a mild Buchananier, any two numbers of the New York *Express* would drive me into Frémontism. . . . House and Senate still in extra session, at a deadlock over the Army appropriations. The House will be beat sooner or later.

September 1, MONDAY. I must record as matter of curiosity the results of my silly experiments with Hashish, or rather with the officinal extract of *Cannabis Indica*. I was incited thereto by Dillingham's story of his experiences, recounted at Brattleboro. Tried it very cautiously and warily in small successive doses, without very positive effect, without any effect that I was sure of, and made up my mind that the drug was inert or that I was insensible to it. Thursday night at twelve, just before retiring, I treated myself to a larger bolus, as big as two peas perhaps, and went to bed and to sleep as usual. At two A.M. I woke from a perturbed, dreamy slumber that seemed to have been indefinitely long, and was instantly aware that I was in an abnormal condition. The physical symptoms were dryness of mouth and tongue, slight sense of local pressure at the pit of the stomach, occasional rapid fluttering action of the heart, slow and weak pulse, and later coldness and slight numbness of the extremities. I think, also, that my face was flushed. There was nothing beside, and all this gave me no disagreeable sensation at all except the leatheriness of my mouth, which was a little unpleasant.

But my mental gear was working strangely, so strangely that it instantly occurred to me that my bolus must have been an overdose, and the next step might be entire loss of self-control, insensibility, or perhaps death. I felt very comfortable and easy, however, quite free from fright. It seemed a grave matter, about which I ought to consider what was best to be done, and the progress of which it was interesting to watch, but which didn't concern me personally a great deal. The prominent feature of my mental condition was that I was distinctly in a dual state. I was two gentlemen in one night shirt: G. T. Strong No. 1 was in an agreeable, mild delirium, unable to control and hardly able to follow the swift current of incoherent images that were passing through his head. G. T. Strong No. 2, rather languid and lazy, looked on, noted the phenomena, tried to remember them distinctly, and to devise some form of words that would describe certain of his (or No. 1's) sensations which he rightly thought could not be expressed in language.

This flow of images was wonderful and unprecedented, each distinct and keen, but instantly giving place to a new one, equally vivid, all disconnected and hurrying on in swift succession. When I closed my eyes, a phantasmagoria of living and moving forms kept pace with this current of delirious thought. Louis XIV, with a splendid group of embroidered coats and lace cravats in the background, stood with a lady holding his arm in a long gallery, all pilasters and carving, and was evidently giving a rebuke to a little footman who'd been caught in mischief. Gone like a flash, and in their place I saw Schomberg's soldiers marching slowly over a desolate withered moor, file after file of old-fashioned uniforms; I knew they were Schomberg's, of course, intuitively. Then a flying crowd of peasants, instantly recognized as Irish *keme* fleeing the Boyne (I'd been turning over Macaulay's *History* just before going to bed); then like a flash a Brattleboro landscape stood before me, so distinct I could have counted the trees on the crest of the nearest hill, but it was gone, and in its place was Millais's "Huguenot" picture, not as picture but as reality, and so on. I could still catalogue the series by scores. All were tangible as if seen by the natural eye, but not strong in color; they were as if seen through smoked glass. The effect of the exhibition would have been delightful but for its hurrying succession, which wearied and bewildered me. A second set of impressions, the most intense of all, but which can't be described, occurred at intervals. I tried in vain to analyze and define them. Some object without form, color, or definability of any kind was present, some word without sound or syllable was spoken, and this unknown word or thing seemed long forgotten but perfectly familiar now it had come back and brought with it a whole world of associations, memories, influences, and I don't know what, shadowy but most weighty, unutterable, uncertain even whether they were good or evil, whether their intensity was of joy or sorrow, but most keen and searching. These were not pleasant by any means; there was something in them that seemed real and earnest and most uncanny. There seemed slowly to present itself something of this same class; the nearest approach to describing it, or rather suggesting what it seemed like, would be to say it was the sensible presence, embodied in something close at hand and drawing closer, of death, bodily death with its accessories. It was as if a corpse in its cerements was drawing near me, and I knew that with its first touch, I should be *It*. There was no illusion of sense, but a hideous horror of loathing and shrinking such as I never felt before.

September 9. We turned out to see the Grand Democratic Torchlight Procession. Large certainly, but rather straggling, and with a large infusion of youthful Democrats who'll hardly grow enough to vote next November! Not very joyous or enthusiastic and greeted by little outside hurrahing. The news from Maine hasn't helped to make them jolly. That rather doubtful state seems to have gone Republican with a rush. Frémont forever![13]

September 10. Three cheers for Maine! The election there is a great fact; it shews which way the cat is jumping and will make her jump farther. Doubtless it has already decided $x+y$ cautious gentlemen, waiters on Providence, uncat-like people to whom the *victoris causa* is always pleasing, to get down from their fence and go for Frémont, in-

[13] In the state election in Maine, with Hannibal Hamlin running for governor, the Republicans triumphed by a vote of roughly 67,000 to 42,500. They won by a still greater margin in Vermont, the vote being nearly three to one.

fluenced solely by a conscientious sense of duty. This x+y is a large figure; it may well be ten thousand in this state alone. Hamilton Fish is said to have seen a great light lately and to be trying the feel of the current with his toes before jumping in. I don't believe his accession will affect the fortunes of any party very essentially. It's said a Frémont electoral ticket will be run in several Southern states, including Missouri, North Carolina, and Virginia. Dubious. It probably won't be permitted by the oligarchy of little barbarous princes to which the white trash of the South is subject.

September 11. Long discourse with Walter Cutting, who's frightened at the Maine news; has a "betting opinion" still, but will give no odds on Frémont, and considers that the South will secede if Frémont's elected. Which the South *won't*, as long as Southern gentlemen can make a little money going to Congress.

September 16. Early train to Boston, breakfast, and then sat on a barrel for two hours reading Mrs. Stowe's *Dred*, for that the Nahant boat had privily changed its hour. . . . *Dred* is a strong and telling book. Ellie is now deep in the first volume, and much exercised thereby. Found all well at Nahant; hotel all but deserted; weather lovely. Small party that evening at Mrs. Paige's: Professor Felton, Agassiz and wife, and Longfellow (to whom I missed an introduction, not knowing he was there). Next day dined at Agassiz's with Felton—very pleasant; Agassiz and his wife most charming people. After dinner on the rocks at low tide (the "sunken ledge") with him for a couple of hours, and was presented to marine notabilia, chiefly of the zoöphyte family, many of which I've long sought to see.

September 21, SUNDAY. Committee of the Whole on the State of the Nation tonight. No talk but of politics as the momentous month of November draws near. Mr. Ruggles has been vice-presidenting the Old Line Whig convention at Baltimore and drawing the platform resolutions of that sedate and venerable Witenagemot or Council of Notables, which has adopted Fillmore and Donelson as "Whig" candidates. It does look like a Historical Society or Congress of Antiquarian Associations, rather than a practical political assemblage, for the Whig party is dead, decomposed, and disintegrated. But Mr. Ruggles gives a pretty clear and plausible statement of its aims and policy, namely:

The pestilent little state of South Carolina, mad with metaphysics and self-conceit, gasconading itself day by day into greater wrath and keener sense of imaginary wrong, means to secede if the North elect Frémont.

It may by its legislature declare itself an independent nation, November 15th, or it may back out a little later, if it can secure Georgia or Virginia as allies, by refusing to go into ballot for President and Vice-President, and forming a Southern Confederacy. If it stand alone, it is easily dealt with; a couple of frigates can blockade its ports, and it will be starved into submission in about two weeks, being as poor and weak as it is insolent and irrational. But should it find aid and comfort from the sympathy of other slave states, *which is not an improbable thing*, if it put itself forward as champion of "Southern rights," the situation becomes a grave one and admits of but two probable solutions: a long and fierce civil war, or what's worse, dissolution of the Union. Now admitting Fillmore's chances to be none, that he will not get an electoral vote, which is likely to happen (though the Know-Nothings profess to have 186,000 registered voters in this state alone), it is desirable, when the South is considering about secession, to have *established* in both Northern and Southern states a party organization, under an old, familiar, national party name, ignoring the sectional questions at issue, opposing both sectional candidates, and proclaiming its cardinal principle to be hostility to all sectional parties. The existence of such a party South as well as North will (according to Mr. Ruggles) furnish a basis for compromise, a nucleus for moderate men, a remnant of political unity to connect New York and Virginia. There is much sense in all this. And this convention, though not great in numbers, seems to have been made up of strong and influential men from all parts. It may play an important part, as a brake on the train, and save us a bad collision.

September 22. With Ellie to see *The Rivals* at Wallack's tonight. Rather a satisfactory performance on the whole, in spite of a most un-Hibernian Sir Lucius O'Trigger and a very dreary Falkland and Julia. But for that dismal pain the author is mainly responsible. A "good comedy" well played is entertaining while it lasts, but after all, these productions, from Congreve & Co. down to Mr. Boucicault, seem to me as shallow, silly, frivolous, and unreal as any compositions I know of. One can imagine comedy that should be to *The Rivals* or *London Assurance* what *Pendennis* and *The Newcomes* are to the old novels of fashionable life.

September 25. Politics engross everybody's thoughts and talk, more and more daily. Hamilton Fish has pronounced at last for Frémont, and favors mankind with an analysis of his motives and reasons that fills two columns of the *Courier*, and is hard reading. Unimportant, except as shewing what an ambitious commonplace man, with some experience and opportunity of observation, thinks is for his own interest. It's significant like the diligence of spiders before rain, the movements of various animals in anticipation of an earthquake or a hurricane. . . .

As for our Southern friends, they're madder every day. *Vide* the Muscogee (Ga.) *Herald* on "Northern Society" as "made up of greasy mechanics and so on," not fit company for a Southern gentleman's body-servant. Also, somebody makes a grand allocution to the young men and braves assembled at a South Carolina militia muster, tells them that if somebody should "smite down the miscreant (John C. Frémont) beside the pillars of the Capitol, in case of his election, not a Southern regiment but would spring to the rescue" of the hypothetical Ravaillac.

Last night to Wallack's again with Ellie; *Old Heads and Young Hearts* one of the best comedies I've seen. Blake as Jessie Rural excellent.

Fought out in an atmosphere of public excitement over "bleeding Kansas," the three-cornered campaign of 1856 aroused the most impassioned feeling. Frémont and the Republican party attacked the repeal of the Missouri Compromise in vehement terms, and insisted that Congress must prohibit slavery in all the territories—Kansas entering the Union as a free state. Buchanan and the Democratic Party upheld the popular sovereignty doctrine embodied in the Kansas-Nebraska Act; the fate of Kansas was to be decided by her own voters. Fillmore, nominated first by the Know-Nothings and late in the summer by the remnants of the Whig Party, took a non-committal position on slavery, but denounced the sectional views and lòyalties of the other two parties. A powerful and indignant uprising of Northern free-soilers gave the Republican Party tremendous strength. The pulpit and the religious press outside the slave states were generally for Frémont; so were the most important newspapers— Bryant's Evening Post, Greeley's Tribune, Samuel Bowles's Springfield Republican, Bennett's Herald, Medill's Chicago Tribune; so were the famous authors—Longfellow, Irving, Emerson, Whittier, and Lowell. The Independent exhorted voters to remember that a Republican success would be a victory "for Christ, for the nation, and for the world." It added: "Vote as you pray! Pray as you vote!" Great meetings, marked by tumultuous enthusiasm, were held all over the North. The colleges, led by Harvard and Yale, were strongly on the Republican side. George William Curtis, who delivered a number of excellent campaign speeches, tried especially to rally young men in an address at Wesleyan University on "The Duty of the American Scholar."

Indignant Southerners met this wave of free-soil feeling with threats of secession. Toombs of Georgia declared that Frémont's election would mean the end of the Union. The Republicans meant to dictate to the South: "I am content that they shall own us when they conquer us, but not before." Slidell of Louisiana asserted that if Frémont won, "the Union cannot and ought not to be preserved." Mason of Virginia avowed that "immediate, absolute, eternal separation" would be the result. But most Northerners, like Strong, scoffed at these utterances of the fire-eaters. They had heard such threats before, and did not believe they would be carried into execution. Southerners could not be kicked out of the Union, declared Senator Wilson of Massachusetts. It was only a minority who were trying to frighten the Northern voters. Said Curtis: "Twenty millions of a moral people are asking themselves whether their government shall be administered solely in the interest of three hundred and fifty thousand slaveholders."

The state contest was also embittered. The Republicans had nominated for governor John A. King, ex-Congressman and diplomat; the Democrats had named Amasa J. Parker, lawyer and judge; and the Know-Nothings, Erastus Brooks, an editor who had become prominent by insisting that Catholic property be taxed.

September 27, SATURDAY. Nothing fresh in politics. George Cornell counts on 50,000 majority for Frémont in this state, allowing 10,000 majority the other way in this city. Dubious. . . . To *Star of the North* last night with Ellie and George C. Anthon. Opera admirably put on the stage and all the parts well filled. Music generally overworked and elaborated so as to obscure its not very brilliant ideas.

September 30. . . . Attended a ward meeting last night—the Eighteenth Ward Republican organization—and was duly enrolled; a respectable meeting in number and style of business. Fry of the *Tribune* office made a long speech, vehement, extravagant, and odd, but with some telling points. Judge Cowles presided. I don't count on success in this election, but I think it's time now for everybody at the North to aid, as far as he can, any decent party that aims at putting down the aggressions and assumptions of our Southern friends, and to try to bring them to reason.

Result of my political meditations as I lay awake last night. *Vide* Walter Scott:

SOUTHERN WAR-SONG
Tune, *Bonnets of Bonny Dundee.*

To the base churls in Congress 'twas Brooksy who spoke
"Ere the West shall be Free there are heads to be broke.
"So let each Southern Gent who loves Niggers and me,
"Come follow the bludgeon of Chevalier B."

Chorus:
Go finish your cocktail, go borrow a ten,
Go lock up your niggers and count up your men.
We'll pepper the Yankees for talking so free,
And it's room for the bludgeon of Chevalier B!

Bold Brooks is excited, he strides down the street,
The children drop senseless, the dogs they retreat.
But the Judge (well-bred man) says, "It isn't for me
To confine a real Gent like the Chevalier B."

As he marched by the office where Patents are kept
Each Yankee Mechanic turned livid and wept.
But the sly coffin-maker, he chuckled in glee
Saying, "Luck to thy bludgeon, bold Chevalier B."

With Free-Soil Canaille the Hotel steps were filled,
As if half of New York had come South to be killed.
There was buttoning of pockets and trembling of knees,
As they watched for that bludgeon of Chevalier B's.

These low "self-made" scrubs, they were full of their prate,
And had reasons and facts such as *gentlemen* hate.
But they fled to their rooms and the entry was free,
At the whisk of the bludgeon of Chevalier B.

He stalked to the bar, through saliva and smoke,
And with the wild Quattlebum gaily he spoke.
"Our District alone will raise regiments three,
"For the love of buck-niggers, big bludgeons and me."

The Quattlebum asks: "The Campaign? It is planned?"
"The spirit of Arnold our March shall command!
"You shall soon hear of Boston surrendering to me,
"Or that high swings the corpus of Chevalier B.

"There are streams besides Hudson, with towns at their mouth.
"If they've men in New England, we've Gents at the South.
"And loyal 'White Trash' (they can't read, don't you see?)
"Who will bite, scratch, and gouge for the Chevalier B.

"There are knives and revolvers that be about loose.
"There are Hounds in our Kennels we've trained up for use.
"The blood-hounds will bite and the pistols shoot free
"At the wave of the bludgeon of Chevalier B.

"Away to the Hills, to the swamps, to the Moon!
"Ere I recognize Frémont I'll couch with the Coon
"And tremble, false snobs, as you sit at your tea.
"You'll catch fits before long from my bludgeon and me."

He waved his proud hand and the toddies were brewed,
The glasses were clinked and the chieftains were "Stewed"
And in slight incoherence, chivalric and free,
Died away the wild war notes of Chevalier B.

    Go finish your cocktail, go borrow a ten,
    Go mortgage your niggers and muster your men.
    It's death to the North where the workies are free
    And hurrah for the bludgeon of Chevalier B. . . .

October 2. I have become a politician. I must immediately read the Constitution of the United States, also that of the State of New York, and make notes of those instruments respectively. Attended this evening a meeting to organize "The Young Men's Eighteenth Ward Frémont Vigilance Committee." About a dozen present—wire-pullers seemingly; men familiar with canvassing, who knew the best places to get posters printed, and were on intimate terms with stump-speakers and "central organizations." Mostly "middle-class people," but fair and intelligent, able to talk clearly and pertinently. Find myself on several committees and quite likely to be a great statesman some day.

Governor Floyd[14] made a speech in front of the Exchange this afternoon. Large assemblage at first, but far from enthusiastic; reason good therefor—at least half were Frémonters or Fillmoreites. A few claquers did the cheering in a perfunctory way. Saw only one man whose applause seemed genuine, and that was a soap-lock, about a block and a half from the orator, who said, "That old feller is making a *big* speech, now I tell yer." People generally listened with sad civility, and I was glad of the example of good breeding and fair play shewn to a secessionist from Virginia, where a free-soil Cicero would be lynched. To my surprise the speech was read from manuscript. What I heard was not impressive. It was spouted with great vehemence—deliberate animation. I hung around

[14] Ex-Governor John B. Floyd of Virginia, soon to become Secretary of War in Buchanan's cabinet.

for about an hour. People were then thinning off lamentably. The *Journal of Commerce* will lie loud tomorrow about the meeting.

Mr. Ruggles has come out in the *Commercial Advertiser* criticizing Banks's statistics delivered a week ago.[15] " 'Pears like" he pulled them to pieces. He's an ugly customer in a quarrel about facts and figures. Don't like altogether the form in which he puts his argument, namely, a reply to a formal request for his opinion from William B. Astor, Theodore Dehon, and "several others." " 'Pears like" being invoked as a sort of oracle. The *Evening Post* is very funny about it, though in a good-natured way. Shouldn't wonder if it were easier to laugh at than to confute. But I wish Mr. Ruggles were not on that side in the battle. Sent my doggerel (*vide supra*) to the *Evening Post*, which published it to my surprise. . . .

October 5, SUNDAY. Mr. Ruggles has urged Hunt[16] strongly to propose the introduction into the liturgy of a prayer for the Union, but it's objected that this is not the proper time. South Carolina might think it personal. It's a weightier objection that prayers for the sick are only put up when the patient is past cure, and this would seem an admission that Toombs and Henry A. Wise are grave symptoms. A "Collect for Civilization" would do better, for civilization is clearly retrograde south of the Potomac. H. C. Dorr suggests a historical solution for the difference of manners North and South. New England and the Middle States were colonized by the middle class, commercial and laboring people. But Virginia, the mother of Southern society, boasts of her aristocratic settlers, and we know what were the manners and morals of that part of the English aristocracy which was likely to emigrate under the Stuarts and the Protectorate; the low-class Cavaliers, the race that produced the Mohocks and Lord Mohun and Colonel Blood, the raff of which Roger Wildrake (in *Woodstock*) has some of the faults with a great many extra virtues. Virginia took instantly to breeding horses; that's a significant fact. Now the Love-lock has degenerated into the Soap-lock. The words "Gentleman" and "Southern Gentleman" signify things different in genre. The two classes exist both North and South, but the latter class gives the tone to Southern society—ready to fight duels, slow to pay debts.

Signs of coalition and bargain between Democracy and the Fill-

[15] As a former Whig and a man of conservative tendencies, deeply alarmed by Southern threats of secession, Ruggles opposed Frémont.

[16] Ex-Governor Washington Hunt had similarly refused to ally himself with the Republicans.

moreites grow stronger. Probably they wait for the Philadelphia election a fortnight hence before deciding on their arrangements. It would be a desperate move, either killing Frémont or strengthening him immensely.

Bronson Alcott, now past his middle fifties, was resident for the time being in Walpole, N.H.; his family supported chiefly by the exertions of Mrs. Alcott and their daughter Louisa in sewing, teaching, and other work. His model co-operative community of "Fruitlands" had come to a swift failure more than a decade earlier. He was not an effective lecturer of the formal kind; but he devised a series of informal "conversations" or discussions, interesting if not particularly instructive, which he offered to select audiences in the East and the Northwest. Since he could be a brilliant though vague and indefinite talker, these lecture-discussions obtained much attention. It was at one of them that Theodore Parker asked Alcott to define his terms, and Alcott retorted: "Only God defines—man can but confine." Alcott's career as an educator of the young, the abrupt ending of which had been such a deep personal tragedy, was many years in the past; his "Concord School of Philosophy" was still before him. Strong was drawn to one of Alcott's meetings.

October 9. This evening at a meeting of our Frémont Executive Committee; thence to the Rev. Brother Bellows's, the parsonage of the Red and White Unitarian establishment in Fourth Avenue (which is a "pied variety" of the St. Sophia) where I spent two hours oddly enough. Some thirty people, generally notabilities, had been assembled to meet the illustrious Alcott, the father, I suppose, of Yankee-Platonism and hyperflutination, and to talk to Great Alcott and be talked to by him; the subject of tonight's discourse being announced in a sphinx of a printed card as "Descent," which left it uncertain whether we were to be enlightened about family history and pedigree from an aesthetic standpoint, the canons of art applicable to bathos, or the formulas expressing the law of gravitation. Bellows introduced Great Alcott in his usual pleasant conversation immediately, but everybody was afraid to begin. At last the Rev. Mr. Osgood plunged heroically into the dark profound of silence, and uttered certain dark sayings, and he and Alcott and Bellows had it all to themselves for an hour or so, belaboring each other with "representative men" and "cosmic men" and "whole men" (analogous, I suppose, to "entire horses"), "pre-existent souls," "ideal archetypes," "genial receptivity," and the "Handle of the Cosmos." The first ray of

light I got came from the Rev. Mr. Osgood, who lifted up his voice after
a pause that was becoming formidable, and affirmed the proposition:

"A Cat is an Individual. A Cat is not a Person."

Afterwards things began to lighten up a little, and I understood
enough of Alcott's talk to see in it signs of genius, some power of illus-
tration, and the expression of a kindly and hopeful temper. If he and the
school he belongs to would spend three hours daily in trying to make
themselves intelligible to plain people and would sign a pledge to use no
word from their polysyllabic technical vocabulary, it would be a useful
discipline to them. It would cut them off from a good deal and diminish
the quantity of their talk, but make the residual balance easier to understand, and would possibly convert it into commonplace. Query: If the
"Handle of the Cosmos" be any relation to the "Pan-handle" of Virginia?

Last night the first "mass-meeting" (under auspices of our poly-
onymous Republican Ward organization) at Demilt Dispensary; a decided success. Much concourse, room crowded till near eleven, many
standing, and all classes represented. I *presided* (Heaven help me) with
dignity and decorum; favored the audience with a prabblement of fifteen
minutes on taking the chair, which was well received, and got through
without making an utter ass of myself, to my own great astonishment.
Oakey Hall failed us. Clarence Seward took his place (son of Senator
Seward) and for so young a man did fairly, considering his manifest careful preparation. He was followed by one Joseph J. Couch of Brooklyn,
not an educated man, but enviably fluent, and solid, substantial, and
clear. The illustrious Chauncey Shaffer followed. I never knew what a
stump-speech was before. It was not exactly like Demosthenes or the
Areopagitica, being made up of slang, funny stories, and an occasional
modulation into a high flight of Bowery theatre declamation, indignation, and "pathos and bathos delightful to see." But it was immensely
effective, kept his audience in an uproar of cheers and genuine laughter,
and shewed considerable tact in dealing with the ticklish ground of the
orator's defection from Know-Nothingism. I was sick and sore with
laughing when he finished.

Heard two acts of *Der Freischütz* Tuesday evening with Ellie at
Niblo's; poorly sung, on the whole. It was sad to hear Agatha struggling
and striving in vain to do justice to that freshet of strong joyous melody,
her Allegro in the second act. She sang her notes, but the contrast between her visible toil and the free, spontaneous inspiration of her music was
too manifest. The orchestral business was all admirable, the glorious

overture could not have been played with more accuracy or truer feeling. Bergmann is a great leader. . . .

October 12, SUNDAY. Political news. The Connecticut state election has resulted in a Republican success, but the result is a little obscure and not quite satisfactory. Florida seems to have gone Fillmore; very "important if true" as a straw that shews how the wind is blowing south of Mason and Dixon's line. . . .[17]

Niggerism has got into the [Episcopal] General Convention at Philadelphia. Murray Hoffman was here this evening, full of the theme and of wrath at his father's defeat. The ex-assistant vestry counsel has been laboring long over a "proposed canon" for the church judiciary, establishing a general system for trial of malfeasant bishops, presbyters, and deacons in all the dioceses; very elaborate and judicious, and very possibly of no practical value, like many of the Honorable Murray Hoffman's most elaborate efforts. It was brought forward and was generally acceptable and was going to pass, when some Southern delegate suddenly discovered that it contained no provision whereby a nigger was precluded from giving evidence in proceedings in a Southern diocese. Every Southern delegation bristled up at once, vigilant against any attack on the peculiar institution, and stood to its arms. It was that Proteus of Abolitionism in a new disguise. Offers to amend by providing that the evidence in each case be governed by the law of the place of trial were respectfully declined. It was "unclean," it was to be distrusted, it was bad and dangerous, it had been tainted at best, and could never be made wholesome for the South, and so the South went against it in a body and squashed it. These are the gentry who call us Sectional.

Old Verplanck has pronounced for Buchanan! Talks like a filibuster, a South Carolinian, Brooks or Captain Rynders. Marvelous, but gratifying. I never knew old G. C. Verplanck to be on the winning side anywhere.

October 15. Another meeting last night, got up by our Vigilance Committee among the "roughs" in Fifteenth Street away down by the East River. The assemblage of freemen was tolerably large, and its quality would have been improved by a little soap and water. Honorable Abram Wakeman, our candidate for Congress, was chief speaker; his speech poor stuff, without even the merit of being limited to the capacity of the audience. . . .

Writing hard tonight, save an hour in a dresscoat at Mrs. Dubois'.

[17] Not true; the Democrats carried Florida by a safe majority.

Her "sociable party" was small and slow like a young mud turtle. Dirty little Erastus Brooks there, looking quiet, stealthy, and malignant. His "dog Noble" sobriquet is much too good for him, even judging from his outer man alone. If men are to develop into animal forms, each according to the law of his individual being, Erastus will be a very ugly, cunning, and vicious rat some of these days.

October 16. Fine weather. Excitement steady and increasing about election returns. Things look far brighter today. Morning papers announced that the Northern and Western counties had changed the result in Pennsylvania to a "Fusion" majority of 10,000. By noon this was changed to 4,000 and upwards the other way, and the next fluctuation was "no decisive result," and the contest so close "that we must wait for the official count." But I've just been to the *Tribune* office, where the bulletin says 3,000 majority against the Democrats pretty reliable.

So the result in that state may be considered as decisive against Buchanan. For even if there should be a couple of thousand for him now, the great reserved Quaker vote next month will be more than enough to sweep it away.[18] But the state seems in a queer kind of condition, and how much of this "opposition" vote belongs to Frémont and how much to Fillmore no man knoweth. The Republican leaders here whisper of a great "mine" that is to be sprung before November and to blow up everything; some intrigue with Know-Nothings, probably. They are a treacherous folk—veritable "Hindoos." I put no trust in any bargain to which they're parties.

Ohio seems all right, though there seem to be strange losses on the Congressional ticket. Indiana has probably given herself over to Democracy. . . .

October 19. Alas for Frémont! Woe is me on account of the prospects of the Republican ticket! Everything is out of joint. Seward and Thurlow Weed have got hold of the cosmos by the wrong handle, as the Great Alcott would express it. We are all exchanging despondencies and condolences and confident predictions of being *nowhere* next November. Perhaps we were unduly elated a fortnight ago, when everything looked

18 Actually the Democrats carried Pennsylvania for their state ticket by a narrow majority, varying from 1,800 votes to less than 3,000 according to the candidates. But narrow as it was, it proved decisive. It chilled the hopes of Republicans for carrying that pivotal state for Frémont, and encouraged the Democrats to expect a victory for Buchanan. The state election in Indiana also went against the Republicans, and Buchanan was now expected to sweep the state (as he did) in November.

so bright and Frémont was so sure of every Northern state, and are immeasurably disgusted by discovering that he has more to do than to walk over the course at his leisure.

Pennsylvania is lost beyond all peradventure, though it may and probably will vote against Buchanan next month. Indiana is hopeless. And the Republican party loses fearfully in the House of Representatives. The "masses" of the North are very far from Abolitionism, whatever it may suit Southern politicians to say. They distrust any party that is' hostile to the niggerocracy and can be misrepresented as Abolitionist. Though the Garrisons and Gerrit Smiths are clamorous in hostility to Frémont, people are apt to look on both as tending the same way, tainted with niggerophily (or philo-nigger-anthrophy), only in different degrees; and there is no doubt that such taint is most repulsive to the instincts of the American people.

For myself, party feeling has not changed my views about the abstract right and wrong of the institution of slavery. I still firmly believe that the relation of master and slave violates no moral law. I can imagine a state of society in South Carolina itself that should make the servile condition infinitely better for the black race than any other, especially if you leave out of view the doubtful possibility of higher development for that race in the future and look merely to their present welfare and happiness.

But slavery may exist in various forms and with various features. There is its Hebrew form, with all the privileges and safeguards with which the Gentile servant was surrounded; and the mediaeval form of serfdom which gave Gurth and Wamba their home in the forests of Rotheswood. It was no part of that system to legalize the selling of Gurth to a Northumbrian baron, Mrs. Gurth to a Squire of Kent. There was classical servitude, under which the slave might be a scholar or an artist and was expressly debarred from no kind of culture or development.

Our slavery system says to some three millions of people: You and your descendants are and shall be forever deprived of every privilege, right, and attribute of humanity which can be directly or indirectly reached by our legislation or our social system. Being slaves, you are, of course, not entitled to the fruit or benefits of your own labor. But in addition to that, you and your so-called wives and husbands and your offspring shall be separated by sale, and the disintegrated fragments of your pretended families shall be scattered from Maryland to Texas whenever we or our judgment creditors can make profit thereby. You shall be shut out from all that humanity has gained in past ages and is gaining still of food for the mind and the heart; you shall be denied any aid toward culture and improvement, moral or intellectual. We will imprison any person who shall give you the key to the outer vestibule of the great treasury of knowledge by teaching you to read. However trustworthy and true you may be, whatever trials your integrity may have stood, you shall in no case be believed under oath. Crimes may go unpunished, civil rights may be lost, but you are incapable of testifying to what you have seen and know as to either. Your owner is irresponsible to society for the exercise of his rights over you, and you must submit without redress to any form or amount of cruelty and oppression and wrong his caprice may dictate. Nothing of manhood or womanhood that man can take from man shall be left you. So far as we can effect it, we decree that 3,000,000 of men and women shall be three millions of *brutes*.

It strikes me that this institution—slavery as it *exists* at the South with all its "safe-guards" and "necessary legislation"—is the greatest crime on the largest scale known in modern history; taking into account the time it has occupied, the territory it covers, the number of its subjects, and the civilization of the criminals. It is deliberate legislation intended to extinguish and annihilate the moral being of men for profit; systematic murder, not of the physical, but of the moral and intellectual being; blasphemy, not in word, but in systematic action against the Spirit of God which dwells in the souls of men to elevate, purify, and ennoble them. So I feel now; perhaps it's partly the dominant election furor that colors my notions. Of course, slaveholders are infinitely better than their system. And we have nothing to say about this system where it is established, and we have no right to interfere with it, no responsibility for it. The question for the North is whether we shall help establish it elsewhere, in the "territories" our nation owns.

October 24. Tuesday night, I vice-presidented at a ratification meeting over the nomination of Mr. Wakeman; meeting very large and spirited. Republicanism has made strong adherents in the laboring-class, rugged, dirty-faced blackguards who listened attentively to the great Wakeman's dish-water oratory, and entered fully into his subject as it seemed. To be sure, it could hardly be otherwise. This is the workingman's party, emphatically the democratic party, resisting the spurious sham Democracy that subordinates labor socially and politically to capital. . . . My belief is that Frémont will carry Pennsylvania and New York, and be elected; if not, that it will go to the House. . . .

Another Alcott *conversazione* last night, or rather an Alcottian soliloquy with occasional stimulative interjections by the audience. It was *de omnibus rebus et quibusdam aliis;* nominally on "Health" moral and spiritual, sanity in the highest sense. The great Alcott is vegetarian, and I think attributes most of the sin and evil in the world to our carnivorous habits. "We are what we eat." "We make our flesh out of the substance of sheep and pigs, therefore, we make ourselves like to sheep and pigs," was the substance of his argument on that head. Generally, it was showy, insubstantial stuff; fanciful analogies, broad generalizations from single facts and doubtful facts, perversions of metaphor into logic. A certain rather literal and unplatonic Dr. Stone would burst in occasionally with medical statistics and physiological laws in conflict with Alcott's transcendental dietetics and therapeutics, but the great Alcott brushed them aside and slipped placidly over them with his eyes fixed on the clouds. According to him, the faculty of Pekin proceed on true philosophical principles when they prescribe pounded elephant bones for debility, that being the strongest of animals. . . .

October 27. After a chilly, wet day the city is steeping and stewing in a tepid mucilage of fog, such fog as prevails in cities, definable as the gaseous form of mud and civic filthiness; Fat Fog, lit up in every direction by the glare of tar-barrels and straw-bonfires that blaze before the multitudinous lager-beer saloons and pot-houses in which we, the people, congregate tonight, as we do every night now, and call ourselves ratification meetings, and the like.

October 28. "I rise, Mr. President, for the purpose merely of stating for the information of this meeting" that I am aweary of ward-meetings, and that my soul is sick of vigilance committees. I suppose it's one's duty in this country to mix in these matters and that like the majority of my friends, I've been criminally negligent all my life in omitting to exercise my sovereign functions otherwise than by voting and in letting the machinery that is practically so much more important than any single vote take care of itself. But it's a very dreary function. A ward-meeting is no Witenagemot. Gas, bad grammar, bad manners, bad taste, bad temper, unnecessary rhetoric, and excitement, and affected enthusiasm about "our" candidate for this or that twopenny office, agonizings and wrestlings over momentous points of order, conscientious misgivings whether we can "legally" take this question till we've taken that other question, dirty little substrata of intrigue and jealousy about chairmanships and the like. It doesn't raise one's estimate of humanity.

November 2, SUNDAY.   Walter Cutting here this evening, with Hoffman, George Anthon, and Mr. Ruggles, very full of his pamphleteering
against Mr. Speaker Banks's statistics. I fear Mr. Speaker Banks is con-
siderably overmatched in this controversy. Last night at the last of our
"Vigilance Committee" series of mass-meetings; heard Joe Blunt deliver
a dull rambling argument on the Kansas matter, and our friend, Richard
J. Deming, like a Western prairie, a vast monotony of flowery flatness
about Webster and the shade of Clay, Scipio and the labyrinth of ages,
and the embodiment of ideas. Afterwards to Century Club, where I heard
the "memorial" strongly commended by sundry people who didn't know
its author.

I heard Benjamin, Bob Winthrop and Ned Bell pronounce a decided
opinion in favor of restoring the slave-trade—the next piece in the "Democratic" programme. Opinions develop fast in this age. Four years ago,
no Northerner would have dreamed such a thing possible.

The Frémont candle flickers up a little in the socket. People seem to
think his chance not so bad; certainly it will not be surprising if everybody
is surprised at his success. He may run far ahead of all inferences from
state politics. Many may vote for him who don't usually vote at all.

November 4, TUESDAY.   Four P. M. Voted after breakfast. Spent an hour
or two at the polls of my election district at the corner of Twenty-second
Street and Third Avenue. Went downtown to a Trust Company meeting,
and then spent two or three hours more in political service. In spite of the
foul weather, there is an immense vote; never larger in this city, I think.
People form in queues, and so far as I've seen, everything is orderly and
good natured; no crowding or confusion. Governor Fish told me he was
two hours in line before he could get his vote in. Peter Cooper and Dr.
Webster must have been still longer about it this afternoon. They were
half an hour off when I left them. There has been some fighting in the
First Ward and a couple of men killed; no other disturbance that I hear of.

Indications are not discouraging. The strength of the Frémont vote
went in early in the day. This afternoon Fillmore is gaining and Buchanan
still more. So it seems, but ordinary inferences from the appearance of
voters are not *perfectly* reliable this time. For example, a party of Irishmen came along this morning asking for Republican electoral tickets.
They were going to vote the Democratic ticket in the Fifth Ward where
they belonged, except for President, and they didn't like to ask for a
Republican ticket there. Frémont, I think, will run largely ahead of his
ticket, and I don't expect over 10,000 against him in this city. The signs

from Pennsylvania are good as far as they go, and the feeling this morning is that Frémont may well be elected. It's a momentous business; thank God, the responsibility of its decision doesn't rest wholly on me. Either way, fearful disaster may come of this election. . . .

11 P.M. Have been downtown exploring and enquiring; learned little that's new and less that's good. Nassau Street and the other streets round the great newspaper establishments (*Tribune, Times, Herald,* and *Sun*) pretty well crowded, in spite of sloppiness under foot and an occasional brisk shower. Bulletins put out from the windows as fast as returns came in and received with vociferations, the dissatisfied parties keeping silence as a general rule. The city is all one way. Buchanan gets hardly less than 20,000 majority, and the river counties will give him as much more, I suppose. So the western counties will have to come out very strong if Frémont is to get this state. Kings County reported Democratic by 6,000, which I don't believe. On the whole, I think Republicanism in a bad way. This storm (it's now blowing hard and the wind is coming round to the northwest) is inconvenient, for it will interfere with the telegraph and the community will have fits if it doesn't know about Pennsylvania and Indiana tomorrow at breakfast time.

November 5. Pennsylvania goes in for slavery extension and Buchanan by 20,000 majority. New Jersey the same way. New York Republican by an immense vote. Maryland probably gives her little all (eight votes) to Fillmore. So Buchanan is elected, unless Fillmore shall have got some Southern state besides Maryland. That would carry the election into the House, a thing rather undesirable. But I shan't be surprised to find that Indiana and Illinois are Democratic, in which case the Sage of Wheatland can afford to give the Snob of Buffalo a little small change in the shape of Louisiana and one or two second-class states in addition.

Consolatory fact that Beastly Brooks (as distinguished from Bully Brooks), the editor of that most filthy and libellous print, the *Express*, and Rat candidate for governor, has experienced a loud call to remain in private life, and that Oscar W. Sturtevant, actually Republican candidate for alderman of the Third Ward, is also allowed to continue by his own fireside. They may both abide, unless a more efficient and discriminating criminal code sends both to the State Prison. Washington Hunt was defeated at Lockport. Wood is doubtless mayor, the Democratic majority in this city being some 20,000. Whiting is nowhere; people think him a little crazy, and some of his performances seem to justify the belief.

Few observers were astonished by the results of the election. In October, as noted above, the Republicans had lost the hard-fought state of Pennsylvania, which was bound by a lucrative trade with the South and which had a conservative body of voters. By pouring large sums of money into Philadelphia, employing a small army of speakers, and making the most of the fact that Buchanan was a Pennsylvanian, the Democrats carried their state ticket by a majority of less than 3,000 in a total vote of 423,000. At the same time they won the less important vote of Indiana. In both states, many Know-Nothings and Whigs voted on the Democratic side. They feared that Frémont's election would mean civil war; they objected to placing a sectional party in control of the government. The November election added three more free states to Buchanan's column—New Jersey, Illinois, and California; while he carried the whole slave domain except Maryland, which stood alone for Fillmore. In all, Buchanan had 174 electoral votes, Frémont 114, and Fillmore 8.

Yet the Republicans, as Strong indicates, were left with solid grounds for optimism. They carried New York by a far more decisive vote than they had anticipated; Frémont's majority over Buchanan was 80,000, and John A. King's majority over Parker was 65,000. Moreover, Frémont had swept all New England and gained the day in most of the Middle West. Considering that the Republican Party had sprung up only since the Kansas-Nebraska Act of two years earlier, its showing was magnificent. "If months have wellnigh won the field," Whittier inquired, "What may not four years do?" It was clear that the Whig Party was dead, and that it would never again nominate a presidential candidate. It was clear, too, that Buchanan was a minority President; the combined popular vote of Frémont and Fillmore far out-topped that which he received.

The country could now turn its attention to other matters. One was another dreadful maritime disaster. The French iron steamer Le Lyonnais, *a new vessel, with thirty passengers and a crew of ninety-five, collided off Nantucket Shoals on the night of November 2 with the bark* Adriatic, *engaged in the coastwise trade. The Lyonnais stayed afloat for two days, while lifeboats and a raft were used to take off the passengers; but a heavy gale sprang up, the boats became separated, and several were lost. In all, only sixteen of those aboard were saved.*

Kansas continued to be a hot-bed of trouble, and sectional animosities did not abate.

1859

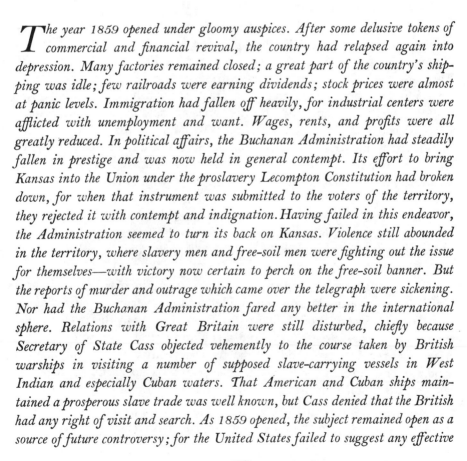

*T*he year 1859 opened under gloomy auspices. After some delusive tokens of commercial and financial revival, the country had relapsed again into depression. Many factories remained closed; a great part of the country's shipping was idle; few railroads were earning dividends; stock prices were almost at panic levels. Immigration had fallen off heavily, for industrial centers were afflicted with unemployment and want. Wages, rents, and profits were all greatly reduced. In political affairs, the Buchanan Administration had steadily fallen in prestige and was now held in general contempt. Its effort to bring Kansas into the Union under the proslavery Lecompton Constitution had broken down, for when that instrument was submitted to the voters of the territory, they rejected it with contempt and indignation. Having failed in this endeavor, the Administration seemed to turn its back on Kansas. Violence still abounded in the territory, where slavery men and free-soil men were fighting out the issue for themselves—with victory now certain to perch on the free-soil banner. But the reports of murder and outrage which came over the telegraph were sickening. Nor had the Buchanan Administration fared any better in the international sphere. Relations with Great Britain were still disturbed, chiefly because Secretary of State Cass objected vehemently to the course taken by British warships in visiting a number of supposed slave-carrying vessels in West Indian and especially Cuban waters. That American and Cuban ships maintained a prosperous slave trade was well known, but Cass denied that the British had any right of visit and search. As 1859 opened, the subject remained open as a source of future controversy; for the United States failed to suggest any effective *alternative for determining the nationality and the innocence of suspected vessels. Much anger and mortification had been produced in the North by the flagrantly open landing of a large cargo of African slaves on the shores of Georgia, imported by Southern citizens. In Central America, meanwhile, filibustering operations continued, the American government seeming powerless to stop them.*

Worst of all was the deepening animosity of the sectional conflict. As the people of New York during January read that civil war was raging with fresh violence in Kansas, and that Slidell of Louisiana had introduced a bill in the Senate to purchase Cuba for the erection of two or more new slave states, feeling ran high. The tariff and the Homestead Bill emerged this month as more distinct issues than ever, with North and South definitely opposed upon them.

January 3, MONDAY.   First of all, God watch over and defend my three through this coming year, as hitherto. Amen. . . . Record of New Year's. . . . There were no special incidents. Mrs. Serena Fearing and Mrs. Julia Talmage, each "receiving" for the first time in her own house, were severally very grand and happy and pleasant to behold. At John Sherwood's I had a pleasant talk with his handsome and buxom sister-in-law, Miss Charlotte Wilson, and at Mrs. William B. Astor's with her very intelligent granddaughter, Miss Ward (Sam Ward's daughter).[1] Henry Cram's wife, who has always spent the holidays heretofore in Philadelphia, was at home this New Year's Day—very nice. Mrs. D'Oremieulx trotted out her little Leon to be admired, and I admired him most cordially. He's in Babbins's style, but more mature by a couple of years, and if possible, handsomer. Scarce a house among the forty-odd, the atmosphere of which did not seem kindly and cordial—and which I did not feel glad to have visited and rather reluctant to leave.

Of course, a very large percentage of this aggregate of radiance and hospitality is social sham. But there is still left a certain very valuable residuum or balance of sincere good feeling which is brought out by this much reviled institution of New Year's Day. And this kind of *sham* hurts no one; social usage that requires everybody to receive everybody else with the shew of kindness and cordiality one day in the year does no harm. Perhaps we should be the gainers if the anniversary came *twice* a year.

[1] Sam Ward had married Emily Astor in 1837; she died in giving birth to their daughter, Margaret Ward, who married John Winthrop Chanler (Columbia 1847).

October 18

News from Harper's Ferry of a strange transaction. Some sort of insurrection, an armed gang getting possession of the United States Armory: railroad trains stopped, x+y hundred fugitive slaves under arms, government troops, marines, and other forces sent on. Seems to have been a fight this morning (and the rebellion quashed, of course), but the whole transaction is as yet most obscure, and our reports probably much exaggerated.

On Sunday night, October 16, John Brown—who had been staying with his followers in two farmhouses rented on the Maryland side of the Potomac— armed his little band of eighteen men, seized the Baltimore & Ohio Railroad bridge across the river, and invading Virginia, captured the United States armory, arsenal, and rifle-works at Harper's Ferry. Making himself master of the town, he cut the telegraph wires and began seizing masters and liberating slaves in the country around. At break of dawn the citizens gathered with their weapons, and militia companies soon joined them. Hot fighting commenced. Brown and a surviving remnant of his force were hemmed in at the engine house in the armory grounds, where they withstood a siege all afternoon. During the evening Colonel Robert E. Lee and a company of United States marines reached the town. As morning broke on Tuesday, they battered their way into the engine house, disarmed the little garrison, and took Brown prisoner. In this criminal attempt to begin a slave insurrection, Brown had lost ten men killed; four, with himself, were seized, and four more escaped—two only temporarily. The whole country was thrown into hot excitement, which in parts of the South amounted to frenzy.

October 24, MONDAY. Mr. Ruggles not yet returned from Richmond. The House of Bishops has given poor Bishop B. T. Onderdonk leave to withdraw his memorial. Some deny it, but I've good reason to believe they have so decided. Their action is probably final, for the case is not likely to be stirred again. His friends are savage against Potter, and also against Hawks, who, they say, misled them by representations that a majority of the bishops could be relied on to favor restoration. Sorry for B. T. Onderdonk, but I don't regret the result. Notwithstanding the strong vote in the Diocesan Convention, the laity are generally opposed to the Bishop's restoration, and it would have bred mischief. The assistant ministers of Trinity Church continue to scold about Morgan Dix's appointment, and incredible as it seems, that truculent Mrs. Higby has broken off her handsome daughter's engagement with Abel T. Anderson's son, who looks like a nice fellow, because she can't let her daughter marry the son of a man who has been guilty of acquiescing in so outrageous a procedure. So I hear from half a dozen sources.

The Harper's Ferry insurrection (seventeen white men and five niggers) is suppressed (after conquering a town of two thousand inhabitants) by a combined movement of state and federal troops. State of Virginia was awfully frightened. The leader, old Ossowatamie John Brown of Kansas, seems cracked; a free-soil Balfour of Burley. Insanity won't save him from the gallows. He will undoubtedly be hanged. Were I his jury, I could not acquit him, and twelve terrified Virginians will have little difficulty about a verdict. This insane transaction may possibly lead to grave results. If Gerrit Smith and other fanatics of the extreme left are compromised by the papers found upon Brown, they may be indicted, and a requisition for them from the governor of Virginia would embarrass the governor of New York a little.

October 25, TUESDAY. Mr. Ruggles here tonight. Returned from Richmond this afternoon. Bishop B. T. Onderdonk's case before the House of Bishops seems, by his account, to have been nearly hopeless from the beginning. Not more than one-third disposed to favor even restoration without jurisdiction. It's the best result for the interests of the church. A bishop under a cloud, charitably tolerated because penitent for past misdeeds, would not do in these days of laxity. This age needs precedents not of mercy, but of rigor. Clemency and lazy, good-natured acquiescence in acquittals and pardons have long been vulgar and cheap. I'm very glad that Mr. Ruggles went to Richmond (he took pains to interfere on neither side of the Bishop's case). He has been prominent there and useful. He has been put at the head of an important committee of thirty-three laymen to systematize, develop, and bring out the financial resources of the church. I tell him he is the Lay-Patriarch of the Protestant Episcopal Church in America.

October 29. Trial of Brown and the other Harper's Ferry conspirators on indictments for treason and murder is pushed vigorously, and it will result in a speedy verdict of prompt execution. The conduct of the prosecution is rigorous, or seems so in these days of rose-water criminal practice. We are accustomed to see defendants in a capital case treated with a hyper-delicacy of double-refined tenderness and consideration, favored with every unreasonable delay and encouraged to insist on every frivolous or fraudulent quibble. The rigor of this Virginia court is right enough, but eminently inexpedient. The court should give Brown the maximum of indulgence and vigilantly shut out his prospective claim to the honors of martyrdom. It should be astute in protecting him by subtlety of quibbling or by inventing pleas of insanity for his benefit. If the slaveholding interest were wise, it would exert itself to secure his conviction on some minor offense, inciting to a riot, or the like, and his punishment by flogging, imprisonment, and the pillory. I'm not sure the South can afford to hang him, though he plainly deserves it.

Sent in my resignation as trustee of Trinity School today.

November 2, WEDNESDAY. Opera Monday night with Charley Strong and Mrs. Eleanor, who dined here. Donizetti's *Maria de Rohan*; thinnest small beer, but less objectionable than Verdi's rotgut and not much worse than Meyerbeer's staple article of stale champagne. It is marvelous that people who think they appreciate Mozart and Beethoven can sit out three hours and a half of the paltry commonplaces that make up this opera. Music is a wonderful thing in every point of view. Gazzaniga sang, and a very nice tenor, Stigelli, and a good baritone, Terri (facetiously called Fulltone Terry). Ullman's force seems strong, but the "season" is a failure, thus far. Speranza, who was imported for the purpose of raising a furore, is an utter failure, and "Lasciate ogni speranza" is written on the portals of the Academy, according to Murray Hoffman. They talk of producing the *Zauberflöte*, and I hope they may, but it will only mire the management deeper. Its music will be thrown away on audiences that tolerate Verdi.

November 4. Just from opera, with Ellie and Mrs. Georgey Peters; *Lucrezia Borgia*, [with] Gazzaniga, Beaucardé, a new tenor, whom I like, though his voice has lost its freshness, and that fattest bull of Bashan, Amodio. I left the ladies in their box, in the second act, and went down to the footlights, where it was rather pleasant to watch Gazzaniga's expressive face in the "Madre mia" terzetto. Rarely heard that very clever little bit of trumpery better done.

November 8. This evening with Ellie to Mrs. Wickham Hoffman's, Nineteenth Street, a small party, chiefly Lenoxions. Mr. and Mrs. Ellery Sedgwick, whom I like, and a few more, including a lively Miss Mary Edgar, Murray Hoffman's latest divinity. Also Pierre Kane and Robert Cutting, bringing news of the election and bewailing Democratic defeat, that is, less than twenty thousand Democratic majority in this city. It may be an important fact if the state has gone decisively for the Black Republicans or (as the South would prefer to designate them) the John Brown Republicans.[2]

November 9. Ellie and I have just returned from a concert (at the City Assembly Room in Broadway above Grand Street), one of the performances commemorating the centennial anniversary of Schiller's birth. It was a great success. It gave me a new sensation, or rather, recalled the sensations of 1843, when each successive Philharmonic marked an era by its new revelations. There was a great, silent, appreciative crowd of Teutons in a good room, listening to an admirable orchestra and a passable chorus doing a programme of the first order. Began with the Overture to *Tannhäuser*. I never heard it as well rendered. Its magnificent lights and shadows were fully brought out. It is something more than a mere prodigy of elaborate construction. I admit it at last to rank among works of the highest order. Ellie said its first movement (the grand "Pilgrim-chant") seems hewn out of granite, a felicitous criticism.

Part Second was Beethoven's *Symphony No. 9*, the Choral Symphony —all but absolutely new to me. I heard it some twelve or more years ago, vilely done at Castle Garden, and afterwards by Satter and Timm on two pianos, but retained not a single phrase. My impressions of it were that it was long, *outré*, and dull, and I was surprised tonight to find that I was able to follow it throughout, and, in some moderate degree, to appreciate it. Beethoven meant it to be his greatest work. The first three parts certainly on the grandest scale; they seem to contain as much thought as any two of his earlier symphonies. But they are not inspired in the same sense with the *Eroica* and C minor. The scherzo, however, is full of fire, and the slow movement that follows it of lovely melodic feeling. The fourth part, with its chorus, seems like an afterthought. It's built on a fine and sharp-cut melody and worked up into striking effects. But Beethoven is not at home with a chorus.

November 13, SUNDAY. Tonight . . . Tom Appleton of Boston, Mignot, Mould, Stone, who brought Leutze, Murray Hoffman, and Henry Dorr. Story of Mr. and Mrs. Sturgis of Boston—the lady, a niece of Dr. Parkman's. Appleton saw them one morning just after Dr. Parkman's disap-

---

[2] The Republicans achieved a signal victory in the state election this fall, though only minor officers were to be chosen. They gained heavy majorities in both branches of the legislature, and chose six out of the nine state officers; though the Democrats and Americans had in general united against them. The election proved that the American or Know-Nothing Party was dying fast, and that its free-soil members were all going into the Republican ranks.

pearance, while he and everyone else supposed the doctor had wandered off in a state of insanity, before any suspicion had attached to Dr. Webster. The lady looked wan and weary, and after some pressing for its cause (she and Appleton had had mesmeric confidence and she was an impressible subject, though not clairvoyant), she said: "I have had such a restless and miserable night. I seemed to be seeking and searching for Dr. Parkman all over Boston, and feel as tired and worn out as if it had been a real search. I hunted through the whole city. I found him at last. He was dead, and cut up into little pieces."

November 14. After dinner to Trinity Church vestry meeting. We sat late. Proposition to change our clerical appointments and transfer Vinton from St. Paul's to Trinity, and "associate" Morgan Dix and poor incapacitated Haight (who has been at Trinity) in the charge of St. Paul's. Dunscomb opposed it strenuously and at great length, in usual style of opacity, but he stood alone. Then (against my advice) Cisco moved that Dix's pay allowances be raised to the full assistant grade. This also carried, though Skidmore and Sands and others were reluctant, and wished a postponement. They urged delay, lest we should still further offend the other assistant clergy. I should have preferred to let it lie over for Dix's sake. I fear he will be damaged if he get the reputation of being a pet of the vestry. . . .

The rector and others were pleased to be distressed this evening about my resignation from the Board of Trinity School. That board passed a series of flaming resolutions on the subject, of which it should have been ashamed; it carried civility to fanaticism. Don't know whether I can adhere to my intention after such a battery of compliment, but I do desire we may be better strangers. It seems the school proposes celebrating its 150th anniversary—in the usual way, I suppose—by boring an assemblage with gab and speechification.

November 18, FRIDAY. Last night there was a sound of revelry on these premises; a little dancing party of fifty-odd, partly "for" the Lenox set, partly "for" Miss Grace Coles, Mrs. Edward Snelling that shall be hereafter (I don't clearly understand, by the by, the force of the preposition "for" used in the connection). Being engineered by Mrs. Ellie, it went off pleasantly, of course. Helmsmüller pianized. George Anthon, and the Kings, and Miss Annie Leavenworth being (conventionally) under deep domestic affliction, couldn't come. There were Miss Ellen Schermerhorn and little Miss Helen Lane, Ulshoeffer, Mrs. John Kernochan, little Miss Gerry, Mrs. Peters . . . , William and Edmund Schermerhorn,

Wickham and Murray Hoffman, Dr. Peters and Dr. Carroll, Cutting, Mignot and Stone, Dick Hunt and his brother Leavitt, Ellery Sedgwick, Tip Hoffman, Hazeltine, and so forth. . . . There was a prolonged German, but it was over by one.

John Brown, captured on October 18, was immediately indicted, and on October 26 arraigned for trial before the Virginia circuit court. He was slowly recovering from his wounds, and so weak that he had to lie on a mattress in the courtroom. The trial was concluded within five days, and on October 31, after deliberating less than an hour, the jury rendered its verdict: "Guilty of treason, and conspiring and advising with slaves and others to rebel, and murder in the first degree." This was entirely just; no other verdict was really possible. In a speech when sentence was passed, Brown declared: "I deny everything but what I have all along admitted, of a design on my part to free slaves." He had rejected the plea of insanity which his counsel wished to make for him. Court at once sentenced Brown to be publicly hanged on December 2. Meanwhile, the South was filled with anger, and much public alarm over the possibility of slave insurrections existed in Virginia. John Brown's letters, conversations, and public statements, given to the public by all the Northern newspapers, had telling eloquence. As Emerson remarked, some of his champions made a dubious impression on people; "but as soon as they read his own speeches and letters, they are heartily contented—such is the singleness of purpose which justifies him to the head and heart of all." Brown summed up his final utterances in one sentence. "It is a great comfort to feel assured that I am permitted to die for a cause." At noon on the appointed day, in the presence of fifteen hundred Virginia troops, he was hanged on the scaffold. Strong's attitude toward the man, his crime, and his punishment was probably typical of that of most Northerners; it was quite as sympathetic as Lincoln's attitude, rather coldly defined in the Cooper Union address.

November 20, SUNDAY.   Reading *inter alia* the record of our New York Negro Plot trial of 1741, to see whether our little community of a century ago was driven as wild by panic about a servile insurrection as the Sovereign State of Virginia has been by the insane raid of John Brown and his company. Not much to choose between the two cases. The overt acts in New York were far less clear and the panic seems to have been as shameful. The evidence that anything deserving to be called a conspiracy existed is imperfect and suspicious. The "plot" may very well have been a mere phantom called up by the fright of those who punished the alleged plotters. Virginia certainly has facts more tangible to scare her from her propriety. . . .

There is no doubt that old St. John Brown will be hanged. Virginia is too badly scared to think of clemency, and why should she think of it? Hanging is the logical consequence of unlawful homicide, and it's at least doubtful whether a flagrant, deliberate case like his can be justly or rightfully made an exception for the sole reason that a pardon would be good policy and raise the credit of the community. That he undertook his mad, mischievous enterprise under a wild impulse of mistaken duty, and so forth, is assuredly no reason for pardoning him, or remitting any part of the penalty he has incurred—though I suppose most people have a vague notion that it *is* and that no man should be hanged for doing what he thought at the time to be right. . . .

However that may be, I fear this savage old wrong-headed Fifth-Monarchy-man has done us a mischief that will be memorable. The South is frightened into frenzy, utterly without reason, but that makes no difference. Fanatics and sedition-mongers at the North are doing all they can to exasperate and irritate—and Virginia is giving them a batch of martyrs to stimulate their sentimentalism and flavor their vaporings on platform and pulpit. This next Congress and the Charleston Democratic Convention and the next presidential election are full of peril. God grant the Union may survive them!

The change in the arrangements of the House of Representatives—the removal of the desks—though in itself a change for the better, is unfortunate at this time. We shall have real debates at the next session instead of prosy speeches to Bunkum and essays for the newspapers delivered to Mr. Speaker and an inattentive, letter-writing house—and honorable gentlemen are going to meet next month in a temper that will make earnest *debate* dangerous.

November 21. Murray Hoffman dined here, and we marched to the Opera House through unexpected pelting rain to hear the *Zauberflöte,* from which I've just returned.

House very full considering the foul weather, and inclined to be amiable and patronize Mozart. It was funny to hear people talking during the entre-acte, comparing this with the *Sicilian Vespers* and pointing out their respective merits and demerits; one was more *this* and the other more *that,* and so on, as if one should undertake an analysis of the relative position in art of *The Tempest* and Sylvanus Cobb, Jr.'s last sensation story for the *New York Ledger*.

It was very fairly done. . . . Scenic effects and properties as contemptible as their silliness deserved. As to the plot, the dramatic element of the opera, human language is unable duly to express its idiocy. Let us hope that to the fashionable public of seventy years ago, for which it was written, it conveyed some gleam of a notion about Truth and Virtue (always with a big T. or V.), Illuminatism, Initiation, *Frei Männerei*, or something else. But it is a question whether real music be not heard at less disadvantage when allied with a mere absurd, incoherent series of stage effects like those of the *Zauberflöte*, with the representation of something that can hardly pretend to be real or historical or in any way connected with the movements and doings of human beings at any era of this planet's existence than when it illustrates and accompanies something unreal that claims to be a sort of caricature of real human passion and action.

November 24. To the *Magic Flute* again last night with Ellie and Mr. and Mrs. D'Oremieulx, who dined here. Ellie was delighted. It finds far more favor with opera-goers than I thought possible. Our oracles of the lobby say that it is "very pretty," and others proceed to distinguish Mozart's music from Verdi's as *undramatic* and *unimpassioned!*

People of Virginia are still making themselves ridiculous by panic and bluster. Charlestown thrown into consternation by the mistake of a sentinel in taking a cow for an invading Abolitionist contemplating a rescue. Cow didn't stand when challenged, was fired upon, and the community got under arms. All this and a great deal more of the same sort would be great fun were it not likely to prove disastrous.

November 25. Threatening snow all day; very raw, chilly, rueful weather, and as we left the Opera House just now, it was beginning to come down. We were Ellie and I, Mrs. Georgey Peters and Sus (who married a sister of Dr. Peters's and seems to be a nice person; lives at Staten Island), and we heard the *Zauberflöte*. Mrs. Professor Joy was on one side of us, and as the box on the other side was vacant, Walter Cutting and his brother Robert, Hazeltine, Mignot, and Jack Ehninger took possession of it, and the ladies had a nice time. *Zauberflöte* is delicious, and Mozart the King of Melody, *jure divino*. His work is so simple and *true* that it seems easy, and one must know something of other composers to appreciate it. But how far below him are even Handel, Beethoven, and Haydn in fertility of deep and various melody; how much *more* has he given us of pure, bright musical thought than any other composer! More than Beethoven himself, though I fully admit Beethoven's C minor, *Eroica*, and A major symphonies to be intense beyond, and far beyond, all other music. . . . People call Mozart's work undramatic. "He's a great composer, no doubt, but he could not write *dramatic* music like Verdi's and Donizetti's." I suppose dramatic music to be music that expresses passion or emotion capable of dramatic representation. And no one has ever done that like Mozart, to my knowledge, unless it may be Weber in the "Leise, leise, fromme Weise," Agatha's scene in the *Freischütz*. Look at "Batti, batti," for example. Never mind its melodic beauty, attend only to its narrative power, to the story it tells. Could words express more clearly the serio-comic, solemn-sham penitence and apology of the flirtatious little Zerlina, perfectly conscious of her power over her clown of a lover, than its first movement, or the triumph of the little coquette, dancing round him and reiterating her "batti, batti" when she has teased and wheedled him into reconciliation and submission, than its final allegro? Is not this unequalled as dramatic music?

November 28. I went downtown, encountering at Eighth Street half the scoundrelism of New York marching in procession with colored lights, Roman candles, torches, and hideous howls to a Fernando Wood ratification mass-meeting at Cooper Institute. I greatly fear the city is about to be disgraced by the reëlection of that knave and demagogue to the mayoralty. Party division will put him in. As a friend of the railroad conductor remarked this evening: "Wood's crowd's bound to win, the other fellers ain't got no *spunk* like what Wood's men's got."

Mr. Philo T. Ruggles (Ellie's uncle) has just gone to smash in a kerosene oil manufacturing company speculation, and has dissipated what I suppose was a snug little fortune acquired as master and referee.

November 30. Washington Irving died suddenly night before last. Peters has been visiting him twice or thrice a week for a long time. He has had asthma and some nervous disorder that made his night wakeful, and was suspected of hypertrophy of the heart. But his death was most sudden and without a minute's warning. He leaves a fragrant memory, personal and literary.

What's to be done about the mayoralty election next Tuesday? There are four candidates, viz:

1. Havemeyer—set up by Tammany Hall
2. George Opdyke—Republican

3. My venerable foolish friend, DePeyster Ogden, nominated by a little knot of people who call themselves Old Line Whigs, the fossil remains of an extinct party.

4. The King of the Dead Rabbits, that indomitable knave and demagogue, Fernando Wood. How shall Wood be kept out? is the question with all decent people. Shall we vote for Havemeyer or Opdyke? If we only knew which would poll the stronger vote, the question could be readily answered. But these miserable party differences will divide the vote of those who want a decent man for mayor, and the *canaille* will carry in their champion. Two to one on Wood. I have been advocating Havemeyer thus far. I prefer him because Opdyke's career in the last legislature was discreditable (witness his abortive move against savings banks), and I have thought Havemeyer the more available candidate. But I may be wrong, and my vote will be reluctantly given for Opdyke if he shall appear to be the stronger man. Reluctantly, not only because I prefer Havemeyer, but because my "Republicanism" has waxed cold of late. The *Tribune* and other Republican papers treat the John Brown case, the Harper's Ferry insurrection, too sympathetically; they disapprove in words, and do all they can to elevate that fanatical law-breaker and homicide into a martyr. If the Republican party endorses murder and every crime of violence and lawlessness that may be perpetrated against the institutions of the South, I shall withdraw therefrom. The *Post* and *Tribune* and our Brownists generally put their sympathy on the ground of their martyr's insanity (or they try to do so), and talk of its being shameful to hang an insane man, but laud and magnify him at the same time as sacrificing himself for a principle as a heroic redemptorist, giving his life for his brethren in captivity: Cuff and Sambo, to wit. But why make this fuss about him, if his raid were a mere freak of lunacy? Well, he'll probably be hanged day after tomorrow, and I only trust and hope his crime and his punishment may not lead to the gravest disaster.

December 2. . . . Old John Brown was hanged this morning; justly, say I, but his name may be a word of power for the next half-century. It was unwise to give fanaticism a martyr. Why could not Virginia have condescended to lock him up for life in a madhouse? Had Edward Oxford been hanged for shooting at Queen Victoria in 1840, his death would have stirred up scores of silly shopboys to regicide (or reginicide), merely from the inscrutable passion for notoriety; for being thought about and talked about—that has much power over man's vanity. This man Brown's elements of popular available heroism and martyrdom are unhappily numerous.

December 4, SUNDAY. George Anthon looked in just before tea in great excitement. The corpus of old John Brown is in the city at No. something in the Bowery. Carpenter, the sexton of St. Mark's, had told George of the fact, confidentially. Carpenter had been employed in his undertaking capacity to attend to putting the relics of that sainted redemptorist on ice, and George Anthon could probably be admitted to a sight of the remains, as a great favor, and wanted me to go, which I didn't. . . .

Old Brown's demeanor has undoubtedly made a great impression. Many heroes of the Newgate Calendar have died game, as he did; but his simplicity and consistency, the absence of fuss, parade and bravado, the strength and clearness of his letters, all indicate a depth of conviction that one does not expect in an Abolitionist (who is apt to be a mere talker and sophist), and that tends to dignify and to ennoble in popular repute the very questionable church of which he is protomartyr. Slavery has received no such blow in my time as his strangulation. There must be a revolution in feeling even in the terrified State of Virginia, unless fresh fuel be added to the flame, as it well may be, within the month. The supporters of any institution are apt to be staggered and startled when they find that any one man, wise or foolish, is so convicted of its wrong and injustices as to acquiesce in being hanged by way of protest against it. So did the first Christian martyrs wake up senators and landed gentlemen and patrician ladies, *tempore* Nero and Diocletian, and so on. One's faith in anything is terribly shaken by anybody who is ready to go to the gallows condemning and denouncing it.

December 5. Drizzle, and what's worse, I think it means to go on drizzling tomorrow. That will make Wood—F. Wood, the king of the Dead Rabbits—inevitable. The clouds in their courses fight against Opdyke and Havemeyer. I shall vote for the latter, though with hesitation.

DePeyster Ogden has withdrawn, but the little squad that calls itself the Old Line Whig Party (refusing to die and take refuge in history, where that party belongs) instantly nominated Havemeyer, and if the weather be fine, will help him with perhaps a score of votes. Notwithstanding that accession to Havemeyer, I should prefer to bet on Wood.

Talked with W. T. J. this morning. He's rabidly Republican, and can see nothing in the present situation but the insolence and folly of Virginia and South Carolina. Also with Charles Augustus Davis, who's insane on the other side, and inclines to throw away his vote and help that scoundrel Wood into position once more because even Havemeyer is not quite free from some taint of free-soilism. . . .

The indomitable Fernando Wood had quickly rallied his following after his defeat in 1857. Unable to regain control of Tammany Hall, he, with the aid of his brother Benjamin, had organized a new group called from its meeting-place the Mozart Hall faction. He had also curried favor with the national leaders of Democracy, taking pains to ingratiate himself with President Buchanan, and in 1858 lending the Stephen A. Douglas organization a large sum to finance the Douglas campaign against Lincoln in Illinois. Mayor Tiemann's administration, though honest and efficient, displeased many businessmen as well as the lower orders of the city. A general union of Democrats, immigrant groups, and the disreputable classes made it easy for Fernando to defeat the opposition, which was divided between Tammany Democrats and Republicans, and to capture the mayoralty for the third time in 1859. He thus became a minor power in national politics, and was able to appear at the Charleston Democratic Convention in 1860 at the head of a contesting delegation of pro-Southern views; while his brother Benjamin, purchasing the Daily News *in 1860, made that a pro-Southern organ.*

December 6. "Fernandy" Wood has won. The day has been wet and bad, but when I voted the decent part of the community seemed out in full force, and Havemeyer certainly ahead. Many Republicans were voting for him as the most available candidate, though preferring Opdyke, and everybody ready to bet two to one on his election. Downtown the talk of the street was to the same effect. The *Evening Post* and *Express*, however, talked of a heavy vote for Wood in sundry districts, and I omnibussed downtown through the drizzle at eight o'clock with some misgivings. Found a vast crowd around the great newspaper offices of Nassau and Beekman Streets, mostly rough and in high jubilation. Returns in from all but four wards, and Wood 1,600 ahead. So *vivat F. Wood, diaboli gratia* mayor of New York. . . .

A grand meeting is to be called to protest against Northern sympathy with John Brown. Like nine-tenths of the community, I am free from such sympathy and strongly disapprove of the way the *Tribune* and other papers are glorifying his memory and purring encouragement to treason and homicide. But I'm tired of Southern brag, and of seeing the North on its knees, declaring it is a good boy, and begging the South not to commit the treason and violence it is forever threatening.

December 9. Have been attending with Ellie and Jem and Murray Hoffman (who dined here) one of Sam Cowell's Drawing Room Concerts (so-called) that are given on the off nights of the French Theatre; "Lord Lovell," "The Cork Leg," and other specimens of genuine British song, the Muse of the Cider-Cellar, Pothouse "Free and Easy's" or Easies. It was intolerably funny. In costume. Not elegant, but decidedly low comedy; buffoonery, in fact. I'm weak enough to enjoy buffoonery when there is any true comic *vis* in it, and when it's free from essential coarseness and hints of dirt. This was excellent of its kind, and thoroughly enjoyed by a full house. As an actor of broad comedy, this man rivals Burton. . . . No speaker yet in the House of Representatives; but the want of an organization does not seem felt at Washington. One branch of the legislature is making buncombe speeches about John Brown and his supposed secret instigators; in the other, Southern members are denouncing a book against slavery by one Helper, and thereby advertising it with all their might. Whoever owns the copyright should be very grateful to them. There is no breach of the peace as yet. Our national gift of the gab has its drawbacks, but it is invaluable as a safety-valve. Heaven grant it or anything may save us from disruption. They say Northern members shew more backbone than heretofore. Perhaps so, but they certainly let themselves be catechized and put on their purgation by fire-eaters and disunionists in a way that seems humiliating.

The whole South seems bewildered with fright and fury. It seems an incredible infamy, but the *Richmond Enquirer* endorses the suggestion of a correspondent that the South secede from the Union and put itself under the protection of Louis Napoleon! England would be the preferable ally, but then Her Majesty is shrewdly suspected of free-soil tendencies. This transcends any atrocity I've heard attributed to Garrison or Wendell Phillips. But the ultraism of either section is enough to sicken one into renouncing our model republic for Naples or Vienna.

George Anthon is happy in the possession of a lock of John Brown's hair, and a small section of his halter; relics of S. Giovanni Bruno, obtained through the sexton of St. Mark's.

No party had a majority in the House, which was composed of 109 Republicans, 88 Buchanan Democrats, 13 Douglas Democrats, and 27 Know-Nothings. A spirited contest for the Speakership at once began. It was rendered more acrimonious and dangerous by a fierce accompanying debate on Hinton Rowan Helper's controversial book, The Impending Crisis of the South: How to Meet It, *which had been published in 1857, and which had been endorsed and promoted by many Republican members. Helper, a North Carolinian, had argued that slavery was a terrible evil to the non-slaveholding majority in the South—and had offered many facts and statistics to support his view. The abolition of slavery, in his opinion, would greatly benefit all but a small aristocratic oligarchy in the South. Many slavery leaders, comprehending how dangerous the book was, declared that they would never permit any Representative who had recommended it to become Speaker. As the debate grew angry, violence ensued. The removal of the old desks, as Strong had foreseen, made for closer contact and for more spirited and intimate discussion. Members were soon indulging in fist-fights. As practically all the Representatives were armed with knives or revolvers, many observers feared a bloody battle. Throughout December and most of January the deadlock over the Speakership continued. John Sherman of Ohio, the Republican favorite, once came within three votes of obtaining the honor. As the contest went on, tempers became badly frayed in Washington, and sectional antagonisms in the country at large increased. Numerous Southern Representatives, supported by newspapers in their part of the country, were threatening secession. Helper's book meanwhile was, of course, selling like hot cakes.*

December 15. Cutting told me that the meeting of the John Brown sympathizers at Cooper Institute tonight, at which Wendell Phillips and others were to spout, would probably be interfered with and broken up. I'm not sure that I've much objection. Lawless disturbance and violence are always bad, of course. And I'm still Northern enough to prize freedom of speech and discussion, if only as a comparatively harmless evacuation of peccant humors, a safety-valve for mischievous impulses. Fanatics— especially mere *talking* fanatics, like Garrison and Phillips—are most effectually neutralized by being severely let alone. And in a free community people of every stamp ought, as a general rule, to have the privilege of meeting and discussing any subject undisturbed, under the protection of the law. Abuses of that privilege should be redressed by legal process, not by a mob. But there may be a practical limit to this right, in the best regulated and most law-loving society. The free-love meetings of two or three years ago would have been broken up had they not been prudently discontinued. Their ostentatious advertisement was an outrage on the general sense of right and decency. This Brown meeting is called to endorse and encourage attempts to stir up servile insurrection, with all its horrors, on our own soil—to sanction what the law of the land calls robbery and murder. If the roughs attended and howled, I cannot harshly censure them.

December 16. There was a row at the sympathetic Brunonian meeting last night, but the police kept it under control. Sundry arrests were made. Jerry Larocque spent the night in a station house.

December 19. About one hundred ornaments of our liberal and enlightened profession—one hundred "gentlemen of the bar"—were congregated in the Special Term room this morning. I scrutinized the crowd, to determine how many there were whom I would be willing to receive as visitors at this house, or rather whom I would not be annoyed and disgusted to receive. There were really not more than *three* who were not stamped by appearance, diction, or manner as belonging to a low social station, and as having no claims to the conventional title of "gentlemen." It was manifestly a mob of low-bred, illiterate, tenth-rate attorneys, though it included many successful and conspicuous practitioners. Such is the bar of New York. May our Columbia College Law School do something to elevate it.

After dinner I went to the Union Saving meeting at the Academy of Music. Crowd most dense and formidable. Happy to extricate myself without broken limbs, for the crush and pressure were serious. Whole house packed full. Even the lobbies and stairways crowded. Bonfires and ancillary meeting outside, and cannon in Union Square. Virginia should be appeased by our act of submission and apology; if she be a magnanimous commonwealth, she will hear our deprecations of her wrath and our cheers for Governor Wise will be a sweet-smelling sacrifice. But I detected little sign of spontaneous enthusiasm or hearty feeling in the plaudits of this vast assembly. It seemed a business meeting, and the points of the orators awakened a response not from the concourse itself, but from a minority of claqueurs.

When I had forced my way within the doors, somebody seemed to be making a speech. It proved to be some clerical gentleman (old Spring?) making a prayer. Then our dear friend James Brooks moved the resolutions and pitched into clerical agitators—the Cheevers, the Beechers, and others —less effectively than their demerits deserve.

Him followed Charles O'Conor with an elaborate argumentation that fully adopted the extremist south-side view of the blessings to the North that are embodied in the Southern institution. He went the furthest length in endorsing slavery as right, necessary, and beneficent. Half his speech must have grated on the perceptions of two-thirds his audience. His want of tact is marvelous; for example, he maintained that every Northerner is a slave till he attains twenty-one years—there is only this difference, that the right to his services cannot be sold in market overt here as in South Carolina. I longed to be John Jay or Horace Greeley or Wendell Phillips that I might take his speech and rasp it to rags. Were I an Abolitionist I would so crush O'Conor that he should never shew his head among civilized Northerners again. But I'm not an Abolitionist—and O'Conor was half right.[3]

When he took his seat, I was nearly flattened out between an obese German and a long Irish gent. The compression was growing more intense every minute, and I made my way to the door after an arduous struggle, with ribs unbroken.

December 20. After dinner to a primary election in Nineteenth Street—the Eighteenth Ward Republican Association. My Republicanism is not ardent just now, and I only went at the urgent request of D. D. Field and Judge Cowles, and because it's of great importance to get the ward out of "bad hands," namely, the faction of one Manierre whom I take for a very Pecksniffian personage, and into "good hands"; I don't know exactly whose, but I am in that crowd, it seems, for my name is on the opposition ticket as delegate to some convention or committee. There was a large attendance. Roughs preponderated, and I heard frequent denunciations of "my" ticket as having "too much kid glove on it, by God!" So, I rather suspect I'm defeated, which I shall not in the least regret.

Called at Mrs. Ruggles's for Ellie and saw Governor Hunt, who spoke at the Union meeting last night.

December 21. . . . J. A. Stevens, Jr., called to say that "our ticket" succeeded last night by a large majority. So the country is probably safe. I'm elected to something, but don't know what and don't much care. I must see more clearly what the Republican Party means to do before I consecrate my vast energy and influence to its service.

The medical students of Philadelphia belonging to the Southern states have held a meeting and resolved to evacuate that city as Northern and unclean and to investigate nosology and the materia medica at Southern institutions. They are to be received with military honors by the silly

[3] At this Union-saving meeting Mayor Tiemann, ex-Governor Washington Hunt, and John A. Dix also spoke, and letters were read from ex-Presidents Fillmore and Pierce. But as Strong indicates, public sentiment in the North was hardening against the proslavery men and the men who refused to recognize that slavery had a moral aspect.

citizens of Richmond and carried gratis over Southern railroads. Probably their prescriptions and prognoses will not be more sagacious and beneficent in consequence of this step. They will know less about calomel and quinine, and vital statistics at the South may be affected ten years hence by their exodus. But the proceeding is rather significant. . . .

Lieber in deep affliction because our Columbia College Law School committee decided that examination on the subjects of his lectures should not be conditions of a degree. So I learn from Mr. S. B. Ruggles. Lieber says his chair is degraded, and so on. Mr. Ruggles sympathizes with him and asks whether we want the Law School to turn out mere attorneys. Of course, high and liberal culture is most desirable, but we are not yet in a position to insist upon it. We cannot yet, in the infancy of the school, require young attorneys and lawyer's clerks to sacrifice a couple of hours daily to political science and legal philosophy. It is a great point gained that so many (upwards of sixty) consent to come in to be taught the practicabilities of their profession.

Pity Mr. Ruggles seems inclined to withdraw himself from the College Board and its committees. So strong a man could afford to overlook the little slight of Fish's election to the presidency of the board.

December 22. After dinner with Ellie, Mrs. Georgey Peters, and Walter Cutting to Wallack's. *Everybody's Friend*, a three-act comedy, by Brougham[4] (I believe), very clever and well-acted by Brougham, Lester and Wallack. . . .

No material change in the state of the nation. It's a sick nation, and I fear it must be worse before it's better. The growing, vigorous North must sooner or later assert its right to equality with the stagnant, semi-barbarous South, and that assertion must bring on a struggle and convulsion. It must come. Pity it could not be postponed some twenty years, when Northern preponderance would be overwhelming. If Northern Abolitionism precipitate the crisis and force the battle on us *now*, it will be a fearful and doubtful contest.

I cannot find out why it is against the law of God for one man to own another. But I am better satisfied every day that slavery demoralizes and degrades the slave-owners. For example, when John Brown's gang was finally defeated and captured, one of them was carried wounded and dying into a certain house at Harper's Ferry. The victors proposed to kill him there and then. A young woman (Miss Christina Foulkes or Fowkes, sister-in-law of the proprietor of the house) threw herself between the

---

[4] John Brougham (1814–1880), Irish actor and dramatist.

wounded prisoner and the muskets of his captors and implored them to spare him—to let the law dispose of him, and said and did all that the kind, merciful instincts of a good girl would naturally suggest. Whereupon these chevalier gentlemen dragged him out and killed him in the street. Northern newspapers noticed this fact, and there was talk of getting up a service of plate for this humane young woman. So she is compelled by stress of popular feeling (no one can doubt that *something* compelled her to deny the generous impulses of her womanhood) to write and publish a letter certifying that she was actuated by no regard for the life of an Abolitionist, but only and exclusively by an apprehension that her sister's carpet might be stained and damaged by an Abolitionist's blood.

December 23. Fine day. Cold. Diligent in Wall Street, though wasted an hour attending a meeting called at Trinity Church to see about raising funds to put Lamson's Church for Americans in Paris on a permanent foundation. . . .

We went to Cowell's again. He is wonderfully clever and funny, but this is my third attendance. It will suffice for the present. The house was full and there were people there we knew. People have begun to find him out and he will become popular. Though he deals in the very lowest of comedy, there is not even a whisper or a look of aught uncleanly in his performance, wherein he has the advantage of our theatrical people generally. For although the stage has greatly improved in that particular, one seldom hears a farce or comedy in which there is not some *double entendre* or questionable joke that would not be tolerated in the presence of ladies elsewhere.

December 25, SUNDAY. Weather appropriate, clear and cold. Yesterday afternoon at three, I attended the "Children's Festival" at Trinity Church, which was crowded. Choral service: carol by the children, with accompaniment of the organ and of the chimes in the steeple, was very pretty. Uptown I worked hard to send off presents and harder at unpacking and·arranging those that kept coming in. Ellie rejoiced greatly over mine to her—certain glass and silver dinner-table decorations that I knew she coveted. She had got for me a very carefully finished and colored cabinet picture of herself (a photograph elaborated into a miniature). Considered as a likeness, it is a libel, I regret to say. All the treasures for the children were duly marshalled on the piano and tables as usual, and a grand display they made.

Also, there is a big Christmas tree in the hall, surmounted by the flag of our country, on which Mrs. Ellie has with great care and labor inscribed "THE UNION FOREVER"! . . .

The first business of this morning was, of course, the introduction of the two little men to the treasures set forth in the music room. The spectacle was overpowering. Both were driven nearly wild with ecstasy and wonder. Then to church; music rather good and Higby's sermon very respectable. Dined at Mr. Ruggles's, taking the two boys with us—both of whom did credit to their bringing up. After dinner, Mr. and Mrs. D. C. Murray and John Sherwood and his very agreeable wife came in. . . .

This has been a happy and sunshiny Christmas. Would that the good and genial influences of the day might make themselves felt in soothing the acrimonies of our national family quarrel—that He Who "maketh men to be of one mind in a house," Whose "Name shall be called Wonderful, Counselor, the Prince of Peace," and Whose advent on earth Christendom celebrates today with traditional usages of reconciliation between parted friends and of re-affirmance of all social and family ties by words and tokens of kindliness, could be heard in our discordant Councils: that the government might now (as surely hereafter) "be upon His shoulders" and no longer administered by contending sectional factions, each inspired by hate, ambition, and selfishness, or, in other words, by the Devil. . . .

This present political crisis promises to divide the Republican party of 1856. Its radicalism will become avowed Abolitionism. Conservative Republicans will have to organize independently. Bob LeRoy identifies himself with the extreme Republican Lefts and went on the platform with a revolver in his pocket when George William Curtis lectured in Philadelphia.

December 28. Lieber came to see me Monday morning in great sorrow and soreness. Perhaps it may be worth while to reconsider our action about his Law School lectures.

December 30. Worked with decent efficiency in Wall Street. Dined on roast oysters at Downing's, and spent the afternoon on duty at Bank for Savings, which I visited this morning also, taking down with me to the Manhattan Bank a carriage-load of specie and bills accumulated during the week.

This was the Women's afternoon, no he-depositors being admitted. The crowd was dense, garrulous, and mephitic. Biddy generally brings a young baby with her, if she has one, thinking that she will be "attended to" the sooner. There must have been thirty babies, at least, when we began, and the aggregate of their howlings was something grand and terrible. But I retained my presence of mind and executed my high office with dignified composure, tempering the rigor with which I enforced the rules by a certain suavity of manner peculiar to myself. I presented, no doubt, a sublime spectacle. . . .

Store in Pearl Street just above Wall (west side) is threatening to tumble down. The front wall has separated from the side wall, the solution of continuity being manifested by an ugly crack that extends from the roof downward through one or two stories. Police have stretched ropes across the street, and a crowd was watching patiently this morning in the cold for the crash. Another storehouse on Broad Street crumbled down from its own weight, and that of its contents, a week ago and killed one or two innocent outsiders who happened to be in its neighborhood.

House of Representatives not yet organized.

December 31. This year and this decade will soon be among the shadows of past times. It seems scarce possible ten years have passed since we went out of the forties. They have been ten years of change. Two more have been given to me—the two little men whose portraits Ellie and I have just been admiring: God protect them both—and two more have been taken away, my mother and my father, since December 31, 1849.

1860

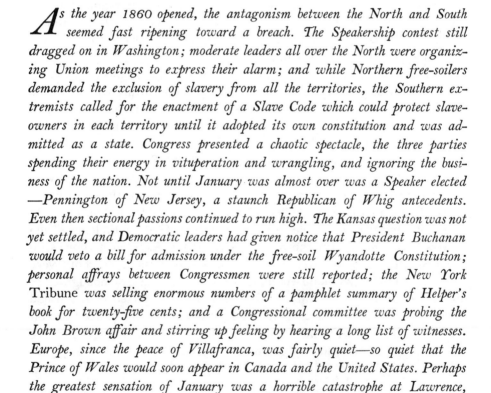

As the year 1860 opened, the antagonism between the North and South seemed fast ripening toward a breach. The Speakership contest still dragged on in Washington; moderate leaders all over the North were organizing Union meetings to express their alarm; and while Northern free-soilers demanded the exclusion of slavery from all the territories, the Southern extremists called for the enactment of a Slave Code which could protect slave-owners in each territory until it adopted its own constitution and was admitted as a state. Congress presented a chaotic spectacle, the three parties spending their energy in vituperation and wrangling, and ignoring the business of the nation. Not until January was almost over was a Speaker elected —Pennington of New Jersey, a staunch Republican of Whig antecedents. Even then sectional passions continued to run high. The Kansas question was not yet settled, and Democratic leaders had given notice that President Buchanan would veto a bill for admission under the free-soil Wyandotte Constitution; personal affrays between Congressmen were still reported; the New York Tribune was selling enormous numbers of a pamphlet summary of Helper's book for twenty-five cents; and a Congressional committee was probing the John Brown affair and stirring up feeling by hearing a long list of witnesses. Europe, since the peace of Villafranca, was fairly quiet—so quiet that the Prince of Wales would soon appear in Canada and the United States. Perhaps the greatest sensation of January was a horrible catastrophe at Lawrence, Massachusetts, on the afternoon of the 10th. The great Pemberton mill collapsed in a sudden crash while some six or seven hundred operatives were at

149

*work; and about two hundred persons, many of them girls, were either crushed
to death or roasted alive in the flames which soon swept the wreckage.*

January 1, SUNDAY.   New Year's Day. God prosper the New Year to
those I love. Church with Ellie and Johnny; an effective sermon by Higby.
Thereafter we took a cold "constitutional" up the Fifth Avenue to Forty-
second Street, a rather vigorous winter day, still and sharp. Tonight is
overcast, with promise of snow tomorrow.

January 5.   With Ellie to the Artists' "Reception" in Dodworth's
Rooms; a vast crowd. Discovered Mrs. D. C. Murray and Mrs. John
Weeks, General Dix, Wenzler, Stone, Rossiter, Mrs. Field (commonly
distinguished as "the murderess," being mixed up a little with the Duc de
Praslin affair),[1] the Rev. Mr. Frothingham, Lewis Rutherfurd, and others.
Many bad pictures on the walls, and some few good ones. Eastman Johnson
and Charles Dix are making progress. Wenzler has a lovely portrait of
one of Dr. Potts's daughters. Stone's portrait of my two little men was
there, and people praised it—to *me*.

Monday the second was kept for New Year's Day. It was a fine specimen of crisp frosty weather, with a serene sky and a cutting wind from the
northwest. I set forth at eleven o'clock in my own particular hack, *en
grand seigneur*, and effected more than twenty calls, beginning with Mrs.
Samuel Whitlock in 37th Street. My lowest south latitude was Dr.
Berrian's and the Lydigs'. There were no incidents. Bishop Potter's draw-
ing-room was perhaps the dullest place I visited. The Bishop is always
kindly and cordial, but nature has given him no organ for the secretion of
the small talk appropriate to a five minutes' call. He feels the deficiency and
is nervous and uncomfortable. Very nice at Mrs. George F. Jones's, and
at Mrs. William Schermerhorn's. At Mrs. Peter A. Schermerhorn's, in
University Place, I discovered the mamma and Miss Ellen, both very
gracious. At Mrs. William Astor's, Miss Ward (the granddaughter of
the house; Sam Ward's daughter by his first wife) talked of her friend
Miss Annie Leavenworth. . . . Mrs. Edgar was charming in her little bit
of a house, the "Petit Trianon." Poor Mrs. Douglas Cruger seems growing
old, is less vivacious and less garrulous. At Mrs. Serena Fearing's I was
honored with a revelation of the baby that was produced last summer.

---

[1] Henry M. Field, brother of Cyrus W. and David Dudley Field, had married
(May, 1851) Laure Desportes, who was innocently involved in the famous Choiseul-
Praslin murder case in France. Rachel Field has told the story in *All This and Heaven
Too* (1938).

Pleasant visit to Mrs. Christine Griffin, née Kean—where little Miss Mary was looking her loveliest. That little creature will make havoc in society a year or two hence, when she "comes out." She is very beautiful and seems full of life and intelligence. Mrs. Isaac Wright in Waverley Place, with her brood of four noble children rampaging about her, was good to see. . . .

Home at six, tired after a pleasant day's work. We had a comfortable session at dinner with Dr. Peters and Mrs. Georgey Peters, Miss Annie Leavenworth, Miss Josephine Strong, Walter Cutting, Richard Hunt, Murray Hoffman, George C. Anthon, Jem Ruggles, and Jack Ehninger. Dinner was successful.

January 7. Walked uptown with George Anthon, who entertained me with the biography of his runaway cousin, Miss "Unadilla" Elmendorf, and incidents of the elopement, which is chronicled in newspaper paragraphs as a "marriage in high life." The girl is illegitimate, and her Lochinvar a noted swindler of tailors and hotelkeepers and a parasite of opera troupes, but full of talent and impudence. He made his way into the barbarous State of Virginia to report John Brown's execution for *Frank Leslie's* or some other newspaper when almost—or quite—every other reporter was repulsed and excluded by the natives.

January 9. To Columbia College meeting, Lafayette Place, at two in the afternoon. . . . I moved that Lieber's opening lecture of his present Law School course be printed, which was carried.

Thereafter to Tenth Street Studio Building to call on Leutze; I spent an hour with him pleasantly. I saw his "Battle of Princeton" picture, and another, a Venetian scene—masqueraders in a gondola, the Bridge of Sighs overhead, the corpse of a state criminal just brought out into another boat, upon which the riotous festive party comes suddenly and unawares. This latter picture is unfinished, but will be among the best things Leutze has done.

January 10. House of Representatives not yet organized, no Speaker elected and government at a deadlock. Members spend their time during the interval between the ballotings in speech-making about John Brown, fugitive slaves, Hinton Rowan Helper's *Impending Crisis*, and the irrepressible nigger generally. That black but comely biped is becoming a bore to me. No doubt he is a man and a brother, but his monopoly of attention is detrimental to the rest of the family; and I don't believe he cares much about having his wrongs redressed or his rights asserted. Our politicians are playing on Northern love of justice and a more or less morbid Northern philanthropy for their own selfish ends by putting themselves forward as Cuffee's champion. But the South is so utterly barbaric and absurd that I'm constantly tempted to ally myself with Cheever and George Curtis.[2]

January 11. News today of a fearful tragedy at Lawrence, Massachusetts, one of the wholesale murders commonly known in newspaper literature as accident or catastrophe. A huge factory, long notoriously insecure and ill-built, requiring to be patched and bandaged up with iron plates and braces to stand the introduction of its machinery, suddenly collapsed into a heap of ruins yesterday afternoon without the smallest provocation. Some five or six hundred operatives went down with it— young girls and women mostly. An hour or two later, while people were working frantically to dig out some two hundred still under the ruins, many of them alive and calling for help, some quite unhurt, fire caught in the great pile of debris, and these prisoners were roasted. It is too atrocious and horrible to think of.

Of course, nobody will be hanged. Somebody has murdered about two hundred people, many of them with hideous torture, in order to save money, but society has no avenging gibbet for the respectable millionaire and homicide. Of course not. He did not want to or mean to do this massacre; on the whole, he would have preferred to let these people live. His intent was not homicidal. He merely thought a great deal about making a large profit and very little about the security of human life. He did not compel these poor girls and children to enter his accursed mantrap. They could judge and decide for themselves whether they would be employed there. It was a matter of contract between capital and labor; they were to receive cash payment for their services. No doubt the legal representatives of those who have perished will be duly paid the fractional part of their week's wages up to the date when they became incapacitated by crushing or combustion, as the case may be, from rendering further service. Very probably the wealthy and liberal proprietor will add (in deserving cases) a gratuity to defray funeral charges. It becomes us to prate about the horrors of slavery! What Southern capitalist trifles with the lives of his operatives as do our philanthropes of the North?

January 17, TUESDAY. Mr. Ruggles is quite ill at Lockport (Governor Hunt's), so ill that Mrs. Ruggles and Miss Bostwick go thither tomorrow. He went to Buffalo, last Thursday was a week, to attend to some railroad receivership and caught severe cold on the journey. Our cars

[2] The Rev. George B. Cheever, author of *God Against Slavery* (1857); George William Curtis, now attacking slavery in his speeches and writings.

in wintertime, with their sloppy floors, red-hot stoves, and currents of chill air from opened doors and windows, are perilous traps for colds and inflammations. He took refuge at Governor Hunt's after two or three days of indisposition, which he was obliged to neglect, and was threatened with congestion of the lungs. He is reported by telegraph "mending slowly" but has been heavily dosed with anodynes and other vigorous medicaments that have weakened and depressed him. We have but just learned how seriously ill he has been, and Ellie feels quite uneasy, but I hope without sufficient cause.

January 19. Mr. Ruggles reported by telegraph "improving," but not strong enough to travel.

January 20. Anxious about Mr. Ruggles at Lockport. A telegram from Jem, received just before dinnertime, announced that "the physicians thought" him improving slowly, which was satisfactory enough, but for the inference, strained perhaps, that Jem did *not* think so.

January 22, SUNDAY. This afternoon lots of people called to ask for news of Mr. Ruggles. I saw D'Oremieulx, D. B. Fearing, and Miss Mary Morris Hamilton. . . . Afterwards George Anthon came in . . . also Dr. Peters. I stated to the doctor what I know of Mr. Ruggles's case, and his prognosis was, on the whole, decidedly encouraging. He thinks the nervous and cerebral trouble in a patient of Mr. Ruggles's peculiar temperament (especially after treatment with narcotics and quinine) likely to occur after any acute attack of disease, and not grounds for serious apprehension.

January 25. Wolcott Gibbs called by appointment tonight. We microscopized energetically, and the performances terminated with a very modest supper of chicken and hock. Gavitt was to have joined us but made default. We studied the Ross 1/12 objective and examined the circulation in the tail of a tadpole and a kitty fish, which I brought uptown with me from the little aquarium shop in Fulton Street this afternoon. Results were satisfactory. My binocular is unquestionably an acquisition. It shews certain structures better than the Ross instrument.

The Rev. Mr. Bellows, who called at breakfast time this morning to ask after Mr. Ruggles, is my authority for the following diplomatic

Scene at the Tuileries. A State dinner. The Honorable Mr. Mason, F.F.V., (our Minister to France), and Don Somebody, the Spanish Ambassador, glowering at each other across the table, during intervals of deglutition, each timidly desiring to establish himself in rapport with the other.

Spain. Breaking the ice: "Parlez-vous français, M'sieu Masón?"

America. With effort: "Ung Poo." (A pause) "Permit me, Sir, to ask whether you speak the English language?"

Spain: "Small." (Conversation closes.)

February 2. After dinner with Ellie to No. 24, where I left her, and then seeing a glow in the southern sky over the roof of the Union Place Hotel, I started in pursuit of the fire. I dog-trotted to Grand Street before I found it. A great tenement house in Elm Street near Grand burning fiercely. Scores of families had been turned out of it into the icy streets and bitter weather. Celtic and Teutonic fathers and mothers were rushing about through the dense crowd in quest of missing children. A quiet, respectable German was looking for his two (the elder "was eight years old and could take care of himself, but the younger had only nine months and couldn't well do so"). I thought of poor little Johnny frightened and unprotected in a strange scene of uproar and dark night and the glare of conflagration and piercing cold, and of Babbins, and tried to help the man but without success. There were stories current in the crowd of lives lost in the burning house; some said thirty, others two. The latter statement probably nearer the truth. Steam fire engines are a new element in our conflagrations and an effective one, contributing to the *tout ensemble* a column of smoke and sparks, and a low shuddering, throbbing bass note, more impressive than the clank of the old-fashioned machines. . . .

There is a Speaker at last. Sherman withdrew, and the Republicans elected Pennington of New Jersey (Bill Pennington's father), who seems a very fit man for the place. Reading Agassiz's *Essay on Classification.* Rather hard reading for anyone not thoroughly learned in a score of -ologies. But I can see and appreciate its general scope and hold it to be a very profound and valuable book.

February 3. Last night's Elm Street fire was a sad business. Some eighteen or twenty people perished. There was another fire in Lexington Avenue (dwelling houses) due to these pestilent furnaces. Two factories have just been blown to bits in Brooklyn by defective or neglected steam-boilers, with great destruction of life. We are still a semi-barbarous race. But the civilizing element also revealed itself this morning at the Tombs, when Mr. Stephens was hanged for poisoning his wife. If a few owners or builders of factories and tenement houses could be hanged tomorrow, life would become less insecure.

February 6, MONDAY. Just from opera, *Puritani,* with Ellie and Mrs. Georgey Peters and Dr. Carroll. Little Patti, the new prima donna, made a brilliant success.[3] Her voice is fresh, but wants volume and expression as yet; vocalization perfect. . . .

Columbia College meeting at two P.M. Resolved to appropriate the President's house and Professor Joy's to College purposes, turn them into lecture rooms, and so forth. A good move. It is contemplated to build a new house for the President on Forty-ninth Street, which I think questionable. I brought up some matters connected with the Law School, which went to the appropriate committee, and instigated King to introduce the question of suppressing these secret societies, which do immense mischief in all our colleges. John Weeks has just taken a young brother of his from Columbia College and sent him into the country, because he found that the youth belonged to some mystic association designated by two Greek letters which maintained a sort of club room over a Broadway grocery store, with billiard tables and a bar. Whether it be possible to suppress them is another question. Result was that King is instructed to correspond with the authorities of other colleges and see whether any suggestions can be got from them and whether anything can be done by concerted action. . . .[4]

February 10. Opera tonight with Ellie and Mrs. Georgey Peters and her papa; *Der Freischütz* in an Italian version. The Germanism of that opera is so intense that any translation of its text is an injustice to Weber's memory, but its noble music can afford to be heard under disadvantages. Max was Stigelli, and very good. Agatha (Colson) was respectable. She knew how her music ought to be sung and tried hard, but had not the vigor it demands. Caspar (Junca) was pretty bad.

Query: if there ever existed a Caspar who could sing "Hier in diesem Jammerthal" as it ought to be sung, or an Agatha who could do justice to the glorious allegro that follows her "leise, leise, fromme Weise"? I enjoyed the evening, also Wednesday evening, when we had Charley Strong and wife in "our box" and heard *The Barber*, delightfully rendered. Little Patti made a most brilliant Rosina and sang a couple of English songs in the "Music Lesson" scene, one of them ("Coming through the Rye") simply and with much archness and expression. This little debutante is like to have a great career and to create a furor in Paris and St. Petersburg within five years. . . .

---

[3] Adelina Patti, now about to enter her eighteenth year, had made her operatic debut in New York in 1859.

[4] Fraternities were well planted at Columbia. Alpha Delta Phi had been chartered there in 1836, and three other fraternity chapters had been organized in the 1840's. Francis Henry Weeks took his degree at Williams College in 1864.

October 24, WEDNESDAY

People begin to look grave and talk anxiously about our prospects. Will this have any serious effect on the vote of New York and Pennsylvania? Panic and pressure in New York and Philadelphia will not have made themselves felt throughout the country in time to influence the elections. Had they occurred earlier, they might have determined the result, for comparatively few Republicans love niggers enough to sacrifice investments for their sweet sake.

October 25. We have reason to be unsettled and alarmed. A large and influential Southern party is working hard for disunion, and in South Carolina, at least, is strong enough to overawe and silence the sensible and conservative minority. Lincoln's election will certainly be followed by a revolutionary movement there. Then we shall see. If no other state join her in secession and if she have time to cool down and recover her senses before any actual collision, and if no accident complicate the situation, this dangerous point may be weathered. But if things take another turn, the black year of 1860 will long be remembered. At best, we must expect an ugly shock and an anxious time before this year is ended.

October 27. Today's special rumor is of a scheme of disunion, fathered by the Hon. Howell Cobb of Georgia, Secretary of the Treasury, who is now favoring us "mudsills" of New York with his presence and talking sedition. His plan is said to be the secession of all the Southern states and of the commercial portions of the Middle and New England states. New York, I suppose, is to be divided by a line crossing the Hudson at West Point. This is lunacy incredible of a man who goes at large. But, I fear there is no doubt that this Honorable Cobb, one of our highest officers of state, is in shameful alliance with the most advanced destructives and secessionists of the South, and stands ready to become a traitor upon the first eligible opportunity for treason. There is reason to fear that our disgraceful old chief magistrate, James Buchanan himself, is in the hands of men like Cobb and ready to become their instrument.

Even anti-Republicans seem to find this a little too much to bear. The attempt to bully us is barefaced. If these threats are in earnest, they will drive all the North into earnest, resolute resistance, with very little distinction of party. If they are merely part of the electioneering programme of the administration and the South, it is a rash and indiscreet programme. The crack of the plantation whip is too audible.

Caleb Cushing foreshadowed something like this in a speech last summer, when he said in effect that Abolitionists need not suppose the civil war which their fanaticism was bringing upon the country would be remote and confined to the South. "No, we will begin it here, in the streets of Boston." But the dream of setting up insurrection against our "State Sovereignties" of New York and Massachusetts in enthusiastic loyalty to the "peculiar institution" and the nigger-owning aristocracy is too extravagant to be entertained by any sane man not under the influence of whiskey, opium, or hasheesh.

October 28. The talk today is that Fusionism may carry this state after all. Then the election goes into the House and would be long contested before a majority could unite on any one of the three. Excitement would be prolonged and sectional fury intensified. I don't feel like voting for Lincoln, but I should be sorry to see New York frightened into voting for anybody else, even if the inevitable crisis were thereby postponed to 1864. It may as well be met now; and were Lincoln to be beat, I believe the Southern states would go into convention, nevertheless, so scared and angry are they.

Old Mrs. Hayward of South Carolina is at the New York Hotel in deep affliction and alarm because it is well known that "the abolitionists" have consigned large invoices of strychnine and arsenic to the slaves of her neighborhood. So Mrs. S. B. Ruggles reports, who saw her yesterday.

Mrs. Sally Hampton spoke the other evening at Mrs. Peters's of Dr. Lieber's having lately presided at a German Republican meeting at Cooper Institute. "So unfortunate for his son" (in business at Columbia or Charleston), "he was doing so well, and, of course, this ruins all his prospects at the South"!!! This is tyranny beyond King Bomba. If severance come, we must console ourselves for its calamity by remembering that we are freed from a most disreputable partner.

The Hon. Cobb, at Duncan, Sherman & Co.'s office, has been openly damning the blindness and stupidity of the capitalists who have taken the United States ten million loan at a premium, and declaring it is not worth fifty cents on the dollar. (So Charley Strong reported on respectable authority.) Pretty talk for a Secretary of the Treasury! I guess he put this loan into the market just at this time in the expectation it would not be taken, and hoping to make capital out of its failure for his own clique of traitors.

October 29. No new features in today's political talk. Perhaps the Fusionists are rather more confident, though the *Herald* gave the latter up for lost a week ago. I hear it said today that New York, New Jersey, and Pennsylvania will vote anti-Republican, which I doubt most omnipotently. There is at least an even chance that we are now on the eve of a great public disaster, a calamity to the whole civilized world. Submission by the North would not avert it long if the Southerners are as unanimously in folly as they seem to be, and I'm not sure the North can submit to be rough-ridden any longer without disgrace.

October 31, WEDNESDAY.   Am just from *Der Freischütz* with Ellie and Mrs. Georgey Peters. The lovely phrases of the finale are not quite out of my ears yet. Formes was Caspar; Stigelli, Max; and Fabbri the heroine. The best performance of the opera I have seen. The Fabbri misconceived her part, took everything too slow and spoiled the glorious allegro of the "Wie nachte mir der schlummer" scene by breaking it up into little bits of light and shadow instead of giving us the sustained rush of joyous melody which Weber meant it to be, and which she could have made it if she tried. But in that scene, perhaps, and in Caspar's drinking song certainly, Weber overrated the capacities of voice, energy, and expression. No mortal ever existed who could render them as they should be rendered and do full justice to their intensity. . . .

No change in the aspect of political matters. Samuel J. Tilden has come out with a letter (anti-Republican) that shows far more depth and ability than I've given him credit for. He has passed for a commonplace, clever, political wire-puller, but he deals with this great question in a statesman-like way. Southern papers and stump orators continue in a blatant way. Fortunately a deal of mischievous gas is liberated and made audible which might be energetic for evil were it pent up. . . .

Republicans refuse to believe secession possible (in which I think they are wrong), and maintain that were it accomplished, it would do us no lasting mischief. I am sure it would do fatal mischief to one section or another and great mischief to both. Amputation weakens the body, and the amputated limb decomposes and perishes. Is our vital center North or South? Which is Body and which is Member? We may have to settle that question by experiment. We are not a polypoid organism that can be converted into two organisms by mere bisection. China is a specimen of that type, but we claim higher rank. Bisection is disaster and degradation, but if the only alternative is everlasting submission to the South, it must come soon, and why should it not come now? What is gained by postponing it four years longer? I feel Republican tonight.

November 2.   Sent Ellie to the opera in charge of her brother Jem and sallied out for a debilitated stroll. Found a great Wide-Awake demonstration in progress; inspected them in Fourteenth Street. Seward was making a speech in "Palace Gardens," and the crowd there was dense, the

Gardens packed full and impenetrable. The show in the street was brilliant—rockets, Roman candles with many colored fire balls, Bengal lights, the Wide-Awakes with their lanterns and torches, and "I wish I was in Dixie." I adjourned to Broadway in front of the New York Hotel to see the procession pass. The Southerners of the hotel groaned and hissed, and the Republican mob in and about the Lincoln and Hamlin headquarters across the street cheered and roared, and the din was deafening. But there was no breach of peace. . . .

Think I will vote the Republican ticket next Tuesday. One vote is insignificant, but I want to be able to remember that I voted right at this grave crisis. The North must assert its rights, now, and take the consequences.

Think of James J. Roosevelt, United States District Attorney, bringing up certain persons under indictment for piracy as slave-traders to be arraigned the other day, and talking to the Court about the plea the defendants should put in, and saying that "there had been a great change in public sentiment about the slave trade," and that "of course the President would pardon the defendants if they were capitally convicted." !!! Is Judge Roosevelt more deficient in common sense or in moral sense? If we accede to Southern exactions, we must re-open the slave trade with all its horrors, establish a Slave Code for the territories, and acquiesce in a decision of the United States Supreme Court in the Lemmon case that will entitle every Southerner to bring his slaves into New York and Massachusetts and keep them there. We must confess that our federal government exists chiefly for the sake of nigger-owners. *I can't do that.* Rather let South Carolina and Georgia secede. We will coerce and punish the traitorous seceders if we can; but if we can't, we are well rid of them.

If I looked remarkably like Kossuth or Mazzini, I could nevertheless travel through Austria with no danger beyond that of a few days' detention, at the end of which, my identity being proven, I should be dismissed with apologies and an indemnity. But I happen to be mistaken for John Jay at least once a week, and it would therefore be utter madness for me to visit that section of our free and happy republic that lies south of Mason and Dixon's line. Before I had traveled half a day's journey through that sunny and chivalric region, some gent who had visited New York would spot me as a damned abolitionist emissary. I should be haled forth from my railroad car and hanged on the nearest palmetto tree.

November 4, SUNDAY. Mr. Ruggles had a long private talk yesterday with General Scott, some portion whereof he imparted to me, including matters I don't care to write here. The General is loyal and union-loving, intensely and without reservation. He wrote to the War Department October 27 or 28, calling attention to the inadequate garrison of Fort Moultrie, only about one hundred men instead of the eight hundred or one thousand required to work its guns, and to the unprotected state of other Southern forts and arsenals, but he has received no answer. Ingraham, appointed some three months since to command of the Home Squadron, is a South Carolina man.

If old Buchanan be really playing into the hands of secessionists, and if disunion come next week, as I think it will, and if his non-feasance enable the fire-eaters to take possession of Fort Moultrie or any other federal fortalice, there will arise from all the North (and, I trust, from no small portion of the South), a reactionary indignant cry for vengeance against traitors in high places that will make old Buck's neck feel insecure for a season.

November 5. With William Schermerhorn to Columbia College Board meeting at two o'clock. Unusual amount of business, mostly unimportant. Treasurer's report. Report from a Committee on Tutorships; we decided to appoint three. . . .

I confidently predict that Lincoln will be elected by the people, and that South Carolina and Texas, and probably Georgia and Mississippi, will thereupon be foolish enough to commit themselves to revolution, which will be a grave calamity. Also that Governor Wise will make several great speeches, and make himself singularly ridiculous. Also, that there will be Northern men enough interested in Southern trade to paralyze our Northern protest against treason and disunion, and that their special organ will be the New York *Express.*[5] Also, that Southern conservatives will be crushed and silenced, though in a majority, and that the Reign of Terror in the Carolinas, Georgia, and other states will be so strengthened that it may become intolerable and be thrown off. I fear the question may have a grim solution in an uprising of the slaves, from Richmond to Galveston, stimulated by their masters' insane talk about the designs of the Black Republican party.

November 6, TUESDAY. A memorable day. We do not know yet for what. Perhaps for the disintegration of the country, perhaps for another

[5] James Brooks's *Express,* founded in 1836 and now supporting Douglas, was a peace-at-any-price organ, reflecting the views of many merchants; in 1861 its defense of the South almost provoked mob violence.

proof that the North is timid and mercenary, perhaps for demonstration that Southern bluster is worthless. We cannot tell yet what historical lesson the event of November 6, 1860, will teach, but the lesson cannot fail to be weighty.

Clear and cool. Vote very large, probably far beyond that of 1856. Tried to vote this morning and found people in a queue extending a whole block from the polls. Abandoned the effort and went downtown. Life and Trust Company meeting. The magnates of that board showed no sign of fluster and seemed to expect no financial crisis. Uptown again at two, and got in my vote after only an hour's detention. I voted for Lincoln.

After dinner to the Trinity School Board at 762 Broadway. Thence downtown, looking for election returns. Great crowd about the newspapers of Fulton and Nassau Streets and Park Row. It was cold, and I was alone and tired and came home sooner than I intended. City returns are all one way, but they will hardly foot up a Fusion majority of much above 25,000. Brooklyn said to be Fusion by 14,000. An anti-Lincoln majority of 40,000 in New York and Kings, well backed by the river counties, may possibly outweigh the Republican majorities in the western counties, but that is unlikely. The Republicans have gained in the city since 1856, and have no doubt gained still more in the interior.

The only signs of excitement and enthusiasm that I saw were in the crowd about the Bell and Everett headquarters (in Broadway below Pine Street).

Election day, as Strong indicates, passed without disturbance in New York; the press even found it dull. Lincoln's election was so universally expected that no one could feel very much excited. As the returns were telegraphed in, it became plain that he had won an overwhelming majority in the electoral college, where he had 180 votes, Breckinridge 72, Bell 39, and Douglas 12. But he had only a plurality of the popular vote, which stood Lincoln 1,866,452; Douglas 1,376,957; Breckinridge 850,082; Bell 588,879. Lincoln had carried all of the free states except New Jersey, where he divided the electors with Douglas. In New England, New York, and Pennsylvania his majorities were impressive. But the most striking feature of the election was the heavy popular vote that Douglas, with the Buchanan Administration and the South opposing him, polled. The question now in everybody's mind was as to the course of the South. Already, on November 5, Governor Gist of South Carolina had recom-

mended to the legislature that if Lincoln were elected, it should provide for a convention to decree the secession of the state from the Union. And on election night the crowds in Charleston cheered the news of Lincoln's triumph as the harbinger of a new Southern confederacy. But Strong remained hopeful.

November 7. Lincoln elected. Hooray. Everybody seems glad of it. Even Democrats like Isaac Bell say there will be no disturbance, and that this will quiet slavery agitation at the North. DePeyster Ogden's nerves are a little unstrung, but they are never very steady.

Republicans have carried every state on which they counted, except New Jersey, and it may be they have carried that, too. They have a very fair show in Delaware!!! Wilmington gives them a majority. Kentucky, Virginia, Maryland, and Tennessee are believed to have gone for Bell, a sore discouragement to the extremists.

Telegrams from the South indicate no outbreak there. There is a silly report from Washington that Governor Wise contemplates "a raid" on that city at the head of a ragged regiment of rakehelly, debauched Virginians. He has few equals in folly, but this story is incredible. I wish it was true and that he would proceed to do it. Nothing could make Southern ultraism more ridiculous. I would not have him hanged for his treasonable attempt, but publicly spanked on the steps of the Capitol.

The next ten days will be a critical time. If no Southern state commit itself to treason within a fortnight or so, the urgent danger will be past. Now that election is over, excitement will cool down rapidly, and even South Carolina will not secede unless under excitement that blinds her to the plain fact that secession is political suicide.

If they were not such a race of braggarts and ruffians, I should be sorry for our fire-eating brethren, weighed down, suffocated, and paralyzed by a nigger incubus 4,000,000 strong, of which no mortal can tell them how they are to get rid, and without a friend in the world except the cotton buyers who make money out of them, and the King of Dahomey. The sense of the civilized world is against them. They know that even the manufacturers and traders who profit by them condemn the institution on which their social system rests. And now their own country decides against their real or imaginary interests, and gives a judgment which they consider (and perhaps correctly on the whole) to be a censure, and which many of them suppose commits the government to a policy hostile to them and endangering their peace and safety.

November 8. . . . . News from the South comes only in brief, but is all one

163

way. Wrath and fiery hatred and malice, privy conspiracy and rebellion, treason and secession, seem the popular doctrine and sentiment in all the Cotton States, and even in North Carolina and Virginia. Colonel Scott (the General's son-in-law), who is a quiet, thoughtful, judicious man, tells me he expects serious trouble in South Carolina and Alabama at once, but he is not sure it will involve the neighboring states.[6] *Per contra*, men like old Stevens, John C. Green, Bidwell, and others, see not the slightest ground for apprehension.[7]

November 9. Much gasconading from the sunny South, condensed in telegraphic reports fortunately. "Palmetto Flag" raised, great speeches, fuss and fury, messages from governors, conventions called, Collector of Charleston resigning, "secession inevitable," and so on. It's a critical time, but things are not so bad as I expected they would be three days after Lincoln's election.

November 10. Trinity Church Committee on St. George's chapel this afternoon. Gouverneur Ogden tells me Betts wants his salary raised to $1,000 as clerk of Columbia College on the strength of our benefaction to the treasurer (Gouverneur Ogden). They are equal in meanness and rapacity. Trustees of a religious or charitable organization should be prohibited from receiving pay for services in any capacity. They should be men who can and will give their time and labor for the public good without reward. If the College needs a financial agent who will make the management of its property his chief business, it should select him from among business men outside the board. If Betts is to have $1,000 for keeping our minutes, each of his colleagues is entitled to $500 per annum, at least, for attending meetings and serving on committees. . . .

News from the South continues to be menacing and uncomfortable. I think the storm will blow over and die away without uprooting anything, but it is a critical time. A trifle may fatally complicate the situation. . . .

November 11, SUNDAY. Miss Puss at tea tonight; afterwards Charley, D'Oremieulx, Dr. Carroll, Jem Dwight, Hoffman, Jem Ruggles, and George Anthon. Political crisis thoroughly discussed. General disposition to concede the right of secession and to regard it with indifference and

[6] Henry Lee Scott, who married Winfield Scott's daughter Cornelia, was a North Carolinian. He had just been retired as Inspector-General in command of the forces in the city of New York.

[7] John A. Stevens was president of the Bank of Commerce; John C. Green was also a banker, and a merchant in the China trade; he is best remembered as a benefactor of the New York Society Library and New York University, and as the philanthropist who endowed the John C. Green School of Science at Princeton.

contempt. I hold secession unlawful and most calamitous, but the South is likely to do this wrong and folly and mischief if it find the North acquiescent and good-natured. I'm sorry, however, to find so many Northerners holding the Union so cheap.

November 12. No material change in the complexion of Southern news. Unless writers of telegraph items lie loudly, secession is inevitable. There is uneasiness here, but mainly as to the possibility of a tight money market from the financial crisis Southern folly is bringing upon the South, which must inevitably react on us more or less. People generally treat the political peril with what seems to me unaccountable indifference. This financial crisis is already beginning in Charleston and Mobile. Suspension of specie payments seems close at hand. They have overtraded, and their crops are short, and they would have been hard up had Lincoln been defeated, and obliged to do their uttermost to get the hogs and housing they need to carry them through the winter. But now that Lincoln is elected and their terrorists are roving about confiscating Northern property and repudiating Northern debts, their credit is paralyzed and they are in danger of a general smash. It would injure us, of course; it may bring them to their senses, or it may make them desperate and reckless.

November 13. Stocks have fallen heavily today, and I think they will fall much lower before this game is played out.[8] One can buy in yet more profitably a fortnight hence. Southern securities are waste paper in Wall Street. Not a dollar can be raised on them. Who wants to buy paper that must be collected by suit in the courts of South Carolina and Georgia?

November 15. Tonight I heard Lieber's lecture at the Law School. Matter good and well arranged; manner bad—dreamy, dozy, and maundering. . . .

No material progress in the political crisis. Stocks have rallied a little here. Perhaps the febrile symptoms and cerebral disturbance of the South seem a shade easier. But the reign of terror in South Carolina continues unmitigated. Mrs. Sally Hampton, now in New York, wants to go home to Columbia, S. C., or thereabouts, and requires an escort, of course. Her husband can't come North without exposing himself to a conviction of "incivisme," and Mr. George Baxter, her papa, cannot go South without danger of being tarred and feathered as a Northerner and a possible Abolitionist. So Mrs. Sally Hampton and her three pretty babies still abide in Second Avenue. Willie Alston and Pringle meant to spend another

[8] Many business men thought the panic worse than in 1857; and numerous firms failed as their Southern paper became worthless.

month here, but their neighbors write them that they must come home. Their loyalty to the South will be suspected if they keep away. So they return, reluctantly. . . .

We are generally reconciling ourselves to the prospect of secession by South Carolina, Georgia, Alabama, little Florida, and perhaps Mississippi, too. We shall be well rid of them. Perhaps the prevalence of this feeling— the cordial consent of the North—will keep them from seceding. I think these porcine communities incline to run out of the Union merely because they think we want to keep them in. One should never pull a pig in the direction one wants it to travel. They have long governed us and controlled our votes by the threat of secession. They naturally think secession will be a crushing calamity to the North and the severest punishment they can inflict on us for electing Lincoln.

November 17. Things in general look bluish-gray. Prophesyings of panic and crisis, and of still worse calamity, are heard in our streets. But people try to amuse themselves; for example, Henry Fearing has just been giving a sumptuous dinner to a dozen men at the New York Club, and Giraud Foster is to give another at the Union. Charles E. Strong, Jem Strong, and H. H. Ward as umpires are to decide which dinner was the more brilliant success, and the giver of the second best pays for both. A very pleasant transaction, no doubt, but just at this time it impresses me disagreeably. It seems like some gorgeous *Heliogabalic Convivium* of the days when the Empire was in decadence. . . .

Memoranda of the crisis. Stocks fell heavily today. The Trust Company declines receiving deposits payable on demand, or for less than six months. A Charleston savings bank has decided to act on a by-law or a provision of its charter authorizing it to insist on ninety days' notice of every draft. Doubt and distrust reign in Wall Street. The best paper is negotiated with difficulty. William and Edmund Schermerhorn, Edward Bancker, and other croakers think we are drawing near to the worst period of crisis and depression this city has ever known. Mr. Samuel B. Ruggles confidently expects another suspension of specie payment before next spring, perhaps before January. *Per contra*, John A. Stevens is sure this flurry will be over, and everything in its normal stride again within thirty days. Everyone admits that our financial condition was never sounder than at this time. But a vague apprehension of some undefined change and revolution has destroyed confidence in securities and property of every kind.

November 19, MONDAY. A most gloomy day in Wall Street. Everything at a deadlock. First-class paper not negotiable; demand for money greater than in October, 1857. Stocks falling. It's said the banks resolved today to buy three millions of exchange on London. This may probably see the machine going again, for the time at least, and enable the West and South to begin moving their grain and cotton. . . .

Very few now deny the probability of secession by the Cotton States, and South Carolina is given up as hopeless. Our national mottoes must be changed to *"e pluribus duo"* (at least) and "United we stand, divided we stand easier." It is generally conceded, moreover, that if federal coercion be applied to a single seceding state, the whole South will range itself against the government.

November 20. Wall Street was a shade less disconsolate this morning. Stocks rallied at the First Board but began to waver and fall again at the Second. The banks cannot bring about a decisive reaction; the disease is too deep-seated.

The revolutionary movement in South Carolina and the Gulf States seems, on the whole, to be gaining strength and consistency. No signs yet of any "sober second thought." Conservatism and common-sense (if any be left in the Cotton States), are still intimidated and silent. Probably the Border States, led by Virginia, will try to mediate and pacify. Dissolution of the Union and re-opening of the slave trade would be disastrous to them, so they naturally desire to make peace. But their mediation will probably be upon the basis of recognition by the North of the extremest Southern exactions (slave trade excepted). The North must consent that slavery be introduced into the territories; Massachusetts, Vermont, Wisconsin, and other states must repeal their "personal liberty" laws that interfere with the Fugitive Slave Law. That plan will not work. Those state laws ought to be repealed, but the South has no right to demand their repeal and make their enactment an excuse for treason, because they are utterly unconstitutional and mere nullities, and no one doubts the United States Supreme Court would so adjudge them.

If these traitors succeed in dismembering the country, they will have a front place in the Historical Gallery of Celebrated Criminals. No political crime was ever committed as disastrous to mankind and with so little to provoke or excuse the wrong as that which these infamous disunionists are conspiring to perpetrate. . . .

November 22. Wall Street has breathed more freely these two days. News this afternoon that all the banks from Charleston to Philadelphia have suspended. I don't know that we need suffer in consequence.

November 23. Mrs. Carson of South Carolina (daughter of Petigru of

Charleston) dined here; conversable, agreeable, and handsome in a mature style. Also Mr. and Mrs. D. C. Murray, Wickham Hoffman, George F. Allen, and Mr. Ruggles. We had much pleasant talk, though the one engrossing subject of the time was excluded, for the sake of our South Carolinian convive. Mr. Ruggles and Allen remained after the rest had gone.

November 24. Stocks all up today and Wall Street very jolly. But they will go lower yet, and Wall Street will look more blue than it has looked these thirty years before A.D. 1860 is ended.

Dr. Peters, and George Anthon, and Charley Peters dined here. After dinner with Ellie and George Anthon to Academy of Music on Robert Cutting's invitation to the rehearsal of *La Juive*; Stigelli, Fabbri, Anna Bishop, Formes, and others. A pleasant and sunny evening. Opera in *dishabille*, and a splendid revelation of Bohemia.

November 25. The Supreme Court in this district has at last reluctantly concluded that it won't do to nullify the decision of the Court of Appeals, reversing their order in the Law School case; so Mr. H. W. Cooper will be sworn in whenever he pleases.

November 26. Today's newspapers indicate no new symptom in our sore national sickness. The tide is still rising, I think, in all the Cotton States. Reaction and ebb are sure to follow, but they may come too late. This growing excitement may do irreparable mischief before it dies out and reaction sets in. The country may be overwhelmed by a flood of disaster and disgrace before the tide begins to fall.

November 27. Nothing new in Wall Street, except that stocks are all down again. Secession certainly gains favor at the South, and grows more threatening every day. But there are symptoms of backing down at the North. There are demonstrations toward repeal of the obnoxious "personal liberty bills" of certain Northern states. It seems likely that Republican leaders and wire-pullers have concluded on a policy of concession and conciliation. I hope it may be in time to prevent terrible mischief.

These "personal liberty laws" are unconstitutional and void. They are mere nullities, and do no harm to the South. What one nigger has South Carolina lost by the legislation of Vermont or Wisconsin? The clamor about them is a palpable humbug. Still they ought to be repealed, being wrong in spirit and interest.

November 28. No political news of importance. The progress of events has startled and staggered some of our notables, who were laughing secession to scorn a fortnight ago. John C. Green, for one, "never dreamed these Southerners would go so far." I think, from all indications, that the Republican leaders are frightened and ready to concede everything, to restore the Missouri Compromise line and satisfy the fugitive slave remedies of the South. A movement that way has certainly begun. But it may be too soon for the North and too late for the South. Suppose it prevail. How will it be received in Massachusetts and Western New York? Will Republicans feel that they have been sold by their leaders, and recalcitrate into more intense anti-Southern feeling? I think they will and that many Republicans will enroll themselves as Abolitionists. But if this crisis pass over without disruption and ruin, if our national life endure another year, I think a strong Union party will come into being and control extremists, South and North both.

November 29. Thanksgiving Day. No political news today. Congress meets Monday. Mr. Ruggles's friend, Senator Dixon,[9] is in town on his way to Washington. Horribly frightened. Connecticut expects him to do something in the Senate, and he is anxiously enquiring, "What shall I do to be saved from the humiliation of admitting that I'm unequal to my high place?"

Tom Corwin was in town Tuesday night with the draft of some "Bill of Rights" which he means to propose, affirming the rights which the South pretends to believe endangered.

There's a bad prospect for both sections of the country. Southern ruffianism and brutality are very bad, but the selfishness, baseness, and corruption of the North are not good at all. Universal suffrage has been acquiesced in for many years. It is no longer debated. But it's at the root of our troubles. What we want is a strong government, instead of a "government of opinion." If there be disunion, a strong government will be demanded and will come into being somehow, both North and South. Democracy and equality and various other phantasms will be dispersed and dissipated and will disappear forever when two hostile families of states stand side by side, and a great civil war becomes inevitable. To which party will God give a great general, when that crisis is upon us?

December 1. Sorry to learn that the Vermont legislature refuses to repeal its personal liberty bill.

A money indemnity for run-away niggers might satisfy the South (if it wanted to be satisfied), but I fear no such arrangement is practicable. Every worthless Cuffee and superannuated Dinah south of the Potomac

[9] James Dixon (1814–1873), Republican Senator from Connecticut.

would be somehow exported into the free states within a year and would have to be paid for.

One hears queer talk in these days of excitement. That white-cravatted, conservative, old, quiet Dutchman, Edward Bancker, thinks every man ought to be hanged that voted for Lincoln, and "means to go South and shoulder a musket." So he tells me, but I think fear for the future of his bank stocks and real estate has slightly deranged his mind, for he is said to have experienced some slight aberrations a few years since, when he had a fierce quarrel with a neighbor about a right of way on Staten Island. Willy Cutting talks mysteriously of an organization to revolutionize the city immediately upon the secession of the South. New York and Brooklyn are to be a free port, and with one or two adjoining counties, Westchester and Kings, I suppose, to constitute an independent principality. Mayor and Common Council to be kicked out, if not hanged, and suffrage to be confined to owners of $5,000 worth of property. A promising prospect.

Why *do* the people so furiously rage together just now? What has created our present unquestionable irritation against the South? What has created the Republican party?

Its nucleus was the abolition handful that has been vaporing for thirty years, and which, till about 1850, was among the more insignificant of our *isms*. Our feeling at the North till that time was not hostility to slavery, but indifference to it, and reluctance to discuss it. It was a disagreeable subject with which we had nothing to do. The battles in Congress about the right of petition, and the Giddings business, made little impression on us. But the clamor of the South about the admission of California ten years ago introduced the question of slavery to the North as one in which it had an interest adverse to the South. That controversy taught us that the two systems could not co-exist in the same territory. It opened our eyes to the fact that there were two hostile elements in the country, and that if we allowed slaves to enter any territorial acquisition, our own free labor must be excluded from it. The question was unfortunate for our peace. But we might have forgotten it had not S. A. Douglas undertaken to get Southern votes by repealing the Missouri Compromise. That was the fatal blow. Then came the atrocious effort to force slavery on Kansas by fraud and violence, with the full support of old Buchanan and his Southern counselors, the brutal beating of the eloquent and erudite Sumner with the cordial approbation and applause of the South, the

project to revive the slave trade, and (a little earlier) a sentimental romance, *Uncle Tom's Cabin*, that set all Northern women crying and
sobbing over the sorrows of Sambo. The Fugitive Slave Law stimulated
sectional feeling by making slavery visible in our own communities, and
above all, the intolerable brag and bluster and indecent arrogance of the
South has driven us into protest against their pretensions, and into a
determination to assert our own rights in spite of their swagger.

December 2, SUNDAY. At supper, Mrs. Carson of South Carolina,
and one Lowndes (a very nice fellow), and Lawrence Williams, Murray
Hoffman, and his brother Wickham, Walter Cutting, George Anthon,
Mr. Ruggles, Dr. Peters, William Chrystie, and one or two more.

Lowndes is quite a young man. Seems a specimen of South Carolinian
conservatism. Is engaged as assistant to Petigru in codifying the laws of
his state, but favors disunion decidedly. His talk is temperate but un-
intelligible. I could make no sense of it, and suggestions that I took to be
truisms seemed to strike him as speculative novelties he was unwilling
to admit. I fear Northerner and Southerner are aliens, not merely in
social and political arrangements, but in mental and moral constitution.
We differ like Celt and Anglo-Saxon, and there is no sufficient force in
"a government of opinion" to keep us together against our will. . . . A
move toward concession and conciliation will undoubtedly be made in
Congress at once by Republican leaders, and will probably prevail. But
it is too late for the South and too soon for the North. The utmost I hope
is that the offer and its contemptuous rejection will put South Carolina
hopelessly and visibly in the wrong, strengthen Union men in the other
Cotton States, and disgust Virginia and Kentucky.

These Southern heretics would be inexhaustible mines of fun, were
the position a little less grave. For example, Governor Gist of South
Carolina writing a grand revolutionary message and recommending all
sorts of measures for "national" defense and "national" finance and so
on, and the enlargement of the State Lunatic Asylum! "National," indeed!
The whole white population of that dirty little spiteful district is con-
siderably less than that of Brooklyn, less than the increase of this city and
county of New York since 1855.

December 4. Interview with Bob LeRoy. Another chapter has opened
in the disastrous history of his family. His father, flagitious old Black
Jake, took a young wife last June—an attractive, refined, well-educated
girl of twenty or thereabouts, daughter of a used-up, insolvent Claverack
lawyer. She sold herself to the old beast for the sake of her family. She

was soon told by the "housekeeper," Mary Ann (a retired strumpet, and formerly in the service of the distinguished Fanny White) that she must not presume on her position, and that if she did so, she should be turned out of doors. The poor wife made some feeble appeal to Black Jake, but without effect, and seems to have acquiesced in her degraded position. This Mary Ann and her husband James (Black Jake's body-servant and confidential adviser) hold Black Jake under their absolute control. Then the lady was reported *enceinte*, over which fact her husband exulted in a style more vehement than refined. A week ago, she was ill, afflicted, it was said, with a disease to which any woman who had married Black Jake would be exposed, and threatened with miscarriage. According to Bob and the Rev. Mr. DeKoven, she died Sunday soon after taking medicine from the hands of this man "James," and was buried yesterday. Bob had seen the nurse, who came to town last evening and who declares there was foul play, and that the physician says she was poisoned. Bob goes to Hudson tonight, resolved on investigation, exhumation, and other steps. If he can get these filthy parasites out of his father's house, his position will be improved. From what he told us, I guess the case was either puerperal convulsion in premature confinement, *or* strychnine poisoning; probably the former.

President's message appears today, and is gobbled up with avidity by everyone. Weak, of course, but perhaps the "Old Public Functionary's" positions are, on the whole, discreet and sensible. The federal government is too notoriously weak to menace with effect. Had Buchanan said, "Secession is treason, and treason is a capital crime, and we have a federal judiciary established for the purpose, among others, of punishing crime, and an executive to hang whomsoever the judiciary shall adjudge worthy of hanging," his position would have been more consistent. But I incline to think it's practically the best thing a *commonplace* president could have said at this crisis. . . .

No concession will avail now, I fear. The Cotton States want to set up for themselves and they will do it.

Buchanan's message to Congress, delivered December 3, was the fruit of anxious thought and numerous Cabinet sessions. He declared that the national crisis had been caused by incessant Northern agitation for the abolition of slavery, which imperiled the security of the slaveholding states. "Many a matron throughout the South retires at night in dread of what may befall her and her children before the morning." The South, he remarked, should have been left alone. He went on to state that the recent presidential election did "not of itself afford just cause for dissolving the Union." The South, in justice to the nation, ought to await some overt act against its institutions before it resorted to secession; it could trust to the facts that the President's power was limited, and that Congress and the Supreme Court had shown themselves friendly to Southern rights. Moreover, the President asserted, secession was unconstitutional, and the Union was rightly perpetual. Under the supreme-law clause, the national government acts directly upon the people, and "the Constitution is as much a part of the constitution of each state and is as binding upon its people as though it had been textually inserted therein." But after denying that secession was either just or valid, Buchanan went on to state that the federal government could do nothing to prevent it. The national government had no rightful power to make war upon a state; and if it did attempt coercion, the resulting civil conflict would cost "a vast amount of blood and treasure" and would make future reconciliation "impossible."

Strong's disgust with this message was shared by most Northerners. But as yet no state had actually left the Union, and Buchanan believed that a conciliatory policy might yet arrest the disruption of the nation. That is, he felt it possible that if the government used only moderate measures, the upper South and Border States would remain in the Union; and that the Cotton States, seeing they could be left alone, would draw back. In any event, he was determined that the first violent step, the "overt act," should not be the work of the federal government. Winfield Scott, in a letter of October 29th to the President, had recommended that six of the forts in the South be garrisoned at once to prevent secessionist elements from taking them over. But Buchanan negatived this proposal. His policy, in the face of Southern preparations for secession and civil war, remained feeble until his cabinet was revolutionized by the resignation of Southern members and the advent of two strong Northerners, E. M. Stanton and John A. Dix. The best that could be said for his course was that it maintained an atmosphere of peace while various leaders made an effort for compromise.

December 5. President's message finds little favor here, or any-where. It's a bad time. This nation is manifestly "coming in two," or three, or more. Hopes of a Congressional compromise diminish. I have lost faith in the magic words, "somehow or other," on which I've thus far relied for a solution of the problem.

1861

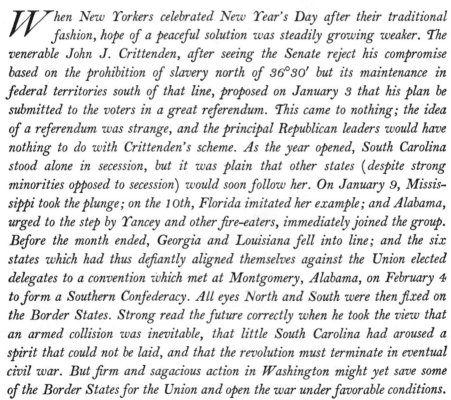

*W*hen New Yorkers celebrated New Year's Day after their traditional fashion, hope of a peaceful solution was steadily growing weaker. The venerable John J. Crittenden, after seeing the Senate reject his compromise based on the prohibition of slavery north of 36°30' but its maintenance in federal territories south of that line, proposed on January 3 that his plan be submitted to the voters in a great referendum. This came to nothing; the idea of a referendum was strange, and the principal Republican leaders would have nothing to do with Crittenden's scheme. As the year opened, South Carolina stood alone in secession, but it was plain that other states (despite strong minorities opposed to secession) would soon follow her. On January 9, Mississippi took the plunge; on the 10th, Florida imitated her example; and Alabama, urged to the step by Yancey and other fire-eaters, immediately joined the group. Before the month ended, Georgia and Louisiana fell into line; and the six states which had thus defiantly aligned themselves against the Union elected delegates to a convention which met at Montgomery, Alabama, on February 4 to form a Southern Confederacy. All eyes North and South were then fixed on the Border States. Strong read the future correctly when he took the view that an armed collision was inevitable, that little South Carolina had aroused a spirit that could not be laid, and that the revolution must terminate in eventual civil war. But firm and sagacious action in Washington might yet save some of the Border States for the Union and open the war under favorable conditions.

Like most Northerners, in the first days of the new year Strong felt a short-lived elation in Buchanan's seeming abandonment of vacillation for a *display of real strength. The reorganization of the Cabinet, following the withdrawal of Cass and several Southern members in December, brought in a number of strong Unionists, who for a time perceptibly stiffened Buchanan's stand. As noted above, John A. Dix became head of the Treasury, and Jeremiah S. Black head of the State Department, while the belligerent Edwin M. Stanton was made Attorney-General. With their encouragement, Buchanan on January 8 sent a message to Congress which had the right ring. It declared that no state had the power to secede, and that the national government had both the right and the duty to use military force defensively against those who resisted federal officers or attempted to seize federal property. But when the unarmed* Star of the West, *sent with men and munitions from New York to reinforce Fort Sumter, was fired upon by the guns of South Carolina, she turned back without delay; no additional move toward reinforcement was made. The Buchanan Administration simply marked time while Southern Senators and Representatives withdrew from Congress, while the Confederacy framed a constitution, and while numerous arsenals and forts in the South were seized. Naturally Strong and others were disgusted by the seeming feebleness of the government. The "wretched old Chief Magistrate," the "O.P.F." (Old Public Functionary or Old Pennsylvania Fossil), came in for endless abuse from all sides. But actually he had little choice, and he was playing a more consistent part than men realized then or for decades to come.*

Humiliated by the apparent weakness of the federal tie, by the "impotent and despicable" role of the Administration, and by the confusion, factionalism, and disheartenment of the people, Strong looked about eagerly for some tokens of rising vigor and energy. His journey to Washington early in the year was partly for purposes of observation, partly to help his father-in-law, S. B. Ruggles, push the project for what ultimately became the Union Pacific Railroad. He did not look in vain. New York and Washington had plenty of invertebrate men, to be sure, but the heart of the intelligent masses was sound. Before January ended he was able to record some encouraging street-talk, and to declare that the folly of the Southern "conspirators" had done more for the Abolitionist cause in ninety days than John Brown, Harriet Beecher Stowe, and Wendell Phillips, with their associates, could have done in a hundred years. This was true. The business leaders of New York City, even those favorable to the South, had been roused to almost unanimous indignation by the secessionist movement. The Journal of Commerce *reported on January 5 that "a large class of conservative men" in the city were ready to take "a decided stand should South Carolina persist in a belligerent course." The popular reception given to Lincoln when he passed through New York indicated a new tone of feeling; and the best men of all parties, as Strong approvingly notes, applauded the firm language of the First Inaugural. As late as March 12, Strong was still humiliated by the spectacle of "a weak, divided, disgraced people"—but the electrifying response to the firing on Fort Sumter swept away all his despondency.*

January 2, WEDNESDAY. Reports from Washington indicate that our wretched old Chief Magistrate begins to exhibit symptoms of a backbone at last. He may perhaps be beginning to understand that he has played into the hands of Southern traitors long enough, and that theirs is too hard a service. It is rumored today that Major Anderson is to be reinforced and that certain ships of war are under sailing orders for Charleston Harbor. Too late, I fear.

I spent yesterday at home. Some eight or ten dined here, and others came in afterwards. It was a pleasant evening. Bob LeRoy appeared very well. The inquest in Columbia County on poor Mrs. "Black Jake" LeRoy is going on, and the testimony thus far looks bad. It convicts Black Jake of the vilest, beastliest tyranny and brutality and strengthens the suspicion of poison.

January 11, FRIDAY. Much to write, too much for one who was up at 4:30 this morning and has travelled a quarter of a thousand miles since daybreak. Even the most insignificant memoranda of these revolutionary days may be worth preserving. We are making history just now fearfully fast.

Thursday, the third, [took] Jersey City ferry and railroad for Philadelphia at eleven A.M. Disgusting steady rain, dull headache. An uninteresting, monotonous ride at best, but most dreary when all the country looks waterlogged and as if deliquescing into primæval chaotic bog, when the very ducks and geese gaze at the traveller with a mute appeal for pity and warm towels, when all one's feelings are harrowed up by sympathy for his unhappy fellow creatures condemned to live in the dismal farmhouses and village homes that are visible from the railroad cars. Reached Philadelphia at three o'clock; Girard House. Most lonely and doleful drive thereto from the railroad depot through miles of monotonous, dirty streets. Rain held up in the evening, and I found my way to Horace

Binney's in South Sixth Street, where I was most kindly received by Horace and Mrs. Eliza and poor Julia Johnson, and urged to take up my quarters with them.[1]

Friday, the fourth. . . . ⟦Took⟧ the railroad for Baltimore at noon. . . . I found William H. Aspinwall on the train at Baltimore, bound for Washington on a Union-saving expedition. Showed me letters from Petigru and others at Charleston, indicating an uncomfortable state of affairs in that metropolis. Washington and Willard's Hotel at 6:15 P.M.; supper. Call on Mrs. Senator Dixon of Connecticut, with Mr. Ruggles, and also on General Scott. Long live the old General!

Saturday. With Mr. Ruggles, inspecting exterior of Treasury, Patent Office, and so forth, and to the Capitol. Settled ourselves in Senate Chamber, first calling on Seward at his house, and calling also on Mr. Speaker Pennington in his gorgeously gilt-and-mirrored Speaker's room. Seward opened the Pacific railroad question in a dignified, statesmanlike speech (which Mr. Ruggles wrote in our little parlor last night). There was opposition from Missouri, from the extreme factions South, of course, and from the Northwest, which wants a route yet farther north. Rice of Minnesota objected and opposed, with a dirty appeal to Southern prejudice and passion for which he ought to be burned in effigy from Boston to St. Paul's. It went off at last without any decisive vote. I left the Senate in disgust and adjourned to the Smithsonian, preferring stuffed penguins and pickled lizards to the dishonest gabble of the Senate Chamber.

Much impressed by the amplitude and grandeur of all the federal buildings, and by the splendid marbles and frescos of the Capitol. We cannot *spare* these structures quite yet. If a partition of federal property is inevitable, let us give South Carolina *all* the pictures in the rotunda, and Clark Mills's equestrian statue of Andrew Jackson. The Smithsonian collections are most fascinating. . . . Evening—with Mr. Ruggles to Seward's. Sat an hour or two with him and Preston King, talking crisis and compromise. Both Senators most jolly, genial, good-natured, and

[1] This was Horace Binney, Jr. (1809–1870), son of the eminent Pennsylvania attorney and himself a successful lawyer since his admission to the bar in 1831, three years after graduation from Yale. He had married Strong's cousin, Eliza Johnson. With their mutual interests in the law, literature, and political affairs, the two men had much in common. At the outbreak of the war, Binney threw himself into activities in support of the Union with a fervor equal to Strong's. He soon became a leading and, Strong later wrote, a steadying member of the Sanitary Commission, president of the Philadelphia Associates of the Commission, and in 1862, chief founder of the Philadelphia Union League Club. Their war-time collaboration deepened the relationship between the diarist and his cousin-by-marriage into an intimate friendship.

free from care, laughing at the vagaries of Toombs and Iverson, talking of conciliation and arrangement as likely to be effected, perhaps—but not worth much effort.

Sunday, the sixth. To church at St. John's. Sat in Seward's pew by his invitation. The Senator did not appear. Reverend Smith Pyne was emphatic and spasmodic in the pulpit. Afterwards, called on us Captain Lewis (of the Navy Yard), Thayer (*Evening Post* correspondent), Stewart, Henry Edwards of Keene, New Hampshire (a nice sensible old gentleman), and others. Many rumors and reports, mostly lying.

Monday. . . . To the Senate Chamber. Very earnest and patriotic speech from Crittenden; labor thrown away. To the House; nothing of much interest there. Heard of the death of William Kent and of the Rev. Henry Anthon. He died Saturday morning after severe suffering patiently endured. I hoped he might yet recover, for Fish, who arrived Saturday night, reported that he was a little better Friday afternoon. Prof. Hackley of Columbia is gone, too. Congestion of the brain. . . . There are men whose death would have been a heavier loss.

Tuesday, the eighth. Neither House in session. . . . With . . . Senator Anthony of Rhode Island to Navy Yard; Captain Lewis, Dahlgren guns, Maynard rifles, fuses, percussion caps, and so forth; all the processes of the foundry and the laboratory duly expounded. Our four hours' scientific session succeeded by a most hospitable lunch. Lewis a decided trump. . . .

Wednesday. Rain; Senate again; message from President. Bitter, acrimonious conversational debate on questions growing out of it between Preston King, Jefferson Davis, and others. "Jim Lane" savage and insolent; Wigfall of Texas venomous as one of his copperhead congeners.[2] Little hope of any amicable settlement. Pacific Railroad came up and I came off, desponding. Evening, another alarm of fire; fires occur every night. . . . Rumors are rife of an attack on the city by a Virginian mob. People are sending off their families to Philadelphia and New York. These incendiary fires are supposed to be part of the revolutionary programme. But old Scott has the case under advisement; that may avert any attack. Burglars are apt to postpone their visit when they know the family expects them. Scott tells Senator Foster that he expects three companies of light artillery from Fort Leavenworth, and one or two of infantry, also the sappers and miners from West Point, to arrive in Wash-

[2] That is, James H. Lane (1814–1866), Senator from Kansas, and Louis T. Wigfall (1816–1874), Senator from Texas; respectively a Republican and a Democratic fire-eater.

ington within a week. With this force as a nucleus, the militia of the District will be of service. If more men be wanted, "I shall write to my friend General Sandford of New York, who has considerable military capacity, and request him to send me the Seventh Regiment. That regiment, sir, can be relied upon. It will stand being brick-batted without drawing a trigger till it is ordered to fire!"

Thursday. Great news at the breakfast table. Steamer *Star of the West,* carrying reinforcements to Major Anderson, fired upon by the savages of South Carolina. Rumor No. 2 was that she had nevertheless made her way into Charleston harbor and fulfilled her mission. Rumor No. 3 (unfortunately correct) that being without heavy guns, she had turned tail and steamed out of the harbor. This will produce great excitement and strengthen the Union feeling all through the North. At Senate heard Jefferson Davis talk treason awhile. Thence to Smithsonian with Eliot and Judge Huntington of the Court of Claims. Spent four hours there, with Professor and Mrs. [Joseph] Henry, not unprofitably. Growing cold and windy.

Evening. Charles Sumner (the Martyr) called to see Mrs. Eleanor; Hawkins, member of Congress from Florida (an unhanged traitor), came to see Mr. Ruggles.[3] The two pairs sat at opposite corners of our little parlor, discoursing *sotto voce.* I was introduced to Hawkins, and had to take his hand, which I dropped with all convenient speed, and then retired to a convenient position, where I waited to see whether the gallant Floridian would not rise up suddenly and scalp the Massachusetts man. But there was no breach of the peace. Sumner tells me he has read the notes of Seward's great conciliation speech soon to be delivered and that it will be effective and conclusive. Much is expected from Seward, but I do not believe he can say anything that has not been said before.

This (Friday) mórning, breakfasted by gas-light, a late supper rather than a breakfast, and was off at a little before six, with Mr. Ruggles, Dr. and Mrs. Peters, and Mrs. Eleanor. Lovely cloudless sunrise, clear and cold. But the sky was soon covered with grey frosty fog that became a heavy and uniform cloud and developed into a snowstorm at Philadelphia. Bitter cold ride. Steamboat at Amboy, and a hearty supper. Home at seven; all well, thank God. Ellie has gone to musical party at Mme. de Trobriand's.

[3] George Sydney Hawkins (1808–1878), a native of New York State now serving his second term in Congress from Florida.

April 6, SATURDAY. *Evening Post,* second edition, says advices have been received at Washington that Major Anderson has been notified by the circumambient traitors of Charleston to vacate Fort Sumter within forty-eight hours, or in default thereof, to take the consequences. The third edition says that *firing has commenced.* Maybe so, maybe not. Any newspaper rumor is probably a lie; the general presumption is against it. But the South Carolinians are doubtless advised of the stir and preparation here, and this may have precipitated the crisis. We shall not be long in suspense. The prevailing opinion today has been, however, that the troops we are sending off from Governor's Island and Fort Hamilton are destined neither for Sumter nor Pickens, but for Texas, to strengthen the hands of Governor Samuel Houston.

Poor Ellie suffering all day from another of these unaccountable headaches.

Century tonight. Monthly meeting. Edward Cooper[4] talking the wildest secessionite doctrine, under a heavy fire of common sense and common honesty from George Allen, Professor Lieber, and Dr. Bellows. The political and private ethics of that school (wherein Floyd and General Twiggs are chief teachers) may be chivalric; they are certainly amazing. They result in this proposition: "No faith is to be kept with heretics." And all are heretics who are unsettled as to the right and the expediency of owning another man's wife and children.

Here is a Southern editor elaborately eulogizing the "Honorable" ex-Secretary Floyd. "But for Floyd's vigilance and sagacity, the whole secession movement would have been a failure. General Scott's plan of reinforcing Fort Moultrie would have killed it dead. But Floyd's official position under Buchanan enabled him to embarrass and prevent the execution of the plan, and he did so very gallantly and chivalrously, keeping the secessionist leaders constantly advised of what the Cabinet was doing or contemplating. Praise and glory to the gallant, true-hearted Floyd!" That is to say, Floyd is to be honored and exalted because he did his utmost to aid and encourage certain traitorous enemies of the Union, while he was a sworn officer of the Union and receiving its pay. . . .

The "decisive move" by the Administration of which Strong speaks was really under way. As early as April 4, Lincoln had decided that he must send a relief expedition to Fort Sumter in Charleston Harbor and another to Fort Pickens in Pensacola Bay, these being the only major forts in the seceded states

[4] Son of Peter Cooper; a Democratic politician and future mayor.

left in Federal hands. *The President had avoided any effort to repossess the numerous posts and fortified places already lost, including Fort Moultrie at Charleston, Fort Pulaski at Savannah, Fort Morgan at Mobile, and the nineteen army posts given up to the Texas authorities by General David E. Twiggs while Twiggs still wore his United States uniform. But he wished to maintain the status quo, and Sumter would have to be evacuated unless stores of food were taken to it. Days and nights of incessant labor got the Pickens expedition ready to sail from New York on the 6th. The Sumter expedition was also to leave on that date, but was delayed, and in consequence of bungled orders was not accompanied by the frigate* Powhatan *as Lincoln had intended. It was not until April 9 that it made a start, and the lack of a powerful warship seriously crippled it.*

Men like Strong in the North regarded the provisioning of Fort Sumter as a test of Lincoln's announcement in his inaugural that no further surrenders of national forts would take place. Radical Southerners, on the other hand, regarded it as an act of aggression which must be met with force. Lincoln took pains to see that the government of South Carolina was notified in advance of the expedition, with information upon its pacific character. But the moment news of the movement reached the South, it was taken as a defiance and a threat. The Confederate Cabinet was called in an excited consultation; and as the relief expedition of three vessels under Captain Gustavus V. Fox slowly voyaged southward, the Secretary of War at Montgomery ordered General Beauregard in Charleston to demand the evacuation of Fort Sumter. If this be refused, he added, "reduce the fort." On the night of April 11, four Confederate officers carried word of these instructions to Major Robert Anderson, commanding the fort. In reply, Anderson promised to evacuate Sumter by noon on the 15th unless he received controlling instructions or additional supplies prior to that date. The supplies were now at hand, while Lincoln's determination not to evacuate was well known. At 3:30 on the morning of April 12, therefore, Beauregard's aides served notice upon Anderson that the Southern guns would open in one hour. Precisely on time, the firing began—and with it four years of war.

April 8, MONDAY. With Charley Strong at the Brooklyn Navy Yard this afternoon. A large force sailed on Saturday for parts unknown, but there is still great bustle and activity there, getting the *Wabash* and other ships ready for sea. Went on board the old *North Carolina* and came off after an interesting two hours, convinced that something is about to be done. . . .

April 9. Great anxiety for news of our armada, by this time in Southern waters, and general gratification, even among the more moderate Democratic malcontents, at this vigorous move, the first sign of national self-assertion. Many believe the fleet destined for Charleston harbor, and that Fort Sumter is not to be given up after all. At the Law School to-night George Allen, Professors Lieber and Bidwell, President King, and others were jubilant over this indication that our great Union, so bragged of for so many years, is not to perish without a struggle.

April 10. This morning's *Tribune* and *Times* announce positively, and as if by authority, that the fleet has gone to Charleston and that Fort Sumter is to be reinforced. Then shall we hear stirring news! But is this force strong enough? It is only about 2,000 men, and the talk has been that 20,000 were needed. Perhaps the Administration counts on a repulse as a tonic and stimulant to the North, but I trust there will be no repulse. God forbid that this effort, forced on the country after long forbearance to maintain the sanctity of law and the authority of government, should be defeated.

April 11. Nothing from the seat of war (wherever that is) except a rumor that Jefferson Davis orders Charleston to make no opposition to the introduction of provisions into Sumter. A politic move, for everything depends on being strictly right on the particular issue in which the first blood is drawn, and many Democrats and Border State men would say the South was wrong in refusing to allow the *status quo* to be maintained by a supply of food to Anderson and his little force. . . .

Dined at William B. Astor's. Dinner given to the worshipful judges of the Court of Appeals, now in session here. There were also Evarts, Charles O'Conor, John Carey (Rev. Mr. Arthur Carey's brother, and one of George Anthon's class in Columbia College, and now Astor's son-in-law, whom I've not seen for twenty years), Governor Fish, Judge Pierrepont, Dr. Rae of Arctic notoriety (who expatiated on flavor of raw walrus blubber warmed at a lamp), and Judge Daly. Mrs. Astor and Miss Maggy Ward gave us the light of their countenances. It was pleasant enough, but their Honors, from Judge Davies *up*, are a little slow.

April 12, FRIDAY. *War* has begun, unless my extra *Herald* lies, and its Charleston despatch is bogus. Busy downtown. . . . Walked up with George Anthon. Evening papers told us nothing material from the South. With Ellie to dinner at Mrs. Annie Cameron's (64 Fifth Avenue) . . . .

Came off at the earliest possible moment, leaving Ellie there, and went to Dr. Berrian's. Committee met there to consider the amount to be allowed by Trinity Church for support of St. George's Chapel. We were a discordant committee, and after much prosing decided that as we could not agree on anything, we had better call a special meeting of the vestry for Tuesday night and leave the question for them to settle.

Walked uptown with Gouverneur Ogden and that wooden-headed Dunscomb. The streets were vocal with newsboys—"Extry—a *Herald!* Got the bombardment of *Fort Sumter!!!*" We concluded it was probably a sell and that we would not be sold, and declined all invitations to purchase for about four blocks. But we could not stand it longer. I sacrificed sixpence and read the news to Ogden and that galvanized pumpkin Mr. Dunscomb by the light of a corner gas lamp. The despatch is a column long, from Charleston, in substance to this effect. The rebel batteries opened on Sumter at "twenty-seven minutes after four" this morning. Major Anderson replied only at long intervals till seven or eight o'clock when he began firing vigorously. At three P.M. (date of telegram) he had produced no serious effect. "No men hurt" in the rebel batteries. No impression made on the "floating battery." Fort Sumter suffering much. "Breaches, to all appearance, are being made." The *Harriet Lane* in the offing, but no other government ships on hand. "Troops are pouring in," and "within an area of fifty miles, where the thunder of the artillery can be heard, the scene is magnificently terrible." That magnificent and terrible sentence sounds as if it belonged to a genuine despatch from the South. Yet I doubt its genuineness vehemently. I can hardly hope that the rebels have been so foolish and thoughtless as to take the initiative in civil war and bring matters to a crisis. If so, they have put themselves in a horribly false position. The most frantic Virginian can hardly assert that this war is brought on by any attempt at "coercion."

April 13.   Here begins a new chapter of my journal, entitled WAR—EXSURGAT DEUS *et dissipentere inimici ejus, et fugerunt qui oderunt eum a facie ejus. Amen!*

This morning's papers confirmed last night's news; viz., that the rebels opened fire at Sumter yesterday morning. During the day came successive despatches, *all one way*, of course, for the Charleston telegraphs are under Charleston control, and in addition to the local taste for brag and lying, there are obvious motives for a high-colored picture of damage done the fort. It tends to prevent reinforcement by any supplementary expedition that might be extemporized if the parties appeared to be at all equally matched.

In substance, the despatches say that firing ceased at six P.M. yesterday, but shells continued to be thrown into the fort all night at intervals of twenty minutes. Cannonade resumed this morning with brilliant success. The fort on fire. "Flames bursting from the embrasures." Raft outside and men passing up water. Great havoc among them. Two explosions in the fort. Major Anderson "believed to be gradually (!) blowing it up." Nobody hurt in the rebel batteries. No impression made on that formidable battle-scow "the Floating Battery." Major Anderson has ceased firing. Then came a fourth edition of the *Evening Post*, with a despatch that he has surrendered. This was while I was at the New York Club. On coming home, I find Ellie in possession of a still later *Herald* extra. The ships are engaged with the batteries; (this we had earlier). Two are sunk. The rest are shelling the city, which is on fire. I take this last item to be invented for the sake of stimulating wrath and fury in the Border States.

To shell Charleston, the ships must have worked their way into the harbor and passed Sumter. If so, they must have silenced the batteries and been able to throw supplies into the fort, which is hardly to be hoped. Had they done so, the object of the expedition would have been accomplished. And I doubt whether they would have fired on the city under any circumstances. But that damnable little hornet's nest of treason deserves to be shelled. It's a political Sodom. . . .

So Civil War is inaugurated at last. God defend the Right.

The Northern backbone is much stiffened already. Many who stood up for "Southern rights" and complained of wrongs done the South now say that, since the South has fired the first gun, they are ready to go all lengths in supporting the government. The New York *Herald* is noncommittal this morning. It may well be upholding the Administration and denouncing the Democratic party within a week. It takes naturally to eating dirt and its own words (the same thing). Would I were in Sumter tonight, even with the chance of being forced to surrender (seventy men against seven thousand) and of being lynched thereafter by the Chivalry of Charleston. The seventy will be as memorable as the "four hundred" of the Light Brigade at Balaklava, whatever be their fate.

It is said the President will assume the right to call for volunteers, whether the law give it or not. If he does, there will soon be a new element in the fray; viz., the stern anti-slavery Puritanism that survives in New England and in the Northwest. Ossawattomie John Brown would be worth his weight in gold just now. What a pity he precipitated matters and got himself prematurely hanged!

April 14, SUNDAY. Fine day. Morning *Herald* announces *Surrender of Fort Sumter* and great jubilation in Charleston. To Trinity Church with Ellie and Miss Rosalie and Johnny. On our way back, I made a detour to the *Tribune* office. The whole story discredited there. Lots of private despatches quoted, inconsistent with surrender, and tending to show there had been no serious fight.

Mr. Ruggles dined with us. This evening Dr. Rae and his pretty wife were here by appointment, with their two young friends from England. . . . There is no doubt that Fort Sumter has surrendered. Despatches received by Mrs. Anderson, Cottenet, and others settle that point. But no reliable details of the transactions have reached us. If it be true, as Charleston telegrams assert, that after forty hours' firing "no one is hurt," *Punch* and the *Charivari* have an inviting topic for jokes at our expense. . . .

From all I can learn, the effect of this on Democrats, heretofore Southern and quasi-treasonable in their talk, has fully justified the sacrifice. I hear of F. B. Cutting and Walter Cutting, Hewitt, Lewis Rutherfurd, Judge Vanderpoel, and others of that type denouncing rebellion and declaring themselves ready to go all lengths in upholding government. If this class of men has been secured and converted to loyalty, the gain to the country is worth ten Sumters. CAM, heretofore strongly Southern in his talk, was declaring his readiness this evening to shoulder a musket in defence of Washington. That is the next point to be thought of. "He is the true Pope who lives in the Vatican." It must be defended at any cost.

At Trinity Church today, Vinton read the prayer, "In time of war and tumults," and the Amen of the white-robed choir boys was emphasized by a suggestive trumpet-stop coloring from the organ.

April 15. Events multiply. The President is out with a proclamation calling for 75,000 volunteers and an extra session of Congress July 4. It is said 200,000 more will be called within a few days. Every man of them will be wanted before this game is lost and won. Change in public feeling marked, and a thing to thank God for. We begin to look like a United North. Willy Duncan (!) says it may be necessary to hang Lincoln and Seward and Greeley hereafter, but our present duty is to sustain

Government and Law, and give the South a lesson.[5] The New York *Herald* is *in equilibrio* today, just at the turning point. Tomorrow it will denounce Jefferson Davis as it denounced Lincoln a week ago. The *Express* is half traitorous and half in favor of energetic action against traitors. The *Journal of Commerce* and the little *Day-Book* show no signs of reformation yet, but though they are contemptible and without material influence for evil, the growing excitement against their treasonable talk will soon make them more cautious in its utterance. The *Herald* office has already been threatened with an attack.

Mayor Wood out with a "proclamation." He must still be talking. It is brief and commonplace, but winds up with a recommendation to everybody to obey the laws of the land. This is significant. The cunning scoundrel sees which way the cat is jumping and puts himself right on the record in a vague general way, giving the least possible offence to his allies of the Southern Democracy. The *Courier* of this morning devotes its leading article to a ferocious assault on Major Anderson as a traitor beyond Twiggs, and declares that he has been in collusion with the Charleston people all the time. This is wrong and bad. It is premature, at least. . . .

Expedition to Governor's Island this morning; Ellie and I, Charley Strong and wife, Dan Messenger, Christie, Miss Kate Fearing, Tom Meyer, and one or two more. Officer of the day was Lieutenant Webb of Maine, whose guests we were. He treated us most hospitably, and had out the band, playing an hour or two for our delectation. Its programme included that jolliest of tunes, "Dixie Land," and "Hail Columbia." We took off our hats while the latter was played. Everybody's patriotism is rampant and demonstrative now. About three hundred recruits on the Island, mostly quite raw. I discoursed with one of them, an honest-looking, simple-minded boy from somewhere near Rochester, probably some small farmer's son. "He had voted for Abe Lincoln, and as there was going to be trouble, he might as well *fight* for Abe Lincoln," so he enlisted two weeks ago. "Guessed they were going to get some hard knocks when they went down South, but then he had always kind o' wanted to see the world—that was one reason why he 'listed."

Great activity on the Island. Guns and all manner of warlike munitions and apparatus are being shipped, generally for Pensacola.

[5] William B. Duncan, a conservative Democratic merchant, had been one of the business leaders who, in 1860, tried to fuse the Douglas, Bell, and Breckinridge parties to defeat Lincoln and thus "save the Union."

April 16. A fine storm of wind and rain all day. The conversion of the New York *Herald* is complete. It rejoices that rebellion is to be put down and is delighted with Civil War, because it will so stimulate the business of New York, and all this is what "we" (the *Herald*, to wit) have been vainly preaching for months. This impudence of old J. G. Bennett's is too vast to be appreciated at once. You must look at it and meditate over it for some time (as at Niagara and St. Peter's) before you can take in its immensity. His capitulation is a set-off against the loss of Sumter. He's a discreditable ally for the North, but when you see a rat leaving the enemy's ship for your own, you overlook the offensiveness of the vermin for the sake of what its movement indicates. This brazen old scoundrel was hooted up Fulton Street yesterday afternoon by a mob, and the police interfered to prevent it from sacking his printing office. Though converted, one can hardly call him penitent. St. Paul did not call himself the Chief of the Apostles and brag of having been a Christian from the first.

This and other papers say the new war policy will strangle secession in the Border States. But it seems to me that every indication from Virginia, North Carolina, and elsewhere points the other way. No news from Slave-ownia today, but most gladdening reports from North, West, and East of unanimity and resolution and earnestness. We are aroused at last, and I trust we shall not soon relapse into apathy. Ellie indisposed again. I begin to be seriously uneasy about the constantly recurring attacks of slight illness—headache and the like—that have visited her of late.

Trinity Church Vestry tonight; special meeting on St. George's Chapel and a very long debate. The appropriation required is large ($6,000 per annum, at least), and in moving it, I premised that the whole question turned on the ability of the vestry to spend that sum. If they have it to spare, the Chapel can be maintained, otherwise not; and a smaller appropriation just keeping up the establishment in its present dead-alive condition would do no good and be simply throwing away so much money, besides bringing a certain amount of discredit on Trinity Church. A smaller appropriation was moved as a substitute and carried by a large majority, Swift and I voting in the negative, with three or four others. . . .

Thence to New York Club. Our talk was of war. Subscribed to a fund for equipment of the Twelfth Regiment and put down my name for a projected Rifle Corps, but I fear my near-sightedness is a grave objection to my adopting that arm. I hear that Major Burnside has surrendered his treasurership of the Illinois Central Railroad and posted down to Rhode Island to assume command of volunteers from that state. Telegram that 2,500 Massachusetts volunteers are quartered in Faneuil Hall, awaiting orders.

GOD SAVE THE UNION, AND CONFOUND ITS ENEMIES. AMEN.

April 17. Dull weather, but it has cleared up tonight. No material change in the complexion of affairs, except that a crisis is drawing very near in Virginia and Kentucky. I count on the loyalty of no Border State, except Maryland. We are on the eve of a civil war that will be bitter and bloody, and probably indecisive.

There was a slight outbreak here today. I was sitting in my office at three o'clock when I heard unwonted sounds in Wall Street, and looking out, saw a straggling column of men running toward the East River. My first notion was that they were chasing a runaway horse, but they soon became too numerous to be engaged in that. They halted in front of the *Journal of Commerce* office and filled the street densely for about a block.[6] There were outcries, which I could not distinctly hear for a minute, and then the American flag was hung out from a window, and the crowd sent up a cheer that stirred one's blood a little, and the surface of the black mass was suddenly all in motion with waving hats. Then a line of policemen came down the street on a dog-trot, and the crowd thereupon moved promptly up Wall Street again, cheering lustily.

They were mostly decently-dressed people, but with a sprinkling of laboring men. I understand they paid a like domiciliary visit to the *Express*, the *Day-Book*, and the *Daily News*, requiring each to put up the flag.[7] They intended to call on the New York Hotel, it is said, but Cranston was forewarned and the American flag was flying from its roof as I came uptown.

April 18. Fine day; drizzly evening. Journalizing is a serious job just now. We are living a month of common life every day. One general proposition to begin with. My habit is to despond and find fault, but the attitude of New York and the whole North at this time is magnificent.

[6] Gerard Hallock's *Journal of Commerce*, long proslavery in tone, had been outspoken in favor of letting the South secede in peace. It argued that two American nations, one free and one slave, might live amicably together.

[7] The *Day-Book*, conducted by John H. Van Evrie, had been violently proslavery and pro-Southern; the *Daily News*, controlled by Ben Wood, a brother of Mayor Fernando Wood, and the *Express*, owned by James and Erastus Brooks, had been only less offensive.

Perfect unanimity, earnestness, and readiness to make every sacrifice for the support of law and national life. Especially impressive after our long forbearance and vain efforts to conciliate, our readiness to humble ourselves for the sake of peace. Still, I expect to hear only of disaster for a long while yet.

The morning papers give us Jefferson Davis's proclamation of reprisals on Northern commerce. Letters of marque are to be issued to any piratical Spaniard who will accept them. Very well. Then we shall have no scruples about retaliating on Southern property, which is peculiar for possessing a capacity for being invited to go away, and legs to take itself off, and arms wherewith to use such implements as may aid it in so doing, if opposed. Davis's proposed privateers can take their prizes into no civilized port. They will have to sink, burn, and destroy. Every maritime power in Christendom will make common cause against them and his "Algerine" Confederacy.

With Bidwell on reference in Carter *v*. Taylor. Little progress. Went to the [City] Hall. The [Sixth] Massachusetts Regiment, which arrived here last night, was marching down on its way to Washington. Immense crowd; immense cheering. My eyes filled with tears, and I was half choked in sympathy with the contagious excitement. God be praised for the unity of feeling here! It is beyond, very far beyond, anything I hoped for. If it only last, we are safe.

The national flag flying everywhere; every cart horse decorated. It occurred to me that it would be a good thing to hoist it on the tower of Trinity—an unprecedented demonstration, but these are unprecedented times; not only good in itself, as a symbol of the sympathy of the Church Catholic with all movements to suppress privy conspiracy and sedition, but a politic move for Trinity Church at this memorable hour of excitement. Somewhat to my surprise, General Dix, Cisco, Skidmore, Swift, and Gouverneur Ogden cordially concurred with me and signed a note to Dr. Berrian, asking his permission to hoist it.

Posted up to the Rector's in Varick Street, but he was out. Again at four, but he was not very well and could not see me. So I left the note and announced that I should call tomorrow morning for an answer. I expected a negative answer, supported by platitudes of fogyism, easily to be imagined. But while I was at dinner came a note from the Rector, who "very cheerfully" complies with our request. Hurrah for Dr. Berrian! His consent to this is the strongest indication yet of the intensity of our national feeling just now. May we dare to hope it will last?

October 13, SUNDAY. General Burnside is in town. Missed tonight's train to Washington. Says there is to be another reconnaissance in force tomorrow—an offer of battle, which the rebels will not accept. Gunboats and transports have been leaving the harbor yesterday and today to rendezvous at Annapolis and Fort Monroe. Twenty thousand men are said to be ready for embarkation on the Chesapeake.

Dr. Hammond, U.S.A., of Baltimore, is in town.[8] Only an Assistant Surgeon, but he has had intimations from the War Department that the last may be first, and that he *may* take Dr. Finley's place. . . . Dr. Bellows thinks well of him.

Another gap now occurs in Strong's diary, occasioned by a fresh trip to Washington; but he fills much of it by a retrospective survey on his return, under date of October 23. The Sanitary Commission was still faced with a critical situation. General McClellan, to be sure, had ably reorganized the army and was imparting to it a fine spirit of discipline. Frederick Law Olmsted, the capable General Secretary of the Commission, was able to report in September that army regulations were being enforced with ten times the zeal previously used and that the results were excellent. "Even the demoralized regiments, with but very few exceptions, are now in better condition, better spirit, in better health, than they were when they received the order for the advance on Bull Run. The very measures which the Commission urged, which it was said could not be enforced, would not be submitted to, and would be useless with volunteers, are now rigidly enforced, are submitted to with manifest satisfaction by volunteers, and are obviously producing the most beneficent results, and this equally in the new and the older regiments."

[8] Here appears a figure soon to dominate many pages of the diary. William Alexander Hammond (1828–1900), the first eminent American neurologist and a great figure in medical education, had been born in Annapolis and had received his medical training in New York. Entering the army as assistant-surgeon in 1849, he served for ten years at various Western posts. Then he resigned to teach and practice in Baltimore, but on the outbreak of the Civil War again enlisted. After organizing a hospital in Baltimore, he attracted attention by his efficient work as inspector of camps and hospitals under Rosecrans in West Virginia. A man of rugged energy, keen mind, and determined will, he seemed just the person to replace the feeble, petulant Finley.

But prodigious labors remained to be accomplished; and they could hardly be carried through until the head of the Medical Bureau of the Army, Surgeon-General Finley, who was accurately described by Strong as "utterly ossified and useless," could be replaced. His personal character was excellent, his former services creditable. But he had been trained to minister to the medical needs of an army of ten or fifteen thousand men; and he recoiled from the radical changes required for the great hosts now in uniform. A lover of routine and red tape, he resented the interference of this novel and anomalous volunteer agency, the Sanitary Commission. Fortunately the Commission had the warm co-operation of General McClellan. Most of its recommendations this fall—its proposal that the head of the Army of the Potomac be allowed to select his own Medical Director, independent of the Medical Bureau, and its suggestion that McClellan also be allowed to create an "Ambulance Regiment" were of special importance—fell upon deaf ears. The War Department ignored them. As a result, the horrors of the Peninsular campaign the next spring were greatly increased. But McClellan supported the Commission's plan of keeping a staff of expert Inspectors of Camps busy in the field, making sure that proper principles of camp sanitation were observed. Both he and the War Department accepted the Commission's recommendations for the erection of a great system of military hospitals built on the "pavilion plan" and properly staffed. The Commission was accomplishing a great deal.

October 23, WEDNESDAY. . . . The Commission no longer occupies its room in the Treasury, having outgrown it. Government has hired for us, in addition to our storehouse, the old rambling three-story "Adams House" for our offices and council room. It is now being repaired, polished up, and papered, and will make commodious headquarters. We met there. Dr. Wood, an excellent, loyal old gentleman, Bishop Clark, Dr. Howe and Dr. Newberry attended, beside our New York members. Colonel Cullum was out of town, and we saw little of that inveterate red-tapist Major Shiras.

The business before us was to kick out the Surgeon-General; to get our hospital plans approved and the work of erecting them begun; to get increased efficiency put into the allotment system, and so encourage volunteers to send their pay home to their families and check the growth of pauperism instead of spending it in the sutler's tent to the detriment of their own condition, moral and sanitary. We worked efficiently toward these several ends and made good progress, though without absolutely attaining either.

As to our groups of one-story pavilion hospitals, we overcame the protest against their cost by demonstrating that it did not very much exceed the aggregate of exorbitant rents paid for old buildings (unfit for hospital purposes and sure to become pesthouses when it shall become necessary to close their windows), and the expense of alterations and ventilating arrangements that would be defective and insufficient at best.

General Meigs (the ablest man I have seen in Washington) spent a morning with us discussing this and other subjects. He is very uneasy about the iron-plated rebel steamer *Merrimac*; thinks we have only two guns that can make any impression on her, the Union Gun at Monroe and another that is not yet mounted. Expects her to sally forth "on the rampage" in a few days, shell the camp at Newport News, pass Fort Monroe, and play the devil. If he is right and she is invulnerable, there is no reason why she should not steam up the Narrows and lay this city under contribution.

Dr. Tripler was an early convert to the hospital scheme and brought over McClellan. They united in endorsing it to the extent of 5,000 beds, but ask for two groups of buildings instead of five. Tripler says they have not medical officers enough to take charge of more than two. We left the plan approved in writing by General Meigs, General McClellan, Dr. Tripler, and Cameron, and only waiting for Lincoln's endorsement, which Cameron insisted upon because of the large outlay involved. Cameron is sadly wanting in moral courage, and the first question he asks about any measure is, "What will the newspapers say?"

The Surgeon-General question is still undecided. Scott, the Assistant Secretary of War, is earnest for Finley's removal and Hammond's appointment. After the Committee adjourned (Saturday evening), Dr. Bellows and I stayed behind for an interview with Cameron Tuesday night. Cameron talked about the newspapers, demurred and hesitated about removing Finley, though admitting his utter imbecility to be most deleterious just now, and pronounced against Hammond most emphatically the moment he was named. "Whatever he did, he should not appoint *that* man." Some official piquè or personal grievance was evidently in his mind. Then I brought up the allotment matter and suggested that the pension agents be charged with the duty of receiving and distributing monies sent home; but Cameron, though admitting the propriety of employing them and the immense importance of the work to be done, was afraid of the newspapers. "There would be a howl" about increasing the patronage of the department; he didn't think he could safely take any action about it. I don't know whether Cameron is corrupt or not, but he is certainly a most cowardly caitiff.

We had an audience of Lincoln from nine to eleven A.M. Thursday (I think it was Thursday). He is lank and hard-featured, among the ugliest white men I have seen. Decidedly plebeian. Superficially vulgar and a snob. But not essentially. He seems to me clear-headed and sound-hearted, though his laugh is the laugh of a yahoo, with a wrinkling of the nose that suggests affinity with the tapir and other pachyderms; and his grammar is weak. After we had presented our views about the Surgeon-General, and after Lincoln had charged us with "wanting to run the machine" and had been confuted, Bishop Clark introduced the subject of exchange of prisoners. Of course, Lincoln replied that such exchange implied recognition of the rebel government as a legitimate belligerent power, and spoke of the flag of truce sent out to recover Colonel Cameron's body after the battle of Bull Run, and of General Scott's reluctance to send it. The General said he had always held that if he fell in battle, he should be quite satisfied to rest on the battlefield with his soldiers.

Poor old Scott, by the way, is sinking. Grows lethargic, sleeps half the day, and entertains certain jealousies of McClellan.[9] His career is finished. Had a talk with poor McDowell. Still sore and morbid about Bull Run.

Another matter was the schismatic St. Louis Sanitary Commission, appointed by General Frémont on his own authority with plenary powers, ignoring our authority derived from the War Department. It's an excellent board of five or six prominent St. Louis men. The Secretary of War, being only too happy to snub Frémont, sent him orders to revoke this appointment or to instruct his local commission to report to us, neither of which he has done yet. Of course, all we want is to keep the peace and secure concert and unity of action; so I telegraphed them to send us one of their number with power to treat and adjust all matters in controversy.

---

[9] Scott was, in fact, ill as well as aged. On these jealousies, see *McClellan's Own Story*, New York, 1887, p. 136 ff. The Assistant Secretary of War mentioned above was Thomas A. Scott (1824–1881), who had been one of the principal architects and executives of the Pennsylvania Railroad, and who performed invaluable services first under Cameron and later under Stanton.

1862

Though Strong chafed much less than most Northerners, his diary in the first weeks of the new year reflects the general impatience for an advance by the Union armies. Since the beginning of November, McClellan had possessed about 140,000 men in or near Washington, a force which he drilled most thoroughly. But although the weather remained fine during November and most of December, he had declined to move forward against the weaker Confederate forces. Finally Lincoln, who shared the popular irritation, issued his famous general order for a frontal movement by both the Eastern and Western armies on February 22. In the East the state of the roads and other factors forbade its execution, and it was not until early in April that McClellan, who had taken his army of about 100,000 men to Fortress Monroe, began a cautious march up the Peninsula between the James and York rivers to reach Richmond. His progress was painfully slow. In the West, fortunately, Grant evinced more energy. The Confederate line was based upon Fort Henry on the Tennessee River and Fort Donelson on the Cumberland, only eleven miles apart. During January, Grant conceived a plan for cutting the line by capturing these two posts, and thus throwing all western Tennessee open to his army. With the aid of a force of gunboats he captured Fort Henry on February 6, and Fort Donelson ten days later, taking more than 15,000 prisoners. John B. Floyd, who had been Buchanan's Secretary of War, barely escaped. These were the first decided successes of the war for the North, and they greatly heartened the people.

January 29, WEDNESDAY. This has not been a session of the Commission. Bellows, Van Buren, Agnew, and I went on to grease the wheels of the New York and Philadelphia delegations and help them to urge reform in the Medical Bureau. The muster was beyond my expectation. From this city we had William H. Aspinwall, Robert B. Minturn, Stewart Brown, F. S. Winston, J. W. Beekman, and others. Our Philadelphia associates sent Judge Hare (Binney's brother-in-law and a notably attractive person), William Welsh, and a platoon of high caste doctors, including John McClellan, Gurney Smith, Stillé, LeConte, and others. We spent two days mostly in council over the details of sundry bills now before the Senate or the House, or got up by some of the Medical Bureau, and settled at last the form of a highly concentrated bill embodying the minimum of revolution. Thursday the new Secretary of War, Stanton, and General McClellan spent a couple of hours with us. The General seems entirely convalescent but looks careworn.[1] Stanton impresses me and everybody else most favorably. Not handsome, but on the contrary, rather pig-faced. At lowest estimate, worth a wagon load of Camerons. Intelligent, prompt, clear-headed, fluent without wordiness, and above all, earnest, warm-hearted, and large-hearted. He is the reverse in all things of his cunning, cold-blooded, selfish old predecessor. Cameron looked like a hybrid between Reineke Fuchs and some large chilly batrachian reptile, but this is a live man, and of a genial robust Luther-oid type. He is most fully committed in favor of reform, but doubts whether he can accomplish anything till Congress acts. He is the most popular man in Washington now, but will it last? The *Demos* begins to carp at McClellan, its idol six months ago.

Senator [Henry] Wilson was with us a good deal; professes to be the special friend and Senatorial agent of the Commission, and as chairman of the Military Committee, he is an important personage. But I distrust him. He is full of little politic stratagems, lacks straightforwardness and sincerity and reliability. He is playing some kind of game with us, which I do not comprehend.

We had a hearing before the House Committee on Monday, and before the Senate Committee on Tuesday. Bellows the chief speaker, of course; he presented the case forcibly and well. Both military committees seemed impressed, if not convinced. But for my experience of the variety of all

---

[1] McClellan had been confined to bed for three weeks in December and January with typhoid fever; "very weak and ill," he wrote later, but with "a clear intellect," so that he was able to give orders at all times.

assurances from politicians, I should feel sure satisfactory measures would be speedily carried. As it is, I expect nothing. It does seem not improbable, though, that old Finley, the Surgeon-General, will be retired or somehow eliminated. He has no friends that I can discover (except "Miss Powell"), and even the medical staff begin to admit he must be thrown overboard. Who would succeed him? Probably old Dr. Wood. This would be great gain, but Wood is far too old and too far gone in the ossification of routine to be fully fitted for the place.

Bellows and I called on the President yesterday to make the modest proposition that if any bill passed giving him power to appoint (doing away with the fatal principle of seniority), he would hear us before making any appointments. It was a cool thing. Lincoln looked rather puzzled and confounded by our impudence, but finally said, "Well, gentlemen, I guess there's nothing wrong in promising that anybody shall be heered before anything's done." We had the unusual good fortune to catch our Chief Magistrate disengaged, just after a Cabinet council, and enjoyed an hour's free and easy talk with him. We were not boring him, for we made several demonstrations toward our exit, which he retarded severally by a little incident he remembered or a little anecdote he had "heered" in Illinois. He is a barbarian, Scythian, yahoo, or gorilla, in respect of outside polish (for example, he uses "humans" as English for *homines*), but a most sensible, straightforward, honest old codger. The best President we have had since old Jackson's time, at least, as I believe; for Zachary Taylor's few days of official life can hardly be counted as a presidential term.[2] His evident integrity and simplicity of purpose would compensate for worse grammar than his, and for even more intense provincialism and rusticity.

He told us a lot of stories. Something was said about the pressure of the extreme anti-slavery party in Congress and in the newspapers for legislation about the status of all slaves. "Wa-al," says Abe Lincoln, "that reminds me of a party of Methodist parsons that was travelling in Illinois when I was a boy thar, and had a branch to cross that was pretty bad—ugly to cross, ye know, because the waters was up. And they got considerin' and discussin' how they should git across it, and they talked about it for two hours, and one on 'em thought they had ought to cross one way when they got there, and another another way, and they got quarrellin' about it, till at last an old brother put in, and he says, says he,

[2] A slip; Zack was President for sixteen critical months.

'Brethren, this here talk ain't no use. I never cross a river until I come to it.' "

I had a private "sifflication" to present on behalf of one George Dower, the husband of little Lewis's excellent, devoted nurse, Ellen. He was convicted a year and a half ago of manslaughter in causing the death of a seaman, he being mate of a merchant vessel, and sent to Sing-Sing for a term of years. The case is hard and doubtful, and I wanted to get his pardon. The papers were referred to the Attorney-General. "It must be referred to the Attorney-General," said A. Lincoln; "but I guess it will be all right, for me and the Attorney-General's very chicken-hearted!"

February 1. The "legal tender" feature in the Treasury Note bill vigorously opposed but can hardly be defeated, I fear.[3] Mr. Ruggles keeps up a damaging cannonade against this disastrous, shortsighted project in the columns of the New York *World.* If it pass, the government should at once hire Union Square as a place to stack its paper money, for no building in the city is large enough to hold what will be spawned within three months.

February 4. Fifty years hence John Brown will be recognized as the Hero or Representative Man of this struggle up to 1862. He will be the Wycliffe of the anti-slavery Reformation. A queer, rude song about him seems growing popular:

> John Brown's body lies a-mouldering in the grave (repeat)
> But his soul's a-marching on.
> Glory Hally Hallelujah,
> Glory Hally Hallelujah,
> But his soul's a-marching on.

[3] The House Ways and Means Committee had reported a bill to make $150,000,000 of Treasury notes legal tender in payment of all debts public and private, and Chase, the head of the Treasury, supported it. Despite the opposition of Eastern bankers, merchants, and economists, it became law on February 25, 1862.

February 8, SATURDAY. Excellent tidings from Tennessee; Fort Henry, a rebel earthwork on the Tennessee River, bombarded and taken. . . . The war news is decidedly encouraging, but we are very blue indeed. Signs of speedy intervention (probably by France with pharisaical England looking cannily on) increase and multiply. The Treasury of the United States is vacuous, and the House has passed the "legal tender" bill. The Senate will not dare to dissent and thereby delay the supply of means. . . .

When Lincoln paid his visit of July 8, 1862, to the Army of the Potomac at Harrison's Landing, home from the Peninsular campaign, the war seemed at its very crisis. McClellan's reverses had caused great discouragement in the North; gold stood at a premium of seventeen per cent; the radical Republicans in Congress were vociferous in their denunciation of the Administration. The time had come when it was necessary to enlarge the objects for which the North was fighting. Lincoln had insisted—and he continued to insist for a short time—that the war was being waged to restore the Union, and for that purpose alone. But a fast-growing proportion of the people and of Congress wished to fight as well for the liberation of the slaves. Congress on July 11–12 passed the Second Confiscation Act, which after sixty days of warning freed forever those slaves of "rebel owners" who in any way came under the control of the national government. The day after its passage Lincoln, driving to the funeral of Secretary Stanton's child, told Welles and Seward that he had about reached the conclusion "that it was a military necessity, absolutely essential for the salvation of the nation, that we must free the slaves or be ourselves subdued." A major change in national policy was impending. The greatest event of the second half of 1862 was to be adoption by the Administration of the emancipation policy; henceforth the war was to be fought for freedom as well as the Union. Abroad as well as at home this lifted the Northern struggle to a higher plane.

*Once more a terrible defeat had befallen the Union in the second battle of
Bull Run or Manassas. John Pope, a West Pointer of Kentucky birth who had
done well at Island No. 10 on the Mississippi, had been brought east and put in
charge of the new Army of Virginia, made up of the united forces of Banks,
Frémont, and McDowell. The commander began his campaign with a boast-
ful general order that deeply offended the brave troops who had fought on the
Peninsula. "I have come to you from the West," he declared, "where we have
always seen the backs of our enemies; from an army whose business it has been to
seek the adversary, and to beat him when he was found; whose policy has been
attack and not defense." Even before this piece of brag had been published,
McClellan had been reluctant to cooperate with Pope; and Halleck had found it
necessary to give him peremptory orders to send troops to reinforce the Army of
Virginia. The veterans of McClellan's force, slowly brought back to the line of
the Potomac, were sulky and listless. As soon as Lee saw that McClellan's
army was being withdrawn from the Peninsula, he resolved to concentrate his
forces and overwhelm Pope before the latter could gain strength. His movements
were attended by complete success. Lee detached Stonewall Jackson with 25,000
men from his main army and sent him to outflank Pope—the irresistible Jackson
by a swift march cutting the railroad and telegraph lines between Pope and
Washington and capturing large quantities of much-needed clothing and food.
Then on August 29 and 30, while consternation reigned in Washington, Lee
and Jackson fell upon Pope's army (superior in numbers, but as yet pitiably ill
organized) at Manassas. The Northern general was well served by one corps
commander, McDowell, but very badly by another, Fitz-John Porter, who
behaved as if he were indifferent and discontented, and failed to give the active
assistance needed. After a hard-fought struggle, in which the Union troops
suffered much more heavily than the Confederates, Pope was compelled to retreat
in confusion. He did not stop until his men were safe in their old entrenchments
in front of Washington, which for a time seemed in danger of capture. On
September 2, he made a doleful plea to the government. "Unless something can be
done to restore tone to this army," he wrote, "it will melt away before you know
it." It was plain that Pope was unfit for his place, and Lincoln forthwith
placed McClellan again in command of all the troops defending the capital.
The hour was one of the bitterest in the whole war, and Strong does not exag-
gerate the general discouragement and anxiety.*

August 31, SUNDAY. Eleven-thirty A.M. Waiting for news. The suspense is trying. Anticipations not brilliant. No further particulars that are at all reliable in morning papers—an ominous stillness. McDowell telegraphs that it's "decidedly" a victory. The adverb produces a negative impression on my mind. . . . Ten P.M. This citizen does not despair of the republic. Most of his friends do. But though things look bad, and there is reason enough for anxiety and apprehension, people are making up their minds to the worst much too fast. I can find no tangible evidence of serious disaster, yet.

At about one o'clock in came Dr. Harris with a telegram from Stanton to the mayor, calling for surgeons to be sent on at once. It is dated yesterday, three-forty-five P.M., but was not received till nine this morning. The Secretary says Friday's battle was a hard one, but the enemy was beaten at all points. It was resumed this (Saturday) morning, and was still going on at the date of the despatch. No suggestion of misfortune. Harris had been working hard and had already secured some thirty surgeons who were to go south by this evening's train. He has considerable capacity for usefulness, in spite of his faults. After conferring with him, I went by appointment to George Anthon's in East Thirty-fifth Street and dined with him, his mamma, Miss Emily, and young Mrs. Reginald Anthon, who evidently contemplates furnishing the nation with a raw recruit before long; and we went after dinner to the upper end of Central Park and walked down. Great progress made since my last visit. The long lines of carriages and the crowds of gents and giggling girls suggested peace and prosperity. There was nothing from which one could have guessed that we are in a most critical period of a great Civil War, in the very focus and vortex of a momentous crisis and in imminent peril of grave national disaster. Being caught in a lively little shower, we walked homeward rapidly and looked out for an extra as we got into the city. But there was none. Took a cup of coffee in the dining room and received George Anthon at about eight o'clock in the evening. He was a messenger of evil. Pope has fallen back on Centreville, if the reports that prevail be reliable. That does not look like decided victory! But the situation is utterly obscure and we can form no opinion about it.

September 3. It has been a day of depressing malignant dyspepsia, not only private and physical, but public and moral. *Egomet Ipse*, George T. Strong, to wit, and we the people have been in a state of nausea and irritation all day long. The morning papers and an extra at mid-day turned us livid and blue. Fighting Monday afternoon at Chantilly, the enemy beat back (more or less), and Pope retreating on Alexandria and Washington to our venerable field-worn fortresses of a year ago. Stonewall Jackson (our national bugaboo) about to invade Maryland, 40,000 strong. General advance of the rebel line threatening our hold on Missouri and Kentucky. Cincinnati in danger. A rebel army within forty miles of the Queen City of the West. Martial law proclaimed in her pork shops. On the other hand, we hear that General [Julius] Stahel and General [Philip] Kearny have come to life again, or were only "kilt," not killed, after all. Everybody talks down McClellan and McDowell. McDowell *is said* to have lost us the battle of Saturday afternoon by a premature movement to the rear, though his supports were being hurried up. He is an unlucky general.

September 4. It is certain now that the army has fallen back to its old burrows around Washington. It will probably hibernate there. So, after all this waste of life and money and material, we are at best where we were a year ago. McClellan is chief under Halleck. Many grumble at this, but whom can we find that is proved his superior? He is certainly as respectable as any of the mediocrities that make up our long muster roll of generals. The army believes in him, undoubtingly; that is a material fact. And I suppose him very eminently fitted for a campaign of redoubts and redans, though incapable of vigorous offensive operations. There is reason to hope that Stanton is trembling to his fall. May he fall soon, for he is a public calamity. McDowell and Pope are "universally despised"; so writes Bellows. Poor General Kearny is dead and no mistake and will be buried in Trinity Churchyard next Saturday; so says Meurer the sexton.[4] He's a great loss. I don't know whether he understood strategy, but he was a dashing, fearless sabreur who had fought in Mexico, Algeria, and Lombardy, and loved war from his youth up. I remember my father talking thirty years ago about young Kearny, who was studying law in his office, and about this strange, foolish passion for a military life. He was under a very dark cloud six years ago and was cut by many of his friends. But, bad as it was, the lady's family were horribly to blame— most imprudent; and Kearny made all the reparation he could. He married her and treated her with all possible affection and loyalty. Whatever his faults, we shall miss him.

[4] The dashing Phil Kearny, riding into the enemy lines at Chantilly, had been killed September 1. Lee, an old friend in Mexican War days, sent the body to General Pope under flag of truce.

Our Sanitary Commission stores were first on the field after the battle of Saturday and did great service, for all the forty-two wagon loads of the Medical Department were bagged by the rebels at Manassas. Dr. Chamberlain, our inspector in charge, was taken prisoner, but the rebels let him go. Stanton is reported rancorously hostile to the Commission; probably because Bellows has talked to him once or twice like a Dutch uncle, with plainness of speech that was certainly imprudent, though quite justifiable.

September 7, SUNDAY. The country is turning out raw material for history very fast, but it's an inferior article. Rebellion is on its legs again, East and West, rampant and aggressive at every point. Our lines are either receding or turned, from the Atlantic to the Mississippi. The great event now prominently before us is that the South has crossed the Potomac in force above Washington and invaded Maryland and occupied Frederick, proclaimed a provisional governor, and seems advancing on the Pennsylvania line.[5] No one knows the strength of the invading column. Some say 30,000, and others five times that. A very strong force, doubtless, has pushed up the Potomac to cut off the rebel communications. If it succeed, the rebellion will be ruined, but if it suffer a disorganizing defeat, the North will be at Jefferson Davis's mercy. I dare not let my mind dwell on the tremendous contingencies of the present hour. It seems to me not quite certain that our next Sanitary Commission meeting will be held at Washington punctually on the 15th!

The nation is rapidly sinking just now, as it has been sinking rapidly for two months and more, because it wants two things: generals that know how to handle their men, and strict military discipline applied to men and officers. God alone can give us good generals, but a stern and rigorous discipline visiting every grave military offence with death can be given us by our dear old great-uncle Abe, if he only would do it. With our superiority in numbers and in resources, discipline would make us strong enough to conquer without first-rate generals, unless an Alexander or Napoleon should be born into Rebeldom.

September 11. Letters from Agnew full of interest. He has been all over our last battlefields under flag of truce; thirty-six hours in the saddle and feels "as if he had a chronic horse between his lower limbs." Our

[5] Lee, learning that Pope had taken refuge within the defenses of Washington, ordered Stonewall Jackson on September 2 to cross the Potomac and lead an advance into Maryland. By September 7 the Confederate army had concentrated at Frederick. On the 15th Harper's Ferry surrendered with 12,000 men and 73 guns.

wounded were left in the field, without shelter, food, or water, from Saturday night till Wednesday morning, because "that scoundrel, Pope" was too busy cooking up his report to think of sending out a flag of truce. Very many perished from starvation and exposure. Our Commission wagons were first on the ground and did good service, thank God; and the relations of our inspectors and agents with the medical staff seem perfectly harmonious. All, from the Surgeon-General down, recognize the value of what we are doing, or rather of what the people is doing through us as its almoner.

Our public interests continue in a state of prostration approaching collapse. We do not know what force the rebels have thrown into Maryland. It is probably large. What a blessing a heavy rain would be that should raise the Potomac above fordable depth! There are clouds in tonight's sky, anxiously watched but probably barren. Newspapers tell us little or nothing about the situation in Maryland. From a letter received by D. B. Fearing from his son, spunky little George Fearing is on Burnside's staff; and from Agnew's letters and from Burnside's telegram to F. B. Cutting today, the following facts are clearly established: McClellan's headquarters were at Rockville Tuesday; Burnside was then at Leesboro; he was at Brookville this morning; he commands our right (40,000 strong?), Sigel the centre, McClellan the left, which, I suppose, rests on the Potomac; no collision as yet; the rebels have *not* occupied Hagerstown.

I suppose we shall soon hear that McClellan has commenced a series of masterly fieldworks and is engaged on an irrefragable first parallel from the Potomac to the Susquehanna, with a series of dashing and brilliant zig-zags toward the enemy. But it is idle to criticize his practice until we can name some stronger and better man to put in his place. It's a controlling fact that the army confides in him, and may mutiny if he be superseded. General Pope's report bears hard on Fitz-John Porter and others; charges them with declining to support him with their commands at critical moments, and seeks to make them responsible for our latest disasters. It's a plausible paper and (were Pope's veracity unquestioned) would be damaging. As it is, the report has generated a swarm of rumors about one general and another committed to Fort Lafayette for treason. Nobody who knows Fitz-John Porter, Franklin, or McDowell (this last affected by rumors for which Pope's report is not responsible) can believe either guilty of positive disloyalty, of conscious, deliberate treason. But may not their partisanship for McClellan have made them unconsciously

George Templeton Strong. Inscribed by the subject: "George Templeton Strong I, while a student at Columbia College, *circa* 1838. His appearance led to the nickname 'Black Hawk,' among his college friends, referring to an Indian chief, then much talked of." *From a watercolor drawing owned by George Templeton Strong III*

The Strong residence, 108 Greenwich Street, Nos. 110 (residence and Aunts Olivia and Jane Templeton) and 112 beyond; Carlisle Street is the cross street in the distance. From a charcoal drawing made in 1950 by Edward Punnett Chrystie. *Courtesy of Kenneth Holcomb Dunshee*

The home of George Templeton Strong. The "Palazzo Strong" or "Schloss am Square" at 74 (later renumbered 113) East Twenty-first Street was built in 1848–49 and torn down eighty years later; it was just opposite the northwest corner of Gramercy Park. In the next house to the west dwelt Strong's parents and spinster sister Mary; Aunt Olivia Templeton lived in the house beyond. *From a charcoal drawing by Edward Punnett Chrystie*

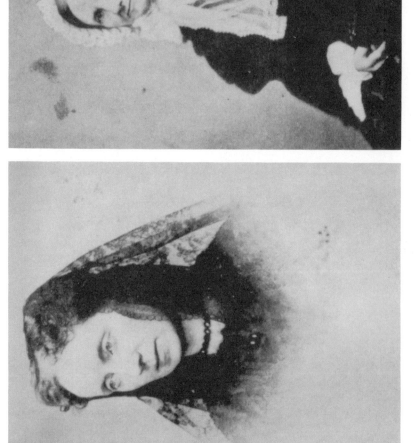

Ellen Ruggles Strong. From a photograph in the Diary, dated July 1864

Ellen Bulkley Ruggles, Ellen Strong's "indomitable grand-mamma." From a photograph in the Diary, dated January 1864

Lewis Barton Strong. From a photograph in the Diary, dated July 1, 1862. "N.B. It does not do him justice." (G.T.S.)

John Ruggles Strong and George Templeton Strong, Jr. From a photograph in the Diary, dated June 25, 1860

John Strong Newberry, George Templeton Strong, and Cornelius Rea Agnew. From a photograph in the Diary, taken at a meeting of Sanitary Commission officers at Washington in October 1863

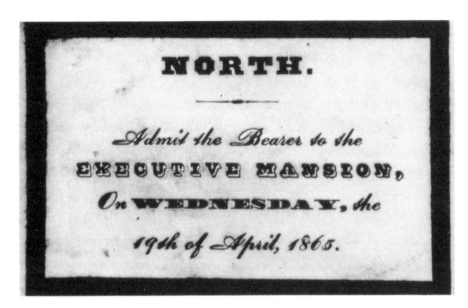

NORTH.

Admit the Bearer to the

EXECUTIVE MANSION,

On WEDNESDAY, *the*

19th of April, 1865.

Strong's card of admission to Lincoln's funeral. From the Diary

Lincoln funeral procession on Pennsylvania Avenue. From a photograph by Brady in the Library of Congress

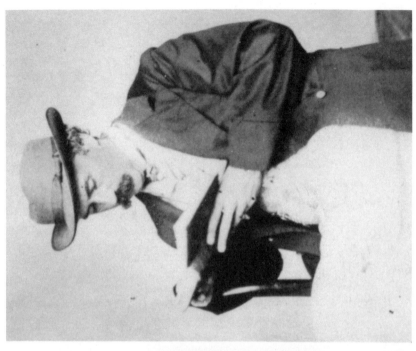

George Templeton Strong. From a photograph in the Diary, dated Washington, October 10, 1863

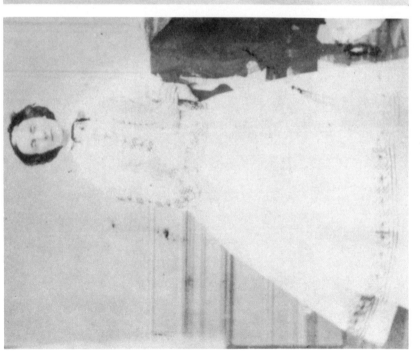

Ellen Strong. From a photograph in the Diary, dated Newport, September 1862

backward in supporting his rival? *Quién sabe? Weissnix.* Jealousies exist among our generals beyond doubt, though one would think them impossible in a time like this. Their existence is a fearful source of weakness and paralysis.

Among today's rumors is this: that General Halleck has ascertained Mrs. A. Lincoln to be the mysterious channel through which so many state secrets have reached the rebels and enabled them to anticipate our action; that he has formally demanded her exportation from the seat of government; and that her *Durchlauchtigkeit* has been sent off west under military guard. Highly probable, to be sure! But I suppose she may be a very tattling woman. Underbred, weak, and vain she certainly is, by all accounts. She may have talked too freely.

Hurrah! There comes a sound of rain. Sabrina fair, nymph of the Potomac, please listen where thou art sitting and never mind the loose folds of thy amber-dropping hair, but hurry up the floods of thy river and make it impracticable for rebel artillery, if you will have the goodness, marm.

September 13, SATURDAY. Agnew returned today and was with us this afternoon. Has been several days on the battlefields around Manassas rendering surgical aid, and with McClellan's advance in Maryland organizing our Sanitary Commission supply trains. His report not encouraging. Many regiments are "asthenic" or worn out. Line of march is traceable by the deposit of dysenteric stool the army leaves behind it. Discipline slack and nerveless; swarms of stragglers marauding, or making up select card-parties by the road side. From other sources I hear of alarming demoralization. McDowell's people are said to have fought badly and to have run with great alacrity a fortnight ago. I fear our army is in no condition to cope with Lee's barefooted, ragged, lousy, disciplined, desperate ruffians. They may get to Philadelphia or New York or Boston, for fortune is apt to smile on audacity and resolution. What would happen then? A new and most alarming kind of talk is coming up, emitted by old Breckinridge Democrats (like W. L. Cutting) mostly, and in substance to this effect: "Stonewall Jackson, Lee, and Joe Johnston were all anti-secessionists till the war broke out. No doubt, they still want to see the Union restored. They are personally friends, allies, and political congeners of Halleck, McClellan, F.–J. Porter, and others. Perhaps they will all come together and agree on some compromise or adjustment, turn out Lincoln and his 'Black Republicans' and use their respective armies to enforce their decision North and South and reëstab-

lish the Union and the Constitution." A charming conclusion that would
be of our uprising to maintain the law of the land and uphold republican
institutions! But we have among us plenty of rotten old Democrats like
Judge Roosevelt, capitalists like Joe Kernochan, traders and money
dealers like Belmont, and political schemers like James and Rat Brooks,
who would sing a *Te Deum* over any pacification, however infamous, and
would rejoice to see Jefferson Davis our next President. Perhaps he may
be. If he is magnanimous and forgiving he may be prevailed on to come
and reign over us. I would rather see the North subjugated than a separation. Disgust with our present government is certainly universal.
Even Lincoln himself has gone down at last, like all our popular idols of
the last eighteen months. This honest old codger was the last to fall,
but he has fallen. Nobody believes in him any more. I do not, though I
still maintain him. I cannot bear to admit the country has no man to
believe in, and that honest Abe Lincoln is not the style of goods we want
just now. But it is impossible to resist the conviction that he is unequal to
his place. His only special gift is fertility of smutty stories. *Quam parva
sapientia mundus regitur!* What must be the calibre of our rulers whose
rule is so disgraceful a failure? If McClellan gain no signal, decisive
victory within ten days, I shall collapse; and we have no reason to expect
anything of that sort from him.

Rebel ravages in southern Pennsylvania may stir up a general arming
and enrolment, but even that would give us only an undisciplined mob
for months to come. O Abraham, *O mon Roi!*

*There is a break in the diary from September 13 to September 24, during
most of which period Strong was in or near Washington. He went south at a
time big with critical events. Early in September, Lee, at the head of about
50,000 ill-equipped troops, had crossed the Potomac and invaded Maryland.
Thousands of his veterans marched without shoes. Stonewall Jackson won an
initial success by capturing Harper's Ferry, and then hurried by forced marches
to rejoin the main army under Lee. McClellan, placed in chief command of the
Union forces, had at first shown his old tendency toward delay and despondency.
But marching to overtake the enemy, he reached Frederick, Maryland, on September 13, and there obtained a copy of a special order issued by Lee four days
earlier, laying bare the whole Confederate plan of campaign. The battle of
Antietam or Sharpsburg took place on the 17th, McClellan throwing his army
heavily against the much weaker army of the Confederacy. According to the*

generally received figures, the Northern forces numbered 87,000 men, the Southern forces 50,000 or 55,000—but McClellan used only 60,000. The Confederate line resisted valiantly, and both sides suffered grave losses—the North 12,400 killed and wounded, the South 11,200. At the end of the fourteen hours of conflict, McClellan had the better of the day, and if he had attacked with determination on the 18th, he might have won a crushing victory. Instead, he failed to renew the fight, and Lee slipped back across the Potomac. Although Lincoln was grievously disappointed by Lee's escape to safety, he was encouraged by this partial victory to resolve to issue the Emancipation Proclamation. On September 22 he announced his intention to the Cabinet, and the next day his great writ of freedom was published to the world. "God bless Abraham Lincoln!" exclaimed the New York Tribune, which had long pressed for this step. Strong was close to the scene of action in these great days; part of the time, in fact, in an office so near Stanton's that he could hear the worried Secretary swearing fearfully.

September 24, WEDNESDAY.   Spent an hour or two at Dr. Bellows's in council with our Sanitary Commission colleagues. Our affairs are prospering. Agnew's report of personal experience in Maryland confirms mine, or rather vice versa, his being so many times larger. The Medical Department is utterly destitute and shiftless as usual, and now confessedly is leaning on the Commission for supplies and looking to it for help to get forward its own stores, waiving all its official dignity under the pressure of work for which it made no adequate provision and in an attitude of general supplication and imbecile self-abasement. *Times is changed,* and scornful dogs have to eat dirty puddings. The fossil old Bureau is not yet galvanized into life, with all Dr. Hammond's energy. Want of independent transportation seems its main difficulty. Hammond is paralyzed by dependence on the Quartermaster Department. We must try to mend this, even at the risk of alienating General Meigs.

Memorabilia of this Sanitary anabasis. To Washington by the accustomed railroad Monday morning the 15th. Found Wolcott Gibbs and Bishop Clark on the train; also Binney and Judge Hare. At Baltimore we came in contact with extras. Battle in Maryland on the 14th. Rebels routed. Grand victory. The politic city of Baltimore was in a confluent eruption of national flags. We bought fifty cents worth of Baltimore *Clippers* and hurled them out of the car windows at the lonely picket guards all along the Baltimore and Washington Road. But as we drew nearer Washington, the glorious news began to dwarf and dwindle. The rebel army was not absolutely disorganized and still showed fight. There were unpleasant rumors, unreliable of course, that Colonel [Dixon S.] Miles had surrendered Harper's Ferry.

Reached Washington and received excellent quarters from the magnates of Willard's Hotel. Binney and Hare, and McMichael and a lot of others, a committee of Philadelphians to wait on the Secretary of War and General Halleck and secure a military chieftain to secure the defense of Pennsylvania, were very blue. Stanton could not be seen but was heard cussing frightfully in an adjoining apartment. Our session began Tuesday morning and lasted till Friday night. Agnew and Harris were sent off Wednesday, I think, in charge of medical stores for the battlefield. We did a good deal of work. Had an interview by appointment with Gen. Halleck. . . . We walked away from Halleck's quarters in dismal silence and consternation. Van Buren broke it with the words "God help us!" That aspiration was never more appropriate. Halleck is not the man for his place. He is certainly—clearly—weak, shallow, commonplace, vulgar. He is a strong friend of the Commission and ready to do whatever it asks, so I am not prejudiced against him. His silly talk was conclusive as to his incapacity, unless he was a little flustered with wine, an inadmissible apology for a commander-in-chief at a crisis like this. He seemed to think it facetious to keep calling Dr. Bellows "Bishop," maundered about certain defects of discipline which he said prevented McClellan from moving more than five miles a day and Buell more than three—"when he moves at all, that is." Someone suggested an order from headquarters as the appropriate remedy (he might have referred to the army regulations now in force), whereupon Halleck became stately and said he wasn't a writer for the newspapers. "No, sir. No, I thank you, sir. That is not my line. I cannot do that," and so on, in the silliest style. His revelations were most imprudent. "People expect me to send a column to Gordonsville or somewhere and cut off the rebel communications. Where are the men? Only 42,000 left for the defense of Washington today. Government has paid bounties to 350,000 men under the new levy. Less than 75,000 have reached Washington. None at all these last two days. So many at Cincinnati, at St. Louis, and other places—less than 50,000 all told. The governors keep them back till each man has his tin cup and his carpetbag, and then a week longer to enable some politician to make a speech to the regiment and shake hands with every recruit individually." We adjourned formally Saturday morning, after an efficient session. Bishop

Clark was as genial and enlivening as of old. He reports a rebel prisoner received in Governor's Island who was scrubbed for two hours with soap and water before they got down to the shirt he wore in 1860. Someone said that blatant, gassy George Francis Train (now blowing at Willard's) abstains from all stimulants and narcotics, from coffee, tobacco, and alcoholic drinks. The Bishop replied it would be a pity to dilute George F. Train with whiskey. From all accounts, Abe Lincoln is far from easy in his mind. Judge Skinner, who knows him intimately, says he wanders about wringing his hands and wondering whom he can trust and what he'd better do. What's very bad, he has been heard to utter the words "war for boundaries," to speak which words should be death. Heaven help our rulers. Never was so great a cause in the keeping of much smaller men. But I still have faith in Abe Lincoln.

Left Washington at five o'clock Saturday afternoon. Baltimore cars densely packed. I rode on the platform and took a dessert-spoonful of cinders dirt out of each ear on reaching that town. Took a car for Harrisburg at half-past nine and arrived there at two or three o'clock in the morning. Met Binney there and got decent quarters at the Jones House.

Sunday morning proceeded with Binney to the State House; the town swarming with Pennsylvania militia and all the paraphernalia of war. Men were drilling in all the streets. The great battle of Wednesday and the withdrawal of the rebels from Maryland were not yet fully understood, and people looked grave enough. The militia, however, were in good fighting humor and would have done all that utterly green, undisciplined men could do. We found [Thomas A.] Scott, Cameron's former Assistant Secretary, on duty as representative of Governor Curtin, and he ordered out a special train for us. Inspected the surrounding country from the State House cupola. Lovely landscape, broad, pure, peaceful river (most fordable, unhappily, as it might have proved) flowing down through a gap in the northwest line of wooded hills, and all flooded with the misty sunlight of an Indian summerish morning.

Off at about ten o'clock through a fertile, rich, thriving region, full of nice farmhouses, big barns and comfortable villages; a most tempting prey for Lee's hungry battalions. At Carlisle and the other places we passed through the whole population seemed to have turned out with anxious faces—many of the women crying, and no wonder. They were yet uncertain whether the pressing danger of devastation was passed. At Chambersburg we were delayed a couple of hours to await a special train from Hagerstown with Governor Curtin. It is a pretty village enough. Found Dr. Cuyler there. Traversed every street a dozen times in quest of Dr. Crane, an inspector, without success. Here we met a telegram announcing a sort of Ball's Bluff blunder on Saturday. A brigade sent across the Potomac by Porter to feel the enemy had got caught in an ambuscade and was driven back. The 118th Pennsylvania regiment was much cut up. As young Horace Binney is a lieutenant in this regiment, the news gave his father some cause of perturbation, but he bore up bravely.

We got to Hagerstown at nine o'clock. Rooms at the hotels not to be thought of; it was not easy to get inside their doors. Soldiers and officers were bivouacking in the streets. By good luck we found Dr. Hartshorne, who put us *en rapport* with Dr. Dorsey, one of the F.F.'s, and a thorough-going loyalist, and in his comfortable house we were received at once, with a frank cordiality and kindness beyond all my experience. They only knew we were Union men and engaged in some kind of work for the army. I never appreciated the meaning of the word hospitality before. The lady of the house is a most thorough-bred kind of person, with the most charming, genial manner. They have a son in the rebel army! But one must go into the Debatable Land to see full-blooded, genuine Union feeling. Ours at the North is a second-rate article. Mrs. Dorsey told me much of the rebel forces that occupied the town some four days; how dirty and wretched they were, how they scampered at midnight on the news of McClellan's approach, and what a smell they left behind them. Stuart, a chaplain from Alexandria, told her they meant to take Philadelphia—"Philadelphia or death."

Next morning, Monday, I made arrangements to put the Medical Director, Surgeon A. K. Smith, in funds for the immediate equipment of his hospital, and then took an ambulance and drove off over the Sharpsburg turnpike with Binney and Hartshorne and a certain indefatigable Mrs. Harris, rival of Miss Dix and agent of some Philadelphia relief association. We soon entered an atmosphere pervaded by the scent of the battlefield—the bloody and memorable field of Antietam ("Antee'tum") Creek. Long lines of trenches marked the burial places; scores of dead horses, swollen, with their limbs protruding stiffly at strange angles, and the ground at their noses blackened with hemorrhage, lay all around. Sharpsburg, a commonplace little village, was scarified with shot. In one little brick house I counted more than a dozen shot-holes, cleanly made, probably by rifle projectiles. Here and there was seen the more extensive ravage made by an exploding shell. The country is most lovely, like Berkshire County, Massachusetts, only more luxuriant and exuberant.

At Sharpsburg, we found the little church used as a hospital for the 118th Pennsylvania; some fifty wounded lay there on straw. The regiment had suffered badly. Young Binney was safe and off on picket duty. His men spoke of his conduct enthusiastically and said he was the last man to leave the ground. His father fairly broke down under this, and no wonder. In the crowd of ambulances, army wagons, beef-cattle, staff officers, recruits, kicking mules, and so on, who should suddenly turn up but Mrs. Arabella Barlow, née Griffith, unattended, but serene and self-possessed as if walking down Broadway. She is nursing the colonel, her husband (badly wounded), and never appeared so well.[6] Talked like a sensible, practical, earnest, warm-hearted woman, without a phrase of hyperflutination. We went to McClellan's headquarters and to Fitz-John Porter's. McClellan has twenty regimental standards and more, and guns, substantial trophies. But for the miserable misconduct that lost us Harper's Ferry, had that unhappy Colonel Miles held out eight hours longer, the rebel retreat would have been a rout. Miles has gone to his account, and whether he was a deliberate traitor or only faint-hearted and incapable will never be known. Left Binney at Sharpsburg, and proceeded in the direction of Keedysville and French's Division Hospital, where we stayed two or three hours. Horrible congregation of wounded men there and at Porter's—our men and rebel prisoners both—on straw, in their bloody stiffened clothes mostly, some in barns and cowhouses, some in the open air. It was fearful to see; Gustave Doré's pictures embodied in shivering, agonizing, suppurating flesh and blood.

Walked with Hartshorne over another section of the battlefield, strewn with fragments of shell and conical bullets; here and there a round shot or a live shell, dangerous to handle. We traced the position in which a rebel brigade had stood or bivouacked in line of battle for half a mile by the thickly strewn belt of green corn husks and cobs, and also, *sit venia loquendi,* by a ribbon of dysenteric stools just behind.

It grew dark, and we watched the light signals from a woody hill in the direction of Harper's Ferry, supped on bologna sausage, drove off at last like mad and got back to our hospitable house at Dr. Dorsey's very late, but not too late for a generous and most acceptable tea. . . . Left Harrisburg at eight this morning.

September 27, SATURDAY. President's Emancipation Manifesto much

[6] Francis C. Barlow was promoted to a brigadier-generalship on September 19, 1862, for his gallant service. The severe wound he received at Antietam was healed in time for him to take part in the Chancellorsville campaign in the spring of 1863.

discussed and generally approved, though a few old Democrats (who ought to be dead and buried but persist in manifesting themselves like vampires) scold and grumble. It will do us good abroad, but will have no other effect.

October 3. A damp, sultry, steaming, unseasonable moonlight night through which I've just taken an active stroll in the mood of a Sioux off on a scalp dance. My condition as to temper has been terrible since I read the afternoon papers. Ellie and Miss Rosalie (who dined with us) can testify to my ferocity. But I pass this over and proceed to the journal proper. We have left Newport bag and baggage and boys, and are at home once more. That is decided cause for congratulation. Went to that wretched place Monday night. The voyage was not unpleasant. Spent three raw, cloudy, cheerless east-windy days there. Lounged on the beach and on the shores of a certain creek. Tuesday spent with Johnny and Temple; Johnny caught no perch, but showed great prowess as a swimmer. Wednesday took out the duo in Nathan's sail boat and fished off the *Dumplings.* Rain and wind. Both boys were sea-sick, but they behaved like little bricks. Many big black-fish captured. Johnny lost a grand eight-pounder just at the gunwale. Dined pleasantly with Charles Kuhn and his piquant little wife. Saw a good deal of Charles Kuhn. His musical furor has not abated, nor have his high notes in Mozart or what-not that he's trying to render—but one forgives everything. . . .

Now for my special present aggravation and irritation. The Triennial Convention of the Protestant Episcopal Church in the U.S.A. is now sitting in St. John's Chapel. Mr. Ruggles is a delegate from this diocese. (So is the Rev. F. L. Hawks.) The afternoon papers announce that some Pennsylvania delegate offered a preamble and resolutions in substance that whereas there is a rebellion against the nation and a schism in the church, therefore, resolved that the church prays that the rebels and schismatics may be brought to a better mind, that the bishops be invited to set forth a form of prayer accordingly, and that the church also hopes and prays that the devices of rebellion and schism be confounded. This motion was tabled two to one after full discussion.

Mr. Ruggles has the House of Bishops and all the convention at No. 24 tonight, and I expected to go there; counted on the evening and looked forward to it. But I could not go anywhere to meet the councillors of the church after this base action of theirs. The position of the people of England toward us, England's utter selfishness and profligacy, gave me one great disillusioning shock a year and more ago. This action, or non-action, of the (*soi-disant*) American Catholic Church gives me another, yet more stunning.

The church in which I was brought up, which I have maintained so long to be the highest and noblest of organizations, refuses to say one word for the country at this crisis. Her priests call on Almighty God every day, in the most solemn offices of her liturgy, to deliver His people from "false doctrine, heresy, and schism," from "sedition, privy conspiracy, and rebellion." Now, at last, when they and their people are confronted by the most wicked of rebellions and the most wilful of schisms on the vilest of grounds, the constitutional right to breed black babies for sale, when rebellion and schism are arrayed against the church and against society in the unloveliest form they can possibly assume—the church is afraid to speak. How would she get on were there a large, highly respectable minority sympathizing with adultery, or homicide, or larceny? Alas, for my dreams of twenty years ago!

I think this shows the existence of a latent anti-democratic or aristocratic feeling as a constituent element of the Protestant-Episcopal or Anglo-American Church. Not a conservative spirit, founded on tradition, inherited from the English Church and dating back to the days of the Stuarts (such as was manifested in 1776), but a revolutionary spirit as against our democratic institutions. It appears in the specially prominent part taken by Southern bishops, presbyters, and leading laymen in the Southern anti-democratic rebellion; and this shameful reluctance of our Northern Council to commit itself against the rebellion points the same way. Were the instincts of the church conservative, they would prompt the most emphatic declaration of sympathy with government. I have no special liking for democratic institutions, but "the powers that be" and that are ordained of God rest on those institutions and the church is bound to uphold them. Her public avowal of lukewarmness in their support puts her back twenty years in influence and popular respect.

October 8, WEDNESDAY. At Columbia College meeting Monday we made a good move—appropriated money for a fencing school. This is the entering wedge, I hope, for the recognition of physical education. We reorganized the Library Committee, and Anderson, Rutherfurd, and I were appointed.

Canvass for fall elections fairly begun. Wadsworth and Seymour candidates for governor. I hope Wadsworth and the so-called radicals may sweep the state and kick our wretched sympathizers with Southern treason back into the holes that have sheltered them for the past year and from which they are beginning to peep out timidly and tentatively to see whether they can venture to resume their dirty work. The result will be an important indication of the way popular feeling tends to flow. I *think* it will show important progress the right way, but we must not be over-confident. Seymour's election would be an encouragement to Jefferson Davis worth 100,000 men.

Thus ends this volume of my journal, in days that are chilly and grey, but not without gleams of light that promise the return of sunshine. So let us hope, and in that hope, let us work. If we work faithfully, and do our duty in freely putting forth all our resources, we can hardly fail, with God's blessing, to crush the rebellion and vindicate our existence as a nation. God enable us so to do our duty. Amen.

The autumn elections of 1862 were of unusual importance. A House of Representatives had to be chosen, and in view of the widespread discouragement over military defeats and the heavy burdens of the war, a considerable reaction against the Administration was expected. In New York the governorship was at stake. When the Democratic Party, meeting in convention at Albany on September 10, nominated Horatio Seymour for the place, all patriots of Strong's views felt a distinct shock. Seymour had wealth and influence; he had made a creditable record during his previous term as governor; and he represented the old up-state Democracy of Van Buren and Silas Wright. But he had been a fierce opponent of the Lincoln Administration, attacking all its repressive measures as unconstitutional and opposing the emancipation of the slaves. He had said again and again that the North could never subjugate the South. All the dissatisfied and disloyal elements of the state rallied behind him. On the Republican side, Governor Morgan had made it plain that he would not run again. The party hesitated for a time between John A. Dix and General James S. Wadsworth, whose record at Bull Run had been distinguished and who stood for an energetic prosecution of the war. Meeting at Syracuse late in September, the Republican Union Convention nominated Wadsworth on the first ballot by an overwhelming majority. A campaign of great bitterness then opened. The Democrats called Wadsworth "a malignant Abolition disorganizer"; the Republicans declared, in the words of Henry J. Raymond of the Times, *that "every vote given for Seymour is a vote for treason."*

October 15, WEDNESDAY. Fine day. News is nix. Went to Jersey City this morning to enquire after Mrs. Herman Ruggles, who is probably in failing health, but is reported better by Miss Rosalie. Van Buren and Agnew at No. 498 Broadway this afternoon. News today of our second $100,000 from San Francisco. I deposited the first yesterday. O pleasing task! We are to send $50,000 to our secessionizing off-shoot at St. Louis, which is a less agreeable duty. Murray Hoffman dined here, and we went to Wallack's old theatre, now a German opera house, and heard the *Entführung aus dem Serail* for the first time and under disadvantage, our seats being within whispering range of the big drum. But many lovely things were perceptible, as in a glass, darkly. I hope to hear it again. There was an exquisite tenor solo, a delicious cosy drinking song, and a lovely finale for the soli and chorus—antiphonal as the Rev. Vinton and his choir boys at Trinity Church. These came out clearly and well defined; everything else somewhat blurred.

Bishop Clark dined here Monday with Vinton, Bellows, Van Buren, Agnew, and Gibbs, and we had a jolly symposium and much good talk, though gold is nearly at 140 premium and McClellan's army immovable as the Pyramids. That general has sent for his wife, his mother-in-law, and his baby, and is going to go into housekeeping, it seems, somewhere near Sharpsburg. He may move next first of May, but I fear he is settled till then. Heaven help us! It is good, however, that the elections yesterday in Pennsylvania and other states seem to show that the spirit of the nation is unbroken. May the voice of New York next month be in accord with theirs, and Horatio Seymour, John Van Buren, Fernando Wood, Richard O'Gor-r-r-man, and the Hon. Washington Hunt (whom as Mr. Samuel B. Ruggles's friend, I regret to see in such dirty company) experience the snubbing a loyal people ought to give them!

The house of clerical and lay deputies is still talking and talking over the great question before it. Ellie goes down to St. John's Chapel every morning and has a good time. A pew there is like a balcony seat at the opera. Prelates and presbyters and notable laics pass through the aisle and stop to gossip a little about the church and the nation. I think the lower house will express itself more decidedly than seemed possible a week ago. The House of Bishops has already taken decided action, I hear. Our very venerable diocesan got up on Monday and moved that no allusion be made in the "pastoral letter" to the state of the country. He is certainly quite "gone in the knees," as horse-people say. His motion was tabled. The Rt. Rev. Hopkins, presiding bishop, brought in the draft of a pastoral letter that did not suit. He is reputed of low-grade loyalty. McIlvaine of Ohio proposed and Whittingham of Maryland seconded another draft as a substitute, which was adopted almost unanimously. This conjunction of McIlvaine and Whittingham, of ultra-evangelical and ultra-Oxford-man, is notable. Times are changed since 1844.

Notable also as a curious coincidence is Dr. Hawks's conspicuous position in this convention as in that of nineteen years ago. Then he was charged with fraud as now with disloyalty. He occupied a large share of time and attention at both these sessions, each more important by far than any other held during the fifth of a century that separates them, and at each his attitude has been apologetic and defensive. In the former, he was using his remarkable faculty of plausible talk to repel allegations of bad faith toward his neighbors at Flushing; now he is trying to make out that he is keeping good faith with his country. He is not on trial now as he was then, but his position is substantially the same. Having resigned the rectorship of Calvary Church and a salary of $5,000, he wants to be recalled. His speeches in convention are addressed to the vestry of that church, and I dare say they will be successful, whatever the convention may decide to do, for members of that vestry are reputed "sympathetic" souls. How Mr. Ruggles, Dr. Higby, and other thoroughly earnest and loyal men can hesitate any longer as to their duty in convention is incomprehensible.

October 17. . . . Election news from Pennsylvania and the West were cold, but I hope the opposition men elected are "War Democrats."

Nothing material from the seat of war, except that McClellan shows signs of life. He has wiggled a little and made a reconnaissance in force as far as Charlestown (the city of John Brown), with loss of one man killed and six missing. Some say this is the beginning of a general advance, forced on him prematurely by the Cabinet and by popular clamor. Last night our Sanitary brethren of the Executive Committee met here, according to rule of rotation, and with the usual slight supper and good talk. Our reverend president has been making a gander of himself, I regret to say, in the course of an address on the war before his Unitarian Convention or Heretical Assenagemote and convocation of philosophical wiseacres now or lately in session here or at Brooklyn or somewhere else. He said much that was good, valuable, and new (to the public, at least), but went out of his way to eulogize the Southern race and is much assaulted and belabored for having done so. He maintained last night, and very plausibly, that he did not go out of his way, and that what he said about the generosity and gentility of Southern traitors and the nobleness of Southern blood was intended to enforce and did enforce his practical conclusion, the necessity for concentrating all our national energies to crush Southern treason. Perhaps.

October 19. Last night with Ellie, George Anthon, and Johnny to Niblo's where we saw Hackett as Rip Van Winkle and as Dr. O'Callaghan in *His Last Legs.* He was funny in both, and the evening was most satisfactory, though it kept Johnny out of his nest till eleven o'clock.

October 23. To Columbia College this morning with George F. Allen in time for chapel. Service satisfactory. Charles Kuhn and Jem Ruggles dined here, and I spent the evening at Dr. Van Buren's. Meeting of Executive Committee of the Sanitary Commission and slight supper thereafter. Olmsted present, also an intelligent, well-mannered Dr. Fowler, a refugee from Montgomery, Alabama. That town cast him out because he was thought overzealous in caring for a hospital full of Union prisoners, of which he was in charge. Sanitary Commission is waxing fat. Its California remittances will foot up not much below a quarter of a million, and may exceed that sum.[7]

Our war on rebellion languishes. We make no onward movements and gain no victories. McClellan's repose is doubtless majestic, but if a couchant lion postpone his spring too long, people will begin wondering whether he is not a stuffed specimen after all. Fat Colonel Burkett tells Augustus King that there will certainly be a grand movement and great results within a week, but I am tired of such talk. One thing is clear: that unless we gain decisive success before the November election, this state will range itself against the Administration. If it does, a dishonorable peace and permanent disunion are not unlikely. The whole community is honeycombed by secret sympathizers with treason who will poke out their heads and flaunt their "red, white, and red" tentacles the moment avowed division of Northern sentiment enables them to do so safely. . . .

October 25. Philharmonic rehearsal this afternoon; Beethoven's Symphony in B flat (No. 2), one of the two that I know but little if at all. I think I had never heard it. Expected little, but it turns out to be a very noble symphony, and for one hour I forgot all about the war and the Sanitary Commission, and was conscious of nothing but the marvelous web of melodic harmony and pungent orchestral color that was slowly

[7] Led by the Rev. Thomas Starr King, Mayor H. P. Coon of San Francisco, Governor F. F. Low, and others, the people of California had rallied impressively to the support of the Sanitary Commission. Of approximately five million dollars collected by the Sanitary Commission during the War, a total of $1,233,890 came from California.

unfolding. Though deep and elaborate, the symphony is very clear, and I swallowed it all without effort on this first hearing. It is Beethoven, every note of it, except perhaps in the first movement, which is Haydn-oid in sentiment. The second movement seems transcendently beautiful; Haydn's purity and heartiness expressed in Beethoven's more copious vocabulary. The scherzo and trio are full of lovely melodic phrases, and the jolliest thing Beethoven ever wrote for an orchestra. . . .

Last night with Murray Hoffman to the German theatre. Heard Boïeldieu's *Jean de Paris* in a German version. That opera has its good points, in the third act especially, but they are too few to compensate one for three hours of mephitic atmosphere and absorption of carbonic oxide into one's blood and bones in that ill-ventilated little theatre.

Today's news is that McClellan is now positively about to advance at last and also that General Curtis has beaten the rebels of North Arkansas once more at Pea Ridge. Also the Rev. Hawks resigns from Calvary Church and makes his hegira to Baltimore this week.

October 29. At Niblo's last night with Ellie and George Anthon; first part of *King Henry IV.* Hackett's Falstaff seems to me beyond criticism, incapable of improvement in a single detail of look, gesture, or intonation—the only perfect impersonation I have ever seen of any character. Such "histrionic art" has real value; it furnishes the best possible commentary on Shakespeare's text. It is wonderful how Hackett can make the part so broadly comic without for an instant forgetting that Sir John is a gentleman in the conventional sense of the term.

October 30, THURSDAY. Private advices from the War Department are that the Virginia rebels are greatly reinforced and that McClellan is to wait a little longer. Alas for next Tuesday's election! There is danger —great and pressing danger—of a disaster more telling than all our Bull Run battles and Peninsular strategy: the resurrection to political life and power of the Woods, Barlows, LaRocques, and Belmonts,[8] who have been dead and buried and working only underground, if at all, for eighteen months, and every one of whom well deserves hanging as an ally of the rebellion. It would be a fearful national calamity. If it come, it will be due not so much to the Emancipation Manifesto as to the irregular arrests the government has been making. They have been used against the Administration with most damaging effect, and no wonder. They have been

[8] That is, Fernando Wood, his brother Ben Wood, S. L. M. Barlow (with his law partner of the firm of Shipman, Barlow, Larocque & Choate), and August Belmont.

utterly arbitrary, and could be excused only because demanded by the pressure of an unprecedented national crisis; because necessary in a case of national life or death that justified any measure, however extreme. But not one of the many hundreds illegally arrested and locked up for months has been publicly charged with any crime or brought to the notice of a Grand Jury. They have all been capriciously arrested, so far as we can see, and some have been capriciously discharged; locked up for months without legal authority and let out without legal acquittal. All this is very bad—imbecile, dangerous, unjustifiable. It gives traitors and Seymourites an apology for opposing the government and helping South Carolina that it is hard to answer. I know it is claimed that these arrests are legal, and perhaps they are, but their legality is a subtle question that government should not have raised as to a point about which people are so justly sensitive.

There go drums through the street. It's a Democratic procession (democratic!) with torches, parading dirty James Brooks's name on a dirty banner. I met this, or its brother, marching down Fifth Avenue on my way to Agnew's, and felt as if a Southern Army had got into New York. . . .

November 3, MONDAY. At Columbia College meeting this afternoon. It was not long. We had the treasurer's annual report and important questions about the Law School, which were referred to our Law Committee. The School is expanding and thriving. Dwight's salary (from fees) is now more than $6,000, and certain of the last graduating class ask for a third year with some further degree at its close—"Master of Laws" or the like. A most promising sign. That school has thriven beyond the utmost we hoped, thanks to Dwight's admirable talent for teaching. Thence to the Sanitary Commission rooms. About $26,000 more from California! Telegrams announce still further contributions coming. . . .

Tomorrow's prospects bad. The Seymourites are sanguine. Vote will certainly be close. A row in the city is predicted by those who desire one, but it is unlikely, though people are certainly far more personally bitter and savage than at any election for many years past. A Northern vote against the Administration may be treated by Honest Old Abe as a vote of want of confidence. He may dismiss his Cabinet and say to the Democrats, "Gentlemen, you think you can do this job better and quicker than Seward and Chase. Bring up your men, and I'll set them to work." It would be like him. And there is little to choose between the two gangs.

After all, Seymour and his tail want the offices—public pay and public patronage. As governor, Seymour will probably try to outbrag the Republicans in energetic conduct of the war. He cares more for his own little finger than for all the Body Politic, and will be as radical as Horace Greeley himself whenever he can gain by it; that is, whenever popular feeling calls for "radical leaders." As yet, the people are sound. They see that stopping the war now would be like leaving the dentist's shop with a tooth half-extracted. There are traitors, of course, now beginning cautiously to tamper with the great torrent of national feeling that burst out April, 1861. And there is also a great mass of selfishness, frivolity, invincible prejudice, personal Southern attachment, indifference to national life, and so on, quite ready to be used as a mud-bank to dam the flood that broke out so gloriously a year and a half ago.

Have we the people, or have we not, resolution and steadiness enough to fight on through five years of taxation, corruption, and discouragement? All depends on the answer to that question.

November 4, TUESDAY. A beautiful bright day, but destined to be memorable, I fear, for a national calamity. Voted this morning, and did not much beside. Indications at the several polling places I visited in the course of enquiry for my own proper civic locality (which I found at last in East Nineteenth Street) were of a rather light vote; no excitement or disturbance, and a fair prospect for the Wadsworth ticket. Came uptown at four, stopping at No. 823 Broadway. George Anthon and Murray Hoffman, Jr., dined here (roast pig). I spent an hour at Bellows's in session with the Executive Committee, returned here, and with Murray Hoffman and George Anthon took a Fourth Avenue railroad car down to the Park to look for election news. Horace Greeley was in our car and not jubilant at all. We found excited crowds around all the newspaper offices of that region—the *Times, Herald, Tribune, World*; everybody craning over everybody's head to get a glimpse of the bulletins. These assemblages were rather unusually clamorous and demonstrative, and all the feeling displayed was on the Seymour side. "Where's Greeley's 900,000 men?" "General Wadsworth can't run for governor, but he *can* run sometimes." "Bully for F'nandy Wood," and the like. Downtown returns indicate overwhelming defeat, the election of Seymour, and a vote of censure on the Administration by the people of this state. The Seymour majority in the city is claimed to be 31,000. The Democrats carry every ward. Fernando Wood and Ben Wood and Winthrop Chanler are sent to Congress,

Walbridge and Conkling defeated.[9] Brooklyn goes the same way. The western counties may save the state yet, but it's improbable. I think the battle is lost and Seymour is governor. God help us. I believe He will, if we be not utterly untrue to our cause.

The Democrats carried the state for Seymour by more than 11,000 majority, and gained a tie vote in the Assembly—a result which sickened many patriots. Henry J. Raymond of the Times, *agreeing with Strong, termed it "a vote of want of confidence in the President." Nor was the showing in other states much better. The Democrats carried New Jersey; they obtained twenty-five new Congressional seats in New York, Pennsylvania, and Ohio; and in the Congressional elections in Lincoln's own state, Illinois, they overwhelmingly defeated the Republicans. Yet the Border States showed an unexpected loyalty to the Administration, and Lincoln retained control of the House of Representatives by a practical working majority. The Senate was, of course, strongly Republican. The reaction was natural under the circumstances, and it exhibited only a temporary and superficial rather than a permanent and deep-seated discontent with the conduct of the war. Lincoln was not greatly perturbed by it, and Strong's early lamentations were soon proved to be excessive—as he himself acknowledged.*

Yet the North could take little comfort this fall from the military situation, which remained nearly static. Lincoln, after visiting McClellan's well-equipped army of more than 100,000 men early in September, had urged a forward movement. Halleck, too, had written McClellan on October 7: "The country is impatient at the want of activity of your army, and you must push it on." McClellan did cross the Potomac, but he went no farther than to place his forces on the eastern slope of the Blue Ridge. Finally Lincoln, his patience exhausted, took steps early in November to place the army under a more energetic commander.

November 5. As anticipated, total rout in this state. Seymour is governor. Elsewhere defeat, or nominal success by a greatly reduced vote. It looks like a great, sweeping revolution of public sentiment, like general

[9] Hiram Walbridge (1821–1870), a merchant who had been in Congress 1853–1855, had run on the Union ticket. Frederick A. Conkling (1816–1891), a brother of Roscoe, who had organized the 84th New York Volunteers, was now in Congress as a Republican, and was an unsuccessful candidate for reelection. Both lived in New York and were personally known to Strong. John Winthrop Chanler (1826–1877), now elected as a Democrat, sat in the next three Congresses.

abandonment of the loyal, generous spirit of patriotism that broke out so nobly and unexpectedly in April, 1861. Was that after all nothing but a temporary hysteric spasm? I think not. We the people are impatient, dissatisfied, disgusted, disappointed. We are in a state of dyspepsia and general, indefinite malaise, suffering from the necessary evils of war and from irritation at our slow progress. We take advantage of the first opportunity of change, for its own sake, just as a feverish patient shifts his position in bed, though he knows he'll be none the easier for it. Neither the blind masses, the swinish multitude, that rule us under our accursed system of universal suffrage, nor the case of typhoid, can be expected to exercise self-control and remember that tossing and turning weakens and does harm. Probably two-thirds of those who voted for Seymour meant to say by their votes, "Messrs. Lincoln, Seward, Stanton & Co., you have done your work badly, so far. You are humbugs. My business is stopped, I have got taxes to pay, my wife's third cousin was killed on the Chickahominy, and the war is no nearer an end than it was a year ago. I am disgusted with you and your party and shall vote for the governor or the congressman you disapprove, just to spite you."

If I am mistaken, and if this vote does endorse the policy of Fernando Wood and John Van Buren, it is a vote of national suicide. All is up. We are a lost people; United States securities, "greenbacks" and all, are worth about a dollar a cord; the Historical Society should secure an American flag at once for its museum of antiquities. I will forge certificates showing that I was not born in America but in *Hingland*—expatriate myself, and become naturalized as a citizen of Venezuela, Haiti, or the Papal States. But I will not *yet* believe that this people is capable of so shameful and despicable an act of self-destruction as to disembowel itself in the face of the civilized world for fear Jefferson Davis should hurt it.

November 8. At Philharmonic rehearsal with Ellie this morning at ten. On my way thence downtown, heard of Dr. Berrian's death last evening. When I met him at Newport last August, he was much broken and unlikely to live many months. He had rallied since then and was not thought in immediate danger till the day he died. Among my earliest recollections is Dr. Berrian perorating blandly in the pulpit of St. Paul's. He always treated me kindly, and after I came into the vestry in 1847, I enjoyed a good deal of his confidence. He was a useful and valuable man to Trinity parish and through it to the diocese, but he was generally held to be the ideal of decent mediocrity, and his name was a convenient and familiar way of expressing the zero point of dull preaching. His sermons were in fact above average merit, which is not saying much for them. Though he never originated a thought, his commonplaces were always reasonable and judicious. He never violated good taste, and his English was accurate. He would have been held a good preacher but for his delivery, which was a monotonous whine. He was most efficient in business and exerted a controlling influence in his own sphere, but worked in such a quiet, "douce" way that few suspected his power. He used this influence wisely, and never (so far as I know) for private and personal ends, and on the whole, Trinity Church will not easily secure a better rector than poor old "Poppy Berrian."

November 10.   The burial was in one of the vaults of St. Mark's Church. Downtown after dinner to Trinity Church vestry meeting; fifteen present. I moved that before organizing we go into an informal ballot for rector, with nominations. Agreed to, the clerk (G.M.O.) putting the question. Result, Morgan Dix 14, and Higby 1 (namely, Dunscomb). We thereupon organized with Dunscomb the warden in the chair, and went into formal ballot. Dix elected unanimously, and a committee of three sent out to notify him. He had been desired to wait in attendance at the Mission Room of St. Paul's, corner of Vesey and Church Streets (as we might require the assistant rector's presence), and was speedily brought in. He said a few words, accepting the place, with the utmost dignity, simplicity, and sincerity of self-depreciation, so sincere and straightforward as to keep all personal considerations quite out of view. And then, after some talking, we adjourned to tomorrow, when the ancient ceremony of "inducting" our new rector is to be performed.

I think our choice was wise. It was certainly spontaneous. There was no lobbying or electioneering. Every one of us voted on his individual conviction, I believe, and without concert. All consultation had been studiously avoided. How could we vote otherwise? There was Higby. His claims were seniority, and a magnificent but unreliable faculty of rhetoric. But he is as unfit for secular business as a yearling child. Hobart is his father's son, but *non compos* for all affairs of this world. Haight is shelved now by disease. Had this vacancy occurred five years ago, he would have filled it, I think. Vinton has no common sense whatever, and as rector would have been incessantly getting the parish into scrapes, while his love of power and exalted estimate of his own rights would have kept him in permanent hot water with his vestry.

November 13, THURSDAY.   Last night's Sanitary session devoted mainly to our relations with the western branches. There are signs of war. The

Cincinnati branch recalcitrates against Olmsted's proposed system of centralization and absolute subordination, and Judge Hoadly goes with Cincinnati. We shall have a row; that branch will lop itself off after the manner of St. Louis, and we shall have to consider whether we have money enough to enable us to occupy that field without its support and with its quasi-hostility. I rather guess we can for a few months at least, thanks to California.

Tuesday at two o'clock we "inducted" the Rev. Morgan Dix according to our corporate usage. The vestry met in the robing room of Trinity Church, came to order, resolved to induct incontinently, and then marched down the north aisle with the Rev. Morgan Dix at our head and all the sextons at our tail, through the north porch and round the tower to the front or "principal" entrance, which was locked. There Dunscomb as warden delivered the key to Dix, with a formal declaration that he thereby transferred the church to his charge as rector. The keys of the chapels were in like manner delivered, and then handed by Dix to the sextons. He unlocked the church door, and we marched back to the robing-room, feeling that we had done something rather striking and effective. The curious crowd that gathered on the sidewalk of Broadway outside the church railings to inspect this mystical process probably supposed we were testing some new patent impregnable anti-burglarious lock. I never witnessed a "livery of seisin" before and gladly keep up any old ceremonial usage, however antiquated and unnecessary. This witnessed our connection with churchmen of 1697, and through them with ages longer past, and so rather impressed me. Dix's election seems pretty generally approved. . . .

California sends $30,000 more to the Sanitary Commission!!!

The war languishes. We are slowly invading Virginia, but there is nothing decisive or vigorous done there or elsewhere. I've a dim foreboding of a coming time when we shall think of the war not as "languishing" and too slow to satisfy our appetite for excitement, but as a terrible, crushing, personal calamity to every one of us; when there shall be no more long trains of carriages all along Fifth Avenue bound for Central Park, when the wives and daughters of contractors shall cease to crowd Stewart's and Tiffany's, and when I shall put no burgundy on my supper table. Much of the moral guilt of this terrible, murderous convulsion lies at our doors. South Carolina would never have dared to secede but for our toadyism, our disposition to uphold and justify the wickedness of Southern institutions. The logic of history requires that we suffer for our sins far more than we yet have suffered. "Without the shedding of blood there is no remission of sins." It is impossible this great struggle can pass without our feeling it more than we have yet felt it. It is inevitable, but in what particular way we shall be visited I cannot foresee.

November 23, SUNDAY. . . . Went to Washington last Monday morning by the seven A.M. train. Bellows, Van Buren, Gibbs, Professor Bache, Binney, and C. J. Stillé were fellow travellers. Dreary, dingy, wet day. No incidents. Got an ill-ventilated, dark, unwholesome room at Willard's Hotel and then went to work and kept at it till Friday night, when we adjourned. A satisfactory and diligent session. I spent all my time between the hotel and the Sanitary Commission office, 244 F Street, except one evening, Thursday, at the Surgeon-General's, where was a little gathering of gentlemen of the Medical Staff and Sanitary Commissioners. Talked with Abbot, Vollum, Gouley, and others, and had a pleasant time enough. Our meetings from ten to two and seven to eleven were most interesting. The reports of inspectors, and so on, submitted and in part read, would make three or four octavo volumes of most valuable information about the progress of the war. Bishop Clark and Judge Skinner of Chicago were absent; Binney present, a most loyal and useful addition to our number. There were also Mr. C. J. Stillé of Philadelphia and Mr. J. Huntington Wolcott of Boston, representing our associates.

Cincinnati sent us two associates, Mr. S. J. Broadwell and Judge or General Bates, to represent the quasi-secession claims of the Cincinnati branch. They favored us with much vehement talk about the relations of East and West and of the Commission and its branches as regarded from an attorney's point of view, but we voted them down unanimously and resolved that the Commission is central, federal, national, and must and will control the action of state organizations calling themselves branches of the Commission. These gentlemen were fluent in talk. They had supposed themselves our equals, but find that they are expected to be mere "hewers of wood," and so on; that is, expected to conform to a general system in the distribution of hospital and other supplies. Had much talk with them, and found them fair but false, governed, perhaps unconsciously, by jealousy of the East. Their principal pretext is the theory that "associate members" of the Commission are full members of the Commission, which mistake may lead to a disastrous schism of the Sanitary church into East and West. We sent a committee to confer with Halleck on the two important points of an ambulance train and independent medical transportation. They had an hour's talk with him that confirmed the impression we received last September that he is second-rate and commonplace. Probably Meigs is the strongest man in the service. Would that he or F. L. Olmsted were Secretary of War! I believe that Olmsted's sense, energy, and organizing faculty, earnestness, and honesty would give new life to the Administration were he in it.

December 2. A long session of the College Law School Committee at Mr. Ruggles's office, conferring with Professor Dwight. That school continues to prosper. It numbers now 135 students and outnumbers the long-established schools of Harvard and Yale. It has been wisely left during its infancy a loose, flexible, undefined, cartilaginous organism, but it is growing to be a big baby and needs phosphate of lime in its bones— a system, that is, and a more formalized existence. Dwight is its vital principle, and we are feeling our way with his counsel toward a scheme of regulations. It would be a delicate and troublesome undertaking were Dwight not the most candid, honest and disinterested of men, a lover of science rather than a lover of self; for the infusion of system into the school will to some extent diminish his prominence and his income both. . . .

Trustees of Columbia College met yesterday afternoon at the Law School, Lafayette Place. Morgan Dix nominated to fill Berrian's place. I resigned off the Standing Committee, Edward Jones having returned from Europe, and nominated him as my successor. There was a good deal of talk about an application for a little money from a Christian Association of undergraduates, but no definite action. For my part, I dislike to see young boys setting up as teachers and "leading in prayer." I don't want to see a line drawn through our undergraduate corps clearly separating saints and sinners. It tends to make the saints pharisees and the sinners reprobate.

At Wolcott Gibbs's last night talking over the scheme of a proposed club to be called the Loyalist or National, or some such thing. Such an organization might make itself most strongly felt. Would I had the time to work at its devising and building and launching, but I haven't.

December 8. Thermometer stood at eight degrees this morning. Columbia College trustees met this afternoon. Morgan Dix unanimously elected to fill Berrian's place. We gave Lieber leave of absence for a month, the Secretary of War and General Halleck having telegraphed him to come to Washington at once. They must want him to advise as a historical expert, either on military usages as to retaliation and other like questions, or on some point of difference with foreign powers.

December 11, THURSDAY. The crisis seems to have come at last. Burnside[10] commenced throwing his pontoons across the Rappahannock at day-light, and being met by a fusillade from the houses of Fredericksburg, opened on that unhappy town with 143 guns from our side of the river. Fredericksburg *fuit*. Meantime, Franklin was effecting a passage some three miles farther down, and gunboats were shelling the rebel right still lower. There the newspaper telegrams of this afternoon stop. We have no news later than noon or thereabouts. This indicates that we have gained no splendid or decisive success. It is consistent with our repulse, with a fall-back by the rebels to a new line, or with the completion of arrangements preliminary to a great battle. We shall see. God help us. I have little faith in the men to whom our destinies seem confided. . . .

Grand meeting got up by our faithful auxiliaries of the "Women's Central Relief Association" to stimulate the contribution of material sup-plies from this city. Mayor Opdyke presided. Our $25,000 worth of pig silver from Storey Co., Nevada (!) was duly displayed; a great row of ponderous, massive, 250-pound chunks of pure metal. Not quite pure, however, for they contain a considerable percentage of gold. It was a splendid symbol of the national feeling that reigns in San Francisco, Stockton, Yubaville, Copperopolis, Volcano, and other places, new to geo-graphical science. Would that Cincinnati were half as loyal! I was on the platform with all the nobs from Minturn and Aspinwall and Dr. Mott and General Anderson down to—well, no matter—down to myself. Bellows made the main speech of the evening, expounding the purposes and methods of the Commission, its relations to government on one side and the popu-lar effort to aid the army on the other. He was clear, compact, and forcible; kept the large audience wide awake for about an hour and a quarter, and was briefly followed by Dr. Adams, Dr. Vinton, and Dr. Hitchcock, who were severally more ambitious and less effective. Dr. Bellows has a most remarkable faculty of lucid, fluent, easy colloquial speech and sympathetic manner, with an intensely telling point every now and then, made without apparent effort. A most enviable gift! The meeting was fuller and went off better than I expected.

Last Tuesday night at Bellows's, Sanitary Executive Committee meet-ing. Another, as usual, yesterday afternoon at No. 823 Broadway, when we

[10] By an order delivered November 7, McClellan was relieved from command of the Army of the Potomac, and Ambrose E. Burnside was appointed in his stead. Burn-side, reluctant to supersede an abler officer and conscious that he was unequal to the post, accepted largely because he did not wish the place to go to Hooker.

considered the Hon. George Hoadly's threatening letter from Cincinnati. He is of low grade—a mere philanthropic attorney—but he may be able to do great mischief. So we decided to convene a special meeting of the Commission here next week. Thereafter Osten-Sacken (of the Russian embassy)[11] and Willy Graham and Mr. Ruggles dined here and went with Ellie and Miss Rosalie to hear the *Ballo in Maschera,* at which performance I was, happily, not required to assist.

December 13. Burnside, having established himself on the right bank of the Rappahannock, seems to have engaged the rebels at nine this morning, advancing his left under General [John F.] Reynolds. The rebels meanwhile have been throwing cavalry round his right, threatening Aquia Creek and the vital umbilical cord of railway on his rear. I knew and predicted they would do it, and I would bet that there is not a gun or a regiment in position to block that old dodge of theirs, so often successful. We know nothing of the progress of the fight. I anticipate only disaster, and an addition to the catalogue of Bull Runs, Big Bethels, and so on already so large. Defeat at this point, with a broad river in our rear, is destruction. But Burnside may be only feeling the enemy.

I have been out exploring for news. There was a bogus extra, but I can get no later intelligence, and dread its arrival. Want of discipline in the army is our great danger, and that is due to want of virility in those who should enforce it—the ultimate cause being the weakness of the President himself. At all our battles, nearly one man out of three has shirked and straggled, and not one man has been shot down by his commanding officer.

Olmsted tells me he called on the President the other evening to introduce some ladies (members of his recent "Honorable Convention" from relief societies all over the country), and Abe Lincoln expatiated on this terrible evil. "Order the army to march to any place!" said Abe Lincoln. "Why it's jes' like *shovellin' fleas.* Hee-yah, ya-hah!" Whereupon one of the ladies timidly asked, "Why don't you order stragglers to be *shot,* sir?" and the query not being immediately answered, was repeated. Olmsted says the presidential guffaw died away and the President collapsed and wilted down into an embodiment of everything weak, irresolute, perplexed, and annoyed, and he said, "Oh, I ca-an't do *that,* you know." It's an army of lions we have, with a sheep for commander-in-chief. O for a day of the late Andrew Jackson!

Other columns are supposed to be cooperating with Burnside's; Sigel's in the direction of Gordonsville, and [John G.] Foster's toward Weldon,

[11] The Baron Osten-Sacken was first secretary of the Russian legation.

or perhaps Richmond itself. His "Army of the Blackwater" is said to be 40,000 strong. There may be good military reasons for this division and separation of our forces. I hope so.

At the Sanitary Commission rooms this afternoon we had Olmsted and Newberry added unto us. We are doing business on a large scale, and must come to the end of our means before many months, unless another California turn up. . . .

Old Gurowski's *Diary*[12] makes some impression on me, due probably, to the intensity of conviction with which he writes, for he records no new facts and no original thoughts. His English is obscure, and his temper, taste, and moral tone are bad. As to his English, want of facility in using that apparatus is quite pardonable in a foreigner, and his temper and taste, however vile, are part of himself. He is an acclimated and naturalized wild-boar from Slavonia, in which region the breed is not yet extinct, and he thinks, writes, and talks like a vigorous Muscovite or Polack porker of the male gender, which he is. He is, moreover, the Thersites of our camps and councils, denouncing and decrying every chief and every measure, but I fear his denunciations are justified, and that Lincoln, Stanton, Seward, McClellan, and all the rest are unequal to their work. God grant Burnside may be an exception.

December 14, SUNDAY. I think the fate of the nation will be decided before night. The morning papers report a general engagement that lasted all yesterday, with no result but a little advance by part of our line, and heavy loss apparently on both sides. Taken together, the little scraps of fact and incident and humor that have come over the wires look unpromising but they might be much worse.

December 15. Sultry weather. Nothing definite from the Rappahannock. There was only skirmishing yesterday. Saturday's business seems to have been on a large scale and not successful. Peace Democrats and McClellanites call it a repulse and say that our main body was engaged. We have reports today that Banks, after showing his fleet south of Hatteras, turned short around and has disembarked at Norfolk. . . .

Poor Bayard, killed last Saturday, was to have been married next Wednesday to a pretty girl of seventeen, daughter of the commandant at West Point.[13] Her trousseau was all ready, and Miss Bessy Fish was to

---

[12] Count Adam Gurowski, the Polish bear, perpetrated three volumes of an abusive diary 1862–1866.

[13] Brigadier-General George D. Bayard, who had taken a gallant part in Virginia operations, was killed at Fredericksburg.

have gone up the river on special service as bridesmaid. Such details help one to appreciate the depth of meaning embodied in the words battle, war, rebellion. Ought we to leave among us men who sympathize with those who have brought these tragedies into our peaceful homes? . . . There is poor Joe Curtis, too, George William and Burrill Curtis's brother, who rose by merit, step by step, from the ranks of the First Rhode Island to its lieutenant-colonelcy.

December 17. Burnside recrossed the Rappahannock, unmolested, Monday night. The operation seems to have been skilfully performed and was ticklish work. Secesh might have smitten us fearfully during its progress. But it is a cognovit. Burnside pleads guilty to failure and repulse. This news, arriving yesterday afternoon, has produced serious depression and discouragement. The battle of Fredericksburg was a defeat with heavy loss, damaging to the national cause. And Banks has not landed anywhere in North Carolina. We are now sure his force is diverted from the vital centre of contest and destined for the extremities—for Florida, Mobile, or Texas. This looks like bad economy of our strength.

The Sanitary Commission sat yesterday morning at No. 823 [Broadway]. Bellows, Professor Bache, Olmsted, Agnew, Gibbs, Van Buren, Binney, Judge Hare, Stillé, dined here yesterday, and Dr. Howe came in *pendente symposis.* It was a satisfactory evening. This morning we resumed our session and adjourned at three o'clock. Our special business has been the Cincinnati imbroglio. We settled this by a reference with power to a committee of heads of western branches. Perhaps our best course, but it will cost our treasury just $50,000 and will not stop the mouths of the Hon. George Hoadly & Co.[14] We had much debate also about the relative authority of the Commission (or Executive Committee when the Commission is not sitting) and our executive officer, F. L. Olmsted, to wit. Were he not among the truest, purest, and best of men, we should be in irreconcilable conflict. His convictions as to the power an executive officer ought to wield and his faculty of logical demonstration that the Commission ought to confide everything to its general secretary on general principles, would make a crushing rupture inevitable, were we not all working in a common cause and without personal considerations.

[14] Judge George Hoadly (1826–1902), a protégé of Chase's who was destined to be a notable reform governor of Ohio, was the chief figure in the Cincinnati branch of the Sanitary Commission.

1863

The great turning point of the war was now being reached. On the eastern and western fronts alike the conflict was at its crisis. Lee's army, elated by its smashing victory at Chancellorsville, reached a strength by June 1 of more than 76,000 men and 272 guns. It confronted Hooker's discouraged army of about 105,000 effective men. In Mississippi, meanwhile, Grant by his bold movement to the rear of Vicksburg had shut Pemberton's force of about 30,000 men into that river city; while Joseph E. Johnston, with less than 25,000 men at Canton, was unable to strike at Grant's force of 75,000. Unless the Southern command moved with speed and skill, Vicksburg would soon be lost and the Mississippi throughout its whole length held by the North, shutting off Texas and its valuable food supplies. Some high Confederate officers, including Beauregard and Longstreet, proposed to transfer heavy reinforcements from Lee's army to Tennessee, build up Bragg's command at Murfreesboro to overwhelming strength, crush Rosecrans, and march against Louisville and Cincinnati. This, they said, offered the best hope of drawing Grant off from Vicksburg. But President Davis, anxious to bring about foreign intervention, thought that a victory on Northern soil might achieve this object. Lee, too, preferred operations in the eastern theatre. Ever since the Antietam campaign, the great Confederate leader had believed that another bold strike north of the Potomac might succeed. An invasion of Maryland and Pennsylvania was therefore determined upon; on June 15 the first Confederate troops crossed the Potomac; and by June 25 the whole army was on or over that river and ready to advance on Harrisburg. Hooker followed, keeping between Lee and Washington. Then came the news of George G. Meade's promotion.

June 29, MONDAY. The hardly credible news that Hooker is relieved and General Meade is in command!!! A change of generals when a great decisive battle seems all but actually begun, and may well be delivered before the new commander is comfortably settled in his saddle! God help us! . . .

People far better pleased with the change of commanders than I expected to find them. Clitz, dining with Henry Fearing at West Point yesterday and, of course, knowing nothing of this change, said that Meade was sure to come out "at the top of the pile" before the war was over.

June 30. Made my way to Union League Club at nine . . . to keep an appointment for consultation over the proposed periodical, and half a dozen of us adjourned to one of the committee rooms. But it was hot and smelt of fresh paint, and I was faint and sweaty and three-quarters sick, and the effort to follow Olmsted's clear, compact, well-considered statement of plans and probabilities made me desperate and fidgety *"comme un Diable dans un bénitier,"* so I excused myself.

July 1. At the Union League Club tonight I found a large assemblage; also, sundry telegrams confirming what the newspapers tell us, that Meade is advancing and that Lee has paused and is calling in his scattered columns and concentrating either for battle or for a retreat with his wagon loads of plunder. Harrisburg breathes more freely, and the Pennsylvania militia is mustering in considerable (numerical) force. Much good they would do, to be sure, in combat with Lee's desperadoes, cunning sharp-shooters, and stark, hard-riding moss-troopers.

July 3. Half-past nine of a muggy morning. We can scarcely fail to have most weighty news before night.

There was a battle at or near Gettysburg on the first, resulting apparently in our favor. We lost a valuable officer in General Reynolds.[1] Fight probably renewed yesterday, but no information on that point. There are no official reports; an unpleasant indication, but the government has maintained the most resolute silence as to all army movements during this campaign. . . .

Evening. No definite news at all. We were told by the bulletin boards at noon that Vicksburg had surrendered, and I believed the story till about one in the afternoon, when it turned out not entirely authentic. Never mind. Do not the *Times, Tribune, Post* and *Commercial* daily certify that the "fall" of Vicksburg is "only a question of time," as distinguished from one of eternity?

[1] Major-General John F. Reynolds, a Pennsylvanian by birth and a graduate of West Point, had been considered by Lincoln for the chief command of the Army of the Potomac. He might have been chosen in Meade's place but that he demanded wide guarantees of freedom of action. He was killed on the first day of Gettysburg as he was leading Wisconsin troops into battle.

July 4, SATURDAY. A cloudy, muggy, sultry Fourth. Awake nearly all last night, tormented by headache and wakened out of each successive cat-nap by pyrotechnic racket. At or soon after daylight, Calvary Church bells began clanging, and cannon firing "a national salute" in Union Square. I arose bilious, headachy, backachy, sour, and savage. Read morning papers. Their news from Meade's army was fragmentary and vague but hopeful. Spent the morning watching over Johnny and Temple, and Johnny's friend, Master Lewis French, firing off no end of crackers, little and big, "columbiads" included. What an infernal noise they make!

At half-past five appeared Walter Cutting with news from the army up to eight last night. There was fighting on the afternoon of the second, renewed yesterday, when the rebels attacked Meade's left centre in great force and were twice repulsed with severe loss. Our cavalry was operating on their flank. Both armies seem to have held their original position. *Gratias agimus Tibi.* This can hardly turn out to have been worse than a drawn battle, and that to an invading aggressive army is equivalent to defeat, as we have good reason to know. Defeat and failure in this desperate undertaking is a serious matter to the woman-floggers. . . .

It would seem that General Daniel Sickles has lost a leg. Wadsworth is wounded. Poor General Barlow (Mrs. Arabella Barlow née Griffith's husband) severely wounded again and probably a prisoner.[2]

July 5. A memorable day, even should its glorious news prove but half true. Tidings from Gettysburg have been arriving in fragmentary instalments, but with a steady crescendo toward complete, overwhelming victory. If we can believe what we hear, Lee is smitten hip and thigh, and his invincible "Army of Northern Virginia" shattered and destroyed. But I am skeptical, especially as to news of victory, and expect to find large deductions from our alleged success in tomorrow morning's newspapers. There has been a great battle in which we are, on the whole, victorious. The woman-floggers are badly repulsed and retreating, with more or less loss of prisoners, guns, and matériel. So much seems certain, and that is enough to thank God for most devoutly, far better than we dared hope a week ago. This may have been one of the great decisive battles of history.

It has been a day of quiet rain. Ellie went to Trinity Church with the

[2] Major-General Daniel E. Sickles, who had offended Meade by taking an excessively advanced position, lost his right leg at Gettysburg; James S. Wadsworth, fighting most creditably as division commander, was little hurt and survived to be slain at The Wilderness. Brigadier-General Francis C. Barlow was shot through the body, left for dead on the field, rescued by the Confederate General John B. Gordon, and restored to the Union forces. He was out of the war for nearly a year.

children. I stayed at home, read, and lay in wait for extras. An extra *Herald* came at noon, another an hour or two later. Both encouraging. At six P.M. appeared Dr. Bellows with a telegram from Olmsted at Philadelphia as follows, to wit: "Private advices tend to confirm report of capture of over fifteen thousand prisoners and one hundred guns. Lee retreating. [Alfred] Pleasanton holds Potomac fords." Olmsted is wary, shrewd, and never sanguine. This despatch was not sent without strong evidence to support it. I carried it down at once to Union League Club and saw it posted on our bulletin board to the intense delectation of a half-dozen people who were hanging about the premises hungering for news.

Mr. Ruggles came in to tea. Afterwards appeared one Hill, of Davenport, Iowa, an ally of Mr. Ruggles in his great ship-canal campaign, and a very intelligent, cultivated person, with no perceptible westernism; also Dr. Peters and Walter Cutting.

At suppertime, ten P.M., a *Tribune* extra. News of victory continued. "Prisoners and guns taken"; x plus y prisoners arrived at Baltimore and "acres of cars" laden with prisoners blocked on the railroad. Lee retreating toward Williamsport. Official despatch from General [William H.] French to General Halleck announcing capture of pontoon train at Williamsport. Significant. The Potomac fords are full just now. Just suppose Meade should bag Lee and his horde of traitors as Burgoyne and Cornwallis were bagged near a century ago. Imagine it! But there is no such luck now.

At half-past eleven, in rushed the exuberant Colonel Frank Howe with a budget of telegrams. Lee utterly routed and disorganized, with loss of thirty thousand prisoners (!) and all his artillery. Details of capture of three or four blockade-running Britishers at Mobile and Charleston I omit as comparatively uninteresting. Now to bed and then for the morning papers. We may be fearfully disillusionated even yet.

July 6. Mugginess continues. Morning papers give us little additional light, if any. Evening papers do. I regret to see no official statement of guns captured. But an extra *Herald* despatch dated at noon today gives us a splendidly colored picture of Lee's retreat and tells how teamsters and artillery men are cutting their traces and riding off for life on their draft-mules; how even [D. N.] Couch's militia regiments are following up the defeated army and bagging whole brigades; and how there is general panic, rout, and *sauve qui peut*. All of which is pleasant to read, but probably fictitious. So is a telegram, no doubt, that I find at Union League Club tonight: "All Lee's artillery captured and thirty thousand prisoners." I take it Lee is badly whipped, but will get across the Potomac with the bulk of his army more or less demoralized. . . .

The results of this victory are priceless. Philadelphia, Baltimore, and Washington are safe. Defeat would have seriously injured all three. The rebels are hunted out of the North, their best army is routed, and the charm of Robert Lee's invincibility broken. The Army of the Potomac has at last found a general that can handle it, and it has stood nobly up to its terrible work in spite of its long disheartening list of hard-fought failures, and in spite of the McClellan influence on its officers.

Government is strengthened four-fold at home and abroad. Gold one hundred and thirty-eight today, and government securities rising. Copperheads are palsied and dumb for the moment at least. S. L. M. Barlow & Co., who are making a catspaw of poor, confiding McClellan and using his unaccountable popularity to stir up disaffection, have lost half their power of mischief. People will soon be cackling, gabbling and gobbling and braying about "George G." as they have been about "George B." George B. is brave, honest, and true, but he has no eye for men, no insight into human character. So he has unconsciously allowed his old friends of days before the war (a long time ago) to use him for their own ends. And as they happen to be Breckinridge Democrats—Constitutional Conservatives—sympathizers and Dirt-Eaters, they have so played him off against the government that he has been for six months past well worth any two rebel generals to the rebel cause. But even their impudence can hardly clamor for his restoration to chief command of the army of Gettysburg. (N.B. I might not object to see him in Halleck's shoes.)

People downtown very jolly today. "This ends the Rebellion." So I was told a dozen times. My cheerful and agreeable but deluded friends, there must be battles by the score before that outbreak from the depths of original sin is "ended." But there does seem to be some kind of obscure Union movement in benighted old North Carolina. Wiseacres profess to know all about it. "Highest authority," "not at liberty to state," and so on, "but I knew it was all arranged with the government through General Foster a week ago" that if General Lee were well licked, North Carolina would secede at once and return to her anxious and heartbroken family. I am not sure I like the prospect. The Returning Prodigal will be represented by a batch of Congressmen swaggering through the corridors of the Capitol with pockets full of revolvers and mouths full of brag and tobacco, ready to play the old Southern game over again. They will fall on their kind old Uncle Sam's neck, of course, and do their best to break it the first time their chivalric sensibilities are stimulated into action, and Uncle Sam will kill the fatted calf and appoint these magnanimous beings Cabinet officers and chairmen of committees on the army. I trust he may not mistake himself for the fatted animal in the pardonable extravagance of his generosity, and so commit national suicide.

The battle of Gettysburg had ended on July 3, when Pickett's charge against Cemetery Ridge broke down with fearful slaughter. Lee expected a counterattack by the Union forces, but it did not come; and after a quiet Fourth, his army that evening began its retreat "under the cover of the night and the heavy rain." Lincoln on the morning of the Fourth had heralded the triumph to the Northern people: "The President announces to the country that news from the Army of the Potomac, up to ten P.M. of the third, is such as to cover that army with the highest honor, to promise a great success to the cause of the Union, and to claim the condolence of all for the many gallant fallen, and that for this he especially desires that on this day He whose will, not ours, should ever be done, be everywhere remembered and reverenced with profoundest gratitude." The Fourth was further signalized by the surrender of Vicksburg. In Pennsylvania Lincoln hoped for a close and destructive pursuit of the fleeing Confederates. He urged Halleck to see that Meade completed his work "by the literal or substantial destruction of Lee's army," when "the rebellion will be over." Halleck, thus firmly and repeatedly prompted by the President, telegraphed Meade to "push forward and fight Lee before he can cross the Potomac." But at the same time he sent despatches of his own informing the general that these directions were "suggestions only," and not orders, and that he was to follow his own judgment. And when Meade, who might have attacked with great effect if not with complete success on July 12 or 13, called a council of his corps commanders, five out of seven advised against a new battle. The result was that on the afternoon of the 14th news came that Lee had brought his whole army intact across the Potomac and was safe. Lincoln's chagrin was intense. He later declared: "Our army held the war in the hollow of their hand, and would not close it." He wrote Meade of his profound disappointment that "your golden opportunity is gone." Strong's diary shows how keenly men of his outlook sympathized with the President's view.

Strong's failure to say anything in particular about Vicksburg also indicates how completely the eastern battle held possession of the minds of New Yorkers.

On the afternoon of July 3, Grant, whose line had steadily closed about the besieged city, and who was ready to begin an assault that the Confederates knew they could never withstand, held a conference with Pemberton, and that evening sent the Confederate general his terms of capitulation. On the morning of the Fourth he was able to telegraph Lincoln: "The enemy surrendered this morning. The only terms allowed is their parole as prisoners of war." Thus closed what was perhaps the most brilliant single campaign of the war. With a loss of fewer than ten thousand men, Grant had inflicted casualties exceeding that number on the Confederates, had captured nearly thirty thousand men and about one hundred and seventy cannon, and had made it possible to seal up the Mississippi River and thus cut the Confederacy in two. Lincoln was soon writing in his famous letter to Conkling: "The Father of Waters again goes unvexed to the sea."

But while these great events were occurring, the city of New York was about to endure the most shameful disorders of her entire history. A Conscription Act had been signed on March 3, 1863, and was now to be put into effect in the metropolis.

July 11, SATURDAY.   The Commission has spent near twenty thousand dollars this week and received as much. It is doing an immense business around Gettysburg. Olmsted reports our losses there inside seven thousand and Bellows twenty thousand!!!

From negative evidence it appears that Lee's retreat was no rout. He shews a firm front at Williamsport and Hagerstown, seeking to recross the Potomac now in high freshet. Meade is at his heels, and another great battle is expected. Olmsted thinks it will be more severe than the last.

I observe that the Richmond papers are in an orgasm of brag and bluster and bloodthirstiness beyond all historical precedent even in their chivalric columns. That's an encouraging sign. Another is the unusual number of stragglers and deserters from Lee's army. Rebel generals, even when defeated, have heretofore kept their men well in hand.

July 12. Despatches in morning papers, though severally worthless, give one the impression when taken collectively that Lee is getting safely across the Potomac and back to Old Virginny's shore, bag and baggage, guns, plunder and all. Whereupon the able editors begin to denounce Meade, their last new Napoleon, as incapable and outgeneralled. . . . People forget that an army of fifty thousand and upward cannot be bagged bodily unless its general be a Mack or a Dupont. But I shall be disappointed if the rebels get home without a clawing.

Draft has begun here and was in progress in Boston last week. *Demos* takes it good-naturedly thus far, but we shall have trouble before we are through. The critical time will be when defaulting conscripts are haled out of their houses, as many will be. That soulless politician, Seymour, will make mischief if he dare. So will F'nandy Wood, Brooks, Marble, and other reptiles. May they only bring their traitorous necks within the cincture of a legal halter! This draft will be the *experimentum crucis* to decide whether we have a government among us.

The drawing of the names of conscripts under the Draft Act had commenced in New York City on the morning of Saturday, July 11. At first the people seemed to take the draft quietly and good-naturedly; no disturbances occurred on the initial day. But on Sunday the names of the men selected were published in the press; and in thousands of homes the meaning of compulsory service was at last fully appreciated. The foreign-born population of the city, especially heavy in the Ninth Congressional District, felt that it had powerful reasons for discontent. For one, most of the foreign-born were Democrats, and they had been assured by Democratic newspapers and politicians that the acts of the Lincoln Administration were highhanded, oppressive, and even unconstitutional. For another, the provision by which well-to-do men could hire substitutes for $300 seemed unjust to the poor. For a third, the Irish and other day-laborers had felt keenly the competition of Negro freedmen now flocking up from the South, and many of them were filled with hatred of the blacks. The hardships imposed by the fast-rising cost of living contributed to the general irritation. When Monday the 13th dawned, it was evident that large groups of the metropolitan population were on the verge of armed resistance to the draft; a mob soon gathered before the draft headquarters at Third Avenue and Forty-sixth Street; and before noon a fierce attack upon this building began. Many factory-workers and employees of the street railroads joined the concourse. Fires were set, flame and smoke enveloped the block, and when first the provost-marshal's guard and then a detachment of police appeared, the mob overwhelmed them and drove them to flight. That afternoon the disorders grew, until a great *part of the upper East Side was in the hands of men inflamed by drink and passion. Negroes were attacked wherever found, and toward evening, as Strong records, the Colored Orphan Asylum on Fifth Avenue just above Forty-third Street was sacked and set on fire.*

July 13, MONDAY. A notable day. Stopped at the Sanitary Commission office on my way downtown to endorse a lot of checks that had accumulated during my absence, and heard there of rioting in the upper part of the city. As Charley is at Newport and Bidwell in Berkshire County, I went to Wall Street nevertheless; but the rumors grew more and more unpleasant, so I left it at once and took a Third Avenue car for uptown. At the Park were groups and small crowds in more or less excitement (which found relief afterwards, I hear, in hunting down and maltreating sundry unoffending niggers), but there was nothing to indicate serious trouble. The crowded car went slowly on its way, with its perspiring passengers, for the weather was still of this deadly muggy sort with a muddy sky and lifeless air. At Thirteenth Street the track was blocked by a long line of stationary cars that stretched indefinitely up the Avenue, and I took to the sidewalk. Above Twentieth Street all shops were closed, and many people standing and staring or strolling uptown, not riotously disposed but eager and curious. Here and there a rough could be heard damning the draft. No policemen to be seen anywhere. Reached the seat of war at last, Forty-sixth Street and Third Avenue. Three houses on the Avenue and two or three on the street were burned down: engines playing on the ruins—more energetically, I'm told, than they did when their efforts would have been useful.

The crowd seemed just what one commonly sees at any fire, but its nucleus of riot was concealed by an outside layer of ordinary peaceable lookers-on. Was told they had beat off a squad of police and another of "regulars" (probably the Twelfth Militia). At last, it opened and out streamed a posse of perhaps five hundred, certainly less than one thousand, of the lowest Irish day laborers. The rabble was perfectly homogeneous. Every brute in the drove was pure Celtic—hod-carrier or loafer. They were unarmed. A few carried pieces of fence-paling and the like. They turned off west into Forty-fifth Street and gradually collected in front of two three-story dwelling houses on Lexington Avenue, just below that street, that stand alone together on a nearly vacant block. Nobody could tell why these houses were singled out. Some said a drafting officer lived in one of them, others that a damaged policeman had taken refuge there. The mob was in no hurry; they had no need to be; there was no one to molest them or make them afraid. The beastly ruffians were masters of the situation and of the city. After a while sporadic paving-stones began to fly at the windows, ladies and children emerged from the rear and had a rather hard scramble over a high board fence, and then scudded off across the open, Heaven knows whither. Then men and small boys appeared at rear windows and began smashing the sashes and the blinds and shied out light articles, such as books and crockery, and dropped chairs and mirrors into the back yard; the rear fence was demolished and loafers were seen marching off with portable articles of furniture. And at last a light smoke began to float out of the windows and I came away. I could endure the disgraceful, sickening sight no longer, and what could I *do*?

The fury of the low Irish women in that region was noteworthy. Stalwart young vixens and withered old hags were swarming everywhere, all cursing the "bloody draft" and egging on their men to mischief.

Omnibussed down to No. 823, where is news that the Colored Half Orphan Asylum on Fifth Avenue, just above the reservoir, is burned. "*Tribune* office to be burned tonight." Railroad rails torn up, telegraph wires cut, and so on. If a quarter one hears be true, this is an organized insurrection in the interest of the rebellion and Jefferson Davis rules New York today.

Attended to business. Then with Wolcott Gibbs to dinner at Maison Dorée. During our symposium, there was an alarm of a coming mob, and we went to the window to see. The "mob" was moving down Fourteenth Street and consisted of just thirty-four lousy, blackguardly Irishmen with a tail of small boys. Whither they went, I cannot say, nor can I guess what mischief the handful of *canaille* chose to do. A dozen policemen would have been more than a match for the whole crew, but there were no policemen in sight.

Walked uptown with Wolcott Gibbs. Large fire on Broadway and Twenty-eighth Street. Signs of another to the east, said to be on Second Avenue. Stopped awhile at Gibbs's in Twenty-ninth Street, where was madame, frightened nearly to death, and then to St. Nicholas Hotel to see the mayor and General Wool. We found a lot of people with them. There were John Jay and George W. Blunt and Colonel Howe and John Austin Stevens, Jr., all urging strong measures. But the substantial and weighty and influential men were not represented; out of town, I suppose.

Their absence emboldened Gibbs and myself to make pressure for instant action, but it was vain. We begged that martial law might be declared. Opdyke said that was Wool's business, and Wool said it was Opdyke's, and neither would act. "Then, Mr. Mayor, issue a proclamation calling on all loyal and law-abiding citizens to enroll themselves as a volunteer force for defense of life and property." "Why," quoth Opdyke, "that is *civil war* at once." Long talk with Colonel Cram, Wool's chief of staff, who professes to believe that everything is as it should be and sufficient force on the ground to prevent further mischief. Don't believe it. Neither Opdyke nor General Wool is nearly equal to this crisis. Came off disgusted. Went to Union League Club awhile. No comfort there. Much talk, but no one ready to do anything whatever, not even to telegraph to Washington.

We telegraphed, two or three of us, from General Wool's rooms, to the President, begging that troops be sent on and stringent measures taken. The great misfortune is that nearly all our militia regiments have been despatched to Pennsylvania. All the military force I have seen or heard of today were in Fifth Avenue at about seven P.M. There were two or three feeble companies of infantry, a couple of howitzers, and a squadron or two of unhappy-looking "dragoons."

These wretched rioters have been plundering freely, I hear. Their outbreak will either destroy the city or damage the Copperhead cause fatally. Could we but catch the scoundrels who have stirred them up, what a blessing it would be! God knows what tonight or tomorrow may bring forth. We may be thankful that it is now (quarter past twelve) raining briskly. Mobs have no taste for the effusion of cold water. I'm thankful, moreover, that Ellie and the children are out of town. I sent Johnny off to Cornwall this afternoon in charge of John the waiter.

July 14. Eleven P.M. Fire bells clanking, as they have clanked at intervals through the evening. Plenty of rumors throughout the day and evening, but nothing very precise or authentic. There have been sundry collisions between the rabble and the authorities, civil and military. Mob fired upon. It generally runs, but on one occasion appears to have rallied, charged the police and militia, and forced them back in disorder. The people are waking up, and by tomorrow there will be adequate organization to protect property and life. Many details come in of yesterday's brutal, cowardly ruffianism and plunder. Shops were cleaned out and a black man hanged in Carmine Street, for no offence but that of Nigritude. Opdyke's house again attacked this morning by a roaming handful of

Irish blackguards. Two or three gentlemen who chanced to be passing saved it from sack by a vigorous charge and dispersed the popular uprising (as the *Herald*, *World*, and *News* call it), with their walking sticks and their fists.

Walked uptown perforce, for no cars and few omnibi were running. They are suppressed by threats of burning railroad and omnibus stables, the drivers being wanted to reinforce the mob. Tiffany's shop, Ball & Black's, and a few other Broadway establishments are closed. (Here I am interrupted by report of a fire near at hand, and a great glare on the houses across the Park. Sally forth, and find the Eighteenth Ward station house, Twenty-second Street, near First Avenue, in full blaze. A splendid blaze it made, but I did not venture below Second Avenue, finding myself in a crowd of Celtic spectators disgorged by the circumjacent tenement houses. They were exulting over the damage to "them bloody police," and so on. I thought discretion the better part of curiosity. Distance lent enchantment to that view.)

At 823 with Bellows four to six; then home. At eight to Union League Club. Rumor it's to be attacked tonight. Some say there is to be great mischief tonight and that the rabble is getting the upper hand. Home at ten and sent for by Dudley Field, Jr., to confer about an expected attack on his house and his father's, which adjoin each other in this street just below Lexington Avenue. He has a party there with muskets and talks of fearful trouble before morning, but he is always a blower and a very poor devil. Fire bells again at twelve-fifteen. No light of conflagration is visible.

Bellows's report from Gettysburg and from Meade's headquarters very interesting. Thinks highly of Meade. Thinks the battle around Williamsport will be tolerably evenly matched, Lee having been decidedly beaten a week ago, but not at all demoralized. But there's a despatch at the Union League Club tonight that Lee has moved his whole army safely across, except his rear guard, which we captured.

A good deal of yelling to the eastward just now. The Fields and their near neighbour, Colonel Frank Howe, are as likely to be attacked by this traitor-guided mob as any people I know. If they *are*, we shall see trouble in this quarter, and Gramercy Park will acquire historical associations. O, how tired I am! But I feel reluctant to go to bed. I believe I dozed off a minute or two. There came something like two reports of artillery, perhaps only falling walls. There go two jolly Celts along the street, singing a genuine Celtic howl, something about "Tim O'Laggerty," with a refrain of pure Erse. Long live the sovereigns of New York, Brian Boroo *redivivus* and multiplied. Paddy has left his Egypt—Connaught—and reigns in this promised land of milk and honey and perfect freedom. Hurrah, there goes a strong squad of police marching eastward down this street, followed by a company of infantry with gleaming bayonets. One A.M. Fire bells again, southeastward, "Swinging slow with sullen roar." Now they are silent, and I shall go to bed, at least for a season.

July 15. Wednesday begins with heavy showers, and now (ten A.M.) cloudy, hot, and steaming. Morning papers report nothing specially grave as occurring since midnight. But there will be much trouble today. Rabbledom is not yet dethroned any more than its ally and instigator, Rebeldom.

News from the South is consolatory. Port Hudson surrendered. Sherman said to have beaten Joseph Johnston somewhere near Vicksburg. Operations commencing against Charleston. Bragg seems to be abandoning Chattanooga and retiring on Atlanta. *Per contra*, Lee has got safely off. I thought he would. . . . Lots of talk and rumors about attacks on the New York Custom-house (*ci-devant* Merchants' Exchange) and the Treasury (late Custom-house). Went to see [John J.] Cisco and found his establishment in military occupation—sentinels pacing, windows barricaded, and so on. He was as serene and bland as the loveliest May morning ("so cool, so calm, so bright") and showed me the live shell ready to throw out of the window and the "battery" to project Assay Office oil-of-vitriol and the like. He's all right. Then called on Collector Barney and had another long talk with him. Find him well prepared with shells, grenades, muskets, and men, but a little timid and anxious, "wanting counsel," doubtful about his right to fire on the mob, and generally flaccid and tremulous—poor devil!

Walked uptown with Charley Strong and Hoppin, and after my cup of coffee, went to Union League Club. A delegation returned from police headquarters, having vainly asked for a squad of men to garrison the clubhouse. *None can be spared.* What is worse, we were badly repulsed in an attack on the mob in First Avenue, near Nineteenth Street, at about six P.M. Fired upon from houses, and had to leave sixteen wounded men and a Lieutenant Colonel Jardine in the hands of these brutes and devils. This is very bad indeed. But tonight is quieter than the last, though there seems to be a large fire downtown, and we hear occasional gun-shots.

At the club was George Biggs, full of the loudest and most emphatic jawing. "General Frémont's house and Craven's to be attacked tonight,

Croton mains to be cut, and gas works destroyed," and so on. By way of precaution, I had had the bathtubs filled, and also all the pots, kettles, and pails in the house. . . . Twelve-thirty: Light as of a large fire to the south.

July 16. Rather quiet downtown. No trustworthy accounts of riot on any large scale during the day. General talk downtown is that the trouble is over. We shall see. It will be as it pleases the scoundrels who are privily engineering the outbreak—agents of Jefferson Davis, permitted to work here in New York.

Omnibusses and railroad cars in full career again. Coming uptown tonight I find Gramercy Park in military occupation. Strong parties drawn up across Twentieth Street and Twenty-first Streets at the east end of the Square, by the G[ramercy] House, each with a flanking squad, forming an L. Occasional shots fired at them from the region of Second or First Avenue, which were replied to by volleys that seem to have done little execution. An unlucky cart-horse was knocked over, I hear. This force was relieved at seven by a company of regulars and a party of the Seventh with a couple of howitzers, and there has been but a stray shot or two since dark. The regulars do not look like steady men. I have just gone over to the hotel with John Robertson and ordered a pail of strong coffee to put a little life into them.

Never knew exasperation so intense, unqualified, and general as that which prevails against these rioters and the politic knaves who are supposed to have set them going, Governor Seymour not excepted. Men who voted for him mention the fact with contrition and self-abasement, and the Democratic Party is at a discount with all the people I meet. (Apropos of discount, gold fell to one hundred and twenty-six today, with the city in insurrection, a gunboat at the foot of Wall Street, the Custom-house and Treasury full of soldiers and live shells, and two howitzers in position to rake Nassau Street from Wall to Fulton!!!!)

Every impression that's made on our people passes away so soon, almost as if stamped on the sand of the sea-beach. Were our moods a little less fleeting, I should have great hope of permanent good from the general wrath these outrages have provoked, and should put some faith in people's prophesyings that Fernando Wood and McCunn, and the New York *Herald*, and the Brookses and others, are doomed henceforth to obscurity and contempt. But we shall forget all about it before next November. Perhaps the lesson of the last four days is to be taught us still more emphatically, and we have got to be worse before we are better. It is not clear that the resources of the conspiracy are yet exhausted. The rioters of yesterday were better armed and organized than those of Monday, and their inaction today may possibly be meant to throw us off our guard, or their time may be employed perfecting plans for a campaign of plundering and brutality in yet greater force. They are in full possession of the western and the eastern sides of the city, from Tenth Street upward, and of a good many districts beside. I could not walk four blocks eastward from this house this minute without peril. The outbreak is spreading by concerted action in many quarters. Albany, Troy, Yonkers, Hartford, Boston, and other cities have each their Irish anti-conscription Nigger-murdering mob, of the same type with ours. It is a grave business, a *jacquerie* that must be put down by heroic doses of lead and steel.

Dr. Peters and Charley Strong called at eleven P.M. They have been exploring and report things quiet except on First Avenue from Nineteenth to Thirtieth Street, where there is said to be trouble. A detachment of the Seventh Regiment, five hundred or six hundred strong, marched to that quarter from their armory an hour ago.

July 17. The Army of Gramercy Park has advanced its headquarters to Third Avenue, leaving only a picket guard in sight. Rain will keep the rabble quiet tonight. We are said to have fifteen thousand men under arms, and I incline to hope that this movement in aid of the rebellion is played out.

The draft riots, which had filled four days with tumult and terror, were indeed ended. General Wool had thrown into the city about eight hundred United States troops, drawn from the forts in the harbor, the Navy Yard, and West Point. Though Governor Horatio Seymour played a dubious part in the affair, making a speech on Tuesday the 14th from the City Hall steps which was altogether too conciliatory and pacific, he cooperated with Wool by ordering all the militia within reach (commanded by General Sandford) to turn out and help maintain order. About two thousand policemen were brought into action and behaved with energy and courage. Moreover, as Strong reports, bodies of citizens organized themselves, obtained arms from the authorities, and with the aid of returned veterans took a hand in restoring order. Pitched battles occurred in Broadway, on Forty-second Street, and along the west-side avenues uptown. A strong set of barricades in Twenty-ninth Street had to be carried by storm. Many of the mob were slain—how many no one knew, for the Evening Post

*recorded that many of the rioters were buried secretly at night, clandestine
parties carrying the bodies across the East River. Some estimates of the total
casualties on both sides ran as high as one thousand, while about $1,500,000
worth of private property was destroyed. The last sharp fighting took place near
Gramercy Park, where on the evening of Thursday, the 16th, United States
forces dealt severely with a body of rioters who were looting residences. Next day
New York was quiet; and in August the drafting of men was resumed without
difficulty.*

July 19, SUNDAY. Have been out seeking information and getting
none that is to be trusted. Colonel Frank Howe talks darkly and predicts
an outbreak on the east side of the town tonight, but that's his way. I
think this Celtic beast with many heads is driven back to his hole for the
present. When government begins enforcing the draft, we shall have
more trouble, but not till then.

Not half the history of this memorable week has been written. I
could put down pages of incidents that the newspapers have omitted, any
one of which would in ordinary times be the town's talk. Men and ladies
attacked and plundered by daylight in the streets; private houses suddenly invaded by gangs of a dozen ruffians and sacked, while the women
and children run off for their lives. Then there is the unspeakable infamy
of the nigger persecution. They are the most peaceable, sober, and in-
offensive of our poor, and the outrages they have suffered during this last
week are less excusable—are founded on worse pretext and less provocation—than St. Bartholomew's or the Jew-hunting of the Middle Ages.
This is a nice town to call itself a centre of civilization! Life and personal
property less safe than in Tipperary, and the "people" (as the *Herald*
calls them) burning orphan asylums and conducting a massacre. How
this infernal slavery system has corrupted our blood, North as well as
South! There should be terrible vengeance for these atrocities, but Mc-
Cunn, Barnard & Co. are our judges and the disgrace will rest upon us
without atonement.

I am sorry to find that England is right about the lower class of Irish.
They are brutal, base, cruel, cowards, and as insolent as base. Choate
(at the Union League Club) tells me he heard this proposition put forth
by one of their political philosophers in conversation with a knot of his
brethren last Monday: "Sure and if them dam Dutch would jine us we'd
drive the dam Yankees out of New York entirely!" These caitiffs have
a trick, I hear, of posting themselves at the window of a tenement house

with a musket, while a woman with a baby in her arms squats at their feet. Paddy fires on the police and instantly squats to reload, while Mrs. Paddy rises and looks out. Of course, one can't fire at a window where there is a woman with a child!! But how is one to deal with women who assemble around the lamp-post to which a Negro had been hanged and cut off certain parts of his body to keep as souvenirs? Have they any womanly privilege, immunity, or sanctity?

No wonder St. Patrick drove all the venomous vermin out of Ireland! Its biped mammalia supply that island its full average share of creatures that crawl and eat dirt and poison every community they infest. Vipers were superfluous. But my own theory is that St. Patrick's campaign against the snakes is a Popish delusion. They perished of biting the Irish people.

July 20. Hot. Atmosphere mucilaginous. City quiet. Nothing special to record. Dined with Agnew at Maison Dorée, and spent a little time at the Club. I see a frequent placard bearing these two words, "Sam, Organize!" It plainly means that there is a movement to revive the old Native American party with its Know-Nothing Clubs; a very natural consequence of the atrocities just perpetrated by our Irish *canaille.* Talking with Americans of the middle and laboring class, even of the lowest social grade, I find they fully appreciate and bitterly resent these Celtic outrages. But the obstacle in the way of a revived Know-Nothingism is that it would be obliged to discriminate between Celts and Teutons. The Germans have behaved well and kept quiet. Where they acted at all, they volunteered against the rabble, as they did, most effectively, in the Seventh Ward. A mere anti-Hibernian party would have no foundation on principle, would seem merely vindictive and proscriptive, and would lead to no lasting result, I fear. For myself, personally, I would like to see war made on Irish scum as in 1688.

July 21. . . . Quiet continues, though the *Express* and that yet more beastly *World* are doing all they can to instigate outbreak.

A vehement south wind all day. Morgan's raid across the Ohio has failed very badly. His whole force is captured, artillery and all, and he escapes by slinking off while negotiations for surrender are in progress. Chivalric Morgan![3]

[3] John Hunt Morgan's cavalry, exhausted by its wild course through southern Indiana and Ohio, was surrounded and largely captured, Morgan himself surrendering July 26. His raid, however, had drawn Federal troops from East Tennessee, relieved the pressure on Bragg's army, and temporarily saved that area for the Confederacy.

1864

*G*rant, by the close of May, had pushed forward to Cold Harbor near the Chickahominy River, nearly midway between Hanover Town and Richmond. He was fighting now to reach the James River below Richmond and to establish his base there, where he could easily be supplied by sea. Lee entrenched himself strongly; and on June 3 Grant made the error of attacking his lines, apparently in a final effort to destroy the Confederate army by a frontal assault. The attack broke down with bloody losses. Grant, who later admitted that it had been a costly mistake, then turned to the policy of approaching Richmond by slow operations of a siege-like character. By now it was clear that Lee was permanently on the defensive, and that Grant's steady blows would soon bring him to a critical pass. In the West, Sherman had meanwhile advanced into Georgia, driving Johnston's much weaker army before him; and on June 8 he began the hard fighting about Kenesaw Mountain which, after three weeks of battle, finally forced Johnston's withdrawal. Atlanta was being brought within reach.

When the Union-Republican Convention opened in Baltimore on June 8, Lincoln's nomination was a foregone conclusion. Prolonged cheers greeted every mention of his name. On the first ballot (June 8) he was given a unanimous vote —though twenty-two Missouri delegates temporarily supported Grant, then changed their votes. The platform called for a victorious conclusion of the war, without compromise, and for the full and final abolition of slavery by constitutional amendment. Lincoln's own choice for the vice-presidential nomination was Andrew Johnson, who also was chosen on the initial ballot. But nearly *all observers agreed that the success of the ticket would depend upon the fortunes of war during the summer of 1864. Lincoln was popular at the North, but not so popular that he could withstand crushing military defeats.*

June 9. After dinner to a session of that ancient and honorable institution the Committee on the Course of Columbia College at Rutherfurd's in Second Avenue. Bradford was there and Barnard, our new president, whom we elected trustee to fill George F. Allen's place last Monday, and whom I met for the first time. We got through with our work expeditiously. McVickar agrees to become an emeritus professor at his present rate of compensation, "which is necessary to him" (!), and Barnard will henceforth represent the Evidences of Natural and Revealed Religion to the Senior class one hour weekly. After we got through, Rutherfurd displayed his spectroscope and revealed to us the sodium line and the lithium line, and so on. It seems a fine instrument, with carefully constructed carbide of sulphur prisms. The strontium lines were gorgeous. Then I walked to Union League Club (monthly meeting) with Barnard and left him there with his friends, Van Nostrand and G. W. Blunt.

Barnard is manifestly a thoughtful, judicious, earnest, kindly man, of high principle, intense loyalty, and great practice in all educational questions. But he is *very* deaf, and his deafness will seriously interfere with his official duties; and he has no presence to help him through. I fear he will find his dealings with our insolent, unruly undergraduates painful and difficult. But they may prove well-bred and magnanimous enough to treat his infirmity with respect. If he possess great tact and win their esteem and confidence, they are likely to do so. If not, they will soon drive him out of the College, for he seems physically incapable of governing a disaffected, disorderly corps of students.

Baltimore Convention nominated Andy Johnson for Vice-President; vice Hamlin dropped. Very well. Unanimity of these nominations encouraging. But it disgusts the *World* newspaper, which condemns and denounces both Lincoln and Johnson as mere plebeians, utterly ungenteel and excessively low. The *World*'s editorial would make an effective L. & J. campaign document. I suppose a certain amount of disapproval and abuse by Marble and Hurlbut of the *World* and by such like coprophagous insects to be as honorable as the Victoria Cross or the Order of the Garter. Of course, its amount would have to be almost inconceivably large, its authors being so despicable, but these renegade Copperheads dignify and ennoble every loyal American by every epithet of indignity they apply to him.

No war news, except that the *Commercial* says Butler is about undertaking some great movement. I fear it will be a failure. Gold 197!!! People are blue. They have found out somehow that Grant will never get into Richmond after all. They may be right, but I do not see why they think so. Certain well-meaning friends of mine in Wall Street help depress public opinion and raise gold by going about bleating like forlorn desolate stray lambs. Take — for example. His daily talk when I ask the news is "Ba-a-a-a!" Snooks says he knows Grant's losses have been per-fect-ly tre-mendous.

June 13, MONDAY. . . . Much business at 823 this afternoon; Agnew, Jenkins, and I. A cord of big bills examined and passed. We are spending money fearfully fast, but I believe to good purpose, and from present appearances our disbursements for June will not much exceed $150,000. May cost us over $262,000! Apocryphal war news most abundant these four days. Newspaper reports, official telegrams, and our Sanitary Commission correspondence indicate one or two facts as established. Grant is destroying his communications with White House and changing his base once more, to the James River. Hunter's success in Western Virginia is fully confirmed and may prove important. Butler has been taking liberties with the city of Petersburg, Virginia, which would have been more completely successful had Gillmore's cooperation been more energetic.

It's a blessed sign that Richmond papers seem in a special fit or orgasm of rage, fury, spite, brag, and insolent indecency just now. The extracts we get from Southern newspapers seldom fail to be significant. They illustrate or indicate the mental and moral tone that slaveholding has given to our Southern aristocracy, falsely so-called. . . . By the by, the proportion of Celtic and Teutonic surnames in the daily newspaper lists of casualties is extremely small, and of those who bear (or who bore) these surnames, very many must have been born Americans. But the Richmond papers and the London *Times* would sneer at our armies "made up of hireling foreign scum," just the same, were every name on our muster-rolls pure Saxon or Norman.

June 15. Very weighty news was posted on the bulletin boards before noon today. Grant "changed his base" to James River on Sunday. He has crossed that river and his headquarters are at Bermuda Hundred.

October 11

Eleven-thirty P.M. George Anthon just rang at the front door to announce that the Pennsylvania news is confirmed and that Indiana and Ohio are reported (by despatch from the *Tribune* office at the Club) to have *gone Union* by great majorities. May it be true! If these state elections have come out right, thousands of men like Hamilton Fish, Gouverneur Ogden, Cisco, and others, will review their decision to vote for McClellan and Pendleton. Waiters on Providence, like James Gordon Bennett, will declare they have always been on the winning side, and the Administration will be sustained unless some great military disaster occur before November 8th and a period of discouragement set in.

Throughout the late summer the chances of Republican victory, as Strong's diary indicates, had seemed small. On August 22, Henry J. Raymond, editor of the New York Times *and chairman of the Republican National Executive Committee, had written Lincoln that he heard from all sides but one report: "The tide is setting strongly against us." This apparently confirmed what the astute Thurlow Weed had already told the President. The political situation reflected the discouraging military position. Grant appeared at a standstill before Richmond and Petersburg, unable to make progress; his first assaults on the Petersburg lines had been repulsed with shocking losses; the Confederates were still strong in the Shenandoah; it was by no means clear that Sherman might not have to turn back from his attempted march to the sea. Reports became current in the North that if McClellan won at the polls in November, his supporters would insist that he take immediate charge of the government. Lincoln feared that he might soon have to face the task of administering affairs during four dark and troublous months while the nation waited for a successor determined to make an ignoble peace. On August 23 he wrote on a sheet of paper two sentences defining his duty and purpose in such an event, and folding it, at the ensuing cabinet meeting asked all the department heads to endorse it without reading the text. The two sentences ran: "This morning, as for some days past, it seems exceedingly probable that this administration will not be reëlected. Then it will be my duty to so cooperate with the President-elect as to save the Union between the election and the inauguration, as he will have secured his election on such ground that he cannot possibly save it afterwards."*

Happily, the situation immediately thereafter changed. Sherman's telegram of September 3, "Atlanta is ours, and fairly won," gave the nation new confidence. Farragut's naval occupation of Mobile Bay shut off another port through which supplies had reached the hard-pressed Confederacy. Sheridan's series of victories in the Shenandoah aroused popular enthusiasm. In September, the elections in Vermont and Maine showed that the Republican Party still had great strength. The price of gold fell; the credit of the United States in Europe improved. On October 2, Secretary Chase wrote John Sherman that not the slightest doubt concerning Lincoln's reëlection remained. "The only question is, by what popular and what electoral majority. God grant that both may be so decisive as to turn every hope of rebellion to despair!" Now state elections took place on October 11. In Ohio the Union ticket triumphed with a majority of 54,751; in Indiana the efficient Oliver P. Morton defeated his Democratic opponent by 20,883 votes; and in Pennsylvania a larger number of Union Representatives were chosen. Maryland, by a narrow majority, adopted a constitution which made her a free state. Altogether, the Union strength in Congress was increased by twenty men.

October 13. . . . Wall Street and No. 823 as usual, and tonight at a meeting of Club. Reports from our Committee on Enlistment. They have done the country substantial service, and the Club was not organized in vain.

Results of the October elections not yet quite clear. Ohio and Indiana are all right, but the "home vote" in Pennsylvania is very close, and both sides claim it. The army vote will carry the state for the Administration, however, for the army is Republican ten to one. On the whole, things look well for Abraham, but Pennsylvania disappoints me a little.

One of the commonplaces of Republican talk is that the exhausted rebels are only holding out in hope of McClellan's election, and that if they see four years more of Lincoln and war coming next November, they will instantly collapse. I doubt it. The pride and rage of their leaders makes surrender unlikely under any circumstances. We have got to destroy their military force and occupy their territory. When that is done, and after a year is spent in doing military execution on bushwhackers and guerrillas, we shall have peace.

The Hon. old Roger B. Taney has earned the gratitude of his country by dying at last. Better late than never. I had begun to fear he was a Struldbrug. Even should Lincoln be defeated, he will have time to appoint a new Chief Justice, and he cannot appoint anybody worse than Taney. Chase may very possibly be the man. Curious coincidence that the judge whose opinion in the Dred Scott case proved him the most faithful of slaves to the South should have been dying while his own state, Maryland, was solemnly extinguishing slavery within her borders by voting on her new anti-slavery constitution. (There seems no doubt it has been adopted.) Two ancient abuses and evils were perishing together. The tyrant's foot has rested so long on the neck of "Maryland, my Maryland," that she has undergone an organic change of structure, making it necessary for her to continue under that pressure, or in other words, loyal to the national government. The Confederacy will have nothing to say to Maryland as a free state.

October 14. Grand rumpus at the Club meeting last night after I left it. The Executive Committee reported and recommended for adoption a preamble and resolution, whereas-ing the infamy of the Chicago platform and inferring the duty of the Club to use its influence and means to promote the election of Abraham Lincoln. There was some little disposition to table the resolution at first. That oracular donkey, the Rev. [Samuel] Osgood, thought its passage would convert the Club into a mere political machine. John Jay, who is always a stumbling block in the way of his own hobbies, by some inscrutable, mysterious law of his factious nature thought so, too. There was a lively debate. The supporters of the resolution had it all their own way, and the resolution was carried at last without audible dissent. But I hear that a few members talk of resigning. Let them depart in peace. A "mere political machine," indeed! What subject of human thought and action is higher than politics, except only religion? What political issues have arisen for centuries more momentous than those dependent on this election? They are to determine the destinies—the daily life—of the millions and millions who are to live on this continent for many generations to come. They will decide the relations of the laboring man toward the capitalist in 1900 A.D., from Maine to Mexico.

October 15. Walk tonight and look in at the Club, seeking news and finding none. Mr. Ruggles looked in before dinner. Just returned from Washington. Abraham, the Venerable, says to him, "It does look as if the people wanted me to stay here a little longer, and I suppose I shall have to, if they do."

October 18. Weather is lovely. Tonight at Dr. Bellows's. He has returned from the Pacific Coast and appeared at No. 823 yesterday afternoon. Tonight there were also Van Buren, Jenkins, and Agnew. The doctor delivered a most instructive and entertaining monologue on his observations and experiences of the last six months in California, Oregon, and Washington Territory, held the floor without much interruption from half-past seven till five minutes ago (eleven-thirty P.M.), and was not in the least tedious or prosy. He has gone deep into the philosophy of California manners and morals, and his view of the probable future of the Pacific States is not discouraging. He expatiates on the Yosemite Valley, the marvellous trees, "the cascades" of the Columbia, and the like. Olmsted is living in great state and dignity as chief of Mariposa. Our (Sanitary Commission) hold on California seems fully confirmed.

Matters political and military look hopeful. Elections in Maryland and Pennsylvania have apparently come out right by small majorities. The Copperheads try to crow over Pennsylvania, but it dies in their throats. News from Grant and Sherman is satisfactory, but I suppose the War Department is in no hurry to give the public, just at this crisis, any news but such as is hopeful.

After prolonged hesitation, the political tide had turned and was flowing ever more strongly in Lincoln's favor. The presidential canvass had been quiet, for both Lincoln and McClellan maintained a dignified silence. After the September and October elections, it was clear that, as Seward remarked, "Sherman and Farragut have knocked the bottom out of the Chicago nominations." Everyone now took Lincoln's victory for granted; and the chief interest of the final weeks of the campaign centered in the question whether Seymour would be reëlected governor of New York. Lincoln himself, resenting a speech by Seymour in Chicago charging that the Administration had been a party to fraud, earnestly desired the governor's defeat; and the Republicans exerted every nerve and sinew in behalf of Fenton, who was making an admirably thorough campaign.

Once more Phil Sheridan made a splendid contribution to Northern confidence in victory. His force had been ravaging the fertile Shenandoah Valley, gathering the ripe crops and driving herds of cattle before it. But Early, after his two defeats, obtained reinforcements, and at dawn of October 19, covered by darkness and fog, delivered a stunning surprise blow. Sheridan that night sent Grant a despatch narrating the result: "My army at Cedar Creek was attacked this morning before daylight, and my left was turned and driven in confusion; in fact, most of the line was driven in confusion with the loss of twenty pieces of artillery. I hastened from Winchester, where I was on my return from Washington, and found the armies between Middletown and Newtown, having been driven back about four miles. I here took the affair in hand and quickly uniting the corps, formed a compact line of battle just in time to repulse an attack of the *enemy, which was handsomely done about one* P.M. *At three* P.M., *after some* *charges of cavalry from the left to the right flank, I attacked with great vigor,* *driving and routing the enemy, capturing, according to the last report, forty-* *three pieces of artillery and very many prisoners." As he put it, disaster had* *been "converted into a splendid victory." T. B. Read celebrated one incident of* *the event in his poem "Sheridan's Ride."*

October 20, THURSDAY. *Laus Deo.* Another victory by Sheridan. News came at noon today. Early's successor, the redoubtable Longstreet, attacked our Shenandoah Army at daybreak yesterday, between Strasburg and Winchester, with alarming vigor. He had probably been reinforced from Richmond. By twelve o'clock we had been driven four miles down the valley, with loss of guns and prospect of disastrous defeat, which might have cost the campaign and the election. At this stage of the transaction, Sheridan appeared on the field from Winchester on his way back after a visit to Washington. Then the tide of battle turned. The retreating lines were halted and formed again: the rebels were repulsed, and at three o'clock Sheridan became the assailant, and drove them back through Strasburg with loss of forty-three guns! He seems a brilliant practitioner, and our best fighting general. There are few cases in history of battle lost, and suddenly restored and converted into complete victory within six hours by the advent of a commander, *sicut deus ex machina.* Of course, the affair may look otherwise when we learn more about it, but our intelligence is official, and this looms up *now* as the most splendid battle of the war. Either we fight better of late, or the rebels fight worse. . . .

Nothing very notable at 68 Wall Street or at No. 823 Broadway. Weather fine. Johnny enters his teens today, through his thirteenth birthday. He still abstains from school and work, but seems better. Meeting of Library Committee (Columbia College) at No. 68. Received a telegram from Knapp at No. 823 and authorized purchase of $10,000 worth of supplies for the hospitals of Sheridan's army, in addition to our stores at Winchester and Harper's Ferry. None too much to provide the "supplementary" relief that's needed, no doubt, by thousands of brave men, lying mutilated, lacerated, and in misery this minute. Victory at Cedar Creek cannot have been recovered without fearful cost. And the Medical Bureau is as worthless now as it was three years ago. Surgeon-General Barnes is an amiable nonentity.

At Union League Club awhile this evening. Discoursed with Captain Marshall, Charles E. Butler, Parke Godwin, and others. Godwin is disposed to protest against confidence in the result of the election. He does not despond, but maintains the necessity of hard work by all loyal men. That is sound doctrine. Every symptom now apparent is unfavorable to the aspirations of G. B. ("Gun Boat") McClellan, and of "Peace and surrender at any price" Pendleton, but the damnable traitors who support them may be keeping some revolutionary movement in reserve for the day of election. The best thing I know of Stanton is that he wanted to send Governor Seymour to Fort Lafayette in July, 1863, and that his colleagues of the Cabinet, and Lincoln himself, hardly kept Stanton from doing it.

I would walk several miles to see Seymour duly and lawfully hanged— as convicted of treason. He is an avowed traitor—*traitoro-phile*.

October 22.   Johnny went with Charley this morning to Point Judith for a couple of days' sojourn. That young scamp has actually been *smoking* on the sly—the premature ruffian!—and has been duly and severely lectured therefor. Nothing very special in Wall Street.

Heard the *Eroica* rehearsed at the Academy of Music, with Ellie. A slovenly performance, but the strength and beauty of the symphony was apparent nevertheless. I suppose it excelled by no extant orchestral work but the peerless C Minor. From beginning to end, it is an intense manifestation of that highest art which cannot be embodied in rules or canons of art. No critic can analyze its wonderful power, and tell why this or that passage is so pungent and burns itself so deep into one's memory and recurs to one so often, solacing a walk uptown or a railroad ride. So Shakespeare's "Come unto these yellow sands" cannot be scientifically distinguished from doggerel, and in "Hark, Hark, the lark at Heaven's gate sings," English grammar is sacrificed to rhyme. But those two songs live and are loved and long will be, because there is in them the same occult vital power that inspires the *Eroica*. I admit, however, that I do not yet appreciate a certain *scratch-cat* passage in the first movement, and the doleful, long-lingering fugue in the second. But faultfinding is ungracious. Is there anything, in all music, instrumental or vocal, fuller of pathos and majesty, more touching and stately than the melody that occurs toward the close of the fourth movement? . . .

At 823 as usual this afternoon, and at the Club tonight. G. W. Blunt gives a bad account of Professor Bache's health. Dr. Lieber talks of probable row and riot here at the November election, and is uneasy because the Democrats are so desperate. But they have no principle, no convictions, no idea to fight for. They are struggling only for possession of the official crib. To be sure, there are among them many Southern refugees and desperadoes. But the Democratic Party as a whole will not try to get up a row. Its leaders are none too good, but they know better.

October 23. . . . Sheridan reports himself pursuing the routed rebels up the valley, and that they are throwing away their arms, and that considerable bodies of them are breaking up and taking to the mountains.[1] This looks as if the character of the war were changing. So does a late article, quite elaborate, that appeared in some Richmond paper. It says in substance, "We have no cavalry, though the South is a people of horsemen. We have only mounted men, useful as scouts and skirmishers, like the Cossacks, but unequal to conflict with the masses of trained cavalry the Yankees have somehow been able to put in the field. Most of them have actually thrown away their sabres. They always run when attacked by Yankee horse. They are not worth their cost, and three-fourths of them should at once be dismounted and put into infantry regiments." A significant confession. It would seem that the estimate generally received at the beginning of the war of the qualities and relative value of a Northern and a Southern soldiery was just and true, but that its worth was not developed till both armies had experienced three years of battle. In July, 1861, a Northern mob and a Southern mob came into collision at Bull Run, and the North was routed. In 1864, Northern veterans are meeting Southern veterans in Georgia and on the Shenandoah, and the case is altered.

October 31, MONDAY. Let me register the notabilia of last week's Sanitary Commission campaign at Washington.

Thither Monday the 24th, by the eight A.M. train. Woods still in full autumn beauty. Ride as dreary and tedious as usual. Bishop Clark joined me at Baltimore, and his lively talk helped me through the last two hours. He seems indisposed to commit himself as to his present views on public affairs. Probably they are of no great importance to anybody. I detected nothing worse than a little pardonable uneasiness about the duration of the war. At 244 F Street, I found a good room awaiting me (poor Bloor's quarters), and a commissariat department fully established for the benefit of this session; so we all breakfasted and dined together. The experiment

---

[1] Resistance in the Shenandoah was now practically ended, and many of Sheridan's troops were soon fighting before Petersburg.

is not wholly successful, but it is an improvement on feeding at Willard's or at Buhler's cockroachy restaurant, and the symposia, though plain and frugal, were jolly.

Session closed Friday night, or rather Saturday morning. There were Bellows, Agnew, Newberry, Clark, Harris, Binney, Stillé (whom we added to the Standing Committee), and Wolcott of Boston. Also a very strong-minded Miss Abby W. May, an elect lady from the patriotic womankind of Boston, who had invited us to invite her attendance. She was attentive, interested, and silent, but her presence obliged us to "go into executive session" now and then, for the discussion of sundry personal questions, and to "clear the galleries" (the sofa in the corner, to wit). Then we lit our cigars. . . .[2]

General Grant wrote us for copies of the report on rebel prisoners to be sent to General Lee. We appointed a committee on my motion (for the sake of perfecting our record, but with no hope of accomplishing anything), to visit City Point and to see whether the rebel authorities could be shamed into allowing us to send supplies to our starving men in their wicked, tyrannous hands, and agents to distribute them and protect them from misappropriation. The President authorized the committee to make the experiment, but just as it was setting off for James River, news came that the rebels had themselves made overtures that way!!! So Bellows, Stillé, and Wolcott concluded to postpone this journey, especially as Grant was making a movement and was likely to be too busy to attend to them. (N.B. This movement failed, and was a worse failure than the newspapers indicated.) I believe these rebel overtures are due to this report by men like Dr. Mott, Dr. Delafield, and others known abroad as entitled to credence and respect and free from all partisan taint. Lee, Davis & Co. see that it is likely to raise a howl throughout Christendom against their barbarism, and hasten to open negotiations on the treatment of prisoners. It is a most important paper. Significant that Lord Lyons asked Bellows for copies to distribute in England.

We had an interesting visit to the Military Cemetery, near the old

---

[2] Abigail Williams May (1829–1888), member of an old Boston family well known for religious and social reform activities, was herself energetic in behalf of her community. She was a founder and chairman of the executive committee of the New England Women's Auxiliary Association, an affiliate of the Sanitary Commission. She had entered the Commission's hospital transport service in 1862 and no doubt had contributed much, both in money and work, to the organization. As she was also a staunch woman's suffrage worker, a species Strong abhorred, it is easy to understand his grudging acceptance of her part in the Commission's affairs.

"Soldiers' Home," where Uncle Abe has his summer quarters; 6,500 walnut headboards painted white, numbered, and recording the name, company, and regiment of the dead soldier sleeping below. These ghastly shapes crowd the beautiful greensward. Suppose the chivalric and venerable Robert Ruffin, who fired the first gun on Sumter, could have seen this sight in a trance or a vision the night before. Would he have touched off his piece without misgivings? We adjourned Friday night. . . .

November 2. . . . Visit from Vinton of the School of Mines this morning —*ci-devant* General Vinton.[3] He is hopeful about the School and seems energetic. It is to open on or about the 15th. Barnard's administration as president of the College is thus far most successful, in spite of his deafness. I predict he will prove the most efficient president we have had for thirty-five years. He must possess singular tact, for Professor Anthon likes him and speaks of him with respect, though he has never before had anything good to say of an official superior.

Standing Committee of the Sanitary Commission tonight at Dr. Bellows's. Newberry with us. The moment election is over, we must declare war against the Medical Bureau, which has been steadily retrograding for six months. If we were to proclaim what we know of its general efficiency and recklessness and of its murderous non-feasances in the Valley of the Shenandoah, the facts could be used by Copperheads so as seriously to weaken Lincoln's chance of reëlection. Of course, we must hold our peace a little longer.

The New York *World* scolds venomously over last night's meeting of War Democrats, and is very hard on General Dix. He is nobody, and a tool of the Administration besides. McClellan stock is low just now, though gold is high, and the *News* and *World* are therefore roaring their loudest.

November 3. Have just returned from the Broadway Theatre after a pleasant evening with Ellie and George Anthon. How long is it since I have taken her to the theatre? This is what used to be Wallack's, in what is now the remote, obscure, downtown latitude of Broome Street. Very good performance of *The Victims* and *Solon Shingle*. One Owens is

[3] Francis L. Vinton (1835–1879), a graduate of West Point in the class of 1856 and of the *Ecole des Mines*, had fought bravely in several campaigns, attained the rank of brigadier, and been so seriously wounded at Fredericksburg that he was unfit for further duty. His friend Egleston was now bringing him into the Columbia School of Mines, where for the next thirteen years he was to be an efficient professor. A man of great personal charm as well as culture, he was to become an intimate friend of Strong's.

the special attraction. His impersonation of an honest old garrulous codger from some rural district of New England or of Suffolk County, Long Island, whose father "fit into the Revolutionary War," is the *ne plus ultra* of histrionic photographing. Every movement and intonation seems carefully studied from a living model.

Nothing notable in Wall Street or at No. 823. Seward telegraphs Gunther the Mayor to beware of a conspiracy to burn this and other Northern cities on or about November 8th. The community is infested by rebel refugees and sympathizers. There are doubtless rebel agents among them, eagerly watching their opportunity to do mischief. Seymour's "friends" are ready to emerge from their tenement-houses and cellars and suburban shanties and from every gambling shop and brothel in the city whenever there shall be an opening for pillage, arson, and murder like that of July, 1863. But I predict no serious breach of the peace next week, though Rebeldom and Copperheadism are cornered and desperate and none too good to bring fire and knife into the streets of New York and Philadelphia, if their wicked cause would be helped thereby, or even for the mere gratification of their malignant spite against us. It looks as if the Administration would be sustained by next Tuesday's election. God grant it!

November 4. . . . At No. 823 this afternoon. Bellows tells me that Governor Morgan tells him "he considers the election over—and won." May he be sustained by the result! This prognosis of a coming election is as trustworthy as that of any political practitioner I know. N.B. The New York *World* is disgusted with Bellows—says he is making "Lincoln speeches" at "corner groceries" (meaning thereby the Cooper Institute), and that if the Sanitary Commission do not get him out of its presidency forthwith, it will be universally recognized as a mere "Black Republican Club."

Meeting of Committee on School of Mines at William Betts's office this morning. Prospects very hopeful. After dinner to Union League Club, and thence with George C. Anthon to inspect the grand Union torchlight procession. It was large, enthusiastic, and most brilliantly pyrotechnic with its rockets and Roman candles. What is more important, it was made up of voters. There were comparatively few boys of sixteen and upwards. Perhaps the Secesh majority in this city may be less than people expect.

[August] Belmont has been publicly invited in the newspapers to take up a bet of two to one that Lincoln will be reëlected. He replies by offering to bet that if Lincoln be reëlected, the war will last through his term of office, and that if McClellan be elected, there will be peace and reconstruction. Very significant as to Herr Belmont's (or Schönberg's) views of the case. The Democratic Party must be short of strong men when it has to put this Dutch banker at the head of its Executive Committee. I have a sort of respect for him as being beautiful Mrs. Belmont's husband, but he is, in fact, a mere successful cosmopolite adventurer and alien, who has made money as the agent of foreign capitalists and has no real affinity with our country or people. They *do* say, moreover, that he is a Jew, half-converted and conforming outwardly; a political Joannes Pfefferkorn (*vide Epist. Obsc. Virorum*). Don't know about that, but his setting himself up as one of our guides and governors is a piece of audacious impudence, whether he be Jew or Christian.

November 5. . . . The city is full of noises tonight. There is a grand McClellan demonstration in progress. Little "Mac" was to "review" his hordes of Celts and rebel sympathizers in person from the balcony of the Fifth Avenue Hotel. I have still respect enough for him left to believe that he must feel himself in a horribly false position. A general who commanded at Malvern Hill and Antietam in 1862 must be tempted to doubt his own identity when he hears Governor Seymour's "friends" hurrahing for him in 1864.

November 6, SUNDAY. General Butler in town. He commands the United States forces here, reporting to General Dix. I hear he proposed issuing an order last night that all officers of state militia regiments report to him. Dix objected and Stanton was telegraphed for a decision. Such an order would be disregarded by Seymour's Copperhead colonels, and they would have the law on their side. It would promote collision with state authorities. But General Butler's personal presence next Tuesday will do no harm. The rabble of New York is not generally well informed, but it knows Butler's name as suggestive of vigorous action against rebels at New Orleans and elsewhere action hampered by very few scruples about form and legal right and thus far successful. The *World* and *News* and *Express* have raved about Butler "the Beast," the tyrant, the lawless minion of a profligate Administration, till such of their party as can read print regard him as the Covenanters regarded Claverhouse; a wholesome fear and dread of Butler underlies all the rebel and Copperhead denunciation of his corruption and abuse of power. It is quite natural that rats should hold terriers unconstitutional and scandalous.

November 7. Rainy day. Columbia College meeting at two. I hope much from Barnard's administration. The new measures he is taking promise to strengthen discipline and raise the moral tone of the under-graduates. There are already signs that the inner life of the College is gaining vigor. Then he appreciates the importance of our getting the hold on the community we ought to have, and is pushing out organic filaments that may become roots; for example, our proposed relations with the Lyceum of Natural History, over which we have pottered at intervals for two or three years, were brought up for action this after-noon, and a committee appointed. This may result in our securing a valuable ally and auxiliary, strengthening our scientific school, and getting control of a very considerable scientific collection.

November 8, TUESDAY.   So this momentous day is over, and the battle lost and won. We shall know more of the result tomorrow. Present signs are not unfavorable. Wet weather, which did not prevent a very heavy vote. I stood in queue nearly two hours waiting my turn. A little before me was Belmont, whose vote was challenged on the ground that he had betted on the election. The inspector rejected it unwillingly, and Bel-mont went off in a rage. Very few men would have been challenged on that ground, but this foreign money-dealer has made himself uncom-monly odious, and the bystanders, mostly of the Union persuasion, chuckled over his discomfiture. . . .

This election has been quiet beyond precedent. Few arrests, if any, have been made for disorderly conduct. There has been no military force visible. It is said that portions of the city militia regiments were on guard at their armories, and that some 6,000 United States troops were at Governor's Island and other points outside the city, but no one could have guessed from the appearance of the streets that so momentous an issue was *sub judice.* . . .

In this city the Democratic strongholds have enlarged their Copper-head majorities, but the total majority seems not to exceed 35,750, which is less than was feared. News from Westchester County looks rather ill, but there is not much of it. Philadelphia reported to have im-proved upon last month's state election. Baltimore and Maryland right by a large vote. Indiana ditto. Gain in New Jersey; Massachusetts all one way. Prospect good in Connecticut. George Anthon has just looked in on his way homeward from the Club. Says the feeling there is that Lincoln is certainly reëlected, but that this state is doubtful and is claimed at the Copperhead headquarters by 5,000 majority. That would be a serious offset against the results of victory. I hope better things.

VICTORIA! Te Deum laudamus. Te Dominum confitemur.
November 9. Laus Deo! The crisis has been past, and the most momentous popular election ever held since ballots were invented has decided against treason and disunion. My contempt for democracy and extended suffrage is mitigated. The American people can be trusted to take care of the national honor. Lincoln is reëlected by an overwhelming vote. The only states that seem to have McClellanized are Missouri, Kentucky, Delaware, and New Jersey. New York, about which we have been uneasy all day, is reported safe at the Club tonight. The Copperheads are routed—*Subversi sunt quasi plumbum in aequis vehementibus.* Poor "little Mac" will never be heard of any more, I think. No man of his moderate calibre ever had such an opportunity of becoming illustrious and threw it away so rapidly. Notwithstanding a certain lukewarmness in the national cause, his instincts and impulses were, on the whole, right and loyal. Had he acted on them honestly and manfully, he would have been elected. But his friends insisted on his being *politic,* and he had not the strength to resist them. He allowed Belmont and Barlow to strike out of his letter of acceptance a vigorous sentence declaring an armistice with armed rebels out of the question, and to append to it its unmeaning finale (which imposed on no man) stating that he assumed the views he had expressed to be what the Chicago Convention really meant to say in its treasonous resolutions. *Fuit* McClellan, Napoleoniculus. Five years hence people will wonder how such a fuss ever came to be made about him.

A very wet, warm day. Copperheads talk meekly and well. "It's a terrible mistake, but we have got to make the best of it and support the government." The serene impudence of this morning's *World* can hardly be matched. It says the mission of the Democratic Party for the next four years will be to keep A. Lincoln from making a dishonorable disunion peace with the South. So a gentleman who has just received a sentence of four years in the State Prison might (if cheeky enough) inform the court and jury that their unjust decision would oblige him to be especially careful during his term that law and order were maintained throughout the state and that no crime failed to meet prompt punishment. The *World* is, moreover, uncommonly proud of the "Democratic masses"

(Governor Seymour's "friends," the liquor dealers, roughs, and brutal Irishry of the city) because they committed no disorders yesterday, *though* so easily tempted to make a general row by the offensive and insulting presence of General Butler with sundry regiments to back him. . . .

George Anthon dined here, and we proceeded to the Union League Club, where was much folk. Discoursed with General Banks among others. It would seem that William E. Dodge is defeated by James Brooks, that most coprophagous of Copperheads, in this congressional district. A great pity, but Dodge's election was hardly hoped for. Would we were quite sure that Seymour is beaten! John Astor says he thinks Seymour's election would be more mischievous than McClellan's, and he may be right. Seymour and McClellan are weak men, but the latter means well. Seymour's instincts are all evil. He is quite as bad as Fernando Wood.

Lincoln's victory was as sweeping as his best friends could have desired. After being a minority President for four years, he now had the satisfaction of receiving a majority of almost 495,000 in the popular vote. He had 212 electoral votes, while McClellan was left with only 21, these being furnished by New Jersey (McClellan's own state), Kentucky, and with a very narrow margin, Delaware. In New York State the result was for several days in doubt, but it finally appeared that Fenton had won the governorship by a margin of 8,293 over Seymour. Never had the American electorate appeared to better advantage. Lincoln, in a felicitous little speech to a crowd of serenaders, made precisely the right comment. " The election, along with its incidental and undesirable strife, has done good," he remarked. "It has demonstrated that a people's government can sustain a national election in the midst of a great civil war; until now, it has not been known to the world that this was a possibility. . . . It shows, also, to the extent yet known, that we have more men now than we had when the war began."

November 10. Election returns improve. New York seems secure by from 5,000 to 7,500, Seymour running a little behind his ticket, and Missouri is claimed for the Administration, leaving poor McClellan only three states. If his wife and her mother, Mrs. Marcy, had not allowed themselves to be talked over by Belmont and Barlow, and brought household influence to bear upon him, he would not be in this plight. They prevailed on him to disregard General Dix's earnest advice and to try to ride two horses, Peace and War, at once. I should not wonder if the old

Democratic party were killed with its candidate—though it has immense vitality. It would be curious if that old and potent organization should die of this election, the result of which has been in great measure determined by the fireside talk of an amiable young wife and a strong-minded mother-in-law. That party can hardly survive another four years of exclusion from office under the national government and in almost every state. Its extinction would be a great blessing. It has been an ancient *imperium in imperio* with its own settled rules, usages, and traditions of political immorality, not worse perhaps than those of other parties, but better established, more powerful, and more fruitful of public mischief.

November 11. No material news, except that it is positively asserted that "Little Mac" has resigned his commission in a pet, and by way of spiting an unappreciative people. . . . By the by, the most infamous paper of the last four years appeared in yesterday's *Daily News*: a congratulatory address to our Mayor, Gunther (an abject Copperhead), on his refusal to approve a resolution of the Common Council recommending illuminations in honor of Sheridan's victories and the fall of Atlanta. It fills two columns with treason and baseness. Charles O'Conor signs it (and it's evidently his handiwork), Horace F. Clark, S. F. B. Morse, [Gideon] Tucker the Surrogate, John W. Mitchell, Hiram Cranston, John McKeon, Richard O'Gorman, and a lot of others (mostly unknown to fame), among whom is the urbane William Betts. May their names be remembered!

I shall find it hard to meet Betts after this at our College committees on the Law School and the School of Mines without letting him know that I think him as infamous as his very small capacity can make him. This flagitious document bears the date October 20, but was suppressed till after the election—an unconscious compliment to the honesty and patriotism of the people. It should be remembered, however, that Betts inherited a large amount of treasonable impulse through his wife, a descendant of the Colonel Beverley Robinson of the last century who was mixed up with Arnold's treason. Betts got his social position by his marriage (I believe he was an adventurer from Jamaica or some other British Colony), and he has dutifully adopted the anti-American tradition of his wife's family. Fortunately, he has no more weight or influence than his cat. He is an attorney and conveyancer of small calibre, with a small amount of literary culture and scholarship on the strength of which he looks down upon the community at large with a supreme disdain. . . .

At the Union League Club tonight. Majority in the state promises to exceed our hopes. This election, peacefully conducted in a time of such bitter excitement, and with a result quietly recognized and acquiesced in by a furious malcontent minority, is the strongest testimonial in favor of popular institutions to be found in history.

November 12. This morning spent at breakfast (Union League Club) in honor of Professor Goldwin Smith of Oxford.[4] About seventy sat down. I was between William C. Bryant and Lieber, and of course had an agreeable time enough. After a period of deleterious deglutition came speeches by Charles Butler, John Jay, General Butler, Evarts, George William Curtis, and others—and the professor, of course. He is a tall, thin, grave man, and speaks slowly but accurately, with intonation a little monotonous but agreeable. He is evidently a scholar and a thinker. General Butler's speech was telling, though a little artificial or stagey in delivery. The Rev. A. C. Coxe spoke, made certain very good points, and shewed his usual want of tact. Avowed that he had little sympathy with the English Liberals (of whom Professor Smith is representative), and said he was "not a political clergyman" and that "he never voted." This little dab at political clergymen brought the Abbé Bellows down on him and when Bellows's turn came, he delivered an opinion that "cocks that didn't fight and didn't vote ought not to crow." Quite smart, but not in the best taste.

Lieber says he wants to have the event of Tuesday known in history as *The Great and Good Election of 1864.* He is always saying things.

Tonight to an adjourned monthly meeting of the Century Club for election of members. Attendance large, as it was understood our minority of Copperhead members meant to blackball Parke Godwin of the *Evening Post.* He was triumphantly elected. Ned Bell, [Francis F.] Marbury, William E. Curtis, and others could not muster half the one-third required to defeat him. . . .

Poor, pretty, little loyal Mrs. Belmont, whom Ellie met tonight at the concert in aid of that everlasting "Nursery," declares herself made very unhappy by newspaper flings at her husband.

November 13, SUNDAY. Vinton preached at Trinity and summed up

---

[4] The brilliant English publicist and scholar (1823–1910), who had played an important rôle in university reform, was one of the principal leaders in the struggle to place British sentiment squarely behind the North. His incisive pamphlets, articles, and speeches had attracted wide attention on both sides of the Atlantic. When the London *Times* pleaded a religious sanction for the peculiar Southern institution, Smith issued a telling pamphlet, "Does the Bible Sanction American Slavery?" His position as Regius Professor of History at Oxford, his slashing style, and his determination made him highly useful to the Union. In his tour of the North in 1864 he met an enthusiastic reception.

strongly against "the esoteric sentimentality of modern pantheism." He does so bounce and swagger in the pulpit and uses such big words that most of his congregation regard him with singular awe. But he would rise still higher in their respect and regard if his sermons lasted less than forty minutes. Tonight Miss Puss here, Charley, D'Oremieulx and wife, Dr. [J. Charles] Peters and wife, John Sherwood, Murray Hoffman, [Charles F.] Blake, Mr. Ruggles, and Charley Post.

A distinguished delegate to the Chicago Convention expatiated to Blake (a fortnight ago) on the dignity and weight of that body. "It was made up, sir, of the most loyal and influential Democratic leaders from Illinois, from New York, from New England, from Ohio, and from Canada. In fact, it represented the whole Democracy." Quite true, no doubt. Had fewer Canadian Democrats (that is, plotting Southern refugees) assisted at that convention, it might have adopted a more patriotic platform, and its party might have escaped absolute annihilation.

> Please to remember the *Eighth* of November,
> Copperhead Treason and Plot.
> We know no reason why Copperhead Treason
> Should ever be forgot.

This election of last Tuesday is quite as important an event in our history as the miscarriage of the Gunpowder Plot in that of Great Britain. Both indicate progress in the same way.

November 14. Uptown at two P.M. with William Schermerhorn to Forty-ninth Street, where the College Library Committee met. Nothing done except to pass on the purchase of a very few new books. We cannot afford to buy many. Dr. Anderson rather objected to the purchase of a very cheap copy of Foxe's *Actes and Monuments* which the librarian had smelt out in some obscure book store, and so did *I*; for that lying, vulgar, narrow-minded old martyrologist is entitled to little respect. But as his book has acquired a certain position in history which entitles it to a place in every collection as a curiosity (on the same shelf with Pinto and the *Malleus Maleficarum*), I proposed that we buy it and that we also import the Rev. S. R. Maitland's *Letters* shewing its worthlessness; which was agreed to. Maitland's book is valuable as a specimen of what can be done by minute, accurate criticism, and we shall have the bane and antidote together. From the library to the School of Mines; Professors Vinton and Egleston there, at work over their arrangements and confident of success. The Gilmore Collection presented by Kemble proves worth far less than its cost, but it is an acquisition, nevertheless. . . .

1865

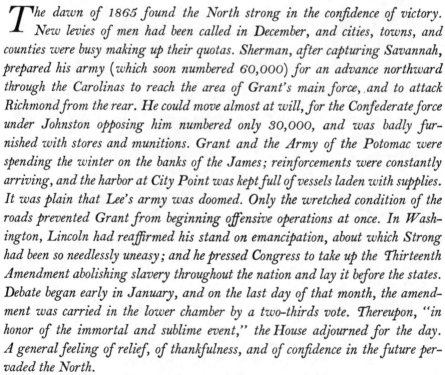

*T*he dawn of 1865 found the North strong in the confidence of victory. New levies of men had been called in December, and cities, towns, and counties were busy making up their quotas. Sherman, after capturing Savannah, prepared his army (which soon numbered 60,000) for an advance northward through the Carolinas to reach the area of Grant's main force, and to attack Richmond from the rear. He could move almost at will, for the Confederate force under Johnston opposing him numbered only 30,000, and was badly furnished with stores and munitions. Grant and the Army of the Potomac were spending the winter on the banks of the James; reinforcements were constantly arriving, and the harbor at City Point was kept full of vessels laden with supplies. It was plain that Lee's army was doomed. Only the wretched condition of the roads prevented Grant from beginning offensive operations at once. In Washington, Lincoln had reaffirmed his stand on emancipation, about which Strong had been so needlessly uneasy; and he pressed Congress to take up the Thirteenth Amendment abolishing slavery throughout the nation and lay it before the states. Debate began early in January, and on the last day of that month, the amendment was carried in the lower chamber by a two-thirds vote. Thereupon, "in honor of the immortal and sublime event," the House adjourned for the day. A general feeling of relief, of thankfulness, and of confidence in the future pervaded the North.

Strong's legal affairs were prosperous, and his household happy, with the three boys and his wife in excellent health. The Sanitary Commission was now at the apex of its usefulness. Its average monthly expenditures had for some *time exceeded a quarter of a million dollars, it maintained a force of more than five hundred in the field, and it was supporting a wide array of "homes and lodges." It had its own flotilla of steamers, its own hospital cars, and its own wagon trains. Over its finances, sustained by a steady stream of popular contributions, Strong presided with efficiency and credit. Only the affairs of the infant School of Mines failed to advance as he wished. He wanted it given a separate incorporation, but other Columbia trustees objected.*

Strong was also giving much time to the Union League Club. As the record shows, he carried on his campaign to interest men of wealth and influence in the School of Mines by enlisting a number of his Union League Club friends as Associate Members. Among them were William Earl Dodge, Jr., N. Pendleton Hosack, Robert L. Kennedy, Franklin H. Delano, Samuel W. Bridgham, George Cabot Ward, and of course his intimate friend, George C. Anthon.

January 2, MONDAY. On New Year's Day duty from eleven till near five, my field bounded by Forty-ninth Street (Mrs. Professor Joy) and Hudson Square (Morgan Dix). It was a pleasant day's work as usual. Mrs. Professor Joy, Mrs. Sam Whitlock, Mrs. William Schermerhorn, all the Dixes, Mrs. Rutherfurd, the Rev. Coxes, were as charming, kindly, and gracious as I have always found them. So were Mrs. Serena Fearing and Mrs. Laura Field. It is really a great privilege to be cordially received once a year by half a dozen such nice women.

At Bishop Potter's, I discoursed with that prelate about the School of Mines. Mrs. Talboys (West Eleventh Street) was very pleasant; Mrs. Augustus Schermerhorn and Miss Ellen in University Place, ditto, as usual. Mrs. Lucretia Heckscher (née Stevens) has been living out of town, and I have not seen her for three years. I established an intimacy with two boys of hers, the elder of whom confided to me, in a fearful whisper, his doubt whether there was any Santa Claus at all. Our usual New Year's dinner table was thus wise:

Mrs. G. T. Strong

Gen. Vinton		Gen. Viele
Miss Kitty Dix		Mrs. Blake
Willy Graham		Col. McMahon
Charley Post		Capt. Bankhead, U.S.N.
Miss Fanny Staples		Mrs. Viele
Charles Blake		Jem Ruggles

Mr. Strong

February 20, MONDAY. . . . At two came an extra—"Evacuation of Charleston!" Grant telegraphs Stanton that the Richmond papers say Charleston was abandoned last Tuesday. We are of little faith, and do not fully receive these good tidings until officially announced. Washington is said to accept them with jubilation, but we distrust them.

February 21. Yesterday's doubtful news confirmed by the *Fulton*, which left Charleston on Saturday night. Charleston was entered and occupied Saturday morning, and the national flag floats over the ruins of Sumter. The Chivalry did not stay to exchange shots with mudsills, but flitted Friday night after firing their cotton storehouses. . . . My deluded Southern friends, who would hear of no compromise four years ago, "not even if you had *carte blanche* to dictate its terms," and who shook hands with effusion and drank cocktails in Charleston bar-rooms on the night of April 12th, 1861, after you had fired the Southern heart and hurled a proud and scornful defiance at Abe Lincoln and his Northern scum by beginning a causeless Civil War, and who telegraphed in the exuberance of your jollity to Washington "With mortar cannon and petard, We tender old Abe our Beau-Regard," what do you think about that day's job now? But I suppose a large majority of the young gentlemen who got more or less gloriously tipsy that memorable night are in their graves before this. Heaven forgive them their share in the colossal crime that has cost so many lives. Wiser, cooler, and better men might have been as blind, mad, and criminal had they grown up as members of a slaveholding caste in a woman-flogging and a baby-buying country. Of course, the whole city has been lit up with flags all day.

Long meeting at two of the subcommittee of Committee on School of Mines; Betts, Rutherfurd, Fish, Jones, and I. Much of our talk deplorably dense and fatuous, but the result, on the whole, not unsatisfactory, and we report in the course of red tape to the "mother committee" on Thursday, and then it will report to the board some of these days.

Sherman's hard-bitten and superbly confident army, leaving Savannah on February 1, was so overwhelmingly superior to the Confederate forces in front of it that it met little opposition as it marched northward. The worst obstacles were the bottomless mud of the roads, the flooded streams, and the ill-mapped swamps. Five large rivers had to be crossed. As General Jacob D. Cox wrote, the problem was one of "bridging chaos for hundreds of miles." Sherman made gestures which convinced the inhabitants of Charleston on the right and Augusta

*on the left that both were threatened. But actually he marched straight through
to Columbia, which he entered over a pontoon bridge on February 17. That night
a great conflagration destroyed much of the capital city. Sherman always con-
tended that huge piles of cotton fired by the retreating Confederates were
responsible for the holocaust. "Before one single public building had been fired by
order, the smouldering fires set by Hampton's order were rekindled by the wind,
and communicated to the buildings around. About dark they began to spread and
got beyond the control of the brigade on duty within the city." The Confederates
blamed the Union troops—who, Sherman admits, "may have assisted in spreading the fire after it had once begun."*

*Sherman's movement had flanked and isolated Charleston, and on February
21 the little Southern army of 14,000 under Hardee evacuated the city. While
the North rejoiced over the humiliation of the starting-point of the "rebellion,"
General Q. A. Gillmore on February 21 took possession of it, with more than
four hundred and fifty cannon and large stores of ammunition. The American
flag had gone up over Fort Sumter at nine o'clock on the morning of February 18,
when a small boat was sent out from Cumming's Point for that purpose. Sherman's forces now rapidly pushed forward to Goldsboro and Wilmington, North
Carolina. Meanwhile, Grant continued his preparations for an irresistible movement against Petersburg and Richmond; and Sheridan was active in the
Shenandoah Valley. The first blow of the year in Virginia, in fact, was struck
by Sheridan on March 5, when, encountering Early's remnant force between
Staunton and Charlottesville, he smashed it to bits, captured most of the survivors, and almost took Early himself. Thunder ringed the Confederacy, and to
such passionate patriots as Strong the days were bright.*

February 23. Committee on School of Mines at Law School at half-
past three o'clock; Fish, Barnard, Betts, Rutherfurd, Edward Jones, and
I. We agreed on our report to the trustees. I fear the measures we recommend will bear no fruit, but I have said my say and done my duty. Fish
and the rest seem to me to be (rightly or wrongly, and it is possible I
am wrong) blind to self-evident considerations. What is worse and more
surprising, they seem influenced by no feeling of ambition to develop
and strengthen the College. When I tell them that our associates think
they would be far more successful in raising funds for an organization
affiliated with the trustees and governed by them, but nominally independent, than for the treasury of Columbia College, Fish replies, "Very

good; then let them go to the 'University,' or set up a school on their own account." Outside wealth and influence and public spirit to help the College, when that help is respectfully offered, does not strike Fish and his colleagues as desirable.

Meeting at Union League Club tonight. We are now duly incorporated.

It is painful to think what Columbia College might become were half a dozen of its trustees earnestly desirous to promote its development. I can do nothing alone. Mr. Ruggles is full of other affairs. The rest are mostly indisposed to get out of their old, well-worn ruts. Having been inert since 17—, they feel bound by corporate traditions and a due sense of corporate dignity to be inert and inefficient and a scandal and offense that deters and repels all rich men who would like to promote the cause of education from giving a dollar to help them.

February 25, SATURDAY. Mrs. Ruggles the elder, Ellie's grandmamma, the noblest of old ladies, died at five this morning. Poor Ellie brought in the news before I was up. I did not in the least expect it, for though Mr. Ruggles spoke to me of the patient last evening as much prostrated and unlikely to survive very long, I thought her immense vitality would carry her on for weeks or months. . . .

February 27. . . . The Rebel Senate declines nigger soldiers by a close vote. Rebel editors are furious and hint that Lee might advantageously "purge" the rebel parliament. The New York *World*'s Baltimore correspondent, "Druid," favors mankind this morning with special and exclusive intelligence as to Lee's intentions. Lee means to seize Jeff Davis and put that potentate in irons. That's step No. 1. For No. 2, he proposes to march on Washington, cross the Long Bridge, march past Willard's Hotel, capture A. Lincoln, and put him in irons. His third move will be to proclaim himself dictator, and in that capacity to call a convention to restore the Union. A very politic and hopeful programme.

March 1. . . . Dr. Peters at the Union League Club tonight, just returned from a seven weeks' exploration at Beaufort, Savannah, and Charleston and Sumter the day after the rebels left it. Conflagration and rifled cannon have left about three-quarters of Charleston standing, but the city is dead. Only low-caste whites and their Ethiops remain there. "Obstructions in the harbor" have been a delusion for many months. There has always been an opening half a mile wide through the piles that barred the channel. This opening *was* obstructed with rope-net entanglements, but they were carried away by tides and currents, and the rebels got tired of replacing them.

Many of the better-most, blue-blooded Savannites still abide in Savannah. Of these one-third secessionize strongly; the rest hate U.S.A. and C.S.A., the Nation and the Rebellion, more or less impartially, and pant for peace after the restoration of law and order anyhow and on any terms. Peters supposes Sherman to be striking for Wilmington as a new base, with 60,000 men as a minimum estimate, and thinks Beauregard cannot confront him with more than 30,000.

March 2, THURSDAY. Trinity Chapel well filled this morning for the Russian service. Part of the chapel was reserved for Russians, Greeks, and Orientals, of whom there were fifty or sixty. The officiating priest, Father Agapias, was in handsome robes. . . . Ogilby says this is the first time the Liturgy of St. Chrysostom has been heard in a Western church (excepting, of course, chapels of embassies at Paris and other Western capitals) since the great schism between Eastern and Western Christendom. If so, this was a very remarkable transaction. It may prove— possibly—a little step on the road toward Catholic unity. There certainly seems to be a moving on the face of the waters just now. Our diocesan committee minutes of every meeting record Congregationalists and Presbyterians applying to become candidates for orders in the church. Even the Unitarians are to hold a council here next month to consider whether they do not believe *something* after all, and if so, to define it in some symbol of faith. . . .

McVickar tells me he found the hard-headed old Scotch sexton of Trinity Chapel quite sulky this morning over the proposed service. Clarke thought it was to be something Popish, and felt conscientious scruples about being accessory thereto. Whereupon Professor McVickar opened a heavy fire on him, with the Council of This and the Council of That, the "Mother Church of Jerusalem" and the "Mission Church of Rome," and the orthodoxy of the Oriental communities and their enmity to the Pope. Clarke was satisfied, or stunned, and said he was glad to learn it was all right, and said he would be happy to countenance the service.

March 4. Standing Committee of Sanitary Commission here this evening; Bellows, Agnew, Van Buren, Stillé, with Wolcott, Jenkins, and Knapp. Appropriated $100,000 for immediate investment in battlefield stores. Made progress with organization of our little *Hôtel des Invalides* in Grove Street. The lease of its building has been taken in my name. We have published an advertisement announcing our intention to use funds for that object, and thus get around Professor Dwight's opinion as to the trusts on which our funds are held.

March 6. The news of Early's defeat by Sheridan was telegraphed by Grant to Stanton, and by Stanton to Dix. . . . It took me an hour to work my way uptown through the crowded streets to our Columbia College meeting at the Law School in Lafayette Place at two o'clock. Little more than a quorum present. Only important business was the report of the Committee on School of Mines. Rutherfurd supported its recommendations forcibly and well. So did Mr. Ruggles. Ogden opposed them ex officio as too *costly*, but withdrew his objections and acquiesced. Zabriskie opposed them in his usual addle-brained way because they were not costly enough to succeed, because they were too costly for the College treasury, and because we ought to inquire and ascertain what professors were paid at Freiburg and Paris before venturing to employ professors in New York. The Bishop made a characteristic speech on both sides of the question. I said a little in confirmation of Rutherfurd. The result was that our resolutions passed without an audible dissenting vote, namely: the conditional pledge of $250,000 to the School and the recognition of the associates as colleagues of the committee. Very well. Now it remains to be seen whether we can get the *other* $250,000 out of the public for the treasury of Columbia College. I have my doubts. Wrote to Egleston this evening.

Today's grand jubilation was a splendid affair, more so than it would have been if held on the fourth, for there are anti-Lincolnites who would have kept aloof lest they should seem to do honor to Lincoln by making the day of his re-inauguration a festival. The crowd was enormous. Even Wall Street was thronged with Brooklynites from the Wall Street ferry. From the Park to Madison Square all New York seemed in the streets, at the windows, or on the housetops. We saw great crowds in the spring of 1861, and when the Prince of Wales honored us with a visit, but that of today seems to me bigger than any of them—perhaps because the impression is more fresh. The procession was three hours and a half long; that is, in passing any one point. I saw portions of it. After dinner, spent an hour at Union Square looking at fireworks. The jets of fire balls—red, white and blue; a dozen or twenty in the air at once—were very brilliant and beautiful. All this extravagant, exuberant rejoicing frightens me. It seems a manifest omen of mishap.

Sorry to say that Andy Johnson, Vice-President of the nation, whom I have held in great respect for four years past, seems to have been disgracefully *drunk* last Saturday and hardly in a condition to take part in the inaugural ceremonies of the new Administration. He has given the

World and the *News* lamentable occasion to blaspheme. Those news-papers denounce and deride the inaugural address by A. Lincoln. It is certainly most unlike the inaugurals of Pierce, Polk, Buchanan, or any of their predecessors; unlike any American state paper of this century. I would give a good deal to know what estimate will be put on it ten or fifty years hence.

It is remarkable that Strong, with his highly cultivated literary taste, should have felt any doubt as to the verdict of history upon the most religious and most eloquent of all Lincoln's state papers, the second inaugural; a piece of prose that will live as long as the English language. It is not so remarkable that the World *and* News, *two embittered Democratic organs, should have been deeply irritated by the President's statement that it might be God's will that the war continue "till all the wealth piled by the bondman's two hundred and fifty years of unrequited toil shall be sunk, and until every drop of blood drawn with the lash shall be paid by another drawn with the sword." Lincoln's "re-inauguration," as Strong calls it, was attended by scenes of patriotic rejoicing throughout the North. Numerous cities, including New York, witnessed the pageantry of grand military and civic parades; while in Washington a huge throng gathered under the shadow of the Capitol dome, now completed with the bronze statue of Liberty surmounting its crest as a symbol of the triumphant vindication of the principle of Union. Before Lincoln delivered his address and took the oath of office administered by Salmon P. Chase, the new Chief Justice, Andrew Johnson was sworn in as Vice-President in the Senate Chamber. This ceremony was unduly prolonged by his own half-maudlin utterances; but he was not to be judged as harshly as Strong's passage implies, for, just recovering from a grave illness, and suffering from fatigue and a bad cold, he had indiscreetly taken too large a glass of stimulant. Vice-President Johnson, far from being addicted to drink, was an eminently temperate man.*

March 8. Wet evening after a fine day. Poor Bob LeRoy's funeral was at Trinity Church at ten o'clock. Ellie went with me; that true little woman never forgets an old friend. I was glad to see so many in attend-ance. . . . Poor fellow, he came home on furlough a fortnight ago, having suffered since June from camp diarrhea of unusual severity, but seemingly not at all pulled down by it. General McCook spoke of him as among the bravest and coolest men he ever knew, and as having utterly abstained from stimulants while on his staff. Poor Bob spoke of his own reformation.

lamented the prevalence of drunkenness among officers in the army, and referred to himself as a living proof that the habit could be broken, no matter how far it had gone (he had suffered at least two attacks of delirium tremens). A day or two after, while he was waiting at a railroad depot to receive Mrs. Charles E. Strong and escort her to her hotel, the morbid appetite came on him suddenly with a force he found absolutely irresistible. This is what he stated on his death-bed. He went involuntarily to the nearest grocery and swallowed two or three glasses of whiskey, one after another, and then adjourned to his club to continue the treatment. Mrs. Charles E. Strong found her way to her hotel without escort as best she could, and Bob returned to his father-in-law's house while the family was at dinner, his wife included, and dropped on the rug before the dining-room fire. He was carried up to bed and resumed the same practice the next day, and the next. But after some four or five days of hard, steady drinking—last Wednesday, I think—he had to give it up and take to his bed, for his diarrhea was much aggravated. His physician (Neill) did not think him dangerously ill till last Saturday morning, when he reported that there was a sudden and alarming change, and that he would call again in an hour or two. He did so, and pronounced the case hopeless. The patient was sinking and stimulants were positively inert. The patient saw the grave looks of those about him and called on his doctor to "speak out like a man" and tell him the truth. "Was he going to die?" Yes. "Would he live through the day?" Probably not. . . . Poor Bob LeRoy! What might not have been made out of him twenty years ago by even the least effort to train him aright? . . .

Kenzua Petroleum Co. Directors sat a couple of hours yesterday afternoon at Mr. Ruggles's office. We commence boring forthwith. May we "strike ile"!

March 9. . . . To School of Mines, where I spent an hour; then to No. 823, where was Marcus L. Ward of Newark, also Mrs. Hoge and Mrs. Livermore of Chicago, who are here working for the Great Northwest Sanitary Fair that is to be opened next June and to surpass all fairs that have been held since the universe was a universe. They are fearful and wonderful women, whose horsepower is to be expressed in terms of droves of horses.

We send a first-class propeller to Wilmington Saturday, as the *Uncas* does not return yet from her last trip, and we cannot delay supplies to that point any longer. I should go with her but for this confounded School of Mines. The next fortnight is a critical period in our *accouche-*

ment of that bantling, and I ought not to go away. Egleston and Chandler spent the evening here, settling drafts of certain circulars.

March 10. . . . Richmond newspapers are in a special spasm of fury beyond any fit they have yet suffered. We must not attach too much weight to what these sensitive, excitable, high-toned, chivalric creatures rave when in nervous exaltation, whether arising from patriotic or from alcoholic stimulus. But this particular paroxysm certainly resembles the death flurry of a whale. The editorial utterances are violent, desperate, incoherent, hurried, and objectless. They amount in substance to this, that there is somewhere a class of "whipped seceders" and "whipped croakers" who desire subjugation and have an appetite for infamy—that these caitiffs want Davis to abdicate, and their pressure is sufficient to make it worthwhile to expend much bad language on them—that they will not succeed in these base designs, because Southerners never, never, *never* will be slaves, and because "our women" ought to take up their broomsticks and drive these wretches into the James River, and so on. There are certainly signs in Secessia of incipient decomposition. The rebellion has, at the very least, another year's fight in it, but it may die of inward disease within thirty days. I trust it will not die too soon and that it will be killed, not merely "kilt." I long for peace, but only for a durable peace, of material that will wear. John Bright writes F. M. Edge that he hopes our war will not end till its work is done, and he sees the case aright.

The rebel hosts continue to be seriously drained by desertion. Not less than fifty deserters have taken refuge within Grant's lines every day for many weeks past, and their average number is probably nearer one hundred than fifty. Companies come in, led by their company officers. All tell the same story of compulsory service, hardships, failure of pay and of clothing and of rations, and of general despondency. The Confederacy has "gone up," they say. "We all know it, and we know it is useless to fight any longer." Lee's soldiers would throw away their arms and disband tomorrow if they dared, and so on. Such statements made by deserters are worth much "less than their face." But when made by hundreds, and corroborated by the actual desertion of thousands, at imminent risk of life and with certain and conscious loss of honor, they are worth a great deal. It is likely, moreover, that for every rebel who flees within our lines, two flee the other way and take sanctuary in the hill country or the "piney woods," supporting themselves by levying contributions on all and sundry as sovereign powers so far as their own personal sovereignty can be made practically available, and thus carrying out the doctrine of secession to its ultimate results. Many counties of Virginia, the Carolinas, and the Gulf States are said to swarm with these banditti, and they are admitted to be even more savage and reckless than the vandal hordes of the North.

The Rebel Congress seems to have reconsidered its refusal to arm the slaves and to have decided, reluctantly, and by a very close vote, that there is no help for it and that Cuffee must be conscripted and made to fight for his chivalric master. So much for the visions of glory the South saw in 1860. This sacrifice of the first principles of the Southern social system is a confession of utter exhaustion; a desperate remedy and a most dangerous experiment. And the experiment is tried at least a year too late. It will take six months to drill and equip any considerable *corps d'Afrique*, and Sherman, Sheridan, Thomas, and Grant are likely, with God's blessing, to give rebellion its death blow within that time.

But the measure has its immediate effects. It disgusts and alienates many slaveholders and many fanatical theorists about slavery, and it is received as an affront by the rebel rank and file—an affront that justifies desertion. They will feel it not only as an affront, but as a disheartening surrender of the principle for which they have fought. They learn that niggers are now to be armed and put into the field as the allies of Southern gentlemen; "that it will depend on the nigger's pluck and muscle and endurance how far he is to share with white men the glory of upholding the Southern cause. It will depend on that and nothing else. Moreover, he is to be rewarded for good service by freedom." But the first of all Southern axioms has been for thirty years past that freedom was a punishment to the slave, servitude his normal condition, and that he loved and looked up to and depended on his owner as a good dog does on his master, and that he despised and rejected emancipation just as a good dog would dislike being discharged from his duty of guardianship and kicked into the street to get his own living as best he could.

March 13.   Did little in Wall Street. Committee on School of Mines met with the associates at the Law School this afternoon. Chandler, Egleston, and Vinton attended, some sixteen in all. It was a kind of preliminary meeting, and no important action was taken. All depends now on the success of our subcommittee on ways and means, as to which I'm not in the least sanguine. . . .

March 15, WEDNESDAY.   Egleston spent the evening here, and after talking of the School of Mines, diverged to his experiences abroad, Trinity Church, theology, religion, theories of education, and so on. His earnestness and enthusiasm are remarkable, and his intensity of feeling as to religion and science both is a phenomenon almost unexampled in these times.

Yesterday brought tidings from Sherman, at last; at Laurel Hill, North Carolina, the 8th instant, and "all right." Gold dropped. Today at noon came news that he was at Fayetteville, North Carolina, and had opened communication with Wilmington. This let gold down to 174⅛; a very deep descent and sudden fall. It almost makes me suspect that operators have further information of an esoteric nature. Bragg has retreated across the Neuse. Sherman seems steering for Raleigh. If he get there safe, his entry may be the signal for a hearty counter revolution. Loyal men abound in Raleigh, and are kept quiet only by Davis's bayonets. And if Bragg stay where he is, he may find it a tight place. He will probably make for Raleigh, too, with Schofield after him. All which looks very nice and hopeful, but let us put off exultation a little longer.

Moreover, the morning papers say that there is sore panic in Richmond and that the evacuation of that pseudo-metropolis is positively in progress at last. This must be the 750th time we have been so informed, on the authority of "escaped prisoners" or "reliable gentlemen" or "intelligent contrabands." I should not think the story worth noting had I not a scrap of information from a disgusted New York Secesher which tends to confirm it. . . .

March 18. Very energetic in Wall Street. Walked off with George Anthon at two, crossed at Wall Street ferry, and explored sundry new districts of Brooklyn. Visited "Fort Greene," a noble public square with fine views in every direction. I hereby prophesy that in 1900 A.D. Brooklyn will be the city and New York will be the suburb. It is inevitable if both go on growing as they have grown for the last forty years. Brooklyn has room to spread and New York has not. The New Yorker of Thirty-fifth Street already finds it a tedious and annoying job to make his way downtown to business and home again. How will the New Yorker of One-hundredth Street get about forty years hence? Brooklyn must outnumber this city before very many years, and then places of amusement and fashionable residences will begin to emigrate across the East River. New York will become "the city" in the London sense of that word. Its Belgravia will be transferred from the Fifth Avenue to King's County. A like change is within my own memory. When I was a boy, the aristocracy lived around the Battery, on the Bowling Green, and in the western streets below Chambers; in Wall Street, Cedar Street, and Beekman Street, on the east of the town. Greenwich Street, now a hissing and a desolation, a place of lager beer saloons, emigrant boarding houses, and the vilest dens, was what Madison Avenue is now. There were the Griswolds in Chambers Street, Philip Hone in Broadway below Park Place, Mrs. Cruger at No. 55, and so on. Between 1828 and 1832, emigration to the regions of Fourth Street, Bond Street, and Lafayette Place set in, and the centres of fashion were moved again, for we are a nomadic people, and our finest brownstone houses are merely tents of new pattern and material. Brooklyn has advantages, too, that will speed the change. The situations on the Heights overlooking the bay can hardly be matched in any great city of Christendom. How often have I wished I could exchange this house for one of them, and that I could see from my library windows that noble prospect and that wide open expanse of sky, and the going down of the sun every evening! . . .

At No. 823; $11,000 in gold from San Francisco. Sold the draft at 164. No war news. No fighting around Richmond. Davis sends his Congress a message, almost equivalent to a *cognovit* of failure and ruin. Southern newspapers are unhappy about the conflagration that destroyed Columbia, South Carolina, when the rebels walked out and our army walked in. It would seem to have been caused by the firing of cotton stored there, and to have been suppressed, at last, by the exertions of our soldiers. But it is attributed to Sherman's "unprincipled diabolism."

George Anthon dined here. After dinner to meeting of the finance subcommittee of the Committee on School of Mines at the Law School, 37 Lafayette Place; Delano, Fish, Dodge, Jones, Tuckerman, Ward, and others. Return rather discouraged. Raising our $250,000 will be uphill work. This fall in gold will depress values, produce a sense of impoverishment, and tell against us. I shall not willingly become interested in the organization of anything *pro bono publico* again. It costs me more worry, anxiety, despondency, and general wear and tear than my feeble work for the public good is worth. For the last few months, I have been as unhappy about the School of Mines as if it had been one of my own children. Let it fail and come to naught and let me devote myself to my own personal interests. But then think of the admirable enthusiasm and self-devotion of Egleston, Chandler, and Vinton! Never was such material put within the control of our board. Not to improve it and make it felt in the community is a breach of trust.

March 21. . . . Great dismay in Wall Street; gold down to 156. It touched 152, I hear. So stocks are down, and men's hearts fail them for fear of a revolution and collapse. United States securities can be bought for less than their face, taking accrued interest into account. This fact will throw cold water on the new 7–30 loan, a curious consequence of our late triumphs and of the general conviction that rebellion is stricken with death.

Fifth Avenue from Forty-ninth Street down was absolutely thronged with costly new equipages on their way to Central Park this bright, bland afternoon. It was a broad torrent of vehicular gentility, wherein profits of shoddy and of petroleum were largely represented. Not a few of the ladies who were driving in the most sumptuous turn-outs, with liveried servants, looked as if they might have been cooks or chambermaids a very few years ago. . . .

Jeff Davis's message seems of graver and more doleful import the longer it is looked at. "Was ne'er prophetic sound so full of woe." He tells his Congress that he and they and all Rebeldom are in a desperate case, and that it is difficult to imagine a worse extremity than theirs, and urges remedies that are not only desperate but impracticable and that would be ruinous if practicable. His Congress has dispersed without administering these remedies or any of them. Strange this paper should have been published. Some say he means to resign, and run—having no doubt put away a pot of money in London or Paris—and to become an illustrious exile, and that this manifesto is meant to justify his abdication. Let him run, if he will. I hope he may get off safe, for if we caught him, we should not hang him, and our omission to do so would be discreditable. . . .

March 23. . . . Jeff Davis's Congress, being snubbed by that potentate in his last message and charged with the responsibility for all the present troubles of the Confederacy, jaws back through a committee report adopted just before adjournment (not on ayes and noes), "sasses" Jeff Davis, and says it's all his fault. As between Jeff Davis and his peers, I believe myself quite impartial, like the spectator of the fight between skunk and rattlesnake. I think that on the face of the papers, Congress has the best of it, and Jeff Davis gets a black eye. Anyhow, Satan is certainly divided against himself, and that is a hopeful sign.

March 24. Sanitary Commission session here tonight; Bellows, Van Buren, Jenkins. Agnew still in North Carolina. Jenkins gives no good account of Knapp's ways at Washington; thinks him cunning, evil-disposed, and untrue. It seems incredible this should be his character, but I fear he is not the embodiment of single-mindedness and unselfishness I used to suppose him. Jenkins has just had a long, semi-confidential talk with [William] Whiting of the War Office, and certain of our western agents have held like discourse with high officials of Thomas's army as to the coming campaign and the points at which we should set about accumulating supplies. Their letters and reports read tonight were interesting. As far as they go, they confirm Whiting's statements, which are generally none the worse for a little confirmation.

Taken together they are encouraging. Sherman and Schofield are about 100,000 strong; Grant 140,000; Sheridan has 15,000 cavalry in southern Virginia; Hancock (or Torbert?) a like force at Winchester and some 8,000 infantry beside.[1] Thomas has 150,000 (I suppose this means our whole force from Nashville and Knoxville to New Orleans). He is to send 50,000 toward Lynchburg and Danville, the Winchester column moving in concert up the Valley, and is to command in person a column of 40,000 marching on Selma. The department thinks it quite likely that Lee will have to capitulate without a battle. The draft and the volunteering thereby stimulated have already mustered into service nearly 100,000, and of these 30,000 are now under arms. We are 100,000 stonger than this time last year.

I hope all this may be true. If we have near 400,000 men in the field, Secessia must be outnumbered two to one, at least, to say nothing of discouragement, discord, financial collapse, and the closing of rebel ports to supplies from abroad. May we get through the next sixty days without any serious reverse or blunder!

March 25, SATURDAY. . . . At Philharmonic rehearsal at three o'clock; Beethoven's Ninth Symphony (the *Choral*), of which I have not heard a note for about five years. A rough performance. Though Eisfeld was not extreme to mark what was amiss, the raps of his baton for the repetition of an ill-rendered passage were many; so many that the orchestra spent an hour and forty minutes on the symphony, though they skipped all the long passage of melodic plain sailing that immediately precedes the "Marcia" subdivision of the fourth movement. On the whole, this great but unequal work gained on me. Its demerits were more distinctly visible, but its merits still more. Never before did I fully recognize the vigor and dash of the second movement, or the noble gravity, the serious sweetness, of the third. That movement is not matched. To me it seems to embody the sentiment of "When to the sessions of sweet silent thought."

March 27. . . . I must record the movements of two chips, because they shew which way the tide is setting. First: The Baltimore correspondent of

[1] Better authority credits Grant with 124,000; but Lee's army was reduced to about 50,000.

the New York *World*, and a bitter secessionist, who has long been prophesying woes to the country and victory to Jeff Davis over the signature of "Druid," writes that within a few weeks or months the Confederacy must cease to exist. It will no longer have a government, an army, or a capital. Its leaders made several mistakes at the outset, and among others this, that the cause of self-government and freedom must be destined always to prevail. Does this statement invite one to vehement cachinnation or to profuse nausea??? Second: At the recent debates in the House of Commons, Palmerston and Disraeli and others were of one mind with Mr. Bright, commending the energy and discretion of Lincoln's Administration under the most trying circumstances, and the most creditable spirit it has shewn in all its dealings with foreign powers! Poor, mean, shabby, fallen, old England restores us the tribute of her shop-keeper's civility and compliments the moment she discerns that we may win our unpromising lawsuit, after all; may "come to our own again," and be a profitable customer or an expensive enemy next year.

March 28. . . . The Kenzua Petroleum Co. directors met at Mr. Ruggles's office this afternoon. Cresson of Philadelphia and Moses H. Grinnell added unto us. Prospects of the company seem good. If it "strike ile," my 10,000 shares of stock may prove worth something, more or less, which would be gratifying. But I expect nothing, and am therefore incapable of disappointment. My stock has cost me nothing, so I have nothing at stake, and any oil of gladness that may flow therefrom, if only half a pint, will be so much clear gain.

Gold seems to have stuck fast in the neighborhood of 154. The prophets of Wall Street are prophesying that it will not soon sink much lower. They hold that we have discounted victory, that the late rapid decline represents the common belief that rebellion is as good as dead already, and that gold will stay where it is for some time after rebellion is actually defunct and gibbeted in chains as a warning to posterity. I do not think so. The wisest financier can only guess how it will be, for the equation is too complex and includes too many unknown and variable quantities—too many chances and contingencies—to be worked out by human wit.

The fray of the 25th before Petersburg was no small affair.[2] Had Lee's veterans fought as they fought last May it might have been a bad

[2] Seeing that he would soon be compelled to evacuate Petersburg and Richmond, Lee determined upon a last attempt to drive Grant back in his immediate front. On March 25, General John B. Gordon in a surprise assault captured Fort Stedman, one of the Union strong points. The Union forces then rallied and drove the Confederates out with heavy losses.

business. But after that first brilliant and successful dash at our line, they shewed little sign of their ancient pluck and tenacity. When once inside "Fort Stedman," many of them seem to have withdrawn into bomb-proofs in spite of their officers and thus to have secured an opportunity to surrender by dint of great resolution. Lee cannot afford many experiments like this. It must have cost him ten per cent of his available force. But what can he do? Grant has him by the throat. Sherman, reinforced by Schofield and Terry, was at last accounts threatening Raleigh, North Carolina, and steadily approaching the last duct that brings nutriment to the garrison of Richmond.

March 29. Committee on School of Mines met at Law School this afternoon and sat near two hours. Certain recommendations to the trustees. Satisfactory meeting. But it is clear one of our associates was a bad choice, Mr. Lewis L. Delafield to wit. He is talkative, conceited, pragmatical, and disputatious. He carries no weight, however, and is only an annoyance.

Afterwards at No. 823. Agnew made a long and interesting report (verbal) on what he did and saw at New Bern and Wilmington. Our supplies sent by the *Chase* reached Wilmington just at the right moment and saved scores of lives. His account of the condition of hundreds of returned prisoners, founded on personal inspection, is fearful. They have been starved into idiocy—do not know their own names, or where they are, or where their home is. Starvation has gangrened their extremities —destroyed their instinctive sense of decency, and converted them into irrational, atrophied, moribund animals. No Bastille and no Inquisition dungeon has ever come up to the chivalric rebel pen for prisoners of war. I do not think people quite see, even yet, the unexampled enormity of this crime. It is a new thing in the history of man. It infinitely transcends the records of the guillotine and concomitant *noyades* and *fusillades*. The disembowelment and decapitation of all men, women, and children of a Chinese city convicted of rebel sympathies is an act of mercy compared with the politic, slow torture Davis and Lee have been inflicting on their prisoners, with the intent of making them unfit for service when exchanged.

I almost hope this war may last till it become a war of extermination. Southrons who could endure the knowledge that human creatures were undergoing this torture within their own borders, and who did not actively protest against it, deserve to be killed.

March 30. . . . Gold touched 149 today. Military matters are as they were. Sherman's army is taking a rest at or near Goldsboro and trying on its new shoes. Lee has made another push at Grant's lines, a small affair compared with that of the 25th, and took nothing by his motion. Sheridan is on the rampage somewhere south of the Appomattox. A column from Thomas seems moving Lynchburg-ward. We are closing in upon Richmond, but Lee has his back to the wall and will fight like a rat in a corner if his men be kept to their work. I do not believe it possible for him to carry his army to Danville or Lynchburg if he wants to. His only hope is in the chapter of accidents. Something may turn up. Richmond editors keep up their spirits, however, and also their vocabulary.

March 31, FRIDAY. Gold 151. News that Mobile was attacked on the 21st. Result not yet known. Also that Grant opened an important movement at three A.M. on the 29th. Sheridan seems to have marched toward Dinwiddie Court House, backed by a strong infantry force. Object probably to cut the "South Side Railroad," and perhaps to draw Lee out of his forts. I hope this rain may not have spoiled the party. We may expect weighty news any minute. There has already been a lively little collision, of which the rebels had the worst. Though all the chances are in our favor, I am anxious, for we are in a premature stage of jubilation that invites disaster.

Agnew opened more of his budget from Wilmington and New Bern. He tells us Sherman's officers say that their campaign was made possible by the order of the rebel government that corn be planted instead of cotton. Four years ago the army could not have been fed. As it was, they marched through a land of groaning corn cribs and granaries, and their men and their animals entered Savannah in better flesh than when they left Atlanta. A notable statement. . . .

From observation at Wilmington, Agnew thinks the Southern "masses" an effete people, unable to take care of themselves now that their slaveholding lords and magnates are gone. A "local committee" at Wilmington is feeding four thousand Wilmingtonians on rations issued by the government. The white trash of even North Carolina is helpless and imbecile, unable to work or to reorganize the community.

So much for that. To come nearer home, the bill for a paid fire department, superseding our ancient, rowdy organization, has passed both houses of the state legislature, to the great disgust and wrath of the existing engine companies. Some of them are reported to say and swear that they will not turn out in case of fire. That is quite enough to justify the change. But as the new department does not yet exist, and the old one is disaffected and mutinous, a large fire might be a very serious business just now. There has been no act of the legislature, in my time, that will work so great a change in this city's daily life.

April 1, SATURDAY. Noon brought an extra, with despatches from Grant, in substance: "Hard fighting yesterday. We took the Boydton plank road, lost it, recovered it, and hold it; also took four battle flags." Not bad so far as it goes, though it leaves much to the imagination. According to Charley Strong, who has returned from City Point and the front after three days there, our officers say the rebels have clearly lost heart, that they fight coldly, run readily, and surrender joyfully. To be sure, this hard pounding on the 31st looks unlike it. But he talked with a Major Miller of General Kimball's staff, who was bagged by the rebels during the Fort Stedman fight. Their commanding officer ("Louisiana Tiger, G–d–you") instantly demanded the major's overcoat, watch, money, and horse, which were surrendered, and hailed the orderly who was taking off the quadruped. "Recollect, now, that's *my* horse, don't you go and turn him over to anybody." After this business transaction, the major asked his captor's name and rank, received the answer above quoted, and was ordered to the rear. But it "rained blue beans," as the Germans say, and also iron cocoanuts and watermelons all along the way to the rebel lines. The fire from both sides was a *feu d'enfer,* and the major's guard preferred taking him into one of the bomb-proofs of Stedman and waiting there till the storm should abate a little. The bomb-proof was already crowded with rebel soldiers. The major proceeded to call the attention of those nearest him to a few leading facts. "The Confederacy had gone up. If they went back to their own lines and took him along, it would be unpleasant for him, but would it be a good thing for them? They would have to do more fighting and probably be bagged at last. Whereas, if they were only in *our lines,* they would be well treated and get not only abundant rations, but twenty dollars each for their arms and accoutrements." They listened eagerly, but they did not like to desert. "Very becoming and proper," said the major, "but why can't I take you in as my prisoners?" The suggestion was received with favor, so he formed them in column by threes and double-quicked them into our lines, 204 men, each with his musket.

The Confederacy was now in its death-throes. Grant on March 24 had issued orders for the grand final movements against Lee to end the war. Though he had now besieged Richmond and Petersburg since the summer of 1864, he did not control the lines west and southwest of these cities; and he feared that

Lee's army would break out along the route of the Richmond & Danville Rail-road, and then either join forces with Johnston's troops or effect its escape into the mountains. A union of the two Confederate armies, he feared, would result in a bloody and painful campaign consuming most of the summer. Grant there-fore thrust forward his left wing, south of Petersburg, in order to cut the branch railroad leading from Petersburg to the Richmond & Danville and seal up the Confederates in that town. Heavy rains slowed down the movement. But on April 1, the Union troops under Sheridan came into collision with the Con-federates at Five Forks, southwest of Richmond; and they carried everything before them. By nightfall the victory was complete. Pickett's troops were routed in utter disorder, and nearly six thousand of them were taken prisoner. This left the main Confederate army, stretched out in a long thin line, in a dangerous position; and next day (April 2) Grant ordered an assault at dawn along the entire front. The Confederate leaders already knew that the struggle to hold their capital was lost. In the first hours of the general assault the Union forces proved irresistible, and before noon Lee had telegraphed to Jefferson Davis: "I see no prospect of doing more than holding our position here till night. I am not cer-tain that I can do that." The Union forces had actually cut his army in two and thrown a powerful wedge between the segments. On the night of April 2, the Confederate forces filed out of Richmond and Petersburg. It was still Lee's hope that he could get away along the southwesterly roads and join hands with Johnston; but April 3 found Grant's army in hot pursuit. So little did Norther-ners grasp the mighty power of Grant's blows that as late as April 1 Strong feared that the Union forces might yet retreat; but, he added, "Grant knows what he is doing."

April 2, SUNDAY. There is reason to hope this day may long be re-membered. To Trinity with Ellie and the two boys. After service (com-munion), we asked General Anderson (of Fort Sumter) to ride up with us and stopped at the *Tribune* office to look for news. There was an extra with a despatch from Lincoln at City Point to Stanton—brief but weighty. Read it to the general, and his *Thank God* was fervently uttered and good to hear. . . .

April 3. Petersburg and Richmond! *Gloria in excelsis Deo.*

New York has seen no such day in our time nor in the old time before us. The jubilations of the Revolutionary War and the War of 1812 were those of a second-rate seaport town. This has been metropolitan and worthy an event of the first national importance to a continental nation and a cosmopolitan city.

The morning papers disclosed nothing decisive. There were two short despatches from City Point giving later news of yesterday's great battle, which looked well, but I omnibussed downtown expecting only to learn during the day more positively that the South Side Railroad was cut; that Lee had returned to his entrenchments badly punished, and that it was confidently expected that he would have to evacuate them at some future period.

Walking down Wall Street, I saw something on the *Commercial Advertiser* bulletin board at the corner of Pine and William Streets and turned off to investigate. I read the announcement "Petersburg is taken" and went into the office in quest of particulars. The man behind the counter was slowly painting in large letters on a large sheet of brown paper another annunciation for the board outside: "Richmond is"— "What's that about Richmond?" said I. "Anything more?" He was too busy for speech, but he went on with a capital C, and a capital A, and so on, till I read the word *CAPTURED*!!! Finding that this was official, I posted up to Trinity Church to tell the sexton to suggest to Vinton to ask the Rector's permission to set the chimes going (which was duly done). When I came back, all William Street in front of the *Advertiser* office was impenetrably crowded, and people were rushing together in front of the Custom House (the *ci-devant* Merchants' Exchange), where Prosper M. Wetmore and Simeon Draper were getting up a meeting on the spur of the moment.

An enormous crowd soon blocked that part of Wall Street, and speeches began. Draper and the Hon. Moses Odell and Evarts and Dean (a proselyte from Copperheadism) and the inevitable Wetmore, and others, severally had their say, and the meeting, organized at about twelve, did not break up, I hear, till four P.M. Never before did I hear cheering that came straight from the heart, that was given because people felt relieved by cheering and hallooing. All the cheers I ever listened to were tame in comparison, because seemingly inspired only by a design to shew enthusiasm. These were spontaneous and involuntary and of vast "magnetizing" power. They sang "Old Hundred," the Doxology, "John Brown," and "The Star-Spangled Banner," repeating the last two lines of Key's song over and over, with a massive roar from the crowd and a unanimous wave of hats at the end of each repetition. I think I shall never lose the impression made by this rude, many-voiced chorale. It seemed a revelation of profound national feeling, underlying all our vulgarisms and corruptions, and vouchsafed to us in their very focus and centre, in Wall Street itself.

I walked about on the outskirts of the crowd, shaking hands with everybody, congratulating and being congratulated by scores of men I hardly know even by sight. Men embraced and hugged each other, *kissed* each other, retreated into doorways to dry their eyes and came out again to flourish their hats and hurrah. There will be many sore throats in New York tomorrow. My only experience of a people stirred up to like intensity of feeling was at the great Union meeting at Union Square in April, 1861. But the feeling of today's crowd was not at all identical with that of the memorable mass-meeting four years ago. It was no less earnest and serious, but it was founded on memories of years of failure, all but hopeless, and on the consciousness that national victory was at last secured, through much tribulation. . . .

After dinner to the Union League Club. Vast crowd, enthusiasm, and excitement. Meeting organized upstairs, Captain Marshall in the chair, and "a few remarks" made by a score of people. Honest, downright old Judge Vanderpoel[3] was very good. "Gentlemen," said the judge, "I tell you that for years before this rebellion, we at the North lived under the tyranny of the slaveholders. I see now that when I was in Congress, almost every important vote I gave was dictated by them and given under the plantation lash. I confess it with shame, and humbly ask pardon of this meeting and of all my fellow-countrymen."

Hamilton Fish was at the Club—I never saw him there before— beaming and gushing, and shaking everybody's hands with fervor. Two years ago he talked nothing but discouragement and practical disloyalty. But (as Sydney Smith irreverently said of bishops), "If you want to know which way the wind blows, throw up Hamilton Fish."

It seems like a Fourth of July night—such a fusillade and cannonade is going on. Thus ends a day *sui generis* in my life. We shall long remember that the first troops to enter Richmond were niggers of Weitzel's corps. It is a most suggestive fact. It's said there were abundant signs of Union feeling in the city. Lee, Davis, & Co. are supposed to be making for Burke's Junction. Lynchburg or Danville is doubtless their proposed harbor of refuge. May Sheridan's cavalry be fresh enough to deal with them according to the example of Blücher after Waterloo. The government of the "Confederate States" has become nomadic. Its capitol and its depart-

[3] Aaron Vanderpoel (1799–1870) had been a Democratic member of Congress in Van Buren's presidency, and later was judge of the superior court in New York.

ments of state and of war are probably in a dirty, damaged, worn-out railroad car, and its "seat of government" probably rests on the saddle which Jeff Davis bestrides.

April 4. Ellie set off for City Point on the steamer *George Leary* with a large pleasant party: Mrs. Paran Stevens and Miss Fanny Reid, John Van Buren and his pretty daughter Miss Annie, Captain Comstock and his daughter, Arthur Leary, Griswold Gray, and Colonel Stoughton. Wish I could have gone. I consented with sore misgivings, but she had earned this little spree by her faithful service on hospital transports on the Pamunkey and the James in 1862. I fear she and her party will be disappointed after all and unable to visit Richmond.

Broadway is a river of flags. Poor Frederic Winthrop was shot through the lungs and is dead. He rose from the ranks to a brigadier-general's brevet. He was a cousin of Theodore Winthrop and brother of Frank Winthrop, with whom I walked uptown after the College meeting yesterday. It's said another despatch came last night, after Howard Potter had left town, announcing the death of General Robert Potter. Tonight's *Post* mentions the report as probably true. God help poor Miss Stevens![4] At Life & Trust Co. meeting this morning, and at three o'clock to a meeting of the Kenzua Co. directors at their new office, 36 Wall Street. Tonight at Union League looking over the collection recently bought by the club of foreign books and tracts on the Rebellion. Nearly all one way, of course.

No news from the front up to half-past one. Everybody was sallying out to look for news every ten minutes and coming back disappointed and wondering whether something hadn't gone wrong. At last came announcements on bulletin boards and an extra with despatches. They indicate that Lee is damaged and demoralized. The country is full of stragglers. We bag prisoners in large handfuls. Lee's course is marked by abandoned artillery and by burned or charred wagons and caissons. Great store of war material found at Richmond, including railroad rolling stock. Unofficial statements are that we have 15,000 prisoners at City Point, that Fort Darling and the rebel iron-clads on the upper James have been blown up, that the Union feeling of North Carolina is so star-spangled as to be actually oppressive, that Sherman's men are so cocky and Johnston's rebels so depressed that three of our foragers commonly form in line of

[4] Brigadier-General Robert B. Potter, a son of Bishop Alonzo Potter, was sorely wounded in the assault on Petersburg April 2, but recovered to live until 1887. He married Abby Austin Stevens.

battle when they encounter not more than thirty seceshers, and always drive them; also, however, that the communication between Goldsboro and Sherman's base is thought to be just a little endangered by Wade Hampton's cavalry.

Guns popping off in every direction tonight. A salute of one hundred guns fired at the foot of Wall Street this morning, and another in front of the Union League Club tonight. Surely the slaveholders' rebellion, with its capital lost, its best army defeated, its soldiers demoralized, its people broken-spirited, and its ports closed to contributions from sympathizing Britons, and its president and chief general both running for their lives, cannot sustain itself or claim to be called a nation much longer. But heaven save us from overtures of peace and reconstruction for the next six months. May Pharaoh's heart be hardened yet a little longer!

April 5. . . . Despatches are still bright. They report Lee's grand army crippled and in great measure disorganized. Unless newspaper correspondents lie most exorbitantly, it is used up and done for. . . .

April 6. . . . Today's news is good and full of promise. Lee is retreating perforce toward Lynchburg. He cannot make for Danville or try to join Johnston in North Carolina, because Sheridan and Grant are moving on a parallel line south of his, and are seemingly ahead of him. He has been obliged to take the wrong side (the north bank) of the Appomattox. . . . Jeff Davis made a moonlight flitting Sunday night and is believed to have taken a special train for Danville. Like the missing Massa in the "Year of Jubilo" [Kingdom Coming]:

> He saw the smoke 'way down the ribber, where the
>   Linkum gunboats lay,
> And he picked up his hat, and he left bery sudden,
>   an I 'spec he's run away! . . .

April 7. . . . At noon came more good news. Lee's army again routed yesterday. More guns and wagon trains captured, and several thousand prisoners, among them Kershaw and Ewell and half a dozen rebel generals beside. Sheridan confident that Lee, with the debris of the "Army of Northern Virginia," will soon be bagged. . . .

April 8, SATURDAY. . . . For the first time in my life, I think, I have heard two of Beethoven's symphonies within twenty-four hours. The Ninth was rehearsed by the Philharmonic corps at the Academy of Music at three o'clock, and this evening I heard the Seventh at Irving Hall with George Anthon, who dined here. It was the last of Theodore Thomas's "symphonic soirées" (why does Mr. Thomas repudiate the English language?). We heard a "Passacaglia" by Bach (whatever that is) "arranged for full orchestra by H. Esser" (whoever he is); the "first time in America." Would it be a serious blow to be told it was the *last*? I honor Bach's name and works, but this seemed a mere exercise in counterpoint, clear and compact, but without significance or interest. Mozart's Symphony for Violin and Viola, with orchestra, was beautiful exceedingly, though there was little orchestra but the strings and hardly a trace of color from the wind instruments. Schumann's Overture to *The Bride of Messina* was rubbish and rot. . . .

April 9. Not a word from the army. This naturally makes one a little anxious. Nor have I yet any news from Ellie and her party. I rather infer from her silence that they have penetrated to Richmond. . . .

★ ★ ★ ★ ★

LEE AND HIS ARMY HAVE SURRENDERED! *Gloria in Excelcis Deo. Et in Terra, Pax hominibus bonae voluntatis.*

April 10, MONDAY.   A series of vehement pulls at the front door bell slowly roused me to consciousness soon after I hurried in last night and routed me out of bed at last. I made my way downstairs in my dressing-gown, half awake, and expecting to find Ellie returned from her James River trip. But it was George C. Anthon come to announce The Surrender and that the rebel army of the Peninsula, Antietam, Fredericksburg, Chancellorsville, The Wilderness, Spotsylvania Court House, and other battles, has ceased to exist. It can bother and perplex none but historians henceforth forever. It can never open fire again on loyal men or lend its powerful aid to any cause, good or bad. There is no such army any more. God be praised!

To bed again, but sleep was difficult. Up early, stimulated thereto by the enthusiasm of John R. Strong, Esq., who was hallooing all over the house, hurrahing for Grant and "singing of anthems" after a fashion; that is, making well-meant efforts to chant "John Brown" and "The Red, White, and Blue." Find the correspondence between Grant and Lee in the morning papers at the breakfast table. It is creditable to Grant, who opened it, and not discreditable to Lee. Lee made a decent shew of coyness, and wrote quite a large number of notes. He was not altogether prepared to admit his position quite hopeless. But he accepted Grant's terms at last. They are most generous. Officers and men to be paroled, officers retaining their side-arms and private property. My first thought was that Grant had been too liberal. I would have waited a day or two longer, when Lee would have been without ammunition and without rations and ready to surrender at discretion. But I was wrong. Grant understands his business. Every officer and every private who goes home on parole under this arrangement will report, for his own credit's sake, that the surrender was unavoidable; that the Confederacy was overmatched; that fighting was useless waste of life; that the rebel cause was hopeless. Each will be a fountain of cold water on whatever pugnacity and chivalry may yet survive in his own home and vicinage. Thus ends Grant's most memorable campaign of eleven months.

Binney came in after breakfast. Then to Wall Street, where appeared at noon tidings (unofficial and not to be counted upon) that Sherman has occupied Raleigh, North Carolina, and a column of Thomas's army penetrated far into Alabama and burned Selma. If untrue they are merely premature, I think; facts a little irregular as to the accident of time.

It has rained hard all day; too hard for jubilant demonstrations out of doors. We should have made this Monday something like the 3rd of April, 1865, I think, had the sun shone, and could we have congregated in the streets without umbrellas. Guns have been firing all day in spite of foul weather. Uptown at two o'clock with William Schermerhorn to Forty-ninth Street for the Library Committee of Columbia College. Discourse with Barnard, Egleston, and Chandler thereafter about the School of Mines. Egleston subject to severe paroxysms of despondency.

On April 7, Lee's army was cut off. It was moving along the road which ran by the way of Appomattox Court House to Lynchburg; and leading elements of Grant's force, crossing the Appomattox River, planted themselves in front of the Confederates and brought Lee to bay. That day Grant sent the Southern commander a polite summons to surrender, and a series of communications passed between the two leaders. Lee knew that his ill-fed, ill-clad, exhausted army was rapidly falling to pieces, and that any battle with the great Union forces gathering in front and on the flank would be hopeless. Further bloodshed would have been criminal, and an interview was finally arranged on April 9. Lee waited in a little house on the outskirts of Appomattox Court House; and a little after noon Grant, accompanied by Sheridan and Ord, was ushered in. The Union general sat down and penned a letter offering to parole all Lee's men, and to permit them to keep their side-arms, baggage, and horses. Lee, donning his glasses, read it, and as he handed it back, he remarked, with what Grant later thought was "some feeling," that the concession as to side-arms would have a happy effect upon his army.

Though small Confederate armies under Johnston and Kirby Smith remained in the field, their surrender was now certain; and the North rejoiced over the triumphant close of the bloody struggle and the dawn of a brighter era. On April 14, at noon precisely, Strong's friend Robert Anderson raised above Fort Sumter, in the presence of a distinguished group, the very flag he had lowered four years before. But before the news of this symbolic act was printed in the morning journals next day, it had been thrown into insignificance by a catastrophic event.

April 11. No further tidings from Ellie, and none from the army. Our appetite for news has been gratified with such powerful stimulants of late that a single day without intelligence of great victory or gain somewhere seems a disappointment.

To Trinity Church at half-past twelve. A meeting of business men yesterday resolved on a *Te Deum*, and arrangements for a service of thanksgiving had accordingly been made, as far as they could be made on such short notice. I found the church already packed, and made my way up the crowded south aisle as certain marine mollusca bore into sandstone. Encountered Miss Kate Wolfe and handsome Miss Mary Ulshoeffer, and got them chairs from the vestry room. Service began a little after one o'clock. The church was then jammed to its utmost capacity, and (I am told) there was a dense crowd at its doors. It was an irregular, special service, conforming to no rubric, but the great assemblage joined in it heartily. The "lesson" was the Beatitudes. Vinton made a very short and a very judicious little address from the pulpit, enforcing the duty of forgiveness and charity. In alluding to the President, he used terms that do his insight credit: "Wise, merciful, resolute, Christian," or their equivalent. Many loyal men hold Lincoln a sensible, commonplace man, without special talent, except for story telling, and it must be admitted that he sometimes tells stories of the class that is "not convenient" and does not become a gentleman and the holder of the exalted place. But his weaknesses are on the surface, and his name will be of high account fifty years hence, and for many generations thereafter. The choir had been largely reinforced and did well, considering there had been no time for rehearsal. . . . The old *Gloria in Excelsis*, the old chant familiar to me since boyhood, was taken up by a thousand voices, sustained by both organs. It was most touching, noble, awe-ful to hear. The "nave-organ" played the assemblage out of church with Handel's "Hallelujah Chorus," "Hail Columbia," and "The Star-Spangled Banner," *fortissimo*.

To No. 823. Much work there. May we hope to wind up soon and muster ourselves out of service? After dinner to the Union League Club, where I presided over the committee on admissions. Copperheads of two years ago, and men who supported Seymour and McClellan last fall, are applying for admission. We rejected half a score of them this evening. Barlow and Belmont, O'Conor and Betts will soon be sending in their names, I suppose. We are discovering now with some surprise that everybody, little Ned Bell included, has been an "uncompromising Union man from the first." What a pity we had not known this a year ago; we should have been saved much uneasiness.

People hold the war virtually ended. It looks so. Lee is out of the game. Napoleon could hardly save Joe Johnston's army. . . . When Joe Johnston is disposed of, Lincoln should announce by proclamation that from and after the —— day of —— next, the Confederacy will be no longer practically recognized as a belligerent power, and that men thereafter taken in arms against the country will be treated as criminals and not as prisoners of war. He might properly do so forthwith, for the so-called Confederate government seems to have abdicated and to be concealing itself with intent to avoid the service of process. That power is reported to have emerged from a railroad car at Danville, Virginia, Monday evening (3rd instant), represented by Davis *Imperator* and two of his pals, all three dusty, deliquescent, and much demoralized. Since that date we know nothing of it. . . .

A rather lively theoretical controversy has arisen of and concerning Jeff Davis: Shall we hang him, when and if we catch him, or shall we let him run? Weight of opinion is clearly for hanging him, but he will save his neck somehow. Justice requires his solemn public execution. Sound policy would probably let him live, in prison or exile. I should vote to hang him. "We'll hang Jeff Davis on a sour apple tree, as we go marching on."

This choral promise and vow, so often repeated by so many thousand soldiers and civilians, should be performed at the first opportunity. Bidwell has long predicted that Jeff Davis, when finally cornered, would kill himself. The best disposition destiny can make of the scoundrel would be to let him be grabbed by some one of the organized bands of deserters and refugees who hold the hill country of North Carolina and Virginia. They would award him a high gallows and a short shrift, and so dispose of a troublesome question.

Even the *World* and the *Daily News* say that Secessia is now conquered, crushed, subjugated, and under our feet. They whine for forbearance and magnanimity toward their friends and fellow-conspirators. To be sure, we should be as merciful as we *safely* can be. The punishment already inflicted on the Southern people is fearful to think of. The death of their best (or worst) and bravest; the devastation, the breaking up of their social system, general destitution, the bitterest humiliation of the most arrogant of mankind, the most splendid and confident expectations disappointed, universal ruin, bereavement, and shame—these are among the terms of the sentence God has pronounced and is executing on rebellious slaveholders. Never, in modern times, at least, has so vast a territory been so scourged. Think, for example, of the scores of hundreds of families, prouder than Lucifer, worth their millions only *four* years ago, whose women and children and old men are now sustaining life on the rations of Yankee charity, whose plantation homesteads have been plundered and burned, whose husbands, brothers, sons, cousins have been killed, and who have to see soldiers that were once "their niggers" mounting guard in the streets of Savannah, Charleston, or Richmond, and prepared to suppress every Southern lady or "high-toned" gentleman who walks his or her own streets without a pass from some Yankee mudsill provost marshal.

April 12. Letter from Ellie at Washington. She has had a glorious time at City Point and Richmond. . . .

April 15, SATURDAY. Nine o'clock in the morning. *LINCOLN AND SEWARD ASSASSINATED LAST NIGHT! ! ! !*

The South has nearly filled up the measure of her iniquities at last! Lincoln's death not yet certainly announced, but the one o'clock despatch states that he was then dying. Seward's side room was entered by the same or another assassin, and his throat cut. It is unlikely he will survive, for he was suffering from a broken arm and other injuries, the consequence of a fall, and is advanced in life. Ellie brought this news two hours ago, but I can hardly *take it in* even yet. *Eheu* A. Lincoln!

I have been expecting this. I predicted an attempt would be made on Lincoln's life when he went into Richmond; but just now, after his generous dealings with Lee, I should have said the danger was past. But the ferocious malignity of Southerners is infinite and inexhaustible. I am stunned, as by a fearful personal calamity, though I can see that this thing, occurring just at this time, may be overruled to our great good. Poor Ellie is heart-broken, though never an admirer of Lincoln's. We shall appreciate him at last.

Up with the Black Flag now!

Ten P.M. What a day it has been! Excitement and suspension of business even more general than on the 3rd instant. Tone of feeling very like that of four years ago when the news came of Sumter. This atrocity has invigor-ated national feeling in the same way, almost in the same degree. People who pitied our misguided brethren yesterday, and thought they had been punished enough already, and hoped there would be a general amnesty, including J. Davis himself, talk approvingly today of vindictive justice and favor the introduction of judges, juries, gaolers, and hangmen among the dramatis personae. Above all, there is a profound, awe-stricken feeling that we are, as it were, in immediate presence of a fearful, gigantic crime, such as has not been committed in our day and can hardly be matched in history.

Faulkner, one of our Kenzua directors, called for me by appointment at half-past nine, and we drove to the foot of Jane Street to inspect apparatus for the reduction of gold ore by amalgamation, which he considers a great improvement on the machinery generally used for that purpose. Returned uptown and saw Bellows to advise about adjournment of our Sanitary Commission meeting next week. Thence to Wall Street. Immense crowd. Bulletins and extras following each other in quick, contradictory succession. Seward and his Fred had died and had not. Booth (one of the assassins, a Marylander, brother of Edwin Booth) had been taken and had not. So it has gone on all day. Tonight the case stands thus:

Abraham Lincoln died at twenty-two minutes after seven this morning. He never regained consciousness after the pistol ball fired at him from behind, over his wife's shoulder, entered his brain. Seward is living and may recover. The gentleman assigned to the duty of murdering him did his butchery badly. The throat is severely lacerated by his knife, but it's believed that no arteries are injured. Fred Seward's situation is less hopeful, his skull being fractured by a bludgeon or sling shot used by the same gentleman. The attendant who was stabbed, is dead. (Is not.)

The temper of the great meeting I found assembled in front of the Custom House (the old Exchange) was grim. A Southerner would compare it with that of the first session of the Jacobins after Marat's death. I thought it healthy and virile. It was the first great patriotic meeting since the war began at which there was no talk of concession and conciliation. It would have endured no such talk. Its sentiment seemed like this: "Now it is plain at last to everybody that there can be no terms with the woman-flogging aristocracy. Grant's generous dealing with Lee was a blunder. The *Tribune's* talk for the last fortnight was folly. Let us henceforth deal with rebels as they deserve. The rose-water treatment does not meet their case." I have heard it said fifty times today: "These madmen have murdered the two best friends they had in the world!" I heard of three or four men in Wall Street and near the Post Office who spoke lightly of the tragedy, and were instantly set upon by the bystanders and pummelled. One of them narrowly escaped death. It was Charles E. Anderson, brother of our friend Professor Henry James Anderson, father of pretty Miss Louisa. Moses H. Grinnell and the police had hard work to save him. I never supposed him a secessionist.

To Trinity Church vestry meeting, specially called, at half-past three at the rebuilt vestry office, corner Fulton and Church. A series of resolutions was read, drawn by the Rector. They were masculine and good, and they were passed *nem. con.*, though Verplanck and Tillou were in their seats— Copperheads both. I looked at the record of our action when Washington died sixty-six years ago. It was a mere resolution that the church and chapels be put in mourning. Our resolutions of today went, naturally, much further. I record to the credit of Gouverneur Ogden, whom I have always held cold-hearted and selfish, that he broke down in trying to read these resolutions, could not get beyond the first sentence, and had to hand them back to the Rector. There was a little diversity of opinion whether we should put our chancel into mourning tomorrow, being Easter Sunday, or postpone it a day longer. We left it to the Rector's discretion. No business was done today. Most shops are closed and draped with black and white muslin. Broadway is clad in "weepers" from Wall Street to Union Square. At 823 with Agnew, Bellows, and Gibbs. George Anthon dined here; with him to Union League Club. Special meeting and dense, asphyxiating crowd. Orations by George Bancroft and by the Rev. (Presbyterian) Thompson of the Tabernacle.[5] Both good; Thompson's very good. "When A. Johnson was sworn in as President today," said the Rev. Thompson, "the Statue of Liberty that surmounts the dome of the Capitol and was put there by Lincoln, looked down on the city and on the nation

[5] The Rev. Joseph Parrish Thompson (Yale 1838), scholarly Congregationalist minister of the Broadway Tabernacle, and one of the first Americans to attain high rank in the study of Egyptology, was esteemed for his eloquence.

and said, 'Our Government is unchanged—it has merely passed from the hands of one man into those of another. Let the dead bury their dead.

April 28, FRIDAY. The best part of an expedition even to Richmond itself is the getting home again and finding Ellie and the children safe and well, as I did at six o'clock. Dr. Vinton's nice son, Frank, was dining here, and there was reading from Haydn's second and sixth Masses and Mozart's No. 1 after dinner that refreshed me after my day of railroading. Tonight's papers announce that Johnston has surrendered everything from Raleigh to the Chattahoochie on the same terms that were given Lee. People will grumble. Sherman opened these negotiations several days ago and brought himself into sore disfavor. His popularity is gone for the present. . . .

Little business has been done in town these ten days. Never, I think, has sorrow for a leader been displayed on so great a scale and so profoundly felt. It is very noteworthy that the number of arrests for drunkenness and disorder during the week that followed Lincoln's murder was less than in any week for very many years! The city is till swathed in crape and black muslin.

[Here follows Strong's record of his trip.]

Tuesday the 18th, to Washington by early train. Called for the Rev. Bellows, and then we picked up Miss Louisa Schuyler and drove through two miles of silent, black-draped streets to the Jersey City ferry, where we found Wolcott Gibbs, Agnew, and his sister-in-law Miss Nash (a chief engineer of last year's Metropolitan Fair). We were invited to take seats in the special car set apart for the delegations on their way to the funeral. There were Moses Grinnell, Colonel Howe, Charles H. Russell, John Jay, William E. Dodge, Judge Pierrepont, and others; also Governor Andrew, with Adams and Ritchie of his "staff." A generous lunch was provided at noon, and the car being "select" was not overcrowded and comfortable; so our journey was less afflicted than usual. . . . In Copperhead New Jersey, few buildings—public or private—shewed sign of public mourning; but Baltimore was all in black. The humble shops and houses, past which the train runs, displayed almost without exception some little black rag, and every street we looked up as we went along was a vista of flags and drapery. I am told the traitorous mansions on Monument Square and the aristocratic quarters generally were profuse in weeds of woe. Perhaps they were put on as mere matter of prudence; perhaps Baltimore aristocracy sees that the cause it favors is hopeless now and finds in this great crime, committed in the interest of that cause and stimulated by Southern teaching, a good opportunity to change its front.

We entered Washington on time, for a wonder. Everywhere like insignia of sorrow. I got a breezy room high up among the higher ranges of Willard's by special favor, for the city is very full. Sanitary Commission met in F Street at eight P.M. Jenkins was plainly unhappy, nervous, and unstrung; he had no quarterly report. He had tried to write his report but had been in a state of mental torpor that made it impossible. Three ladies attended our session, Miss Schuyler and Miss Nash of New York, and Miss Abby May of Boston.

Wednesday the 19th was a bright cloudless day. All places of business closed, of course. Learned that members and officers of the Sanitary Commission (and of the *soi-disant* Christian Commission also) had places on the official programme and were expected to attend the ceremonial in the East Room, a privilege eagerly sought by all sorts of people but not solicited or invited by any of us. We went in a body to the office of the Secretary of the Treasury in the Treasury building. A delegation of our "Christian" friends reported at the same place, including that evangelical mountebank and philanthrope, Mr. G. H. Stuart of Philadelphia. They were an ugly-looking set, mostly of the Maw-worm and Chadband type. Some were unctuous to behold, and others vinegary; a bad lot. A little before twelve we marched to the White House through the grounds that separate it from the Treasury, were shewn into the East Room and took our appointed place on the raised steps that occupied three of its sides—the catafalque with its black canopy and open coffin occupying the centre. I had a last glimpse of the honest face of our great and good President as we passed by. It was darker than in life, otherwise little changed. Personages and delegations were severally marshalled to their places quietly and in good order; the diplomatic corps in fullest glory of buttons and gold lace; Johnson and the Cabinet, Chief Justice Chase, many senators and notables, generals and admirals, Grant, Farragut, Burnside (in plain clothes), Davis, Porter, Goldsborough, and others. About 650 in all.

The appearance of the assemblage was most distinguished. Most of those present were men of visible force and mark, with whom the bedizened diplomats contrasted unfavorably. The latter looked like gorgeously liveried flunkies. Of the religious service, the less that is said the better, for it was vile and vulgar; Bishop Simpson's whining, oratorical prayer most nauseous. When this was finished, the coffin was lifted and the assemblage followed it silently, reverently, and in perfect order. All that was perfectly and admirably managed and executed, and it was all most solemn and decorous, save and except the spoken words. So ended the most memorable ceremonial this continent has ever seen. I count it a great privilege to have been present. There will be thousands of people ten years hence who would pay any money to have been in my place.

After standing nearly four hours, we were too tired for a march in procession to the Capitol. So we slipped off, and Gibbs and I watched the latter half of the funeral cortège as it moved thither along Pennsylvania Avenue. A great body of freedmen brought up the rear, marching in well-ordered ranks and looking quite as respectable as the Caucasian civilians who preceded them. We dined at Nelcker's (Buhler's) and held an evening session.

Two incidents in the East Room were worth noting: the Italian Minister (who looked like a green and gold scarabaeus on its hind legs) leaving his place to march across the room and shake hands with Grant in a very marked way; and Johnson, stepping quietly up to the side of the coffin, looking down a few moments solemnly and thoughtfully upon the dead face—a subject for some future Delaroche.

Thursday the 20th was wholly given to business. After the evening session adjourned, there was a conference about Jenkins. Knapp and he dislike and distrust each other so thoroughly as to neutralize each other and demoralize the Washington office. Jenkins is among the best and most unselfish men, but he has little executive ability. He knows it, and the knowledge frightens and paralyzes him. He wanted to resign six months ago. We decided to let him know his resignation would be accepted now. Newberry should succeed him, but he declines the appointment. Knapp would not do. We must take Blatchford, who has been long in our service at Boston and for the last few months at Washington. He is efficient and accurate, but so formal in manner and quiet in speech that I have not rated him very high. We called at Seward's today; he is doing well.

Friday the 21st. "Executive session"; that is, the three ladies were locked out. Jenkins resigned. I am sorry for him. He shewed himself morbid and sore and thinks Knapp has ousted him by some subtle intrigue, which is a great mistake. Blatchford elected and accepts.

Bellows, Stillé, Binney, and I waited on Andrew Johnson, *Gratia Dei* President, at two o'clock by appointment at his temporary executive chamber in the Treasury building. Before its door hang the two flags that decorated Lincoln's box at Ford's theatre that fatal Friday night. One of them shews a rent several inches long made by the assassin's spur as he leaped down on the stage. We discoursed [with] Maunsell Field a few minutes while waiting for admission to our audience. Field was present during Lincoln's last hours. Being admitted, we find fat Preston King and a couple of military men with Johnson. We were graciously received. Bellows said a few words as to who and what we were, and the President replied in substance that he knew all about the Commission and would further its operations by all the means in his power. We made our interview as brief as might be. Most favorably impressed by Johnson. The "incoherency" of the 4th of March is doubtless correctly accounted for as an accident, for he looks utterly unlike a free drinker. He seems dignified, urbane, and self-possessed; a most presentable person. Heaven prosper his handiwork. Left cards for Seward; he is improving. Mr. Fred Seward is not out of danger. Our Sanitary Commission session closed tonight.

Agnew brought away many anecdotes of Lincoln after a talk with Dr. Stone, his friend and physician. The story of his dream the night before his death as retailed in the papers, is true. It was of a "fine ship entering harbor under full sail." He had had that very dream before every great national success—before New Orleans, Gettysburg, Fort Fisher, Charleston, and other successes—and he was certain he should hear of some great piece of good news within forty-eight hours. A poet could make something out of that. When one McKim, a notable abolitionist, complimented him on some thought or phrase in his Emancipation Proclamation, Lincoln said very slowly, "Well, I should be a quack if I accepted any praise for that. It was Chase gave me that notion."

Saturday the 22nd of April unsettled and showery in the morning. Went at two o'clock with Newberry (Johannes Neuleigendis) to the government mail boat, the *City Point*, and down the river, stopping at Alexandria. Great crowd. . . . At one A.M. there was a knocking at stateroom doors and general commotion. Everybody tumbled up and turned out. A picket boat had brought us to and was lying alongside. Officers came on board and searched every stateroom for Booth and some of his accomplices, but in vain. We were all inspected and called on to shew our papers.

Sunday the 23rd, up early. Stopped at Fortress Monroe and then proceeded up the James River. . . . At City Point, we transferred ourselves to
the *Red Jacket*, a boat of lighter draft, and went forward. On to Richmond
at last. . . . Landed at Rocketts at seven o'clock in the evening. We found
the Spottswood Hotel after a march of a mile and a quarter at double-quick,
mostly through the burned district, a wide area of ruin still smoking.

*When the war ended, Strong was still only forty-five years old; but
the heavy burden he had carried during the conflict—the fourfold
burden of the Sanitary Commission, his law office, the Columbia trusteeship,
and the Trinity vestry—had weakened his constitution. He had only ten years
to live, and henceforth we find frequent mention of ailing health in his diary.
Nevertheless, he tried to labor as hard as ever, and neglected none of his re-
sponsibilities. In the Wall Street office he not only carried his full share of the
routine legal work, but undertook important and arduous cases, such as the
suit (1866) of the Bank for Savings v. Field, in which his argument before
the Supreme Court was specially praised by Justice Nelson; the argument
(1867) of the Seamen's Savings Bank against hostile legislation proposed at
Albany, which involved an elaborate address before a subcommittee of the
Assembly Committee of the Whole; and the partition (1868) of the many
properties held in common by the Schermerhorn family, a "formidable job."
He took time to prepare a full and exact financial history of the Sanitary
Commission, which was published in 1866. His enthusiasm for the Columbia
Law School and the School of Mines showed no abatement, and he was as
ready as ever to put his shoulder to the wheel for their benefit and the general
improvement of the college. To Trinity Church he gave endless hours of unrequited toil. And in this decade he performed his greatest services to music,
assuming the presidency of the Philharmonic Society, and founding an organization to offer the best in sacred compositions, the Church Music Association—
a body which scored an unexpected success.*

It was with heartfelt thanksgiving for the victory of the Union cause, and with profound relief that the bloodshed, destruction, and demoralization of the conflict were over, that Strong turned his face towards the days of peace. Neither he nor any other American fully appreciated the debit accounts still to be settled by the nation, or the magnitude of the tasks of reconstruction both North and South.

June 1, THURSDAY. Most shops and offices closed, this being the national day of mourning for the President's murder. Attended service in Trinity Church awhile. . . .

After dinner to Union League Club. General Hooker expected there to receive a sword presented by California. Rooms crowded, gas-lights many, carbonic acid and caloric predominant. So after a couple of hours spent investigating a volume or two of the Townsend *opus magnus*, the great corpus of newspaper cuttings, I came off. The excerpts preserved in these folios from the *World*, *News*, and *Express* of the summer of 1863 are stupendous monuments of the Northern treason that was trying to paralyze us by riot and arson in concert with Lee's invasion of Pennsylvania. There has seldom been a much baser exhibition of dirt-eating scoundrelism.

Yesterday afternoon our financial subcommittee (*in re* School of Mines) met at the Law School. There were Delano, Howard Potter, W. E. Dodge, Jr., George Cabot Ward, and I. Decided to put off our $250,000 enterprise until next fall, wisely, I think. It is too late in the season. Many have left town. Those who remain will be languid and unimpressible until they have recovered from the succession of shocks and excitements that they have undergone since the first of April last. The people has (I think) just been bringing forth a new American republic—an amazingly big baby—after a terribly protracted and severe labor, without chloroform. It is too weary and prostrate as yet to listen to appeals on behalf of crystallography and "stochiometry." We can conjure no money out of it in the name of science just now. It will be a tough job in the best of times. . . .

Jefferson Davis, "yeoman," as his indictment presumes to style him, is, or soon will be, at Washington awaiting arraignment and trial in due course of law. He is reported to say that "the United States will never hang him," but his past mistakes should make him hesitate about any more predictions. His prophesyings of four years ago have proved disastrous to himself and to all who put faith in him. He told his people that the North would never undertake a war against secession and that France and England would have to become active allies of the South or perish for want of cotton. His people believed this flattering tale and rebelled. Most of them regret it just now!

Southern statesmanship is among the ancient delusions this war has blown away. Southern leaders have displayed energy, activity, audacity, intense purpose, perseverance under discouragement—all the virtues of the belligerent, carnivorous animal. No grizzly bear ever shewed greater ferocity or less rational forethought. Their administration of affairs has been most plucky and resolute, but without a trace of science, except in military strategic engineering work learned at West Point years ago. It has been a series of blunders worthy to succeed their first great blunder of rebellion. All the calculations on which that fatal move was founded, after thirty years of preparatory study and intrigue, have proved untrustworthy. Their most extreme and desperate measures have reacted against their course; that is, starving their prisoners. Any intelligent child could have told them that whatever they thereby gained in the course of exchanges would be far more than counterbalanced by the invigoration this atrocity gave Northern war-feeling and by the trouble it inflicted on Northern allies of rebellion. . . . Another gross blunder was their perseverance to the last in swaggering about death before reunion with the hated Yankees. Had they made anything like a show (however fraudulent and illusory) of willingness to talk about "reconstruction" on any terms—the conservation or restoration of slavery, for instance—at any time before Lincoln's reëlection, they would have enabled Northern traitors to make a fearfully damaging diversion in their favor. There would have been ruinous division here. Lincoln would have been defeated. The national government would have passed into the hands of friends of the South. Buchanan would have come back to life in the person of that unhappy McClellan, bringing with him Southern independence on easy terms and a continental chaos. . . .

Although the diarist says nothing about it, at the end of May President Johnson launched his reconstruction policy with two proclamations, one of limited amnesty and one laying down the mild conditions under which North Carolina might remodel her government in a way satisfactory to the executive. Throughout the summer and fall reconstruction went forward under the very moderate Lincoln-Johnson plan, while such radical Republicans as Sumner and Thaddeus Stevens chafed angrily. The absence of comment in Strong's record is evidence that, like most sensible Northerners, he was satisfied with the scheme. Meanwhile, the Sanitary Commission was nearing the close of its heavy labors. Its heads ordered that the manufacture and procurement of supplies be stopped on July 4, and followed this step by issuing a farewell address to their agents throughout the nation. Strong still had accounts to supervise, and the stores on hand still had to be distributed, but his hard work was finished. In New York, public-spirited citizens were awakening to the need for municipal reform, for during the war the evils of overcrowded slums, foul streets, inadequate sewage disposal, and endemic disease had grown to horrible magnitude.

June 3. . . . Bellows, Agnew, and Blatchford here last night. Blatchford reports 225,000 men camped around Washington and in special need of Sanitary Commission supplies, signs of scurvy being prevalent. During this process of mustering out, it is specially difficult to get requisitions duly honored. Hospital population on the 30th was 89,000, of which not much less than half is within sight of the dome of the capitol.

There is a score or so of paroled pauper rebel colonels and captains at the New York Hotel, sponging on Copperhead Cranston for rooms and meals, and negotiating with their Northern friends the subsidies that give them pocket money and one good solid drunk per diem. Certain people caress them, ask them to dinner, and give them old clothes. Mr. George Deas is there, who resigned his commission in April, 1861. He hailed Willy Cutting the other day in front of this rebel hotel. "Willy! Willy! How are you? Don't you remember me? I'm George Deas!" Cutting bowed, said he knew nobody of that name, and walked on. It's Deas that tells this. Good for Cutting. The world has moved since the New York Club squabble four years ago, when he was furious against any formal club censure of Deas. Deas and his colleagues—haughty, high-toned, superior, aristocratic creatures all—consent to pocket elee-mosynary five-dollar greenbacks and to put on cast-off Yankee breeches, without perceptible pain or struggle and without much expression of thankfulness.

June 4, SUNDAY. Mr. Ruggles dined with us. He recovers slowly from his recent illness. He was here again this evening; also, Dr. Peters and his wife, Miss Lily Clymer, Charley Strong, George Anthon, Graham, and Dr. Duncan, who kept us entertained with reminiscences of Georgia and South Carolina for just four hours. He is very queer and quaint. "As to the fellows that had charge of our prisoners," says the gracious Duncan,

"Hell is too cool for them anyhow. I'd have it heated up hotter than Nebuchadnezzar's fiery furnace when he got up that Jew-bake, and then I'd put an extension on to Eternity." He thinks South Carolinians the loudest talkers and poorest fighters in rebeldom; Wade Hampton a mere braggart and bully. Description of Sherman on the march through South Carolina, looking about him at columns of smoke rising near and far and farther, five, ten, and twenty miles away: "That's Slocum; *that* must be Howard; that's probably so and so. Boy! If you can find a deserted house anywhere around just set it on fire, and let them know where we are." Georgia woman watching the progress of a cavalry regiment past her door, *loquitur*: "Why-y! Did you-uns come all the way down hee-ah, critter-back?"

June 5. Long session of College trustees this afternoon. Preliminary session of Law School Committee, and recommendations that [John] Ordronaux be given certain duties among undergraduates of the Senior class—lectures on physiology as a foundation for his Medical Jurisprudence course in the Law School. The Committee on Honors also met—the Bishop, Rutherfurd, Betts, and I. We decided *not* to recommend that Professor Silliman of Yale, Frederick DePeyster of the Historical Society, and Charles Edward Anthon of the Free Academy be made LL.Ds. Silliman has lost caste, more or less, with certain of his scientific fraternity by reports about California petroleum. I know nothing of the merits of the case. But if we confer these honorary degrees at all, we should do so only where they are plainly fit and proper.

Barnard read an elaborate and valuable report on the inner life of the College for the last year, which was well received and ordered printed. He gave us also copies of the new catalogue of alumni. It's full of errors. I brought up the appropriation for the School of Mines next year—$27,000 (from which must be deducted estimated fees of students, say $16,000), *and it was carried*, Barnard and Mr. Ruggles fighting for it with great spirit. That dogmatic donkey, Mr. Zabriskie, opposed (he has lately restored his name by act of legislature or in some other way to its original Slavonic Zbrowski) and so did Bradford—smart, keen, and fluent, and always wrong on every question. Just before we adjourned, Haight surprised us with resolutions that a committee enquire and report whether the professorships of history (Lieber) and higher mathematics (Davies) should not be abolished, and that there be a special meeting on the 19th instant. This move is extraordinary and will probably produce a shindy. It has not been made without consultation and grounds for expecting it to succeed, but I do not understand its motive.[6] Davies is a mere fifth wheel to our academic coach. He is rich and independent of his salary, and that is not a full salary. It would seem to be a move against Lieber, Davies being joined to give the move an aspect of impersonality and general retrenchment in the undergraduate course. Lieber is fairly vulnerable only because the discipline of his lecture room is abominable. But it cannot be worse than that of Renwick's in my day and of McVickar's afterwards. He has done great public service during the last four years. That fact would dispose certain members of the board—Betts, Beadle, and Zabriskie—to decapitate him, but Haight seems a loyal man, and unlikely to have moved his resolutions on that ground. A committee of five was appointed.

June 8. At 823 today was an Andersonville prisoner, who said he had seen his brethren there on their hands and knees around the latrines of that infernal pen, grubbing among faeces for undigested beans and grains of corn wherewith to mitigate the pains of slow starvation.

The movement against Lieber is even more formidable than I supposed. Mr. Ruggles came in to talk of it at breakfast time. Haight's committee (of which Mr. Ruggles is a member) met yesterday. Haight and Barnard are bitterly bent on legislating Lieber out of office on two grounds. He has but four hours' work a week and doesn't earn his salary; and, secondly, and mainly, his lecture room is in chronic scandalous disorder, insubordination, and row. I suppose this latter averment quite true. The most audacious pranks are said to be played in that room, and the intercourse between the Professor and his classes, as reported, is often conducted in a dialect nearly allied to that of Billingsgate and Mackerelville. Lieber's mode of dealing with his mutinous boys is doubtless very bad indeed. He has no tact at all. But he has been backed by no exercise of legitimate college discipline. President Barnard has made no visits to his room. He might thereby have stopped its disorders. It is

---

[6] President Barnard, who felt personal hostility for Lieber, was anxious to bring about his dismissal. The two had long distrusted each other. Lieber, a strong Unionist, remembered that Barnard, as head of the University of Mississippi, had defended slavery and just after Sumter had even justified the Confederate cause. Lieber was now a Radical Republican; Barnard believed in moderate policies. Lieber held liberal ideas on religion. Barnard attacked the German theological seminaries as schools of atheism. Lieber lectured to his students on history; Barnard, who criticized Lieber's methods of instruction in sweeping terms, thought lectures unsuited to undergraduates. The need for more money to support the new School of Mines gave Barnard an opening for his proposal that Lieber be removed, and his chair of history and political economy be consolidated with the chair of English and philosophy.

quite certain that two or three sentences of dismissal would have made this cowardly crew of undergraduate Fifth Avenue blackguard boys as still as mice. But only last Monday Barnard informed us in his elaborate report on the state of the college that he has not been obliged to order a single student before "the Board" [faculty] during the past year. . . .

Lieber's activity in public affairs since 1860 will tell against him in the board. Copperhead old Verplanck has been growling to me and to others about the political heresies Lieber is teaching in the College and the Law School. Lieber upholds the nation and cares little for state rights in comparison. I fear all clerical trustees will follow the lead of Haight and Barnard. If so, Lieber must go overboard.

June 9. Hotter. Tonight showery. Visit from Lieber this morning to talk of the college attack on him. He is more phlegmatic than I expected to find him, and proposes to see no other trustee, except Mr. Ruggles, Charles King (to whom he has written), and possibly the Bishop. He says he is too old for lobbying and that this move is, in his opinion, wholly on political grounds. Of course, he would like to go out, if he must go, in the capacity of martyr. . . .

June 10. . . . The *World* and other papers publish letters from Southern correspondents stating that Southern Niggerdom refuses to work for wages, holding freedom to mean the right to support by government, or by somebody, without labor. I suppose these statements true as to the course adopted and the theory held by some of our Africo-Americans. We cannot wonder that they should take up any delusion whatever, after being studiously and systematically assimilated to brutes by the legislation of their masters, generation after generation, for so many years. There are predictions of a social or servile war, a war of races, but it is unlikely. If the Negroes go to work and earn their living, they will fall naturally into their proper place, and hold it to the great advantage of all parties. If they decline to do so, they will starve and perish and disappear, and emigration will supply the labor needed to develop the wealth of secession soil.

June 12, MONDAY. With William Schermerhorn to Columbia College this afternoon by the Third Avenue Railroad for a meeting of the Library Committee. Barnard with us, and the spasmodic librarian Mr. Jones. I like Barnard so much that I cannot believe he is behaving ill in this matter of Lieber's, but it would seem he is. After getting through with what very little we found to do, Schermerhorn and I adjourned to the School of Mines, and Chandler shewed us casts, recently acquired, of paleontological forms. . . . Also, we inspected the new building; that is, the old paper factory which the School is to occupy next session. A most dirty, dilapidated, disreputable structure. If our cabinets become very heavy, they will certainly break it down. . . .

June 13. . . . Newspapers report that society in certain regions of Georgia and Alabama has gone to chaos and disintegration—all asthenic, passive, dry gangrene and death. Most property there, public and private, is destroyed. The bare soil is left. That soil could support ten times its population, but it is left untilled. Cuffee will not work because Mass'r has no money to pay him. Cuffee is distrustful and suspicious, and gives no credit. Mass'r belongs to a First Family, was not born to work, and would rather starve than work; and he and his house seem to be starving, partly for the sake of spiting the Yankees. If Mass'r have any money put away at the North or in London, he means to leave the country. "It is not our country any more. You d——d Yankees have conquered it, and we are aliens. Take your country, and let us get out of it, leaving our curse behind us." Parts of Secessia may have to pass through a period of absolute anarchy and barbarism, longer or shorter, before they become Christianized and civilized.

Per contra, Gouverneur M. Wilkins read me a letter from one Trumbull, a nephew of his in Mississippi, stating the measures in progress in his district to reëstablish order, and they seemed healthy and hopeful. But very many Southern aristocrats, probably a majority of them, are utterly broken and ruined and incapable of any resolute effort to recover their lost position. . . .

June 16. . . . Strolled sweatily tonight on the east of the town, in the obscure region of First Avenue and Allen Street. The population of that district is prolific and its nursery is the sidewalk. Poor little children— what a blight and misfortune to them to have been born in a city! Brought to awhile at Union League Club, where was George Anthon, and so home. A Galveston newspaper announces that "it 'pears like subjugation,"—and wonders whether a (*soi-disant*) nation of so many millions was ever subjugated so suddenly. Southern papers and correspondents of Northern papers tell a dismal story of social disorganization and of probable famine in the chivalric states. Everything has been carried away from Southern plantations, except their mortgages. The Southern white race can do nothing for itself, being used so long to make niggers attend to its work.

June 17. . . . Proof given on the assassination trial that "Honorable" Ben Wood, Fernandy Wood's brother, the traitorous proprietor of the *Daily News,* received a check for $25,000 from the treason fund of the rebel refugees and plotters in Canada. I do not perceive the relevancy of this fact to the issues on trial, but it is valuable as a contribution to put in histories. Mr. Ruggles seems not to have returned from Washington. Very unfortunate. The special committee on Lieber was to meet today and the College Board meets Mondays. Lieber continues to pepper me with notes and memoranda. He writes today that he inclines to think Barnard sympathizes somewhat with the move to displace him. The unsuspicious Teuton! Barnard got it up. . . .

Texan newspapers are frank, naïve, and funny. "It seems unaccountable," they say, "but we are actually subjugated. Let us do the best we can under the circumstances." Shall we get through the next year without a social war in the Carolinas and the Gulf States?

June 19, MONDAY. Columbia College trustees met specially at two o'clock to consider the case of Lieber and Davies. Haight's committee reported resolutions abolishing the chairs of both, and that Lieber be continued in the Law School at his present salary of $4,000 till next May. This would be very well, were it not apparent that he will then be cut off altogether, or his salary made nominal. No reasons reported. Haight did not wish to assign reasons. Mr. Ruggles made a speech on both sides of the question. He has misgivings as to Lieber's capacity to manage our unruly undergraduates and thinks we may secure him better terms in the Law School by not opposing too strongly his excision from the College. Barnard favored us with a characteristic specimen of his copious, viscid oratory, letting out that the main reason for the movement was disorder in Lieber's room. I made a brief, dull argumentation against the report, but it was evident I stood alone. Bradford moved postponement, a motion almost always carried unanimously in this board. King supported it in his usual bungling, jolly way, but it was carried *by Fish's casting vote,* 7 to 7, Dr. Hutton and perhaps Anderson not voting. It was delightful to see the promptitude with which Ogden and Copperhead Betts and Zabriskie rose on a division being called for. Dix voted to postpone. Then there was a question whether the postponement be to the 6th of July or to the 20th of September. The former day was adopted by Fish's casting vote again. They mean to make quick work of it, and it is clear that the board has been privily manipulated so as to secure an abundant working majority. John Astor and the Bishop were not present.

Lieber has made enemies of many trustees by his silly, sensitive vanity. He has been offended with Fish ever since Barnard's inauguration and has not spoken to him because there was no mention, in some little address delivered by Fish on that occasion, of the honor and dignity the College and its new President derived from official connection with him, Lieber. When Mr. Ruggles was preparing some report or resolution for the Chamber of Commerce in which Agassiz, Guyot, and Lieber were to be mentioned as representing physiological, ethnological, and political science, Lieber actually wrote him several letters begging that he might be named *first* of the three. Isn't it amazing? I have no doubt he has affronted and alienated Barnard, who seems a kindly disposed man, by some offensive display of vanity. According to Fish, Governor Aiken of South Carolina says Lieber taught pure Calhounism while a citizen of that state. I believe this statement untrue. But Lieber is to all practical intents and purposes *dismissed* with his present salary continued till next May. There is no saving him. Stanton and Seward may be stimulated to raise a breeze about it in the newspapers, but it would be useless.[7]

Tonight Agnew, Blatchford, and Parrish were here for a Sanitary Commission conference. We decide to draw in our tentacles, dismiss agents, close relief stations, curtail work and expenditure everywhere and at once, and to be diligent in gathering and arranging material for a final report, the last dying speech and confession of the Sanitary Commission. Thank God the time for the Sanitary Commission's release and disembodiment seems so near at hand at last!

June 20. This evening young Lee here, and a very agreeable Major Nichols of Sherman's staff, full of anecdotes of the great march from

[7] Barnard had written Hamilton Fish that Lieber's instruction was practically thrown away. Lieber himself had constantly complained "of the listlessness, inattention, imperfect performance, and general ill behavior of his classes," yet these same students were attentive, diligent, and interested auditors of the other courses. An incipient student revolt against him had been barely prevented. Inasmuch as he taught only four hours a week, declared Barnard, his chair could easily be abolished or merged with another. Lieber made no formal answer to the president's charges, though he was full of private complaints. With the help of his friends in the board, Fish, Strong, Ruggles, and King, he was transferred to the Law School, where henceforth he was to occupy the chair of constitutional history and public law at an undiminished salary of $4,000 a year. Lieber was doubtless a failure as a teacher of undergraduates; as a teacher of the whole nation through his books, pamphlets, articles, and lectures, he was a distinct success, and Columbia University has never ceased to cherish his memory. Strong appreciated his best qualities.

Atlanta to Raleigh.[8] He confirms the story told by all Sherman's officers
that the braggarts of South Carolina were the slowest fighters, and are
the most abjectly whipped rebels in all Rebeldom. They did nothing but
whine, he says, as Sherman's column marched over their plantations.
(N.B. A rebel prisoner who called at 823 today to ask after a little tobacco,
observed to Collins that if he'd known New York was such a hell of a
big place he wouldn't never have fit agin it.)

Joe Dukes, *ci-devant* South Carolinian, now New York lawyer, and
always opposed to secession, tells Charley Strong of letters he receives
from the South on which he prophesies a war of extermination by the
white race on the black, or else vice versa, and more probably the latter.
He holds that the two races cannot long remain in peaceful contact under
their altered relations, and that a struggle must soon begin which will
wipe out one or the other. It does not seem likely, but no one can form
an opinion on the question without intimate knowledge of the South as
it was and as it is. Secessia has no more hope from her present population
than our Southwest frontiers have from the Comanches. They are alike
incapable of civilization and progress and must be displaced to make
room for a better breed. It is to be hoped that the displacement may be
through a peaceful process of immigration, gradually changing the stock
by intermarriage; but it may be destined to come with tragical abrupt-
ness, and bring with it all the horrors of San Domingo. . . .

I rather expect a depopulation of the South by pestilence. The vital
forces of men and women are lowered by a profound sense of failure,
defeat, mortification, and subjugation, especially damaging to so arrogant
a race. Add to this a very general privation of the means of living, and
in many regions (as reported), destitution and starvation, even unto
death, and there seems abundant provocation for an epidemic of the
deadliest type.

The political pots of Washington are simmering ominously and are
not unlikely to reach boiling heat before long. Advanced Republicans
grumble over President Andrew Johnson's reconstruction policy, and say
he is selling his party, after the manner of dirty old Tyler, twenty-five
years ago. I do not "see it in that light," and have faith in the President's
judgment and honesty. But a split in the party seems certainly coming,

[8] Brevet Major George Ward Nichols, one of Sherman's aides, had kept a diary of
the campaigns in Georgia and the Carolinas, from which he extracted this year material
for a capital book, *The Story of the Great March*.

and Copperheads chuckle over the prospect, to my serious aggravation.[9] Next winter will probably find Sumner, Wilson & Co., organized as an opposition, and "conservative" Republicans sustaining the Administration, in alliance with Northern "democrats" and malignants and restored penitent Congressmen from the Carolinas, with bowie knives about their persons. Next session of Congress will be an anxious time. "Darkey Suffrage" is a dark and troublesome question, and it must be met. That freedmen, who have as a class always helped the national cause to the utmost of their ability, at risk of their lives, should have political rights at least equal to those of the bitter enemies of the country who are about to resume those rights, sullenly and under protest, only because they are crushed, coerced, and subjugated, is (abstractly considered) in the highest degree just and right. But the average field hand would use political power as intelligently as would the mule he drives. The current phrase that "those who have helped the country with bullets should be permitted to help it with ballots" is mere nonsense. . . . Were I President, I should aim at securing political rights to property-holding Ethiopians and to such as could read and write.[10]

June 22. Mr. Ruggles gave a dinner at Delmonico's to jolly old Charles King, who sails for Europe tomorrow in a French steamer. That Anglophile of other days vows he will not pass under the British flag. His wife and daughters may go and see England if they like, but he will stay on the Continent. . . . Lieber is down upon Barnard. I fear my first estimate of Barnard was too high. . . .

June 27. . . . Gibbs is interested in Lieber's case, and I think understands its pros and cons.

At Union League Club tonight, looking into the pamphlets of three years ago, especially at half a dozen fat volumes I had bound up and gave the club when its library was first launched. Two lamentable diatribes entitled "American Bastilles," or some such thing, I found particularly refreshing. They are detailed personal narratives by disloyal Marylanders bagged in September, 1861, and detained near six months in Fortress Monroe, Fort Lafayette, and Fort Warren. They had mere army rations

---

[9] An acute prophecy; Henry Winter Davis, Ben Wade, Charles Sumner, and Thaddeus Stevens were already publicly denouncing the President's policy, while the old-time abolitionists were full of wrath.

[10] This had been substantially Lincoln's policy. In his letter to Michael Hahn, the free-state governor of Louisiana, on March 13, 1864, Lincoln had suggested that the suffrage might be extended to some of the colored people—"as, for instance, the very intelligent, and especially those who have fought gallantly in our ranks."

to eat—their coffee was not good—they had no liquor except what they bought and paid for and except the baskets of champagne sent them by New York and Boston sympathizers. "Tadpoles" (query: mosquito larvae?) occurred in their drinking water, and worst of all, they were mixed up with mere common men from North Carolina, captured at Fort Hatteras! Their pork was intolerably fat and their soup thin, poor fellows. Their pamphlets are well-defined specimens of Slave-ownia Secesh literature, which embodies the characteristics of (1) the Northern gent, who tries to mask his vulgarity by deportment and swagger and much talk about his own exalted gentility; (2) the Swashbuckler, Alsatian, "bully-ruffian" or "Mohock" of 160 years ago; and (3) the sharp attorney of the present day, whose clients are found in the Tombs, and whose vocation it is to keep thieves and burglars from being consigned to Black-well's Island by invoking law in their behalf. The typical Southerner is a snob—a bully, a "shyster," and (I fear) an assassin.

June 28. To Columbia College Commencement at the Academy of Music. Discoursed with sundry agreeable people in the reception room, and then marched in august procession down the parquet with Barnard and the faculty and Fish and Governor Morgan, and the other fashion-ables, to the sound of soft music, and took my seat on the stage. Sat through six or eight orations and poems. I will not answer for the Greek and Latin salutatories, but all the rest were very small trash, and the efforts of the poets to be smart and funny would have given a cassowary the dyspepsia. . . . There should be a stern censorship of Commencement speeches. The only decent thing I heard was Mendelssohn's exquisite little melody, "Ich wollt' mein Lieb ergöss sich," rendered by a most respectable orchestra—an improvement on the Commencement brass bands of my college days. As each orator made his final bow, there came a concentric fire of bouquets from all parts of the house. The fair artil-lerists sometimes made bad practice. A four-pound bouquet hit me on the leg, and a ten-pounder took the Rev. Morgan Dix in the eye, producing a contusion of the left spectacle. When the cannonade ceased, the orators gathered up these graceful tributes and carried them off, and then came back for a second armful, looking like "Posy John," the peripatetic florist of Broadway. This absurd practice ought to be stopped somehow. The graduating class appeared in academic head-gear, "Oxford caps," for the first time. On the whole, I thought what I heard of these "com-mencement exercises" no credit to the College, but rather a lamentable proof that we, the trustees, are doing our duty most imperfectly. . . .

1866

*T*he year 1866 opened with all the political barometers predicting a storm, for the quarrel between President Johnson and the Radicals over Reconstruction was about to become violent. Strong continued to be much engrossed by duties outside his law office; that is, by Columbia, Trinity, the Bank for Savings, and the Sanitary Commission, now fast winding up its affairs. At last, however, he had some time for social relaxation. On January 7 he and Mrs. Strong went to a musical party at Professor Joy's on Forty-ninth Street, where the guests included President Barnard, the astronomer Lewis Rutherfurd, the sculptor John Rogers (of the well-known statuette groups), and Bayard Taylor. "Would there were more houses in the city like Joy's!" exclaimed Strong. "Its elegant, refined appointments are a standing protest against the barbaric costliness of our Fifth Avenue drawing-rooms." Four days later the Strongs themselves gave a reception. "It's so long since I have attended upon any large fashionable gathering," wrote the diarist, "that I felt like an owl in daylight. I recognized scores of faces, but could not recall the names that went with them, and went about asking everybody in a whisper who everybody else was." Music was furnished by Karl Wehli, the Austrian composer and pianist, who sent up his own Chickering for his selections. Among those present was Anson Burlingame, the American minister to China. Later in the month came a reception by President and Mrs. Barnard, their Forty-ninth Street rooms well filled. "Barnard and his wife 'entertain' with a simple, agreeable heartiness of manner. I esteem him more and more highly." But the noise during the music annoyed Strong. "Our civilization is still of

314

low grade. An assemblage of average New Yorkers will gossip and cackle during one of Mozart's melodies or Beethoven's symphonies."

Inflation gripped the nation, causing great distress among middle-class folk like the Strongs. At Columbia College, the faculty suffered so much from the rise in the cost of living that a special committee of the trustees on salaries decided, on January 15, to give the whole academic staff permanent increases, and also to make a temporary 25 per cent addition to salary for the next two years. Strong thought this bare justice in view of "the present ruinous pauperizing cost of everything." He also thought that Chandler, as head of the School of Mines, ought to have an increase of $1,000 a year. "He is the most self-sacrificing and earnest of men, to say nothing of his scientific ability and attainments." Despite his busy life, the diarist maintained his own scientific tastes, attending meetings of a small Microscopical Society at Clinton Hall. Early in the year we find him still deeply distressed by the divorce case which involved his cousin Peter. He was meanwhile much interested in a lawsuit which the Bank for Savings had carried to the Supreme Court—one concerning a clause of the internal revenue laws; and he presently journeyed to Washington to argue the case before Chief Justice Chase.

January 11, THURSDAY. Dined at seven. Accompanied Johnny through another stage of Caesar's campaign in Gaul (I suspect that great captain of lying horribly as to the magnitude of the forces opposed to him), and then went to the annual meeting of the Union League Club, which adjourned at half-past ten. Did not wait to learn the result of annual election. John Jay is doubtless elected president. I voted against him, as did others. . . .

January 12. Standing Committee of the Sanitary Commission at Twelfth Street tonight. . . . We decided this day to publish the evidence of Andersonville prisoners collected by our Second Commission or Committee of Investigation at Annapolis. It has been asleep these ten months in the hands of the Rev. Walden of Philadelphia, and I had forgotten all about it when I received a letter from William Henry Rawle offering to prepare it for publication and to write a report to be published with it. We accepted his offer *nem. con.* Of course, we shall be blamed for opening an old sore, for not letting bygones be bygones, and so forth. But I see little sign of fraternal feeling south of the Potomac, so little that it is not worth considering. The truth of our former report (which was, by the way, a rather weighty and memorable paper) was denied by Richmond papers, by rebel representatives on the floor of their so-called Congress at Richmond, and by the Honorable Mason in the London *Times*. So we are fully entitled to confirm it by another batch of depositions, even if we thereby offend the sensibilities of Rebeldom. The treatment of national prisoners at Libby and Andersonville is an important historical question. . . .

R. B. Minturn's funeral is tomorrow afternoon at two at the Church of Holy Communion. I would attend, but a meeting of the Law School Committee is called for that hour. The services will be most fully attended. No man in New York will be so missed by the charitable and public-spirited people of the community and by the poor and needy.

We were allies in 1854, in the cause of St. Luke's Hospital. In 1857 he became party to an attack on the corporate rights of Trinity Church, and I rather withdrew myself from his acquaintance till 1861, when a common feeling about rebellion and treason had brought us heartily together again. For Minturn was not only a most generous giver to every worthy object, private and public, but a patriotic supporter of the national cause with his money and his personal influence. Whatever faculty of hating was in his kindly temper was bestowed on rebels and their sympathizers.

January 19.   The House has passed the bill for Negro suffrage in the District of Columbia, and by a two-thirds vote. I think the Senate will pass it, and I do not expect a veto from Johnson. The whole question is full of difficulties and conflicting rights. No statesman ever had a more knotty problem set him by destiny. But whatever doubts there may be as to South Carolina and Mississippi, I approve of Negro suffrage in the District, for it will de-Southernize and nationalize the atmosphere of the national capital.

The cleavage between the Radical Republican extremists in Congress and President Johnson was steadily growing wider. As yet, however, no open and irreconcilable break had occurred, and most Republicans still hoped to stand behind the Chief Executive. A majority of them, as Rhodes says in his history of this sad era, were down to mid-February nearer to the policy of Johnson than to that of Charles Sumner and Thaddeus Stevens. But the course taken by the Southern States made it difficult for the President to rally the popular support that he needed. During the period from October, 1865, to

March, 1866, the Southern legislatures passed a series of laws dealing with the freedmen—the so-called "black codes"—which seemed to Northern observers very unfair. They gave the black man a grudging and partial measure of civil rights; while they applied to him a variety of harsh criminal provisions. The new laws on vagrants and contract labor seemed likely, in various parts of the South, to permit the establishment of a system of peonage in place of slavery. Negroes were forbidden to hold public meetings, their movements were restricted, and in some states they were not allowed to bear arms. Their position in the courts was also generally made inferior to that of the whites. These "black codes" were in general well meant, for the Southerners had a problem of frightful complexity with which to deal. But the North, which failed to understand this complexity, viewed them as cruel and malignant. The observations of Strong were typical of those of a host of other observers.

January 25. . . . *How* shall we deal with our Southern malignants? What shall we do with them? We cannot afford to let them back into the Congressional seats they left so unceremoniously and defiantly and truculently five years ago. We cannot leave our black soldiers, now mustered out, to the mercy of their late masters. We have the Southern wolf or hyena by the ears. Letting go would be ruinous. Holding on awhile is inconvenient. I prefer to hold on awhile, as the less of two evils, and belong (I suppose) to the Radical Party. It seems clear that no Northern man, no Yankee, can live at the South in any moderate safety yet. Negroes are oppressed, tortured, and murdered by their *ci-devant* owners. We may have to undertake another civil war. If we do, it will be waged in most grim and bitter earnest, with no scruple about the summary hanging of rebels and traitors. Troubles and taxes have taught us much. We disincline to hang J. Davis because he and we were equally untaught as to the value of civil order and the criminality of rebellion, five years ago. We know better now. Woe to the next gentleman that sets up a rebellion.

January 27, SATURDAY. . . . To Philharmonic concert. Mozart's Symphony No. 1 in D, and the *Melusina* overture were delightful. Mr. Wehli's piano was very good. But for *finale* we had Berlioz's overture or symphony entitled "Episode in the Life of an Artist," with a page of printed programme setting forth that the artist must be supposed to have fallen in love, to have become much worried, nervous, and bothered thereby, to have taken a narcotic, to have passed a restless night, and to have dreamed that he saw the beloved object at a ball (second movement), that he went into the country and heard shepherds tootle pastoral melodies (third movement), and that he murdered his beloved object and was about to be hanged (fourth movement). (I hope his dream came true and he was hanged.)

> " 'S death, this would make a man spew!"
> Mr. Smith, in *The Rehearsal.* . . .

February 1. Every symptom of Southern temper is bad. It seems to grow worse rather than better. The South is crushed for the time, but the more bitter and vindictive for its humiliation, and fuller than ever, even, of sectional, anti-national, traitorous impulses. Nothing but physical exhaustion keeps the Southern Hyena from instantly flying at our throats again. The beast is whipped into temporary submission, but utterly untamed. It will not be domesticated in our day, if ever.

> "Stern looks the Fiend, as frustrate of his Will,
> Not half sufficed, and greedy yet to kill."

There is a quarrel among his keepers, much to be regretted. The Republican party is cracked, and the crack is spreading and widening. Andrew Johnson seems more and more inclined toward what is called conservatism, and Raymond leads a "Conservative" party in the House. His party is small, but will grow in the sunshine of executive favor. The "Radicals" are firm. I am sure their doctrine is gaining ground with the people. Every change I notice in anyone's political sympathies is that way. Almost every one has changed a little during the last six months, and become a little more Radical or Conservative. The constitutional amendment (as to the basis of representation) passed the House yesterday, 120 to 46.[1] Expediency, abstract right, and common sense agree in calling for some amendment of the Constitution there anent, and this seems a judicious amendment. The President is said to disapprove it. The Hon. Thaddeus Stevens belabored the President in debate yesterday, loudly, coarsely, and unwisely. Brooks, Win Chanler, and the Devil chuckled over Stevens's oratory, no doubt.

February 3. . . . Bidwell and Charley keep tormenting me to go to Washington for this Savings Bank case on Monday. . . .

February 10, SATURDAY. I have seen the face of the Supreme Court

---

[1] That is, the Fourteenth Amendment, defining citizenship, declaring that no state might abridge the privileges or immunities of citizens, and stipulating that any state which denied the ballot to male citizens over twenty-one should have its representation in Congress proportionately reduced.

of the United States, and yet live (though with a slight headache). Got home last night at six-thirty, too tired to journalize.

To Washington *Monday*, 5th inst., by seven-thirty train. Severely cold. River so ice-blocked that the ferry boat had to back into her dock when half way across, and take a fresh start. She reached Jersey City at last, crashing her way through a great ice field that stretched northward without visible boundary. Railroad ride was arctic. Everything sealed up with clear frost all the way to Washington; every little water-course, dead, Gunpowder Creek and other streams sheets of ice.[2] Washington itself for once in a state neither of dust nor of mud, but of congelation. People said to be skating on the Potomac, and that river frozen nearly across. Comfortable room at Willard's, but in a corner of that caravansary so remote that I was two days learning the way to it. Came near providing myself a hatchet wherewith to "blaze" the corners of the multiplex corridors.

Discoursed with Judge [William F.] Allen (whom I like much and find worthy of all regard and respect), Benjamin Silliman, William E. Dodge (who is likely to oust Jem Brooks from his seat in the House); Maclure (just from New Orleans), Sam E. Lyon, [William M.] Evarts, Burrill, and others.

Tuesday was clear and growing mild. Washington streets, and Pennsylvania Avenue in particular, began assuming one of their two normal conditions, namely, that of mud. After breakfast, Judge Allen told me I must take part in the argument of our case, and must *reply*, because (relying on Bidwell to reply) he had prepared himself for the opening. My hair stood on end at the suggestion. But he reminded me that the Supreme Court allows counsel only two hours each, and will hear two counsel on the same side. If he alone were heard for the plaintiff, he would be compelled to confine himself to one of his two hours in opening, and the other in reply, while the defendant, represented by Mr. Attorney-General Speed and the Assistant Attorney-General (Ashton of Philadelphia, a very respectable fellow), would be entitled to the attention of the Court for four hours between them. Whereas, if I consented to take part in the argument, he could open, and I could reply, for two hours each. So I thought it my duty to give a despairing assent. With Judge Allen to the Capitol and Supreme Court room.

[2] Strong had recorded on January 8 "the coldest day for sixty years," with a wind that "blows lancets and razors." His house that day, with both furnaces in full blast and fires in every story, had an interior temperature of 38.

At eleven o'clock, there was the voice of one crying: "The Honorable the Chief Justice and the Associate Justices of the Supreme Court of the United States!" Mr. Chief Justice Chase and his associates in their judicial robes marched solemnly into the courtroom, everyone rising. The Court bowed to the Bar, and *vice-versa*, and the crier "made an oyez," finishing it off with "God save the United States of America and this Honorable Court!" I wish more of these Old World formalities survived among us. Judge Allen then moved my admission as attorney and counselor of the Court, and "introduced me." I bowed, and was bowed to by the Bench, took the usual oath in the courtroom (that I would demean myself decently as an officer of the Court and obey its directions), and then went to the Clerk's office and took the special "iron-clad" oath that I had never designedly given Rebellion any aid or comfort, which oath I took most honestly and heartily, with no mental reservation whatever—thank God.

Then the Court proceeded to hear the "Bankers and Brokers Cases" under the Internal Revenue Act.[3] Mr. Attorney-General opened and closed for the Collector; Judge Allen, John Burrill, and Evarts *in contra*. All three acquitted themselves well, Evarts *very* well. I have heretofore thought him overrated. This case was disposed of sooner than was expected. Our case was called a little after two. Judge Allen opened, with great ability, and the Court adjourned at three.

Wednesday (cloudy, dull, and drizzly). Judge Allen resumed and finished his opening. Ashton thereupon argued for the defendant at great length. His argument was clever and lawyer-like though disingenuous, and his manner and delivery forcible and impressive. Not more than one-fifth of it was devoted to the merits; all the rest was on the question of jurisdiction. Then the Attorney-General took up his parable, and made a good, effective stump or platform speech, mainly on the question of jurisdiction, maintaining the propositions of his printed brief (as did

---

[3] Now generally referred to as the Bank Tax Cases, and others. The issues concerned the constitutionality of the national banking system established in 1862, and the validity of the various state laws which laid taxes on the notes and business of the national banks, and on the federal securities held by state banks as part of their capital. At least nine cases dealt with these general issues, of which Strong's was The Society for Savings *vs.* Coite (6 Wall 611). The Supreme Court took a firm position in defense of national power. It held that the notes, operations, and shares of national banks could not be taxed without explicit Congressional permission, for such banks were an agency of the national government. It also held that investments by state banks (or others) in federal securities could not be taxed by the states. Attorney-General James Speed of Kentucky (1812-1887), who had been appointed by Lincoln in 1864, delivered the principal argument for the government.

Ashton) and reminding me strongly of the arguments of the Crown lawyers under Charles I and James II, when questions of Prerogative and Dispensing Power were discussed in Westminster Hall. They had the audacity to insist that the Internal Revenue Act, giving authority to the Commissioner of Internal Revenue to decide "on appeal" questions as to taxes levied by his subordinates, *ousted* all courts of law and equity, state and federal, of all jurisdiction over those subordinates, and their official head, and subjected all the business and all the property of the country to the discretion of an irresponsible executive officer. I could not have believed my ears had not this monstrous proposition been clearly enounced in the Attorney-General's brief and maintained in all its atrocity in twenty printed pages of "black on white." I could not but remember what Macaulay says of the Solicitor-General's argument (Sir William Williams) in the *Trial of the Seven Bishops.* "The audience stood aghast at the effrontery of the venal turncoats." I have no reason to suppose Mr. Attorney-General Speed a "turncoat," but his effrontery is unmatched within the last hundred years.

I hoped the defense would keep the Court occupied till the hour of adjournment. But I saw the Attorney-General was beginning to run emptiness and would soon dry up. I was sickening for a lunch after my early breakfast; was faint and heart-sunken. My hopes were in vain. The Attorney-General sat down at two o'clock, the Chief Justice bowed toward me, by way of invocation, and I got on my legs as one gets into a cold plunge bath. Once up—the ice broken—I was self-possessed and comfortable, and trotted out my little notions and lectured the Supreme Court "like a Dutch uncle" (why Dutch?). I was heard with the utmost courtesy and attention. Court adjourned at three P.M. On the Capitol stairs I crossed Judge Nelson diagonally and took off my hat. He stopped me most kindly, shook hands, introduced me to Judge Clifford, said sundry civil things, and as we parted remarked *sotto voce,* "I think you were a little nervous when you *began* your argument, Mr. Strong, but you will be all right tomorrow morning."

In fact, I was not nervous or alarmed. I was merely suffering physical depression for want of an oyster or two. But how kind this was of old Nelson; how good in the learned old judge to think of an encouraging word for the goose and greenhorn of an advocate! We generally forget the importance and value of such kind offices. This makes me Nelson's backer and supporter to my life's end!

Next morning (*Thursday*) I took up my parable once more. I had expatiated the day before on the distinction between banks and savings banks and tried to shew that they differed generically, and not as species of the same genus. (This was the best part of my argument, and perhaps presented certain considerations that Allen had not brought home to the Court. Judge Wayne was struck by a point I made on the construction of paragraph 79 and asked me to read the section again. It is a decisive point. Allen had made it when opening, but he had so much matter on his hands that he was obliged to talk very fast, and it had made no impression.) When Court opened I spent a little time on the verbal construction of the act, and then took up the question of jurisdiction. I think I treated both decently well. I had made some little progress in discussing the Attorney-General's atrocious position that all courts of law and equity are ousted of jurisdiction over assessors and collectors by the Internal Revenue Act, when Chase, C.J., and Nelson, J., laid their heads together a moment, and the former said, "I don't think we need hear you any further on this branch of the case, Mr. Strong."!!! Was ever Attorney-General so snubbed? But it was a blow to me, for I had meant to say a great many fine things about Charles I and James II, Dispensing Power, Strafford, Courts of High Commission, centralized despotism, and the like. So I had nothing left to do but prose a little on the quite unimportant question of our right to an injunction as "provisional remedy against which Ashton had told the Court the Internal Revenue Department had always objected." I suggested that such "objections" were an unpleasant novelty, and that we were entitled, anyhow, to directions from a court of equity as to the administration of our trust—with its 50,000 *cestuis que trust*. And there the case stands. The Court is with us on the question of jurisdiction. Nelson, the weightiest member of the Court, on the merits, and I think Wayne, too. But we shall be beat, of course. It's my luck. . . .

Went with Allen to the Congressional Library and spent an hour looking over Gould's gorgeous monograph of the *Trochilidae* with a sense of great relief and comfort, such as one feels when set free from the hands of his dentist. To the Sanitary Commission office, looking into affairs which need action by the Committee. . . .

Congress was faced with the question whether enlarged measures for the protection of the liberated Negroes in the South were necessary. Deciding that they were, it passed early in February a bill greatly increasing the authority of the chief protective agency, the Freedmen's Bureau, and extending its life for one year. When this came before the President, he gave it careful study and took expert advice. Then he vetoed it on the ground that it was unconstitutional, adding as "another very grave objection" the fact that it had been passed by a Congress in which eleven states of the Union still had no representation. He avowed, however, that he shared the desire of Congress to give the Negro adequate protection. The veto message was very strong and made a deep impression. When the Radicals in Congress attempted to repass the bill over the veto, they failed of the necessary two-thirds.

February 20. Today's sensation was Johnson's veto of the *Freedmen's Bureau* Bill. It seems a tough paper, not easily to be answered. It goes far toward demonstrating certain provisions of the bill not only impolitic and open to most mischievous abuse, but plainly repugnant to the Constitution. Johnson states his objections clearly and cogently. Had he contented himself with stating them, all but a few extremists would heartily approve this message (though the New York *World's* delectation over it disgusts all who love the nation more than they love the South). But after giving his sufficient reasons for this veto, in statesmanlike style, Johnson goes out of his way to lecture Congress for not letting in Southern Representatives, wherein I think he shews himself impertinent, and what's worse, radically unsound. I am sorry, for I do not want to lose my faith in Andy Johnson.

February 22, THURSDAY. A "legal holiday" now, so all banks are closed; Custom House, Treasury, and many stores. Wall Street is left as a lodge in a garden of cucumbers. After an hour or two there, I walked uptown. Weather genial, with the least little trace of spring flavor, and I found my overcoat a burthen. Broadway so packed with people who wanted to see the sojers that I had to work my way home by side streets.

Tonight is the grand reception of Lieutenant-General Grant at the Union League Club. Ellie was to have gone, escorted by Frank Howe and his wife. I would not have been squeezed in the crowd for fifty dollars. But she was feeling out of order at dinner time, and gave up the reception. I went off after dinner for a Standing Committee meeting of Trinity Church. But I found at Madison Square an almost impenetrable crowd watching the most brilliant beautiful fireworks. Stopped with the crowd till it was evident either that the Committee had got a quorum and did not want me, or that its members, if less than a quorum, had dispersed.

The "Freedmen's Bureau" bill failed of a two-thirds vote in the

Senate (30–18), so the "Radicals" are defeated, and you can distinguish
a Copperhead a hundred yards off by the light that beams from his countenance. Confounded be their breed! The veto was wise, but I wish it did
not give these caitiffs such keen enjoyment. H. W. Beecher says in the
course of a long lecture or address defending it and the President's
general policy, that an executive officer declining power and patronage
so immense as Congress offered Johnson by this bill is something new
under the sun. It's quite true. But the more extreme Republicans in
both Houses are furious. Senator Anthony of Rhode Island writes Mrs.
Charley Strong in depths of despair. "The party is broken up," he says.
"No such scene in the Senate since Buchanan's time, when Senators from
seceding states were going out." But he is an easy man to scare. It is
clear, however, that moderation and temper are needed to keep the party
from a split, and that "Radical" leaders have shewn little sign of either,
since this bombshell burst among them.

February 23 . . .

Affairs of state look stormy. The vital force of government has for
some time been decomposing into negative and positive, and these
hostile electricities have now so accumulated apart, and intensified each
other by mutual reaction, that their flash and crackle begins to be alarming, and there may well be a grand detonating discharge before equilibrium
is restored. God grant the discharge may not smash the apparatus!

There was a "Conservative" meeting at Cooper Institute last night
to "sustain the President." It was large and enthusiastic, and got up by
men of weight, political purity, and unquestioned loyalty, Republicans
and War Democrats. An important move. Seward was chief speaker, and
his speech reminds one of his "ninety day" prophesyings five years ago.
"All is just as it should be. Everything is serene. The Ship of State has
weathered the storm and is as good as safe in harbor. To be sure, there
is a little debate between her officers whether she should proceed to her
anchorage on this tack or the other, but nobody will be hurt whichever
way they settle it. Don't worry yourselves, my friends and fellow citizens!
Our safety, comfort, and prosperity are *res judicata*. The universe is
estopped from disturbing us in their enjoyment." Three cheers for
Seward!

This meeting was significant. It shewed that discord in the National
or Union party (i.e., the North, *minus* Copperheads) is beginning to
formulate itself. But far more significant was Mr. President Johnson's
long speech yesterday at the White House addressed to a mob that waited

on him and asked for a few remarks. It is a very long speech and full of repetitions. Its bouquet seems to me (as to others) to be that of Old Bourbon, largely imbibed by the orator just before taking the rostrum. Anyhow it is bad, egotistical, diffuse, undignified, intemperate, unwise, and sure to do great mischief. He avowed himself at war with radicalism, and denounced Sumner of the Senate and Stevens of the House and Wendell Phillips, who is a mere private lecturer and sophist (if you will), as disunionists and traitors. He talked of Senators going about "with assassination in their hearts," and of his own indifference to such hypothetical designs; of the exceedingly moderate sum he needed for food and raiment, and talked much bosh beside.

This speech is a national calamity. It hurts us badly, and it will disgrace us abroad. The *Saturday Review* will make it the subject of an entertaining and scholarly leading article. Johnson made several good points, for the "Radical" policy he assailed is plainly open to grave objections. But so is his own. The problem is most difficult. Those who disagree about its solution ought to meet and confer with the utmost candor, forbearance, and temper. Neither party has shewn a trace of temperance or conciliatory disposition. And war being now declared, I fear it is manifest that the "Radicals" of Congress first drew the sword. This may result in an impeachment of the President within thirty days!!! The possibility had occurred to me, but I had not entertained it till a word from Blatchford this evening shewed that the same possibility or conceivability (remote enough to be sure) had occurred to him. Imagine it!!!!! Agnew says he would testify if called upon, as a professional expert. that the inspiration of this speech came from alcohol and from no other exciting cause. His acquaintance with toxicology satisfies him that Andrew Johnson was more or less *drunk* on inspection of what A. Johnson said. *Eheu!*

Johnson had made a most unfortunate speech, as Strong notes, on Washington's Birthday—though it was not made without provocation. When the Radicals in Congress failed to obtain a two-thirds vote for the Freedmen's Bureau Bill, they resentfully carried a joint resolution which declared that no Senator or Representative should be admitted from any state of the former Confederacy until Congress had declared that state entitled to representation. This gratuitous resolution was a slap at the President. It passed the House on February 20. Congress then adjourned over Washington's Birthday. On the night of the 22nd, a mass-meeting of the President's supporters proceeded to the White House to congratulate him. Secretary Hugh McCulloch advised Johnson not to make an address, and the President said: "I shall thank them and that's all." But his old liking for a stump speech overcame him. He was soon delivering a wildly irresponsible harangue, in which he called the Joint Reconstruction Committee "an irresponsible central directory"; charged that it had "usurped all the powers of Congress"; asserted that Sumner, Stevens, and Wendell Phillips were trying to destroy "the fundamental principles of this government"; and even intimated that some of his enemies would like to have him assassinated. The speech did him infinite harm, although the charges of his enemies that he was drunk when he made it had no foundation whatever. S. B. Ruggles placed his finger on the real source of Johnson's error: he was always a little intoxicated by a crowd.

How great was the change in public sentiment became evident when Johnson found it necessary to veto another Congressional measure. This was the Civil Rights Bill, which made the freed Negroes citizens of the United States, with all civil rights, prohibited anyone from interfering with such rights under color of a state law, and set up a firm national machinery for dealing with any interferences. Johnson on March 27, as Strong notes below, vetoed the bill as unconstitutional, inexpedient, and generally objectionable. His reasons were for the most part sound. But some moderate men who had formerly supported him now deserted his cause. The bill was easily repassed by a two-thirds vote in both houses. So high did feeling now run that the announcement of the vote provoked an excited tumult of applause in the Senate. A deep gulf had opened between the President and the Congressional majority.

March 1. All indications are that Johnson's policy gains ground with the people, and that the extreme Left in Congress is losing heart. But Southern representatives will have to "stand disconsolate," like Tommy Moore's *Peri,* at the gates of the Congressional Paradise, a little longer. There is still a working majority to keep them "out in the cold." Sooner or later the gates must open, I suppose, for we cannot always hold these barbarians as a conquered people. Their representatives will have to be admitted, and the wolves swarm in to help the dogs guard the sheepfold. What will happen then? . . .

All England is in great trepidation over the "bare-armed" (query: legged?) Fenians, and doing all we shocked her by doing a year or two since, and even more than that. Habeas corpus suspended! Military rule!! Domiciliary visits!!! Patriots by the score actually sentenced to imprisonment at hard labor!!! and all these wrongs done upon a people suspected of designing to assert their independence!!! O John Pecksniff Bull, what a diaphanous old humbug you are! Meanwhile, there is stir, no doubt, among the Fenians here and in Oireland, too. "Brian Boru's body lies a-moulderin' in the ground, but his sowl's a-marching on!"

March 2, FRIDAY. Suppose Andy Johnson, President of the United States, return to Congress the next bill Congress may send him for approval, with a message to this effect: "Gentlemen of the Senate and the House. I must decline signing this bill, because it has been passed by Senators and Representatives from a certain number of the states that form the political entity known as the United States, while the Senators and Representatives of certain other of those states were not allowed to sit with you. Had you refused to receive them as colleagues because they had been rebels, I should have no right to take their exclusion into account, for you are sole judges of the qualifications of members of your own Houses. But you have undertaken to exclude from his seat in Congress every man who professes to represent Virginia or Alabama, because the state he professes to represent was in rebellion a year ago. This you cannot do. Virginia and Alabama and South Carolina have been whipped into recognition of their proper relation toward the nation. While those states are unrepresented in the national Congress, I hold the acts of the body that calls itself a national Congress to be nullities. I ignore them and I ignore you. Go on with your debating club if you like. Your debates do not concern me. I hold that the nation is for the present without a Congress, and I shall, therefore, proceed to execute my own proper official duties to the best of my ability, acting on the theory that no Congress is now in session." I do not see why Andrew Johnson is not bound in logical consistency to take this ground, and I fear a majority of Northern people would sustain him in doing it—so anxious are we to have affairs settled, however illusory and temporary such settlement may be, and however dangerous and disastrous.

Mr. Ruggles says A. Johnson's violent, unbecoming speech to the Copperhead mob that swarmed around the White House February 22nd reminds him of the *Fille du Régiment.* The heroine of that opera is recovered from her low estate of *vivandière* by her noble relatives and trained in all the convenances of gentility, and she dutifully walks in that path till she hears one day the regimental drums as the regiment marches by the hotel in the faubourg. Then she breaks out into demonstrations of affection for her old friends and companions, and outrages all the usages of aristocratic life. So A. Johnson, stump orator by profession, accidentally made President, and stirred up by sharp collision with Congress on a grave political question, forgets the demands of official dignity, goes back to his old habits, and makes a vehement, reckless, stump speech, being stimulated thereto, at the moment, by the clamor of a rabble demanding an allocution or (what we call) "a few remarks."

Extreme Republicans denounce A. Johnson most savagely. "When he dies," quoth ——, "there will be one comfort. Judas Iscariot will not be quite so lonesome"!!! Another says, "It's bad enough to have a tailor for President, but a drunken tailor, and a drunken Democratic tailor, is beyond endurance." I see nothing to justify such extravagant bitterness.

March 5. College trustees at two o'clock; Barnard absent. He has narrowly escaped a severe inflammation of the bowels, and is still in bed. The "special order," namely, consideration of report on financial policy and establishment of a sinking fund and building fund, was laid over on account of his illness. My term and Anderson's on the Library Committee having expired, we tried to introduce the principle of rotation in office. I electioneered for Morgan Dix as my successor, but was badly beat and reëlected. Mr. Ruggles got through a resolution directing that committee to enquire and report what sum is necessary to make the library tolerably complete as a working library in language, mathematics, and science. Zabriskie made a prosing speech and got a committee appointed to consider the expediency of purchasing land for a permanent College site. He expatiated on the superior value of land on the west side of the town as compared with that of land on the east side. Told him he had thereby stirred up a hornets' nest, and after adjournment, Hamilton Fish, Lewis Rutherfurd, Edward Jones, William Schermerhorn, great landholders on the east side, mauled him mercilessly. I got the year for raising our outside subscription of $250,000 for the School of Mines, to be duplicated by the College, extended to March, 1867. Dr. Jay told me formally—and authorized me to state—that he would turn over to the College his splendid library of natural history and his collection of shells (among the finest in the world), whenever the College may have a fireproof building to receive them. O were I William B. Astor or A. T. Stewart for a single hour!

March 13. . . . The Supreme Court of the United States decides against us in the Savings Bank Case!!! Nelson and Grier dissented, however, so that the weight of the Court is with us. The decision is amazing. Section 79 of the Internal Revenue Act defines banks and bankers and banking business. If we are within that definition I'll eat my head. . . .

March 23. . . . Library Committee—Barnard, Schermerhorn, and I— with the Rev. Beverley R. Betts, librarian, met at my office at three. Resolved to ask the trustees for a little more money; $2,000 a year for the next three years, in addition to the permanent appropriation contemplated by the "Financial Scheme." I wish we may get it. The Rev. Beverley is certainly the meekest and softest and least masculine of male mankind. Were a sea anemone or a jellyfish endowed with the faculty of speech, it would talk as he does.

Prices and gold seem settling downward a little, thank Heaven! Gold is at 128. Unless they shew much alacrity in sinking, I shall be forced to sell out, emigrate, and make Florence or Karlsruhe a city of refuge till better and cheaper times come (if they ever come), and this tyranny be overpast. That's a pet project of Ellie's. But the mere suggestion of it is as a pint of ice water poured under my coat collar and down my back. I may have to come to it, or to something worse. But I have no right to complain, for my belongings (such as they are) infinitely exceed my deserts, or rather my undeservings.

Johnson and Congress do not seem coming together again. Another veto is said to be expected. English papers are loud in Johnson's praise, which fact disposes me to instinctive distrust of his policy. It is the more strictly constitutional policy, no doubt—but it was no strict adherence to the English Constitution that saved England in 1688. No nation can live and prosper that is absolutely bound—in every emergency—by constitutional forms. The best thing old Eldon ever said was that "political liberty could not be durable unless the system of its administration permitted it to be occasionally parted with in order to secure it forever. Otherwise, liberty contained the seeds of its own destruction." We must not be too nice and scrupulous about the Constitution in dealing with these barbaric, half-subdued rebel communities, or we shall soon find that there is no Constitution left for Reverdy Johnson to analyze in the Senate, and Mr. Marble to glorify and exalt in the columns of the New York *World*.

March 26. Spent most of this morning at the *Evening Post* office correcting proofs of Savings Bank Memorial to Congress. Gold 125. The Savings Bank Memorial is a respectable paper, but far unworthy its subject, which certainly involves first principles of political economy and may involve the worst consequences of legislative stolidity.

March 28. . . . Another veto! A. Johnson has put his foot on the Civil Rights Bill. So the crack spreads and widens. His message is less strong than that against the Freedmen's Bureau, but very able, perhaps sound, possibly a little disingenuous. I fear that these vetoes shew Johnson's sympathies and prejudices to be wrong and dangerous. I am losing my faith in him, by no logical process, but by instinctive distrust of any one who is commended by the *Express* and *Daily News* and *World*, the London *Times*, and the Richmond papers. The "restoration" he wants will crush the National Party just as that of the Stuarts suppressed all Commonwealth men. Seward, Stanton, and Sumner will have to look sharp lest they share the fate of the regicide judges as unconstitutional, bloody, murderous devastators of the South, and Lincoln's bones may be dug up like Cromwell's. There should be no "restoration" till all possible safeguards have been set up. The question "would you make the South a Poland?" causes me no shudder. I reply, by all means, if it be expedient.

April 2, MONDAY.   Session of College Trustees from two to six this afternoon. Time spent mostly in skirmishing over Gouverneur Ogden's financial "ordinance" to create an "accumulating and sinking fund." . . .

Connecticut election is decided before this. Its result is waited for with anxiety. Marshall O. Roberts tells Mr. Ruggles that the current of feeling at the West sets strongly against the President. Maybe so. The loose, reckless denunciations of the President as without personal honesty and integrity which I hear uttered by "Radicals" (with whom I, on the whole, sympathize) tempts me to wish it may not be so. They are chargeable with most bitter intolerance and uncharitableness. But the opposing party, the Democrats and Copperheads of the *World* and the *Express* and *Daily News*, sin against charity no less, and are, moreover, utterly dead (and rotten) in all the trespasses and sins of political profligacy. Their peculiar boast is that Christian morals and the Christian religion have nothing to do with their schemes of public policy.

April 5. . . . They are jawing away at the veto in Congress and making much use of the *argumentum ad hominem* founded on Mr. President Johnson's talk when a Senator and disgusted with old Buchanan's exercise of the veto power. This is small business. The "Radicals" are strong on the merits, but they will fail to override the veto.

April 6. . . . This evening Rev. J. F. Young of St. John's came in to introduce Dr. James Pech, graduate of New College, Oxon., and Music Doctor, pupil of Chopin and Czerny, and a most agreeable man, who is to be nominated Monday night as organist of St. John's. After a couple of hours' talk . . . I took them into the parlor, where was Dame Ellen, and he sat down to the piano and gave us specimens of Pergolesi and of Chopin and of his own handiwork. . . . He seems so unexceptionable and admirable, of so high a grade of thought and culture and of accomplishments so various, that he must have some grave faults that will appear in time. If not, he will be worth his weight in gold, or even in greenbacks, to the music of the parish. . . .

April 9. With William Schermerhorn to Columbia College this afternoon; Library Committee. Nothing important. . . . We nearly burned up the College Friday night. Fire broke out in the assay room of the School of Mines (on the ground floor), owing to defect in a flue connected with the assay furnaces. . . . Damage about $2,000, covered by insurance.

April 11. Savings Bank trustees this afternoon. Sundry civil things said about the memorial to Congress, and a solemn vote of thanks passed. Walked up thence with Hamilton Fish and suggested to him the rather wild notion of putting up a long shanty—a rope-walk or park barracks— on the College grounds, parallel with Fourth Avenue, for the benefit of the School of Mines. Its rooms are overcrowded already, and the faculty declare there is no place to put the class that will enter next fall.

April 13, FRIDAY. The railroad-car drivers have struck, so omnibusses are overcrowded, and getting uptown and down is harder than ever. They held a mass-meeting this afternoon around the Washington statue on Union Square and afterwards marched in procession up Fourth Avenue. I heard one of their orators, an unwashed loon. He spoke grammatically, fluently, and sensibly, and with good manner and action. Would that I enjoyed the same gift! I hear of no rioting yet and of but few cases of assault on newly enlisted drivers. The police seem wide-awake.

Standing Committee of Trinity Church last night at Trinity Chapel schoolhouse. The irrepressible descendants of Anneke Jans are organizing another campaign against the church. One of them writes Dunscomb that she understands the church is buying up the claims of the heirs, and that she, being a church woman, would like to settle her claim without controversy, and is prepared to deal with the church liberally and generously. Some talk about Nelson J. Waterbury,[4] whom G. M. Ogden had retained for the church or for Columbia College, to lobby against the tax bill pending before the legislature of the state, which, if passed, would confiscate three-sevenths of the income of both institutions. General Dix said that Waterbury called at his house during the riots of July, 1863, to tell him that the draft could not be enforced, and that the Governor (Seymour) would order the New York militia regiments to resist its enforcement and to fire on any Federal forces employed to enforce it, or to suppress the riots. Dix ordered the caitiff out of his house. Pity he had not sent him before a drumhead court-martial and hanged him. The city would have been rid of one scoundrel.

After committee meeting to the Union League Club. The Copperhead papers, in despair and anguish, advise the President to summon Southern senators and representatives to Washington and to put them into their seats and keep them there by military force. They feel their party dissolving for want of office, and therefore advise the desperate remedy of a *coup d'état*. The suggestion will be remembered against them. May it speed the dissolution of that wicked, corrupt old party organization. Its decomposition would be great public gain.

April 19. . . . Committee on School of Mines sat nearly three hours yesterday at the Law School, reading and discussing the testimonials of Sterry Hunt, Kimball, and Newberry, candidates for the chair of geology and paleontology. Hunt's are very strong and include letters from Sir Roderick Murchison, Sir Charles Lyell, Professors Dana and Silliman, and others. He had had them printed and sent them to Barnard with a letter in which he said that understanding there would certainly be an election this spring, and inasmuch as he could not suppose there could be any one whose claims to the place were equal to his own, he had declined several advantageous offers from the West. This damaged him badly. Then Barnard, who abominates him, as do all the faculty, remarked quite casually and by way of parenthesis that he understood Hunt proposed, when elected, to procure a division of the chair, keeping geology as his own department, Hall to take paleontology. This settled Hunt's case, as far as the Committee is concerned. Barnard is a very sagacious old practitioner, and his opposition to Hunt is founded on most sufficient reasons. . . .

---

[4] Waterbury was a Tammany leader. He had been judge-advocate during the war, and had prepared a report on the enrollment of troops (1863) which upheld Governor Seymour's contention that New York's draft quota was excessive.

June 12. . . .

Colonel Badeau dined here and gave us many most interesting reminiscences of Grant's campaigns and Lee's surrender. Badeau's narratives are always perfectly modest, simple, and free from egotism. Being on Grant's staff, he naturally thinks his chief the best and greatest of men, and I certainly do not feel called on to dispute that proposition. . . .

June 16. Fine weather. Four cases of cholera yesterday. First, war —then, famine prices—next, pestilence. . . .

June 22. . . . "Keble Commission" at Dr. Haight's tonight. He is out of town. There were only the Rev. Houghton and Seymour, Mead of Albany, Professor Drisler, and I. We did nothing, and the undertaking will probably die out quietly. Last night at Standing Committee of Trinity Church. Drisler tells me ground is broken for the new School of Mines building. Barnard and Chandler lose no time. Ogden, by the way, spoke to me last night of Chandler's admirable accuracy in details of business. The professor, being dean of the faculty, is brought into frequent contact with the treasurer of the College.

July 2, MONDAY. . . . Europe is entering on a time of trouble. But our affairs are in no comfortable state. "Reconstruction" makes little headway, and party discords grow more and more bitter. No Congress was ever so berated as this. There are special backers of Johnson who think he has failed and thrown away his chances for want of decision at the right moment. Do they mean that he should have taken the advice of the *Daily News* and followed the example of Cromwell? They decline to say. There is to be a formal bolt from the Republican party. A convention is called for August 14th in which "every state" is to be represented. It will probably generate an intermediate anti-radical, semi-Copperhead faction, styling itself "Conservative"; in fact, the party of "the King's friends." Meanwhile, Southern arrogance and brutality have revived, lifted up their ugly heads, and seem nearly as rank as ever. The First Southern War may prove not the last. These blind barbarians are actually protesting against immigration of Northern capital. They fear the debasement of "their people." Free speech is hardly less perilous among them today than it was six years ago. Slavery being dead (we may hope it is), improvement in Southern manners is now possible. But it has not yet begun.

July 9. European news interesting. Austria and Italy fought 24th June, on a rather large scale at Castrozzi near Villa Franca. Victor Emmanuel was badly beaten, with loss of guns and prisoners. . . .

Mr. Ruggles is a little ill—not seriously, I hope, but any ailment seems perilous when its subject is sixty-six years old. This is "bronchitis," or a severe cold. . . . Vague report of a revolt in Cuba. Like enough to be true. So mean and cruel a power as Spain will get little sympathy in any trouble.

July 16, MONDAY. . . . News from Europe very important. After a series of minor defeats, Austria seems to have found her Waterloo "near Sadowa." Her army is reported demoralized or destroyed, with loss of more than one hundred guns and 14,000 prisoners. The success of Prussia is attributed to her new breech-loading rifle, which made the Prussian fire sixfold more rapid and effective than that of Austria. It is said that Austria asks the mediation of Napoleon, and agrees to surrender Venetia, and that there will be a Congress.

July 18. . . . Dawdling feebly over books of the class last to be understood by feeble men. Strange *Peter Wilkins* is so little known. Its author is almost equal to Defoe in Defoe's special knack of so describing details as to make them seem veritable. He is far beyond Defoe in fancy, and still further in purity of feeling. Poor "Robert Paltock of Clement's Inn" ought to have become a great name in English literature. It's preserved now only in a single scrap of accidentally preserved bookseller's MS and was unknown till 1835. What was Robert Paltock's difficulty? Did he take to drink?

July 24. . . . A very clever story or novel by Charles Reade is appearing by instalments in the *Atlantic Monthly*. *Griffith Gaunt* is its title. I am interested in its plot. I've felt no interest in the plot of any novel for twenty years, at least. All the parties to this plot are (at its present stage) in a very bad way. I cannot guess how Mr. Charles Reade will disentangle them. But he is a clever novelist.

Cholera prevalent. Bought twenty pounds of sulphate of iron and diffused it in water-closets and wash-hand basins. N.B. Sadowa was among the most terrible battles in modern history.

The exceptionally hot, stifling summer of 1866 found Strong in wretched health, complaining of weakness and languor. Probably one cause of this was overwork. Beside his law business and labors for Columbia and Trinity, he was much concerned with the issuance of an official history of the Sanitary Commission. The principal author was Charles J. Stillé of Philadelphia; but Dr. Bellows was to write on California's effort, Dr. B. A. Gould on vital statistics, and Strong himself on the financial history of the Commission. They ran into difficulties when Bellows turned in a chapter of "slovenly slip-slop of the lowest grade," done in haste, and they made him rewrite it. Stillé's own work, "a ton of MS," was too diffuse. As for Strong's chapter, he toiled upon it until he was sick of the sight of paper and ink. The whole city, as the heat grew worse, was in fear and trembling over the expected visitation of cholera. It duly arrived, and by the end of July had both Brooklyn and Manhattan in its grip. Mrs. Strong early in the summer visited Mrs. Paran Stevens in Newport, coming home pleased with her entertainment, but vowing that she would not be bothered by Mrs. Stevens's fourteen servants for all that lady's wealth. Strong was relieved when Ellen and the three boys departed for the cool and salubrious town of Brattleboro.

A variety of matters helped fill up the diary during the summer. Strong comments occasionally on the European war. Most Americans, he remarks, did not care a rap whether Austria or Prussia was in the right, and did not give a fig which won. But there was general sympathy for Italy and her desire to gain Venetia. A poignant paragraph on July 12 deals with the death of Willy Alston, Strong being present at his bedside. He was killed, as Strong puts it, by the breaking of the Mason will in 1853; for that misfortune compelled him to go to South Carolina to look after his plantation; he then naturally enlisted when the war began, and in service on Magruder's staff he lost his health. Early in July General Dix came to Strong to talk of a disagreeable business. A special money collection had passed into the hands of an assistant minister at Trinity; he had failed to give it to the church; and when inquiry was made, he confessed he had forgotten it. Now another special collection was missing. The assistant minister had forgotten again! Strong was much interested in Dr. H. von Haurowitz's book on the Militärsanitätswesen *of the United States in the Civil War. But he could not compliment the German author on his accuracy. Haurowitz asserted that General Pope had been a bishop, and he placed Richmond on the Potomac.*

The all-absorbing topic of the summer was the fast-intensifying struggle between President Johnson and the Radicals of Congress. The political crisis became more ominous every day. Behind Johnson were rallying the moderate Republicans, and the Democrats; but they were unable to form an effective coalition. The President's cause was badly injured when, late in July, a convention of Radicals in New Orleans was attacked by a mob, and some of its members, together with a number of Negroes in the neighborhood, were killed.

Johnson sent a dispatch to the Attorney-General of Louisiana which contained no reprobation of the "massacre," and which the Nation *therefore pronounced infamous. Nor was the President's cause particularly helped by the great gathering of conservative men of both parties which met in Philadelphia in mid-August. Though Ben Wood and C. L. Vallandigham were excluded, the body seemed to many observers to have a strong Copperhead seasoning. The able and disinterested men there—John A. Dix, Henry J. Raymond, Samuel J. Randall, Orville H. Browning—were overlooked. When the Massachusetts and South Carolina delegates entered arm in arm, the spectacle was derided as hypocritical. No proper effort was made by the President's followers to nominate candidates for Congress on a basis which would combine Democrats and magnanimous Republicans. And the mismanagement of Johnson's battle reached its climax when, late in the summer, he departed on his famous "swing around the circle" (August 28 to September 15), visiting a dozen great northern cities. His rough-and-ready speeches, and his general public demeanor before audiences which rudely heckled him, seemed to the country a humiliating spectacle.*

July 26. Cholera has taken root at last and grows rankly. It is severe in certain districts of New York and Brooklyn, inhabited by the unwashed, and very severe, indeed, among soldiers at Governor's Island and Hart's Island, and among paupers at Bellevue Hospital and Ward's Island. *"Susurrat obscurior fama"* that there are many cases in the city beside those registered by the Board of Health. . . .

The town is very dull. People are interested only in the foreign news and in the Philadelphia Convention that is to be held next month. This convention will be a "bolt" from the Republican party in the interest of the President's peculiar policy. Some say it will be controlled by Copperheads, and that it is a Copperhead movement. Vallandigham, Fernando Wood, and my reconstructed client, "Vernon K. Stevenson," are nominated, or talked of, as delegates from the "Democracy." Will the convention receive those vermin? If it reject them, and if its members be mostly moderate, fair-minded patriotic men, from North and South, their conference can hardly fail to do good, though it may result in no definite action. But if a single well-known Northern Copperhead Peace-Democrat be prominent in the convention, it will surely come to naught.

July 30, MONDAY. . . . Atlantic cable laid and working. Not the least symptom of any tendency to jubilation over this closer alliance with

England; nothing like the cordial, exuberant demonstrations of Anglo-philism that were called out so spontaneously, from Maine to Minnesota, by the cable of 1858. There is ample reason for our change of feeling. Wonder how long this cable will last. Thirty days? I do not care if its wire be burned up tomorrow by the heavy currents it must require. The first news it brings is of peace between Prussia and Austria! Steamers bring us earlier news of fight. Austria beat, as usual. The map of Europe is going to be largely changed.

Congress has adjourned. Whether its "Radical" majority has done the country good or ill will be more apparent twenty years hence. But Andrew Johnson has played his cards badly. He might, I think, have prevented this split in the national party to which, as I hope and believe, he belongs. . . .

August 1. . . . The people of New Orleans have been cutting up rough. There was a "Convention" dispersed by rioters. Some forty people were killed. It was almost a rebellion. A. Johnson's course in the premises seems to have been unwise. I begin to fear that Sumner and Stevens may be right about him. A few more outrages like this will teach all Northern men (Copperheads excepted) that these Southern wolves are not yet so humanized as to be fit to share the government of the sheepfold. Will this generation of Southerners ever be fit for it, brought up as they have been under the ruffianizing influence of slavery? . . .

August 3. Cholera increases in the city, and is very virulent "on the islands." I hear there were sixty cases among the women of Black-well's Island yesterday. The Magic Cable has sent us no foreign news for three days past. There are people who whisper that it never will send any foreign news! that it does not *work*, and that its signals are irregular, and often so faint that the attending hierophants have to guess at them. . . .

August 6, MONDAY. Cholera multiplies. Cases are confined as yet to our disgraceful tenement houses and foul side streets—filthy as pigsties and even less wholesome. The epidemic is God's judgment on the poor for neglecting His sanitary laws. It will soon appear as His judgment on the rich for tolerating that neglect—on landlords for poisoning the tenants of their unventilated, undrained, sunless rookeries, poisoning them as directly as if the landlord had put a little ratsbane into the daily bread of each of the hundred families crowded within the four walls of his pest-house. And the judgment will be not on the owners of tenement houses alone, but on the whole community. It is shameful that men, women, and children should be permitted to live in such holes as thousands of them occupy this night in this city. We are letting them perish of cholera and then (as Carlyle suggests somewhere) they will prove their brotherhood and common humanity by killing us with the same disease—that capacity of infection being the only tie between us that we could not protest against and decline to recognize.

Another material change in the aspect of Broadway. Taylor's showy restaurant becomes the office of an Express Company. Chapin's Universalist or Unitarian Church (east side of Broadway between Prince and Spring streets, built some twenty years ago, used of late as a picture gallery) is being demolished. So things go. Let 'em go!

August 7. . . . The feud between Johnson and the "Radicals" grows more and more deadly every day, and threatens grave public mischief. His "Philadelphia Convention" seems likely to receive into brotherhood and full communion the Woods and Vallandighams of the North, and also any and every bitter rebel from the South who may call himself half-converted to a toleration of the national government, though avowedly so half-converted by the *vis major* and by nothing else. I am becoming an anti-Johnsonite, though with slow, unwilling steps. His policy seems to me wrong, and his practices bad. I fear the memories of his boyhood, when he was a Southern "poor-white," are ineradicable, and that he stands in awe of the chivalry. Yet his course from 1860 to 1865 does not look like it.

August 13. . . . Cholera decreases in New York, but seems to hold its own in Brooklyn. Dr. Peters has looked through the "Battery Hospital" and thinks it well managed.

Cable news important. Louis Napoleon tells Prussia that the changes in North Germany brought about by this war make it necessary that the boundaries of France be "rectified." This indicates another war at hand— France *vs.* Prussia, in which case, Heaven prosper the needle-gun!

August 14. . . . Philadelphia Convention met this morning. Rebels and Copperheads mostly. General Dix is in bad company.

August 15. . . . Philadelphia Convention in session. Fernandy Wood and Vallandigham decline to take their seats, lest they should thereby diminish and weaken the moral influence of the Convention. A good and hopeful sign. But if the Convention do its work, the Woods and Vallandighams and Seymours will be our chief rulers next year. All the patronage and power of Johnson's administration will be used against the Republican party, to which (and to John Wilkes Booth) Johnson owes his great place.

August 19, SUNDAY. The Philadelphia Convention has adjourned, after a smooth session. All debate was discouraged and suppressed. It would have been dangerous and revealed deep latent elements of discord between the South and the country. Southern gentlemen were politic enough to sit mute and bide their time. The Convention has put forth a strong, well-written address. Not a difficult thing to do, for the constitutional argument of the Johnsonists is unanswerable, except by the proposition that *Salus Populi Suprema Lex*. I predict that the fall elections will sustain the President. He has a strong case on the merits; the Radical project of Negro suffrage must find little favor with any but theorists, and the great law of reaction will tell in his favor. Perhaps it may prove best that the President's policy prevail. But I find my faith in A. Johnson growing daily weaker.

Cholera, by the by, now a little stronger. . . .

August 20. . . . Morning papers full of political bitterness. The *Tribune* calls A. Johnson "Judas"—"Judas Johnson." That is mere Billingsgate, I think. Were he a politic scoundrel, he would make fewer speeches (imitating Grant's most popular talent for silence) and would not have declined by his veto the vast power and patronage offered him by the Freedmen's Bureau Bill. The Philadelphia Convention was clearly a most important transaction. If the so-called Radicals go into the fall campaign as advocates of Negro suffrage, they will be badly beaten. Their only true ground is a change in the basis of Congressional representation such as will put the voter of South Carolina on equal ground with the voter of New York. On that position they may succeed.

August 22. To Columbia College this afternoon with a box of specimens for the School of Mines; New England and Nova Scotia gold and copper sent me by Nelson Derby. Found Chandler there, at work as usual, superintending the new building and its fixtures. It's nearly under roof now, about half its roof finished. When the whole is finished, the flooring and fitting up of the interior will advance fast.

I hear of Newberry at Buffalo, attending the American Association for the Advancement of Science and taking high ground for and against sundry glacial theories. Why don't he come here and advise with Chandler, Barnard, Egleston, and others about the details of this new building?

To Union League Club this evening in desperation. Looked through sundry stupid periodicals, and listened awhile to a dozen old codgers (G. W. Blunt and his congeners) who were prosing vehemently about A. Johnson and the Philadelphia Convention. I had read all their talk in the newspapers every day for the last month, so I soon tired and came home.

September 5. . . . The President "progresses" and speechifies. Every speech costs "my policy" many votes, I think. No orator has used the first personal pronoun in all its cases (I—me—my) so freely since the days of Erskine, the "Counselor Ego" of the *Anti-Jacobin.* It is an unhappy mistake and may paralyze all his efforts to do the country service. I believe his intentions honest, whether his policy be wise or unwise, but this exuberance of egotism will surely weaken his influence. Seward helps him little. His auxiliary harangues are smart and plausible, but very shallow. Seward is a clever politician and has often secured many votes, but he has never secured any deep general faith in his sincerity and single-mindedness.

September 9, SUNDAY. . . . Went to Brattleboro Thursday by eight A.M. train. Lovely day and the country gorgeous to behold. . . .

No news in town. The temper of Brattleboro very decidedly radical, and so is that of all Vermont, it seems. The late election shews a heavy Republican or "radical" gain—five thousand at least. It is a weighty indication. . . . If the fall elections sustain Congress, the President will have his own unruly tongue to blame for the result. I think he had the inside track three months ago, but he has lost it by his exhibitions of petulance and egotism during this stump pilgrimage. *Per contra,* the last Philadelphia Convention did his opponents little good. The Rev. S. H. Tyng comes out against them, following Beecher's example, but neither of those reverend gentlemen has much weight on a strictly political question, though they were formidable in any controversy involving considerations of religion and morality, such as was that about slavery. The honors they won in that great battle against anti-Christian ethics have turned their heads and tempted them to enlist in another campaign with which, as clergymen, they have nothing to do. The *Herald* and its congeners have denounced them for years as "political parsons." They have now, for the first time, become "political parsons" indeed, putting themselves prominently forward on a mere question of state policy, and the *Herald* and all Copperheads caress and applaud them. Wonder if the Rev. Beecher does not feel a little uncomfortable when he reads the eulogies with which the New York *World* disgraces him.

Talked with Governor [John A.] Andrew at Brattleboro (he made an address at the Fair) and found him apparently a backer of Congress. John Schermerhorn, at the Lawrence, is fervent in extreme "Radicalism," and though he is of no great account, "straws shew—and so on and so on." . . . There is reason to think that Grant and Sherman do not enjoy this stumping tour, and Sherman slipped a little sentence into one of the speeches he had to make at some town or other which intimated, very quietly, that he was traveling with the President *by order*. And one of the presidential papers—either the *Times* or *Herald*—publishes in the report of its "own correspondence" an alleged remark of Grant's that this progress was not to his taste. "He didn't like attending a man who was making speeches at his own funeral." Possibly true, probably false, but rather smart. I cannot yet stir myself up to any earnestness on either side of this great dispute, though I incline to uphold Congress. Its merits depend on an issue of fact, namely, whether the temper of the late rebels be or be not such that they can safely be restored to their old places in the national councils. . . .

September 12. . . . The Republicans have carried Maine by 30,000 majority, gaining largely on the vote of 1864, in spite of the office-holder influence. This recalls the times of "Tippecanoe and Tyler, too."

> O have you heard from Maine-Maine-Maine-
> Have you heard from Maine?
> She went hell-bent for Governor Kent (bis)
> And with him we'll beat little Van.
> Van-Van-Van! Van is a used up man—and so on.

This most unexpected result, coming on the heels of the Vermont election, perplexes Democrats and Johnsonizing Republicans. The *World* says it is of no importance, because Maine is only a New England State. But the *Herald* thinks otherwise and seems getting ready to change front. It announced a day or two since, very distinctly, that IT would support no Democratic candidate for governor of this state except General Dix. Now the nominating convention has thrown Dix overboard, for Copperheads of the Seymour type could vote for no man who had shewn himself actively and efficiently patriotic during the war. John T. Hoffman, mayor of New York, is Democratic candidate for governor. He is a respectable person, but I shall vote against him with a clear conscience, which I could not have done against General Dix, for Dix, though not a great man, and without a perfectly consistent political record, means always right. On the whole, I think I am a "Radical." I have wavered between the President's policy and that of Congress. But A. Johnson's stump-philippics have uprooted all my faith in him. He is doubtless honest, but he wants common sense, to say nothing of statesmanship and decency.

September 13. . . . To Union League Club. Monthly meeting. Crowd. Sundry loyal Southerners present (the New York *World* calls them "mean whites"). Charles Butler was slowly delivering a long speech on the political situation. It was not a lively speech and the atmosphere was asphyxiating, so I did not stay to hear his peroration. I fear the Club is degenerating. Few of the first-rate men who used to attend its meetings in 1863 attend them now. The meetings are larger, but they are made up mostly of people who look and talk like low politicians and wire-pullers.

September 14. Went to a German bookseller's in North William Street, among canary birds and lager-bier saloons, to order a copy of certain numbers of *Unsere Zeit* (Brockhaus, Leipsic), which Lieber writes me contain an account of the Sanitary Commission. "No. 4," said the shopman, "why that's the number of which Secretary Stanton has ordered ten copies." Wonder whether he thinks we wrote the article—as he thought in 1864 that we had written everything that had appeared in foreign medical journals on the same subject. Lieber and I are in correspondence on things in general. Though a place-holder, he denounces the President, whom he calls "Moses" Johnson.

Visit from Dr. Peters this evening. He says that French physicians recognize a disease which they call the "malady of forty years." It attacks, Dr. Peters says, men who have led a dull, monotonous-lifed routine. They suddenly or gradually lose vital force and get somehow all wrong. This disease is partly physical, partly moral. Its only remedy is total change of scene and atmosphere. So Peters says I *must* go abroad, or go somewhere out of New York for a few months. He guarantees that I will come back fresh as a daisy, and as good as new. His prescription is pleasant, but he might as well advise me to jump over the City Hall. I am not in funds for a foreign tour.

September 17, MONDAY. A sultry evening. Have just inspected the grand Democratic or Conservative meeting in Union Square. It was got up regardless of expense, particularly in the way of pyrotechny. There was an uninterrupted succession of rockets, Roman candles, "flower-pots" and "bombs," and there were sundry great elaborate "pieces" besides, which I did not wait to see fired. One was blinded by calcium lights (as they call them) and by the most refulgent red Bengolas and white Bengolas blazing in permanence at a dozen points. Chinese lanterns by the hundred were quenched and killed by these fervent fires. The principal platform (which looked down Broadway) was elaborately canopied. Brass bands were playing. People had been hired to sing and sang very badly. "The" cannon boomed at intervals. There was a great assemblage of all sorts and conditions of men. It would not have been so very much smaller had it been convoked to bear witness to the respect and affection of the American people for the memory of Christopher Columbus or Captain Hendrick Hudson. For the show was really brilliant and fine. The scenery of *The Black Crook,* at Niblo's, which is so highly commended, can hardly be more brilliant than was the view from the south side of Fourteenth Street in front of the Maison Dorée. I doubt if half as much money has ever been laid out upon the apparatus and accessories of any mass-meeting in New York. . . .

Today's cable news is that Austria and Prussia are like to come to blows again. . . . By the by, what a wonderful achievement is the dredging and dragging up from the depths of ocean the lost cable of last year, splicing it and establishing it as a second nerve of sensation between Europe and America! This looks as if cable communication would last.

Peters, who came and saw and prescribed last evening, tells me that many Democrats and Copperheads are disposed to give up the game. They think the Vermont and Maine elections the first blasts of a great northern gale that will sweep the whole country in November. I hear the same story from many other quarters. The *Herald* has changed front, and wonders Johnson does not see that he ought to adopt the "Congressional policy." The Hon. H. J. Raymond wavers. An editorial in this morning's *Times* assails the Albany Convention for forcing on "conservative Republicans" a Peace Democrat as candidate for governor, namely, Mr. John T. Hoffman, mayor, and so on, and personally entitled to all respect. Newsboys on railroad trains say they sell three copies of the *Tribune* for one copy of any other paper. This morning's *Tribune* certifies that its circulation is increased by near 60,000 since August 1. But, of course, any such certificate is of little value.

Visit from Stephen P. Nash about a question submitted to the Standing Committee of the diocese and referred to a subcommittee (Nash, old G. C. Verplanck, and myself); namely, whether a new parish should be set up in Morrisania (Westchester County) without the consent of one Appleton, now rector there. After reading the voluminous papers pro and con, I answer the question in the negative. So does Nash. Have read also two or three hundred MS pages of Knapp's Report on the Special Relief Service of the Sanitary Commission. It's a most slovenly, cacographic MS.

September 18. . . . Ellie is to come home next Monday. Thank God. It is not good for a man to be alone.

Bellows thinks national affairs very hopeful. He tells me things that indicate great wrath throughout the rural districts east and west called

forth by Johnson's appointment of Copperheads to post offices and col-
lectorships. . . .

September 24. . . . Barnard is in great glory over the new School of
Mines building.

All political signs are hopeful now. Very many Democrats say their
game is lost. But let us see what Pennsylvania says October 9th. If there
be Republican gain there, it will be nearly decisive as to the result of the
November elections.

September 25. After Wall Street to School of Mines; Barnard, Chandler, Egleston. All looks well there. . . . I am told Governor Hunt (Washington Hunt) is fatally stricken with some cancerous affection; also, that
the Rev. [Francis L.] Hawks is very ill with what's supposed to be
Bright's disease. Secessia will lose in them two backers who "gave it all,
they could no more, though poor the offering be." Hunt gave his friends
a grin like that of a galvanized corpse. Nobody ever cared much for him.
Hawks's elocution has endeared him to many New Yorkers. But I suppose
him a humbug. His information on any subject was malleable and ductile;
he could spread out a pennyweight of gold into a square rood of gold leaf.
But even I, George T. Strong, could see the utter shallowness and folly
of his discourse about Mexican antiquities, and about certain MSS he
knew of, and meant to secure, ten years ago. His talk proved that he
knew nothing about its subject, that he was merely "blowing" at random.
But he was very clever and keen when discussing his clerical colleagues
—Dr. Anthon, Dr. Taylor, Dr. Berrian, and others.

September 30, SUNDAY. . . . Tonight General Dix here, Graham, Mr.
Ruggles, Dr. Peters. What choice Dix would make among the several
good things offered him by the Administration has been much debated in
the newspapers. He takes the mission to Paris, sails in the latter days of
October, and holds the naval office and its emoluments provisionally,
meanwhile. Dr. Hawks died Thursday morning. His funeral yesterday at
Calvary Church was attended by crowds.

With Ellie and General Vinton to Theodore Thomas's "open-air
concert" Friday evening. Very respectable. Mendelssohn's A Symphony
and the *William Tell* Overture among the pieces produced.

It seems admitted by everyone that the President's indiscretions have
blighted his "policy" and mired his party. We shall see how that is next
November. I fear the "President's party" is the old malignant "Democracy," most falsely so-called. He is certainly active in displacing Lincoln's
appointees and putting very bad Copperheads into office as postmasters,

collectors, and the like. I want to think well of Johnson. The statements on which one's opinion of him must be founded are obscure and conflicting. But I begin to fear that his name is destined to infamy.

October 9. . . . No news yet from Pennsylvania or from any of the state elections of today. We shall know something of their result tomorrow morning. God send us good news. If the country would avoid ruin it must sternly repudiate A. Johnson and his "policy." To that conclusion have I come, with slow, reluctant, amorous delay, for until this summer I held A. Johnson among the greatest and best of men. The carmagnoles of this recent stumping tour of his, the indecent demagogical blather he let off at every railroad station throughout the West, satisfied me that he was no statesman and that the people could not trust him as a leader. But I still believed him honest. He has so used his appointing power of late that I begin to believe him in dishonest league with rebels, and with rebel sympathizers. Loyal men (like George P. Putnam) who stood by the national cause in its darkest days are displaced, and the vilest Copperheads succeed them. This is exasperating. Mr. Ruggles thinks these state elections will prove a great cataclysm drowning A. Johnson and his "policy." God grant it!

October 10. Election news from Pennsylvania and other places is good. The national majorities fall off a little in large cities like Philadelphia and Cincinnati, for they have to contend against the Administration. The post office and the custom house and the navy yard have always been formidable reservoirs of ballots. They are reinforced now by an army of internal revenue assessors, collectors, cashiers, clerks, and detectives. These officials are the semi-Johnson party. The old Democratic Copperhead party seems a little numerically stronger from the alliance of these hirelings. But I guess the country sees the case aright and understands it.

The result of the October elections in 1866 was awaited throughout the country with the keenest interest. Four important states voted on the 8th, and they elected one-third of the membership of Congress. Moreover, the moral effect of their action upon the remaining thirty-two states would be very great. The battle between the Radical Republicans and the Johnsonian Conservatives and Democrats had been fought with a desperate intensity and had steadily grown more exciting. In Ohio and Iowa, the followers of President Johnson knew that they had no chance of carrying the state as a whole; but they hoped to win a few new Congressional seats, or at any rate hold their own. In

Indiana, their chances were better. As matters stood, the Republicans had eight Congressional seats there, the Democrats three; and the Democrats cherished expectations of a substantial gain. But the fiercest struggle was in Pennsylvania. Great mass-meetings, vociferous processions, and countless street affrays had marked the campaign. The Johnson Administration was charged with filling the Philadelphia navy yard, custom house, mint, and other offices with its adherents. Fenian discontent was expected to help it, for the Administration had displayed sympathy with the Irish.

But the vote revealed a sweeping victory for the Radical Republicans. They carried Pennsylvania by about 16,000 majority, Indiana by about 13,000, and Ohio by about 40,000. Iowa was almost unanimously with them. Their representation in Congress was strengthened. The result filled men like Strong with exultation. It was evident that the voters (who had been fed some highly misleading arguments by the Radical propagandists) had rejected Johnson's policy. "They have decided that massacre and insurrection shall not be tolerated as part of our political machinery," trumpeted the Nation. The Fourteenth Amendment, the main purpose of which was to guarantee equal civil rights to the Negro, had been placed before the legislatures of the country by Congress in June. Several of its provisions—notably its disqualification of large numbers of former Confederates from office-holding—were repugnant to the South. The great question now was whether the Southern States would accept the amendment, and so escape some worse penalties. Already various Radical leaders were talking of impeaching Johnson. One, Ben Butler, had in fact announced that he would go into Congress for the special purpose of pushing impeachment forward; and this would place one of the Radical leaders, Ben Wade, in the White House.

Cisco tells me that the Vestry (at its meeting 8th inst., which I failed to attend) resolved to sell St. John's Park to Vanderbilt. Consideration $1,000,000, of which the church gets $400,000, and the lot-owners $600,-000. I fear this will stir up a perilous storm of abuse and misrepresentation against us. "A bloated corporation"—"adding another to its untold millions, by destroying an old landmark, the garden spot of downtown, one of the few breathing places left to the city poor"—somehow "intriguing with the lot-owners to secure their concurrence"—"no reasonable man can doubt that members of the vestry pocket at least half the money," and so forth. Forty flagrant lies will be told about the transaction and thirty-nine of them will be firmly believed except by a minority of rational people. It is in fact a dangerous step for a wealthy corporation to take. Our only safety is in keeping every dollar of the $400,000 out of our own treasury, and applying that sum forthwith to some church-object outside Trinity Church; as for example, to the erection and endowment of a Free Church or two, over which we might retain some nominal control, or the establishment of scholarships with stipends in Columbia College, the right of nomination to be given to all the New York parishes. No one would more gladly apply this money to the extinction of our debt than I, if it could safely be done.

October 15, MONDAY. On Thursday at six o'clock in the evening I left the foot of Canal Street on the *Dean Richmond*. This boat and her colleague the *St. John* are, I suppose, the most spacious and costly boats ever built for river navigation. This boat is like four stories cut off the Fifth Avenue Hotel and set afloat on the Hudson. There was no one I knew on board; the night was dreary; so after tea and a cigar, I took to my stateroom and woke at Albany, after a series of uneasy cat-naps. Breakfast at Delavan House. Central Railroad for Utica at seven-thirty, then north by the Black River Railroad, and at Trenton Falls at twelve-forty. The solemn splendor of the autumn woods all the way from Albany, and at Trenton Falls, was a spectacle to be thankful for. The grass in every field and meadow looked as fresh and green as last June, and the pines and hemlocks retained their dark verdure quite undimmed, and both helped bring out and intensify the gold and orange, scarlet and purple of the deciduous foliage. . . .

Explored the ravine of the Falls after dinner, with an intelligent contraband, "William," a professional guide over those perilous paths for twenty-two years. I should not have ventured on them without his watchful aid and care, for I was shaky as to my knees, and notwithstanding the chains fixed in the rocks for pedestrians to hold on by, I felt nervous and almost dizzy at more points than one. The "Narrows," for example, where the waters of West Canada Creek rush down, boiling and furious and all alive with destructive power, through a narrow gorge which a desperate man running for his life would try to leap, and so close to the wet slippery pathway that you could dip your hand or foot into the torrent. You feel that if you touched it with a finger you would surely be dragged in and ground to powder. It is, I dare say, far more fearful than "The Strid," on Wharfe, commemorated by Wordsworth and Samuel Rogers. Back to my inn through lovely woodland paths. Visited one

Borden, who collects fossils and minerals, and bought $20 worth for the School of Mines cabinet. Saturday morning I turned my face homeward. . . .

This has been a fine fall day. Felt perfectly well when I went downtown, but that wretched sensation at the pit of the stomach returned soon after I entered Wall Street. Still it was so mitigated that I am sure this little spree has done me good. At three o'clock to School of Mines with that nice young fellow Charley Post. Inspected all the premises with Chandler and Egleston. Very satisfactory. Chandler commended my contributions from Trenton Falls, especially a big trilobite, and a specimen of well-formed quartz crystal growing out of semicrystalline lemon-colored carbonate of lime, mixed up with flakes of what seems to be black asphaltum. I had taken it for granted that Borden shaved me horribly in the sale of these specimens, but Chandler says they are worth more than I paid for them.

October 16. . . . John Van Buren died on the *Scotia* last Sunday. "Debility," following a slight touch of paralysis experienced at Alexander Duncan's place in Scotland; and also, it would seem, some disease of the kidneys.

October 18. . . . Yesterday with Ellie to School of Mines at two o'clock. There was a little celebration of the opening of its third year. Barnard made a little speech, so did Newberry (who appeared very well), and Egleston pronounced a brief eulogium on the undergraduate corps. This was in the chapel. Then we looked through the rooms, and partook of oysters and coffee.

October 26. . . . Ellie has just come in from a farewell visit to the Dixes. Mrs. Dix and Miss Kitty sail tomorrow. The Ambassador is to join them in Paris a month hence. This is a grave loss to poor Ellie; the two houses so near and so pleasantly intimate.

But I think General Dix's appointment to the naval office in New York and to the French Embassy have not raised him in public esteem, coupled, as they are, with his endorsement of the President's "policy" of surrender to the South. I like him much and respect him highly, but he has been too much in office. He has held high positions under Buchanan, Lincoln, Johnson. Official existence under conditions so diverse proves tact and sensibility. But it furnishes no evidence of faith in any political principle. I fear Dix, much as I like him, has none at all. He was a "Free-Soiler" in 1848, a proslavery Democrat in 1860, an administration man in 1861, noncommittal as between Lincoln and McClellan in 1864, and now, in 1866, a servant of A. Johnson.

October 31. . . . Meeting of Committee on School of Mines. Only Barnard, Edward Jones, and I with Egleston, Chandler, and Newberry. We must call on the trustees for some $4,500 more to fit up our geological room with cases and so on. A painful necessity.

November 1. . . . Thank Heaven, Mr. Zabriskie (alias Zbrowski) has gone to Europe! May his stay there be pleasant, prosperous, profitable, and above all, *protracted.* I wish he could be made king of Poland. His exodus is a great blessing to the College.

Very sudden death of Charles A. Heckscher. Little Gallatin married to Miss Amy Gerry. . . .

November 5, MONDAY. . . . At Union League Club tonight. An extemporized meeting, and an oration by John Jay, Esq., which I did not hear. People seem hopeful as to tomorrow's election, though it will probably be very close. The only bad symptom is that the *Herald* supports Fenton. Its candidates are apt to be beat. Home; General Vinton here, as lively and clever as usual.

I am more annoyed than need be, perhaps, by this stolid inaction of the College Board, and feel myself tempted to have nothing more to do with College concerns. Our corporate disease is deep-seated and incurable. The board undertakes to do a great deal that should be left to the faculty, but two-thirds of the trustees care nothing for the College and are disinclined to do any work for it. They have not the least inclination to push its interests actively and keep its affairs in public view. To attend our monthly meetings, when attendance is perfectly convenient, is to them the whole duty of a trustee. At these meetings they are always disposed to vote down or postpone any movement toward extension or invigoration, on any objection, however frivolous and unsubstantial. For they are not in earnest about the expansion and development of the College and its schools. I'm a conservative, but I believe the College would gain ground if its charter were annulled and its trustees elected annually by its alumni.

November 10. Miss Helen Stanly spent last evening here. The young lady goes to Europe with her invalid mamma on the 24th. Everybody is going to Europe. The tide of emigration and immigration has turned. She says Governor Curtin tells her the Senate will not confirm General Dix as Minister, which must afflict the young lady. I predict the General will be confirmed, though Congress will doubtless meet in a bitter bad humor.

Tuesday's elections were a victory, thank God. We were routed in the city, of course, but Fenton is reëlected by a majority of near 15,000. All the states that voted on that day (New Jersey included, Maryland and Delaware excepted), voted a condemnation of the President's "policy." Another Congress will be controlled by a two-thirds majority of so-called Radicals, and competent to override any presidential veto. May it use its great power with discretion and moderation. The ex-rebel states seem utterly to repudiate the "Constitutional Amendment." Rather than ratify it, they will remain without representation. That is bad, and full of peril. But it would be far worse and more dangerous to open the doors of Congress to Wade Hampton and Robert Lee.

November 12. College Library Committee met this afternoon; Schermerhorn, Barnard, Anderson, and I. Used up about half our annual appropriation of $1,000 for the College and $1,000 for School of Mines, and then walked through the School with Chandler. I took care that Anderson and Schermerhorn saw the desolation of the geological room.

As the October elections had foreshadowed, the campaign of 1866 ended in a decisive victory by the Radicals, and an irretrievable defeat for the President. His program was now dead; the extremists were in the saddle, and meant to ride hard. The Republicans carried every state outside the old Confederacy except three along the border—Maryland, Delaware, and Kentucky. They obtained more than a two-thirds majority in both houses. Thaddeus Stevens, Ben Wade, and Charles Sumner could pass what legislation they pleased over Johnson's veto. News was already coming in which indicated that enough of the Southern and Border States would defeat the fourteenth amendment to cause its rejection. In the end, in fact, twelve states refused to ratify it, and ten would have sufficed to set it aside. When Congress gathered at the beginning of December, it was therefore in an angry mood. The Radical leaders agreed that the South must be placed under military control and required to accept Negro suffrage; and legislation to that end was rapidly whipped into shape. As Strong writes below, the Congressional majority was ready to "cut up Southern institutions, root and branch." Thaddeus Stevens meanwhile introduced the Tenure of Office Act, the main purpose of which, as it shortly appeared, was to furnish a basis for the impeachment of the President.

One of the books of the autumn in which Strong was particularly interested was C. J. Stillé's History of the Sanitary Commission, *which received favorable reviews on all hands. It was praised as lucid, interesting, and comprehensive. What was more, it afforded an opportunity for eulogies of the Commission. "We are satisfied it will be admitted, and perhaps a hundred years hence more readily than now," stated the* Nation, *"that the Sanitary Commission, from the very first hour of its conception, represented the American people more fully and fairly in its best and noblest mood . . . than either the government or the politicians." Strong's full account of the finances of the agency was mentioned with credit. He had reason to feel pleased, too, by the continued steady progress of the School of Mines, the assured success of which was greatly encouraging the progressive group among the Columbia College trustees. No member of the board had taken a keener or more intelligent interest in the School than Strong.*

November 14. . . . The Chicago *Times*, the chief Copperhead organ of the Northwest, extreme in its antipathy to Niggers and its tenderness for treason, a most fetid and poisonous ally of Rebeldom, declares editorially that the Democratic party, whereof it is a well-deserving pillar, must change front or perish. It must repudiate A. Johnson & Co., and proclaim as its first principle "Impartial Suffrage in the Southern States," or die and decompose and become extinct like the megatherium. Thus and thus only can it extinguish and annihilate Radicalism. This is funny. . . . But there will be much kicking and swearing in the "Democratic" ranks before they are aligned on this new position, if they ever can be. The editorial deserves notice only as shewing how badly their leaders are scared by the fall elections, and for the cynicism with which it avows that if any one set of principles fail to secure the party place and power, it must try another.

November 18. . . . "The South" more and more mulish against the Constitutional Amendment.[5] Its newspaper editors bray and brag and bluster and write blatant fustian "leading articles" that remind one of 1860. The Democratic party (so-called) is in perplexity. Its politic leaders seem taking kindly to the suggestion of adopting black suffrage as a "Democratic" war-cry. . . . But this move would be risky, *periculosae plenum opus aleae*. It would alienate many Southern swashbucklers, and many of the nigger-haters whose votes swell the anti-national majorities of New York and Brooklyn. All the brutal Irishry—all the great multitude of low corner-grocers, of brothel-bullies, of professional gamblers, and their decoy ducks—will care little for a Democratic Party that advocates nigger suf-

---

[5] Only one of the states of the old Confederacy, Tennessee, ratified the Fourteenth Amendment in 1866. The other ten, angered by the third section, which was intended to make all former Confederate leaders ineligible for office, rejected the Amendment. This meant that it could not become part of the Constitution until they were forced to reverse their action.

frage. On the other hand, Northern votes will no longer sustain a party that seeks to excommunicate black men from civil rights, and has been a most abject flunkey of Rebeldom all through the war. Democracy seems in a bad way.

November 24, SATURDAY.   General Vinton dined here and we went to Theodore Thomas's second concert at Steinway's new music hall. William Schermerhorn sat with us. We had the pretty *Nozze di Figaro* Overture, an inane piano concerto by Schumann (*pereat iste*), and then Beethoven's Ninth Symphony, for which precious gift to mankind let all who love music thank God. I never heard it so well performed. Ellie had heard it, but without seeing much in it or remembering much of it. To Vinton and Schermerhorn it was new. I feared this roughest and toughest of all Beethoven's symphonies would rather bore them, as I am sure it bored me on my first experience of it, and my second. But all three were enthusiastic over every movement of the symphony, and I suppose their sympathy magnetized me into special clairvoyance of its manifold beauties. It is less fresh—more labored—than the C Minor Symphony, the A Major, and the *Eroica*, but surely among the greatest of musical works. I tingle all over, this minute, as I think of some of its phrases. . . .

November 26. . . . Political affairs seem troubled. The Constitutional Amendment will not be adopted. It is dead, and its death is generally recognized. A. Johnson shews no disposition to conciliate Congress or to make any concession. He is refractory and lavishes his official patronage on Copperheads of the worst and most "septic" type. Congress will meet in bad humor. Its extreme "Radicals" will get up an impeachment if they can. A. Johnson disgraces his high place and deserves to be impeached, but these ultraists, as, for example, B. F. Butler, are no less violent in talk and revolutionary in aspiration than A. Johnson himself. They must be careful not to bring on a popular reaction. To retain public favor they should be most studiously moderate and dignified in all their action. If they undertake to out-scold or out-babble A. Johnson or to put him down by extreme measures, our popular weathercock will soon be pointing the other way.

November 28. . . . Our movements on the frontier of Mexico look as if we might be mixing ourselves up with the affairs of that rotten cadaver, without reason and at risk of war with France. I fear A. Johnson wants a foreign war. Perhaps L. Napoleon will not be forced into it, but he must be sulky and sore-headed since Sadowa, and will probably not stand a great deal of kicking.

December 1.   Frosty. Long council with Mr. Derby this morning. He has just brought Mary home from a visit to Boston. At three o'clock with Jem Ruggles to Philharmonic rehearsal at Steinway Hall. Beethoven's Fourth Symphony is the most radiant and joyous of all his symphonies. Nos. 1, 2, and 8 are sunshiny, but none of them so bright as this. Its final movement is as full of healthy fun and high spirits as anything Haydn ever wrote. . . .

After dinner to Century Club. . . . Large assemblage. Macdonough was absent, so I was made secretary pro tem. Newberry was unanimously elected a member. Then we went downstairs to our oysters. I discoursed with sundry people—Dr. Barnard, Mr. Ruggles, Joy, Rood, W. E. Dodge, Jr., H. R. Winthrop, Henry C. Dorr, George Cabot Ward, Silliman of Merchants' Bank, Jem Dwight, Kirkland, Kensett, Stone, the Harrisse (?) of Thursday evening, Bellows, the illustrious Bancroft, Jack Ehninger, S. P. Nash, Edward Slosson, Wolcott Gibbs, Lucius Tuckerman, Isaac G. Pearson, and so forth. The bivalves were in good condition; so was a great bowl of sauterne punch. . . .

December 3, MONDAY. . . . Ellie has gone with Mrs. Wallack to witness her husband's debut for the season in *She Stoops to Conquer*.[6] Last night there were here Murray Hoffman, Mr. E. H. Derby, Mr. Ruggles, General Barlow, with a brother of his, Dr. Peters, and others.

"Extras" at two o'clock with President's message. It urges admission of Southern Congressmen temperately and fairly. The Congressional majority seems ready to go all lengths against the President. The temper of its caucus at Washington last Saturday was bad and ominous. I trust they may remember that it is excellent for the Republican or Radical Party to have a giant's strength, but tyrannous to "use it like a giant," and (what will touch them more nearly) that such use thereof may bring about a calamitous revulsion of public feeling.

December 13. . . . Congress seems going ahead with vigor. It is quite clear that the Southern States (so-called) spurn and repudiate the Constitutional Amendment, and Congress seems disposed to try another method of reconstruction, which will cut up Southern institutions, root and branch.

December 15, SATURDAY. . . . This has been a day of refreshing—a gracious season of good music. Heard the Fourth Symphony rehearsed (with Ellie) at Steinway Hall at ten o'clock in the morning. The room was scarcely half-full and Beethoven's sparkling music came out perfectly clear and bright, none of it being absorbed or muffled by a great area of

---

[6] This was Lester Wallack (1820–1888), who had opened Wallack's Theatre at Broadway and Thirteenth in 1861, and who there appeared in many parts.

skirts and shawls and furs and all sorts of feminine fixings. The Philharmonic orchestra seems in very good condition this season. Tonight with Ellie, Temple (!), and Mrs. Ruggles to the Philharmonic concert. Full house. Fourth Symphony. Violin concerto in F, op. 64, Mendelssohn. Violin by Mlle. Camilla Urso. A good-looking young lady violinist apparently of the first force is a novelty. I could detect no feminine shortcomings in her work. She seemed to me to play admirably well, but then I'm no judge of execution on any instrument. Ellie's judgment of her execution agreed with mine and affirmed it. The composition was—*me judice*—refined and elegant, but nothing more.

Then (Part II) came Wagner's "Introduction to the Opera *Lohengrin*." I heard its opening movement at the rehearsal of a fortnight ago, supposed it was Hector Berlioz's *Carnival* Overture, and inferred that Hector Berlioz was experimenting on a new mechanical method. I did Hector B. injustice. This "Introduction" was as bad as anything he ever wrote and vastly less entertaining. Wagner writes like an "intoxified" pig, Berlioz like a tipsy chimpanzee. Then we had a concert for the piano (Mozart), by Miss Sophie Groeschel—well played, but not up to the Mozart standard; a polonaise by Miss Urso, and then Overture *Le Carnival Romain*, op. 7 in A by Berlioz. This was the finale. I can compare it to nothing but the caperings and gibberings of a big baboon, over-excited by a dose of alcoholic stimulus.

December 24.   Monday and Christmas Eve. . . . Presents came in, were unpacked and arranged in the middle room, the boys being sent off to bed. But they were hallooing till near nine o'clock in high excitement. Then, or an hour later, we had our traditional roast oysters. . . .

December 28.   At 21 West Twelfth Street tonight; Bellows, Blatchford, and I. Chief subject of discourse our incubus of a claim agency at Washington. There are still some sixteen thousand claims on hand, which we have undertaken to see through the Pension Bureau, and so forth, to collect gratuitously. We work them off at the rate of about twelve hundred a month, but by this process the plain and easy cases are being sifted out. In the course of a few months, we shall come down to a nearly insoluble residuum of hard cases, some of which may take ten years to settle from the difficulty of securing the necessary papers and vouchers. . . . Binney's hesitating, modest doubts as to the prudence of undertaking this claim business on any large scale, or at all, are abundantly justified. The record of the Commission is thus far decent and creditable, but its career may close in disgrace from the failure of its work in this subordinate and altogether supererogatory department of its relief service.

Mr. Ruggles has just happened in at eleven-thirty this evening. Spent an hour and smoked a cigar in the library. Talked of the Paris Exposition, and so on. Were I not a vestryman but a mere average Christian, I should say d— the "Exposition." It is a skillful operation of Louis Napoleon's (that imperial Barnum) designed to bring people from all the nations of the earth to his imperial capital to spend money in the shops and the lodging houses of that infamous city. The device will succeed. Paris is all "engaged" already. Its citizens are preparing to abandon their homes for a time that they may let them to Englishers and Yankees, Russians, Turks, Jews, and dwellers in Mesopotamia. On the whole, I am rather glad I have not money enough to go to Paris this spring. I should like well enough to visit Paris or any other ancient capital, but I do not want to see Paris in days of joy and jubilation and profit. I know a little of the record of Paris in the day of Marat and Couthon and Barère, and nowhere in Europe for a thousand years of war and revolution and insurrection did the great central fire of hate and murder and all abominations ever break through the crust of social charity and humane instincts so violently and so cruelly as in Paris seventy years ago. That city has been a maleficent blow-hole of poisonous gas over all Europe and over all the world since the days of Henry IV. Louis IX seems to have been the last Christian ruler of France. *He* was a soldier and a gentleman (*vide* Joinville). This Louis Napoleon seems to be neither.

December 31, MONDAY. . . . Nothing very notable in Wall Street. A.D. 1866 is just in *articulo mortis*. It will be midnight, and another day and another year will begin within five minutes. God bless Ellie and my boys through 1867, and may His mercy rescue me from the depression and paralysis that has made 1866 so barren of good works and enable me to try to do my duty.

1868

*T*he great drama of Reconstruction was now reaching its climax, and the American public watched with eager interest the highhanded activities of the Radical leaders in Congress. They were intent on impeaching and trying President Johnson—a fact demonstrated when, immediately after the New Year, the Senate refused to concur in President Johnson's removal of Secretary of War Stanton, thus in effect challenging the Chief Executive to violate the Tenure of Office Act by a second removal. Many Radical leaders were equally intent on disciplining the Supreme Court, for it was believed that five of the nine judges regarded the Military Reconstruction Act as unconstitutional, and in the case of ex parte McCardle—a Vicksburg editor charged, in effect, with obstructing the reconstruction of Mississippi—a decision hostile to Radical policy was feared. The House in January hastily passed a bill forbidding fewer than two-thirds of the Supreme Court judges to pronounce any law unconstitutional. In the South, the first weeks of the year found "black and tan" or mixed Carpetbag, Scalawag, and Negro conventions sitting to complete constitutions which, embodying Negro suffrage provisions, would be submitted to the voters for adoption. That of Alabama went to the people early in February. Thad Stevens, Ben Wade, Charles Sumner, and others of the Radical Junta seemed temporarily in control of the destinies of the nation, trampling down all opposition. Yet it was by no means certain that they could long maintain their sway; it was not certain that the Republicans, even with the aid of the magical name of U. S. Grant, could carry the presidential election in the fall.

Of the lesser topics of the day, the most painfully interesting to Strong was *the high, the almost intolerably high, cost of living, which bore heavily on workingmen and the middle class alike. People were also discussing the Alabama question, which would have to be settled before good feeling could be restored between Britain and America; the speculation in gold; the activities of the Tweed Ring, the Erie Railroad Ring, and other nefarious combinations; and the activities of the Fenians on both sides of the Atlantic.*

January 10, FRIDAY. . . . The Rt. Rev. [John Henry] Hopkins has died at Burlington, Vt.; presiding bishop or senior prelate, and volunteer champion of slave-breeding. He was smart, but had a latent crack somewhere in his cranium. Being a virulent Copperhead, he was rather detested in his diocese. His talents and acquirements were respectable, but made of none effect by lack of common sense.[1]

January 13. . . . To College this afternoon. Saw Newberry, Egleston, and Chandler. "Irish Elk" not yet quite set up. Every room in the School fairly hums with industry and earnestness. . . .

Have looked carefully through Dr. [Austin] Flint's volume of Medical Reports (Sanitary Commission). So far as I can judge, it is exceedingly well edited. Many of the papers seem valuable, especially the report by Professor Jones of Nashville to the Rebel Medical Bureau on the condition of prisoners at Andersonville, an elaborate and able paper, barring some tendency to repetition. . . . I fear that, as a body, our rebels were a depraved set.

January 15. . . . Affairs at Washington look stormy. A disastrous explosion of some sort is very possible. The Senate finds (under the Tenure of Office Bill) that Stanton was removed without sufficient cause, so he has gone back to the War Office. Grant let him in without opposition or protest, thereby causing intense disgust in the great soul of A. Johnson. A. Johnson is reported this evening to have given Grant a piece of his mind about it, and to have objurgated him *coram concilio*, that is to say, in presence of the Cabinet. Grant's course seems rather to indicate his final adhesion to the Congressional side. The President is said to have issued an order that no one connected with the executive departments, or the army, recognize Stanton or any of his works. (The President didn't.)

[1] Bishop Hopkins, whose eccentric defenses of slavery on biblical grounds have previously been mentioned in the diary, had been so conciliatory in attitude toward the South during the war that just after it he was able to take a leading part in Episcopal reunion. Oxford had given him a D.C.L. in 1867.

Meanwhile, Congress is pushing on new and more stringent measures of Reconstruction, and for bridling the Supreme Court, all of which the Democrats denounce as unconstitutional and revolutionary. Honorable F'nandy Wood let off a good deal of foul language in the House this morning, and railed at this "infamous" Congress, refused to apologize, and was reprimanded by the Speaker, in pursuance of an order. The impudent demagogue will parade this Radical indignity with great effect before his enlightened constituency, the roughs, blackguards, and rum-sellers of New York.

All this makes up a threatening prospect. They are having a bad time in England, too, with their Fenians. It is unpleasant to believe (rightly or wrongly) that certain squads of semi-humanized gorillas, with the outward aspect of unwashed Celtic Christians, and with faculties so far developed that they can use phosphorus and gunpowder, are crawling about the streets at night, trying to blow things up. . . .

January 17. . . . Mr. Ruggles here, from Washington last evening, bringing an invitation to Ellie from Secretary McCulloch and his wife to sojourn with them awhile—very kind of them.[2] Mr. Ruggles's scheme of monetary unification, which is to reduce the coinage of Christendom, and perhaps of Heathendom, too, to one uniform standard, has met an unexpected check. This scheme involved the reduction of the dollar by two or three cents, so that the half-eagle should be the equivalent of, for example, the new twenty-five franc piece. Such reduction would be unobjectionable. But certain Congressmen, with an appetite for anything fraudulent, want to make the proposed new dollar a legal tender in payment of debts contracted when the dollar was worth 100 cents. And if that amendment be adopted, Mr. Ruggles will, of course, have nothing more to do with the measure, though he has given it so much labor and research. It is amazing and alarming that so atrocious a movement for the partial repudiation of all debt, public and private, should be even suggested among our lawmakers. But Congress is full of rascals.

I have "no confidence in either party," like Colonel Sibthorpe (*vide Punch*) nor in any member of either House. If the Radicals are right in their radicalism, I believe it is by accident. Mr. Ruggles reports a very savage and despiteful state of feeling between the two parties at Washington—so grim as materially to affect social intercourse and check the current of the life-blood of "society" through the capillaries of tea-

---

[2] Hugh McCulloch was Secretary of the Treasury.

drinkings, receptions, dinners, and so on. But the "Diplomatic Set" still keeps up its independent circulation.

January 18. . . . . Washington affairs are unchanged. "All quiet on the Potomac," as the newspaper despatches used to report in 1861 and 1862. Congress seems unterrified by the alleged popular reaction against "Radicalism." I think there *is* such reaction and that it will prove formidable. Meanwhile, A. Johnson seems to have suppressed himself for the present, and to be "laying low," in a passive condition, waiting for Congress to make a false move. That is his best policy. Almost every positive affirmative step of his for the last two years has done harm not only to the country, but to himself and to his party, if he have any party. "Andrew's Adventures in Blunderland" would be a good title for a political squib. But it would be hard to write anything with that title that would not suggest most disadvantageous comparisons with that wonderfully clever and original little *Kinder-märchen, Alice's Adventures in Wonderland.*

January 19. . . . . This evening Mr. Ruggles was here; General George Ruggles and his wife—she was a Miss L'Hommedieu of Cincinnati, and is a little beauty; Charley; "Dismal Jemmy" Lawrence; a clever Mr. Stanly from eastern parts; a M. Nagelmacher from Belgium—Liège—who is making the grand tour of this continent, and hopes to shoot many "boofalo" next spring.

Cable announces that that windbag, George Francis Train, and two of his fellow-passengers were arrested as suspected Fenians on their steamer's touching at her Irish port, and haled off to dungeons by the hired myrmidons of British tyranny.[3] O proud Bird of our Country, and O shades of Gineral Jackson, Mister Freeny, and Brian Boroimbe, shall such things be unavenged? Mr. George F. Train would not have missed this experience for $10,000 in gold. But a certain amount of folly, on either side of the Atlantic, may make the event produce great disaster. There will doubtless be several splurging star-spangled speeches about it in the House tomorrow, and probably some resolutions breathing battle, murder, and sudden death. As far as I'm concerned, the bloated aristocracy of Britain are heartily welcome to Mr. G. F. Train, and I would take it very kindly if they would relieve us of a few more of our braying, mischievous vagabonds. Of course, I assume that the British

---

[3] This irrepressible promoter and adventurer (1829–1904) had actually espoused the Fenian cause. He was arrested, briefly jailed, and then when the American minister insisted that he be either tried or discharged, was released.

government is not so absurd as to have arrested these men for any conspiracy or malfeasance, contemplated or committed in *this* country, and that they are secured because they are believed to design some breach of the peace on British soil. Their arrest and arraignment for a conspiracy in America would be a *casus belli*.

January 20. . . . Of course, the morning papers are in high cackle over George Francis Train and his brethren in bonds. An American army must go and overrun England at once, as England is dealing with Abyssinia, and get Train & Co. out of jail. Meanwhile, George F. Train is doubtless in the highest feather, eating his victuals with uncommon relish and appetite, writing the most stern and appalling protests, and hurling a haughty and disdainful defiance (on paper) at the Ministry and the Lord Lieutenant and the other mercenary, etc., etc., minions of an effete, etc., etc., despotism. But N.B. If the Irish or English authorities have made a false move in the premises, and if we *are* entitled to demand the liberation of these land-louping peddlers of sedition, let us adopt the precedent given us by our loving cousins and allies in the matter of Mason and Slidell, and help Britannia to a slice of humble pie. To *that* end I would make a row over the wrongful detention of an American bedbug, no matter how much the offensive conceit of the insect might be thereby stimulated. This little speck of possible trouble has sent gold up. Professor Tyndall's best thermo-electric pile is not more sensitive than that metal. Indeed, gold has the advantage, for its index rises at the mere contingency of future friction or collision.

January 21. . . . Read tonight volume one of Colonel Badeau's *Military History of General Grant*, a copy of which he has sent to Ellie. Very good —clear, compact and untainted by bunkum and fine writing. He is "down upon" General McClernand, justly, I think, and not particularly eulogistic of Halleck and Burnside. Rosecrans suffers somewhat. Sherman is the most prominent figure after Grant, and probably *ex debito justitiae*.

January 22. . . . Cable reports the great Train out of jail again and that he has "sued the British Government" (?!) for false imprisonment. Damages £100,000, which is £99,999, 19s. 11 ¾ d. more than the aggregate value of a whole ship load of Trains, at retail prices. . . .

January 23. . . . Miss Rosalie dined here and went with Ellie and me to Steinway Hall, for *The Creation*. Not very crowded. Chorus admirable, orchestra very good. Soli respectable, but a little deficient in strength and spirit. The tenor was perhaps an exception. "In Native Worth" was charmingly sung, as it well deserves to be, and was encored. We missed

Parepa's fire and power and brilliancy, especially where the soprano sings against the chorus, as in "The Marvelous Works." But her substitute, Mrs. or Miss Brainard, was of average merit, or above it. The audience seemed appreciative, and did not *talk*. . . .

January 29. . . . Dined at the bachelor quarters of Charley Strong, William Robinson, and John Cadwalader.[4] Present the triumvirate, and Tappan. It's a nice little house in East 26th Street. C., Tappan, and I went through the weather to see *The White Fawn* at Niblo's—a grand new show piece, manifestly got up at very great cost, and said to surpass *The Black Crook* itself, which drew crowded houses for a year and a half. Ballet, spectacle, machinery, and pink legs are its chief constituents. The dialogue is senseless, the plot undiscoverable, and the music common-place—plagiarism from the *Grande Duchesse* excepted. But the dresses, properties, decorations, and the like, are novel and lavish, except the costumes of the ballet girls, which are the reverse of lavish in quantity, though various and pretty in design and color. A grand procession of fishes, oysters, and lobsters is very grotesque and carefully equipped. The final tableau or "transformation scene" is particularly elaborate and pretty. A scene shifter would call it gorgeous. In a meretricious sort of way it is quite artistic, with its slowly shifting masses of color, chang-ing lights, and groups of good-looking young women (with very little on) nestling or hanging about everywhere. But the whole production depends for its success mainly on the well-formed lower extremities of female humanity. It is doubtless the most showy, and the least draped, specimen of what may be called the *Feminine-Femoral* School of Dramatic Art ever produced in New York. House packed—men mostly—and enthusiastic.

Curious "progress" has the drama made since the days of old Samuel Johnson, E. Burke, J. Reynolds, and Davy Garrick!

January 30. . . . The Republican majority at Washington evidently means to persevere in its Radical policy and "fight it out on this line,"

---

[4] This was John Lambert Cadwalader (1836–1914), a graduate of Princeton and of the Harvard Law School who was now practising law in New York. A brilliant and energetic man, he was Assistant Secretary of State under Hamilton Fish 1874–1877, making a distinguished record. Later, as a partner of Charles E. Strong, he maintained and enlarged the great reputation of the law firm established by John Wells and George W. Strong and long headed by the latter's son, the diarist. Charles Strong had joined the two men in bachelor quarters after selling his house on East 22nd Street in the spring of 1866; his wife and daughter went to live in Europe in the early summer of that year, where he periodically joined them.

undaunted by signs of popular reaction. It seems prepared to ride over President and Supreme Court both, unless they get out of its way. This looks like a courageous adherence to principle very rare among our politicians. Democrats maintain, of course, that it is merely a desperate effort to keep power in the hands of the so-called Radicals by consummating a lawless reconstruction of the Southern States under military rule, and with a view to nigger supremacy, before the next presidential election. Each of these theories may be more or less accurate. Meanwhile, the "Reconstructing" Conventions seem to work hopefully, and without sign of undue haste or of any vindictive temper. It is easy to write reports of the proceedings of "black and tan conventions"—"whitey-brown committees"—"Meade's Minstrels"—and the like. Specimens of the Negro dialect and pronunciation can be recorded or invented by any newspaper correspondent, and they seem quite funny when connected with the debates incident to the framing of a Constitution. But I guess the *patois* of the Poor White is ruder even than Cuffee's, and many of these black barbers and artizans shew better taste and temper than some of their chivalric colleagues, and quite as much good sense—or as little, whichever you please.

February 1. . . . . General Vinton dined here and we went with Ellie to the Philharmonic concert. House most uncommonly full. Every standing place occupied. We went very early and experimented on the amphitheatre, or top gallery, which is apt to be almost empty. Being early, we got good front seats there, but its whole area was flooded with people a few minutes later. Our experiment was successful. It's the best place in the house. The music comes up from the orchestra through free space, clear and sharp, instead of being muffled and deadened by passing over bales of furs and velvets and broadcloth, as it has to do before reaching the balcony or the rear parquette seats. The difference is like that between looking at a landscape with one's near-sighted eyes and with an eyeglass. The crash of the orchestra is not so heavy in the amphitheatre, the object seems smaller, as it were, but it is better defined, and all its details can be followed. There is a little less noise and a great deal more music.

Only three pieces produced. Spohr's Overture, Schumann's piano concerto, op. 54, with Mills at the piano (excellently played, but inane and long-winded as it seemed to me), and the Ninth Symphony. The chorus did its ungrateful work fairly, but the quartette was clearly insufficient and broke down a little once. or twice. There are great points in this symphony, especially its noble, saintly adagio, but as a whole it is unequal to the others. Its spasm and oddities foreshadow the degradation Beethoven's peculiarities have undergone at the hands of those who think themselves his scholars and successors.

February 2. . . . A rather good Anti-Fenian riddle, got up by some bloody and bloated British oligarch, is well received: viz.: "When my first makes my second, he calls himself my whole." Give it up? Ans.: "*Patriot.*" N.B. Osten-Sacken says Barnard tells him that the valuable gift of Ye Tsar of Moscovia to ye School of Mines is in port. It is understood to consist of certain books of price, and a fine suite of Russian minerals. Long live the Czar! and may the batteries of his next Sebastopol prevail against its besiegers! If this Imperial contribution to our library and cabinet prove important, as I hope it will, we must convert it (by "correlation of forces") into an agent for getting the School fame and credit through the newspapers. "Another proof of Russia's cordiality toward America," and so forth *ad libitum.* After the uncommonly good sale the Czar has just made of the rocks and glaciers and icy bogs and lonely islands and foggy coasts of Walrussia, he is very likely to have felt jolly and generous, and to have sent us a brilliant "donation" if any. . . .

February 3. College trustees met this afternoon; not a great deal of business. On Barnard's motion, we ordered Newberry's private collection to be insured for $10,000, or about half its estimated value. This was clearly right, as we have its use for nothing, and it passed *nem. con.* Then we went into an election for trustee to fill Bradford's place. Dr. Beadle and I were tellers. . . . Fourth ballot: Nash 7, Emott 7; fifth: Nash 9, Emott 4, Denning Duer 1; so Nash was elected. I voted for him on the 1st, 4th, and 5th ballots, and for Pierrepont on the 2nd and 3rd. It's a good choice. . . .[5]

Alumni will growl at the election of Nash, who is not an alumnus. But what have alumni done for the College? They have founded some little prize for scholarship, and they keep alive a little alumni association. The most valuable "donation" ever made the College by a private person, viz.: the Herbarium and Botanical Library, we owe to Dr. Torrey, an outsider. When we were trying to raise funds from the public for the nucleus or germ of our School of Mines, very few alumni did anything.

[5] Stephen P. Nash proved a progressive trustee, who later contributed much to the establishment of a graduate School of Political Science; John W. Burgess speaks of him as a man of superior intelligence and organizing ability, "chafing to move forward."

I remember only Agnew, Travers, and myself. It was William E. Dodge, Talboys, Cotheal, John Caswell, George Cabot Ward, and other outside barbarians who gave us substantial aid. A dozen wealthy and distinguished alumni to whom I applied turned up their noses at me and pooh-poohed the College and all its doings. So our graduates have no right to grumble if we choose trustees from without their ranks. . . .

It is a question worth considering, what can have been the special weakness or error of its trustees, from the date of its reorganization after the Revolution down to the present time, that has kept it so low in public favor, compared with Harvard, Princeton, and Yale, and has almost wholly turned away from its Treasury the great current of private munificence—donations and bequests—that has sustained and enriched those institutions, and created scores of new ones, many of them worthless enough, to be sure. It must be confessed that Columbia College has been, at least till within the last ten years, a "one-horse concern," and that if it has risen of late to higher grade, its rise is due simply to the increased value of its endowment, to the increase of its income by reason of the progress of the city, and not to anything its trustees have done. . . .

February 4. . . . Gold is UP, and there are experts who say it will rise to 150. There is uneasiness about the *"Alabama* claims," and possible breach with England, and also about home affairs. People vaguely apprehend some grave mischief from the discord between Congress and the President. In the *Alabama* correspondence it is curious to observe that each party decorously abstains from all allusion to what each probably feels to be among the weightiest considerations connected with his case. Great Britain is painfully aware that if she refuse to admit her liability in damages for the "escape" of that petted pirate from her ports, it will be a terrible precedent against her the next time she finds herself involved in war, and that pirates equally maleficent will, in that case, "escape" in swarms from every "neutral" port and play Old Scratch with British commerce. Of course, Seward understands this with equal clearness, and never forgets, while he concocts his voluminous despatches, how extremely difficult it will be to keep privateers from dodging out of American harbors whenever an "Eastern difficulty" or any other difficulty shall give them a chance to go forth against British merchantmen, with the advantage (which the *Alabama* did not possess) of sailing under some recognized national flag and turning their prizes to substantial profit. But both diplomats are silent on this point. English reasoning against making the recognition of the South as a belligerent part of any case to be submitted to arbitration (*vide* letter of "Historicus" to London *Times*[6]) is founded on the doctrine of estoppel. It will be held cogent by special pleaders, if any of that race have survived "Law Reform," but I think a statesman would give it very little weight.

If A. Johnson be the selfish, ambitious, profligate partisan his adversaries think him, I do not see why he should not make the *Alabama* a *casus belli.* The right being clearly with us, and long negotiations having come to naught, he could plausibly justify himself in declining further negotiation and proceeding to levy our damages by reprisals or by an assault on the new Dominion of Canada. A war with England would unite the whole people, property holders and taxpayers excepted, in cordial support of his Administration. Many of that class would join in its support, with all their hearts, for the old reverential love of England that was so strong during the ten or fifteen years before 1861 is quite extinct now. All the Irishry of the land would lay itself, its votes, shillelaghs and dudeens, at the feet of the New Deliverer of the Isle of Saints. The Administration would become invincible. Congress would have to concur or perish. There would be a grand shindy and general ruination on this side the water, and some little tribulation, I think, on the other side thereof. But I guess that A. Johnson, with all his passions and prejudices, understands that national bankruptcy is a bad thing.

February 7. . . . The New York Republican Convention having endorsed Grant, he is almost sure of the nomination at Chicago. The New York *World* considers it certain and settled that he will be the Republican candidate, and opens fire on him accordingly with the filthy missiles its party loves. It says Grant is a "commonplace man. Has no military talent—a very dull fellow, indeed. He is hated by the army. He is generally drunk. He never goes to church," and so forth. . . .

February 8. . . . Walked uptown with George Anthon. Spent an hour at Society Library looking over a large collection of books, a thousand or two, given it by Robert Kennedy. These books were part of the stock of [the owner of] a circulating library at Newport for about fifty years, perhaps longer. He died, and Kennedy bought all his books that were printed before 1820. They are mostly American, and *such* rubbish! But they may—or some of them may—acquire a bibliomaniacal value hereafter, and these idiotic novels, plays, and poems possess a certain value

[6] "Historicus" was later disclosed to be William Vernon Harcourt; and British recognition of the belligerency of the Confederacy was in time admitted by all to have been proper and necessary.

even now, as being the current co-temporary literature our grandfathers bought and read. . . .

February 10, MONDAY. To Forty-ninth Street at half-past three, for College Library Committee: Barnard, Schermerhorn, and I and our very meek librarian, Mr. Betts, who seems diligent and faithful in his little orbit of small duties. We "passed" certain lists of books to be bought, and then Barnard invited Schermerhorn and me into the President's room to talk of the vacant [Latin] professorship, and the coming election. Barnard is in a twitter of fidgets. He has written me about it, and I have responded that I could not see why he was so anxious, that the election of Morris would be no grave calamity. But it now appears that he fears feud and discord in the board, like the squabble about Wolcott Gibbs fourteen years ago. I see no signs of it. . . .

February 12. Ellie is in Washington, dining with diplomats from the uttermost parts of the earth—Blaque Bey included[7]—with generals, heads of departments, and other swells. N.B. The New York *Herald* has swung around again, and upholds Grant for the presidency. Bad for Grant.

Sorry to find that disloyalty to President Barnard is whispered among College trustees. His action as to the salaries of professors has given offense. I think it was a mistake to raise the salaries of the college faculty, but Barnard did not press that measure unduly, and if any one trustee be responsible for the proceeding, it is the Bishop. When this extra allowance comes up for renewal, there will be a fight over it.

February 14. In all my reading I have seen nothing worse than the spite and fury of the "Democratic" newspapers. The New York *World* seldom refers to *Abraham Lincoln*, except as "The late lamented," or "our Martyr." Rebel newspapers were hardly so bitter during the war.

February 17. . . . Political affairs look ill. Reconstruction makes no headway. The new Constitution of Alabama seems rejected and defeated, because a majority of Alabamians, black and white, stayed away from the polls. Such is the result under the last Reconstruction Act. But it is now proposed to recognize this Constitution, though repudiated according to the terms of the law under which this election was held, and to admit such Congressmen and such electors as shall be chosen under its provisions. This seems a strong measure, though I admit that no measure can be much too strong for the hating and hateful half-suppressed rebels and nigricides of the South. They are of a race "that cannot be domesticated," as Agnew said years ago.

[7] The Minister from Turkey.

April 25. . . . The New York *World* is quite smart in its wicked Copperhead venom. Alluding to some probably false story about General Butler's financiering with commissaries and the like for his own private profit during the war, it says: "Now this Butler was more Sutler than any other Beast in the field!" That little drop of concentrated virus is quite too pungent to have been distilled from the poison glands of a mere commonplace North American Copperhead Snake. It is not unworthy of the most maleficent and malignant cobra that ever squirmed in the jungles of Bengal. . . .

April 27. . . . Johnny and Temple heard *Richard III* read by Mrs. [Fanny] Kemble this evening. They enjoyed and appreciated it, though Temple "does not see why Mrs. K. should holler so." . . .

April 29. Last night with Ellie to the theatre appurtenant to the Union League Clubhouse, whilom "Jerome's Theatre," and heard Mrs. Fanny Kemble read *Cymbeline*. It was an admirable reading, but perhaps a little stagey and overdone, here and there. I am specially fond of that play, for Imogen has always seemed to me the most lovable and the very noblest of all Shakespeare's portraits of noble and lovely women. And while Mrs. Kemble read, I was obliged to fix my thoughts, sometimes, as firmly as I could, on the fooleries and buffooneries of *La Belle Hélène*, to keep myself from snivelling. Her great talent and her careful study of the text make her reading an instructive commentary upon it. She brought out many points that were new to me; for example, Imogen's question in the last scene, "Why did you throw your wedded lady from you?"—so delightfully appropriate to her loving, generous, and loyal wifely nature. I have always understood this as a cry of passionate joy uttered as she throws herself into her husband's arms. But there is far more delicacy and truth in Mrs. Kemble's rendering. She gives it in a faint, broken whisper —as the instinctive utterance of one hardly yet half conscious and only just beginning to recover from the blow that has stricken her down— without the least trace of complaint or resentment and without any intensity of expression.

Pity Mrs. Kemble is such a Tartar. The ladies (Mrs. Cooper, Mrs. Barlow, and others) at whose request she read last night, for the benefit of some charity which they administer, addressed her a very civil note, proposing to send a carriage for her, and to meet her at the door, and introduce her into the house. Mr. Tighe tells me he saw her answer. "She would be happy to read for the benefit of the (whatever it was); she needed no introduction, and she could pay her own hack-hire. Yours resp'y."

In the same key was her reply to one of the Fields, at Stockbridge, who remarked by way of civility, "Madam, you ride that horse better than I can." The reply was; "Of course. You are afraid of the horse, and the horse is afraid of *me*."

Poor Pierce Butler! I fear his married life was stormy.

May 2. . . . . Evarts has actually got through his oration in defense of the President. Strange so clear-headed a man should not have seen that the merit and weight of a forensic argument are apt to be inversely as its bulk. Witness Somers's speech in the Seven Bishops case, and Erskine's in the Greenwich Hospital case. Each was the foundation of a great name, a great fortune, and the highest rank a professional man can aspire to, and neither occupied much more than an hour, if so much. Evarts has talked through the sittings of four days. His argument might have been made powerful by compression into one-twentieth of its bulk, or by evaporation of its wordiness. In its diluted form, it seems inert, as an ounce of Epsom salts dissolved in ninety gallons of dishwater.

May 4, MONDAY. Spring weather, flavored with a dash of east-wind-vinegar.

Trustees of Columbia College held a rather long session. Barnard was a little prolix about the Russian minerals, and how some of them were lost by perils of the sea, and how the Russian government promised to make the loss good, and how he rather thought it would, and why he thought so, and so on. Also, about the Senior class, how it's in a state of discord, and how the management of Commencement will have to be taken off its hands, and so forth. Report of Committee on Greek Prize Scholarships. My colleague and venerated father-in-law got himself into a heat because they were to be called *"Anthon* prize scholarships"—couldn't see why they should be so designated, "especially as there were to be two of them," and moved to strike out the prefix, which motion prevailed. "Why," quoth Mr. Ruggles, "is *everything* we may hereafter do to promote Greek scholarship necessarily to be called after the late Professor Anthon?" I must say that the query seemed to me worthy the Gouverneur Ogden of fourteen years ago. It was perfectly understood that these prizes were to be established in memory of the old professor, and it was eminently proper they should be established in his name. *Dis aliter visum.* I am vexed by the result, and especially vexed that the objection should have come from Mr. Ruggles. I contented myself with an expression of decided dissent, and the two anonymous scholarships were duly established. . . .

May 7. . . . Arguments of Counsel in the Impeachment Case are closed. Senators will probably emit gas among themselves for a fortnight at least before coming to a vote. Result of that vote cannot be confidently predicted. Johnsonists assert that sundry Republican Senators will vote to acquit, and that a two-thirds vote against the accused cannot be had. Maybe so. The violence of the New York *Tribune* and its denunciation of every Republican Senator so voting, as a traitor to his party, looks as if the Honorable Horace Greeley felt a little anxious about the issue. He forgets that Senators, sitting as judges, must decide *secundem allegata et probata*, and ignore everything else, even party obligations. He thinks the managers have made out their case, and so do I. And I believe Johnson's conviction and degradation desirable and expedient. His sentence would be *veri justum aequum et salutare*, according to my best judgment. But I'm not disposed to rail at everybody who thinks otherwise.

May 9. We closed the [Law School] examination at eleven last night. *Evöe!* That bore is finished. We privately examined two of the class, Goodhart and Hervey, who seemed shaky, and passed them both, but not without misgivings about the former.

When the public examination was finished, and we were drawing long breaths and rising to go, Mr. David Judson Newland, of the graduating class, got on his legs, and addressed Professor Dwight with a few remarks, evidently committed to memory. They were condensed and well worded. "He was deputed by the class to declare their respect and affection for the Professor. Most members of the class came to the school from first-class colleges. They could, therefore, testify from personal knowledge that such teachers as Professor Dwight were rare. And he begged to present on behalf of the class this slight testimonial of" etc., to wit, a handsome silver tea service. The Professor's surprise and deep feeling were clearly genuine. He replied in broken sentences, with eyes full of tears, and very briefly. "Ten years ago," said the Professor, among other things, "I lost an only son, and I think I shall never have another. The memory of this loss has made me love young men and love the work of training them." These words may seem unreal to any one who did not hear them spoken, but they evidently came from the depths of the speaker's heart, in unpremeditated simplicity. . . .

May 10. . . . The old "table-moving" fancy seems reviving. Miss Louisa brought here a new device called a "planchette," now in fashion.

It's a little board that moves freely on little rollers, with a pencil stuck through it. . . .

May 11. . . . Benjamin R. Winthrop told me not long ago that poor Theodore Winthrop of Big Bethel memory had converted his sister, Mrs. Laura and her husband, "to infidelity." I denied the allegation. But that brave, brilliant, and unfortunate young fellow used to avow his disbelief in the commonly received doctrines of Christianity with more frankness and freedom than good taste. I well remember his doing so, on these premises, and the avowal was quite gratuitous. He was clever and bright and energetic in talk, and exercised much influence over his associates. . . . [8]

May 12. . . . I notice more building this season than usual. Work is begun on the site of the Society Library (afterwards Appleton's), southeast corner of Broadway and Leonard Street. The southeast corner of Cedar and Broadway and several old buildings adjoining it are coming down, and a grand insurance building is to take its place. Thus is swept away Guerin's ancient lunching place, which we law students used to haunt. . . .

May 13. Stormy day, and at last a steady deluge of rain, like a summer shower indefinitely prolonged. Hence a scanty attendance at Law School Commencement at the Academy of Music. It was barely half full. Mr. Ruggles, Judge Blatchford, Edward Jones, Governor Fish, and I, of the trustees, looked as imposing as we could behind the footlights. Barnard presided, of course, and said *auctoritate mye hyc commissa,* and so on, as usual. But he was educated at Yale, "one of those *habebam* colleges in New England," as Bull Anthon used to call them. Blatchford brought old Judge Nelson of the Supreme Court, U.S.,[9] who sat with us and looked leonine and learned enough to represent Ellenborough and Kenyon and Mansfield and Marshall all in one. "Alumni address" by L. Bradford Prince had its good points, but was rather anserine. He complimented the Faculty of the School and particularly Dwight, "without whom," he said, "the School would resemble *Hamlet* with the part of the Prince of Denmark omitted"— a line of observation which probably did not gratify Lieber. It was none the pleasanter because it was true. . . .

[8] For Theodore Winthrop's death in battle, see the diary for 1861. The posthumous publication of *Cecil Dreeme* and two other novels, and of *The Canoe and the Saddle* and *Life in the Open Air*, had given him an enduring if minor niche in American literature.

[9] Judge Samuel Nelson, born in Washington's first Administration, had been one of the most conscientious and industrious members of the Supreme Court since 1845. He was a graduate of Middlebury College. Samuel Blatchford (1820–1893), a graduate of Columbia College in 1837 and a long-time friend of Strong's, had been appointed federal judge for the Southern District of New York by President Johnson in May, 1867.

Something must be done about this Law School, and our Committee is to meet this week and consider what should be done. It has become too strong and useful to remain, as it is, entirely dependent on Dwight's life and health. It is *his* School. Were he to die or resign tomorrow, it would evaporate and evanesce the next day. If it is to be permanent, he must have a staff of associates and coadjutors and they must be of high grade and well paid. He has Lieber as professor of constitutional law and political history. We pay Lieber $4,000 a year, and his last year's work consisted in dispensing scraps from his memory and his note books to *six* of the graduating class, who chose to attend his "optional" course. I don't believe he gave the School forty dollars' worth of work. We shall have to throw him over and make his salary useful. [Dr. John] Ordronaux is probably of little account, but then he comes comparatively cheap. [Charles Murray] Nairne with his "Ethics of Jurisprudence" costs the School nothing, so he and the School are probably square.

May 14, THURSDAY. Something like spring again. Met Evarts, just from Washington and cocksure of his illustrious client's acquittal. Mr. Derby writes from Washington that Sumner is much cast down, but still hopes for conviction by one or two votes. General Burnside, who is rather violently anti-Johnsonian, writes that he is disgusted by the requests addressed to him by prominent politicians from New England and the West to use his influence with Sprague and Anthony of Rhode Island in sundry illegitimate ways. . . .

May 15. Law School Committee sat from eight to eleven, this evening, at the School.

Poor Lieber! The Committee was hardly kept from recommending that he be suppressed altogether. Dwight saved him by insisting that his name carries weight and brings students to the School, though they mostly decline hearing his lectures after they have joined it. But he certainly doesn't earn half his pay. It will not be easy to get him into working relations with any readjustment of his duties and his salary. He has plenty of learning and ability, and a keen appreciation of the money value of any position in the College. But he has little common sense. He is such an *owl*, so wise and lazy, and so puffy with self-importance, that I fear we shall have to choose between leaving him as he is, and dropping him altogether.

May 16, SATURDAY. Another day of dull uncertain weather. Before two o'clock it was generally known that H.E. the President was acquitted, and the streets were full of newsboys, whose extras confirmed the report.

It was close work—19 to 35. I don't know why this result should "dis-integrate the Republican Party" as the *World* and other malignant Copper-head organs joyously predict it will. It .nerely proves that many prominent Republicans are superior to party obligations and influences, whereas the Democrats have voted together on every interlocutory question and on the final decision, as a strictly partisan corps. Johnson's term will soon end, and this narrow escape warns him that he must be wary for the future. . . .

May 17. . . . I think with Mr. Ruggles that this acquittal is worth many thousand votes to the Republican Party, for it excludes A. Johnson from the prestige of martyrdom. But it was an error. As the *Tribune* suggests, the right claimed by the President to ignore any law he deems unconstitu-tional enables him to dispense with "any statute for about two years, or until a case can be made and carried up to the Supreme Court." For example, he may honestly hold a protective tariff unconstitutional, and prohibit collectors at every port from enforcing it. He can nullify all legislation for at least half his term of office, and excuse himself, at last, under the plea of *ignorantia legis*. It would seem that Senators were misled by the words "high crimes and misdemeanors," and that the Managers made little effort to set them right. Counsel and the Court seem to have taken it for granted that crimes and misdemeanors must be made out analogous at least to those of which Grand Juries and Courts of Oyer and Terminer take cognizance. I suppose the word "misdemeanor" to be used not in its technical sense, but as synonymous with misbehavior—official misconduct—grave departure from sound public policy. I suppose the functions of the Senate on an impeachment to be partly judicial but partly legislative, too. It is the grand inquest of the nation, assembled to see that the republic takes no detri-ment. . . .

Strong's view of the impeachment proceedings was that which the Radical leaders had taken. Senator Sumner had declared that "this proceeding is political in character—before a political body—and with a political object." Happily for the best interests of the republic, more than one-third of the Senators had taken a different view. William M. Evarts, who made the ablest speech in defense of the President, asked what high crimes he had committed. Had he betrayed a fortress, surrendered a fleet, or sold public offices? On the contrary, he had done nothing but attempt—unsuccessfully—to remove an insubordinate Cabinet member. Why the effort, inquired Evarts, to dispel the conception that the Senate was sitting as a court of justice? This was but a confession that if the Senate were a court, it could find no sufficient grounds for a judgment against the President; it was essentially an effort to get the Senate to enact a bill of attainder. And if the President were removed, Evarts warned, then all balance among the three departments of government would be lost. Congress would become omnipotent, with the executive and judiciary its mere tools.

The first vote in the Senate was taken May 16 on the eleventh or omnibus article of impeachment, which not only dealt with various charges connected with the removal of Stanton, but asserted that President Johnson had termed the Thirty-ninth Congress "a Congress of only part of the states," thereby implying that its legislation was invalid. This touched the pride of the Senate, and the article was thought to offer the best chance of obtaining a conviction. When the roll was called, thirty-five Senators voted "guilty" and nineteen "not guilty." Of the staunch nineteen, seven were Republicans—Fessenden, Fowler, Grimes, Henderson, Ross, Trumbull, and Van Winkle. The pressure brought to bear on Grimes of Iowa, Henderson of Missouri, and Ross of Kansas had been terrific. Lincoln's old friend Lyman Trumbull of Illinois, and Lincoln's one-time Secretary of the Treasury, Fessenden, also showed great courage. It was said later that had more votes been needed to save Johnson, one or two Republicans would have cast them. The verdict, sustained by later ballots, was a sore humiliation to Ben Wade, who had hoped (as president of the Senate) to succeed to the White House, to Thaddeus Stevens, vengeful and arbitrary, and to Sumner, who had actually called Johnson "the impersonation of the tyrannical Slave Power." It left men like Strong, who deemed Andrew Johnson too erratic, undignified, and blundering for his high office, dissatisfied. But it preserved the dignity and authority of the presidency, kept the power of the executive in balance with that of the legislative branch, and saved Johnson from a stigma which he in no wise merited.

Strong was now, in characteristically unselfish fashion, giving a great part of his time to Columbia, and striving earnestly to improve the Law School and School of Mines. On the day that news of the vote in the Senate came, he tried to convince S. B. Ruggles of the necessity for erecting a fire-proof building to house the library, the fine geological specimens accumulated by the School of Mines, and Dr. Torrey's Herbarium. Such a building would cost only $75,000, he thought, and Columbia would soon be repaid the cost by an increase in valuable donations. The diarist was worried about the precarious position of Francis

Lieber, who since his transfer to the Law School remained a poor teacher if a great publicist. Nobody could foresee that in little more than four years Lieber would be dead.

May 18. . . . The Messiah tonight with Ellie, at Steinway Hall. That ineffable music was fairly rendered. Parepa did her part full justice. . . .

May 19. Law School Committee sat two hours and a half this afternoon. We agreed to recommend the appointment of an assistant professor with very narrow function (a small step the right way) and also that a change be made in Lieber's department, which he can rightly understand as a notice to quit at the year's end—to be enforced unless he can so modify his style of work meanwhile that students can be induced to attend his lectures.

Steinway Hall tonight. Second evening of the "Musical Festival." Bach's Suite No. 3 in D. Third movement very strong, like Beethoven in ruffles and a bag-wig. . . . Mendelssohn's *Reformation Symphony* produced here for the first time. Its second movement, a sort of scherzo, is delicious, but what it has to do with the "Reformation" I cannot guess. . . .

After this, I came home—for nobody offered me fifty dollars to stay and listen to Berlioz's "Dramatic Symphony," *Romeo and Juliet*, and I would not undergo that majestic work for a cent less.

They are beginning to pull down old St. George's in Beekman Street, a venerable landmark. All the west side of Broadway between Eighteenth and Nineteenth Streets is coming down—a row of twopenny little two-story shops. Cheever's Meetinghouse, west side of Union Square, is in course of rapid demolition. Tiffany & Co. are to build on its site. It will be an improvement—the change will. Real jewels will be sold there instead of bogus ones. Cheever's pew-holders paid high prices for their bogus acquisitions. Tiffany's customers will pay still larger sums, but they will secure a genuine article.

May 21. After Wall Street, I went to School of Mines. Saw Chandler, Newberry, and Egleston, severally full of work and of hope. Our collections begin to grow precious, and I shudder when I think of this old barn of a building, with white hot assay furnaces in its cellar and of the remediless mischief that may befall us at any moment. . . .

May 22. . . . Hurrah for Grant and Colfax, nominees of the Chicago Convention, for whom I hope to deposit a little vote next November, if I'm alive, and out of the State Prison. Colfax's character is decent, considering that he's a politician, and my faith in Grant's honesty and ability is very strong.[10]

Mrs. Secretary McCulloch here this afternoon; a nice jolly woman, full of talk about affairs at Washington, and especially about the impeachment case. She upholds A. Johnson, of course, and I said nothing to his disparagement.

I'm in discourse with the Schermerhorns (William and Edmund) about a partition, between themselves, John Jones Schermerhorn, and Mrs. Augustus Schermerhorn's family, of the great estate they now hold in common. It would be a serious undertaking. . . .

May 23. I went to Steinway Hall for a "Miscellaneous" Concert, of the "Musical Festival" series. Cherubini's Introduction to 3rd Act of *Medea* was very good. Thereafter, I sat through a symphony in A by F. L. Ritter, conducted by that maestro in person. It was well enough, but who is F. L. Ritter that we should have to hear his commonplace compilations, while so many orchestral works of great composers are but half known to us or wholly unknown? . . .

General prophesying that Grant and Colfax will sweep the country. No ticket can be put up that has a chance against them. On this point Republicans are positive and unanimous. But I remember 1844, when "the Whigs took Clay and made a *bust* of it." Clay was nominated with enthusiasm and unanimity. Like Grant, he "would only have to walk over the course." But the Democrats dug up, out of his congenial dirt and darkness, one J. K. Polk, and somehow or other contrived to carry the day. Then there was the famous match between General Scott and the nonentity, Franklin Pierce. Grant's prospects are hopeful, but we must not be too sanguine. Every Yahoo of a Democratic editor will pelt him with dirt for the next six months, and some of it may stick. The influence of the Administration will be used against him with little reserve or scruple, and it is tenfold stronger than it was in old times before the war. The Democratic nomination may be a specially lucky hit. Grant's friends may over-eulogize him and thereby disgust the "masses." Many things may happen before next November. Grant is not elected till the electoral votes are counted and the result announced.

May 24, SUNDAY.   Rain. Rain. Rain. And headache. Fate seems against

[10] The Republican Convention, meeting in Chicago on May 21, adopted a brief platform endorsing the Radical reconstruction policy, and nominated Grant on the first ballot by unanimous vote of the 650 delegates present. Five ballots were required to nominate Schuyler Colfax of Indiana for Vice-President.

my going to church. This evening Mr. Ruggles here and Murray Hoffman, Wolcott Gibbs, Alexander (the ostracized Unionist of Baltimore), Rueful Jeames, Bramwell, Jem Ruggles, and one Ashworth, an English yachts-man. . . .

Gibbs had a story—positively authentic—of the Reverend [Samuel] Osgood, one of our Unitarian philosophers, traveling uptown in a crowded horse-car, and haranguing the crowd, *more suo*, under cover of conversation with a friend. When he gets out, some wild Western man who had been sitting opposite accosts his neighbor thus-wise: "Stranger, who is that man that's just *gitted*?" "That's the Reverend Dr. Osgood, etc." "Wal, stranger, I should say he was lookin' out for a vacancy in the Trinity." !!! Somewhat profane, but not infelicitous. Finite limits can hardly be assigned to Reverend Osgood's self-appreciation.

This Mr. Alexander, by the by, seems much more of a man than I have thought him. It seems that reports are multiplying that the Democracy will adopt Chief Justice Chase as its candidate. "Prominent Democrats" have confirmed these reports. They have been current some time, but I have held them incredible, and do so still. The Party would thereby repu-diate its record, and its platforms of the last twenty years at least, and would throw overboard all its Vallandighams, Seymours, Touceys, *et id genus omne*. It would become a new party—"of like substance," at least, with the Republican, and far in advance of the Republicans of 1861. Thus purged of Copperheadism, reformed and penitent, supporting Chase, that "d——d Abolitionist" of a few years since, renouncing all its traditions, the Demo-cratic Party might entitle itself to the confidence and respect of the country, after some little probation. But it will do no such thing, and I am surprised to find intelligent people talking as if they thought such a somerset pos-sible. Would it were possible! What a blessed event for the country it would be if the old Copperheads and Peace Democrats were rejected by both parties and finally consigned to the Limbo of political insignificance, wherein are no offices! Their infamy should consign them to some still lower depth. Many of them were doubtless honest, but they were most sadly misguided—"sair left to themsell"—and the country can never safely trust one of them again. When I think of Toucey, and Horatio Seymour, and even of poor Washington Hunt, who was so sound and useful outside of politics, and so warm a friend of Mr. Ruggles, I tend to become vitriolic and vindictive, and think not unfavorably of guillotines and committees of *Salut Publique*.

1872

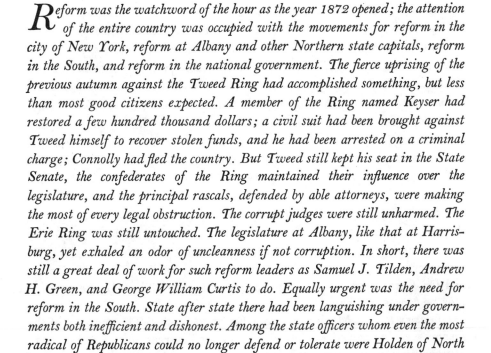

*R*eform was the watchword of the hour as the year 1872 opened; the attention of the entire country was occupied with the movements for reform in the city of New York, reform at Albany and other Northern state capitals, reform in the South, and reform in the national government. The fierce uprising of the previous autumn against the Tweed Ring had accomplished something, but less than most good citizens expected. A member of the Ring named Keyser had restored a few hundred thousand dollars; a civil suit had been brought against Tweed himself to recover stolen funds, and he had been arrested on a criminal charge; Connolly had fled the country. But Tweed still kept his seat in the State Senate, the confederates of the Ring maintained their influence over the legislature, and the principal rascals, defended by able attorneys, were making the most of every legal obstruction. The corrupt judges were still unharmed. The Erie Ring was still untouched. The legislature at Albany, like that at Harrisburg, yet exhaled an odor of uncleanness if not corruption. In short, there was still a great deal of work for such reform leaders as Samuel J. Tilden, Andrew H. Green, and George William Curtis to do. Equally urgent was the need for reform in the South. State after state there had been languishing under governments both inefficient and dishonest. Among the state officers whom even the most radical of Republicans could no longer defend or tolerate were Holden of North Carolina, impeached and turned out of office for dishonesty; Scott of South Carolina, one of the state's "forty thieves"; Warmoth of Louisiana, who had accumulated wealth while the people were robbed; and Reed of Florida, who was *being put on trial for the theft of railroad bonds. The reconstruction policy of Grant had proved a failure.*

In national affairs, a "Liberal Republican" movement originating in Missouri was gaining important adherents in other states. Its object was to defeat President Grant for a second term, put an end to corruption, introduce civil service reform and other administrative improvements, and inaugurate a more liberal policy toward the Southern people. Carl Schurz of Missouri, Lyman Trumbull of Illinois, former Secretary Jacob D. Cox of Ohio, and Horace Greeley of New York were among the leaders who hoped for a brighter era in Washington. An investigation of the New York custom house early in the year disclosed a shocking system of blackmail and graft, while it was generally known that other branches of the government were run by machine politicians for selfish ends. It was already plain that the country would witness a Republican schism and a bitter presidential campaign.

Strong began the new year with a lament that because of a slow omnibus he did not reach a meeting of the Columbia trustees in time to vote to put Abram S. Hewitt in a vacancy of the board. Had he arrived promptly he could have tied the vote; as it was, the place went to Anthony Halsey, who lacked Hewitt's commanding abilities. Strong recorded thirty calls on New Year's Day; a delightful Saturday evening concert on the 6th by the Philharmonic; and that same evening, news at the Century Club that Ned Stokes had fatally shot Jim Fisk on the stairway of the Broadway Central Hotel, the sequel of a miserable quarrel over a strumpet named Josie Mansfield.

January 7, SUNDAY. . . . The great Fisk died this morning. No loss to the community—quite the reverse—but it's a pity he should have escaped the state prison in this way. He seems to have died surrounded by his congeners, amid the sobbings of Tweed, David Dudley Field, Jay Gould, and Dr. Carnochan. Stokes is in custody, and it is difficult to see on what plea he can escape hanging.

January 8. . . . Much talk about Fisk and Stokes. The remains of the former were conveyed to the railroad depot in great state for interment at poor little Brattleboro. What a scamp he was, but what a curious and scientifically interesting scamp! When he "took to the road" a very few years ago and opened his campaign against society he was penniless. By talent and audacity he raised himself to the first rank among business scoundrels, and (I suppose) to great wealth—certainly to opportunities of great wealth—but then he was reckless in spending. He was opera impresario, "commodore," financier, roué, mountebank, corrupt to the core, with great faculty of corrupting others, judges included, colonel of a regiment of militia, which he uniformed at his own cost and the splendid band of which he supported. He paid its first cornet-player $10,000 a year, it is said. Illiterate, vulgar, unprincipled, profligate, always making himself conspicuously ridiculous by some piece of flagrant ostentation, he was, nevertheless, freehanded with his stolen money, and possessed, moreover, a certain magnetism of geniality that attracted to him people who were not particular about the decency of their associates. He was liberal to distressed ballet dancers and munificent to unfortunate females under difficulties. Let us put this generosity down to the credit side of the scamp's account. The item may be more important than it seems to *us*. His influence on the community was certainly bad in every way, but it is also certain that many people, more or less wise and more or less honest, sorrowed heartily at his funeral. . . .

January 9. . . . Talk of possible war with Spain. May I see no more wars!

That beast John Graham enters an appearance before the Fisk coroner's jury, and is more blatant and insolent than ever. Before any witnesses are sworn, he makes a speech "protesting against the coroner's introducing a murderous atmosphere into the jury room." He should have been collared by policemen and dragged out of it. I am ashamed to live in a community of Fisks, Tweeds, Vanderbilts, John Grahams, and D. D. Fields. Connolly, by the by, has cut and run.

An investigating committee uncovers a most nasty mess of corruption in the custom house, with "Colonel" Frank Howe seemingly ensconced in it, like a burrowing coprophagous beetle.[1]

January 11. . . . Oakey Hall withdraws "for a few days" from malversation in office, and John Cochrane is acting mayor. Hall's private affairs require attention. This is thought a prelude to his resignation; perhaps. Prospects of city reform do not improve. A squabble between two Republican factions interests the legislature more deeply.

January 15, MONDAY. . . . Annual meeting of Century Club Saturday

[1] The principal culprit in the custom house corruption was a hanger-on of Grant's named George K. Leet, who by the President's favor obtained control of the "general order" business (the holding of certain imported goods in a general order warehouse kept by a private citizen under authorization by the government, with large fees attached). Leet made a fortune while performing no real service. But the custom house was also a citadel of machine politics in the state.

night. Edward Slosson bequeaths the Club some thirty or forty pictures, mostly by American artists. Average is fair. Election was nearly unanimous, save that Theodore Weston retained his place by only 97 to 92, which should be a warning to him. —— was there, drivelling about "art" and "tone." From a fribble he is solidifying into a bore. Also —— (Sir Mungo Malagrowther), who acts on the spirit of the rule *nil de mortuis,* and so forth, by never saying anything *de vivis nisi malum.* Also Egleston, in one of his fits of depression. Discoursed with the Rev. Mr. Osgood, William C. Bryant, and other magi, and came off before supper. . . .

They say Stokes will set up that he slew Fisk in self-defense, that he lived in hourly dread of Fisk's myrmidons, and that Fisk instigated the nocturnal assault from the effects of which D. B. Eaton has not yet recovered.[2] Then why did he not have Fisk bound over to keep the peace? Such evidence is absurdly inadmissible, as it strikes me. But it will be got in somehow and will give John Graham a field for indecent gymnastics such as he has never yet enjoyed. And the jury will disagree.

January 19. . . . Tonight with Ellie, Temple, and Louis to Booth's theatre for *Julius Caesar.* Booth as Brutus. Performance fairly good, every part rather above average merit. Perhaps Mark Antony exhibited as too enlightened to rant and roar, but he was effective in his funeral oration. So were Brutus and Cassius in the Tent Scene. So was pretty little Portia in her five minutes' work. Caesar's ghost was a good piece of supernaturalism, and the setting of the play—the *mise en scène* (I hate writing French words)—was unsurpassable.

January 25. . . . Johnny arrived Tuesday, after a voyage that was long and rough, but which he endured without seasickness. Eyes much better; general health and spirits excellent. Very fluent, unreserved, and vivacious in telling his experiences. No trace of moodiness or apathy, *laus Deo.* He went to College this morning and was cordially received by Dr. Barnard and others. He is as nice as he can be. . . .

[2] Dorman Bridgman Eaton (1823–1899), formerly a law partner of Judge William Kent, had been counsel for the Erie Railroad. As a result of that bitter controversy, he was seriously injured by unidentified assailants in the night attack Strong mentions. Upon recovery he resumed practice and threw himself into a crusade for civil service reform. In 1870 he gave up his practice to devote himself entirely to reform activities. President Grant appointed him chairman of the national Civil Service Commission in 1873. He wrote important books on municipal administration and civil service and by bequests endowed professorships of the science of government at Harvard and Columbia.

Custom House Investigating Committee drags slowly along with its work and causes much skipping in the morning papers. The New York *World* and the New York *Tribune* have entered into a partnership for the throwing of dirt at Grant. But their projectiles are so mephitic, fetid, ammoniacal, hippuric, cacodylic, and abominable that they do Grant little harm. They merely disgust and alienate the public. The specially smart malignity and virulence of the *World* must make friends for Grant every day. . . .

January 30. . . . Read Robert Dale Owen's new book on spiritualism, *The Debatable Land.* It is more readable and less irrational than most books of its very low class. His testimony as to personal experiences as to things seen, heard, and felt cannot be summarily disposed of in a lump as legerdemain or delusion, except by some ruling that would exclude all human evidence as to any new and strange occurrence. It must go to the jury for what it is worth, and I dare say cross-examination would shew it to be worth very little indeed. . . .

February 2. Philharmonic rehearsal this afternoon. Very large attendance. Sarasate [the Spanish violinist and composer] did a violin concerto by Max Bruch. . . . The Schumann symphony is really respectable. . . .

February 3. . . . The Assembly at Albany is "going for" Cardozo and Barnard at last, and its Judiciary Committee is instructed to take up the charges of the bar association against those learned judges. Only one legislator voted against the reference and that was the notorious Tom Fields, who has a natural antipathy to investigations. So far, well. We are living in a day of ruffianism and of almost universal corruption. Life and property are as insecure here in New York as in Mexico. It is a thoroughly rotten community. "The whole head is sick and the whole heart faint. From the sole of the foot even unto the head, there is no soundness in it but wounds and bruises and putrifying sores. Run ye to and fro through the streets of Jerusalem and seek in the broad places thereof, if ye can find a man, if there be any that executeth judgment, that seeketh truth." Unless some peaceful and lawful remedy be found, a dangerous convulsion cannot be far off. To degrade venal judges and restore confidence in the courts is manifestly the first step toward reform. . . .

February 6. . . . Columbia College trustees met yesterday afternoon. Mr. "Zbrowski" writes from Paris resigning his seat once more, and we accepted his resignation. So I hope we are at length finally rid of that insufferable noodle. There was considerable debate on the question of setting up an adjunct professorship in Nairne's department. Decision affirmative, and I think unwise. Anthony Halsey took his seat as trustee. Had not seen him since our college days and found him pleasant, as he was of old. He tells me that N. W. Chittenden is practising law in San Francisco. I had supposed him to have died several years ago.

February 10. . . . A little fluster about possible war with England. John Bull talks foolishly about repudiating the Treaty of Washington, because our claims under its provisions are too large. That strikes me as the very question which arbitrators were selected to decide.

Indictments brought in today against Mayor Hall, Sweeny, the Pecksniffian Nathaniel Sands, and others.

February 14, ASH WEDNESDAY. . . . Yesterday's atmosphere was succulent. Toward evening it deliquesced into pouring rain, and at about nine in the evening the Lacrymosa of Mozart's Requiem at Steinway Hall was accompanied by a vehement hailstone chorus on the roof, much more than *sotto voce*, with lightning and low thunder. Concert (Church Music Association) was crowded. I knew nearly every other person in the room. Policeman told me "with amazement and awe" that by half-past ten "there was nearly five hundred carriages in Fourteenth Street, sir, and half of them was private." Fifteenth Street also blocked with vehicles.

The *Struensee* Overture came out well, and is certainly handsome. The harp passages are fresh and effective. I like it better than any other orchestral work of Meyerbeer's. The Requiem traveled well. The Dies Irae was as impressive and aweful as anything I know in music, and the Lacrymosa embodied another sentiment with almost equal power. And then that gem of a Benedictus, so pure, sad, and elegant! . . .

February 20. . . . At Columbia College yesterday afternoon with William Schermerhorn, Barnard, Haight, and H. J. Anderson, the Doctor Angelicus, or Simplicissimus. Then we spent an hour in the cabinets of the School of Mines. The College library is now all but useless.[3] We incline to make it useful in spite of the treasurer, whose way it is to oppose

---

[3] On this subject see Brander Matthews' testimony in *These Many Years*. He writes that at this time the Columbia library was open only one or two hours a day, in the afternoon when most students had gone home; that he for one never entered it during his undergraduate career, and he thinks no classmate did so; that the collection of fewer than 15,000 volumes was kept in glazed cases all carefully locked; and that the librarian, allowed $1,000 a year for purchases, took pride in returning to the college treasury as large a part of this as possible.

every little disbursement no matter how necessary for our students, while he pants to run up a debt of a million or so for a new site and new buildings.

February 26. . . . Oakey Hall's trial began today.

Died, at Geneva, Mrs. M. H. Grinnell. . . .

The legislative committee is diligently investigating the judicial career of Judges Barnard and Cardozo. Results, if any, are kept very close. E. H. Owen (!!!) and Fullerton attend on Cardozo's behalf, and Bidwell (!!!!) is retained "for consultation."[4] This is for the sake of his white cravat and his high character, for there can be nothing to consult about, and there has been no consultation. Cardozo wants to be able to talk about "my eminently respectable counsel, Mr. Bidwell and Mr. Owen." As to Fullerton, he and his client are well suited to each other. Bidwell took this retainer reluctantly, feeling bound by the strict rule that forbids a refusal, unless there be an actual prior retainer on the other side. But I think he was wrong, and that that rule applies to none but judicial proceedings. On investigations by legislative or congressional committees, and the like, counsel do not appear professionally and as sworn officers of a court, but merely as experts in badgering witnesses; and they have a perfect right to accept or decline that function. This committee is no tribunal. I regret that Bidwell should have befouled his fingers by touching—even formally—such filth as Cardozo. The immaculate Barnard is weak enough to publish a "protest" against Mr. S. J. Tilden's acting as a member of this committee, because Tilden has publicly denounced him and is not impartial. Impartiality is the first qualification of a judge, but it is not essential to a prosecutor, or to him who collects evidence for a prosecution.

February 28. . . . Went to a state dinner at William Schermerhorn's. We were honored by none of the ladies but Mrs. Fanny Bridgham. There were Samuel, her husband, R. M. Blatchford, Alexander Hamilton, Fred Sheldon, Rives, General McDowell, Robert Hone. . . .

After three days' hard work, eleven jurors have been bagged for Oakey Hall's trial. The defendant's pertinacious fight over every minor point does not look as if he felt the confidence in his case which he pro-

---

[4] Marshall Spring Bidwell (1799–1872), who had been born in Massachusetts but reared in Canada, had been compelled to leave Upper Canada after the rebellion under William Lyon Mackenzie. He became one of the leaders of the New York bar, and a man of prominence in society and philanthropic affairs. For his long career as a member of Strong's law firm, see the earlier volumes of this diary, and the Introduction. Bidwell's integrity and standing were indeed in striking contrast with the reputation of his client.

fesses with so much flourish. . . . The case made against Judge Cardozo before the legislative committee is said to be fearfully damaging.

Yesterday afternoon a long session of Philharmonic directors at Steinway and some effusion of pepper sauce. Vocalists give us no end of bother, and we seriously incline henceforth to do without them, if we can. Remmertz, the respectable barytone, was engaged for our next (fourth) concert by Herr Rietzel as a Committee of One with power at $100. The other directors rightly thought this sum exorbitant and wanted to rescind the bargain, but I advised them that they could not do it.

March 3, SUNDAY. . . . I hear that the genial climate of Nassau has reinvigorated the Rev. Vinton and that he will inflict himself upon Trinity Church again by Easter at latest. I am glad he is better, of course, but what a pity he could not have received a loud "call" to some tropical parish in Nassau, or Tobago, or Trinidad, or Tierra del Fuego, where one would have niggers for "underlings" and could bully them at his own sweet will!

March 5. At three to the first of Edmund Schermerhorn's series of musical "matinées" in the afternoon. About fifty present, among whom were Miss Nilsson, old Robert Ray, Count Costi, Osten-Sacken, and the usual set. Edmund has advanced from the quartettes and septettes of last year to an orchestra of twenty-five! mostly Philharmonics. Pech is the leader, of course. We had Bennett's Overture to *Die Naiaden,* which is pretty; Haydn's B-flat Symphony, No. 12, a dear old friend, and one of the loveliest and healthiest orchestral works extant—sweet, sound, and simple as an oread. Then Mrs. Imogen Brown sang certain truck from *Traviata,* and we closed with a "potpourri" by some Frenchman from the *Freischütz,* which was pungent and delicious. A most brilliant afternoon. Talked with nice, kind Miss Louisa Schuyler. . . .

College trustees met yesterday. A bare quorum and a most unsatisfactory meeting. Professor Egleston had asked for another assistant for the reason, among others, that his mineralogical and metallurgical collections are growing so fast that it takes the whole time of one man to determine, arrange, and label them. The Standing Committee made a most elaborate report adverse to the application and recommended, as a remedy for the professor's difficulty, that "foreign exchanges" be stopped and our advantageous arrangement with the Smithsonian terminated! In other words, "the child is so vigorous and grows so fast that we really cannot afford to find it in clothes, and we must stunt and dwarf it by putting it on half-allowance." And this while we are saving up money for a site and for buildings and have near $200,000 already hoarded. I wonder the committee did not recommend a public notice that no contributions to the cabinets or the library will be hereafter received. I moved that consideration of the report be postponed, which passed, and I suppose it will never be called up. This seemed to me rather better than a recorded vote endorsing the positions of the committee, and it was manifest that their recommendation would have been adopted.

What a Boeotian board it is! How easy it is to see why Harvard and Yale are securing millions of new endowment from year to year almost, while we lie still, except as we are aroused by the falling in of leases.

March 7, THURSDAY. Church Music Association rehearsal tonight with Ellie; satisfactory. Evening was devoted to Kyrie of Beethoven in D, and Gloria, down to the Quoniam. These movements were worked at very hard and in detail, many passages repeated four or five times, and single parts (bassi, and so on) drilled separately. Then we tried part of the refreshing *Lorelei*. These movements of the Mass begin to glimmer out into form and comeliness as one knows them better. . . .

Wall Street is more infested than ever with roving presbyters from the ends of the earth—clerical privateers—each setting forth the claims of his own local Zion, and each declining to stop his noise and move on for anything less than a ten dollar bill. Three of these "frères mendicants" came for me this morning, and my pocketbook feels "as if an elephant had stomped on to it." I object to these centralizing tendencies. The rural districts should have the privilege of doing a little for themselves, instead of making this metropolis their foraging ground. . . .

It is a majestic spectacle, the mayor of New York on trial for stealing or for helping certain pals of his to steal, and defended by a great array of counsel, who are pettifogging their case with technical quibbles against every offer of evidence. . . .

March 8. . . . Yesterday afternoon Oakey Hall and his battalion of counsel were dumbfounded by the appearance of A. J. Garvey, the plasterer, who was supposed to be in foreign parts. He was called by the prosecution, took the stand, and was sworn. Had the late estimable Mr. Watson risen from the dead and come forth as state's evidence, he would not have struck more terror to the souls of Hall and Company. But the estimable Stoughton soon rallied, found room for an objection to a question, and then talked against time till the hour of adjournment. There was great need of consultation as to the treatment of this unexpected and most uncomfortable symptom.

This morning there were more objections and "nice sharp quillets," maintained with vehemence. But Judge Daly seems to dispose of them fairly and well. From what the respectable Garvey has said on the stand today, he would seem ready to make a clean breast of it, to reveal the "Mysteries of New York," and "display Satan's Invisible World." Slippery Dick Connolly is reported to have slipped off, leaving his bail liable for half a million and absquatulated—"G.T.T."[5]

Grand subject for a historical picture on a large scale—the Awful Apparition of Garvey, Oakey Hall turning pale, John Burrill and Stoughton and dirty Tom Buckley and others making a ghastly effort to grin and look unconcerned, Daly watching the scene with the impartial serenity of a rather sagacious old owl, a courtroom full of briefless barristers in high excitement and delight.

March 11. . . . Hall's trial suspended today because of a juror's illness. His counsel have irreparably damaged whatever breechcloth of reputation he has left by their continual objections and obstinate resistance to the admission of evidence. They love darkness rather than light, because their client's deeds are evil. A single sunbeam blackens him as certainly as it does a sensitive plate. . . .

It would seem that the Erie Ring has come to grief. A little talk with General Dix about it this evening, but I do not understand the situation precisely. There has been a conspiracy and a *coup d'état*. The General is president, and the company is rid of the scoundrelly cabals that have ruled and swindled it so long. But Jay Gould (the dethroned president) and D. D. Field will doubtless fight hard to recover their opportunities of peculation, and they will be backed by Cardozo, Barnard, and Ingraham, judges they own.[6]

March 12. . . . Died, the incendiary, agitator, and humbug, Mazzini.

[5] "Gone to Texas"; but Connolly had gone first to Canada and then Europe. Andrew J. Garvey, a plasterer, had been one of the leading rascals of the Ring, and as executive officer so-called to Tweed, had prepared a great part of the fraudulent claims which Mayor A. Oakey Hall admitted. Garvey's sudden introduction into the trial was a *coup de théâtre* indeed. When the autumn storm burst he had fled to Europe, but his wife (intent on saving part of his money) brought him back and delivered him up to the prosecutor as state's evidence. He at once began telling how the frauds were planned and the money divided.

[6] Jay Gould was president of the Erie Railroad down to March 15, 1872. In a complex series of transactions, various American and British investors anxious to place the railroad in honest hands combined forces and brought about the election of a new directorate, which chose the eminent John A. Dix as president of the road. Daniel Sickles and S. L. M. Barlow had been prominent in the change. In midsummer of this year Peter H. Watson, former Assistant Secretary of War, succeeded Dix.

Jay Gould appears to have begun the day with a notification to all agents of the Erie Company that he insisted on his rights as president and should treat yesterday's meeting of directors as illegal and its action as a nullity. But the fourth edition of the evening's *Post* announces that he resigned at two-thirty this afternoon and that the Erie Ring has finally collapsed, after doing the country infinite disgrace and mischief throughout Christendom. Fisk's sudden death seems to have destroyed it, as Watson's led to the destruction of its ally, the Tammany Ring.

March 14, THURSDAY. . . . By Mrs. John Taylor Johnston's kind invitation went this afternoon to see her husband's beautiful gallery (8 Fifth Avenue), which he liberally throws open on Thursday afternoons.[7] How superb it is, how rich he must be, and how much wiser of him to spend his money this way than on race horses, four-in-hands, and great ostentatious parties! There are Church's "Niagara," Cole's "Voyage of Life" series, several fine things from the old Düsseldorf collection of twenty years ago, Gérome's "Death of Caesar," Müller's admirable "Conciergerie" (duplicate in the Luxembourg), and many other covetable pictures. Not one of them struck me as bad. J. T. Johnston is quite an enviable person. But I dare say he has his troubles and anxieties and sore spots like other people.

The Republicans recovered New Hampshire from the Democrats on Tuesday, which victory is rather a disappointment to the anti-Grant wing of the successful party and makes Grant's renomination nearly certain. His unfriends (the *Tribune* and *World* especially, a most unnatural alliance!) have so overdone their harping and nagging that every fair man must incline to side with him. These newspapers have certainly made me quite a partisan of Grant's.

March 15. . . . Philharmonic rehearsal at two-thirty. *Eroica*, Mendelssohn's *Fingal's Cave* overture, and Bargiel's *Prometheus*. In our box, Ellie, Johnny and Temple, Mrs. Noble, Mrs. Talboys, Rosalie, Dick, Jack Ehninger. I could write an essay on the *Eroica*. It is ranked by no orchestral work except Beethoven's immortal C Minor Symphony. One feels, after hearing it, as though he had fully dined on a score of most exquisite courses, with due allowance of champagne (in the third move-

---

[7] John Taylor Johnston (1820–1893), the first president of the Metropolitan Museum, had been trained for the bar but had turned to railroading. As head of the Lehigh & Susquehanna and the Central Railroad of New Jersey, he had accumulated a large fortune. His private collection of pictures was at this time probably the best in America. Financial reverses caused him to sell most of the collection in 1876, but he remained head of the Metropolitan until 1889.

ment), the raciest old Madeira (in the fourth), and so on. One is hardly able to imbibe any more music. . . .

March 17. . . . Jay Gould has resigned from direction of the Erie Railroad.

March 21. Trinity Church Standing Committee met this afternoon. Cisco has secured for us the Barbey house (built by William T. Blodgett) on Twenty-fifth Street, west of Trinity Chapel, as a rectory. The price with furniture is $75,000; cheap, but we must ask the vestry for an additional $15,000. . . .

Bidwell was subpoenaed to attend the Judiciary Committee now investigating Barnard. With characteristic timidity, he "really could not undertake to state the general opinion of the New York bar as to Mr. Barnard," and so was not examined after all.

Owners of the fatal *Westfield* are already nearly ruined by judgments for damages growing out of the massacre of July 30. Each of their ferryboats is now placed in custody of a gallant deputy-sheriff, who should be well paid for thus facing death in the discharge of his duty, for levying on an active volcano, as it were, and going into possession.

The valiant Sir Charles Dilke has now fired off the first anti-monarchical gun in the House of Commons. He moved for an enquiry and report as to the cost of the Crown. He lost 274 to 2.[8] But this ridiculous minority will not discourage the extreme Radicals. They have certain plausible half-truths on their side. It requires no thought or study to take in their arguments. Every coal-heaver or navvy or semi-brutal agricultural laborer can understand them. The Radical movement seems to me sure to grow stronger year by year.

March 25, MONDAY. . . . Saturday evening, Edmund, Pech, the Rev. Cooke, and General C. C. Dodge were here. Dodge desires to take hold of the Church Music Association; he will be useful. A rather anxious council, followed by a deliberative and aesthetic tea, over the asperities and the arduosities of the Beethoven Mass. Agreed to introduce four experimental "saxophones," or other wind instruments, at next rehearsal to guide and steady the aberrant voice parts of the chorus. . . .

Marrin, who has been looking after our Life and Trust Company bill at Albany (the fate of which bill is as yet uncertain because certain

[8] Sir Charles Dilke had been conducting an agitation against the monarchy, in the course of which he made a violent speech at Newcastle. When he tried to carry his crusade into the House of Commons, Gladstone sternly indicted him, and the House howled down both him and his single supporter. The really strong English movement was not republican but laborite.

honorable members oppose it in the hope of being bought off) tells me that this "reform" legislature is at least as corrupt as the worst of its predecessors, and I believe him. Judge Barnard will, it is said, be unanimously elected colonel of the militia regiment recently orphaned by the untimely death of James Fisk, Jr.!!! I fear our trouble lies deeper than the venality of legislature and judiciary. I fear the community has lost all moral sense and moral tone, and is fast becoming too rotten to live. We are seriously threatened by social disintegration and a general smash. I wish I could flee into the wilderness as Lot fled from Sodom and take refuge in some dull but decent New England village. No rich and crowded community can long survive universal suffrage.

March 27. . . . Erie stock has gone up like a balloon, and great fortunes have been made by people whom *I* think quite rich enough already.[9]

Maledictions on the memory of the doctor who steered safely through measles and whooping cough the maternal grandfather of the man who invented the income tax! I am engaged over those pestilent "returns."

The New York *Times* publishes transcripts of the bank accounts of Cardozo and Gratz Nathan, and they present coincidences that are curious and instructive. Connolly having evaporated and disappeared and his evidence being essential to the conviction of Brady and Haggerty, the voucher-stealers, their trial cannot be brought on, and Cardozo (perhaps not improperly) admits them to bail. So they will go unpunished. But it is comfortable to think that the scoundrels have been locked up for several months.

The Rev. Vinton is not to return before the fifteenth of April, *Deo gratias*. He will not afflict us on Easter Sunday.

April 1, EASTER MONDAY. The College trustees met this afternoon; only a quorum. The Boeotian report . . . about Egleston's cabinet was called up. Mr. Ruggles, the Bishop, and Dr. Haight had severally a little to say against it, and I spoke briefly on the same side. Ogden was prolix in its support. The result was that the more offensive recommendations were withdrawn, especially the stolid proposition that the professors be instructed to purchase henceforth such minerals only as are "necessary for purposes of instruction" and to purchase no mere "curiosities." Then the Committee on a New Site reported progress and asked for power to

[9] The spectacular rise in Erie stock, a result of the dramatic change in management, made more than a million for Jay Gould himself. Actually the financial condition of the road was so desperate that two million dollars had to be raised at once to save it from bankruptcy. General Charles C. Dodge, mentioned above, was one of the sons of the eminent merchant and philanthropist William E. Dodge.

purchase whenever they should find a site to suit them; a modest recommendation, which was objected to and laid over. . . .

March went out like a roaring and a rabid lion. A cold outrageous northeast storm poured and blustered all yesterday. Nevertheless, Trinity Church was jammed full, standing room and all, long before the service began. Morgan and Messiter had got together an orchestra from outside the Musical Protective Union (some of whose members were so disgusted with the attempt to extort money from the church last Thursday that they resigned and appeared in the organ loft yesterday). It was an excellent orchestra. . . .

April 3. . . . Died, Professor S. F. B. Morse, the Father of Telegrams, at eighty-one. Strange how little sensation was produced by the first telegram from Washington to Baltimore (or vice versa) on May 27, 1844. I have no recollection of the event. Probably book-buyers of 1480 remembered nothing about the appearance of the Mazarin Bible or the Mainz Psalter. Flags at half-mast all day and everywhere, partly for Morse and partly for General Anderson's funeral. The reliquiae of that good man and faithful soldier were removed from the Second Avenue cemetery for final interment at West Point. . . . The Republicans carried Connecticut by an increased majority.

April 8. . . . Poor Vinton returned from Nassau yesterday and had to be carried from the steamer to his house. The Rector saw him this morning and thinks badly of the case. The patient's liver is congested, and he is jaundiced. There is dropsical effusion in his legs and abdomen. He "has not slept for five weeks," and his stomach cannot retain food—all which looks rather grave. But the Rev. Mr. Vinton's stamina are iron— or brass. . . .

April 10. . . . Through the rain yesterday afternoon to a College library meeting. Long talk with Barnard and Dr. Haight. Every screw in the College is loose. Both undergraduates and faculty have slipped down far below concert pitch. I fear Barnard is a King Log.

This anti-Grant or "Liberal Republican" movement looks like fusion with the so-called "Democratic" party. Black Marble of the *World* and Goose Greeley of the *Tribune* are in sweet accord. Greeley means right, I think, but he is ruined by overweening vanity and a most plentiful lack of practical common sense. During the war, and during the period of suspense that preceded it, his paper was somehow a constant embarrassment and damage to the national cause, weakened it, and retarded its final triumph more than all the Copperhead presses of the North. Now he has allowed himself to be seduced by the old Copperheads of eight years ago and fondly hopes that they will make an honest President of him! It's a comfort to think that they will find him a very fractious and uneasy bedfellow. This bolt may prove to be a serious matter. Personal hatred of Grant seems at the root of it. I cannot understand how he has not merely alienated so many of his old supporters but converted them into bitter enemies. Mere coldness and hardness of manner, ungeniality, and taciturnity, do not justify or account for active and savage hostilities.

April 12. Meeting of the anti-Grant Republican Bolters at Cooper Institute tonight looks formidable in numbers but is doubtless strongly reinforced by Copperhead auxiliaries. General Dix and other prominent men are in the movement. Strange they take no warning by the plaudits and the caresses of the New York *World*. If they succeed, they will break up the Republican party and throw the government into the hands of the doughfaces, Copperheads, and traitors of 1860.

The first public rehearsal of the Church Music Association at Steinway yesterday afternoon, a rehearsal satisfactory beyond expectation, was devoted to Beethoven's Mass and lasted from three thirty-five until near six. That is an extraordinary work. Even those portions of it which I do not understand (and they are many) keep my attention riveted. Obscure passages in other works . . . drive my thoughts miles away. But this music, hard and unmelodic as it is, collars me with its first chord and holds me tight till its finale, as the Ancient Mariner held the Wedding Guest. It's very strange, almost uncanny. One carries away few definite memories of phrases in the Mass. I cannot now distinctly recall any part of it but the grand opening of the Kyrie, and the awful "Ante Omnia Saecula." One can find no words to define the peculiar something which distinguishes Beethoven's second from all other compositions, even from the Ninth Symphony, which belongs to the same period of Beethoven's development.

April 15, MONDAY. . . . Yesterday, Ogilby preached at Trinity—"with acceptance." The Rev. Vinton is reported rather better but extensively hydropic. In the evening, Dickon was here, Carroll, General Dix, one Hazard of Boston, [E. S.] Nadal of the *Nation*, and a dozen more. General Dix gives an appetizing account of the pickings and stealings wherein the Fields (*père et fils*) reveled while counsel for the Erie Ring, and pals of Jay Gould and the late Jem Fisk, Jr. Carroll wants the adjunct professorship of belles-lettres, and the like, in Columbia College, but he will not get it; for though he is just the man for the place, our fogies and noodles will hold his connection with the press a disqualification. . . .

1873

The Crédit Mobilier investigation was the sensation of the day in national affairs, as the trial of William M. Tweed was the focus of attention in New York. Never in American history had so great a scandal in the national government been disclosed as that which a House committee under Luke P. Poland of Vermont was laying before the public. The Crédit Mobilier was a corporation promoted by Oakes Ames, a Massachusetts manufacturer and Congressman, with T. C. Durant and other associates, for the purpose of keeping in the hands of a small group all the profits derived from the building of the Union Pacific Railroad. This road was heavily subsidized by the government, and the Crédit Mobilier carried out the construction work in such fashion that the federal endowment, or much of it, was drained into private pockets. In 1867–1868 Oakes Ames, fearful that Congress might interfere with the arrangement between the Union Pacific and Crédit Mobilier, distributed at least 160 shares of the highly valuable Crédit Mobilier stock among fellow-members of Congress at bargain rates—some Representatives paying for it out of the colossal dividends. In January and February, 1873, the newspaper headlines were full of revelations highly injurious to various public figures. Among the men whose reputations suffered worst were Schuyler Colfax of Indiana, James Brooks of New York, and Senator James W. Patterson of New Hampshire. Oakes Ames barely escaped expulsion, and was formally censured by House vote. . . .

The great boom which followed the Civil War had ended. Ever since the failure of the Atlantic Bank the previous April, the atmosphere had been uneasy. On September 8 the New York Warehouse & Security Company suspended; Kenyon, Cox & Co., in which Daniel Drew was a partner, failed on the 13th; on the 18th Jay Cooke & Co. went down, and on the 19th Fisk & Hatch. Men had looked upon Jay Cooke's house as a financial Gibraltar. It had done more than any other agency to market the nation's securities during the Civil War, and was currently building the Northern Pacific Railroad. The panic on the Stock Exchange became so severe that before noon on the 20th its governing committee closed it for ten days. Bankruptcies became the staple of news, factories and mills shut down, railway construction stopped, and business fell to a low ebb. On the heels of the panic came a great depression, destined to last for six years— years of unemployment, widespread poverty, grave labor disturbances, and radical political movements.

At first the people called the panic "a Wall Street affair" and poured denunciation on the heads of stockbrokers and railway speculators. It soon became evident, however, that its roots went deep into the national and international situation. Over-expansion in the building of iron mills and factories in various Western lands; too rapid extension of the railway systems of Europe, the United States, and Argentina; the dislocation of trade by the new Suez Canal; the heavy losses in the Chicago and Boston fires; and above all, the cumulative evil effects of the American Civil War, the Franco-Prussian War, and other conflicts, were among the principal causes of the crisis. In Europe and America alike the speculative boom had gone to excessive lengths. On both continents banks had lent money too wildly and brokerage houses had marketed securities recklessly. A battle at once developed in Washington between inflationists and conservatives, Grant after some hesitation taking his stand with the latter. And in the era of deflation and retrenchment which now opened, an appalling list of governmental and business scandals was exposed to the public sight. Strong could be thankful for his $6,000 salary.

September 26, FRIDAY. Business active at No. 187. We must borrow $25,000 at least to carry us over November 1, and it may be hard to do it in these times. If we cannot do it, I must try to prevail on our Rector and assistant ministers to receive their salaries on the "truck system"—namely, in hassocks, surplices, prayerbooks, and the like. It is fearful to think of the vestry office besieged, and me, the comptroller, rent limb from limb by a mob of hungry and furious presbyters, deacons, organists, sextons, Sunday School teachers, and female annuitants. *Spero meliora.*

Wall Street is very quiet. No mob there and none in Broad Street or Nassau Street. Closing the Stock Exchange acts as an anaesthetic and suspends our financial convulsions. But the community cannot be kept under chloroform indefinitely.

September 27. . . . All quiet along the Broad Street sidewalks. Affairs unchanged. . . . How to move the crops is becoming a grave question. Banks are suspending throughout the land. If Trinity Church suspend, I shall be gibbeted in church history as the Romulus Augustulus of comptrollers.

September 30. . . . Most admirable sermon (published) before the alumni of the Theological Seminary by Morgan Dix. Nobody treats of Catholicism as contrasted with Romanism and with Protestantism half so clearly, forcibly, and lovingly. But there are expressions in this sermon that can be sorely misrepresented by those who wish to misunderstand and misrepresent them.

October 2. . . . Strange to say, currency is at a premium of 2 or 3 per cent. The banks pay no large checks but certify them. So he who *must* have greenbacks to any considerable amount goes to a broker with his certified check and buys them as he would buy gold. Queer, anomalous, and all wrong.

Saw Shepherd Knapp of the Mechanics Bank, who says Trinity Church shall have all the "accommodation" necessary to keep her afloat till the November rents come in. He thinks everything is serene. But Skidmore this evening prophesies hard times all winter. If not too hard, they will do us good.

October 4. . . . An "evangelical" happy family is in session here. Specimens of diverse and hostile genera and species of Protestantism waiving their mutual hates for a season and meeting under a flag of truce for the sake of a grand international talking match. There seems a "revival" of religious activity just now, notably in France, where . . . pilgrimages (of a nineteenth century type) are fashionable once more, with parlor-car pilgrims, second-class pilgrims, smoking-car pilgrims, deadhead pilgrims, and the reporters. No doubt a reaction against Communism and archiepiscopocide; and so far good.

October 6. Renovation of St. Paul's interior all but finished. It is a great improvement. . . . Columbia College trustees met this afternoon at the old Schermerhorn Great Jones Street palazzo. How odd it is that our clerk should happen to be blind, our president deaf, and our treasurer dumb (Teutonice, *dumm*). The fact is symbolical of our corporate character. Our members, myself included, are somehow assimilated to these chief vital organs and made like them. . . . We are all fogies, dullards, and fainéants together, and I see no help for it. . . .

Petition received this afternoon from a half-dozen strong-minded young ladies, chaperoned by the strong-minded "Mrs. Lillie Devereux Blake," for admission to the College classes. To my surprise, the Rev. Haight thought the petition should be respectfully considered, so it was referred to some fossil committee or other. The mere suggestion of young ladies among our Freshmen and of "sweet girl-graduates" on the stage at commencement shocks all my conservative instincts, but I cannot shut my eyes to considerations in its favor, strange as the innovation would be. Morgan Dix, by the by, says that the school of the Sisters of St. Mary finds great favor with the "strong-minded" womankind, because the "Sisters" carry out the theory of "women's rights" in doing their noble work thoroughly and well without masculine aid. This Mrs. L. D. Blake has a couple of pretty little daughters under their care. Poor old Horace Greeley's Miss Gabrielle is another of their pupils and is said to be extremely clever and nice. These young ladies submit kindly to the influences of the church. Some of them have a special talent for caricature and caricature everybody —the "Sisters" included (not so very difficult).

October 8. Clear, cold morning, but rapidly moderating. The bloated corporation of Trinity Church got a note for $20,000 at thirty days "done" at Mechanics Bank, and was thankful for the favor. It is walking in dry places just now seeking rents and finding none, or but few, and payments on account. There will be hard times this winter. . . .

October 10. . . . Talked of the savings bank with John C. Green and finance in general with him and with Palmer of the Leather Manufacturers Bank. They think our troubles not quite over yet. Gold is down to eight and a fraction today, its lowest point for some twelve years.

Mr. Ruggles looked in on me in Fulton Street, and I exhibited to him the renovated interior of St. Paul's. He was in the best spirits, but I regret to say that he looked much thinner and older than when I last saw him in June just before he went to Delhi and fearfully changed from what he was a year ago. His brilliancy and geniality survive, in his brighter moments at least, but he is manifestly infirm and old. *Eheu*, what a loss that will be!

October 17. Professor Van Amringe called to talk of a proposed incorporation of Columbia College alumni, with a view to the possible future

concession to them of some share in the government of the College, and
wanted me to be chairman of a committee. . . . I told him I would heartily
give my best aid and counsel to any such movement, but that I could do so
far more efficiently if I were not on the committee or in any way identified
with the undertaking. Any change in the College government can hardly
fail to be an improvement. . . .

October 21. Sale of Philharmonic boxes at the Academy of Music this
afternoon. They brought panic prices, and many were left unsold. An
additional $300 for the Church Music Association came in this morning,
and "we may be happy yet." It would be a great pity to let so fine and well-
trained a chorus disperse. . . . His Lordship [the Bishop] of Zanzibar
attended [chorus rehearsal] and was interested. He discoursed with me
during the interval (a pause for refreshment and respiration), and I found
him most amiable.

October 27. . . . Wall Street continues in feverish, nervous malaise. Its
pulse keeps going up to 120 under hourly rumors of defalcation in this or
that great corporation, railroad, or others. Faith in financial agents is gone.
Every treasurer and cashier is "suspect," and no wonder after the recent
epidemic of fraud. The anticipated resumption of silver specie payments
seems indefinitely postponed. Factories and employers throughout the
country are discharging hands, working half time, or reducing wages. There
is a prospect of a hard, blue winter. We read in the papers of a "shrinkage
of values," but I see no sign of it in the bills I have to pay. Heaven help me!

October 29. . . . Visit from an infuriated lover of harmony, protesting
against gross fraud in the sale of Philharmonic seats at Heuser's music shop.
He proposed writing to all the newspapers and calling an indignation
meeting, in which purposes I subtly encouraged him under the semblance
of soothing his angry passions. . . . The more fuss about this swindle the
better. Schirmer and Heuser both have acted most dishonestly and scandal-
ously and in direct violation of their instructions. . . .

Guns are firing an accompaniment to some grand ratification meeting
somewhere. But the political campaign is sleepy and apathetic, and the city
registration is 25,000 short. This points to a "Democratic" victory, and
the present financial distress, moreover, will tell against Administration
candidates. Prospects for the coming winter look darker and darker.

October 30. . . . The great manufacturing house of the Rhode Island
Spragues went down today, throwing an army of operatives out of employ-

ment. This will have consequences.[1] Taintor is convicted. His defense—
namely, that his president and directors were *particeps criminis*—was
promptly ruled out. Stokes's third trial results in a verdict of manslaughter
and a sentence of four years at Sing Sing.

"General" Wade Hampton makes a great speech at Richmond and says
the South is now where Prussia was after Jena, and that as Prussia speedily
broke her chains and smote her tyrants so will Secessia be avenged of her
enemies, both nigger and Yankee, "the blacks and their blacker allies."
It seems impossible to whip the brag out of these Gascons.

October 31. First Philharmonic rehearsal at two-thirty; a tolerable
house. . . . Beethoven's Fourth Symphony, Max Bruch's Introduction to
Lorelei, and Liszt's "Preludes."

November 3. Columbia College trustees met this afternoon. Not much
done. Reconsidered the reference to a committee of the application of certain young ladies to be admitted as students and unanimously agreed to
decline the honor. Barnard's proposition to enlarge the School of Mines
building (150 students now!!) was referred to the Committee on the Site,
and the question of sending a representative to see that the coming transit
of Venus is in all respects regular and decorous was similarly disposed of.
Admiral Sands and other Washington magnates wish us to do this, and it
will be a scandal to leave it undone. But what can be expected from our
board? . . .

Wall Street feels better. The Spragues (of Rhode Island) show a good
list of assets, though it does include certain "cats and dogs," and Claflin's
house is plucky still. It's notable that the five-penny and six-penny fares
on our street railroads have fallen off a third. There is an example of
retrenchment for me to follow. . . .

November 4, TUESDAY. As it is a "legal holiday," my office did not
open. I voted. Looked in at the great Barnum show. Infinite claptrap, but
many of the animals are fine specimens, and the menagerie is worth
visiting. Barnum's shewbills, by the by, present a life-sized portrait of him
as Phoenix T. Barnum, with a pair of wings appended to his shoulders. . . .

November 5. As I expected, there are anti-Administration gains and
victories, East and West. The New York *World* is jubilant. As Dr.

[1] Senator William Sprague, who had married Salmon P. Chase's beautiful daughter
Kate, was the most prominent figure in the textile manufacturing business founded by
his grandfather of the same name. The failure of the A. & W. Sprague Manufacturing
Co. involved about $20,000,000, and reduced the Sprague fortune to a mere remnant.

Johnson would have said, "This merriment of Democrats is mighty offensive." But the absolute Democratic gain is small, if there be any. Republicans have stayed at home disgusted, reasonably or not, and left the country to take care of itself.

Had a talk with the Rev. Haight about vacancies on the College board created by the death of good old Dr. Torrey and the Rev. Spring, especially the Rev. Spring. I vote for no Presbyterian preacher-man as trustee. . . .

November 7. Gold is 106¼. We seem not far from specie payments. . . .

Times grow harder and harder. I think our Church Music Association concerts must be given up.

The Republican defeat is a Flodden or Bull Run. But it may scare that party into better behavior and so prove a blessing in disguise.

Died, old General Delafield, DeRham *père*, the fair Miss Laura Keene, Gaylord Clark, and at Boston, C. A. Lombard.[2] DeRham, they say, left his native Switzerland as plain Mr. Rham, but after arriving in New York, adopted a prefix as being euphonious and genteel. He always looked, though, like an old marquis of the Ancient Regime. Gaylord Clark was for many years editor of the old *Knickerbocker* magazine and was the most refined and genial of our American humorists, though not so strong in the grotesque as John Phoenix, Artemus Ward, and Orpheus C. Kerr.

November 10. . . . Vestry meeting tonight. Read comptroller's annual report. Morgan Dix nominated to the vacancy at St. Paul's the Rev. Mr. Mulchahey of Ohio, a most bog-trotting, potato-munching, whiskey-drinking, "dudeen-shoughing," shillelah-brandishing name. But the gentleman is highly spoken of. Publication of the Rector's proposed annual "Manual of Trinity Parish" was informally approved. All my motions and recommendations were adopted good-naturedly and *nem. con.* My "bosses" of the vestry certainly treat me very kindly indeed.

This afternoon, the Rev. Cooke, Horsley, Gerard, Stephens, and I took counsel together at my office in re The Church Music Association. Edmund Schermerhorn couldn't come but sent me a kind note full of timidities and nervousness. The question we had to consider was whether

[2] Richard Delafield (1798–1873) had twice been superintendent at West Point and from April, 1864, to his retirement in August, 1866, chief of the Army Engineer Corps; Laura Keene (c. 1826–1873), the beautiful English-born actress, had great comic talent, and will long be remembered as chief actress in *Our American Cousin* the night Lincoln was murdered.

the Church Music Association should be dropped and left to perish and its chorus disbanded, or should be kept alive by another "season" of concerts. When we came together, the Church Music Association was in imminent peril of dissolution. I was disinclined to undertake the pecuniary risk of running it, and Ben Stephens was of the same mind. But it appeared that our subscriptions suffice to carry us through the season with strict economy. Probably the "shrinkage of values" will enable us to secure our soli and others, possibly even our orchestra, at reduced prices. There is a chance that some of our subscribers may repudiate. If so, we shall know it when the first instalment is called in, and we must then issue a circular to our honest and solvent subscribers, tell them why we can give but one concert or two (as the case may be), report to them the names of the defaulters, and return to them whatever little dividend may be left of their respective subscriptions. . . . I hope I shall not be saddled with another deficit.

November 13. . . . Great wrath over the capture of the *Virginius* and the summary execution of her filibustering crew by Cuban volunteers. "A speck of war."[3] Strange we should be nearly ready to make war on Spain for the summary execution of people who were proceeding to Cuba with homicidal intent and who went forth taking their lives in their hands. For only last Tuesday a pretty girl of seventeen, a couple of children, and a half-dozen poor laboring men, all pursuing their lawful avocations on the public highway, were massacred by the engineer of a steam hoisting machine at Harlem without notice, without provocation, and without even the formality of a drumhead court-martial. And nobody seems indignant or excited over this butchery.

November 15. Philharmonic concert this evening. . . . The house was very full. It would be indiscreet to enquire what was the percentage of deadheads. I gave away some half dozen boxes, thereby, I think, gratifying sundry nice people. Concert was delightful. . . .

Naval preparations are active. Gold rises from 107 to 110. If war

[3] American indignation over the *Virginius* affair was not, as Strong at first supposed, exaggerated. The filibustering vessel was captured by a Spanish gunboat, taken into Santiago harbor, and held there. Her crew of Americans and Britons were landed, and without proper trial fifty-three of them were shot. It was doubtful whether the Spaniards had any right to capture a vessel flying the American flag when on the high seas. Certainly they had no right to shoot the captured Americans as if they had been pirates; they were at worst prisoners of war. The British warship *Niobe* hastily steamed into Santiago harbor and forbade further executions. Only Secretary Fish's astute management of the crisis prevented war.

come, we shall probably gobble up Cuba at last, and what should we do with it? We certainly do not want these bloodthirsty little blackmuzzled Cubans as fellow citizens. As well annex and try to adopt and assimilate a large nest of lively black and yellow hornets. . . .

Mr. Ruggles was at the concert this evening. I talked with him during the entr'acte. I fear infirmity is gaining on him. He is five years older than he was six months ago.

November 17. Work at the Navy Yard is lively. A Spanish war is not improbable. The slogan of "Free Cuba" would rally many waverers around the Administration flag, where they are wanted in time for the next election. Waiving the technical questions raised by the capture of the *Virginius* under American colors on the high seas, there have been wars on slighter provocation than ours. Alva's style of work is so obsolete as to have become offensive, and one doesn't want a slaughterhouse set up next door and under his very nose. Poland had to be abated as a nuisance, and Cuba may require the same treatment.

November 19. Everyone expected Boss Tweed's jury to disagree—they were out so long—but they brought that scoundrel in guilty this morning; thank Heaven. Sentence is postponed till Friday. Pity he can't be hanged. But he'll get a new trial, I suppose, and probably get off altogether, the rank, old felonious dog-fox!

War-jaw is still loud in all the newspapers.

November 21. Most belligerent despatch from Madrid. Our blameless representative there (the delectable Dan Sickles) has been threatened by a mob of truculent Jack Spaniards. Between the Carlists and the *Intransigentes* and the ignorant, arrogant, savage plebs of Spain, the Republican chiefs are in a tight place. Having two civil wars on their hands already, they want nothing less than a foreign war besides. But any concession to us may raise a storm that would blow their heads off. The greatest activity continues at our Navy Yards, and a rather formidable fleet will soon be ready for business. God avert war! I have seen quite enough of war times to last me my life.

November 22. Boss Tweed the *Meister-Dieb* sentenced to twelve years and a moderate fine. Good as far as it goes.[4]

[4] This was Tweed's second criminal trial. The sentence was to twelve years in prison and a fine of $12,750; but the court of appeals shortly reduced the sentence to a year and a fine of $250! Thus Tweed was enabled to leave Blackwell's Island penitentiary in January, 1875. But he had other gauntlets to run, and finally died in the Ludlow Street jail (1878).

1874

*T*he bleak early months of 1874 were marked by demonstrations of the
unemployed in many cities, by a sharp struggle in Washington between
inflationists and anti-inflationists, and by largely futile efforts on the part of
businessmen to get the wheels of industry turning faster. Strong recorded in his
diary for January 8 that Union Square had been filled with a mob of laborers
demanding that the city find them work. "Why should not our horde of briefless
and poverty-stricken lawyers require the public to get up suits for their benefit
and relief?" he asked—for many fellow-attorneys were suffering severely. The
efforts of the inflationists to increase the stock of paper money at first met some
success, but when they pushed their movement too far, trying by a Finance Bill
to raise the amount of greenbacks to $400,000,000, with a corresponding
increase in National Bank bills, President Grant on April 29 met them with a
veto. For this act all "sound money" men enthusiastically praised him. Industrial
conditions continued bad, however, with general lack of confidence, a weak
market for goods, and a high bankruptcy rate. In the Middle West the Granger
movement for drastic state regulation of railroads succeeded in passing some
highly controversial laws; that of Wisconsin, signed in March, provoked much
protest in the East.

Strong was now admitting that Grant was a very poor President. His
efforts to get various unfit men into the Chief Justiceship, rendered vacant by the
death of Salmon P. Chase, disgusted the diarist. He named and then withdrew
Attorney-General George H. Williams, who was not only incompetent for the
post, but open to charges which affected his financial integrity. Strong dealt

401

with this misstep in emphatic language. It was "a nomination that should never have been made," he wrote; "Williams is a tenth-rate man." Then Grant startled the country by nominating for the Chief Justiceship none other than Caleb Cushing, a learned but crafty, erratic, and time-serving politician and jurist widely hated and generally distrusted. When Cushing's enemies showed that he had written in 1861 to "my dear friend" Jefferson Davis, recommending another friend to the Confederate President, this nomination was crushed. Grant then turned to Morrison R. Waite of Ohio, who as E. L. Godkin put it, was in the front rank of second-rate lawyers. The "moiety scandal" in the Treasury Department was laid bare early this year, showing that Ben Butler had used Secretary of the Treasury Richardson (a henchman of Butler's Massachusetts machine) to make large sums out of the government.

January 15, THURSDAY. . . . Died yesterday in Washington, Charley Bristed! His last letter to me not a fortnight ago, I think, spoke of his being unwell. . . . In spite of certain foibles and oddities, "Carl Benson" is a great loss. We have few such scholars, and nobody more honest of purpose and resolute in expression. Hatred of snobbery, and especially of Southern swagger and presumption, was one of his strong points. He was partial to me, and I infer from things I have heard of his saying that he strangely overestimated me, though he was somewhat disposed to criticize people sharply.[1]

January 16. . . . "O Cupid, king of gods and men," what have I heard today!!! First, from Gouverneur Ogden at lunch; second from Duncan, who had it as a matter of incontrovertible verity from Cisco; and third from Miss Mary Bostwick (who called to ask after poor Ellie) and had it from Mr. Tom Ogden—Morgan Dix is engaged to Miss Soutter, Mrs. Ned Bell's younger sister.[2]

January 17, SATURDAY. . . . To Philharmonic concert; only Temple, Johnny, and Louis, and a couple of Temple's and Johnny's musical pals in our box. There was a full house. The *Melusine* Overture was played, and a long piano concerto by Hanselt, performed by Mills, which was melodic but protracted. Schubert's "Fantaisie," orchestrated, is very

[1] Charles Astor Bristed, frequently mentioned heretofore, was not yet fifty-four. He had published several books in recent years, including *The Interference Theory of Government* (1867) and *On Some Exaggerations in Comparative Philology* (1873). A man of wealth and leisure, he had of late spent most of his time in Washington.

[2] Morgan Dix was to marry Emily W. Soutter, daughter of James T. Soutter, on June 3 of this year.

melodic and brilliant but excessively protracted and full of damnable iteration. Phrases so lovely are outraged and insulted by being rubbed into one over and over again. Then there was some Chopin played by Mills. Chopin is wholly beyond me. During the second part of the program, the Schumann symphony was played. Schumann's diction is masterly; pity he has nothing new to say.

Morgan Dix's engagement is the town talk. The fact rests not on Ned Bell's authority alone, but on that of the lady's brother; so I suppose it must be admitted. Opinions differ about it (if that be of any consequence). There are some who say "how very injudicious; disparity of age (twenty-three and forty-five). It will destroy his usefulness," and the like. Others dwell on his lonely life and his genial instincts, his fondness for young people and children, and so on. I prefer to side with the latter. The disparity of age is nothing. As to the young lady, I know that her sister, Mrs. Bell, is charming and kindly, with the special attractiveness that belongs to the best Southern women, or women of Southern descent. . . .

January 20. . . . Chang and Eng, the Siamese twins, died last week at their home in North Carolina, surrounded by their wives and children. One died of paralysis, it would seem, and the other, though in good health, survived but a couple of hours. Their physician, if they had any, did not venture on amputation, cutting the Mezentian bond. . . .

One Waite of Ohio nominated for chief justice, a respectable nobody. What has got into Grant?

January 22. . . . Standing Committee tonight. After our calendar was cleared off, Ogden suggested that I withdraw for a little, and when I returned, I was informed that the committee had agreed to recommend an increase of the comptroller's salary from $6,000 to $8,000 (very acceptable, Heaven knows!). I returned thanks and the committee "made compliment," and I said with great sincerity that I hoped the increase might take effect from a future day—say May 1—and not immediately. I had two reasons for this: first, we are hard up and in debt and shall be so till we get our May rents; and second, it's my business to oppose all increase of expenditure, and so I have been doing. Tonight, several applications were laid over indefinitely, on my suggestion, because we are short of funds. I thought that common fairness required me to apply the same principle in my own case, and also that I should be able to fight propositions for extravagant and improvident outlay more effectively hereafter if it were known to the vestry that I had demurred to a grant in my favor. But Cisco, Skidmore, Arnold, and others "shut me up," said I had nothing to do with it, and insisted on their recommendation that the increase take effect from the first of January. I have to thank Gouverneur Ogden for this. He undertook the measure without the slightest suggestion from me, and has been extremely kind and unselfish about it.

Waite is confirmed as chief justice. "Now God be with him," saith Uncle Sam; "since better mote not be. But I think we have in this our realm five hundred good as he." Waite may make his mark yet, however. . . .

January 23. . . . Died at London, Mme. Parepa Rosa, a magnificent singer and greatest in the best music—Handel, Haydn, and Mozart.

January 24. Orders were sent out from police headquarters last night to all the station houses that the police keep an eye on the churches. The German and French Communists or "free-thinkers" (calling themselves unemployed workmen) were said to have designs on them. We were called upon this morning at No. 187 by policemen enquiring about St. Paul's and Trinity.

January 26, MONDAY. . . . Trinity Church has become, not exactly a den of thieves, but a "fence" or receptacle of stolen goods. A certain young man . . . has long been a devout and punctual worshipper there, and specially edifying in his outward demonstrations of reverence. . . . Saturday, he asked Augustus Meurer, the sexton, to lock up a little satchel or traveling bag for him till he should call for it. Yesterday, a detective intervened and requested Augustus to submit the same to his inspection. It was found to contain about $1,000 worth of jewelry, burglariously abstracted from the safe of the youthful saint's former employer, and the saint was incarcerated. . . .

February 6. A Philharmonic rehearsal tonight. In the Strong box were Temple and Louis, Rosalie, Miss Sarah Lazarus, and Dick. He returned this morning from Cleveland, where he "stood up with" Col. John Hay, who has married a Miss Stone.[3]

February 7. . . . Edwin Booth has gone into bankruptcy (!!!), whither I must expect to follow him. But I hear vague and second-hand rumors concerning "Minnesota." It will certainly begin paying up "next summer," which is, being interpreted, at the Greek Kalends. Such is Mr. Ruggles's report.

[3] Hay married Clara Stone, daughter of Amasa Stone, railway builder and for a time managing head of the Lake Shore & Michigan Southern.

February 9. Vestry meeting tonight was brief. I retired and was promoted from six (thousand) to eight (thousand), *nem. con.* I am very much obliged. Cisco, by the by, though a very good friend of mine, grows more and more arrogant and censorious, and finds fault with everything and everybody. . . .

Died, Saturday evening, old James W. Gerard. He had been failing for at least a year. In spite of much flippancy and a profusion of bad jokes, he used to be a most dangerous antagonist, especially before a jury. As a low comedian, he would have rivaled the late Mr. Burton, but he was a learned lawyer and a potent advocate, nevertheless. He loved music with all his heart and was among its chief patrons and promoters here thirty years ago. But his zeal was not always according to knowledge—witness his frequent strident ejaculations: "Ah, bravo, bravo, very fine, very fine indeed; brav-iss-i-mo! Bra-a-ah! Extremely staccato!" Witness also his fatal liberality to organ-grinders, so often productive of torture to other residents on Gramercy Park. He was thoroughly public-spirited. Even before he left the bar (in 1868), he was active and useful in public school affairs and in other civic matters, and to him, I believe, we are indebted for valuable improvements in the police department.[4] In all this work he sought neither place nor profit, nor even notoriety or distinction, but the general good alone. Strange that so honest and sagacious a man should have gone so far astray during the war. But he is entitled to be forgiven that one grave error.

February 11. . . . Died yesterday at Rome, Mrs. Arabella Mott, wife of Dr. Aleck B. Mott, much to be regretted. That pestilent Roman fever, I suppose. The lady was always nice to me, though she had a sharp tongue. . . .

Last night's Church Music Association concert went off well. The house was full and good-natured. It seemed to like parts of the Schumann Mass. I am glad to have heard the last of that leaden work. Weber's Jubel Overture and Gade's "Erl-König's Tochter" were delightful, of course.

February 13. Philharmonic rehearsal at two-thirty this afternoon. In my box were Rosalie, Mrs. Newman (who was Miss Ellen Rogers), Mrs. DeNeufville, Mrs. Harry Parker, Charles Carroll, and Temple.

---

[4] James W. Gerard, eighty years old at the time of his death, had been not only one of the best lawyers of the city, but an unwearied worker to aid juvenile delinquents and paupers, and (as school trustee and school inspector) a vigorous advocate of better education.

Wieniawski did a brilliant and beautiful Mendelssohn concerto, and a dry, hard, scrapy something by Bach. Then a director's meeting. The projected performance of Beethoven's Ninth Symphony with the Church Music Association chorus seems likely to fall through. The two hundred members of that chorus want two reserved seats each. We have not a quarter of that number to give them. Were this difficulty got over, two of the directors (at least) are unwilling to give the Ninth Symphony at all. It will involve expenses, and they think, moreover, that the Church Music Association chorus cannot do it. Possibly they are right. . . .

February 17. Spent last evening at the rectory on Twenty-fifth Street at a "reception" for the Rev. Mulchahey (a nice person, it would seem). Present were the Bishop, a dozen of the vestry, and a half-dozen of the clergy of the parish. O how slow it was!

Died, at two-thirty in the afternoon on Sunday, Dunscomb, aged eighty-six. He was taken ill on Friday and retained consciousness, though without speech, till Sunday morning. He had belonged to Trinity Church vestry as vestryman, warden, clerk, and comptroller for forty-four years but had been unable to attend a meeting since December, 1872. He was, I think, the most impenetrably dense, wooden, and stolid old gentleman I ever knew, but he was painstaking and thoroughly honest and served Trinity Church faithfully and did his duty doggedly, according to the very best of his perception and judgment. More can be said of no man. I wish one-tenth as much could be said of me. As I am now sole warden, the capacity of the vestry to meet and transact business depends on my life; so I have called a meeting for Thursday to fill the vacancy. I tell the Rector that my precious life should be watched and protected night and day till Thursday by a powerful bodyguard of sextons and lay visitors. After Thursday, I shall relapse into my original insignificance.

Bristed leaves his "adopted" daughter, Miss Cecile, the income of $41,000. That rather odd and self-willed young lady has left Mrs. C. A. Bristed and gone to Mr. and Mrs. Frank Weeks. Poor Johnny, the eldest son, is still insane.

Novel epidemic running through Western towns and spreading eastward. It suggests the "Childrens' Crusade" a little and also the viragoes of Paris marching on Versailles eighty odd years ago. Its symptoms are bands or mobs of pious women who run to and fro, hold prayer meetings, and sing psalms in grog shops or before the doors thereof, warning off thirsty customers and "wrestling with" the proprietor. These evangelical monads sometimes so work on the dispenser of drinks that he staves his lager-bier barrels and retires or even catches the infection, joins the train of anti-Bacchantes, and howls with the loudest of them. While these orgies are in progress, the meetinghouse bells are tolled, business is suspended, and folks come into town from all the countryside to witness the "function," or pilgrimage, as it were. The phenomenon is working on a large scale, but I think its effects will be transient. We must not speak *too* disrespectfully, however, of any movement however grotesque and ungraceful that is directed against the terrible mischief of drunkenness.

February 18. Dunscomb's funeral was at Trinity Church at three-thirty this afternoon. The attendance was very much larger than I expected. I was pallbearer with Curtiss, Sackett, Cisco, and others. Dix officiated with six other of our clergy. Interment was in the vault under the floor of the north robing room. The service was choral. . . .

The Philharmonic directors met here and smoked at five-thirty this afternoon. We agreed to abandon the Ninth Symphony for this year. There is not time for thorough choral rehearsals. Moreover, its announcement at the beginning of next season might increase our subscriptions, whereas its production at the end of this would profit us nothing.

February 20. . . . Special vestry meeting yesterday afternoon. Skidmore was unanimously promoted to be warden. We provided that plans and estimates be obtained for the new additional Trinity Church schoolhouse on 56 New Church Street and that action be taken against Erben for his failure to complete the organ for St. John's, now two months past due. Thereafter a Standing Committee meeting. There was the question whether we shall oppose or agree to opening of Desbrosses Street. So am I "King of the Cats" (*vide* Grimm's *Märchen*), that is, first on the vestry list. Of the twenty-three gentlemen who constituted the vestry in November, 1847, only two survive—William Moore (resigned) and Bleecker (extruded).

February 24. . . . The skeleton of a great dome is slowly developing above the north front of the new post office. Its arching iron supports, with their elaborate braces, look like the remains of some huge fossil radiate.

February 26. . . . Referee's office, one P.M., for Pech's case. The hour came but not the man, but at half-past there appeared unto us a scrub of a little Jew office boy, who said that plaintiff's counsel were "drying a gace in the sessions" and couldn't come. So we dispersed. . . . Standing Committee meeting tonight; chief business—the proposed opening of Desbrosses Street, which we agree to oppose—wisely, I think.

Through the snow yesterday to a Leake and Watts meeting at the garrulous Frederic De Peyster's. As usual, no quorum. Only the Dutch De Witt and the Presbyterian Paxton attended, besides Knox the treasurer, who don't count. For practical purposes, that board is nearly null. The mayor and recorder (ex officio trustees) never attend. It's hardly possible they should, and the rest are very uncertain. The orphan house runs of itself somehow, but I fear it may suddenly come to grief sooner or later for want of due supervision and disgrace us all.

March 2. . . . College trustees met at two this afternoon at Great Jones Street. The large Committee on the Site reported progress and certain resolutions concerning alterations and enlargements of the existing college buildings, the accommodations for the School of Mines, and the like. The first of these resolutions was in substance that the growth of the School be stopped should the School outgrow its proposed enlarged accommodations and that we would do no more for it in any event. On this we had a lively debate. Ogden and Barnard talked at great length pro and con. The Rev. Mr. Haight left the chair, put old Robert Ray into it, and let off one or two vehement little anti-science speeches that were founded on half truths and did his judgment little credit. I thought the resolution sure to pass, but I was resolved to bear my testimony against it; so when everyone else had got through, I spoke for three minutes about my willingness to limit the number of School of Mines students by raising the standard of qualifications for admission and about my unwillingness to be a party to putting on our minutes a resolution deliberately and avowedly dwarfing either the undergraduate corps, the Law School, or the School of Mines. I said I thought such a resolution without precedent in the history of any American college, and I might have said much more about it. That our board listened to the proposition for five minutes is quite enough to account for the fact that Columbia College lies still while Yale and Harvard and Amherst grow. The resolution was lost, and some of them said its loss was due to my little speech. I hope they were right.

The *World* and *Times* call attention to the disgrace brought on this city and on the state by the public funeral honors lavished on that corner grocery politician and swindler of savings banks, Mr. "Hank Smith," late police commissioner, and among the nastiest of the larvae that have lived by burrowing in the great dunghill of our civic corruption and have fattened thereon. There is a plentiful lack of moral sense in this community.

March 4. . . . Yesterday, the Leake and Watts board took a little doze at the Rev. De Witt's in Ninth Street. First step toward the inevitable removal of the orphan house to Westchester County or Long Island. A committee was appointed to enquire and report anent the expediency of such removal. In the afternoon (very hot) with Morgan Dix, Braem, and Ostrander, at 50 Varick Street, conferring with "Mother Harriet" and "Sister Eleanor" about the infirmary. (I can't yet make these new titles fit my tongue quite readily, and I say "Madam" when I should say "Mother.") These seem nice, kindly, efficient women, wholly free from Pharisaism and ostentation of sanctity and quite capable of enjoying a small joke.

March 6. . . . Her Majesty's Ashantee expedition seems in a doubtful sort of way. Prayers put up for it in all London churches. I guess it will come out all right.[5] But we have not forgotten England's attitude toward us ten years ago in our time of trouble. We should shed few tears over the failure of this foolish foray into the malarious swampy fastnesses of a horde of howling, gibbering savages with whom England and English soldiers have no legitimate business at all. We should be honestly and heartily sorry were England visited by famine or pestilence or harried by a Prussian invasion. But that she should be mortified and humiliated just a little would not afflict us a bit.

March 8, SUNDAY. . . . Temple and a select party of his friends were doing wind quartettes all the afternoon. That boy's musical talent is remarkable. Here has he been instrumenting for full orchestra the accompaniment to Schubert's *Erl-King* ballad!!! I don't doubt that his score bristles with blunders, but as Dr. Johnson says somewhere, "You are not surprised that a dog dances badly; you wonder that he dances at all." If I had but a little more money for Temple and his brothers, how happy I should be with them. They are three noble fellows.

March 9. . . . Died, at Buffalo, old Millard Fillmore. There was "mair tint" at Bull Run.

March 11. . . . New Hampshire elections and opposition gains. Though this result is complicated with local issues, Grant's administration is losing ground, I fear. We are dissatisfied with many things, with corruption, extravagance, and Ben Butlerism at Washington, with the currency, the tariff, and the disgraceful customhouse spy system. Staunch Republicans

[5] The Ashanti tribesmen had begun hostilities against the British early in 1873; a small force under Sir Garnet Wolseley, after some severe fighting, occupied their capital early in 1874, and compelled them to sue for peace.

would go over to the opposition in battalions if the opposition bore another name, but they cannot shake hands and rub noses with "Democrats" of 1860–65.

Died, Charles Sumner, an able, accomplished, and unwise man. The bludgeon of that caitiff and ruffian "Bully Brooks" made him a first-class confessor in the anti-slavery cause and has now promoted him to the dignities of martyrdom, for they say that memorable brutal assault was the remote cause of his death. But he never had much hold on the people. He was too self-conscious and, perhaps, too cultivated and scholarly for the American people. Ever since he deserted his party in 1872 he has been a lone man, out of humor with everyone, himself included. . . .

March 12. Flags at City Hall and everywhere else at half-mast in honor of Sumner. Who could have predicted this fifteen years ago? To do him justice, he shewed immense pluck in his fight for a principle when he seemed in a hopeless minority, and in enduring obloquy and hatred for its sake from all the South and half the North. . . .

March 16. . . . "Temperance" crusade, so-called, continues active and abundant in spasm. Query: if there be not in this, as in other developments and vagaries of ultra Protestantism, something inherited from the Manichaeans and Paulicians. . . . Manichaeans, sixteenth century Puritans, and modern Evangelicals clearly agree in regarding all enjoyments derived from matter as of the nature of evil, and the old Manichaeans justified their view by attributing the creation of matter to Ahriman. . . .

March 17. . . . The New York *Herald* reports "Bald Mountain" in western North Carolina setting up as a volcano. Probably a canard or sell.

March 18. . . . Rumors continue of subterraneous singults and borborygmi in North Carolina. That region of tar and turpentine would be much endangered by a volcanic outbreak. The rebel eruption, checked by external applications of cold steel, must have struck in. Or perhaps the buried fire-eaters are uneasy in their graves and seek to convert their conquered pine woods and plantations into *campi phlegraei.* . . .

March 19. Wet morning; evening oppressively warm. Wrote Governor Dix about certain crude, mischievous legislation wherewith we are threatened by Albany. Nash, Palmer, and I took counsel together and agreed on the outline of our report upon Wiswall—in substance, that his wife's allegations are not proven, but that his indiscretions in financial and other matters have impaired his usefulness. The lady is now suing for divorce by little Jerolomon, her attorney.

June 25. . . . The pragmatical Pharisees of prohibitionism and sabba-tarianism have set up Myron H. Clark (!) against Governor Dix (who will doubtless be the Republican candidate), because Dix has room in his brains for more than one idea at a time and does not believe the enforce-ment of total abstinence to be the sole end and aim of civil government. . . .

June 30. Less scorching than yesterday, when Fahrenheit reached three figures, and I nearly exuded into nonentity. George Carleton the publisher dined here. We perspired terribly. He is a clever man and an observant traveler. . . .

July 15. The other half of the inflammable city of Chicago is burned up. Another Indian War is setting in. The "Black Hills" are to be invaded, and the Sioux braves are mustering in great force to defend that sacred soil as yet unprofaned by palefaces. . . .

July 17. No letter from Ellie, who doubtless spent yesterday with the 24,999 other "fash'nables" (the newspapers report them 25,000) assisting at the Saratogian Collegiate Boat Race which didn't come off because of high wind and rough water. . . .

July 19, SUNDAY. The great "intercollegiate" race, postponed for two successive days, was run yesterday morning, and Columbia came in first by several lengths, undisputed victor. I hoped for nothing better than a second or third place. Grand row and jubilation at Saratoga, and flags hoisted all over the city—City Hall included—as soon as the tidings came. Even the Brokers' board hurrahed and carried on like mad. The trustees have never given the sleepy College such an advertisement as it has received from these half-dozen undergraduates and "Miners." Their suc-cess is an interesting physiological fact, moreover. It shews that the kid-gloved boys of Fifth Avenue can develop better muscles than the rustics of Vermont and Maine. Perhaps diet has something to do with it. The former live on beef and mutton; the latter eat a good deal of salted meat, salt fish, things fried, corn bread, hot cakes, and heavy pies, like their fathers before them. . . .

July 21. No letter from Ellie today. I fear the dinner she was to have given on Sunday to the College victors may have proved too much for her. John Astor enthuses about these athletes and wants to get up some testimonial for them. They were received in grand style at the Forty-second Street depot at two-forty this afternoon. I would have liked to be present, but there was to be a banquet or collation at the Windsor Hotel, and as I am among the few trustees in town, I should have been imperatively called upon for "a few remarks" and should have seen my dinner-table brayings reported at length in all the morning papers.

July 23. . . . After many dark insinuations and innuendoes, Mr. Theodore Tilton publishes in form and at great length his charge against the Rev. H. W. Beecher—namely, the seduction of Mrs. Theodore Tilton, with specification of time, place, and circumstance. Tilton is probably a cad or *vaurien*, certainly a goose, and his word counts for little with me. He prints a letter from the Rev. Mr. Beecher, expressing profound penitence for some wrong or other, but the letter is written under manifest excitement, and its language may be exaggerated and hyperaesthetic and refer to something far less grave than the alleged crime to which Tilton makes it apply. Most people incline toward Beecher's side, those excepted who always wish to believe anything against a notable preacher. But his abominable misconduct in the Richardson and McFarland case is now remembered, to his grave prejudice. As to Tilton, nobody has anything to say for him. His own statement befouls him beyond disinfection by chlorine or carbolic acid. He is a cur of low degree.

I guess the investigation now in progress under direction of the authorities of "Plymouth Meet'n House" will shew that Mrs. Tilton is a gushing pietist and pulpit worshiper over whom Divus or Sanctus Beecher secured a sort of influence which rather alienated the lady from an uncongenial husband who was tending toward spiritualism and free-love-ism, and writing about the communications of Mrs. Victoria Woodhull with the spirit of Demosthenes. Probably Beecher did not seek this influence and went in merely for a little pious evangelical flirtation and fun. But it would seem that Tilton, having found out the state of affairs, pitched into St. Beecher and shed tears, and the Saint said and wrote that he was very sorry and shed tears, and the lady did the same. At that point the whole nasty business should have been wiped up and never mentioned again, but Tilton is a fool. Though most erratic and unsound, Beecher is manly, able, and eloquent and many silly women besides Mrs. Tilton have made an idol of him. There are those who say he is a bad man and that he "keeps" a batch of "singular Christian women," but I do not believe it.

July 25. . . . And now comes Mrs. Theodore Tilton, puts in her appearance, and gives her tale to the newspapers, with much of the high-flavored cant and high-falutin' verbiage to which the Chosen People of Brooklyn seem partial. But it reads rather like a true story. If it be true and if her husband's recent sayings and doings be truthfully reported, he is either a "looney" or an even shallower fool than I thought him, and a malignant, mischievous fool, moreover. But the whole case is not yet disclosed. Tilton's talk about what he means to prove against Beecher is orgulous and minatory, but it is probably mere "thrasonical huffe-snuffe." If Beecher has recruited a little harem for himself from among the Plymouth sisterhood (as many believe—I *don't*, for one), he has doubtless manoeuvred too warily to be caught by a feather-brained coxcomb like Theodore Tilton.

July 28. These days are doleful. Mr. Ruggles returned from Saratoga yesterday, improved in health and spirits, and reports Ellie stronger and every way better. He proposes to take up the Life & Trust Company loan. To help him do so I endorsed his note in the Bank of Commerce, due January 20, a proceeding not at all to my taste. . . .

The Beecher pot still boils. People begin to say that whether Tilton be lying or not, Plymouth Church is a cage of unclean birds. Beecher's profound abasement for some wrong or other by him done to Tilton is the ugly feature of Beecher's case. But for that, no one would listen to the brayings of Tilton or the gabble of the drabs who uphold him. Beecher explains it by the fact that he advised Mrs. Tilton to separate from her husband, and then he discovered that he had been misinformed and had advised her wrongly. But Mrs. Theodore Tilton avers in her manifesto that her life was embittered by Theodore's "free-love" affiliations, teachings, and practices, and that he caused her home to be infested by vermin of the Victoria Woodhull species whom he patronized and cultivated. Now would any clergyman, or layman either, declare himself humiliated, prostrated, driven to despair, and ready to welcome death by learning that when he advised a separation for reasons like these, he had been misinformed as to some detail or other? The Rev. Mr. Beecher is not reputed a hysterical patient. Till this mystery be cleared up, he must be content to rest under a cloud of suspicion. His political record in the "bleeding Kansas" times and his sermons about Sharps' rifles are remembered against him now. Many Southern and Western newspapers take his guilt for granted.

July 29. . . . Tilton is arrested for libel. . . .

July 31. . . . The general character of the Beecher-Tilton stench continues the same. Newspapers still reek with it, and everyone dwells darkly on the mystery of Beecher's contrition and attrition and longings for death. People don't get themselves up in sackcloth and ashes and scrape themselves with potsherds for any small matter. Every day that passes without satisfactory explanation of this phenomenon does Beecher irreparable damage and lessens the chance of any explanation being generally received at last.

It will be remembered that in the autumn of 1872 Victoria Woodhull had published in Woodhull and Claflin's Weekly *an article accusing Henry Ward Beecher of improper relations with the wife of Theodore Tilton; she was a member of Beecher's congregation, and Tilton had succeeded Beecher as editor of the* Independent. *The great preacher took no immediate notice of the charges, but as ugly rumors and stories continued to circulate he finally, on June 30, 1873, issued a formal denial. Still Victoria Woodhull continued her campaign, and the accusations gained national currency. Beecher then, in 1874, appointed a committee of six members of Plymouth Church to conduct an investigation of the charges. Efforts were made to get Mrs. Tilton to repudiate her husband and to give the committee a denial of the Woodhull story. Tilton himself had long kept silence, but he now made a drastic move: On July 20, 1874, he appeared before the authorities of Plymouth Church and made a sworn statement of Beecher's adultery, supporting it with much documentary evidence. This statement, as Strong notes in his diary for the 23rd, was at once published in the press, and one of the most famous scandals in American history became full public property. Mrs. Tilton, always emotional and now quite distracted by the crisis into which she was plunged, deserted her husband and took her stand by the side of her pastor. A storm of denunciation from Beecher's innumerable admirers beat upon Tilton's head. As noted above, he was charged with libel. In this extremity, he brought suit against Beecher for criminal conversation, demanding damages of $100,000; and his friend Frank Moulton (another member of Beecher's congregation) supported him, both Moulton and Mrs. Moulton swearing that Beecher had confessed his guilt to them. This trial, which began on January 11, 1875, lasted until July 2 of that year, with the whole country hanging on the evidence and arguments. It ended in a division of the jury, nine to three in favor of acquittal. Students of the trial have shown this same general division of opinion.*

The Nation, *in its incisive article on the scandal in the issue of August 20, 1874, took the view that Mrs. Tilton, maltreated by her husband, had contracted an affection for Beecher which presently seemed to her overwrought mind to be unlawful, and that she made a hysterical confession of this over-fond-*

ness for Beecher in a way which Tilton, his fortunes declining, could and did use in virtual blackmail of the pastor. But in a supplementary article on August 27, E. L. Godkin added: "The lying in every direction seems to be tremendous and unblushing. . . . It has come to be a 'conflict of veracity' between people whose moral standard is evidently not that of respectable men, and the best thing the public can do is let it drop."

August 5. . . . Poor Mrs. Theodore Tilton, being examined by the Plymouth investigators, tells a most pitiful story of neglect, insult, and outrage passively endured for years. She may or may not be the patient Griselda she describes herself, but she is evidently a weak vessel, perhaps badgered, bullied, and tormented into something approaching imbecility by the pranks of her demented husband. . . . Theodore Tilton now declines the jurisdiction of the Plymouth committee and means to take his case into the courts, a sensible proceeding if he have any case to take there. The Rev. Mr. Beecher continues silent as the Sphinx. This remarkable Mrs. Theodore Tilton seems to admit having written letters or certificates affirming the Rev. Mr. Beecher's criminal intimacy with her. But she says (or seems to say) that they were written at her husband's dictation for the sake of peace and because he had a kind of mesmeric influence over her. They are all lunatics together.

August 6. . . . The mystic and enigmatic Mr. Moulton consents at last to appear unto Plymouth and to open his budget. He is said to have acted as confidant and adviser of both parties while this mess was brewing, and to be an exceptional case of sanity. He required the consent of both as a condition precedent to his appearing. It has been given, and he may throw some light on the doings of these very queer people.

August 9. . . . Forster's life of Charles Dickens does not raise the "inimitable" in my estimation. With all his endearing and charming philanthropic sentiment, he seems to have been personally egotistical, self-conscious, and far from unselfish.

August 22, SATURDAY. Home again [from Mt. Desert]. . . .The can-can *à l'église de Plymouth* is not yet danced out but grows faster and more furious. Tilton has sued the Rev. Mr. Beecher (that great gospel-gun) for criminal conversation, damages at $100,000. Doesn't he wish he may get them? Moulton publishes a statement damaging the Rev. Mr. Beecher. Unless Moulton be a loud liar, the Rev. Mr. Beecher is a convicted Tartuffe. But these saints of Plymouth Church and their friends act and talk so unlike common low-caste Christians that one can't be quite sure they mean what they seem to say. Strange that the New York *World* after reviling the Rev. Beecher so long and so savagely should now be defending him through thick and thin. As to the gushing, saintly, "white-souled" epistolographic Mrs. Tilton, she hardly seems an accountable being. . . .

Architectural Notes: Roof of the hideous, top-heavy Union Telegraph building, corner of Dey Street and Broadway, is now sheathed in iron scales, and the huge brick and granite nightmare seems nearly complete. The metal skeleton of the hybrid between the dome and steeple at the south end of the new post office ("mulatto monkeyshines," they call it) begins to be likewise clothed upon. The Delaware & Hudson Company's building (R. M. Hunt's, corner Cortlandt Street and New Church Street) advances and promises pretty well. The grand tower of the new *Tribune* edifice has made no progress. In our old Trinity school building all the new tracery is set up and looks well enough. The new building rises slowly. Erben has nearly finished his work on the Trinity Church organ, but the *vox humana* as yet "speaks not to the goose-fleshed throng."

August 27. . . . The *Nation* prints a sensible article on Beecher and Tilton convicting the Rev. Mr. Beecher of fatuity, timidity, and foolish faith in Tilton and Moulton, but acquitting him of Tilton's charges. Though not quite conclusive, it is weighty. But I fear we have not yet got to the bottom of this most noisome mess. The present aspect of the Rev. Mr. H. W. Beecher is certainly undignified, at least, just now. It reminds one of Mr. Chadband, Mr. Pickwick, and Mr. Augustus Moddle (in *Chuzzlewit*), combining certain traits of all three. But however the case may turn out, the Rev. Mr. Beecher has Brooklyn worshippers who will continue to bow down before him.

August 29. The Plymouth committee read to a crowded meeting of Plymouthers last night a long report or judgment, whitewashing the Rev. Mr. Beecher, of course, but so unjudicial and partisan in tone that it will do him more harm than good. Outsiders will resent its unfairness and lean against him because of it, however illogically. These committeemen are, of course, disqualified from trying this case, not only as being Beecher's special liegemen and fautors, but also as holders of costly pews that would lose half their value were Beecher ousted from his platform. The precious report was received by a great audience with laughter and triumphant cheers. The somewhat questionable Mr. Frank Moulton was so rash as to attend the meeting and to signify his dissent as a minority of one from its prevailing sentiment. He was hissed and hooted down; and after the proceedings were closed and after the Plymouth saints had sung the doxology, they "went for" Moulton with pious ejaculations of "Give him H——!"—much as Cyril's deacons and Parabolani and Nitrian monks used to go for Jews and pagans. The police saved Moulton's bones. Beecher should pray to be saved from his friends.

August 30, SUNDAY. . . . It seems that some of Beecher's shoulder-hitting saints, or progressive Christian b'hoys, brought carnal weapons —to wit, revolvers— with them to the Plymouth meet'n house on Friday night, and that Moulton escaped with his life rather narrowly. The Rev. Mr. Beecher may be innocent; he is certainly not proven guilty. But his preaching and influence had certainly raised up around him a crop of scallywags, snobs, cads, and liars that it would be hard to match.

August 31. . . . Political skirmishing is active. "Democrats" are sanguine. But I think that Dix, the probable Republican candidate for governor, will run well, in spite of the 30,000 anti-lager fanatics who will do their devilmost to defeat him.

September 2. . . . Omens of "Democratic" gains this fall. God forbid the restoration of that party to power. But I should like to see the Republicans watched and menaced by a strong minority. They have enjoyed absolute undisputed control too long for their own good. Sporadic riots and lynchings among Southerners are exaggerated by the newspapers into a war of races and a reign of terror for effect on the fall elections.

In poor sorely-punished South Carolina, the doctrine of the rights of man and universal suffrage is settled by a *reductio ad absurdum.* Semibrutal black voters are in a great majority and, under the leading of knaves and carpet-baggers, control the state and are sinking it into deeper ruin every day. Perhaps the unfortunate result of this experiment may open people's eyes and sooner or later bring about reaction at the North where it is sorely needed. As to South Carolina, it seems as if her white folks would have to emigrate in a body unless they can save themselves by a revolution. The nigger majority is confiscating all their property by fraudulent taxation for the benefit of political operators and demagogues, or rather "zoogogues." It may come to a war of races in bitter earnest.

September 4. . . . More bills! *Billi et billiores, etiam billissioni!!!* I had to draw upon my poor little Trust Company reserve fund, and how I am to pay my taxes and the doctors, *non constat.* Thought of absconding, but it is better to stick to the comptrollership, "though billmen ply the ghastly blow." With $18,000 a year and a house, it is wonderful I should be always hard up. I spend very little on myself. Probably our housekeeping may be too loose and lavish.

Southern symptoms are bad. Black spirits and white refuse to mingle for any political purposes. They distrust and hate each other worse and worse as time goes on, far worse now, I think, than nine years ago. An explosion may come any day and a social war. United States troops are ordered down to keep the peace, but they can't garrison the whole Southern country and watch thousands of square miles of powder magazine.

September 8. Ellie returned from Cornwall last evening for a couple of days in town, and she was much better, stronger, and more cheerful, at least till dinner time today, when the fact that I have resigned the Philharmonic presidency seemed to produce a depressing effect. . . .

The catalogue of the Columbia College library is printed and is on sale; a goodly volume, but the collection includes tons of rubbish. . . .

Horsley opens an active Church Music Association campaign and hopes for another season. May he succeed! Cooke, Edmund, and I are out of that boat now, thank Heaven!

Died, Peter Remsen Brinckerhoff.

September 11. Letter from Mr. Ruggles today. Glad to see that his handwriting, which has been shakey ever since his illness, is now clear and firm. . . .

Newspapers are full of politics and nothing else. For governor, the Republicans probably put up Dix and the Democrats Tilden. Not a bad nomination, but the shattered Tammany Ring will recalcitrate.[6] The "Liberal Republicans" make no nominations. The hydrocephalites or hydromaniacs run the Hon. Myron H. Clark, I believe. He is a nonentity, a mere aquatic larva. Dix is very strong, but Republicans are languid and there is disaffection in the ranks, so the result is doubtful.

September 14. . . . F. Moulton prints another long statement—diffuse, irrelevant, and unclean—doing as much damage to himself as to Beecher, and that is saying a good deal. Were Beecher strong in conscious virtue, he would make haste to get Moulton and Tilton indicted for libel or for conspiracy.

September 15. Disturbances at New Orleans that may be premonitory of the gravest mischief.

September 16. . . . Visit . . . from the Rev. Mr. Cooke. The Rev. Wiswall means to make war on Trinity Church vestry next Easter Tuesday. An

---

[6] The nomination of Samuel J. Tilden, chief hero of the successful fight against the Tweed Ring, was one of the highest merit, and proved the reformation of the Democratic Party in the state.

obscure Sunday newspaper, the *Call*, prints a column of scurrility about the expected campaign. . . .

Died, the Hon. B. R. Curtis of Boston, a lawyer of the first grade. . . .

Order reigns at New Orleans, the bogus state government (so-called) having collapsed before the "White League," which will not much help the Northern "Democracy." The governments of South Carolina and Louisiana are, I fear, mere nests of corrupt carpet-baggers upheld by a brute nigger constituency. But have we here in New York any right to look down on them? Our civic rulers are, as a class, utterly base, and a Celtocracy is as bad as a niggerocracy, and in some respects worse. "When God will devast and punish a people or a kingdom . . . He bereaves them of wise, honest, and godly rulers and counsellors . . . then are the common people secure and merry, and they go on in all wilfulness. . . . Therefore, I fear the axe is laid to the root of this tree that it soon must be cut down. God of His infinite mercy, take us graciously away that we may not live to see such calamity!" Amen.

September 17. . . . Trouble not yet over in Louisiana, if it be true that Grant sides with the collapsed government and intends employing horse, foot, and dragoons to reinflate it. I don't clearly see how he can do otherwise, and there is probably not much to choose between the two gangs or factions, but we are steering close to another civil war, big or little as the case may be.

Tilden is "Democratic" candidate for governor. I thought this a strong nomination that would give Dix trouble, but Cisco pooh-poohs it and says a weaker man could not have been put up. Cisco knows more than I do, but his political prophesyings fail sometimes. Tilden's record during the black winter of 1860-61 is against him, and he will get no cordial support from the scoundrelly survivors of the Tammany Ring which he helped to smash in November, 1871. But I should hate to see even a Democrat defeated because of that good service to the city.

September 23. Radiant weather continues. No news except that General Dix is nominated by acclamation. I sent the Rev. Mr. Morgan Dix quite a long letter. . . .

Horsley has secured one Sanford for president of the Church Music Association. He is said to be rich, unemployed, and an earnest lover of music. Richard Grant White and one or two more are to be vice-presidents. Another season seems probable. I hope so. I should be sorry to see that fine chorus collapse and disintegrate. Horsley evidently means to run the machine himself, with these laymen as ornamental assessors. He is likely to blunder in his choice of music. English audiences and American audiences differ in taste. We can't stand much Handel, the *Messiah* excepted. Horsley proposes bringing out the Dettingen "Te Deum." I predict it will be pronounced a bore.

October 1.   At Diocesan Convention all day. . . . Little or nothing done outside of the annual routines. The "regular" tickets for the Standing Committee and the Missionary Committee prevailed, with but two or three scattering votes in opposition. I think Morgan Dix was scratched by four malcontents. I was made a trustee of the Episcopal fund. The Bishop's address was two hours long, mainly devoted to the inculcation of tolerance and the mischief of "restrictive" legislation on questions of ritual and things indifferent. It was Dix's Ascension Day sermon, *cum commento*, capable of great compression, like sponge. I won't say like gas, for it was thoughtful, scholarlike, and wholesome. But it might all have been said in half the time. I rather protested against being made trustee as aforesaid, for there are plenty of people who grumble about Trinity Church having too much to say and to do in the diocese.

Discoursed nice old Prof. Bartlett, whilom of West Point, Gen. Morell, the ophidian Honorable Henry E. Davies, the Honorable Hamilton Fish, Bishop Tozer, Bishop Young of Florida, the Right Rev. Horatio Potter of New York, and others. And who should appear but my old classmate, the Rev. William E. Snowden, whom I have not seen since 1838! He has been settled all this time in North Carolina, but has now come North.

October 3. . . . Much arranging for the General Convention next week. It will cost Trinity not less than $8,000—feed included.

October 4, SUNDAY. . . . The Rev. Mr. Beecher has got Tilton and Moulton indicted for libel—a sensible proceeding.

Mr. Ruggles means to take his seat in the General Convention, in spite of remonstrances and entreaties. The session promises to be stormy. He will be sure to speak and excite himself, and there is an even chance of his bringing on a second seizure like that of October, 1872.

October 8. . . . I resigned from the American Geographical Society, since I am unable to perceive the advantage of paying certain annual dues for nothing at all.

The General Convention met yesterday. Much clack and waste of time over rules of order and much grumbling over the acoustic (or dys-acoustic) properties of St. John's. Cambridge Livingston's cunningly devised system of crosswires to destroy reverberation by breaking the sound waves seems a total failure.

The "church congress" met and has, I believe, adjourned. It looks like a fizzle. But it was a happy provision for the harmless discharge of peccant wind, which, if confined and pent up, might cause distress and incite to mischievous action.

October 13. . . . Much evolution of gas at the Convention; salutary. The more they talk, the less they will legislate. Mr. Ruggles does his share, of course, and most imprudently. But he is wholly irrepressible. . . .

October 15. Went through the workshops and manufacturing lofts of Tiffany's Union Square house with the intelligent Magauran. About five hundred men and women are employed there. Processes and apparatus interesting; some of the products are artistic and splendid. . . .

The Convention went into secret session yesterday—hammer and tongs—over Seymour, bishop-elect of Indiana, and have been at it, I believe, all today. I guess his election will be confirmed.

I signed a petition with Cisco, Nash, J. P. Pirsson, Edward Matthews, *et multis aliis,* praying for deliverance from legislation on ritual. . . .

Democrats claim great gains in Ohio and Indiana. Discouraging for Dix.

October 17. The General Convention is still within the veil dissecting Dr. Seymour and clapperclawing over ritualism. . . .

Horsley has filled up his Church Music Association subscription list. His new president, S. S. Sanford, led off with a subscription of $1,500. Good for Sanford! The vice-presidents (there is no committee) are a queer assortment: General Barnard, Richard Grant White, Clarence Seward, the Rev. Mr. Stanton, and J. Wrey Mould(!). I am glad the Association has passed safely through the critical process of casting its skin.

October 19. The General Convention thinks its oysters too small. So I assumed the responsibility of ordering bigger oysters and also of issuing them daily instead of every other day. Anything to inspire the Council of the Church with the spirit of peace and harmony, which is the fruit of good living and eupepsia.

Western elections have disheartened the Republicans and also the third termites, whoever they are. I never saw any of them. General Dix's prospects are not brilliant. . . .

October 26, MONDAY. I became a borrower today for the first time in my life. Loan of $3,000 from Charley Strong on the pledge of the Bank of New York stock. There have been unusually heavy demands on me this year, but I must economize in earnest, and I have begun clipping and trimming my little personal expenses.

Total lunar eclipse Saturday night. The sky was veiled with inopportune cirri, and the orb was visible only as through a glass darkly; so I went to bed without waiting for the phenomenon.

November 2. College trustees took their monthly nap this afternoon, and it lasted two hours and a half. Betts, now almost quite blind, resigned the clerkship, and Halsey was elected clerk. Poor Betts is so infirm and his sight so bad that I had to give him my arm down the stairs and help him into his carriage. Barnard mumbles and maunders worse than ever.

November 4, WEDNESDAY. Yesterday's election was a Waterloo or Sedan to the Republicans. Total rout, North and South. General Dix was badly whipped. Some 80,000 votes changed in this state since 1872. Wickham is mayor, of course. New Jersey is Democratic, and so is the governor of Massachusetts! There has been no such discomfiture since Bull Run. One consolation is that Ben Butler's Massachusetts constituency invites him to try how the door of the house shuts from the outside and then to resume his seat by the domestic hearth. This revolution does not mean that people have changed their principles and gone over to Democracy so-called. It means that people are bored by the dullness of business ever since the panic of last year, that they are disgusted by abuses of power and bad management in Louisiana and other Southern states, by stories (half true, at least) of corruption and extravagance at Washington, and they are nervous about a "third term" and "Caesarism.". . .

November 6. . . . Mr. Ruggles brought in Hunt of New Orleans, who might fill Lieber's place. He seems well read and scholarly, is a churchman, national as to his politics, a gentleman, of good family, and looks just like Mephistopheles.

The insatiate General Convention devoured, absorbed, ingulphed, ingested, bolted, gobbled, munched, masticated, ingurgitated, deglutinated, and, I hope, digested and assimilated 80,000 oysters!!! And the Rev. Mulchahey tells me that the "Hospitality Committee" expects the long-suffering corporation of Trinity Church to pay its deficit of some $7,000 (hotel bills).

Election returns are painfully monotonous. As they come in more fully, they merely magnify the revolution of Tuesday. Some Northern Democrats and many downtrodden Southerners will probably misunderstand it. They will fancy that the good old days of 1860 have come back, and they will put on airs, exalt their horn, sharpen their bowie knives, and oil their revolvers. The amiable Isaiah Rynders, who crawled out into the light the other day, gave us a specimen of this kind of thing in certain rhetorical and parabolical allusions to "niggers." Very little of this would suffice to stir up an intense anti-Democratic reaction, which might possibly—and only possibly— carry Grant into a third term if he would take it.

The Republican defeat this fall was indeed overwhelming, constituting the greatest party overturn since 1860. The Democrats swept Samuel J. Tilden into the governorship of New York by a majority of about 50,000, thus almost reversing the vote which had made John A. Dix governor in 1872 by 55,000. New Jersey went Democratic, and Massachusetts chose a Democratic governor, partly by way of rebuke to the Republicans for nominating the impudent Ben Butler. In the South new gains were made by the Democratic or Conservative Party, presaging a return to full white supremacy. The Senate remained Republican, but the new House would be Democratic—and its investigating committees were certain to make the most of the opportunity to explore Republican misconduct and corruption. A remarkably able group of Democrats were chosen to the House, including Abram S. Hewitt of New York, Julius H. Seelye of Massachusetts, and Henry B. Payne of Ohio. It was evident that the Democratic Party, under such men as Tilden and Allen G. Thurman, had a great opportunity. If it could prove its adherence to reform it stood a handsome chance of carrying the country in the presidential election of 1876.

November 11. . . . Morgan Dix returned today on the Cunarder *Russia* with the Frau Rectorinn. While in London, he went to the illustrious Poole's to order some clothes. The urbane salesman said, "Certainly, sir, with great pleasure, sir; but then we don't take orders, sir, from strangers, sir, without some kind of reference, sir." "Oh-ah—of course, very proper," said the Rev. Morgan Dix, and produced from his pocket a letter of introduction from Bishop Potter to the Archbishop of Canterbury. The salesman hummed and hesitated and then said: "Yes, sir, a most flattering endorsement, sir. It would carry great weight, sir, in clerical circles, sir, but it won't do here, sir." So the Rev. Mr. Dix had to go into the City and get a letter from his banker. . . .

November 12. . . . In the evening to the Law School; Mr. Ruggles, Nash, Ogden, and I, with the professors. Sundry radical changes in the organization of the School were discussed, and sundry unpleasant truths spoken out at last as to the great dissatisfaction of many trustees with our present arrangements. The School has proved too successful and has grown far too unwieldy for any one professor, however able, but Dwight cannot bear to have anyone associated with him. . . .

1875

*S*trong began the last year of his diary in apparent good health and good
spirits. New Year's Day, clear, chill, and windless, fell on Friday. He made
a fair number of calls, going to the houses of Mrs. John Sherwood, Mrs.
William Schermerhorn, Mrs. Morgan Dix, and others. He enjoyed Mrs.
Strong's party that night for "Miss Puss," Charley Strong's pretty daughter.
At the Trinity Corporation office he was active as ever. His interest in public
affairs continued strong, and he was outraged by the arrogant conduct of the
Grant Administration in New Orleans. The recent election had left the control of
the lower house of the legislature in doubt, and the President had resolved on heroic
measures. He ordered General Sheridan to the state; on the 4th of January,
some 1800 federal troops were posted about the State House; and at a critical
juncture, General R. de Trobriand marched in, seized five objectionable members—objectionable, that is, to the Grant party—and expelled them from the
chamber. Everyone recalled that even Charles I had not been able to deal
quite so highhandedly with Parliament. While a wave of indignation swept
over the North, the Cabinet itself took a stand against Grant, Secretary Fish and
others being ready to resign if the President persisted in his course.

January 2, SATURDAY. Nothing very new, except that the Spanish
Republic is dead, and Alfonso XII sits on the uneasy throne of Spain—poor
young gentleman. . . .

January 7. Grant's Louisiana blunder is doing him and his friends
great harm. Prominent Republicans denounce it, and indignation meetings

are to be called here and elsewhere, "without distinction of party." Strange that the canny and politic Hamilton Fish can acquiesce in the wild capers of the Administration! That bold dragoon, Gen. Philip Sheridan, wants the President to proclaim all the white folk of Louisiana (except the carpet-baggers) "banditti" and to let him, General Phil, dispose of them as he did of Early and his men and afterwards of the Pi-egans. But I don't think a *la stoccata* will so carry it away quite yet. I have stood up for Grant through evil report and good report for ten years, but he is "coming it rather too strong" now. There are reasonable people who think it Grant's deliberate purpose to stay in the White House after his term expires, if he can do so, *per fas aut nefas*, but it seems preposterous.

January 9. . . . Signed (at the *Evening Post* office) the "Indignation Meeting" call. I am sorry to do it after swearing by Grant so long. Grant is said to be "not at all scared" by the storm he has raised. He is not easily scared by anything. Whatever may go to smash, *impavidum ferient ruinae.* His heart is hardened, and he "will fight it out on this line" as he once did in a better cause. As old Pepys, my prototype, says, "Pray God send all well!" . . .

January 11. . . . I hear that George Anthon, at Yonkers, has had a small boy added unto him, and to Mrs. Constance Harrison a little girl. May they thrive and prosper!

Tonight's vestry meeting was of brevity unprecedent—only forty minutes! But we gave the committees many "chores" to do. General Dix was with us for the first time in two years, and we added him to the Standing Committee, making it nine instead of eight. But this does not increase the *quorum.* In discourse with a half dozen of us, the General remarked: "It's only the other day that they murdered a score or two of niggers at Vicksburg. Why didn't these gentlemen get up an indignation meeting about *that?*" Which was a rather fatuous remark, methought. But our dear, good, astute, old sagacious General likes to be on good terms with administrations and remembers the teaching of his catechism about "honoring the civil authority," which has foreign missions and other good gifts for its friends.

January 13. . . . Mr. Morris's opening in Tilton *v.* Beecher reads like a summing up and consumed two days and a half. The look of the case may change and probably will when Evarts has his innings, but Beecher's contrite and despairing letters can never be so explained away as to free him from the gravest weight of suspicion.

January 15. . . . Grant's Louisiana message is less truculent than was expected, but palliating and trying to excuse what seems a great wrong.

Tilton *v.* Beecher. Frank Moulton was on the stand and his direct examination is not yet closed. He testifies to full and free admissions by the defendant. This threatens to be as protracted as the Tichborne case, and it is watched with something like the same interest. Plymouth Church will stand by its shepherd whatever the trial may disclose and whatever be the verdict. But outside that fane, opinion sets strongly against Beecher, and no wonder. To use his own cant or peculiar religious patois, he put too much "inwardness" into these fatal letters of his and recorded his "heart-experiences" too copiously. Unprejudiced people can give them only one construction. The plaintiff's position is, however, so assailable and his record so bad that he can expect only nominal damages in any event. Were he seeking a divorce, he would fail.

January 17, SUNDAY. . . . Two long grave conferences with Temple. I didn't scold a bit, though I was fairly entitled to do so, for Temple has been behaving ill and in an underhand, tortuous way; but I read him several fine moral lessons. I was much discouraged at first, for I could elicit nothing but a tendency to sulk, to invent plausible excuses, and to find fault with everybody. The radical cause of his troubles, of his "playing hookey" and shirking work at Mr. Everson's and now at George Anthon's, was but too apparent. He does not recognize the unpleasant truth that it generally devolves on every son of Adam to do work he doesn't like. My parenthetical suggestion of calling in grandpapa and Uncle James as a *conseil de famille* to advise me as to what the deuce I should do with him produced considerable effect, I thought. He was silent for a time and then remarked that he "didn't see the use of that." I thought he would not. At last, to my great joy, he volunteered a suggestion, or proposition, that he should do his Greek with me in the afternoons or evenings and pledge himself to regularity and effort, and I promised to watch him and see that he shirked school no longer. On these terms a treaty was concluded. I may find my share of its obligations a bore, but it looks like Temple's last chance.

January 18. . . . School work tonight with Temple. The young scapegrace knows more Greek and far more algebra than I. He's as bright as he can be. All he needs is perception of the duty of work.

January 19. Died William H. Aspinwall, at sixty-seven, whom I regret.[1] They say he never got over the death of his brother John, and he

[1] The eminent merchant had been still active in business. Probably no man had done so much to build up the Pacific and Latin-American trade of the United States. During the Civil War he had given vigorous support to the Union, and had gone to England to urge the British to stop the building of the Laird rams.

has suffered for several months under a complication of disorders, including disease of the heart, which seems to have been the immediate cause of his death. He was always particularly civil and good to me, and while I was in college, he offered to take me into the countinghouse of Howland & Aspinwall—a most special favor and distinction. Perhaps I should have become a partner and blossomed into a millionaire.

January 20. . . . Grant has blundered again: "Federal myrmidons," that is, a squad of U.S. infantry, summarily eject the sheriff of Vicksburg from his shrievalty and install somebody else in his place. This is a cheap and easy substitute for the costly, tedious, and antiquated machinery of a *quo warranto.* But unless Grant is careful, he will be outflanked by an impeachment.

January 22. Visit from Egleston—in his usual nervous, perturbed, and *wronged* condition. He *will* order work done at the School of Mines without the least authority and then wonder that there should be any demur about paying the bills; he is confident that he will die soon.

January 23. Whom can we trust, and who can feel sure of even his own honesty? Henry Nicoll, after forty years of honorable practice, after having won the unquestioning confidence of every businessman in New York, after coming to be universally regarded as the embodiment of old-fashioned integrity, caution, and conservatism—Henry Nicoll is in every man's mouth today and in the newspapers, besides, as having used, or embezzled, several hundred thousand dollars of the trust funds in his keeping!!! Townsends, Bradhursts, and Hickson Fields are among the chief sufferers. This is a public calamity, weakening everybody's faith in anybody. The Devil must certainly be unchained in these days. What will come next? Will Bishop Potter pocket the fund "for the relief of decayed and insolvent clergymen," and run away?

January 24. . . . Bad account of the Nicoll case; assets doubtful. W. H. Aspinwall is said to have lost a great deal of money during the last year or two. . . .

January 25. Died Charles Kingsley, also Maunsell Field, who worked with me in my father's office in 1842.[2] I liked him greatly then, but he underwent a kind of fatty degeneration afterwards and became heavy, pompous, oedematous, and puffy, though always quite efficient in business. His marriage turned out ill, and I don't think his life was prosperous or

[2] Maunsell B. Field, who had held minor diplomatic posts before the war and risen to be assistant secretary of the Treasury under Chase, left a volume of *Memories* which was published posthumously.

very happy. He had a passion for knowing notable people, not with ulterior designs, but for their own sake, and I suppose the crowning mercy of his life was his accidental presence when Mr. Lincoln died.

January 27. Two College committees met today; namely, the School of Mines this afternoon, at William Betts's (Betts, the president, Agnew, and I), and "On the Course," at the Bishop's this evening. . . . Our excellent president's prosing grows more and more afflictive. He prosed tonight a full hour on a matter as to which we were all of one mind. When he dried up and ceased at last, we were all in a kind of magnetic trance, and nobody seemed able to say anything. I broke the spell by a motion that was unanimously adopted at once (I had some difficulty in rousing myself to move it) and then came away as fast as I could. . . .

January 28. My auditing committee finished its labors and signed its report. Its examination has been searching—thank Heaven. An annual examining committee would probably have saved George A. Jones and Henry Nicoll from misapplication of trust funds and from disgrace and ruin. But I confess that as our Fulton Street office is organized I do not see how I could steal a dollar if I wanted to. I was much flattered and gratified by a casual remark of Cambridge Livingston's: "Why, I thought Henry Nicoll was like Edgar S. Van Winkle, and *you*, and a few other people about whom nobody has any doubt at all." God keep me from falling!

February 1, MONDAY. . . . College trustees met at two this afternoon. Judge Blatchford was in the chair, and Mr. Ruggles was present for the first time (I think) since October, 1872. A proposition was made by Barnard to suspend chapel services during examinations. Spirited speech by Mr. Ruggles against that proposition, and it was lost, *nem. con.* Barnard's position on the board is painful. He is prime minister and chief administrative officer, but he can never count on a majority and is constantly thwarted and snubbed by adverse votes. He doubtless wishes he could afford to resign, and I, for one, wish so, too.

Certain recommendations from the Law School Committee were carried, and I moved a resolution which I had promised Dwight to move, though expressly declining any promise to vote for it. It was to diminish the amount of Latin hereafter to be required as a condition of admission to the School. I moved it, stating that I should vote against it, and it was lost, Mr. Ruggles making another quite brilliant little speech against it and in maintenance of classical culture.

We went into an election to fill a vacancy on the board. There were twelve votes, and James W. Beekman was unanimously elected. This lay dissenter takes the place of some deceased Presbyterian or Dutch Reformed cleric—whom precisely, I don't remember. I want the College made a church college, and with that view I vote for the promotion of dissenting laymen to places long filled by dissenting parsons, quasi ex officio. As these laymen die off, they can be easily and silently replaced by churchmen. When Halsey, our clerk, read the names of men who had been nominated for the vacant trusteeship, it was sad to hear him slur over Henry Nicoll's name as being a name, strictly speaking, before us but for which, of course, nobody could vote. I should have voted for him a month ago.

February 3. . . . Tilton *v.* Beecher. Tilton still on the stand. The drift of public opinion seems setting more and more decidedly against Beecher.

Our grand little dinner for the Rector and the Rectoress yesterday was rather pleasant. Ellie knows how to entertain. People seemed to enjoy themselves and talked like ten square miles of tropical forest full of parrots and parroquets. I was glad to have John Astor here, to whom I'm indebted for many sumptuous dinners. I fear their splendors have deterred me from asking him. A half-conscious but wholly snobbish feeling that I could not rival the gorgeousness of his dinners has interfered with the performance of my "social obligations." But our table was handsome enough for any reasonable Christian, and nobody seemed to feel the absence of a service of gold plate. I don't believe that John Astor himself missed it much. The dinner was quite good enough, too. . . .

February 8. Continued monotony of rancorous cold, aggravated by the mockery of brilliant but lifeless sunshine. Many seals reported in the Lower Bay, and their visit is attributed to this severity of the winter. If it last much longer, we shall be invaded by walruses and polar bears. . . .

February 10, ASH WEDNESDAY. . . . Henry Nicoll resigns from the Bar Association. Poor Henry Nicoll!

February 12. . . . The long record of the Astor House is closed. They are selling off its gear and plenishing at auction, and it will be converted to business uses.

February 13. . . . Dined here, Hamilton Fish, Jr., and the Austrian Fritsch; both pleasant.

Died, Major Joseph Delafield, aged eighty-five, one of our vestry. He had been confined to his room for many months, but the immediate cause of his death was this lethal pneumonia, of which everybody seems to die now-a-days.

March 27. . . . It's said that Fitz-John Porter's application for a rehearing is denied. I fear this is just.

Scribners—A. and W.—have got up their new shop. It's doubtless the largest and shewiest bookstore in America, probably in the world.

March 30. Easter Tuesday. Clear and un-springlike. I found an unusual confluence of voters at Trinity Church. The polls closed at one; result: 189 votes unanimous, and *not a single name scratched*!!! . . . So the politic machinations of Wiswall prove a mare's nest. So I expected, but it was right to take precautions. Wiswall and Mrs. L—— tell Henry Erben that they are too busy just now for anything but floating hospitals and "tea-parties" at the academy; but *next* year they will try to attend to the vestry. . . .

March 31. . . . I spent most of the morning, after signing checks for April 1, pasting newspaper cuttings into a big scrapbook—materials for future memoirs of Trinity Parish. I have a vast mass of newspaper cuttings, besides, from poor old Dunscomb's desk, and Henry Dorr called this morning with a great bundle of like matter. So I have enough to keep my paste pot busy to the end of my days. Dorr is a most loyal parishioner of Trinity; he's our antiquarian. He has rummaged in the Historial Society and in the Society Library for material that appears in the appendix to Dix's sermon on the centennial of St. Paul's and in the last year book of the parish. Pity he is the ideal of a bore.

April 2. . . . The vestry met this afternoon and organized. Contoit was put on the Cemetery Committee—vice Swift disappeared; otherwise, there was no change. Then we organized a Standing Committee meeting. Our new colleague, Dr. Wilkes, took his seat. He is a descendant, or else a great-something-nephew of the London John Wilkes—a connexion of the Scotch Lord Jeffrey—and a gentlemanlike person.

One or two of my friends have set their hearts on buying lots near Central Park for $360,000 to build a new chapel for parishioners who have moved uptown, and incurring a debt of three-quarters of a million dollars. *Das geht nicht.* The strongest point made against us in 1856 and 1857 was that we built Trinity Chapel for wealthy people who ought to provide themselves with churches. It could readily be answered, but it was a telling *ad captandum* criticism. We had much better add transepts to Trinity and increase our church accommodation downtown.

Interest in that weary Tilton *v.* Beecher revives a little, the reverend defendant having taken the stand himself. He is a cool and powerful witness. Fullerton's examination will not shake him; but it will tax even his subtlety, unction, and histrionism to produce an exculpatory commentary on his *epistola poenitentialis*.

April 6. Died, the Hon. James J. Roosevelt, aged eighty. His gross personal prejudices and partialities spoiled him for a judge of the Supreme Court; and he was too servile a white nigger not to disgrace the U.S. district attorneyship, even in the days of Buchanan and the plantation whip. He slipped and fell some little time since, breaking the neck of the thigh bone. For some reason or other his stomach thereupon refused all food, and he literally starved to death. So one of his nephews tells me.

April 9. Went to Cemetery Committee meeting this afternoon. Cisco called, eager for the purchase of a dozen lots on Fifty-ninth and Fifty-eighth Streets for a new chapel. It's the finest situation in the city, just west of Fifth Avenue and fronting the Park, and we may secure them for $300,000 and build at our leisure. But I look with trepidation on a new debt of near a million, especially while a couple of hundred thousand dollars must soon be laid out on that insatiable cemetery. Our building Trinity Chapel was one of the chief and the heaviest weapons used against us in 1855–57. It was a costly church for rich, uptown people who ought to build their own churches. "But we must retain our corporators." Answer: We had 189 of them last Easter Tuesday, but I fear Cisco will push this through; he says the Rector is with him. . . .

The *Tribune* tower is finished off at last with a jaunty little steeple, like a seventeenth century peaked hat. Our Trinity Church School house tower looks well, though the gargoyles at its angles are hypertrophied. When a new idea has forced its way into the head of Upjohn, Jr., he is apt to "run it into the ground," or (as in this case) into the air.

April 26, MONDAY. At daybreak Sunday morning, the Union League Club house took fire. The storm retarded the fire signals, and the combustion was not suppressed till this costly building was denuded of its roof and every storey singed and soaked. . . .

Dick [Derby] came in at noon with sad news from Boston. George [Strong Derby] died Sunday afternoon at five P.M. . . . His father and mother were telegraphed at Norfolk on their way home from Florida. They did not even know that poor George was ill. He was one of the nicest and best fellows that ever lived.

May 1. . . . In Tilton *v.* Beecher, the defense rests from its labors at last, and there will probably be a few months of rebuttal. Fullerton, for the plaintiff, offers to waive all objections to Mrs. Tilton if called by the defense. Evarts replies from a high moral standpoint. He cannot possibly call Mrs. Tilton because it would be against the policy of the law, and so on. This affords food for meditation, but I am too tired of the case to care anything about it any more.

May 3. To the University Place meeting house for John C. Green's funeral. . . .

A dozy meeting of the College trustees began at two o'clock—two hours in Boeotia. Amazing, how some of us dread and shrink from any profaning contact of the College with the community. Here have the board of health and one or two equally respectable bodies been allowed the use of a room in the School of Mines for evening meetings at a cost of gas amounting to less than $6.00 all told. One would think the newspaper reports of these meetings an advertisement of the School and that we should seek to make the College buildings a center for all the reputable scientific and literary organizations of the city. But —— demurs and objects, and the Standing Committee will doubtless agree with him. . . .

May 7. . . . In Tilton *v.* Beecher, Mrs. Tilton makes an appeal to the court—quite spontaneously and *not* on the suggestion of the counsel—to be allowed to take the stand and vindicate her reputation. To which Judge Neilson, of course, replies, *"Non possumus"*—a good dodge but rather thin. H. C. Bowen's rebutting evidence hits the Rev. H. W. Beecher very hard; while the Rev. Mr. Beecher has sworn that his deep contrition for injuries to Theodore Tilton, his wish for death, and all that, were founded on his having advised Bowen to divest Tilton from his editorship of the *Independent*. And now comes Bowen and swears that Beecher never gave him any advice or suggestion of the kind.

May 13. . . . Johnny has passed his [bar] examinations with flying colors. . . .

June 12, SATURDAY. I finally broke down two days after my last entry, Saturday, the 15th, being unable to eat, hardly able to stand, and suffering constant sharp pain. I authorized Ellie to send for Dr. Peters, which I should have done a month before. Peters appeared and forthwith told me frankly that I was in very considerable danger, and that if I had delayed sending for him another week, he could probably have done nothing in the premises. The trouble was not dyspepsia but a liver enlarged to about three times its normal bulk, like that of a Strassburg gander, and threatening "induration," cirrhosis, and dropsy. I don't think the danger of all this quite over yet, but Peters thinks it diminishing and that, though I'm still on a lee shore, I am slowly clawing off in a hopeful way. He continues vigilant and most vigorous in his requirements as to diet and medicine.

So for the last month I have been in a state of combined torpor and medication, sustaining a passive or negative existence on pills and milk. The former were and are blue and cannabis, the latter (I believe), the "sincere milk" of the cow, furnished by an honest purveyor. Both my front and rear elevations have been tastefully frescoed with tincture of iodine; but I laid it on too freely, and the result was a pustular eruption that nearly drove me mad with itching. I longed to denude myself of all my clothes and all my flesh; and had that been practicable, I should probably have been found actively going over my ribs with sandpaper. My principal bother is now weakness, with a constant sense of almost intolerable fatigue. A few days ago, I tried for a drive in the Park with Ellie; but the vile pavement of Fifth Avenue caused me such pain that I had to turn about, and I got home feeling faint and prostrate. . . .

Jem's baby was baptized by Morgan Dix last Sunday at Trinity chapel, "James Francis Ruggles, Jr." Johnny was one of its godfathers. He—Johnny, not the baby—has gone in for a season with E. H. Owen, as he is thirsting for work in court. He is ambitious to be an advocate, not a mere conveyancer, and is full of ardor for any fray that may turn up.

I have had as many visitors as I wanted, including several of my bosses; for example, Gouverneur Ogden, Morgan Dix and the Governor, Cisco, and others.

Edmund Schermerhorn is president of the Philharmonic, an admirable choice for the Society but bad for Edmund, who will worry and fidget himself into a serious fit of illness before his first term is ended.

The case of Tilton v. Beecher is nearly run out at last. Beach is closing for the plaintiff. . . .

A weighty discovery is said to have been made by one Crookes of London, namely, that light has motive power, not of attraction, but of repulsion. Perhaps. If this discovery hold water, light will prove the centrifugal force and the cause of the behavior of comets' tails when near the sun.

Strong's physical suffering in these days was sharpened by an estrangement between him and his son Temple that became acute in the early part of April. The cause and progress of the difficulty cannot be known because the pertinent passages have been obliterated from the diary. Temple left home to earn his own livelihood with only vague prospects. Though he saw his mother daily, the rebellious youth avoided his father, who wrote on April 30: "Strange he should prefer a garret to the luxury and the indulgence of home. But I suppose it is the same feeling that makes boys long to be Robinson Crusoes and get shipwrecked on desert islands. Were he not a Bohemian to the backbone I should be sure he would sicken of this experiment within a month. Strange and sad that this unforeseen rupture should have occurred and should have become something very like permanent, incurable schism in less than thirty days. I fear I shall never hear poor obstinate, ungrateful, disobedient Temple's oboe tootling up-stairs any more."

June 16.   Warmer, but this summer is thus far backward and not torrid. I am still stupefying in this library (the Gandercoop or New Strassburg), weak as a baby and regaining strength imperceptibly, if at all. I made a sortie Monday night to a vestry meeting—only a short drive—where I was cordially received by my colleagues, the pillars of the church. A leave of absence was voted for me till October 15—a very kind deed. If I could lay my hands on a few hundred dollars, wouldn't I spend the summer in England! Dix is acting comptroller during my hypothetical absence. Our excellent old ex-Governor, ex-Major-General, ex-Secretary, ex-Ambassador, and the like, can no more live without some office, little or big, than a pagurus without his univalve. An order was taken for the purchase of land for a chapel on the south side of Houston Street, just east of the Bowery. It's the ancient Quaker burying ground, but I believe all the old Quakers have been dug up and transplanted. Our offer is $80,000 for the land, but we must probably pay a little more.

June 23.   Much warmer. I have been losing ground this last week, am as weak as I was a month ago, and have lost taste for all food save milk, of which emollient fluid I ingurgitate two full quarts per diem. Peters is to bring Dr. Alonzo Clark to inspect me tomorrow.

June 25, FRIDAY.   A hot day. Peters brought the great Dr. Alonzo Clark yesterday, who manipulated my liver with great energy but pronounced no definite judgment that I heard of. I have been improving the wrong way, like bad fish in warm weather. One day last week, I had a woeful day of headache, nausea, and malaise, which left me as weak as a sea anemone at low water. Since then, there has been no improvement.

This was the diarist's last entry; he died on July 21.

INDEX

(Adapted from the 1952 four-volume edition of Strong's Diary)